Invisible Citizens

Foundations of Archaeological Inquiry

James M. Skibo, series editor

INVISIBLE CITIZENS

Captives and Their Consequences

Edited by **Catherine M. Cameron**

The University of Utah Press
Salt Lake City

Foundations of Archaeological Inquiry
James M. Skibo, series editor

 The Defiance House Man colophon is a registered trademark
of the University of Utah Press. It is based upon a four-foot-tall,
Ancient Puebloan pictograph (late PIII) near Glen Canyon, Utah.

12 11 10 09 08   1 2 3 4 5

Library of Congress Cataloging-in-Publication Data

Invisible citizens : captives and their consequences / edited by
Catherine M. Cameron.
      p.   cm. — (Foundations of archaeological inquiry)
      Includes index.
      ISBN 978-0-87480-936-7   (pbk. : alk. paper)   1. Human remains
(Archaeology)   2. Social archaeology.   3. Slaves.   4. Slave trade.
5. Captivity.   I. Cameron, Catherine M.
      CC79.5.H85I68 2008
      930.1—dc22   2008031475

Contents

Figures

Tables

1

Introduction

Captives in Prehistory as Agents of Social Change

Catherine M. Cameron

Throughout history, warfare and raiding have forced captives from one society into another. Captives, mostly women and children, were often enslaved. They formed an almost invisible stratum in many societies, strangers in strange lands, without kin and largely outside the social systems in which they lived. Captives were victims of war and oppression, but they were also, often, agents of change.

Captives have been overlooked in anthropology and archaeology in part because violence and warfare have been understudied in non-state societies (Keeley 1996; LeBlanc 2003) and partly because the horrors of the Atlantic slave trade made scholars understandably reluctant to discuss slavery in non-Western cultures (Donald 1997:35–40; Kopytoff 1982; Kopytoff and Miers 1977:3–7; Patterson 1982:xi). Anthropologists often downplay or ignore evidence for capture and enslavement. Yet captives have been taken throughout time, and slaves have existed in significant numbers in many, perhaps most, societies.

The premise of this book is that the mingling of societies and customs that resulted from the taking of captives must have had a profound effect on cultural development—effects that archaeologists should explore. Archaeologists tend to treat social group boundaries in the past as if they were relatively fixed and impermeable. Yet if adults or even subadults from other cultures were frequently introduced as captives through warfare, raids, or trading, then social boundaries in the past were not fixed; people of different cultural traditions *often* lived together in the same communities. Captives may have profoundly influenced developments in language, technology, social practices, and ideology.

The perspective taken by contributors to this volume is that captive-taking is a phenomenon that plays out at a broad geographic scale, creating "predatory landscapes" in which economic, social, and political interactions were defined or heavily influenced by the practice (see especially the chapters in this volume by Stahl, Bowser, and Robertshaw and Duncan). Captive-taking and trade in captives is a phenomenon that enmeshes societies of different sociopolitical levels, as well as those that are geographically distant, in a vast network of moving bodies—bodies carrying foreign cultural information. Social, ethnic, and political boundaries may be maintained despite immense demographic movement across their borders. We believe that captive-taking should be seen as an extension of other processes that move people around the landscape, such as marriage, migration, and refugee situations, although the lines dividing these processes are likely to be faint.

The terms "captive" and "slave" require clarification. Slavery in classical and colonial societies has been the focus of much scholarly study, with the definition of "slave" the subject of considerable discussion (Bonnassie 1991:16–25; Copley 1960:4–9; articles in Engerman et al. 2001; Davis 1966:31–35; Patterson 1982:13). In this volume, we are most interested in how captives interacted with and potentially transformed their captor's society. It is less important to determine if captives fit definitions of "slave" than to determine how they were integrated into the alien society and what roles they played within it. As discussed below, captives were integrated into their captor's society in a variety of ways. Some became part of a highly stigmatized slave class, while others were adopted or otherwise became full members of the society. Women, often the target of raids, could become wives or concubines, or they might labor as domestic servants or agricultural workers. Scholars who study slavery have acknowledged this range of statuses, yet often disagree about the extent to which captives could ever be truly integrated into an alien society.

For the purposes of this volume, we are interested in adults or subadults who are forcefully removed from their natal society and injected into a new one, bringing with them knowledge of an alien culture. The distinction between adopted captive and slave is not always clear-cut, and the terms "captive" and "slave" are used somewhat interchangeably here. Slaves born into servile status are of less interest in this discussion, except to the extent to which they maintain and transmit alien cultural practices. However, individuals born into slavery may not have been numerous in non-state societies. Some scholars argue that because of the brutal lives they endure, slave populations tend not to reproduce themselves adequately; as a result, slave populations have to be frequently replenished with captives taken during warfare and raids (Klein 1983:73; Lovejoy 2000:7; Meillassoux 1983:51–54). Other scholars disagree (Patterson 1982:133–134), although differences in fertility levels for slaves in state-level versus non-state societies should be examined.

This chapter introduces the issues that are pertinent to understanding captive-taking and its influence on cultural development. It begins with a consideration of the silence that surrounds the practice of captive-taking, the influence of this loss of memory on contemporary accounts of the past, and especially the wisdom of recovering these horrifying practices. Next, the scope and scale of captive-taking are explored; evidence suggests that it was almost ubiquitous in the past and involved large numbers of people.

Captive-taking as a strategy for gaining power is evaluated, as well as the motivations that fuel this strategy, and then captive-taking is considered in a landscape perspective, including the profound effects that captive-taking had on both the captor and donor society. The selection of captives is also examined; captives are generally the most vulnerable members of society, especially women and children. Also considered are the various ways that captives were integrated into captor society and the role of captives in cultural transmission. Finally, several methods for identifying captives in the archaeological record are assessed, with the acknowledgment that this topic requires a great deal more work.

Silence, Memory, and the Invisible Captive

Captive-taking and enslavement were widely practiced and almost universally accepted two centuries ago (Hochschild 2005:2), yet today they have been banished from the collective memory of many groups or spoken of only in whispers. Ann Stahl (this volume) considers slavery as both past practice and present memory, reflecting on the amnesia that surrounds internal African slavery. This amnesia extends beyond Africa. Although variably expressed, capture, enslavement, and trade in human beings were, as Taylor (2005) points out, not only widespread in the past: even today such practices involve millions of people. Few people now are unaware of or deny the Atlantic slave trade, and scholars of Classical times acknowledge the vast numbers of slaves held in ancient Greece and Rome, but only a handful of scholars have recognized or explored practices of capture and enslavement in indigenous societies elsewhere. As Kopytoff (1982) lamented more than twenty-five years ago, in the early twentieth century anthropologists began to ignore or downplay the historical existence of slavery in many parts of the world. But it is not just scholars who have forgotten practices of slavery. Stahl (this volume) shows that African societies have almost erased a once pervasive custom from their active discourse, although it can be seen in practices of divination, dance, and witchcraft. Similarly, Brenda Bowser (pers. comm., 2007) reports that women in contemporary Amazon Basin settlements will speak only in whispers, if at all, about practices of wife-capture that occurred here until the middle of the twentieth century.

Kopytoff (1982) points out that the social evolutionists of the nineteenth century—such as Taylor, Morgan, and even Marx—incorporated slavery into their studies of social development. But for several reasons, slavery was eliminated from the field of anthropology during the early twentieth century. Kopytoff (1982) argues that during this period small-scale societies were studied as if they lacked a history, and societies that anthropologists visited were, of necessity, those in which warfare and captive-taking had largely been eliminated through European intervention. Field anthropologists tended to promote the most positive aspects of "their" societies, increasing the penchant for seeing these groups as harmonious and free of conflict. A decline in Classical education resulted in a focus on plantation slavery that eventually became the model through which slavery was defined.

Kopytoff's analysis also offers another explanation for the loss of memory among societies in which slavery was once practiced.

> Slavery had, for the most part, become a matter of memory, and informants' accounts of it were given in a new social and political setting. Some informants softened the picture to cater to known Western sensibilities. But a more important reason was usually internal: former slaves had become voluntary retainers and quasi relatives as a matter of public myth that benefited all concerned.... and no informant was going to rock that boat. Also, slaves were often addressed by kinship terms (such as "child" or "nephew"). To modern Westerners, the kinship metaphor suggests nurture and closeness; in Africa and elsewhere, it conveys authority and subordination.... (Kopytoff 1982:215)

Memory is a tool that individuals use for negotiating their place in society, and that societies use for creating group cohesion and establishing boundaries and status relative to other groups. The process by which captive-taking and enslavement went from being widely practiced and generally accepted to almost universally reviled is a fascinating one. Brooks's (2002:123–126) study of the Southwest Borderlands shows this process in operation. Although laws against enslaving Native Americans were enacted in Spain, they were twisted to allow the practice in the New World. Captive Native Americans were incorporated into Spanish households using terms of fictive kinship, but still lived lives of servitude and low status. Both Brooks (2002:124–126) and Brugge (1993:97) describe the creation of *genízaros*, a class made up of captives and their descendants. Brugge (1993:97) demonstrates how slavery went underground—how the incorporation of captives, mostly women and children, was disguised. Priests recorded captives as "adopted" by their captors, and those purchased by their ultimate masters from Native American owners were described as "ransomed" or "redeemed." Yet the variety of euphemisms by which they were known (*pieza*, game bagged by hunters; *chusma*, galley slave; *criado*, servant) made their servile status evident. Brooks (pers. comm., 2006) found that even today, rumors of Native American or servile origin plague individuals in Hispanic families in New Mexico and southern Colorado.

For the present volume we are obligated to consider our motives and the wisdom of insisting that memories of enslavement and servitude be revived. Who gains and who loses in such scholarly endeavors? Individuals and the social groups they represent may want to forget that their ancestors were violent aggressors who sold their own children and enslaved and violated women. Others may not want to acknowledge that their ancestors were once slaves, a status whose stigma has been erased in very few parts of the world. My goal in studying captive-taking has been to recognize the contributions and accomplishments of captives in cultural development and transformation. I believe that our explanations of culture change are at least incomplete and potentially incorrect if we ignore the presence and contributions of captives. Does this justify resurrecting the memory of practices that have been comfortably forgotten? We hope that it does.

Ubiquity, Antiquity, and Scale of Captive-Taking

While slavery is a well-studied practice, captive-taking is not (but see Ames 2001; DeBoer 1986; Donald 1997; Santos-Granero 2005). When captive-taking is reported in historic and ethnographic accounts, the emphasis is often on male enemy combatants; women and children who were taken captive at the same time are often mentioned only in passing. Patterson (1982) shows that captive-taking during raids or warfare was the major means of enslavement in kin-based or tribal societies and in the formative stages of the development of large-scale slave-holding societies like ancient Greece and Rome (Patterson 1982:113; see also Goody 1980:24). This section explores the antiquity and geographic scope of the practice of captive-taking. The discussion is brief and not systematic, yet the scale of captive-taking it implies is startling.

Antiquity

Slavery—like its sister, prostitution—is ancient. In a comprehensive study of slavery, Orlando Patterson says the institution "has existed from before the dawn of human history, right down to the twentieth century, in the most primitive of human societies and in the most civilized. There is no region on earth that has not at some time harbored the institution. Probably there is no group of people whose ancestors were not at one time slaves or slaveholders" (1982:vii). Similarly, Taylor says, "Following Marx and Engels, I suggest here that there are good reasons for supposing slavery to have been a major structural feature of the majority of human social formations at least since the advent of farming" (2005:225).

Some scholars have argued that European colonization, with its emphasis on an industrial mode of production and enormous labor needs, increased the prevalence of warfare and introduced or increased the practice of captive-taking and enslavement in otherwise tranquil societies (for warfare, see Ferguson and Whitehead 1999; for the American Southeast, Gallay 2002:29; for the Northwest Coast, see discussion in Donald 1997:35–40; for New Zealand, see Vayda 1961). Other scholars, however, warn against the assumption that slavery was introduced or dramatically increased by European colonists everywhere. For example, Goody states that in Africa "slavery was undoubtedly ancient and not simply a product of the European trade" (1980:28). He notes that Mesopotamian cuneiform tablets, the world's first writing, document the sale

of slaves (Goody 1980:18; see also Baker 2001; Siegel 1947).

In western Europe, Keeley (1996:38) reports evidence for warfare beginning in the Mesolithic and becoming especially prevalent during the Neolithic. Based on the ethnographically and ethnohistorically known practices presented here, enslavement of captives seems likely. Similarly, Kristiansen (1998:116–117) reports that a Late Iron Age settlement in northwest Bohemia contained human remains with evidence of trauma that indicates the use of slave labor in mines. He also suggests that an increase in the numbers of hillforts in England during the middle of the first millennium BC may been a defense against slave raids in the region (Kristiansen 1998:302). Slaves likely served as the major labor force for the hillforts and their associated agricultural lands. Lenski (this volume) explores practices of captive-taking and slavery that characterized relations between early Germanic tribes and their Roman neighbors during the centuries surrounding the beginning of the common era.

In South America, DeBoer (1986) uses both archaeological and ethnographic data to show the antiquity of raiding for women in the Peruvian Amazon (see also DeBoer, this volume). Santos-Granero (2005) uses early travelers' accounts to demonstrate the precontact practice of captive-taking and enslavement among stratified non-Arawak Amerindian groups in tropical South America and the Caribbean, arguing that it differed from practices described in postcontact, largely unstratified groups. Other archaeological studies discussed below (in "Seeing Captives in the Archaeological Record") from the Northwest Coast, the American Southwest, the Northeast and Southeast, Mesoamerica, Africa, Europe, and the Pacific not only confirm the antiquity of captive-taking, but suggest avenues for its archaeological investigation.

Based on extensive evidence of captive-taking and enslavement in prehistory, Taylor's position seems appropriate: "The task of the archaeologist may be not to try to find evidence of slavery in a particular place and time, but to assume access to coerced labour as *a priori*, in the same way as access to drinking water is assumed" (2005:232). As chapters in this volume show, archaeologists are recovering evidence of precontact captive-taking in several parts of the world.

Geographic Scope

Studies of slavery show how widespread capture and enslavement were, but they ignore the large category of captives who were adopted or incorporated into captor society. If these individuals are included, captive-taking had an enormous geographic scope. Orlando Patterson (1982:346) found that of anthropologist George Murdock's sample of 186 world cultures, 66 were coded as slaveholders. These groups range geographically from northeastern Siberia to New Zealand, and from central Uganda in Africa to the Great Plains of North America. In other words, more than a third of the world's societies were slaveholders. Similarly, Goody (1980:25) also used Murdock's *Ethnographic Atlas* to look at the distribution of slavery in societies of different socioeconomic types. He found it was rare (3 percent) in hunting-gathering societies, but 17 percent of societies with incipient agriculture had slavery, as did 34 percent of societies dependant on fishing, 43 percent of those reliant on advanced agriculture, and 73 percent of pastoralists.

Because he was coding for slaveholding, Murdock almost certainly did not include societies in which captives were adopted into families rather than relegated to a separate slave class. Similarly, Nieboer's (1910) "study of slavery among the savage tribes" specifically excludes groups like the Iroquois or the Huron, whose captives were adopted (1910:55–56). With regard to the Ojibway, Nieboer (1910:52–53) says of prisoners of war, "the marriageable women became slaves.... [but] we know that a slave system without male slaves is not slavery proper"; he therefore excluded the Ojibway from his study. DeBoer (this volume) finds the same distinction in Jorgensen's (1980) cross-cultural study of tribes in western North America. Jorgensen shows that two-thirds of the groups he studied raided for captive women, but most of these groups were not recorded as raiding for slaves. DeBoer (this volume) reports Driver's (1966:144) finding that wife-capture was common in North America and may have been universal. These studies suggest that if groups without formalized systems of slavery were included as captive-takers, the proportion of cultures with captives from other societies increases significantly.

Numbers

Slaves made up a substantial portion of the population in many societies. Patterson (1982: App. C) calculated the proportion of slaves in "large-scale slave systems" and found that slaves constituted one-third of the population in places such as ancient Greece. Lenski (this volume) reports that slaves constituted at least 20 percent of the population of Roman Italy. Slaves in ancient Greece and Rome were acquired from the distant corners of the known world and often transported hundreds or even thousands of miles (Lenski, this volume; Thompson 2003:3–4). Patterson (1982:353) found that in many Islamic states slaves constituted 15 to 20 percent of the population. In Korea, slaves reached 50 to 75 percent of the population during some periods, and in ancient China, "hundreds of thousands" of war captives were either enslaved or resettled as colonists somewhere else (Patterson 1982:108–109). Bonnassie reports that in Europe after the fall of Rome, from the fifth to the eighth centuries CE, war was constant, and "it remained fundamentally a manhunt. The Anglo-Saxon conquest was accompanied by the large-scale enslavement of the Celtic population. All those Britons who had neither been massacred nor taken refuge...were reduced to slavery" (1991:32). He also notes that the Catholic Church was the largest slaveholder (Bonnassie 1991:28–29; see also Lenski, this volume). Similarly, for northern Europe, during the period 1000 BC to AD 1000, Woolf (1997:68) argues that female slaves were the most common of four possible social categories (which also included free women and free and unfree men). During the era of the Atlantic slave trade, the proportion of the enslaved population was extraordinarily high (up to 90 percent) for some areas (Patterson 1982: App. C).

In less complex societies, proportions of slaves could also be significant. Among the chiefdom-like polities of the coastal Philippines, imported foreigners comprised up to 50 percent of the population of some groups (Junker, this volume). In the Northwest Coast of North America, Donald (1997) found that slaves in tribal societies such as the Tlingit and the Makah constituted about 15 percent of the population and were sometimes transported or traded over distances of more than a thousand miles; for the Greater Lower Columbia River portion of this region, Ames (this volume) suggests slaves comprised 20 to 25 percent of the population. Donald (1997) compared captive-taking and enslavement on the Northwest Coast with data from the Northeast, where war captives that were not killed were adopted in order to bolster the population. The numbers of such "adoptees" was large. For example, two-thirds of the seventeenth-century Oneida were actually of Huron or Algonquian origin (Donald 1997:262; Trigger 1976:826). Although scholars disagree about the status of these captives as slaves or family members (Starna and Watkins 1991), the mingling of individuals from different cultures is clear.

Captive-Taking and Power

Although doubts about the importance and effectiveness of slaves in economic production have characterized the slavery literature in some parts of the world, it is increasingly clear that captive-taking is frequently a strategy for gaining power. Captives are subordinate, powerless individuals who instantly increase the status and wealth of their captors. They are movable property and thus a profitable trade item. In fact, Patterson (1982:113) suggests that exchange of slaves was one of the earliest forms of trade. Carneiro (1991:179) even argues that the switch from killing war captives to maintaining them as slaves is a major evolutionary step in the development of complex societies (much like the classical social evolutionists, such as Tylor and Morgan; see Kopytoff 1982:209). Robertshaw and Duncan (this volume) provide examples of this transition, describing how small-scale societies became politically complex as a result of slaving (see also Robertshaw 1999).

Some scholars have argued that captives may have been *symbols* of wealth and power, but they were generally not a means of surplus production or a source of economic power for their masters. Others scholars have rebutted with evidence that captives could be highly profitable. Watson (1980:14) calls slavery in China "luxury slavery" because slaves consumed more than they produced. These slaves (mostly girls) were sold as children by their impoverished parents to the rich, and Watson (1980:14) argues that they functioned primarily as status symbols for their owners. A similar argument has been made for captives in several parts of North America. For example, among the tribes of the Northwest Coast, captives were held primarily by titleholders, and traditional views saw them as status symbols of little economic importance. This argument has been vigorously rebutted by Donald (1997), who has shown that captives' labor was valuable and that they could produce a significant surplus for their owners (see also Ames, this volume). Northwest Coast captives also were sold for profit and were an important trade item. Some scholars have argued that captives in the North American Southeast were of no economic importance (see Perdue 1979:12 for the Cherokee), but others contend that they were valuable in economic production (Anderson 1994:101).

There appear to be two entwined avenues for the creation of power that are key to producing contexts in which captive-taking is practiced. First are situations where power is directly related to the numbers of followers a leader can amass. In these situations, captives can rapidly increase group size. This strategy was implemented especially in societies where population was low or geographically dispersed. Second, captive-taking satisfies a need for labor, and leaders acquire captives as tools for increasing production and output of surplus goods that will bring them wealth and power. This strategy is perhaps most familiar since it formed the basis of the Atlantic slave trade.

These strategies for gaining power are not exclusive, and both create contexts for captive-taking depending on demographic, political, social, and environmental conditions. The chapters in this volume and other studies show how these factors interact. In many African societies where population was low and land abundant, power was derived through control over people rather than acquisition of territory (Watson 1980:11; see also Robertshaw and Duncan, this volume). Captives from warfare and raiding, especially women, could be incorporated into society as wives or concubines, increasing the population and prestige of the group, although slaves were also critical sources of labor, especially for agriculture. Robertshaw and Duncan (this volume) suggest that the low productivity of hoe agriculture in Africa necessitated huge numbers of slaves.

Examining the chiefdom-like polities of the coastal Philippines in the twelfth through sixteenth centuries, Junker (this volume) shows that captive-taking was a result of demographic and environmental conditions, including low population levels and a fragmented geography, which hampered efforts to centralize political power. Power was based on ties of personal loyalty, command of labor, and the circulation of prestige goods—and captive-taking, primarily of women, was a way of increasing a chief's or ambitious individual's number of dependents and labor pool. This strategy for gaining power and prestige became embedded in cultural values, with warriors who took many captives becoming enshrined in oral history. (Such warrior cults are also found in other parts of the world; see, for example, Trigger 1969:52 and Sioui 1999:169–174 for the American Northeast.) Similarly, Habicht-Mauche's study (this volume) of Plains-Pueblo relationships shows the value of Pueblo women to Plains men, who used them to increase the production of buffalo hides. Pueblo captives (or marriage partners?) increased group size, supplied necessary labor for hide production, and added to the wealth and status of their Plains captors/husbands. Brooks found that in the Southwest Borderlands, the control of captured women and children ensured prestige as well as labor for both Native American and Spanish men (Brooks 2002:34). Finally, Lenski (this volume) shows that Roman slaves imported into ancient Germanic societies caused differentiation of labor and expansion of production among these groups.

Captive-Taking
in a Landscape Perspective

Captive-taking was carried out at a large geographic scale involving societies in an asymmetrical web of predators, victims, and long-distance trading partners. Larger, more complex societies commonly raided smaller acephalous societies for captives, but this pattern was not always so simple, and roles could be quickly reversed (Goody 1980; see also the chapters in this volume by Junker, Robertshaw and Duncan, and Stahl).

Sociopolitical level, population size and distribution, local geography, and other factors define the predatory landscape, including boundary zones between captive-takers and donor societies, and places/times where captive-takers were actively expanding the predatory zone. In many parts of the world, captive-taking even had a season, occurring at times when travel was easy and other activities did not compete with preparations for raids, warfare, or kidnapping expeditions (for example, see Morey 1975 for South America, and Robertshaw and Duncan, this volume, for Africa).

Two aspects of the geography of captive-taking should be considered. First, the taking of captives—and the raiding and warfare of which it was a part—altered cultural landscapes by changing settlement patterns, remaking ethnic affiliations, stimulating sociopolitical development, and reworking social relationships. Second, predator societies and the groups they raided formed two sides of an asymmetrical but often dynamic relationship. Although full of negative connotations, the relationship between captors and victim societies could become a system of mutual interdependence. Like marriage arrangements and trade, captive-taking could function to maintain social boundaries, permit economic interactions, and establish kin relationships between groups that could be exploited in times of need (Brooks 2002). Whether negative or positive, captive-taking resulted in sweeping transformations of cultural landscapes, as illustrated by chapters in this volume and other studies.

In his study of Africa, Goody (1980:28–30) shows that slavery was especially common where state-level societies were bordered by acephalous tribes that could be conveniently raided for captives, but that acephalous societies also were slaveholders (Braimah and Goody 1967:11, cited in Goody 1980:27; Goody 1980:24–27). Stahl (this volume) cites recent studies showing that acephalous African societies not only held slaves but also raided for slaves. Border areas between societies were vulnerable to raids by predatory societies and could expand or contract through time and with changes in social or political relationships. Robertshaw and Duncan (this volume) discuss the "moving frontier of slavery" that resulted from the expansion of Islamic culture.

Koranic teaching dictated that individuals within territories conquered by Muslims could not be enslaved, so Muslims raided for slaves beyond their furthest territorial boundary. Robertshaw and Duncan also catalog the impacts of slave trade on the African landscape, including migration of vulnerable societies to inaccessible areas and construction of fortifications. Stahl (this volume) notes that the slave trade caused people to alter their travel patterns to avoid kidnapping and enslavement, which affected the scale of social interactions. Robertshaw and Duncan (this volume) discuss an increase in political complexity and centralization in response to the threat of slavers. For example, they describe the transformation of several small-scale African societies into more complex polities as a reaction to, and eventual participation in, the slave trade. They also note the creation, loss, or homogenization of ethnicities as groups resist or join in the profitable slave trade.

Changes in settlement patterns, depopulation of regions, mixing and elimination of ethnic groups, the restructuring of group boundaries, and changes in sociopolitical development are also evident in the North American Southeast during the early historic period, when warfare and the slave trade were widespread (Anderson 1994; Callender 1978; Gallay 2002; Hudson 1976; Usner 1992). Gallay (2002) found that as a result of wars engendered by the slave trade, "huge areas became depopulated, thousands of Indians died, and thousands more were forcibly relocated to new areas in the South or exported from the region" (Gallay 2002:6). Groups banded together in formations such as the Creek Confederacy that functioned for defense but also aggression, and social identities were refashioned for the same purpose. Gallay notes that ethnic identity for Native people in the Southeast, as in many other parts of the world, was only one source of identity that could be called on by individuals during intergroup interactions. Settlement patterns resulting from the historic slave trade also appear in the archaeological record, providing evidence that prehistoric raiding and trading of captives may have been pervasive. Anderson (1994: 133) reports archaeological evidence that "large areas of the Southeast underwent depopulation and abandonment at one time or another over

the course of the Mississippian [the period from AD 900 to 1600]." The similarity between the historic and prehistoric land use patterns suggests that warfare and captive-taking may have had significant effects on the cultural landscape of the Southeast long before Europeans arrived.

The geographic scope of slave-raiding can be significantly increased with the use of boats, as Junker's (this volume) study of the historic-period Philippines shows. Here maritime slave-raiding transported captives, mostly women, great distances across Southeast Asia. The cultural landscape was peopled not only by polities that needed slave labor, but also by upland foragers or swidden agriculturalists, ethnically distinct sea-faring populations who could be hired to conduct slave raids, and aggrandizing individuals who willingly took on the costs of raiding expeditions independent of local political leaders. Raids were undertaken against competing maritime polities or upland groups, and the booty included both slaves and prestige goods. Similarly, Santos-Granero (2005:46–47) describes the long-distance maritime raids undertaken by Kalinago warriors of the Lesser Antilles against groups in the Greater Antilles and the Guiana coast that netted numerous women and children captives as well as a few adult men.

Although captive-taking has caused violent disruptions across wide geographic areas, it has also resulted in structured interactions that became part of social negotiations among groups. Brooks (2002; see also Brooks, this volume) has described the complex web of relationships in the American Southwest Borderlands during the historic era among indigenous people and the Spaniards in which raiding for and trading of slaves, primarily women and children, figured prominently. Here, captive-taking structured and transformed interactions among the many groups that inhabited this region. The borderlands were social as well as geographic, and Brooks explains how ethnic boundaries were maintained or modified as captives moved across them. Strategies differed, and in some groups the status of captives as outsiders clarified and defined group social boundaries (see Brooks's [2002:246–247] discussion of the Navajo; also Perdue 1979:17 for this same effect of captives on the Cherokee). Other groups adopted captives to reverse steep population declines (Brooks 2002:364).

Brooks (2002) shows how raiding and captive-taking in the Southwest Borderlands were built on traditional customs of intercultural marriage and adoption in both indigenous and Spanish cultures, both of which view control over women and children as a source of power and status. DeBoer (this volume) also emphasizes the links between marriage patterns and captive-taking. Using ethnographic data on wife-capture from both North and South America, DeBoer shows that captive women came from the perimeter of the area in which men would normally take wives, essentially extending this catchment zone. He notes that this pattern produces a seamless flow of human bodies over large areas, mixing genetic and cultural information.

Captive-Taking as a Selective Process

Warfare and pillaging might seem to sweep up everyone in their path, but captive-taking and enslavement are actually selective processes. Captives most often come from the lowest strata of society as defined by gender, age, and social standing. Situations that create vulnerable groups of individuals include the juxtaposition of powerful states and weaker non-state societies, economic downturns, processes by which families or individuals become disenfranchised, and social or religious dictates concerning categories of individuals who might be captured and enslaved (Goody 1980:24; Patterson 1982:105–171; Robertshaw and Duncan, this volume; see also Arkush and Allen 2006; Kelly 2000; Keeley 1996:86–87). Stahl (this volume) also urges us to look beyond the warfare, raiding, and kidnapping to the more subtle ritual and juridical proceedings that functioned to produce slaves (see also Lovejoy 2000:3–4).

Women and children were everywhere the most common victims of capture and enslavement. In fact, DeBoer (this volume) likens the process of captive selection to the treatment of livestock, with the unruly adult males being killed and the reproductive-aged females retained. Young males who can be trained as warriors or used to replace members lost to war are also selected (Brooks 2002:187; DeBoer, this volume). Overlapping categories of vulnerable individuals also include orphans or those with weak kin ties, outcasts, criminals, and the poor. Although women and children are generally highly valued captives, representing a significant gain to their captors and a loss to their natal society, in other situations both captor and donor societies benefit in the transaction (see Brooks 2002). For example, donor societies might use the slave trade as a means of sloughing off members (at a profit) during trying economic times or disposing of unproductive members to larger societies more able to absorb them.

Such patterns in the selection and acquisition of captives are widely evident. For example, in the Northwest Coast, Donald (1997) found that because women and children were easy to capture and transport, they were much more likely to become slaves; when raids occurred, initial efforts were made to kill the men or drive them away. Because they were the most vulnerable and least protected members of society, slaves were often captured more than once and could be moved from group to group with each new raid (see also Lenski, this volume, for the same pattern of recapture in ancient Germanic societies). Some individuals on the Northwest Coast became slaves as the result of gambling, inability to pay off a debt, or the threat of starvation (see also MacLeod 1925; Lenski [this volume] also finds debt slaves in ancient Germanic societies). In some cases, debt slaves were treated differently than slaves acquired in war, and these individuals had the hope of eventually buying themselves out of slavery. Sometimes people were enslaved as punishment for a crime (Donald 1997:119). There are also reports of men selling their wives into slavery in order to humiliate their in-laws (Donald 1997:120), although these cases were apparently rare.

In the Northeast, endemic warfare among many tribes produced a vast number of captives (see Peregrine, this volume), and Heidenreich (1978:386) suggests that it was primarily captive women and children who were given formal adoption into Huron families. Similarly, among the Illinois, Callender (1978:676) reports that male captives were usually burned to death, whereas the women and children were distributed among the households that had lost members to warfare. Some of these women and children were adopted, but others were kept as slaves.

In the Southwest, historic accounts show that when indigenous people fell on hard times, they might sell themselves into slavery. Udall (1969: 43) reports that when the Hopi of northeastern Arizona faced starvation, some walked more than 200 miles east to the Spanish villages along the Rio Grande in New Mexico to sell themselves into slavery or indentured servitude. Although some of the migrants returned, others never did. An anonymous report by a nineteenth-century Indian agent provides a first-hand account of such an event, describing how when supplies dwindled, men stayed at Hopi while women and children made the long journey east to become slaves to the Spanish (Anonymous, n.d.).

Among the Kalinago of the Caribbean, gender and age determined the fate of captives (Santos-Granero 2005:47). Adult male captives were executed, but subadult males were raised as house servants before eventually being killed and eaten. Young women became either concubines of their master or maidservants to their master's wife.

In Africa, kingdoms waged war against small-scale societies, extracting and enslaving many captives (Robertshaw and Duncan, this volume). Slaves in Africa could also be acquired by other means, as Kopytoff and Miers (1977:12–14) explain. Orphans were sometimes sold, children and adults were bartered for grain in times of famine, outcasts and criminals might voluntarily submit to slavery in exchange for a fresh start in a new area, and debt hostages or pawns might not be retrieved, forcing them to endure a lifetime of slavery. The Batomba of West Africa believed that an infant whose first teeth appeared in the upper jaw would bring disaster (Baldus 1977:439–440). Abandoned by their parents, these children were taken in and raised by the Fulbe, functioning as slaves.

As Stahl (this volume) points out, Africa ritual and juridical proceedings, especially witchcraft accusations, were a common way in which people became enslaved. Witchcraft accusations, in particular, were used to justify trafficking in humans (see also Lovejoy 2000:4 for judicial proceedings resulting in enslavement). Rather than being an ancient phenomenon, witchcraft accusations in Africa may be more recent, intro-duced as part of the experience of the slave trade (Stahl, this volume).

Integration into Captor Society

The extent and nature of the influence that captives had on the societies into which they were introduced depended in part on how they were integrated. As Patterson notes, "Although the slave might be socially dead, he remained none-theless an element of society. So the problem arose: how was he to be incorporated?" (1982:45; see also Kopytoff and Miers 1977:15). The ways in which integration took place ranged from full adoption and assumption of the captor's culture, to segregation into a special and highly exploited slave class with limited or no individual rights (Kopytoff and Miers 1977:29–32; Meillassoux 1991:23–35; Patterson 1982:38–65; see also Robertson and Klein 1983b:5–8). This section explores first some of the parameters that surround the incorporation of captives into captor society, and then some of the reasons that have been proposed for different kinds of integration.

Patterson (1982) describes slavery as "social death" in which captives are stripped of all previous identity and remade as subordinates in their captors' society. Peregrine's study (this volume) of the indigenous groups of the Western Great Lakes region of North America provides a detailed description of the torture and dehumanizing practices by which captives were separated from their prior social persona. Although Peregrine believes that Western Great Lakes captives became full members of captor society, such complete acceptance is unusual. In many societies the next step is the reintroduction of captives as non-persons with no claim to the benefits of membership in the social group, completely at the will and whim of their master. Following Meillassoux, Patterson says:

The slave is violently uprooted from his milieu. He is desocialized and depersonalized. This process of social negation constitutes the first, essentially external, phase of enslavement. The next phase involves the introduction of the slave into the community of his master, but it involves the paradox of introducing him as a nonbeing. This explains the importance of law, custom, and ideology in the representation of the slave relation. (Patterson 1982:38)

Meillassoux (1991:138–140) shows that in kin-based societies slaves were not only aliens from society, but actually "anti-kin" who were excluded from any claim on inheritance, succession, ancestors, or any other benefits of kinship. The benefit to the master was that slaves could be trusted in ways that kin could not, which in some cases opened an avenue for advancement for these non-persons. Captive women were especially valued in many parts of the world because men could take them as wives without payment of bride-price (see below).

As shown through a comparison of Peregrine's study (this volume) and patterns reported by Patterson (1982) and Meillassoux (1991), there is a wide range of possibilities for how captives become incorporated into captor societies. Scholars are not in agreement about factors conditioning these different modes or even how they operated. Some scholars studying African slavery emphasize the eventual incorporation of alien captives into kinship systems (Kopytoff and Miers 1977), and others their essential kinless-ness (Lovejoy 2000:2–3; Meillassoux 1991). Watson (1980) presents a compromise view, arguing for the existence of two modes of slavery: "closed" and "open." In a closed system, which was common in Asia, slaves are never under any circumstances admitted to the kinship system. In an open system, common in Africa, slaves could eventually be absorbed as members of society. Watson (1980:11–12, following Goody 1971:32) believes that the difference between these two systems lies in sources of wealth. In Asia, land was the primary source of wealth, and there was no incentive to invite aliens into kinship systems that would give them access to land. In Africa, land was plentiful, and wealth was derived through control over people. Here captives acquired during warfare and raiding, especially women, could be incorporated into society as wives or concubines, increasing the population and prestige of the group. (See Nieboer's [1910] argument that slavery exists only in societies where capital is unnecessary for gaining subsistence, as well as MacLeod's [1929] critique of this idea; see Donald's [1997:41–44] review of Nieboer's and MacLeod's proposals; see

also Kopytoff and Miers's [1977:66–67] discussion of the development of slavery.)

Watson's dichotomy, perhaps most useful for state-level societies, does not work for all groups that practiced slavery. In comparing the ways in which captives were incorporated in the Northwest Coast with those in the Northeastern and Southeastern parts of North America, Donald (1997:255–271) found significant differences. In the Northwest Coast, captives became slaves unless they were ransomed, and the much despised slave status was passed on to their children. Among the Iroquoian societies of the Northeast, captives not killed were adopted into Iroquoian society (see also Peregrine, this volume). Constant warfare caused enormous drops in population, and Iroquoian groups adopted captives to increase their numbers. As noted above, historic accounts suggest that captives sometimes comprised as much as two-thirds of the population of some tribes (Donald 1997:262; Starna and Watkins 1991:38; Fenton 1978:315; see also Trigger 1969, 1976). Donald (1997:260–268) reviews different interpretations of the status of Iroquoian adoptees. Early explorers' accounts, and those of the many scholars who use these accounts, report that captives who were adopted by the Iroquois became true members of the family with all rights and privileges of kinship. Other scholars (Starna and Watkins 1991) argue that adoptees retained an outsider status and could properly be called slaves. Donald (1997:271) finds the evidence equivocal.

Donald (1997:268–270) cites Hudson (1976), who describes the treatment of captives in the Southeast as different for men and women. Men were slaves—valued mostly as items of prestige, forced to do menial tasks, and often sold to another group or put to death. Women and children, in contrast, were frequently adopted, and Hudson says that they "lived free and relatively normal lives" (Hudson 1976:254–255). A similar view of Southeastern slavery is provided by Perdue (1979), who studied the practice among the Cherokee. Although her focus was primarily on the historic period, Perdue (1979:6), like Hudson (1976), reports that the Cherokee generally did not kill women and children. Captives who were not killed faced two fates: either they were adopted into families and the kinship system to replace members of the group who had died, or they remained outside the kinship system. The latter were slaves, called *atsi nahsa'i,* or people with no rights, and they were under the absolute control of their masters. Neither Perdue (1979) nor Hudson (1976) see slaves as economically important to Southeastern groups, but this point (discussed below) may not be settled, as Donald (1997) has shown for the Northwest Coast.

Based on Donald's (1997) three examples, the ways in which captives are incorporated, at least in non-state societies, does not seem to be closely tied to the subsistence base or social system of the captors (see also Patterson 1982:181, who argues that the mode of subsistence has no effect on how slaves are treated; see also Siegel 1945). The three cases represent different points on the continuum of incorporation for captives, although the subsistence and social systems were not remarkably different. For each group (Northwest Coast, Northeast, and Southeast), a significant portion of subsistence was based on hunting and gathering, although horticulture was practiced by the Northeastern and Southeastern groups. The Southeast groups had stratified chiefdoms, while the Northeast and Northwest Coast groups were less highly stratified. Raiding or warfare among all three groups was often undertaken to obtain captives, and warfare was endemic in each group. Despite these similarities, adoption was not practiced in the Northwest Coast at all, was common in the Northeast, and seems to have been used primarily with women in the Southeast. The Southeast and Northwest Coast groups both had individuals who functioned as slaves, but a similar status of "adoptees" was not as clear as for the Northeast. Of the three, only the Northwest Coast groups excluded women from adoption, and only the Northeastern tribes clearly allowed adoption of men.

Gender and age are important factors in determining how captives are incorporated into society. As demonstrated by the three cases presented by Donald (1997)—as well as examples in South America, Africa, and elsewhere—women and children are far more likely to become integrated into a captor society through marriage or adoption than adult males. Captive women could become wives or concubines at no cost in bride-wealth or other payment (for example, see

Robertshaw and Duncan, this volume). Alien women had no kin and therefore no divided loyalty (Kopytoff and Miers 1977:31). In matrilineal societies, men had more direct control over the children of their captive wives, whereas the children of their free wives belonged to the mother's matrilineage, and the children of their sisters were of uncertain loyalty. Children seem to have been prized captives because they could be easily acculturated (Kopytoff and Miers 1977:21, 53). Only in places like the Northwest Coast, where slavery was hereditary and highly stigmatized, were aliens *never* admitted into the society of their captors.

Although captive women, children, and sometimes men might be adopted or married into the society of their captors, the chapters in this volume provide compelling evidence that their position was often at the lowest and most precarious rung of the social ladder. Santos-Granero (2005) describes the rituals and practices in tropical South America and the Caribbean by which captives, mostly women, were physically marked as subordinate individuals. Bowser (this volume) describes how captive women in Amazonia might marry their captor but later be sacrificed or die of neglect. Those that survived were subordinate individuals. Habicht-Mauche (this volume) suggests that on the American Plains, captive Pueblo women may have become drudge wives, secondary to senior local women. Brooks (this volume) repudiates the frequent ethnographic and historic accounts of captive women who "refuse to leave their captors," showing that their captive status (sometimes physically marked with tattoos or mutilation and emphasized by the children they had with captor husbands; see also Santos-Granero 2005) severely limited their options for returning home. At the same time, their liminal status and association with powerful captor men may have offered opportunities for attaining power and social advancement that they might not otherwise have had (see also Brooks 2002; DeBoer, this volume; Socolow 1992).

The Roles of Captives in Cultural Transmission

Captives were active agents of culture change. Although they occupied low-status positions, they brought with them new ideas about religion, health care, agricultural production, hunting, plant gathering, craft production, food preparation techniques, and much more. How and under what circumstances these ideas were adopted by the society of their captors should be the subject of much future research, and the chapters in this volume begin that process. In this chapter, patterns of cultural transmission in the ethnographic, historical, and archaeological literature are discussed, including some identified by contributors to this volume. This section outlines the many activities that captives likely engaged in, showing that there are few arenas of active endeavor that did not involve captives. The potential for involvement of captives in cultural innovation is then examined, as well as the limitations imposed by the different ways they were incorporated into captor society. The place of captives as liminal individuals with a special role as cultural intermediaries or curers also is explored. Finally, the ways captives affected social boundaries within and between societies is discussed. It is evident that in some cases captives strengthened social boundaries through active agency or their mere presence.

Activities of Captives

Captives could be found laboring in almost every active niche of society. For example, Kopytoff and Miers report that African slaves provided "labor to till the fields, retainers in the compound, soldiers for warfare, paddlers for trading canoes and war canoes, trading agents, servants and officials at court, and even victims for human sacrifice" (1977:14). Captives were involved in food production, household chores, and craft production, and also provided service as retainers, soldiers, and mediators between their captors and other groups (including their natal group). Captives in non-state societies typically undertook the same tasks as ordinary members, although they might do the more difficult or unpleasant of those tasks and work longer and harder at them.

Food production seems to have been a primary occupation of captives in many parts of the world. Ethnographic studies from Africa and North America report that captives/slaves toiled in agricultural fields, fished, hunted, gathered plant foods, and prepared meals (Ames 2001:4; Donald 1997:134–136; Hudson 1976:253, 264; Kopytoff and Miers 1977:14; MacLeod 1928:641; Robertson and Klein 1983b:10–11; Uchendu 1977). Captives in both areas also performed daily household tasks such as gathering wood and water, freeing their masters from these burdensome duties (Donald 1997:124; MacLeod 1925:378; Robertson and Klein 1983:11; Starna and Watkins 1991:51). Gender-specific tasks would sometimes be assigned to captives regardless of gender, an added humiliation (Ames 2001:4; Donald 1997:134–136; Hudson 1976:253; Meillassoux 1991:100–101; Robertson and Klein 1983b:10).

The role of captive labor in craft production is a particular focus of this volume because these material goods are often visible in the archaeological record. Patterson (1982:255) points out that at least for state-level societies, including ancient Greece, craftwork was considered dull and menial, and was relegated to the lowest strata of society whenever possible, often slaves. This was also true of slaves in early colonial North America, including some who arrived from Africa as skilled craftspeople and others who were trained in craft production upon their arrival (Usner 1992:54–56). Captives also were involved in craft production in the Northwest Coast region, sometimes even of ceremonial objects. They produced everything from cloth and baskets to canoes and houses (Curtis 1913:74, cited in Donald 1997:38, 75, 126–128, 130–136, App. 1; MacLeod 1928:640). Similar patterns of captive-produced crafts and even tributary goods are evident in the Southeast (Anderson 1994:101; Hudson 1976:264–267; Perdue 1979:15) and Africa (Harms 1983:100; Keim 1983:145; Klein 1983:85). In this volume, chapters by Junker and Habicht-Mauche provide examples of the key role of captives in the production of craft goods that their masters used as sources of wealth and power.

Captives often served as retainers, servants, porters, and especially soldiers. In Africa and North America, captives were owned primarily by the wealthy, and large numbers of captives were obvious markers of the master's power and prestige, as well as convenient labor for accomplishing necessary tasks and attending to their master's or mistress's every need (Ames 2001:3; Donald 1997:127, 131; Dunbar 1977:169, 171; MacLeod 1928:641; MacCormack [Hoffer] 1974:181, cited in Robertson and Klein 1983b:15; Perdue

1979:3, 15; Ross 1966:92, cited in Donald 1997: 132; Starna and Watkins 1991:51; see also Santos-Granero 2005 for South America). Captives were also pressed into service as warriors, making up large portions of armies and raiding parties, sometimes even going to war against the society into which they had been born (Brooks 2002: 127; Donald 1997:83, 89, 127; Meillassoux 1971:53; Nwachukwu-Ogedengbe 1977:142; Trigger 1969: 49; Uchendu 1977:130–131).

Potential for Cultural Transmission

Scholars who study slavery have recognized that captives had the potential to play a strong role in culture change (e.g., Keim 1983:150). Women may have been especially influential in transmitting culture because they had roles in rearing their own and often their captor's children (Klein 1983:85; Patterson 1982:88). The different ways in which captives were integrated into captor society very likely affected both their ability to introduce new ideas and practices, and the acceptance of those ideas and practices by captor society. Evidence that captives sometimes identified strongly with the society of their captors (DeBoer, this volume) likely also had an effect on cultural transmission.

Captives were stripped of their natal identity as they were remade as members of their captor's society (Patterson 1982; Peregrine, this volume; Santos-Granero 2005). They were often from a much hated alien society, and it is likely that they were forced to abandon any practices that evoked the alien group (distinctive pottery forms or designs, particular styles of clothing or body decoration, unique foods) and embrace those of their captor. In societies where captives became part of a subordinate slave class, any natal practices that they might retain would likely be considered inferior or inappropriate. Furthermore, captives may have chosen to shun natal practices in order to improve their position in their new society. As DeBoer (this volume) points out, captives often appear eager to blend in to the society of their captors, and they sometimes become demonstrative advocates for the captor's cultural practices, actually helping to fix the social boundaries they have just crossed (see also DeBoer 1990). We should be alert, however, to hidden acts of resistance in the material goods produced by captives, including symbolic references to their place of origin. For example, slaves in the American South stitched symbolically coded messages into quilts to guide their compatriots along the Underground Railroad to freedom (Tobin and Dobard 1999). Some of the quilt codes were derived from African symbol systems.

The extent to which captives promote their captors' cultural practices as a strategy of self-preservation rather than a genuine approval of the new society may vary. Socolow (1992:88–89) discusses a Spanish woman in South America who was captured by Indians as a child, but was then taught the Spanish language by other captive women, an obvious effort to maintain natal identity despite their captivity. Socolow's example highlights the fact that if large numbers of captives from the same or similar cultural traditions were held together, they may have been better able to maintain some natal traditions and practices (as has been found among slaves of African origin in the American South [e.g., Ferguson 1992], even though American slaves came from a variety African cultures).

Captives bring a wide variety of novel and alien practices with them as they enter captor society. It is likely that practices that did not actively evoke their natal group (technological sequences of vessel forming or house building, for example, or food preparation techniques) might be introduced either consciously or unconsciously and would not elicit active suppression from their captors. For example, because women generally function as horticulturalists, scholars should explore the extent to which captive women may have introduced new plant species, propagation techniques, or soil preparation methods. As discussed below, people are especially receptive to novel curing methods or new ideologies. In part because they are aliens, captives may be able to introduce new medicines, treatment regimes, and novel religious practices more readily than other cultural habits (see DeBoer, this volume; Lenski, this volume).

In societies where captives were adopted or become wives or concubines, opportunities for introducing cultural innovation were likely greater, although as aliens, captives might still be subject to suspicion and sanctions. For example, Junker (this volume) shows that the large numbers of women captured in the Philippines during maritime raids were rapidly integrated into their captors' society, most often as wives but also as laborers. Many became producers of earthenware pottery and textiles, using natal design styles for the goods they produced for their masters. In a fascinating twist on our usual assumptions concerning stylistic innovation, Junker shows that new design styles were likely developed in the small-scale societies that were subject to raids by the larger polities. In other words, the direction of design innovation was from the smaller groups to larger centers, and the agents of change were captive women.

Similarly, Habicht-Mauche's study (this volume) of the bison hunters of the Southern Plains of North America shows the value of nonlocal Pueblo women in producing bison hides used by Plains men as status items in ceremonial exchange. Although the focus of these bison-hunting societies was hide production, Habicht-Mauche found that captive Pueblo women also brought Pueblo pottery-making practices with them. Although the bulk of their labor may have been focused on hide production, where one suspects that deviation from established patterns of production would have been frowned upon or suppressed, their presence is most apparent in other crafts that may not have been as strong a focus of cultural expression or repression.

Captives as Cultural
Intermediaries and Curers

Captives, whether stolen as children or adults, lived between two cultures: that of their birth and that of their captors. Because of this liminal position, and because they were generally multilingual, captives often served their masters as cultural intermediaries during interactions with other groups, sometimes even maintaining regular communication with their natal groups, whether for their own or their captors' benefit (e.g., Socolow 1992:88). Some captives attained considerable power in such roles, and their abilities as mediators may have increased their influence within the society of their captors (e.g., Perdue 1979:7). In North America, one of the most famous cultural intermediaries was Sacagawea, a Shoshone girl who had been captured at age ten by the Hidatsa and served as a media-

tor and guide for the Lewis and Clark Expedition (see Brooks 1998). Similarly, the captive Aztec Malantzin became the consort of Cortes and served as an interpreter for his invasion of Mesoamerica (Brooks 1998). Brooks (2002:75–76, 101–102) provides a number of historical accounts of captives in the Southwest, both men and women, also playing roles as intermediaries.

DeBoer (this volume) shows that partly because captives were aliens, they were sometimes seen as possessing powerful medicinal or sexual powers (also Socolow 1992:87), and he provides examples of the spread of curing ceremonies introduced by captives in both North and South America. Meillassoux (1991:139) notes that slaves in some African societies could become dangerous miracle workers because they were able to use powerful potions or talismans without fear that their descendants would be cursed. In effect, they had no descendants: they were either forbidden to have children, or the children they had were permitted no kin relationship with them.

More formal religious practices were also spread by captives. Lenski (this volume) shows that captives were involved in the introduction of Christianity to the Germanic tribes during the early centuries of the current era. In a study of the African kingdom of Dahomey, Bay (1983:347) found that female captives introduced Islam to portions of the Dahomey royal family, and that captive royal wives also introduced other alien or novel religious practices.

Captives and Social Boundaries

Captives are aliens, and as such they may have strengthened or defined social boundaries both within captor society and between societies. The presence of aliens brought cultural differences between groups into sharp relief, and captives were often a catalyst for defining ethnic boundaries. For example, with regard to Cherokee slaves, called *atsi nahsa'i*, Perdue says:

> The *atsi nahsa'i* also functioned as deviants in Cherokee society. Deviance is a logical and necessary element in all societies because it confirms common values and group identity. The members of a society frequently establish their identity not by proclaiming what they are, or the norm, but by carefully defining what they are not, or deviance. (Perdue 1979:17)

Brooks (2002:246–247) describes how captives in nineteenth-century Navajo society, simply by their presence as outsiders, helped to cement the tribe's social solidarity. Captives were only partially assimilated or adopted, and were excluded from ritual practices; some rituals actively defended Navajos against aliens such as the captives among them.

Captives sometimes became active promoters of captor culture, using their advocacy to strengthen their own social position and in the process more clearly defining group boundaries. DeBoer (this volume, 1990) describes captive women among the Shipibo-Conibo who were more assiduous replicators of their captors' pottery designs than the Shipibo-Conibo women themselves. He also describes a captive man who became a "zealous missionary" for the culture of his Shipibo captors even after he returned to his natal group. This man's advocacy almost certainly drew the cultural boundaries between aggressor and captor societies more clearly.

Seeing Captives
in the Archaeological Record

To understand the important role that captives played in past social, political, and technological development, we must be able to identify them in the archaeological record. This is difficult, however, especially for non-state societies, because captives were usually integrated into their masters' households and undertook the same types of activities as other household members (albeit more of the difficult or unpleasant tasks). As a result, there are few categories of material culture that can be exclusively associated with captives. As both Martin (this volume) and Alt (this volume) show, however, human remains provide some of the best evidence for the presence of captives. Other lines of evidence for capture and enslavement include productive capacity (see Ames, this volume), iconography (see Alt, this volume), oral history, and linguistics. Captives were so frequently the product of wars and raiding that indicators of warfare should alert archaeologists to the possibility of captives. The presence of nonlocal artifacts or those with nonlocal designs, forms, or production methods, in conjunction with other evidence, also can be used to infer the presence of captives (Junker, this volume;

Habicht-Mauche 2000, this volume; Robertshaw and Duncan, this volume; Trigger 1976).

Human remains can be used to identify captive populations through evidence of physical differences or differences in bone chemistry or DNA, signs of physical abuse, differences in treatment of the dead, or skewed sex ratios (Martin, this volume; see also Ames 2001, this volume; Donald 1997:202–205; Kohler and Turner 2006; Lowell 2007). Donald (1997:202) suggests that the different physical types represented by groups in the Northwest Coast might be evidence of slavery. Slaves were not permitted to flatten the heads of their children (Donald 1997:78), but this trait would not distinguish a slave taken in adulthood. However, the Conibo of South America practiced head elongation and directed raids at people who did not, potentially distinguishing captives from captors. Similarly, DeBoer (this volume) cites an example of burials found among the Seneca of the Northeast that had heads flattened in the manner of the Cherokee of the Southeast, suggesting the presence of captives brought from a great distance. Alt (this volume) describes burials at Mississippian sites that have isotopic signatures and dental characteristics that suggest they were not local and were likely captives; furthermore, captive female sacrificial victims at the Mississippian site of Cahokia were apparently selected for their youth, good health, and uniform height.

In many societies, slaves were forced to distinguish themselves from the rest of the population through distinctive dress, treatment of hair, or other physical markers. Santos-Granero (2005) describes how in South America the status of captives was abundantly marked by physical modifications, including tattoos, short hair, clothing and ornaments, and genital mutilation (see also DeBoer, this volume, for discussion of markers of captive status). Of course, many of these characteristics would be difficult to see in all but the most well preserved burial populations. Patterson (1982) notes that in many societies slaves were either forced to wear, or forbidden from wearing, certain ornaments or special kinds of clothes. For example, Northwest Coast slave women were generally forbidden to wear the labret (lip plugs) worn by free women (Donald 1997:77; Patterson 1982:58), while female captives among the Kalinago in the Caribbean were forbidden to wear the cotton leg bands that signified free women post-puberty. Among some African groups, slaves were not allowed to scar themselves as free people did, although scars sometimes identified outsiders within populations who did not practice scarring (Patterson 1982:59). Roman slaves were often branded or tattooed as a mark of their status (Lenski, this volume). Patterson (1982) describes the practice of shaving the head or cutting the hair of slaves, a practice also associated with mourning for the dead and an indication of a slave's social death. Among Northwest Coast tribes, slaves were generally required to cut their hair short (Donald 1997:77), as were Germanic slaves (Lenski, this volume) and Kalinago captives in the Caribbean (Santos-Granero 2005). Starna and Watkins (1991) suggest that mutilation of the fingers, including amputating them and tearing out the nails, was a sign of enslavement among the Iroquois. While dress and hair style would generally not be recoverable archaeologically, mutilation of the hands might be.

Skeletons also may retain evidence of hard work and physical abuse, and Martin (this volume) has identified a subpopulation of women in the La Plata Valley of the American Southwest with cranial and post-cranial trauma that is consistent with the type of nonlethal violence often perpetrated on captives/slaves (see also Donald 1997:203; Martin 1997; Wilkinson 1997). Such injuries suggest a subclass of enslaved women who were physically brutalized. Martin (this volume) provides important evidence for the effects of such brutality on the physical and mental health of captives and their ability to function normally.

Also providing evidence of captives are differences in treatment after death. Martin (this volume) shows that the mortuary contexts for the La Plata female subpopulation were different and much less formal than that of other burials. Similarly, ethnographic evidence in the Northwest Coast shows that slaves were not formally buried as were other members of the group; instead their bodies were simply tossed aside (Ames 2001:5; Donald 1997:203; Hajda 2005:573). In contrast, Alt (this volume) describes numerous remains found in ritual contexts in Mississippian societies of individuals who appear to have been captives used as sacrificial victims. Some Northwest Coast slaves may also have been used as sacrificial victims, with their bodies placed beneath totem poles or house posts (Donald 1997: 171–172, 204; MacLeod 1929:108–111). Use of captives in sacrifice was common elsewhere, too (for example, in Africa among the Igbo [Uchendu 1977:129], among the Kongo of Zaire [MacGaffey 1977:241], among the Vai of Liberia and Sierra Leone [Holsoe 1977:287], among the Duala of Cameroon [Austen 1977:315], and in the kingdom of Dahomey [Law 1997]). Among the Huron, captives who suffered torture heroically were often eaten (Heidenreich 1978:386; Sioui 1999:174; Tooker 1991:38–39; Trigger 1969:51). Tracing this practice into the past, Trigger (1976:158) reports archaeological evidence of increasing cannibalism at archaeological sites in the Northeast around AD 1550 as well as evidence for increasing warfare. Of course, captives killed quickly after capture would not have been able to contribute to their captors' society and are of less interest for the purposes of this volume.

Skewed sex ratios in the archaeological record also suggest the presence of captives. Since most captives were women, either an excess of women or decreased frequencies of women in burial populations could suggest groups that took captives or those that were victims of raids. Kohler and Turner (2006) found an excess of women during the thirteenth century at two large groups of sites in the American Southwest, Chaco Canyon and Aztec Ruins, and a lower proportion of women at other sites in the vicinity of Aztec. They argue that these skewed sex ratios indicate raiding for women by residents of the large site clusters. In another Southwest study, Lowell (2007) found an excess of women at Grasshopper Pueblo in west-central Arizona and at adjacent sites during the late thirteenth and fourteenth centuries. Although she attributes the imbalance to an influx of female war refugees, it is also possible they were captives. Scholars studying Northwest Coast slavery have associated skewed sex ratios with slavery in prehistoric burial populations, following the work of Cybulski (1990 [cited in Donald 1997:203]; see also Ames 2001:5, this volume; Cybulski 1990, 1992; Donald 1997:203–204). Cybulski (1990, 1992) studied two Northwest Coast populations and found more women in the population with the highest historical rate of slavery, suggesting a continuation of the prehistoric practice of capturing and enslaving women. Similarly, skewed sex ratios also suggest captured women at the Crow Creek site, a village in South Dakota that dates to about AD 1325 (Keeley 1996: 68). Archaeologists found the remains of more than five hundred men, women, and children who had been killed during an attack on the village, but there were far fewer young women than would be found in a normal population structure. Keeley (1996:68) suggests some women had been taken captive by their attackers.

Ames (this volume) uses archaeological evidence for household productive capacity to document the presence of slaves. Using data from the Northwest Coast, he shows that productive capacity supports arguments that slavery was an ancient practice and that slaves were essential to the maintenance of the status of elite titleholders in these societies.

Material indicators of captives and enslavement are few. Taylor (2001) reports that in Europe, approximately fifty iron shackles and gang-chains are known from the later pre-Roman Iron Age and the Roman period (see also Kristiansen 1998: Fig. 185; and especially Lenski, this volume). Taylor (2001:29) notes that the chains might have been an efficient method of transporting both the slaves and iron; at the destination point, the iron could be easily reforged into other objects. Similarly, in Africa, ivory was tied to slaves both to restrain them and transport the ivory (Taylor 2001:29). Trigger (1969:48) notes that Iroquois warriors carried a special leather thong for binding prisoners, and Fenton (1978: 306) shows a decorated vegetal fiber cord that he describes as a "prisoner tie" (it also had other uses). Neither of these objects would be likely to preserve in the archaeological record, however. Stahl (this volume) suggests that archaeologists in Africa look for shrines and other artifacts of divinatory practices that are material remains of the ways in which African people negotiated the predatory landscapes created by the slave trade. Similar ritual features might also be found elsewhere in the world.

Iconography is another useful avenue for identifying captives and slaves in the archaeological record, although women may be underrepresented in prehistoric images (see DuBois 2003 for an analysis of slaves in ancient Greek imagery). Taylor (2005: Fig. 2) shows a remarkable Upper Paleolithic figurine from southern Russia that is more than twenty thousand years old and seems to show a woman pregnant and bound by the hands. Alt (this volume) discusses Mississippian images of warriors and captive or execution victims. She notes the prevalence of male captives in these images, even though other evidence suggests the capture of women and children. Recently, Redmond and Spencer (2006) used images on carved stone slabs to discuss the treatment of war captives of the Zapotec, a state-level people of ancient Oaxaca, Mexico (see also Brooks 1998). A rope around the neck symbolizes the captive's status (Redmond and Spencer 2006: 355). The captives depicted on stone slabs seem to be exclusively male, seem to have been warriors (based on dress, hairstyle, ornaments, etc.), most seem to have been mutilated, and many may represent corpses. Apparently ancient Oaxacan sculptors were more interested in depicting defeated male captives (who may have been ritually killed) than the many women who likely remained among them as slaves. In a historical example, Brooks (2002) discusses a painting on a buffalo hide that depicts a raid on a Native American (probably Apache) encampment by Spanish-outfitted *genízaros* (individuals of mixed ethnicity). In this image, women and children are behind a palisade, defended by men; the *genízaro* slavers have clearly come for the women and children. In the Northeast, the Iroquois beheaded their captives, who are depicted as headless in pictographs (Fenton 1978:316). Kristiansen (1998:160) discusses stelae and gold from Late Bronze Age European sites with images that suggest an exchange of slaves. A recent volume on Amerindians' use of human body parts as trophies includes numerous images of captives from throughout the Americas, including sculptures, statuary, and rock art (Chacon and Dye 2007).

Oral history and language are both important sources of evidence for the antiquity of slavery. Averkieva (1966, cited in Donald 1997:45) reported that slaves appear in Northwest Coast oral traditions as a normal part of the social scene, suggesting that they had considerable antiquity. Donald (1997:177–179) discusses various Northwest Coast oral accounts in which slaves play roles and suggests a close association between salmon, copper, and slaves. He also examines Northwest Coast languages that have terms for "slave" (Donald 1997:205–209) and argues that in these languages the terms seems to be very old, and not recent loan words. Brooks (1998, 2002) shows that origin narratives and ceremonies for incorporating outsiders confirm the presence of female captives in the Southwest and other parts of the Americas. Starna and Watkins (1991:48–49) find that the Iroquois have root words that mean "slave." Although their discussion is not directed at proving the antiquity of slavery among these groups, these words suggest that slavery existed prior to the historic period. Santos-Granero (2005) found that in both South America and the Northeast United States, words for captives were often the same as those used to describe animals, especially pets. Keim (1983:145) reports that oral traditions among the Mangbetu-related people of northeastern Zaire provide considerable information about different roles played by male and female slaves (see also Kusimba 2006:219–221).

Captive-taking and enslavement are the outcome of warfare and raiding, and evidence of warfare in prehistoric non-state societies should prompt archaeologists to look for evidence of captives. For example, Allen (2006) reports that warfare in Polynesia was common prior to European contact, suggesting that captives would also have been common. Evidence of warfare in New Zealand includes fortifications and weapons, and although war captives are not mentioned by Allen (2006), Vayda (1970) describes how prisoners of war were either killed or enslaved, and provides accounts of women prisoners of war who became slaves. Archaeological studies of Maori sites could help confirm the presence of captives.

Finally, artifact distributions, primarily ceramics, have been used to identify captives. Habicht-Mauche's (this volume, see also Habicht-Mauche 2000) identification of Pueblo-style pottery made in Southern Plains villages during the protohistoric period suggests a subpopulation of Pueblo women who may have been captured during raids by Plains bison hunters. These women made pottery using local materials, but with production techniques learned in their pueblos—the only methods they knew. Similarly, Trigger (1976) uses the distribution of sites and pottery to suggest patterns of warfare between the Huron and other groups during the period when bands in this area were becoming tribes. He suggests that the homogeneity of pottery types found at proto-Huron villages (prior to the sixteenth century AD) was a result of the movement of captive women from village to village (1976:159). Trigger also suggests an "index of female movement" using foreign pottery at Iroquoian sites. When foreign-style pottery is found at a site, Trigger argues that it was likely produced by a foreign woman living at the site because the Huron rarely carried pots very far. Although these foreign women could have been acquired brides, refugees, or even prisoners of war, Trigger argues that if the women were refugees or a group that was forced to resettle, foreign pottery would be found at the site to which the refugees fled, as well as the host's pottery at the villages from which they came. Blood feuds, on the other hand, which involve more give-and-take (and presumably the capture of women on each side), would result in small to moderate quantities of each adversary's pottery at the sites of each group (Trigger 1976:161).

Conclusions

Captives have been largely ignored by archaeologists, most of whom tend to operate as if social boundaries are fixed even though they know better. Capture, as well as marriage and migration, moved people across landscapes, mixing genetic material and cultural practices. Captive-taking was usually an aspect of warfare and raiding, and it was a potent source of power. Because of their low social position, captives add a new dimension to any social hierarchy they enter, creating relationships of dominance and subordination that may have a significant effect on economic and political development. Where population was low and power was derived from how many followers a leader could amass, captives increased group size, provided wives without bride-price, and boosted the labor force. Captive-taking could play out on a vast scale, creating predatory landscapes where warfare and raiding affected virtually every aspect of human interaction, from settlement patterns to trade routes.

Captives were agents of social change, and the chapters in this volume explore the factors that conditioned the kind and amount of influence they exerted. Some of these factors included the captives' gender and age, and how they were integrated into captor society. In most places and times, captives were overwhelmingly women and children, and given women's intimate role in childrearing (including their master's children), female captives were likely to have been especially influential. Captives, especially older children and adults, arrived with a repertoire of practices (technologies, decorative ideas, rituals, methods of communication) that they were likely to use in their new homes unless these practices were actively suppressed. Which of these practices they continued to use would depend in part on how captives were integrated into the society of their captors. The degree of integration varied widely, ranging from segregation into a despised slave class, to incorporation as wife or concubine, to adoption as a subordinate, or to full membership in society. These different levels of integration almost certainly affected the kind and level of captives' influence. Other factors must also have affected cultural transmission, including the desire of captives to lose their alien traits and embrace the culture of their captors. In other situations, captives may have sought hidden or subtle ways to honor their natal culture.

Captives are difficult to see in the archaeological record because for the most part their sub-ordinate status and alien origin leave few traces. Chapters in this volume suggest avenues for identifying captives in the archaeological record, exploring their activities, and assessing their achievements. Human remains, artifacts, iconography, the material remains of religious practices, oral history, and other avenues show promise for identifying captives in the past and recognizing their contributions to cultural development.

Captives were a common and accepted part of human society in most parts of the world throughout history. Perhaps the fact that captive-taking and enslavement are almost unanimously reviled today, although they were widespread only two hundred years ago, is evidence of human progress. Even though women and children continue to be snatched and sold throughout the world (Taylor 2005), these practices are now almost universally outlawed, and a tragic and tainted aspect of human history has been largely forgotten by descendants of captive-takers and their victims. While we must consider the reasons for this loss of memory, as well as our motives for studying captive-taking, we should not forget the contributions of captives to cultural development and change. This volume is a step toward the study and commemoration of those contributions.

Acknowledgments

My thanks must go first to Jim Skibo and Jeff Grathwohl, who invited me to organize a Foundations of Archaeological Inquiry (FAI) conference at Snowbird, Utah, in the fall of 2006, leaving the topic up to me. Without their invitation, I might never have acted on my long-standing interest in captives and slavery in the past, an interest sparked by Tien Fuh Wu, the fictive aunt of my childhood who was sold by her father at age five and endured five years of slavery in San Francisco. Abundant thanks are also due to the participants in the FAI conference, whose chapters form this volume. (Noel Lenski was not able to join us at Snowbird, but we are very fortunate to have his contribution.) An enormously stimulating group, they provided two days of intense and challenging dialogue. We ended the session by developing a series of "focus questions" which each of us used to shape our respective chapters. This chapter is intended to outline these common goals, and I hope it achieves this aim.

The conference was funded in part by the University of Utah Press FAI series and in part by a generous grant from the Wenner-Gren Foundation.

This chapter benefited not only from the comments of my conference colleagues, but also from the comments of colleagues at the University of Colorado and elsewhere. These include Doug Bamforth, Frank Eddy, Art Joyce, John Hoffecker, Jim Hester, Steve Holen, Steve Lekson (who read and commented on several versions of the paper), Irina Panyushkina, Payson Sheets, and Richard Wilshusen. Finally, many people who have endured my excited monologues on captives have suggested references and new avenues for research. Attempts to thank them would likely be incomplete, so to these kind folks, many thanks for your help and for listening.

References Cited

Allen, Mark W.
2006   Transformations in Maori Warfare: Toa, Pa, and Pu. In *The Archaeology of Warfare: Prehistories of Raiding and Conquest*, edited by

Elizabeth N. Arkush and Mark W. Allen. University Press of Florida, Gainesville.

Ames, Kenneth M.

2001   Slaves, Chiefs and Labour on the Northern Northwest Coast. *World Archaeology* 33(1):1–17.

Anderson, David G.

1994   *The Savannah River Chiefdoms: Political Change in the Late Prehistoric Southeast.* University of Alabama Press, Tuscaloosa.

Anonymous

n.d.   The Starving Time. In Part III, Hopi, manuscript on file, Huntington Library, Pasadena, California. This is an account written by an Indian agent of his life at the Hopi villages. It apparently dates to the mid-1800s.

Arkush, Elizabeth N., and Mark W. Allen (editors)

2006   The *Archaeology of Warfare: Prehistories of Raiding and Conquest.* University Press of Florida, Gainesville.

Austen, Ralph A.

1977   Slavery Among Coastal Middlemen: The Duala of Cameroon. In *Slavery in Africa: Historical and Anthropological Perspectives,* edited by Suzanne Miers and Igor Kopytoff, pp. 305–334. University of Wisconsin Press, Madison.

Averkieva, Julia

1966   *Slavery Among the Indians of North America.* Translated by G. R. Elliot. Victoria College, Victoria, B.C.

Baker, H. D.

2001   Degrees of Freedom: Slavery in Mid-First Millennium BC Babylonia. *World Archaeology* 33(1):18–26.

Baldus, Bernd

1977   Responses to Dependence in a Servile Group: The Machube of Northern Benin. In *Slavery in Africa: Historical and Anthropological Perspectives,* edited by Suzanne Miers and Igor Kopytoff, pp. 435–458. University of Wisconsin Press, Madison.

Bay, Edna

1983   Servitude and Worldly Success in the Palace of Dahomey. In *Women and Slavery in Africa,* edited by Claire C. Robertson and Martin A. Klein, pp. 340–367. University of Wisconsin Press, Madison.

Bonnassie, Pierre

1991   *From Slavery to Feudalism in Southwestern Europe.* Cambridge University Press, Cambridge.

Braimah, J. A., and J. R. Goody

1967   *Salaga: The Struggle for Power.* Longmans, London.

Brooks, James F.

1998   Amerindian Societies. In *Macmillan Encyclopedia of World Slavery,* vol. 1, edited by Paul Finkelman and Joseph C. Miller, pp. 52–55. Simon and Schuster/Macmillan, New York.

2002   *Captives and Cousins: Slavery, Kinship, and Community in the Southwest Borderlands.* University of North Carolina Press, Chapel Hill.

Brugge, David M.

1993   The Spanish Borderlands. In *Encyclopedia of the North American Colonies,* vol. 2, edited by Jacob Ernest Cooke, pp. 91–101. Charles Scribner's Sons, New York.

Callender, Charles

1978   Illinois. In *Handbook of North American Indians,* vol. 15, *Northeast,* edited by Bruce G. Trigger, pp. 673–680. Smithsonian Institution, Washington, D.C.

Carneiro, Robert L.

1991   The Nature of the Chiefdom as Revealed by Evidence from the Cauca Valley of Colombia. In *Profiles in Cultural Evolution: Papers from a Conference in Honor of Elman R. Service.* Anthropological Papers no. 85. Museum of Anthropology, University of Michigan, Ann Arbor.

Chacon, Richard J., and David H. Dye

2007   Heads, Women and the Baubles of Prestige: Trophies of War in the Arctic and Subarctic. In *The Taking and Displaying of Human Body Parts as Trophies by Amerindians,* edited by Richard J. Chacon and David H. Dye, pp. 32–44. Springer, New York.

Copley, Esther

1960   *History of Slavery, and Its Abolition.* Reprint.
[1839]   Negro History Press, Detroit.

Curtis, Edward S.

1913   *The North American Indian.* Vol. 9. Plimpton Press, Norwood, MA.

Cybulski, Jerome S.

1990   Human Biology. In *Handbook of North American Indians,* vol. 7, *Northwest* Coast, edited by Wayne Suttles, pp. 52–59. Smithsonian Institution Press, Washington, D.C.

1992   *A Greenville Burial Ground: Human Remains and Mortuary Elements in British Columbia Coast Prehistory.* Canadian Museum of Civilization, Quebec.

Davis, David Brion

1966   *The Problem of Slavery in Western Culture.* Cornell University Press, Ithaca, NY.

DeBoer, Warren R.

1986   Pillage and Production in the Amazon: A View through the Conibo of the Ucayali

Basin, Eastern Peru. In *World Archaeology* 18(2):231–246.

1990   Interaction, Imitation, and Communication as Expressed in Style: The Ucayali Experience. In *The Uses of Style in Archaeology*, edited by Margaret W. Conkey and Christine A. Hastorf, pp. 82–104. Cambridge University Press, Cambridge.

Donald, Leland

1997   *Aboriginal Slavery on the Northwest Coast of North America*. University of California Press, Berkeley.

Driver, Harold

1966   Geographical-historical versus Psycho-functional Explanations of Kin Avoidances. *Current Anthropology* 7(2):131–182.

DuBois, Page

2003   *Slaves and Other Objects*. University of Chicago Press, Chicago.

Dunbar, Roberta Ann

1977   Slavery and the Evolution of Nineteenth-Century Damagaram (Zinder, Niger). In *Slavery in Africa: Historical and Anthropological Perspectives*, edited by Suzanne Miers and Igor Kopytoff, pp. 155–180. University of Wisconsin Press, Madison.

Engerman, Stanley, Seymour Drescher, and Robert Paquette (editors)

2001   *Slavery*. Oxford University Press, New York.

Fenton, William N.

1978   Northern Iroquoian Culture Patterns. In *Handbook of North American Indians,* vol. 15, *Northeast*, edited by Bruce G. Trigger, pp. 296–321. Smithsonian Institution, Washington, D.C.

Ferguson, Brian R., and Neil L. Whitehead (editors)

1999   *War in the Tribal Zone: Expanding States and Indigenous Warfare*. 2nd ed. School of American Research Press, Santa Fe, NM.

Ferguson, Leland

1992   *Uncommon Ground: Archaeology and Colonial African America: 1650–1800*. Smithsonian Institution Press, Washington, D.C.

Gallay, Alan

2002   *The Indian Slave Trade: The Rise of the English Empire in the American South, 1670–1717*. Yale University Press, New Haven.

Goody, Jack

1971   *Technology, Tradition, and the State in Africa*. Oxford University Press, Oxford.

1980   Slavery in Space and Time. In *Asian and African Systems of Slavery*, by J. L. Watson, pp. 16–42. University of California, Berkeley.

Habicht-Mauche, Judith

2000   Pottery, Food, Hides and Women: Labor, Production, and Exchange within the Protohistoric Plains-Pueblo Frontier Economy. In *The Archaeology of Regional Interaction in the Prehistoric Southwest*, edited by Michelle Hegmon, pp. 209–231. University Press of Colorado, Niwot.

Hajda, Yvonne P.

2005   Slavery in the Greater Lower Columbia Region. In *Ethnohistory* 52(3):563–588.

Harms, Robert

1983   Sustaining the System: Trading Towns along the Middle Zaire. In *Women and Slavery in Africa*, edited by Claire C. Robertson and Martin A. Klein, pp. 95–110. University of Wisconsin Press, Madison.

Heidenreich, Conrad E.

1978   Huron. In *Handbook of North American Indians,* vol. 15, *Northeast*, edited by Bruce G. Trigger, pp. 368–388. Smithsonian Institution, Washington, D.C.

Hochschild, Adam

2005   *Bury the Chains*. Houghton Mifflin, Boston.

Holsoe, Svend E.

1977   Slavery and Economic Response Among the Vai (Liberia and Sierra Leone). In *Slavery in Africa: Historical and Anthropological Perspectives*, edited by Suzanne Miers and Igor Kopytoff, pp. 287–304. University of Wisconsin Press, Madison.

Hudson, Charles

1976   *The Southeastern Indians*. University of Tennessee Press, Knoxville.

Jorgensen, Joseph G.

1980   *Western Indians: Comparative Environments, Languages and Cultures of 172 Western American Indian Tribes*. W. H. Freeman, San Francisco.

Keeley, Lawrence H.

1996   *War Before Civilization: The Myth of the Peaceful Savage*. Oxford University Press, Oxford.

Keim, Curtis A.

1983   Women in Slavery among the Mangbetu c. 1800–1910. In *Women and Slavery in Africa*, edited by Claire C. Robertson and Martin A. Klein, pp. 144–159. University of Wisconsin Press, Madison.

Kelly, Raymond C.

2000   *Warless Societies and the Origin of War*. University of Michigan Press, Ann Arbor

Klein, Martin A.

1977   Servitude Among the Wolof and Sereer of Senegambia. In *Slavery in Africa: Historical and Anthropological Perspectives*, edited by Suzanne Miers and Igor Kopytoff, pp. 335–366. University of Wisconsin Press, Madison.

1983 Women in Slavery in the Western Sudan. In *Women and Slavery in Africa*, edited by Claire C. Robertson and Martin A. Klein, pp. 67–88. University of Wisconsin Press, Madison.

Kohler, Timothy A., and Kathryn K. Turner
2006 Raiding for Women in the Prehispanic Northern Pueblo Southwest? A Pilot Examination. *Current Anthropology* 47(6):1017–1025.

Kopytoff, Igor
1982 Slavery. *Annual Review of Anthropology* 11: 207–230.

Kopytoff, Igor, and Suzanne Miers
1977 Introduction: African "Slavery" as an Institution of Marginality. In *Slavery in Africa: Historical and Anthropological Perspectives*, edited by Suzanne Miers and Igor Kopytoff, pp. 3–81. University of Wisconsin Press, Madison.

Kristiansen, Kristian
1998 *Europe Before History*. Cambridge University Press, Cambridge.

Kusimba, Chapurukha M.
2006 Slavery and Warfare in African Chiefdoms. In *The Archaeology of Warfare: Prehistories of Raiding and Conquest,* edited by Elizabeth N. Arkush and Mark W. Allen, pp. 214–249. University Press of Florida, Gainesville.

Law, Robin
1997 The Politics of Commercial Transition: Factional Conflict in Dahomey in the Context of the Ending of the Atlantic Slave Trade. *Journal of African History* 38(2):213–233.

LeBlanc, Steven A.
2003 *Constant Battles: The Myth of the Peaceful, Noble Savage*. St. Martin's Press, New York.

Lovejoy, Paul E.
2000 *Transformations in Slavery: A History of Slav-*
[1983] *ery in Africa*. 2nd ed. Cambridge University Press, Cambridge.

Lowell, Julie
2007 Women and Men in Warfare and Migration: Implications of Gender Imbalance in the Grasshopper Region of Arizona. *American Antiquity* 72(1):95–124.

MacGaffey, Wyatt
1977 Economic and Social Dimensions of Kongo Slavery (Zaire). In *Slavery in Africa: Historical and Anthropological Perspectives*, edited by Suzanne Miers and Igor Kopytoff, pp. 235–260. University of Wisconsin Press, Madison.

MacLeod, William C.
1925 Debtor and Chattel Slavery in Aboriginal North America. *American Anthropologist* 27(3):370–380.
1928 Economic Aspects of Indigenous American Slavery. *American Anthropologist* 30(4):632–650.
1929 The Origin of Servile Labor Groups. *American Anthropologist* 31(1):89–113.

Martin, Debra L.
1997 Violence Against Women in the La Plata River Valley (AD 1000–1300). In *Troubled Times: Violence and Warfare in the Past*, edited by Debra L. Martin and David W. Frayer, pp. 45–76. Gordon and Breach/Overseas Publishers Association, Amsterdam.

Meillassoux, Claude
1971 Introduction. In *The Development of Indigenous Trade and Markets in West Africa*, edited by Claude Meillassoux, pp. 3–86. Oxford University Press, London.
1983 Female Slavery. In *Women and Slavery in Africa*, edited by Claire C. Robertson and Martin A. Klein, pp. 49–66. University of Wisconsin Press, Madison.
1991 *The Anthropology of Slavery: The Womb of Iron and Gold*. University of Chicago Press, Chicago.

Meillassoux, Claude (editor)
1971 *The Development of Indigenous Trade and Markets in West Africa*. Oxford University Press, London.

Morey, Nancy Kathleen Creswick
1975 Ethnohistory of the Colombian and Venezuelan Llanos. Ph.D. dissertation. Department of Anthropology, University of Utah, Salt Lake City.

Nieboer, H. J.
1910 *Slavery as an Industrial System: Ethnological Researches*. 2nd ed. Martinus Nijhoff, The Hague.

Nwachukwu-Ogedengbe, K.
1977 Slavery in Nineteenth-Century Aboh (Nigeria). In *Slavery in Africa: Historical and Anthropological Perspectives*, edited by Suzanne Miers and Igor Kopytoff, pp. 133–154. University of Wisconsin Press, Madison.

Patterson, Orlando
1982 *Slavery and Social Death*. Harvard University Press, Cambridge, MA.

Perdue, Theda
1979 *Slavery and the Evolution of Cherokee Society, 1540–1866*. University of Tennessee Press, Knoxville.

Redmond, Elsa M., and Charles S. Spencer
2006 From Raiding to Conquest: Warfare Strategies and Early State Development in Oaxaca, Mexico. In The *Archaeology of Warfare: Prehistories of Raiding and Conquest*, edited by Elizabeth N. Arkush and Mark W. Allen, pp.

336–393. University Press of Florida, Gainesville.

Robertshaw, Peter
1999   Women, Labor, and State Formation in Western Uganda. In *Complex Polities in the Ancient Tropical World*, edited by E. A. Bacus and L. J. Lucero, pp. 51–66. Archaeological Papers no. 9. American Anthropological Association, Arlington, VA.

Robertson, Claire C., and Martin A. Klein (editors)
1983a   *Women and Slavery in Africa*. University of Wisconsin Press, Madison.

Robertson, Claire C., and Martin A. Klein
1983b   Women's Importance in African Slave Systems. In *Women and Slavery in Africa*, edited by Claire C. Robertson and Martin A. Klein, pp. 3–25. University of Wisconsin Press, Madison.

Ross, Alexander
1966   *Adventures of the First Settlers on the Columbia River*. Citadel Press, New York.

Santos-Granero, Fernando
2005   Amerindian Torture Revisited: Rituals of Enslavement and Markers of Servitude in Tropical America. *Tipiti* 3(2):42–69.

Siegel, Bernard
1945   Some Methodological Considerations for a Comparative Study of Slavery. *American Anthropologist* 47(3):357–392.
1947   Slavery During the Third Dynasty of Ur. *American Anthropologist* n.s. 49(1):1–54.

Sioui, Georges E.
1999   *Huron-Wendat: The Heritage of the Circle*. Translated by Jane Brierley. UBC Press, Vancouver, B.C.

Socolow, Susan Migden
1992   Spanish Captives in Indian Societies: Cultural Contact along the Argentine Frontier, 1600–1835. *The Hispanic American Historical Review* 72(1):73–99.

Starna, William A., and Ralph Watkins
1991   Northern Iroquoian Slavery. *Ethnohistory* 38(1):34–57.

Taylor, Timothy
2001   Believing the Ancients: Quantitative and Qualitative Dimensions of Slavery and the Slave Trade in Later Prehistoric Eurasia. *World Archaeology* 33(1):27–43.
2005   Ambushed by a Grotesque: Archaeology, Slavery, and the Third Paradigm. In *Warfare, Violence, and Slavery in Prehistory: Proceedings of a Prehistoric Society Conference at Sheffield University*, edited by Michael Parker Pearson and J. J. Thorpe, pp. 225–233. Archaeopress, Oxford.

Thompson, F. Hugh
2003   *The Archaeology of Greek and Roman Slavery*. Duckworth, London.

Tobin, Jacqueline L., and Raymond G. Dobard
1999   *Hidden in Plain View: A Secret Story of Quilts and the Underground Railroad*. Anchor Books, New York.

Tooker, Elisabeth
1991   An Ethnography of the Huron Indians, 1615–
[1964] 1649. *Bureau of American Ethnology Bulletin* 190. Syracuse University Press, NY.

Trigger, Bruce G.
1969   *The Huron: Farmers of the North*. Holt, Rinehart and Winston, New York.
1976   *The Children of Aataentsic I: A History of the Huron People to 1660*. McGill-Queen's University Press, Montreal.

Uchendu, Victor C.
1977   Slaves and Slavery in Igboland, Nigeria. In *Slavery in Africa: Historical and Anthropological Perspectives*, edited by Suzanne Miers and Igor Kopytoff, pp. 121–132. University of Wisconsin Press, Madison.

Udall, Louise
1969   *Me and Mine: The Life Story of Helen Sekaquaptewa*. University of Arizona Press, Tucson.

Usner, Daniel H., Jr.
1992   *Indians, Settlers, and Slaves in a Frontier Exchange Economy*. University of North Carolina Press, Chapel Hill.

Vayda, A. P.
1961   Maori Prisoners and Slaves in the Nineteenth Century. *Ethnohistory* 8(2):144–155.
1970   *Maori Warfare*. Polynesian Society Maori Monographs 2. Reprint. A. H. & A. W. Reed, Sydney.

Watson, James L.
1980   *Asian and African Systems of Slavery*. University of California, Berkeley.

Wilkinson, Richard G.
1997   Violence Against Women: Raiding and Abduction in Prehistoric Michigan. In *Troubled Times: Violence and Warfare in the Past*, edited by Debra L. Martin and David W. Frayer, pp. 21–44. Gordon and Breach/Overseas Publishers Association, Amsterdam.

Woolf, Alex
1997   At Home in the Long Iron Age: A Dialogue Between Households and Individuals in Cultural Reproduction. In *Invisible Peoples and Processes: Writing Gender and Childhood into European Archaeology*, edited by Jenny Moore and Eleanor Scott, pp. 68–74. Leicester University Press, London.

2

The Slave Trade as Practice and Memory

What Are the Issues for Archaeologists?

Ann Brower Stahl

The spectre of slavery has never ceased to haunt African consciousness.
— ACHILLE MBEMBE

Slavery has been, until recently, the "great un-spoken subject" (Mbembe 2001:21) within African studies generally and African archaeology more specifically. A change of conscience, heart, or perhaps courage seems to have been ushered in by the *fin de millénaire* (Oostindie 2001: 9), resulting in a proliferation of publications on the African slave trade by historians, anthropologists, and somewhat more belatedly, archaeologists.[1] This has coincided with a swell of "memory work" centered on the Atlantic slave trade in the form of commemorative ceremonies, monuments, and heritage/slavery tourism associated with the two-hundredth anniversary of Britain's abolition of the trade (L. Brown 2002; Comité National pour le Bénin du Projet "La Route de l'Esclave" 1994; Dann and Seaton [eds.] 2001; Ebron 2002:189–212; Oostindie [ed.] 2001; Seaton 2001; Tibbles 2008; Wallace 2006). Although we should consider *why* the concern with slavery has increased at this historical juncture (what compels our attention to the topic now, when for so long it has been shrouded in silence?),[2] I focus instead on what is to be gained, and how, from archaeological engagements with questions of slavery in Africa. What issues confront us as we seek to learn more about the practices and consequences of slavery? Who are the

constituencies for this knowledge, and what is its role in contemporary memory work? How does a primary focus on the Atlantic trade shape archaeological archives, and with what implications for our understanding of internal African slavery? To address these questions adequately, we need to approach the study of slavery as both (past) practice and (present) memory.

I explore two entry points into these issues before offering reflections on how to operationalize an archaeology of the slave trade as practice and memory. The first is heritage tourism in West Africa and its implications for what is brought to the fore and what is silenced through its associated memory work. Tourism has centered primarily on the coastal sites from which enslaved captives were transported by Europeans—sites like Gorée Island off the Senegalese coast near Dakar (Katchka 2004) or the castles of Ghana's Central Region (Anquandah 1999; Essah 2001). Alex Haley's (1976) *Roots* prompted pilgrimage tourism to Juffure, an interior Gambian village to which Haley traced his ancestry (Ebron 2002:204–206; Wright 1981); however, tourist circuits in other countries have only recently, with UNESCO sponsorship, been expanded into the interior regions from which many/most captives originated. Launched in 1994, the UNESCO

25

Slave Route Project promotes research, education, and tourism centered on the slave trade, and is conceived as a memory project aimed at ending the silence surrounding slavery (UNESCO 1994, 2006a). At the same time, the cultural tourism that it promotes takes the form of "root work" (Gilroy 1993:19, 1996), which endeavors to connect diasporan Africans to an authentic Africa conceived in terms of essentialized identities (Hartman 2007). This kind of root work finds resonance in archaeological investigations that project extant identities and cultural practices into the distant past, reinforcing enduring silences with respect to both the complexities of the slave trade and the dynamism of African societies.

Second, I explore how existing archives condition our knowledge of slavery in Africa, and discuss research strategies designed to generate archaeological archives relevant to questions of slavery. Recent literature stresses the extent to which historical and anthropological archives were forged through colonial contexts while simultaneously being bound up in the production of social difference (e.g., through conventions of mapping, censuses, and associated forms of governmentality [Cohn 1996; Comaroff and Comaroff 1992; Dirks 2001; Hawkins 2002; Pels 1997; Stoler 1989, 2001, 2002, 2006]). By extension, we need to approach these archives as culturally conditioned products rather than straight-forward repositories of facts (Dirks 2002; Mathur 2000; Trouillot 1995:26, 52–53). For example, we need to consider how a perception of Africa as a reservoir of enslaveable labor conditioned colonial documents, as well as the ways in which ethnographic conventions diverted attention from slavery's dynamics and effects. Archaeological sources can provide an alternative archive, but here too we must consider how our discipline's tendency to reify boundaries between social groups (Trigger 1984, 1989:148–206) and frame archaeological knowledge in terms of spatially and temporally bounded "cultures" conceived through a progressive developmentalist lens has shaped archaeological archives (Stahl 1999b, 2004). These conventions arguably hamper our ability to address questions surrounding the effects of slavery and the slave trade on African societies. Thus, just as scholars of colonialism have emphasized the need to develop new archives (Comaroff and Comaroff 1992:33–34; Stoler and Cooper 1997: 11–18), archaeologists need to reflect on how past research goals and assumptions have shaped existing archives, and to envision how we might invigorate an archaeology of slavery by defining new research goals and alternative conceptual framings (see also Kusimba 2004; Robertshaw and Duncan, this volume).

Slavery and Memory Work

Any consideration of the slave trade must begin with an appreciation of the complex emotions and resonances of this traumatic episode (Argenti and Röschenthaler 2006; Austen 2001; Ferme 2001:82; Schramm 2005; Tibbles 2008). As Mbembe observed, the slave trade is a haunting, durable presence in African-American discourses on history and identity (Bailey 2005; Ebron 2002: 201; Gilroy 1993:3; Hartman 2007). The collective amnesia surrounding how Europe—or, more broadly, the West—was produced through flows of humans, goods, and wealth bound up in the slave trade (Williams 1964) has long been a source of frustration and anger among African and African-descendant peoples (Gates 2001; Gilroy 1993, 1996; Oostindie 2001:11–12; Trouillot 1995:74–83). This amnesia is intensified by white guilt and the complex, racially charged politics of knowledge production centered on the slave trade (Argenti and Röschenthaler 2006; Austen 2001:240; Boukhari 1998; Cooper 1979:103; Hall 1996), a problem that has plagued even ostensibly radical scholarship (e.g., British cultural studies [Gilroy 1993:10–15]). The anger and frustration of Africans and diasporans is conditioned by inattention to the slave trade's legacies in relation to colonial and neocolonial processes, the modern world system, and enduring racisms (Appiah 1991; Gilroy 1993, 1996:26; Hartman 2007; Magubane 2004; Mudimbe 1994:212; Stoler 2006). In this respect, the UNESCO Slave Route Project's commitment to investigate the "global transformations and cultural interactions" generated by the slave trade and to promote a "tourism of memory" (UNESCO 2006a) is laudable. Yet we need to attend to the complexities of memory work in relation to the slave trade, pausing to ask ourselves, "Whose memories, how, and with what effects?" (e.g., Dann and Seaton 2001).

Any discussion of memory work must take account of a central paradox surrounding African slavery. On one hand, it stands as a primary symbol of the victimization of African peoples, and thus a core experience. At the same time the slave trade has been "…essentially *forgotten* by Africans. Very few Africans accord it any foundational character whatever" (Mbembe 2001: 21; also Argenti and Röschenthaler 2006:33–36; Bailey 2005; Haenger 2000:xiii; cf. Shaw 2002). Reflecting on the silences surrounding the slave forts of her home country of Ghana, Ama Ata Aidoo (2001:30) observed that it was African-American intellectuals who stirred consideration in newly independent Ghana of "that sorry part of the recent history of Africans and people of African descent." Historians and anthropologists have commented on the silences surrounding slavery in Africa, whether with regard to the external or internal trade (Austen 2001; Dumett 1990:7; Greene 2003; Haenger 2000:xiii, 169; Shaw 2002:1; cf. Baum 1999; C. Brown 2003; Piot 1996). For some, this silence flows from the denial of traumatic events (Fogelson 1989:143) or operates as a form of "strategic amnesia" (Argenti and Röschenthaler 2006:34).[3] But as recent literature demonstrates, memory can take nonverbal forms—for example, as embodied in divinatory practices in Sierra Leone that Shaw (2002) interprets as "habit memories" of the slave trade. Shaw (2002:7) builds on Bourdieu and Giddens in apprehending "practical memory" that is "'forgotten as history'…precisely because [it is] embedded in habits, social practices, ritual processes and embodied experiences" (see also Ferme 2001:9, 17; Stoller 1995). These memories evoke the terror and moral dilemmas associated with the slave trade, and are often bound up in practices centered on witchcraft (e.g., Parish 1999, 2000; Parker 2004, 2006; Shaw 1997). In short, these practical memories connect "present and past experiences of predatory commercial flows" (Shaw 2002:12) and, as such, operate as an alternative archive from which to discern the processes and effects of the slave trade. Similarly, Argenti (2006) interprets masked dance in Cameroon Grassfields as a "somatic sequela" of the slave trade and forced labor, exploring how dance embodies tensions between elder and junior males that are deeply rooted in predatory practices of the past. Röschenthaler (2006) stresses the dynamic character of cult associations in the Cross River area of Nigeria in relation to embodied memories of both the enslaved and the enslavers (see also Lovejoy and Richardson 2003).

Among diasporic Africans this paradox of remembering while forgetting shapes the fractured terrain of memory work, fissured as it is among those who embrace an absolutist, nativist perspective on the unity of African cultural identity grounded in a shared racial essence, and those who stress the plural character of African-descendant peoples as a starting point for reflecting on black identity (Gilroy 1993:187–192, 1996:21; Mbembe 2001:22–24). In the first instance, the slave trade stands simultaneously as a symbol of "what the West has done to Africa" (Mbembe 2001:24) and as an episode that masked the achievements of African peoples (Asante 1990; for a critical discussion, see Gilroy 1993:1–19, 187–223). The second stance potentially opens the way to a more nuanced historical consideration of the slave trade and its effects on what Gilroy (1993) describes as the "double consciousness" of African-descendant peoples. Yet we need to attend to how framing slavery and the slave trade as issues only for "black" or African-descendant peoples obscures the role that slavery and the slave trade played in the identifications of "white" or European-descendant peoples (Bell 2005; Gilroy 1993:13–17, 30, 49). This elision has its roots in the Enlightenment project of analytically cordoning off a domain of the modern, but as Shaw observed:

> while on the European and American sides of the Atlantic, the economic logic of the slave trade helped construct a modernity that was defined (for those who were white, affluent, formally educated, and male) in terms of "rationality," in this part of the West African Atlantic the imperative to produce slaves helped construct a contrasting memory of a vampiric modernity through images of the very occult forces that modernity was supposed to have superseded. (Shaw 2002:17)

Thus, if the slave trade has been forgotten by Africans, it has been doubly so by Europeans (Dresser 2001; Gilroy 1993), a point that recently has been brought into relief by controversies surrounding memory projects centered on the slave trade in Britain (e.g., Bristol, Liverpool [Seaton 2001; Tibbles 2005; Wallace 2006]). We should be wary of engaging in projects that, explicitly or not, obscure these connections and perpetuate a sense that memory work surrounding slavery is an issue for descendants of the enslaved only (Gilroy 1993:49; Hall 1996).

The fractured terrain of memory work among diasporans is also conditioned by the profound sense of betrayal that flows from the knowledge that Africans participated in the slave trade (Hartman 2007), with implications, as Mbembe (2001) outlines, for identifications:

> As a result, the appeal to race as a moral and political foundation for solidarity will always depend, in some way, on a mirage of consciousness so long as continental Africans have not reconsidered the slave trade and other forms of slavery, not only as a catastrophe that befell them, but also as the product of a history that they actively helped shape by the ways in which they treated each other. (Mbembe 2001:26)

Thus we should anticipate that the institutionally supported "demands for remembrance" in the form of slave trail heritage tourism will likely enter into what Argenti and Röschenthaler (2006: 34) characterize as a "peculiarly asymmetrical dialogue" with the "fathomless, implacable silence" (Argenti 2006:49) on the subject of slavery in many African societies.

These issues complicate simplistic models of memory as "recall," underscoring the extent to which its operations involve processes of remembering and forgetting that are not only individual and psychological but also collectively performed social processes (Bloch 1998:67–84; Connerton 1989). Though aspects of recall are surely conditioned by a shared human capacity, anthropologists have argued that the operations of memory are shaped by culture and history. Bloch illustrates this through contrasting examples of three groups: the Sadah, the Bicolano, and the Merina. The Sadah are a Muslim Yemeni group for whom the particular events of history are external to their essential identity, which is rooted in descent from the Prophet Muhammad; the Sadah

do not view themselves as made *by* history, but rather see themselves "in history in the way a rock is in the middle of a stream" (Bloch 1998: 80). The Bicolano are an impoverished Filipino group who see themselves at the mercy of outside forces and therefore altered by history; they neither "construct an imaginary pre-colonial, pre-compromise state to which they want to return" (Bloch 1998:73) nor stress an essentialized identity, seeing themselves instead as having negotiated the historical forces to which they have been subject. The Merina (Madagascar) represent an intermediary between these "Platonic" (stressing transcendental truth; Sadah) and "Aristotelian" (stressing a transformational dialectic; Bicolano) examples. For the Merina, transformation in life gives way through the course of living to the durable and fixed world of ancestors in death. This is captured by the tendency of Merina who immigrate to France to embrace French practices but insist "at amazingly great expense" (Bloch 1998:80) on being interred in family tombs in Madagascar upon death. What these examples show is that there is "no one way of relating to the past and the future and therefore of being in history. There is, therefore, no one way by which one wants to inscribe memory in the public world" (Bloch 1998:80–81). Further, Bloch (1998) argues,

> There is not a generalised need of human beings to remember the past. And in any case… the devices which select from the past what is to be remembered also inevitably involved selecting what of the past is to be obliterated…. When we consider the social actor's attitude to the distant past it becomes clear that one's effort involves not simply finding ways of remembering better, as is the aim of psychologists' imaginary actor, but also, and equally, finding ways to forget it. (Bloch 1998:81)

In contrast to this anthropological emphasis on the need to contextualize the practices of memory, the sense of memory evoked by the UNESCO Slave Route Project glosses the complexities of memory's operations. Here memory is portrayed as a form of "storage" (Trouillot 1995:14) consistent with what Stoler and Strassler (2000:7) term a "hydraulic model" of memory: "that memories are housed as discrete stories awaiting an audience, repressed or unrecognized sources poised to be 'tapped.'" Resistance studies that endeavor to recuperate the agency of dominated groups often assume that event-centered memories of past domination persist, but have simply not been retrieved; however, as Stoler and Strassler (2000) document in their study of memory among former domestic servants under the Dutch in Indonesia, memory more often takes the form of "unrehearsed recollections" of minutia. Although these recollections conjure the "uncomfortable space" in which servants lived,

> Their recollections of touch, taste and smell were not shaped into tidy plots, much less congealed as anti-Dutch resistance narratives. Moving fluidly between the 1930s and the Japanese occupation, between the present and the 1950s...these accounts refused the colonial as a discrete domain of social relations and politics, or experience and memory. (Stoler and Strassler 2000:38)

In similar fashion, we should ask, rather than assume, what form memories of the slave trade might take, and recognize that the traumas of the slave trade thread through the understandings and memories of more recent social, political, and economic traumas endured by African peoples (e.g., forced labor, repressive forms of colonial governance, warfare, etc. [Argenti 2006: 49; Ferme 2001; Stoller 1995; Werbner 1998]).

The UNESCO Slave Route Project

UNESCO initiatives have contributed to the production of historical memoryscapes (Ebron 2002: 164, following Appadurai 1996; see Kirshenblatt-Gimblett 2006) that are intimately linked to heritage tourism (Benson and McCaskie 2004). In the late 1970s, UNESCO inscribed several West Africa sites associated with the Atlantic slave trade on the World Heritage List (WHL): Gorée Island, Senegal, in 1978;[4] and the Forts and Castles, Volta Greater Accra, Central and Western Regions in 1979.[5] Sites on and around James Island in the Gambia River were added in 2003 based on their significance to the "beginning and the conclusion of the slave trade, retaining its memory related to the African Diaspora" (UNESCO 2006b). The WHL status of these sites prompted restoration programs that were embraced by Af-

rican nation-states as a way to boost tourism, but at the same time they opened up struggles over ownership, restoration, and interpretation (Austen 2001; Boachie-Ansah 2005:47; Bruner 1996; Essah 2001:45–47; Katchka 2004; Kreamer 2004, 2006; Osei-Tutu 2004, 2007; Reed 2004; Richards 2005; Singleton 1999). In Ghana, for example, struggles ensued over efforts to stabilize and restore Elmina and Cape Coast castles. Whereas government and museum officials saw this as part of a conservation effort, ex-patriot African Americans living in Ghana and some African Americans in the United States saw restoration efforts as an attempt to sanitize the fort's dark history (Aidoo 2001:31; for detailed recountings see Bruner 1996; Essah 2001; Kreamer 2004, 2006; Osei-Tutu 2004:63–67, 2007; Reed 2004; Richards 2005; Schramm 2005; Singleton 1999:151–158). Further struggles ensued over the content of the *Crossroads of People, Crossroads of Trade* exhibit mounted in the Cape Coast Castle Museum in 1994, in which a focus on diasporan history prevailed over other aspects of the castle's and Ghanaian history, effectively diminishing "the voices of the Ghanaians in the representation of this site" (Kreamer 2006:462; also Schildkrout 1996; on Asen Praso, see Benson and McCaskie 2004:108–109).

Approved by the General Council of UNESCO in 1993 (Resolution 27 C/3.13), the Slave Route Project is a more recent, multidisciplinary international initiative that supports an objective study of the "fact of the slave-trade" and the cultural interactions resulting from it (UNESCO 1994; e.g., Comité National pour le Bénin du Projet "La Route de l'Esclave" 1994). Project monies fund research and education with the aim of producing and disseminating new knowledge. The project is explicitly framed as one centered on memory (Diéne 1998), sponsoring exhibits such as the *Lest We Forget* virtual exhibition (Schomberg Center for Research in Black Culture 2006) launched in 2004 in conjunction with the UN's International Year to Commemorate the Struggle against Slavery and Its Abolition. It also promotes "cultural tourism of memory" through

> identification, restoration and promotion of sites and places of memory of the slave trade and slavery in Africa, the Americas and the

Caribbean. This includes the identification and preservation of archives—written and oral traditions—relative to the slave trade (Slave Trade Archives project) and the development of a tourism of memory. (Slave Route Project 2006)

A concern to curate and make accessible primary source materials was a key focus of the Slave Trade Archives Project (1999 to 2005). Though the project's success varied by country, it resulted in the digitization of some 200,000 documents and images, some of which have been made available on the Web (Slave Trade Archives Project 2005). Less formalized efforts have been directed at constructing archaeological archives relevant to the Slave Route Project. In Ghana, this focused on an inventory of sites related to the slave trade, particularly those in interior areas that could serve as the basis for extending heritage tourism along "slave routes" that trace the paths of captives from their homelands to the interior markets where they were sold, ending at the coastal castles from which enslaved people were transported (cf. Bénin; see Lokossou 1994).

Though UNESCO initiatives are framed in universalizing rhetoric, African Americans are the primary constituency of Slave Route Project memory projects and tourism initiatives (Katchka 2004:5, 8; Osei-Tutu 2004:62–63, 2007; Reed 2004).[6] As Gilroy observes,

> A battle is still raging between those who make the pluralising inner logic of the diaspora idea their starting point for theorising black identity, refusing its simple negation in return to the motherland or fatherland, and others who seek to terminate the fragmentation and dissipation of Africans abroad and favour the ruthless simplicity of undifferentiated racial essences as a solution to growing divisions in black communities. This essentialism rearticulates black cultural nationalisms that have been appropriated without much modification from the standard European sources. (Gilroy 1996:21)

Heritage tourism centered on the slave trade is clearly inspired by the latter, with significant implications for the direction and forms of memory work circulating around sites in its networks.

Memory Work in the Present: Slave Routes, Tourism, and Identifications

African diasporic heritage tourism is often framed by its organizers and approached by its participants in a reverential, redemptive (Gilroy 1993:4) way, couched in narratives of return (Bruner 1996; Katchka 2004; Reed 2004).[7] In this sense, heritage tourism is a form of pilgrimage (Benson and McCaskie 2004:94; Ebron 2002:189–212; Higgins 2000; Kreamer 2006:459–460). It is often orchestrated as a Turnerian ritual process "in which stages of separation, liminality, and reintegration with transformation were used to press the participants to rearticulate their identities within particular narratives of family and homeland" (Ebron 2002:190; see also Bruner 1996; Hartman 2007; Reed 2004). As part of a broader "transatlantic agenda" (Osei-Tutu 2004:60–63; also Hasty 2003), the government of Ghana in 2007 launched an initiative that builds on notions of pilgrimage to coincide with the fiftieth anniversary of Ghana's independence and the two-hundredth anniversary of British abolition of the slave trade. Termed Project Joseph, the initiative is named for the biblical figure in the book of Genesis who was cast into slavery by his siblings, but who rose to prominence and later achieved reconciliation with his siblings (Osei-Tutu 2004:64). The project has ambitious goals modeled on the requirement that all Muslims should visit Mecca at least once in their lifetime; Project Joseph seeks to encourage all diasporan Africans to travel to Ghana, where they will "reverse the journey" by traveling from "the coast to areas where people were hunted" (Ghana Tourism 2006). The slave route journey is framed as a painful yet uplifting form of memory work: "For our Pilgrims there will definitely be sadness and anger in the homecoming pilgrimage but yet it will be an upliftment, a catharsis, a self re-discovery—a Strengthening" (Ghana Tourism 2006). Pilgrims will

> visit the Slave markets, the slave baths, the rest stops on the long journey from the hinterland to the slave lodges, slave forts and slave castles from where people departed to suffer the agonies of the inhuman "middle passage".... Along the pilgrimage route our pilgrimage will also experience the rich culture of

Ghanaians. We will seek to expunge the years of being denied who they are and reintroduce them to their roots…. They will establish a kinship with their brothers and sisters here in the homeland. (Ghana Tourism 2006)[8]

Sites designated as "shrines to the suffering of our people" (Ghana Tourism 2006) include the historically documented slave market at Salaga (Johnson 1986), the "last bath" at Assin Manso on the Pra River, where captives bathed before proceeding to the coast, as well as the walled settlement of Gwollu in northwestern Ghana, constructed as a defense against slave raiders (see photos in Perbi 2004; also Benson and McCaskie 2004). Pilgrims in 2007 attended a healing ceremony in Ghana's capital city; traditional rulers of groups that participated in the slave trade came together with rulers from groups whose people were hunted in a ceremony of rapprochement. Longer-term plans of Project Joseph include the production of a "gene map" that will help returnees/pilgrims identify the "villages of the ancestors" (Ghana Tourism 2006). Consistent with the broader theme of connecting diasporan Africans with Ghana, James Fort in Accra will house the African Excellence Experience, highlighting the biography of diasporan Africans who triumphed over adversity (Frederick Douglas, Harriet Tubman, Toussaint L'Ouverture, and Martin Luther King, among others). A special visa to be issued to diasporans after their initial visit to Ghana will allow visa-free entry to the country, and a land ownership program is envisioned as enabling diasporans to "have real ownership of a piece of the Homeland" (Ghana Tourism 2006). The project is conceived as a memory project for Africans by Africans since "Almost all of what has been written to date, has been written by the 'Europeans'. It is time that Africans told the story of this very African tragedy" (Ghana Tourism 2006).

Forged in relation to contemporary racisms in the United States and Europe, memories of the slave trade serve as a resource in processes of identification in the present (Hartman 2007). Viewed through the lens of race, the project becomes one of reconciling siblings (brothers and sisters)[9] as a step in reconnecting a group whose original unity was shattered through circumstances of history. Yet to a striking degree, these institutionally sponsored memory projects centered on the Atlantic trade are informed by essentialist, absolutist notions of identity (Gilroy 1993:1–15, 187–192). Like Afrocentricity, these memories "may be useful in developing communal discipline and individual self-worth and even in galvanising black communities to resist the encroachments of crack cocaine, but [they] suppl[y] a poor basis for the writing of cultural history and the calculation of political choices" (Gilroy 1993:188) because they merely reverse the valences but do not probe the processes through which African peoples have been marginalized. Heritage tourism becomes linked to a quest for origins that is itself "an expression of particularly and peculiarly modernist intellectual habits" (Gilroy 1996:22, also 1993:19). This form of memory work leaves intact, and arguably reinforces, the durable "lattice" of essentialized understandings (Smith 2004) that shape present-day practices of inclusion and exclusion (Hartman 2007).

Academic memory work is equally complicit in reproducing this lattice. Conventional historical and archaeological research enables essentialized forms of "root work" when it portrays Africa's past through an "ethnographic" lattice of discrete, bounded cultures differentiated from one another by durable cultural practices perceived in relation to a scale of cultural complexity. By extension, an imagined past in which so-called acephalous or decentralized societies are perceived as separate from (and precursors to) "middle range" societies, distinct in turn from "states," fosters the notion that many African societies stood outside the progressive march of history (for critiques, see Sharpe 1986; Stahl 1999b; Yoffee 1993). This separation is reinforced by a disciplinary division between historic and prehistoric archaeology defined in relation to the presence of Europeans and documentary sources (Lightfoot 1995; Rubertone 2000; cf. Hall and Silliman 2006; Reid and Lane 2004), in which dynamic, coastal, complex societies are encompassed by history, while "simpler" interior societies remain enmeshed in tradition (Robertshaw 2004; Stahl 2001b:31–33). The perceived "traditional" character of interior societies is further reinforced when archaeologists analogically project ethnographic images of African societies into the distant past (Lane 2005;

Stahl 1993, 2001b:19–40). These disciplinary practices have profoundly conditioned our understanding of slavery in Africa. Until recently (e.g., DeCorse [ed.] 2001; Kusimba 2004) slavery entered our view in the form of a tragic coastal trade that siphoned the ancestors of diasporic Africans from the continent through the transatlantic trade (Benson and McCaskie 2004:107), but it has been perceived as of little relevance to the study of so-called traditional societies of interior Africa. Taken together, these conventions shape a culture history of Africa that reproduces essentialized, progressive developmentalist perspectives on the continent and its peoples (Connah 1998; Stahl 2005).

As I argue below, we can more powerfully address the historical marginalization of the continent and the lingering racism that conditions the lives of African-descendant peoples by pursuing an archaeology of the slave trade focused on the processes through which durable, essentialized forms of difference have been produced and sustained. At the same time, alternative forms of memory work need to take account of the complexities of memory and identification within Africa, where the descendants of those enslaved in the internal slave trade live alongside those of their captors (C. Brown 2003; Soumonni 2003: 12).

Remembering While Forgetting: Internal African Slavery

The national and international initiatives summarized above are explicitly engaged in memory work, but remembering is intimately bound up in forgetting (Fabian 2003), just as mentions always involve silences (Trouillot 1995:48–53; see also Hartman 2007:155–172). The diasporic focus of memory projects centered on the Atlantic trade (Benson and McCaskie 2004:106–107; Reed 2004:13–14) perpetuates a deeper silence surrounding internal or domestic African slavery that until recently also characterized academic work (C. Brown 2003:219; cf. Perbi 2004). The facts surrounding internal slavery are the source of some controversy. It is clear, for example, that the term "slavery" is an inadequate gloss for the complex relations of dependency that characterized African societies in the early twentieth century. Rattray (1969:34) identified five terms

to describe "various conditions and degrees of voluntary or involuntary servitude in Ashanti" (see also Dumett 1990:12–15; Haenger 2000:1–3). Some distinguished a more benign "lineage slavery" that augmented families by incorporating enslaved individuals from a harsher slave "mode of production" in which slave labor was central to the political economy (Haenger 2000:61–62). Historians have split on whether internal slavery emerged late—as a response to the cessation of the Atlantic trade and an absorption of captives for which the external market had disappeared (e.g., McSheffrey 1983)—or whether the use of slaves in Africa predated the Atlantic trade (Grace 1975). There is, nevertheless, broad agreement that internal slavery intensified with the shift to the so-called "legitimate trade" as captives were used to produce and transport agricultural commodities after 1807 (the date of British abolition of the slave trade) (Baum 1999: 154; C. Brown 1996; Cordell 2003; Falola 2003: 111; Grace 1975; Johnson 1986:349–355; Haenger 2000; Klein 1971, 2003; Law 1995; Lovejoy 1983: 136, 160, 1989:388; Perbi 2004). Though we have no precise estimates of the scale of internal slavery, historians have suggested that anywhere from 15 to 35 percent of the population in some areas of West Africa were enslaved in the first decade of the twentieth century (Hubbell 2001:43; Lovejoy 1989:391–392; Lovejoy and Hogendorn 1993), with the Sokoto Caliphate representing the third largest slave society in modern history (after the United States and Brazil; Lovejoy 1989: 392, 2005). Estimates for other parts of Africa are lacking, but areas that fed the Atlantic trade internally consumed large numbers of slaves (e.g., Asante, Yoruba, Igbo; Falola 2003:113; Kea 1982: 20; Lovejoy 1989:393; Lovejoy and Richardson 2003; Wilks 1975). Today, the descendants of the enslaved are often (though not always; M. Brown 2004; O'Hear 2006) stigmatized and remain among the powerless and disadvantaged in contemporary Africa (C. Brown 1996:77, 2003:223; Haenger 2000:33, 56, 162–163; Parker 2006:358; Rattray 1969:42; Robertson and Klein 1983). As such, they remain outside the constituency for internationally sponsored programs of memory and healing.

The reasons for the continuing silence surrounding the internal trade are surely complex.

Africanist scholars have been concerned with distinguishing practices of internal slavery from those of chattel slavery in the western hemisphere and have thus highlighted the incorporative practices of absorption that distinguished African slavery (e.g., Kopytoff and Miers 1977; Lovejoy 1983:109–134; Perbi 2004:8–12; for a critique, see Cooper 1979:121–125; Falola 2003:109–110; Klein 1978:601). The enslaved in Asante, for example, were often incorporated into their master's family, and it was a serious offense to inquire into or disclose the origins of another (Rattray 1969:40). Yet the incorporation of slaves was often (maybe always) partial, as witnessed in the lingering stereotypes, ritual proscriptions, and marriage prohibitions that speak to enduring social distinctions associated with the practices of internal slavery (C. Brown 1996; Cooper 1977: 223–224, 264; Falola 2003:112, 120; Haenger 2000: 162–163; Lentz 2006:29; Parker 2006:358; Rattray 1969:43–44; Robertson and Klein 1983; Röschenthaler 2006). These processes resonate in the production of history, as rumors of slave origins are alternately circulated and suppressed within specific contexts and societies (e.g., Greene 2003; Hartman 2007:195; O'Hear 2006:269–273; Stahl 2001a:43–44). Cultural subordination was often part and parcel of the process of assimilation, but Cooper reminds us of the extent to which memory accompanied the loss of ancestry that slavery entailed: "remembering where they came from and asserting the value of the way of life of their homelands, slaves struggled *not* to be absorbed" (Cooper 1979:125). Though oral histories—particularly those associated with the powerful among society—are often silent on internal slavery (cf. Lentz 2006:29–32, 48–49), memories of the internal trade often take an embodied form in dance, ritual, and particularly the practices surrounding witchcraft (Argenti and Röschenthaler 2006; Parker 2006).

Although literature on the Atlantic trade stresses the terror and alienation experienced by enslaved peoples, portrayals of internal slavery have tended to "strip the process of its terror" (Cooper 1979:118 n. 61). As Meillassoux (1973: 450) stressed, these enslaved peoples originated in acts of violence that stripped them of their social identity, after which they were instated as marginal members of another society, often in a place far removed from their home where escape was unlikely (Klein 1978:606; cf. Hubbell 2001: 25; Smith 1955:39, 43).

The silences surrounding internal slavery are reproduced in the memory work of heritage tourism centered on the external slave trade (e.g., Benson and McCaskie 2004; Hartman 2007:164). Archaeology's contribution to heritage tourism has been to identify sites that can be incorporated into slave trails that serve the "root work" of diasporic memory (Ebron 2002). In this way, archaeological sites are drawn into forms of memory work that reproduce essentialist logics in the present, as seen also in recent, highly publicized efforts to identify the "tribal affiliations" of prominent African Americans through genetic testing based on the problematic assumption that biological, cultural, and linguistic variation comes in tidy, unified packages (e.g., Gates et al. 2006; cf. MacEachern 2000).[10] Extant ethnic groups are treated as durable, bounded entities locked in a drama that pitted raiders against the raided. This perspective is belied by robust evidence for the fluidity and malleability of ethnicity in recent centuries (e.g., Gilbert 1997; Lentz 1995, 2000a; Lovejoy and Trotman 2003; Miller 2004; though cf. Lentz and Nugent 2000 on the "limits of invention"), at the same time as it is reinforced by archaeological reconstructions that project historic ethnic groups into earlier centuries. The fact that many of the sites incorporated into slave trails are known primarily for their involvement in the internal trade of the nineteenth and early twentieth centuries—and therefore post-date the transatlantic trade—is among the silences perpetuated by heritage tourism (e.g., the site of Gwollu, fortified against Samori's attacks in the terminal nineteenth century; Mendonsa 2001: 44; Perbi 2004: Plate iv). But we might (and arguably should) envision an alternative kind of "route work" (Gilroy 1993:19, 1996) that eschews the "simple stories" (Benson and McCaskie 2004: 93) of slavery tourism and instead explores the processes and practices associated with slavery and slaving, both internal and external, and attends to their effects on contemporary social and political economic forms and practices of identification. This requires new archives that inform on the practices of slavery and their ramifying effects.

"Route Work"
Through Alternative Archives

The image of "route work" implies both connections—spatial and temporal (Gilroy 1993)—and movement or process. It implies a different endpoint from which one began. In this sense, it usefully underscores the need to consider African societies as dynamic, connected entities (Mitchell 2005) rather than tradition-bound isolates in which to root essentialized identities. It opens to inquiry the ways in which the taken-for-granteds of African ethnography—ethnic units, marriage and kinship systems, ritual, productive practices, political organization, settlement, physical environment, and more—were actively configured through the centuries of the external and internal African slave trade. It problematizes our use of these taken-for-granteds as analogical props to envision a deeper past (Stahl 2001b:19–40, 2004). In this view, the practices captured in twentieth-century ethnography represent historical products rather than timeless configurations (see Dirks 1996). At the same time, route work should also bring into view how western/European societies and their practices were reconfigured through their involvement in the African slave trade, both external and internal (as masterfully captured, for example, by Mintz 1985). Cast in this light, the study of African slavery ceases to be a "special topic," one that we choose to be interested in or not, and becomes instead a necessary component to investigating the dynamic, ramifying landscape of social, political, and economic relations that configured the modern world. Such investigations contribute to a historiography of the present (Pels 1997:177) and meaningfully connect with an emerging anthropology of colonialism that works to trace the processes through which the practices and forms of the modern world took hold and are maintained (see contributions in Cooper and Stoler 1997; Stoler [ed.] 2006; also Comaroff and Comaroff 1992).

Approaching African societies as dynamic and emergent—enmeshed with, though not determined by, ramifying connections within and outside the continent (Mitchell 2005)—requires that we approach existing archives with a fresh eye and work to develop archaeological archives that foster an appreciation of that dynamism. As such, archaeologists need to build on innovations in other disciplines by considering the implications of new archives in history and anthropology for our understanding of slavery as material, social, and historical practice.

Archival Innovations
in History and Anthropology

One of the most dramatic developments in Atlantic slavery studies in recent years was the 1999 publication of the transatlantic slave trade database sponsored by the W. E. B. Du Bois Institute for Afro-American Research at Harvard University (Eltis et al. 1999). The database promises to transform our understanding of patterning and variability in the Atlantic slave trade at the same time as it conjures new concerns surrounding history-making and memory (Austen 2001). The interactive database provides information on an estimated two-thirds of all transatlantic slaving, totaling 27,233 voyages between 1527 and 1866, and representing the activities of British, French, Dutch, Danish, Brandenburger, Spanish, Portuguese, and North American slavers. The CD-ROM represents a pioneering use of technology to bring information that was formerly the province of specialists and scattered among diverse archives to a wide audience (Smallwood 2001:257). Though the database suffers from issues of sampling and unevenness of information (Smallwood 2001:261), it has invigorated studies of the Atlantic slave trade, particularly with respect to demographics (how many enslaved Africans were transshipped, and of what gender and age?) and regional variability in the trade's organization (Bailyn 2001; Nwokeji 2001; Solow 2001). Research based in the Du Bois database suggests that children were more common among enslaved captives on Atlantic slavers than previously recognized (Campbell et al. 2006; Diptee 2006; Lovejoy 2006). These insights have led to renewed considerations regarding the contexts in which, and processes through which, African men, women, and children were enslaved and transferred to shipping points (Diptee 2006: 186–190). Explorations of the database have led historians to consider the periodicity of the trade in relation to food supplies and shortages. Slavers were concerned with the regularity and predictability of food supplies while periodic drought and famine led to upsurges in the availability of the enslaved (Behrendt 2001; Diptee 2006:186). This has prompted historians to consider agricultural ecology as a variable shaping the practices and patterns of the Atlantic slave trade. The insight that port of origin correlates most closely with Middle Passage mortality rates has raised new questions regarding regional differences in health and nutritional status (Klein et al. 2001). Though much of the information contained in the Du Bois database was previously "known," its compilation in CD-ROM format has produced a new archive from which to consider the processes and practices of the Atlantic slave trade.

By virtue of its sources (slavers' records), the Du Bois database yields a coastal perspective on the Atlantic slave trade. Yet recent historical and anthropological studies of interior societies expand archival perspectives on the processes of enslavement as well as the conditions and effects of internal slavery. Two themes stand out in recent literature: (1) a growing appreciation of the varying ways in which societies participated in and were affected by the slave trade; and (2) the extent to which the social institutions and practices once taken as timeless features of an African ethnographic present emerged through long histories of global entanglements, particularly through the "tumultuous era of the Atlantic slave trade" (Baum 1999:5; Hawthorne 1999:117–118, 2003a; Ogundiran 2002:457; Parker 2004, 2006: 377; Piot 1999).

Recent historical studies have questioned conventional wisdom regarding the involvement of societies of different scale in the slave trade. States and complex societies were conventionally seen as those who acquired slaves through raiding or warfare, whereas relatively egalitarian, so-called "acephalous" societies were assumed to be the sources of slaves (Goody 1971). Recent studies call for a reassessment of this conventional understanding (Hubbell 2001), first because of temporal variation (a society that was a source of slaves at one point might become a supplier of slaves at another; Van Dantzig 1982), and second because it is now evident that some so-called acephalous societies raided for slaves (Baum 1999:109; Hawthorne 1999, 2003a, 2003b; Hubbell 2001; Swanepoel 2004, 2006). In a study of decentralized societies in coastal Guinea-Bissau,

Hawthorne (2003b:154) argues that involvement in slaving offered a measure of protection against being enslaved (also Swanepoel 2006:267), yet did not inexorably lead to increased political centralization (Hawthorne 1999:113; cf. Mendonsa 2001:23–25, 55). At the same time, members of societies engaged in slaving were not necessarily immune from enslavement themselves (e.g., Lovejoy and Richardson 2003). By emphasizing the complex interactions that linked states and so-called acephalous societies, these studies call into question the social evolutionary assumptions that have shaped archaeological archives and underscore the importance of apprehending the connections between, and dynamism of, societies of varying scale (e.g., Holl 2001; Hubbell 2001; Mitchell 2005; Robertshaw 1999; Stahl 1999b, 2005).

Recent literature similarly stresses the dynamism of African social institutions and practices in relation to global processes, including the slave trade. For example, Baum's (1999) study of Diola religious practices explores the proliferation of new cults and spirit shrines associated with Diola participation in the Atlantic slave trade, chronicling the role of religious authorities in its legitimation and regulation. There is similarly an enhanced understanding of the complex processes that produced enslaveable people. While the importance of raids and warfare has long been appreciated, recent research highlights the ways in which enslaveable people were produced through ritual and juridical proceedings that were "refashioned for the production of slave exports" (Hawthorne 1999:110, also 105–106). Witchcraft accusations were a common pathway to enslavement (Baum 1999; Hawthorne 1999:106), and a number of recent studies explore witchcraft as a phenomenon quintessentially bound up in modernity and rooted in experiences of the slave trade (Comaroff and Comaroff 1993; Geschiere 1997; Moore and Sanders 2001:10–13).[11] Though witchcraft practices and beliefs surely preceded the slave trade, there is evidence that they intensified in relation to the looming threat of enslavement or in contexts where large numbers of enslaved captives presented a danger to their captors (Parish 1999, 2000; Parker 2004, 2006; Röschenthaler 2006; Shaw 1997, 2002). Ritual innovation (Shaw's [2002:84] "ritual reformation") was common as people struggled to cope with the challenges of a predatory landscape in which "terror had become a taken-for-granted aspect of the environment in which people's lives unfolded" (Shaw 2002:41; see also Baum 1999; Ferme 2001). Parker (2004, 2006) stresses the cross-cultural and transregional dimensions of this process in the Gold Coast region. Here ritual practices of northern peoples who were perceived as uncivilized and enslaveable by their southern Akan neighbors nonetheless inspired a series of Akan anti-witchcraft cults. Similarly, some power associations and secret societies were bound up in the slave trade. For example, the secret Ekpe society in southeastern Nigeria provided a measure of protection against enslavement for its members and simultaneously produced, through exclusion, those subject to legal enslavement (Lovejoy and Richardson 2003:105–106; cf. Ferme 2001: 37, who observes that the Sierra Leonean forests and associated secret societies provided a refuge from the trade). We should, however, be cautious about generalizing; whereas shrines and oracles were intimately bound up in the production of enslaveable people in some contexts (C. Brown 1996:56; Lovejoy and Richardson 2003:104), in others they served as refuges for dissatisfied or maltreated slaves (Haenger 2000:46), underscoring the need to engage in contextually specific analyses of local practices.

Ethnic and religious identifications similarly served to distinguish the enslaveable. Whereas the spread of Islam in West Africa produced a moving frontier of enslaveable people (Cordell 2003:32–35; MacEachern 1993), other areas appear to have served as stable reservoirs of circumscribed, raidable populations (Mendonsa 2001:23, 27–28). In the Gold Coast, people of northern origins, who were often visibly marked by distinctive scarification patterns, were subject to harsher, more durable forms of enslavement than were ethnically Akan peoples, who were placed in slavery through family debt or misfortune (Austin 2003; Haenger 2000:30, 57; Parker 2004, 2006:354, 356, 358). Alternatively, ethnicity and language could protect individuals from enslavement, as for example among the Efik of Old Calabar, whose creolized practices operated to distinguish the Efik from those they enslaved (Lovejoy and Richardson 2003:104–105).

At the same time we need to keep in view that individuals often had multiple associations and connections, and were thus able to "define themselves through belonging in multiple ways," a view that runs counter to the "unidimensional, homogenous, comprehending, and stable 'ethnicity' that underlies most existing discussion of African identities" (Miller 2004:86). In this regard, we should anticipate that malleable ethnic identification, sometimes combined with migration, may have helped some individuals avoid enslavement.

The practices of internal slavery reshaped gender relations through its effects on labor allocation and control of property, particularly, though not exclusively, in contexts where captive women were taken as wives. Ferme (2001:18, 81–88) explored how the entangled character of slavery and marriage among the Mende in Sierra Leone profoundly affected gender relations, with enduring implications for forms of social dependency in contemporary contexts. Nineteenth-century changes in craft production among the Makara in Mali were associated with the use of male slave labor to cultivate indigo (formerly a female domain) and to weave cloth, which altered the balance of property relations among husbands and wives (Roberts 1984). These examples underscore the fact that contemporary gender relations are the result of complex historical dynamics shaped in part by slavery, and that its legacies were felt among enslaved and free alike.

Whereas earlier studies of slavery treated kinship as a priori and given—at most a framework into which internal slaves were absorbed (e.g., Kopytoff and Miers 1977)—Cooper (1979:104), among others, has stressed that "absorptionist analyses" reify kinship. Instead we need to open these forms of sociality to investigation (Ekeh 1990; Haenger 2000:9). Internal slavery implied a new social calculus (Argenti 2006; Ferme 2001: 82–88). Kinship practices were flexible and could provide either protection from enslavement or a pathway toward it. For example, Lovejoy and Richardson (2003:104, 108, 111) adduced evidence for the ways in which local institutions, including familial relations, distinguished enslaveable outsiders from protected insiders among the Efik of Old Calabar. Although family ties were not always sufficient to protect those involved in the slave trade from enslavement, those so protected were more likely to be returned to their families if enslaved. But family ties could also lead to enslavement when, as an example, less powerful family members were used to settle family debts and liabilities, a practice that may have intensified on the Gold Coast with increasing monetization and new forms of lending (Austin 2003; Bailey 2005:53; Haenger 2000:58). Detailed biographies of enslaved individuals recorded by mid nineteenth-century Basel missionaries in the Gold Coast enabled Haenger (2000:32–56) to apprehend the "complex geometry of family organisation" in which blood ties often existed between slave and master lineages, as, for example, in the case of Rosine Opo, who was "on the one hand, a female slave, the daughter of a man bound to [a mighty chief], and on the other, the wife of two free men and the mother of a whole host of children" (Haenger 2000:51; see also Smith 1955:39–43). Such cases underscore that status and identity were not fixed, but operated instead through inclusionary and exclusionary practices that could vary through an individual's life history. Recent literature similarly stresses the mutability of social reckoning within societies. Tengan (2000), for example, argues that Dagara lineage and patriclan structures atrophied under pressure of frequent migration in a period of intense slave raiding. The Dagara developed instead a house-based structure that linked residential units who did not necessarily share common ancestry (though cf. Kuba and Lentz 2002:388–392). These examples point to the need to consider the ways in which family and identity were recast through processes shaped by the slave trade.

The Dagara example highlights the relationship between social organization and settlement dynamics. As amply developed by Robertshaw and Duncan (this volume), shifting settlement strategies emerged in response to the predatory landscape of recent centuries. Some groups moved into settings that were difficult for horse-mounted slavers to access and/or constructed dwellings that impeded assaults through fortification or restricted entrances (Bah 2003; de Barros 2001:71–73; Guèye 2003; Hawthorne 2003b: 157; Klein 2003; Kusimba 2004, 2006; Kusimba et al. 2005; Mendonsa 2001:24, 39–44, 51–53; Soumonni 2003). Clearly we cannot assume a simple

directional relationship between settlement and specific patterns of social reckoning; however, an archaeological focus on settlement patterning can inform on spatial responses to the threat of predatory landscapes in recent centuries. Though specifics may elude us, evidence for altered settlement patterns may highlight cases in which ethnographically documented forms of social calculus emerged through processes of the slave trade era (e.g., Hubbell 2001:29; Mendonsa 2001:53, 55; Tengan 2000).

The implication of these recent historical and anthropological studies is that practices once viewed ahistorically (Parker 2006:377) must be considered anew in relation to dynamic historical processes (e.g., Kuba and Lentz 2002; Lentz 2006). As Klein (2003:73) observes, those living in raided areas "changed the structure of their community, the crops they grew, the ways they related to strangers and to each other, all in the interest of protection." The practices of societies involved in raiding changed as well, particularly as they worked to incorporate the enslaved into the social fabric of their communities, whether as kinsmen—albeit socially disadvantaged ones— or as a despised labor force in a slave mode of production. In short, recent historical and anthropological studies forcefully underscore a point made decades ago by Walter Rodney (1970: 259): that the production of slaves had everyday consequences.

Towards an Archaeology of Slavery as Practice

"One of the sinister and poignant features of slavery is that it is a phantom industry that leaves scant traces; its capital lies in people, long since dead, not machinery" (Seaton 2001:117). In referring to slavery's phantom memory, Seaton draws a contrast with industrial production, the visibility of which seems ensured by durable material residues such as factories and machinery. But the production and consumption of slaves also involved material practices and had wide-ranging material effects that can be investigated through archaeological sources (e.g., contributions in DeCorse [ed.] 2001; Ogundiran and Falola 2007). Because the interior African societies drawn into slavery's ramifying networks occupied a "parched documentary landscape" (Cohen and Odihambo

1989:16), archaeological sources are particularly important in considering slavery's processes and effects (DeCorse 2001b). Yet despite its potential, the archaeological archive on African slavery is thin, in part because, to date, slavery has been treated as a special topic within historical archaeology, which has focused primarily on coastal settings involved in the European trade (e.g., Bredwa-Mensah 2004; DeCorse 2001a; Hall 1993; Hall and Markell 1993; Kelly 1997; Schrire 1995; though cf. Reid and Lane 2004). Whereas historical archaeological studies have deepened our understanding of slavery in coastal contexts, we arguably need a more comprehensive and robust engagement with questions of slavery (Kusimba 2004). This requires us to broaden the archive beyond sites directly linked to the slave trade (i.e., forts, castles, and plantations), artifacts that speak to its horrors (implements of torture and bondage), and the state-level societies that until recently dominated historical studies of slaving and slavery (MacEachern 2001:148). What we need is a more encompassing understanding of the material effects that the production and consumption of enslaved peoples had on societies of varying scale, both within and beyond Africa. Accomplishing this requires us to cease treating slavery as a special topic and begin to explore it as a dynamic and ramifying landscape of social, political, and economic relations that was simultaneously produced by and productive of the modern world.

An archaeology of slavery requires a focus on those societies perceived as quintessentially timeless: the so-called acephalous or stateless societies that were long presumed to be outside the currents of history (Johnson 1986:346–347). This is a yawning gap in the archaeological archive because, until recently, there was virtually no archaeological research focused on these societies (MacEachern 2001:148).[12] Natalie Swanepoel's (2004, 2006) recent work in Sisalaland, northern Ghana, is thus a welcome addition that demonstrates the value of archaeological investigations in addressing how people living in a nineteenth-century decentralized society responded to the "predatory zone" (Swanepoel 2004:13–21) in which they were enmeshed. It also requires us to be attentive to the complex connections (e.g., in relation to processes of production, consump-

tion, and social differentiation) between societies that were the source of both slaves and raw materials or finished products consumed by raiding societies. The complexity of these relations has been adeptly highlighted by MacEachern (1993, 2001) in his analysis of iron production and slaving in the Mandara region of Cameroon (also de Barros 2001; see discussion in Robertshaw and Duncan, this volume). All of this has implications for our units and scales of analyses as we endeavor to produce archaeological archives relevant to the study of slavery in Africa.

What, then, might an archaeology of slavery as practice look like? Robertshaw and Duncan's (this volume) lucid review of the characteristics of African slavery allows me to focus here on future projects. Given its wide-ranging effects, our appreciation of the transformative character of the slave trade and slavery requires systematic research strategies aimed at comparatively analyzing material practices through time and across space. As Swanepoel (2004:31) observed, we should conceptualize this not as an "archaeology of the slave trade," but rather as an "archaeology of daily life during the slave trade." However, "doing" an archaeology of slavery raises the issue of material signatures (Alexander 2001; cf. Kusimba 2006:218). How will we know slavery when we dig it up? This problem bedevils every new set of questions that archaeologists ask—for example, with respect to gender or, more recently, ritual and memory (Mills and Walker 2008). Yet as we have repeatedly learned, posing new questions often prompts new investigatory approaches (Stoler 2006:146). Those of us who work in areas of Africa where the slave trade is amply documented can take slavery to be a "fact" (Robertshaw and Duncan, this volume) and perhaps even a "total social fact" in the same vein as Gosden (2004:24) argues for colonialism in that it "infiltrated all areas of people's lives." Given its "phantom quality" (Seaton 2001: 117), slavery seldom comes into focus in the form of concrete material traces (DeCorse 1991; though cf. Cox et al. 2001). If, however, slavery can be considered a "total social fact"—part and parcel of the social, political, and economic landscapes that produced the material traces we recover from archaeological sites—we need not be preoccupied with its concrete traces so much as its ramifying effects (Robertshaw and Duncan, this volume). We might usefully conceptualize slavery as a phenomenon that comes into our vision peripherally, indirectly through its effects on a range of practices. Viewing slavery as a process rather than a thing similarly aids our investigative approaches. For example, enslaveable people were defined through exclusionary practices; therefore, material practices of distinction (Bourdieu 1984; Stahl 2002) and boundary making are one avenue through which to investigate changing terrains of risk and vulnerability. As amply demonstrated in the historical and anthropological literature, populations perceived as enslaveable were commonly viewed as less than human (Cordell 2003; Parker 2006:371), an ideological construct that was often based on visible distinctions in lifestyle. Spatial variability in practices may therefore provide insight into the social boundaries that conditioned a population's vulnerability to enslavement. These observations suggest two avenues for investigating the processes and effects of slavery: a genealogical approach to practice, and a focus on material practices of inclusion and exclusion.

A genealogical approach (Gosden 2005; Pauketat and Alt 2005) explores patterns of continuity and discontinuity through time and across space in order to discern commonalities associated with a community of practice (i.e., people who share a series of bodily dispositions, notions of style, and so on; in short, people who share a sense of how to proceed on a daily basis; Fenn et al. 2006; Minar 2001; Minar and Crown 2001; Sassaman 2001; Van Keuren 2006). Although discontinuities in practice can result from a variety of processes—including some, like migration, that archaeologists routinely invoke to explain change—slaving should be considered among the possible explanations for discontinuity. For example, discontinuities in technological practices might signal an influx of people from a different community of practice as, for example, when captives are put to work in craft production. In other instances, discontinuities in practice may occur without a change in personnel as in cases where groups adopted new forms of protective architecture in the face of predation. In this case, we might expect a change in the form, but perhaps not the techniques, of construction.

Thinking genealogically about practice involves a consideration of material sequences (in terms of production sequences or *chaînes opératoires*—of ceramics, metals, houses; Childs 1991; Dietler and Herbich 1998; Gosselain 1992; Lemmonier 1986) and forms with a view to understanding historical connections between practices at spatially and temporally distinct sites (Gosden 2005). Existing archaeological archives, cast as they often are in typological terms that stress homogeneity within and differences between types or sites, are ill-suited to this task.

Constructing genealogies of practice requires that we generate comparable (in terms of contexts, sample size, etc.), temporally seriated data sets that can illuminate continuity and change in specific practices through time (e.g., practices of production, consumption, settlement, exchange, and so on), beginning with sites occupied in relatively recent periods and extending our investigations to successively earlier sites (Stahl 1999a, 2001b). These seriated data sets provide the basis for constructing genealogies of practice in an area through time. In a study of ceramics, for example, we might document stylistic change in the form and decoration of pottery despite an underlying continuity of technological style (e.g., in the practices of clay preparation, molding, etc.; Gosselain 1992, 2000). Or we might discern changes in architectural forms and site placement despite continuities in other aspects of material culture. In other contexts we might identify simultaneous changes in a range of practices. By adopting a systematic investigative approach across regions, we can build comparative insights into the genealogies of practices across space and through time (Pauketat and Alt 2005). Though we may not be able to draw direct causal links between slavery and changes in strategies of settlement, subsistence, production, or consumption (MacEachern 2001; Singleton 2001; also Robertshaw and Duncan, this volume), we can nonetheless posit connections when viewed in relation to the broader landscape of enslaving connections that conditioned daily life in Africa in recent centuries.

Several recent studies demonstrate the potential for a genealogical approach to technological sequences or operational chains (Childs and Herbert 2005:282–287; Dietler and Herbich 1989,

1998; Gosselain 1992, 1998, 2000; Lemmonier 1986; Pfaffenberger 1998) to inform on the materiality of slavery. For example, evidence from the Bassar region of northern Togo attests to experimentation with new clays by local potters as Bassar peoples were forced into refuge zones under pressure of slaving and their access to trade wares diminished (de Barros 2001:74–75). Technological studies may also be used to discern instances where enslaved peoples maintained distinctive practices despite their apparent incorporation into the societies of their enslavers. Based on the notion that technological processes are relatively conservative (Gosselain 2000:192–193, 209–210), Barbara Frank (1993:396) makes a case for the visibility of enslaved female potters in the Kadiolo region of southern Mali who "forced by circumstance to lose their social identity, chose to keep their skills as potters and to continue making pottery in the distinctive way their mothers taught them." Whereas decorative style and form were malleable and created a semblance of homogeneity across the Mande area, enslaved women passed on to their descendants distinct approaches to the fashioning of vessels that endure today (also Habicht-Mauche, this volume; though cf. Herbich 1987 on the complications of post-marital transmission of technological skills; see Robertshaw and Duncan, this volume for changes in craft production linked to the slave trade but not necessarily to the use of enslaved labor in production).

Following Frank's lead, we might, therefore profitably investigate the potential effects of incorporating slaves on a wider array technological practices, particularly since historical sources suggest that enslaved craft specialists were often put to work producing goods for their new masters. For example, the Zaberma put captives to work producing arms and protective gear for their army. The number of captives engaged in mining, metal, and leather work was so large that 20 percent of the Zaberma army devoted its time to supervising captive workers (Echenberg 1971:247). A detailed investigation of the operational sequences and technological styles of metallurgy through time in the area occupied by the Zaberma would help to discern whether the practices of enslaved metal workers were continuous or discontinuous with earlier practices in the region. Comparative profiles of operational sequences and technological styles in time and space can thus help us to discern instances in which captives introduced distinctive approaches to the crafts in which they were engaged.

Genealogical approaches to subsistence practices can also help us to discern the effects of slaving on daily life. Historical and ethnographic sources suggest that some groups altered their subsistence regimes under the predatory pressure of slaving (e.g., Cordell 2003:40–42; Ferme 2001:45; Hawthorne 2003b:164; Klein 2003:73). In some instances, this was associated with movement into new environmental settings (Hawthorne 1999:107, 2003b:158; Soumonni 2003). In other cases, agricultural regimes were altered through the adoption of new crops, particularly introductions from the western hemisphere, maize (*Zea mays*) and cassava (manioc; *Manihot esculenta*). Though it seems clear that these crops spread in the context of the slave trade, details of how and when they spread remain sketchy (Alpern 1992). Historians have suggested that maize may have been valued by armies as a transportable staple (Dickson 1964), while cassava is known for its ability to thrive untended and to remain in the ground for long periods, both advantages for populations confronted with insecurity and/or labor shortages (Cordell 2003:40–42; Ohadike 1981). Gathering of wild plant foods was another strategy pursued by populations whose agricultural strategies were compromised by predation. We might similarly anticipate changes in the degree of reliance on domestic animals and in the composition of hunted fauna as people responded to the pressures of slaving (e.g., Kusimba 2006:239 describes a shift from cattle to goat herding under predatory conditions of recent centuries in southeastern Kenya). By adopting a comparative approach to rigorously analyzed floral and faunal assemblages recovered from sites distributed through time and across space, we can begin to develop an appreciation for the ways in which subsistence practices were adjusted in the face of predation and warfare.

Genealogical approaches to settlement patterning should prove similarly informative. Architectural forms can be linked to the turbulence of daily life, though not in simple, directional fashion. Whereas some groups constructed fortress-like walled dwellings in the face of pre-dation (Baum 1999:93; Echenberg 1971:243; Hawthorne 1999:107; Hubbell 2001:31–32; Swanepoel 2006:273–276), others opted to flee and build expedient structures requiring minimal labor (Guèye 2003:54–56; Stahl 2001b:200–203). Settlement morphology was also altered in response to slaving (Robertshaw and Duncan, this volume). Consistent with Horton's (1976:91–92) view that "compact villages" were a defensive strategy, dispersed settlements located close to cultivated fields gave way in some areas to nucleated settlements after the seventeenth century (Hawthorne 2003b:158; Mendonsa 2001:39–44; Swanepoel 2006:274; cf. Robertshaw 1999:131). In other instances, groups resettled in terrain that was difficult for slave raiders to access (e.g., marshes; Hawthorne 1999:107, 2003b:158; Soumonni 2003; see Robertshaw and Duncan, this volume, for additional examples). Travel patterns were altered as people endeavored to minimize the risks of kidnapping, with implications for the extent of social interactions and attendant social fields (Baum 1999:121; Kusimba 2006:225, 239; Stahl 2001b:189–214). These processes of site relocation should draw our attention to how sites were abandoned (Cameron and Tomka 1993), particularly as instances of rapid abandonment related to warfare (e.g., Stahl 2001b:169, 187) may signal contexts in which populations were threatened with enslavement (Kusimba 2006). When combined with careful study of site abandonment processes, a comparative, genealogical approach to architecture and settlement promises to yield insights into the strategies of populations encompassed by predatory landscapes (e.g., de Barros 2001; Kusimba 2004, 2006; Kusimba et al. 2005; Swanepoel 2004, 2006).

Because the production of social boundaries was intimately related to people's vulnerability to enslavement, material practices of inclusion and exclusion provide a promising avenue for investigating the processes and effects of enslavement. With respect to internal slavery, the maintenance or dissolution of "foreign-ness" (in material cultural terms) provides a potential pathway into how practices of inclusion and exclusion may have been linked to the control of labor and wealth (e.g., Cooper 1979:123–124; see Cooper 1977: Chap. 6, for an extended discussion of the significance of cultural practices in the struggles over slaves' place in coastal Swahili society). Though different forms of servitude are masked by the word "slavery" as applied to Africa, they share the term's referent as a "foreigner brought by force into a society" (Cooper 1979:105). While some have stressed the benign, incorporative qualities of internal slavery (Kopytoff and Miers 1977), there were limits to incorporation, even when female slaves were incorporated through marriage. The limits of incorporation came into sharp relief at times when families were faced with debt or a need for individuals to be sacrificed on the death of a prominent person (Haenger 2000). Though the role of slaves varied within Africa, a shared feature of all enslaved persons was their subordinate status, which Cooper argues has too long been ignored in the literature on African slavery: "Africanists have tried too hard to say what 'rights' slaves did or did not have or what the 'status of slaves' in a particular society was, and not hard enough to analyse *how* such rights and statuses became customary or *how* they changed" (Cooper 1979:117, emphasis added).

Consumption practices may be a particularly productive way to investigate processes of inclusion and exclusion shaped by slavery. By building genealogies of consumptive practices in reference to time and space (Stahl 2002), we may glean how the enslaveable were distinguished through material practice. As an example, Lovejoy and Richardson (2003) make an intriguing case based on a study of Efik peoples around Old Calabar who participated in the slave trade that consumption of imports and an associated "creolization" of practice was part of a broader set of cultural markers that "helped to distinguish the Efik from those they dealt in as slaves" (Lovejoy and Richardson 2003:105). Efik peoples adopted European-style dress and home furnishings, part of a broader range of habits or practices that simultaneously protected Efik peoples from being enslaved and marked a boundary between the Efik and those who could be enslaved. This perspective encourages a reconsideration of the material practices documented by DeCorse (1992, 2001a) at Elmina, one of the primary castles involved in the slave trade along the Gold Coast. DeCorse's excavations at the African settlement adjacent to the castle yielded large numbers of imported objects, including imported ceramics, glassware, and items of personal adornment, which were taken to signal the wealth of Elmina's residents. Despite impressive quantities of imports, DeCorse argues for continuity in food ways and architecture. A preference for hollow-ware vessels (bowls) over plates suggests continuity in cuisine (e.g., consumption of stews). Whereas houses were built from stone, their layout was consistent with local conventions, taking the form of an enclosed compound organized around a central courtyard. Though DeCorse's argument for continuity is sound, Lovejoy and Richardson's (2003) analysis of Efik practices suggests that the consumption of imports at Elmina was about more than signaling wealth. When viewed in relation to Elmina's context as a transshipment point for the Atlantic trade and a site where slaves were consumed in the internal trade, the transformation in taste (Bourdieu 1984; Stahl 2002) signaled by the embrace of imports was a material practice that distinguished free residents of Elmina from both the enslaved in their midst and those condemned to the Middle Passage, thus drawing attention to the local operations of power.

Ritual practice is another promising site through which to consider practices of inclusion and exclusion (Kuba and Lentz 2002). Carolyn Brown (1996) argues that in northern Igboland the relevant distinctions between enslaved and free did not emerge primarily through the kinds of labor in which slaves and their masters engaged, for in many instances they were engaged in a similar range of tasks (clearing bush, digging yam mounds; see also Smith 1955:44). Instead, the key distinction centered on the exclusion of enslaved individuals from ritual practices central to community life (e.g., burial practices and sacrificial practices associated with shrines; see also Lentz 2006:29). It was these exclusions rather than labor issues that were a focus of local emancipation struggles in the early twentieth century.[13]

The predatory landscapes of recent centuries were negotiated through ritual practice. As outlined above, recent literature on shrine and divination practices underscores the dangerous associations of slavery and its links to witchcraft. An archaeology attuned to material traces of shrines and divinatory practices has the potential to inform on the dynamics of these practices through time (Lentz 2000b; Stahl 2008; see Lyons 1998:354–357 on the material signatures of anti-witchcraft practices, though not in reference to slavery). Ogundiran's (2002) analysis of divination practices and reconfigurations of the Yoruba pantheon through the period of the Atlantic slave trade provides a robust example of a genealogical (what he terms "biographical") approach to ritual practice. By tracing the changing uses and associations of beads and cowries in archaeological contexts, Ogundiran makes a substantive case for how the cowries that entered Yorubaland in massive quantities in exchange for slaves were recontextualized and incorporated into ritual practice. The fact that cowries served as an important currency in the period of the Atlantic trade (Johnson 1986) at the same time they came to operate as a primary form of bride-wealth among societies subject to intense predation (e.g., in northern Ghana; Goody 1969:130, 133–34; Mendonsa 2001: 143) suggests additional avenues for extending Ogundiran's (2002:457) call to historicize material culture associated with the slave trade. That objects acquired through the sale of slaves became a prerequisite for marriage transactions raises intriguing questions about the processes through which the circulation of women between kin groups became dependent upon tender ultimately acquired through the slave trade.

To sum up, extant archaeological archives are insufficient to address questions surrounding the processes and effects of slaving and slavery in Africa, and efforts to "find slavery" will likely be frustrated by a paucity of material traces (DeCorse 1991). If, however, we consider slavery as part of a broader landscape of intersocietal entanglements—a total social fact for the last number of centuries across wide swaths of Africa—our focus is directed instead to its implications for a range of practices: subsistence, craft production, consumption, settlement dynamics, and more. Viewed in this light, questions of slavery's effects cease to be a special topic and need to be routinely incorporated into our research designs. Considered individually, changes in the aforementioned practices might result from any number of causes, making it difficult to establish a direct relationship to slavery and slave trading

(Robertshaw and Duncan, this volume). But this is not a problem confined to the study of slavery, for archaeologists are invariably confronted with multiple explanations or interpretive possibilities (Minar and Crown 2001:370). As in the case of archaeological interpretation more generally, the strength of our interpretations is enhanced by invoking multiple lines of evidence or, in this case, evidence relating to a range of practices affected by slavery or the slave trade.

Discerning slavery's effects also requires that we treat ethnographic sources as outcomes rather than privileged sources of insight into enduring patterns of "tradition" (Stahl 2004:256–259). Working back in time from these sources, a comparative genealogical approach to practice across space and through time will help us to investigate the production of predatory landscapes and their effects on the lives of African peoples in recent centuries. When combined with a focus on material practices of inclusion and exclusion, these research strategies will yield insight into how some populations were made vulnerable to predation while others were protected. Though sharply focused images of slavery and its effects will likely elude us, by bringing slavery within range of our peripheral vision and endeavoring to discern its operations and effects as a routine component of our research designs, archaeological investigations hold considerable potential to address the silences that surround both the international slave trade and internal African slavery. Viewed as an alternative form of "route work" (Gilroy 1993:19, 1996), an archaeology of slavery as practice fosters an appreciation of the dynamism of African societies and illuminates the processes through which durable forms of difference and inequality have been produced and perpetuated, both within and outside the African continent.

Concluding Comments

Whereas the "spectre of slavery has never ceased to haunt African consciousness" (Mbembe 2001: 21), it has not, until late, similarly haunted "European" consciousness. The *fin de millénaire* has prompted new reflections on the slave trade and its legacies, with a concomitant concern to make available and expand archives relevant to the slave trade. New facts about the slave trade will surely result, but we need to attend as well to how these facts contribute to memory work in the present. Trouillot (1995:19–22) reminds us that history is produced and circulates in multiple spaces, with implications for how we envision present and future. A heritage tourism rooted in identifications based on an essential "African-ness" leaves intact the binaries produced through the long history of the Atlantic slave trade. Similarly, archaeological investigations that uncritically project contemporary ethnicities and cultural practices into Africa's past obscure the processes through which those groups and practices took form (Stahl 2004). Both divert attention from the social, political, and economic processes that simultaneously produced "Africa" and "Europe" (Gilroy 1993:17, 49; Mintz 1985; Stoler 2006:133–135; Wolf 1982) and how those processes thread through the continued marginalization of the African continent and its peoples.

By trafficking in essentialized images of African culture, the memory work of cultural tourism in its present form colludes with conventional archaeology to reproduce the lattice and logic that makes cultural tourism one of the few bases on which to ground economic development in Africa. Both draw on notions of enduring tradition in ways that occlude the dynamic character of African societies and the complexities of the continent's entangled histories. As if by sleight of hand, the processes through which the West and Europe were produced through their engagement with Africa slip from view. At the same time, a heritage tourism focused exclusively on the Atlantic trade entails profound silences regarding the internal trade (Benson and McCaskie 2004) and its enduring legacies for patterns of inclusion and exclusion in contemporary African life, a silence made possible in part through the inattention of archaeologists to questions of internal slavery. These are patterns forged through the complex, entangled history of an Atlantic system that simultaneously produced multiple forms of modernity and the obdurate categories of human difference that are its inheritance (Gilroy 1993; Mehta 1997; Stoler 1989, 2002). Envisioning an archaeology that systematically engages slavery's practices and memories—one that keeps its ramifying connections clearly in view—opens the way for our discipline to contribute meaningfully to alternative forms of "route work" that explicitly engage those inheritances and their enduring legacies.

In sum, though we cannot reduce African history to the slave trade, neither can we ignore its ramifications. To address these, we require new research strategies, expanded archives, and a sustained engagement on the part of archaeologists working in diverse settings (i.e., coasts and interiors, plantations and villages, decentralized and state-level societies). We need an archaeology that avoids parochialism and is attuned to the connections that gave rise to the modern world (e.g., Hall 2000; Hall and Silliman 2006;

Mitchell 2005) while simultaneously rejecting the artificial boundary perpetuated by a disciplinary distinction between historic and prehistoric archaeology (Connah 2007; Robertshaw 2004). And finally, we need an archaeology enriched by an appreciation of how the legacies and entailments of slavery in the present complicate the terrain of memory work in which we are all engaged, tourists and academics alike. The challenge that confronts us is to develop robust, empirically grounded insights into the practices of slavery as we attend to the forms and saliencies of its memories.

Acknowledgments

Sincere thanks to Cathy Cameron for organizing the very stimulating Snowbird seminar that preceded this volume. Her invitation prompted me to think and write about issues that I otherwise would not have, and fostered productive conversations with colleagues working in different world areas whose comments helped crystallize my thinking around a number of issues. I am grateful to Carola Lentz, Nicholas David, Pete Robertshaw, and Maresi Starzmann for perceptive commentary on an earlier draft and for directing my attention to several key references. The perspectives explored in this chapter were also shaped by seminar discussions with graduate students in the "Archaeology of Colonialism" in fall 2006 and by collaborative teaching with Deborah Elliston, from whom I have learned much.

Notes

1. Although pioneering studies of slavery's effects on Africa date to the 1950s and 1960s (e.g., Curtin 1969; Daaku 1970; Dike 1956; Fage 1969; Rodney 1970), attention to slavery among historians and anthropologists of Africa bubbled up in the later 1970s and 1980s (e.g., Cooper 1979; Inikori 1982; Klein 1978; Lovejoy 1983, 1989; Meillassoux 1975; Miers and Kopytoff 1977; Watson 1980), becoming a more prominent concern through the 1990s (Argenti and Röschenthaler 2006; Baum 1999; Manning 1990; Shaw 2002). Until recently, archaeological attention to questions of slavery has centered on named sites in the slave trade (e.g., DeCorse 1992, 2001a; Kelly 1997, 2001), with less attention to questions of the slave trade and its effects in interior regions of Africa (cf. contributions in DeCorse [ed.] 2001; Kiyaga-Mulindwa 1982). See Alexander 2001; Kusimba 2004; and Robertshaw and Duncan, this volume, for a fuller

consideration of the archaeological literature on slavery in Africa.

2. As Trouillot (1995:19) reminds us, "historical relevance does not proceed directly from the original impact of an event," thus encouraging us to consider "the symbolic and analytical relevance of slavery for the present." A florescence of commemorative projects centered on the slave trade, accompanied by expressions of regret by European nations, coincided with what Oostindie (2001:10) describes as a "colonization in reverse" as African-descendant peoples moved to the "mother countries." See also Wallace 2006.

3. Notably, "strategic remembering" also occurs. Memories of slave origins can gain relevance in contests over chieftaincy, and memories of slave possession may be offered as evidence of past status (Carola Lentz, pers. comm., Feb. 2007; see also C. Brown 1996; Lentz 2006; O'Hear 2006).

4. The inscription for Gorée Island describes it as the "largest slave-trading centre on the African coast" (http://whc.unesco.org/en/list/26, accessed 10/12/06) despite the growing evidence that Senegambia was the source of far fewer slaves than other regions of Africa and, perhaps not coincidentally, was the region with the highest rate of shore-based attacks on slave ships (Bailyn 2001:246; Eltis 2001:40, 42, 44). See Austen's (2001) discussion of the struggles over Gorée's role in the slave trade in relation to issues of memory (also Katchka 2004).

5. Note here the discrepancy between published works that cite 1972 as the date of inscription (Aidoo 2001:31; Singleton 1999:154) and the date of 1979 based on the WHL Web site.

6. For example, the UNESCO-supported 2006 African Diaspora Heritage Trail Conference held in Bermuda was intended to "stimulate the develop-

ment of African Diaspora Heritage Trail destinations, programs and products—all crafted from the perspective of people of the African Diaspora working to conserve the vast achievements of their cultures" (African Diaspora Heritage Trail Conference 2006).

7. This is surely consistent with heritage tourism more generally—for example, with European-descendant peoples making trips to their "ancestral homelands." The European Union has devoted significant funds to the development of heritage sites intended to foster a unified European identity through its "Culture 2000" initiative, which has recently been extended for an additional six years (2007 to 2013) with a projected budget of 400 million euros (European Union 2007). However, the violence and force of the slave trade contribute to the intense emotions associated with heritage tourism for diasporic African peoples (e.g., Hartman 2007; Higgins 2000).

8. The Web sites of private tour companies offer itineraries for "the pilgrimage" that end with a welcoming ceremony at Elmina (e.g., Prime Resorts and Tours Promotions, http://www.primetoursghana.org/primetours/panafest/default.asp).

9. The Ghanaian minister of tourism and diasporan relations, Mr. Jake O. Obetesebi-Lamptey, has embarked on a campaign to encourage Ghanaians to greet African-American tourists as *Ayenmi* (Brothers) rather than *Obroni*, the term used to refer to light-skinned foreigners (see also Ebron 2002:205, who notes that African Americans and Europeans in the Gambia are similarly referenced by the single term *toubob*). The header on the Ghana Tourism web page on Project Joseph reads, "Akwaaba Ayenmi," or "Welcome Brothers." (http://www.ghanatourism.gov.gh/main/advertdetail.asp?id=1)

10. We need to consider the ways in which newly developed techniques in genetic history make use of typological constructs (of race, ethnicity) that are blunt instruments for the study of human variation, obscuring the variability within, and overlap between, groups. The resulting biohistory intersects with deeply rooted social imaginations, both in its production and its effects on processes of identification (e.g., Santos and Maio 2004; see also Goodman et al. 2003; MacEachern 2000).

11. The term "witchcraft" is an English gloss that carries meanings and connotations from European contexts. As Moore and Sanders (2001:5–6) observe, "Witchcraft in Africa is a complex historical phenomenon that is specific to local contexts, has evolved and changed markedly over time and is specifically tied to African forms of modernity."

For a discussion, see Moore and Sanders 2001: 3–6.

12. DeCorse's path-breaking edited volume (2001) included seven case studies exploring the consequences of the Atlantic slave trade across West Africa. However, with the exception of Kelly (2001), questions of slavery were not central to the initial designs of these research projects; rather, contributors were prompted by DeCorse to explore how archaeological patterning in their study areas may have been affected by the transatlantic slave trade. The complement of papers is thus consistent with, and shaped by, a broader preoccupation in African archaeology with so-called Middle Range societies or chiefdoms (McIntosh 1999; Stahl 2005). Despite the innovative insights that emerged from these papers, none focused on the acephalous, or decentralized, societies that were often the source of slaves in West Africa.

13. The sensitivity surrounding this issue was brought into relief when British officials appointed a former slave as warrant chief, who subsequently decreed that "wealthy slaves could be buried with full rites of free born (including sacrifice of a cow)" (C. Brown 1996:71).

References

African Diaspora Heritage Trail Conference
2006   Linking our Futures. http://portal.unesco.org/culture/en/ev.php-URL_ID=31848andURL_DO=DO_TOPICandURL_SECTION=201.html.

Aidoo, Ama Ata
2001   Of Forts, Castles, and Silences. In *Facing Up to the Past*, edited by Gert Oostindie, pp. 29–34. Ian Randle Publishers, Kingston, Jamaica.

Alexander, John
2001   Islam, Archaeology and Slavery in Africa. *World Archaeology* 33(1):44–60.

Alpern, Stanley B.
1992   The European Introduction of Crops in West Africa in Precolonial Times. *History in Africa* 19:13-43.

Anquandah, Kwesi J.
1999   *Castles and Forts of Ghana*. Ghana Museums and Monuments Board. Atalante, Paris.

Appadurai, Arjun
1996   *Modernity at Large*. Minnesota University Press, Minneapolis.

Appiah, Kwame Anthony
1991   *In My Father's House: Africa in the Philosophy of Culture*. Oxford University Press, New York.

Argenti, Nicholas
2006   Remembering the Future: Slavery, Youth and

Masking in the Cameroon Grassfields. *Social Anthropology* 14(1):49–69.

Argenti, Nicolas, and Ute Röschenthaler

2006 Introduction: Between Cameroon and Cuba: Youth, Slave Trades and Translocal Memory-scapes. *Social Anthropology* 14(1):33–47.

Asante, Molefi Kete

1990 Afrocentricity and Culture. In *African Culture: The Rhythms of Unity*, edited by Molefi Kete Asante and Kariamu Welsh Asante, pp. 3–12. African World Press, Trenton, NJ.

Austen, Ralph A.

2001 The Trade as History and Memory: Confrontations of Slaving Voyage Documents and Communal Traditions. *William and Mary Quarterly* 58(1):229–244.

Austin, Gareth

2003 Human Pawning in Asante, 1820–1950: Markets and Coercion, Gender and Cocoa. In *Pawnship, Slavery, and Colonialism in Africa*, edited by Paul E. Lovejoy and Toyin Falola, pp. 187–224. Africa World Press, Trenton, NJ.

Bah, Thierno Mouctar

2003 Slave-Raiding and Defensive Systems South of Lake Chad from the Sixteenth to the Nineteenth Century. In *Fighting the Slave Trade: West African Strategies*, edited by Sylviane A. Diouf, pp. 15–30. Ohio University Press, Athens.

Bailey, Anne C.

2005 *African Voices of the Atlantic Slave Trade: Beyond the Silence and the Shame*. Beacon Press, Boston.

Bailyn, Bernard

2001 Considering the Slave Trade: History and Memory. *William and Mary Quarterly* 58(1): 245–251.

Baum, Robert M.

1999 *Shrines of the Slave Trade: Diola Religion and Society in Precolonial Senegambia*. Oxford University Press, New York.

Behrendt, Stephen D.

2001 Markets, Transaction Cycles, and Profits: Merchant Decision Making in the British Slave Trade. *William and Mary Quarterly* 58(1):171–204.

Bell, Alison

2005 White Ethnogenesis and Gradual Capitalism: Perspectives from Colonial Archaeological Sites in the Chesapeake. *American Anthropologist* 107(3):446–460.

Benson, Susan, and Thomas C. McCaskie

2004 Asen Praso in History and Memory. *Ghana Studies* 7:93–113.

Bloch, Maurice E. F.

1998 *How We Think They Think: Anthropological

Approaches to Cognition, Memory, and Literacy*. Westview, Boulder, CO.

Boachie-Ansah, J.

2005 Archaeological Research at Kasana: A Search for Evidence on the Historic Slave Traffic in the Upper West Region of Ghana. *Journal of Environment and Culture* 2(1):35–57.

Boukhari, Sophie

1998 Maintaining the Ignorance. *UNESCO Sources* 99 (March):2.

Bourdieu, Pierre

1984 *Distinction: A Social Critique of the Judgement of Taste*. Translated by Richard Nice. Harvard University Press, Cambridge, MA.

Bredwa-Mensah, Yaw

2004 Global Encounters: Slavery and Slave Lifeways on Nineteenth Century Danish Plantations on the Gold Coast, Ghana. *Journal of African Archaeology* 2(2):203–227.

Brown, Carolyn A.

1996 Testing the Boundaries of Marginality: Twentieth-Century Slavery and Emancipation Struggles in Nkanu, Northern Igboland, 1920–29. *Journal of African History* 37(2):51–80.

2003 Memory as Resistance: Identity and the Contested History of Slavery in Southeastern Nigeria, an Oral History Project. In *Fighting the Slave Trade: West African Strategies*, edited by Sylviane A. Diouf, pp. 219–225. Ohio University Press, Athens.

Brown, Laurence

2002 Monuments to Freedom, Monuments to Nation: The Politics of Emancipation and Remembrance in the Eastern Caribbean. *Slavery and Abolition* 23(3):93–116.

Brown, Margaret L.

2004 Reclaiming Lost Ancestors and Acknowledging Slave Descent: Insights from Madagascar. *Comparative Studies in Society and History* 46(3):616–645.

Bruner, Edward M.

1996 Tourism in Ghana: The Representation of Slavery and the Return of the Black Diaspora. *American Anthropologist* 98(2):290–304.

Cameron, Catherine M., and Steve A. Tomka (editors)

1993 *Abandonment of Settlements and Regions: Ethnoarchaeological and Archaeological Approaches*. Cambridge University Press, Cambridge.

Campbell, Gwyn, Suzanne Miers, and Joseph C. Miller

2006 Children in European Systems of Slavery: Introduction. *Slavery and Abolition* 27(2):163–182.

Childs, S. Terry

1991 Style, Technology and Iron Smelting in Bantu-speaking Africa. *Journal of Anthropological Archaeology* 10:332–359.

Childs, S. Terry, and Eugenia W. Herbert
2005   Metallurgy and Its Consequences. In *African Archaeology: A Critical Introduction*, edited by Ann Brower Stahl, pp. 276–300. Blackwell, Oxford.

Cohen, David William, and E. S. Atieno Odhiambo
1989   *Siaya: The Historical Anthropology of an African Landscape*. James Currey, London.

Cohn, Bernard S.
1996   *Colonialism and Its Forms of Knowledge: The British in India*. Princeton University Press, Princeton, New Jersey.

Comaroff, Jean, and John L. Comaroff (editors)
1993   *Modernity and Its Malcontents: Ritual and Power in Postcolonial Africa*. University of Chicago Press, Chicago.

Comaroff, John L., and Jean Comaroff
1992   *Ethnography and the Historical Imagination*. Westview, Boulder, CO.

Comité National pour le Bénin du Projet "La Route de l'Esclave"
1994   *Le Bénin et La Route de l'Esclave*. ONEPI, Contonou, Benin.

Connah, Graham
1998   Static Image: Dynamic Reality. In *Transformations in Africa: Essays on Africa's Later Past*, edited by Graham Connah, pp. 1–13. Leicester University Press, London.
2007   Historical Archaeology in Africa: An Appropriate Concept? *African Archaeological Review* 24(1–2):35–40.

Connerton, Paul
1989   *How Societies Remember*. Cambridge University Press, Cambridge.

Cooper, Frederick
1977   *Plantation Slavery on the East Coast of Africa*. Yale University Press, New Haven, CT.
1979   The Problem of Slavery in African Studies. *Journal of African History* 20(1):103–125.

Cooper, Frederick, and Ann Laura Stoler (editors)
1997   *Tensions of Empire: Colonial Cultures in a Bourgeois World*. University of California Press, Berkeley.

Cordell, Dennis D.
2003   The Myth of Inevitability and Invincibility: Resistance to Slavers and the Slave Trade in Central Africa, 1850–1910. In *Fighting the Slave Trade: West African Strategies*, edited by Sylviane A. Diouf, pp. 31–49. Ohio University Press, Athens.

Cox, Glenda, Judith Sealy, Carmel Schrire, and Alan Morris
2001   Stable Carbon and Nitrogen Isotopic Analy-

ses of the Underclass at the Colonial Cape of Good Hope in the Eighteenth and Nineteenth Centuries. *World Archaeology* 33(1):73–97.

Curtin, Philip D.
1969   *The Atlantic Slave Trade: A Census*. University of Wisconsin Press, Madison.

Daaku, K. Y.
1970   *Trade and Politics on the Gold Coast, 1600–1720*. Oxford University Press, London.

Dann, Graham M. S., and A. V. Seaton
2001   Slavery, Contested Heritage and Thanatourism. In *Slavery, Contested Heritage and Thanatourism*, edited by Graham M. S. Dann and A. V. Seaton, pp. 1–29. Haworth Press, Binghamton, NY.

Dann, Graham M. S., and Anthony V. Seaton (editors)
2001   *Slavery, Contested Heritage, and Thanatourism*. Haworth Press, Binghamton, NY.

de Barros, Philip Lynton
2001   The Effect of the Slave Trade on the Bassar Ironworking Society, Togo. In *West Africa During the Atlantic Slave Trade: Archaeological Perspectives*, edited by Christopher R. DeCorse, pp. 59–80. Leicester University Press, London.

DeCorse, Christopher R.
1991   West African Archaeology and the Atlantic Slave Trade. *Slavery and Abolition* 12(2):92–96.
1992   Culture Contact, Continuity, and Change on the Gold Coast, AD 1400–1900. *African Archaeological Review* 10:163–196.
2001a   *An Archaeology of Elmina: Africans and Europeans on the Gold Coast, 1400–1900*. Smithsonian Institution Press, Washington, D.C.
2001b   Introduction. In *West Africa During the Atlantic Slave Trade: Archaeological Perspectives*, edited by Christopher R. DeCorse, pp. 1–13. Leicester University Press, London.

DeCorse, Christopher R. (editor)
2001   *West Africa During the Atlantic Slave Trade: Archaeological Perspectives*. Leicester University Press, London.

Dickson, K. B.
1964   The Agricultural Landscape of Southern Ghana and Ashanti-Brong Ahafo: 1800–1850. *Bulletin of the Ghana Geographical Association* 9(1):25–35.

Diéne, Doudou
1998   The Slave Route: A Memory Unchained. *UNESCO Sources* 99 (March 1998):7. Accessed 10/21/2005 at http:unesdoc.unesco.org /images/0011/001113/11347e.pdf.

Dietler, Michael, and Ingrid Herbich
1989   *Tich Matek*: The Technology of Luo Pottery

Production and the Definition of Ceramic Style. *World Archaeology* 21(1):148–164.

1998 *Habitus*, Techniques, Style: An Integrated Approach to the Social Understanding of Material Culture and Boundaries. In *The Archaeology of Social Boundaries*, edited by Miriam Stark, pp. 232–263. Smithsonian Institution Press, Washington, D.C.

Dike, K. O.

1956 *Trade and Politics in the Niger Delta, 1830–1885: An Introduction to the Economic and Political History of Nigeria.* Oxford University Press, London.

Diptee, Audra A.

2006 African Children in the British Slave Trade During the Late Eighteenth Century. *Slavery and Abolition* 27(2):183–196.

Dirks, Nicholas B.

1996 Is Vice Versa? Historical Anthropologies and Anthropological Histories. In *the Historic Turn in the Human Sciences*, edited by Terrence J. McDonald, pp. 17–51. University of Michigan Press, Ann Arbor.

2001 *Castes of Mind: Colonialism and the Making of Modern India.* Princeton University Press, Princeton, NJ.

2002 Annals of the Archive: Ethnographic Notes on the Sources of History. In *From the Margins: Historical Anthropology and Its Futures*, edited by Brian Keith Axel, pp. 47–65. Duke University Press, Durham, NC.

Dresser, Madge

2001 *Slavery Obscured: The Social History of the Slave Trade in an English Provincial Port.* Continuum, London.

Dumett, Raymond E.

1990 Traditional Slavery in the Akan Region in the Nineteenth Century: Sources, Issues, and Interpretations. In *West African Economic and Social History: Studies in Memory of Marion Johnson*, edited by David Henige and T. C. McCaskie, pp. 7–22. African Studies Program, University of Wisconsin, Madison.

Ebron, Paulla A.

2002 *Performing Africa.* Princeton University Press, Princeton, NJ.

Echenberg, Myron J.

1971 Late Nineteenth-Century Military Technology in Upper Volta. *Journal of African History* 12(2):241–254.

Ekeh, Peter P.

1990 Social Anthropology and Two Contrasting Uses of Tribalism in Africa. *Comparative Studies in Society and History* 32:660–700.

Eltis, David

2001 The Volume and Structure of the Transatlantic Slave Trade: A Reassessment. *William and Mary Quarterly* 58(1):17–46

Eltis, David, Stephen D. Behrendt, David Richardson, and Herbert S. Klein (editors)

1999 *The Trans-Atlantic Slave Trade: A Database on CD-ROM.* Cambridge University Press, Cambridge.

Essah, Patience

2001 Slavery, Heritage and Tourism in Ghana. In *Slavery, Contested Heritage and Thanatourism,* edited by Graham M. S. Dann and A. V. Seaton, pp. 31–49. Haworth Press, Binghamton, NY.

European Union

2007 Overviews of the European Union Activities: Culture. http://europa.eu/pol/cult/overview_en.htm. Accessed 1/12/07.

Fabian, Johannes

2003 Forgetful Remembering: A Colonial Life in the Congo. *Africa* 73(4):489–504.

Fage, J. D.

1969 Slavery and the Slave Trade in the Context of West African History. *Journal of African History* 10:393–404.

Falola, Toyin

2003 Slavery and Pawnship in the Yoruba Economy of the Nineteenth Century. In *Pawnship, Slavery, and Colonialism in Africa*, edited by Paul E. Lovejoy and Toyin Falola, pp. 109–135. Africa World Press, Trenton, NJ.

Fenn, Thomas R., Barbara J. Mills, and Maren Hopkins

2006 The Social Contexts of Glaze Paint Ceramic Production and Consumption in the Silver Creek Area. In *The Social Life of Pots: Glaze Wares and Cultural Dynamics in the Southwest, AD 1250–1680*, edited by Judith A. Habicht-Mauche, Suzanne L. Eckert, and Deborah L. Huntley, pp. 60–85. University of Arizona Press, Tucson.

Ferme, Mariane C.

2001 *The Underneath of Things: Violence, History, and the Everyday in Sierra Leone.* University of California Press, Berkeley.

Fogelson, Raymond D.

1989 The Ethnohistory of Events and Nonevents. *Ethnohistory* 36(2):133–147.

Frank, Barbara E.

1993 Reconstructing the History of an African Ceramic Tradition: Technology, Slavery and Agency in the Region of Kadiolo (Mali). *Cahiers d'Études Africaines* 33(131):381–401.

Gates, Henry Louis, Jr.

2001 Preface. *William and Mary Quarterly* 58(1): 3–5.

Gates, Henry Louis, Jr., et al.

2006 *African American Lives*. PBS Home Video, Hollywood, CA. (See also PBS Web site: African American Lives: Learning from DNA, http://www.pbs.org/wnet/aalives/science_dna.html)

Geschiere, Peter

1997 *The Modernity of Witchcraft: Politics and the Occult in Post-Colonial Africa*. Translated by Janet Roitman and Peter Geschiere. University of Virginia Press, Charlottesville.

Ghana Tourism

2006 Ghana Joseph Project. http://www.ghanatourism.gov.gh/main/advertdetail.asp?id=1. Accessed 10/12/2006.

Gilbert, Michelle

1997 No Construction Is Permanent: Ethnic Construction and the Use of History in Akuapem. *Africa* 67(4):501–533.

Gilroy, Paul

1993 *The Black Atlantic: Modernity and Double Consciousness*. Harvard University Press, Cambridge, MA.

1996 Route Work: The Black Atlantic and the Politics of Exile. In *The Post-Colonial Question: Common Skies, Divided Horizons*, edited by Iain Chambers and Lidia Curti, pp. 17–29. Routledge, London.

Goodman, Alan H., Deborah Heath, and M. Susan Lindee (editors)

2003 *Genetic Nature/Culture: Anthropology and Science beyond the Two-Culture Divide*. University of California Press, Berkeley.

Goody, Jack

1969 *Comparative Studies in Kinship*. Routledge and Kegan Paul, London.

1971 *Technology, Tradition and the State in Africa*. Cambridge University Press, Cambridge.

Gosden, Chris

2004 *Archaeology and Colonialism: Cultural Contact from 5000 BC to the Present*. Cambridge University Press, Cambridge.

2005 What do objects want? *Journal of Archaeological Method and Theory* 12(3):193–211.

Gosselain, Olivier P.

1992 Technology and Style: Potters and Pottery among Bafia of Cameroon. *Man* n.s. 27(3): 559–586.

1998 Social and Technical Identity in a Clay Crystal Ball. In *The Archaeology of Social Boundaries*, edited by Miriam Stark, pp. 78–106.

Smithsonian Institution Press, Washington, D.C.

2000 Materializing Identities: An African Perspective. *Journal of Archaeological Method and Theory* 7(3):187–217.

Grace, John

1975 *Domestic Slavery in West Africa: With Particular Reference to the Sierra Leone Protectorate, 1896–1927*. Frederick Muller, London.

Greene, Sandra

2003 Whispers and Silences: Explorations in African Oral History. *Africa Today* 50(2):40–53.

Guèye, Adama

2003 The Impact of the Slave Trade on Cayor and Baol: Mutations in Habitat and Land Occupancy. In *Fighting the Slave Trade: West African Strategies*, edited by Sylviane A. Diouf, pp. 50–61. Ohio University Press, Athens.

Haenger, Peter

2000 *Slaves and Slave Holders on the Gold Coast: Towards an Understanding of Social Bondage in West Africa*. Edited by J. J. Shaffer and Paul E. Lovejoy. Translated by Christina Handford. P. Schlettwein Publishing, Basel, Switzerland.

Haley, Alex

1976 *Roots*. Doubleday, Garden City, NY.

Hall, Catherine

1996 Histories, Empires and the Post-Colonial Moment. In *The Post-Colonial Question: Common Skies, Divided Horizons*, edited by Iain Chambers and Lidia Curti, pp. 65–77. Routledge, London.

Hall, Martin

1993 The Archaeology of Colonial Settlement in Southern Africa. *Annual Review of Anthropology* 22:177–200.

2000 *Archaeology and the Modern World: Colonial Transcripts in South Africa and the Chesapeake*. Routledge, London.

Hall, Martin, and Ann Markell

1993 Introduction: Historical Archaeology in the Western Cape. *South African Archaeological Society Goodwin Series* 7:3–7.

Hall, Martin, and Stephen W. Silliman

2006 Introduction: Archaeology of the Modern World. In *Historical Archaeology*, edited by Martin Hall and Stephen W. Silliman, pp. 1–19. Blackwell, Oxford.

Hartman, Saidiya

2007 *Lose Your Mother: A Journey along the Atlantic Slave Route*. Farrar, Straus and Giroux, New York.

Hasty, Jennifer

2003 "Forget the Past or Go back to the Slave Trade":

Trans-Africanism and Popular History in Postcolonial Ghana. *Ghana Studies* 6:135–161.

Hawkins, Sean

2002   *Writing and Colonialism in Northern Ghana: The Encounter between the LoDagaa and "the World on Paper."* University of Toronto Press, Toronto.

Hawthorne, Walter

1999   The Production of Slavers Where There Was No State: The Guinea-Bissau Region, 1450–1815. *Slavery and Abolition* 20(2):97–124.

2003a *Planting Rice and Harvesting Slaves: Transformations along the Guinea-Bissau Coast, 1400–1900.* Heinemann, Portsmouth, NH.

2003b Strategies of the Decentralized: Defending Communities from Slave Raiders in Coastal Guinea-Bissau, 1450–1815. In *Fighting the Slave Trade: West African Strategies*, edited by Sylviane A. Diouf, pp. 152–169. Ohio University Press, Athens.

Herbich, Ingrid

1987   Learning Patterns, Potter Interaction and Ceramic Style among the Luo of Kenya. *African Archaeological Review* 5:193–204.

Higgins, Chester, Jr.

2000   Pilgrimage to the Past: An African-American's Lifelong Search for Identity. *Archaeology* 53(1):38–43.

Holl, Augustin

2001   500 Years in the Cameroons: Making Sense of the Archaeological Record. In *West Africa During the Atlantic Slave Trade: Archaeological Perspectives*, edited by Christopher R. DeCorse, pp. 152–178. Leicester University Press, London.

Horton, Robin

1976   Stateless Societies in the History of West Africa. In *History of West Africa*, vol. 1, edited by J. F. Ade Ajayi and Michael Crowder, pp. 72–113. 2nd ed. Longman, London.

Hubbell, Andrew

2001   A View of the Slave Trade from the Margin: Souroudougou in the Late Nineteenth-Century Slave Trade of the Niger Bend. *Journal of African History* 42:25–47.

Inikori, J. E. (editor)

1982   *Forced Migration: The Impact of the Export Slave Trade on African Societies.* Hutchinson University Library, London.

Johnson, Marion

1986   The Slaves of Salaga. *Journal of African History* 27:341–362.

Katchka, Kinsey A.

2004   Re-siting Slavery at the Gorée-Almadies Memorial and Museum. *Museum Anthropology* 27(1–2):3–12.

Kea, Ray A.

1982   *Settlements, Trade, and Polities in the Seventeenth-Century Gold Coast.* Johns Hopkins University Press, Baltimore, MD.

Kelly, Kenneth

1997   The Archaeology of African-European Interaction: Investigating the Social Roles of Trade, Traders, and the Use of Space in the Seventeenth- and Eighteenth-Century Hueda Kingdom, Republic of Benin. *World Archaeology* 28:350–369.

2001   Change and Continuity in Coastal Bénin. In *West Africa During the Atlantic Slave Trade: Archaeological Perspectives*, edited by Christopher R. DeCorse, pp. 81–100. Leicester University Press, London.

Kirshenblatt-Gimblett, Barbara

2006   World Heritage and Cultural Economics. In *Museum Frictions: Public Cultures/ Global Transformations*, edited by Ivan Karp, Corrine A. Kratz, Lynn Szwaja, and Tomás Ybarra-Frausto, pp. 161–202. Duke University Press, Durham, NC.

Kiyaga-Mulindwa, D.

1982   Social and Demographic Changes in the Birim Valley, Southern Ghana, c. 1450 to c. 1800. *Journal of African History* 23:63–82.

Klein, Herbert S., Stanley L. Engerman, Robin Haines, and Ralph Shlomowitz

2001   Transoceanic Morality: The Slave Trade in Comparative Perspective. *William and Mary Quarterly* 58(1):93–118.

Klein, Martin A.

1971   Slavery, the Slave Trade and Legitimate Commerce in Late Nineteenth Century Africa. *Etudes d'histoire africaine* 2:5–28.

1978   The Study of Slavery in Africa. *Journal of African History* 19(4):599–609.

2003   Defensive Strategies: Wasulu, Masina and the Slave Trade. In *Fighting the Slave Trade: West African Strategies*, edited by Sylviane A. Diouf, pp. 62–78. Ohio University Press, Athens.

Kopytoff, Igor, and Suzanne Miers (editors)

1977   *Slavery in Africa: Historical and Anthropological Perspectives.* University of Wisconsin Press, Madison.

Kreamer, Christine Mullen

2004   The Politics of Memory: Ghana's Cape Coast Castle Museum Exhibition "Crossroads of People, Crossroads of Trade." *Ghana Studies* 7:79–91.

2006   Shared Heritage, Contested Terrain: Cultural

Negotiation and Ghana's Cape Coast Castle Museum Exhibition "Crossroads of People, Crossroads of Trade." In *Museum Frictions: Public Cultures/Global Transformations*, edited by Ivan Karp, Corrine A. Kratz, Lynn Szwaja, and Tomás Ybarra-Frausto, pp. 435–468. Duke University Press, Durham, NC.

Kuba, Richard, and Carola Lentz
2002 Arrows and Earth Shrines: Towards a History of Dagara Expansion in Southern Burkina Faso. *Journal of African History* 43:377–406.

Kusimba, Chapurukha M.
2004 Archaeology of Slavery in East Africa. *African Archaeological Review* 21(2):59–88.
2006 Slavery and Warfare in African Chiefdoms. In *The Archaeology of Warfare: Prehistories of Raiding and Conquest*, edited by Elizabeth N. Arkush and Mark W. Allen, pp. 214–249. University of Florida Press, Gainesville.

Kusimba, Chapurukha, Sibel B. Kusimba, and David K. Wright
2005 The Development and Collapse of Precolonial Ethnic Mosaics in Tsavo, Kenya. *Journal of African Archaeology* 3(2):243–265.

Lane, Paul
2005 Barbarous Tribes and Unrewarding Gyrations? The Changing Role of Ethnographic Imagination in African Archaeology. In *African Archaeology: A Critical Introduction*, edited by Ann Brower Stahl, pp. 24–54. Blackwell, Oxford.

Law, Robin (editor)
1995 *From Slave Trade to "Legitimate Commerce": The Commercial Transition in Nineteenth Century West Africa*. Cambridge University Press, Cambridge.

Lemmonier, Pierre
1986 The Study of Material Culture Today: Toward an Anthropology of Technical Systems. *Journal of Anthropological Archaeology* 5:147–186.

Lentz, Carola
1995 "Tribalism" and Ethnicity in Africa: A Review of Four Decades of Anglophone Research. *Cahiers des Sciences humaines* 31(2):303–328.
2000a Colonial Constructions and African Initiatives: The History of Ethnicity in Northwestern Ghana. *Ethnos* 65(1):107–136.
2000b Of Hunters, Goats and Earth-Shrines: Settlement Histories and the Politics of Oral Traditions in Northern Ghana. *History in Africa* 24:205–219.
2006 *Ethnicity and the Making of History in Northern Ghana*. Edinburgh University Press, Edinburgh.

Lentz, Carola, and Paul Nugent
2000 Ethnicity in Ghana: A Comparative Perspective. In *Ethnicity in Ghana: The Limits of Invention*, edited by Carola Lentz and Paul Nugent, pp. 1–28. St. Martin's Press, New York.

Lightfoot, Kent G.
1995 Culture Contact Studies: Redefining the Relationship between Prehistoric and Historic Archaeology. *American Antiquity* 60:199–217.

Lokossou, Clément
1994 La route de l'esclave et les circuits touristiques. In *Le Bénin et la Route de l'Esclave*, Comité National pour le Bénin du Projet "La Route de l'Esclave," pp. 124–129. ONEPI, Contonou, Benin.

Lovejoy, Paul E.
1983 *Transformations in Slavery: A History of Slavery in Africa*. Cambridge University Press, Cambridge.
1989 The Impact of the Atlantic Slave Trade on Africa: A Review of the Literature. *Journal of African History* 30(3):365–394.
2005 *Slavery, Commerce and Production in the Sokoto Caliphate of West Africa*. Africa World Press, Trenton, NJ.
2006 The Children of Slavery: The Transatlantic Phase. *Slavery and Abolition* 27(2):197–217.

Lovejoy, Paul E., and Jan S. Hogendorn
1993 *Slow Death for Slavery: The Course of Abolition in Northern Nigeria, 1897–1936*. Cambridge University Press, Cambridge.

Lovejoy, Paul E., and David Richardson
2003 Anglo-Efik Relations and Protection against Illegal Enslavement at Old Calabar, 1740–1807. In *Fighting the Slave Trade: West African Strategies*, edited by Sylviane A. Diouf, pp. 101–118. Ohio University Press, Athens.

Lovejoy, Paul E., and David V. Trotman
2003 Introduction: Ethnicity and the African Diaspora. In *Trans-Atlantic Dimension of Ethnicity in the African Diaspora*, edited by Paul E. Lovejoy and David V. Trotman, pp. 1–8. Continuum, London.

Lyons, Diane
1998 Witchcraft, Gender, Power and Intimate Relations in Mura Compounds in Dela, Northern Cameroon. *World Archaeology* 29(3):344–362.

MacEachern, Scott
1993 Selling the Iron for Their Shackles: Wandala-Montagnard Interactions in Northern Cameroon. *Journal of African History* 33(2):241–270.
2000 Genes, Tribes, and African History. *Current Anthropology* 41(3):357–384.

2001 State Formation and Enslavement in the Southern Lake Chad Basin. In *West Africa During the Atlantic Slave Trade: Archaeological Perspectives*, edited by Christopher R. De-Corse, pp. 131–151. Leicester University Press, London.

McIntosh, Susan Keech

1999 Pathways to Complexity: An African Perspective. In *Beyond Chiefdoms: Pathways to Complexity in Africa*, edited by Susan Keech McIntosh, pp. 1–30. Cambridge University Press, Cambridge.

McSheffrey, G. M.

1983 Slavery, Indentured Servitude, Legitimate Trade and the Impact of Abolition in the Gold Coast, 1874–1901: A Reappraisal. *Journal of African History* 24:349–368.

Magubane, Zine

2004 *Bring the Empire Home: Race, Class, and Gender in Britain and Colonial South Africa*. University of Chicago Press, Chicago.

Manning, Patrick

1990 *Slavery and African Life: Occidental, Oriental, and African Slave Trades*. Cambridge University Press, Cambridge.

Mathur, Saloni

2000 History and Anthropology in South Asia: Rethinking the Archive. *Annual Review of Anthropology* 29:89–106.

Mbembe, Achille

2001 The Subject of the World. In *Facing Up to the Past*, edited by Gert Oostindie, pp. 21–28. Ian Randle Publishers, Kingston, Jamaica.

Mehta, Uday

1997 Liberal Strategies of Exclusion. In *Tensions of Empire: Colonial Cultures in a Bourgeois World*, edited by Frederick Cooper and Ann Laura Stoler, pp. 59–86. University of California Press, Berkeley.

Meillassoux, Claude

1973 Etat et conditions des esclaves à Gumbu (Mali) au XIXe siècle. *Journal of African History* 14:429–452.

Meillassoux, Claude (editor)

1975 *L'esclavage en Afrique précoloniale*. Maspero, Paris.

Mendonsa, Eugene L.

2001 *Continuity and Change in a West African Society: Globalization's Impact on the Sisala of Ghana*. Carolina Academic Press, Durham, NC.

Miers, Suzanne, and Igor Kopytoff (editors)

1977 *Slavery in Africa: Historical and Anthropological Perspectives*. University of Wisconsin Press, Madison.

Miller, Joseph C.

2004 Retention, Reinvention, and Remembering: Restoring Identities through Enslavement in Africa and under Slavery in Brazil. In *Enslaving Connections: Changing Cultures of Africa and Brazil During the Era of Slavery*, edited by José C. Curto and Paul E. Lovejoy, pp. 81–121. Humanity Books, New York.

Mills, Barbara, and William Walker (editors)

2008 *Memory Work: The Materiality of Depositional Practice*. School of Advanced Research Press, Santa Fe, NM.

Minar, C. Jill

2001 Motor Skills and the Learning Process: The Conservation of Cordage Final Twist Direction in Communities of Practice. *Journal of Anthropological Research* 57(4):381–405.

Minar, C. Jill, and Patricia Crown

2001 Learning and Craft Production: An Introduction. *Journal of Anthropological Research* 57(4):369–380.

Mintz, Sidney W.

1985 *Sweetness and Power: The Place of Sugar in Modern History*. Viking, New York.

Mitchell, Peter

2005 *African Connections: Archaeological Perspectives on Africa and the Wider World*. AltaMira Press, Walnut Creek, CA.

Moore, Henrietta L., and Todd Sanders

2001 Magical Interpretations and Material Realities: An Introduction. In *Magical Interpretations, Material Realities: Modernity, Witchcraft and the Occult in Postcolonial Africa*, edited by Henrietta L. Moore and Todd Sanders, pp. 1–27. Routledge, London.

Mudimbe, Victor Y.

1994 *The Idea of Africa*. Indiana University Press, Bloomington.

Nwokeji, G. Ugo

2001 African Conceptions of Gender and the Slave Trade. *William and Mary Quarterly* 58(1):47–68.

Ogundiran, Akinwumi

2002 Of Small Things Remembered: Beads, Cowries, and Cultural Translations of the Atlantic Experience in Yorubaland. *International Journal of African Historical Studies*, 35(2/3):427–457.

Ogundiran, Akinwumi, and Toyin Falola (editors)

2007 *Archaeology of Atlantic Africa and the African Diaspora*. Indiana University Press, Bloomington.

Ohadike, D. C.

1981 The Influenza Pandemic of 1918–19 and the Spread of Cassava Cultivation on the Lower

Niger: A Study in Historical Linkages. *Journal of African History* 22:379–391.

O'Hear, Ann
2006   Elite Slaves in Ilorin in the Nineteenth and Twentieth Centuries. *International Journal of African Historical Studies* 39:247–273.

Oostindie, Gert
2001   Stony Regrets and Pledges for the Future. In *Facing Up to the Past*, edited by Gert Oostindie, pp. 9–18. Ian Randle Publishers, Kingston, Jamaica.

Oostindie, Gert (editor)
2001   *Facing Up to the Past.* Ian Randle Publishers, Kingston, Jamaica.

Osei-Tutu, Brempong
2004   "Slave Castles" and the Transatlantic Slave Trade: Ghanaian and African American Perspectives. *Ghana Studies* 7:59–78.
2007   Ghana's "Slave Castles," Tourism, and the Social Memory of the Atlantic Slave Trade. In *Archaeology of Atlantic Africa and the African Diaspora*, edited by Akinwumi Ogundiran and Toyin Falola, pp. 185–195. University of Indiana Press, Bloomington.

Parish, Jane
1999   The Dynamics of Witchcraft and Indigenous Shrines among the Akan. *Africa* 69(3):426–447.
2000   From the Body to the Wallet: Conceptualizing Akan Witchcraft at Home and Abroad. *Journal of the Royal Anthropological Institute* 6(3):487–500.

Parker, John
2004   Witchcraft, Anti-Witchcraft and Trans-Regional Ritual Innovation in Early Colonial Ghana: Sakrabundi and Aberewa, 1889–1910. *Journal of African History* 45:393–420.
2006   Northern Gothic: Witches, Ghosts and Werewolves in the Savanna Hinterland of the Gold Coast, 1900s–1950s. *Africa* 76(3):352–380.

Pauketat, Timothy R., and Susan M. Alt
2005   Agency in a Postmold? Physicality and the Archaeology of Culture-Making. *Journal of Archaeological Method and Theory* 12(3):213–236.

Pels, Peter
1997   The Anthropology of Colonialism: Culture, History, and the Emergence of Western Governmentality. *Annual Review of Anthropology* 26:163–183.

Perbi, Akosua Adoma
2004   *A History of Indigenous Slavery in Ghana from the 15th to the 19th Century.* Sub-Saharan Publishers, Legon, Accra, Ghana.

Pfaffenberger, Bryan
1998   Mining Communities, *Chaînes opératoires* and Sociotechnical Systems. In *Social Approaches to an Industrial Past*, edited by A. Bernard Knapp, Vincent C. Piggott, and Eugenia W. Herbert, pp. 291–300. Routledge, London.

Piot, Charles
1996   Of Slaves and the Gift: Kabre Sale of Kin during the Era of the Slave Trade. *Journal of African History* 37:31–49.
1999   *Remotely Global: Village Modernity in West Africa.* University of Chicago Press, Chicago.

Rattray, R. S.
1969   *Ashanti Law and Constitution.* Negro Univer-
[1929] sities Press, New York.

Reed, Ann
2004   Sankofa Site: Cape Coast Castle and Its Museum as Markers of Memory. *Museum Anthropology* 27(1–2):13–23.

Reid, Andrew M., and Paul J. Lane (editors)
2004   *African Historical Archaeologies.* Kluwer Academic/Plenum Publishers, New York.

Richards, Sandra L.
2005   What Is to Be Remembered? Tourism to Ghana's Slave Castle-Dungeons. *Theatre Journal* 57:617–637.

Roberts, Richard
1984   Women's Work and Women's Property: Household Social Relations in the Maraka Textile Industry of the Nineteenth Century. *Comparative Studies in Society and History* 26:229–250.

Robertshaw, Peter
1999   Seeking and Keeping Power in Bunyoro-Kitara, Uganda. In *Beyond Chiefdoms: Pathways to Complexity in Africa*, edited by Susan Keech McIntosh, pp. 124–135. Cambridge University Press, Cambridge.
2004   African Historical Archaeology(ies): Past, Present and a Possible Future. In *African Historical Archaeologies*, edited by Andrew M. Reid and Paul J. Lane, pp. 375–391. Kluwer Academic/Plenum Publishers, New York.

Robertson, Claire C., and Martin A. Klein
1983   Women's Importance in African Slave Systems. In *Women and Slavery in Africa*, edited by Claire C. Robertson and Martin A. Klein, pp. 3–25. University of Wisconsin Press, Madison.

Rodney, Walter
1970   *A History of the Upper Guinea Coast, 1545–1800.* Oxford University Press, London.

Röschenthaler, Ute M.
2006   Translocal Cultures: The Slave Trade and Cultural Transfer in the Cross River Region. *Social Anthropology* 14(1):71–91.

Rubertone, Patricia E.
2000   The Historical Archaeology of Native Americans. *Annual Review of Anthropology* 29:425–446.

Santos, Ricardo Ventura, and Marcos Chor Maio
2004   Race, Genomics, Identities and Politics in Contemporary Brazil. *Critique of Anthropology* 24(4):347–378.

Sassaman, Kenneth E.
2001   Communities of Practice in the Early Pottery Traditions of the American Southeast. *Journal of Anthropological Research* 57(4):407–425.

Schildkrout, Enid
1996   Kingdom of Gold. *Natural History* (October): 36–47.

Schomberg Center for Research in Black Culture
2006   *Lest We Forget.* Virtual exhibition sponsored by Schomberg Center, New York Public Library and UNESCO Slave Route Project. http://digital.nypl.org/lwf/ Accessed 9/7/2006.

Schramm, Katharina
2005   The Transatlantic Slave Trade: Contemporary Topographies of Memory in Ghana and the USA. *Transactions of the Historical Society of Ghana*, n.s. 9:125–140.

Schrire, Carmel
1995   *Digging through Darkness: Chronicles of an Archaeologist.* University of Virginia Press, Charlottesville.

Seaton, A. V.
2001   Sources of Slavery—Destinations of Slavery: The Silences and Disclosures of Slavery Heritage in the UK and US. In *Slavery, Contested Heritage and Thanatourism*, edited by Graham M. S. Dann and A. V. Seaton, pp. 107–129. Haworth Press, Binghamton, NY.

Sharpe, Barrie
1986   Ethnography and a Regional System: Mental Maps and the Myth of State and Tribes in North-Central Nigeria. *Critique of Anthropology* 6(3):33–65.

Shaw, Rosalind
1997   The Production of Witchcraft/Witchcraft as Production: Memory, Modernity, and the Slave Trade in Sierra Leone. *American Ethnologist* 24(4):856–876.
2002   *Memories of the Slave Trade: Ritual and Historical Imagination in Sierra Leone.* University of Chicago Press, Chicago.

Singleton, Theresa A.
1999   The Slave Trade Remembered on the Former Gold and Slave Coasts. *Slavery and Abolition* 20(1):150–169.
2001   An Americanist Perspective on African Archaeology: Toward an Archaeology of the Black Atlantic. In *West Africa During the Atlantic Slave Trade: Archaeological Perspectives*, edited by Christopher R. DeCorse, pp. 179–184. Leicester University Press, London.

Slave Route Project
2006   UNESCO Programmes http://portal.unesco.org/culture/en/ev.php-URL_ID=28093andURL_DO=DO_TOPICandURL_SECTION=201.html. Accessed 10/12/06.

Slave Trade Archives Project
2005   The Slave Trade Archives Project Final Report. Project 516INT5061. UNESCO, Paris. Digital access at http://portal.unesco.org/ci/en/ev.php_URL_ID=18318andURL_DO=DO_TOPICandURL_SECTION=201.html. 10/12/06.

Smallwood, Stephanie E.
2001   Review of *The Trans-Atlantic Slave Trade: A Database on CD-ROM. William and Mary Quarterly* 58(1):253–261.

Smith, Adam T.
2004   The End of the Essential Archaeological Subject. *Archaeological Dialogues* 11:1–20.

Smith, M. F.
1955   *Baba of Karo: A Woman of the Muslim Hausa.* Philosophical Library, New York.

Solow, Barbara L.
2001   The Transatlantic Slave Trade: A New Census. *William and Mary Quarterly* 58(1):9–16.

Soumonni, Elisée
2003   Lacustrine Villages in South Benin as Refuges from the Slave Trade. In *Fighting the Slave Trade: West African Strategies*, edited by Sylviane A. Diouf, pp. 3–14. Ohio University Press, Athens.

Stahl, Ann Brower
1993   Concepts of Time and Approaches to Analogical Reasoning in Historical Perspective. *American Antiquity* 58(2):235–260.
1999a   The Archaeology of Global Encounters Viewed from Banda, Ghana. *African Archaeological Review* 16(1):5–81.
1999b   Perceiving Variability in Time and Space: The Evolutionary Mapping of African Societies. In *Beyond Chiefdoms: Pathways to Complexity in Africa*, edited by Susan Keech McIntosh, pp. 39–55. Cambridge University Press, Cambridge.
2001a   Historical Process and the Impact of the Atlantic Trade on Banda, Ghana, c. 1800–1920. In *West Africa During the Atlantic Slave Trade: Archaeological Perspectives*, edited by Christopher R. DeCorse, pp. 38–58. Leicester University Press, London.
2001b   *Making History in Banda: Anthropological*

Visions of Africa's Past. Cambridge University Press, Cambridge.

2002 Colonial Entanglements and the Practices of Taste: An Alternative to Logocentric Approaches. *American Anthropologist* 104(3): 827–845.

2004 Comparative Insights into the Ancient Political Economies of West Africa. In *Archaeological Perspectives on Political Economies*, edited by Gary M. Feinman and Linda M. Nicholas, pp. 253–270. University of Utah Press, Salt Lake City.

2005 Introduction: Changing Perspectives on Africa's Pasts. In *African Archaeology: A Critical Introduction*, edited by Ann Brower Stahl, pp. 1–23. Blackwell, Oxford.

2008 Dogs, Pythons, Pots and Beads: The Dynamics of Shrines and Sacrificial Practices in Banda, Ghana, AD 1400–1900. In *Memory Work: The Materiality of Depositional Practice*, edited by Barbara Mills and William Walker, pp. 159–186. School of Advanced Research Press, Santa Fe, NM.

Stoler, Ann Laura

1989 Rethinking Colonial Categories: European Communities in Sumatra and the Boundaries of Rule. *Comparative Studies in Society and History* 31(1):134–161.

2001 Tense and Tender Ties: The Politics of Comparison in North American History and (Post) Colonial Studies. *Journal of American History* 88(3):829–865.

2002 Developing Historical Negatives: Race and the [Modernist] Visions of a Colonial State. In *From the Margins: Historical Anthropology and Its Futures*, edited by Brian Keith Axel, pp. 156–185. Duke University Press, Durham, NC.

2006 On Degrees of Imperial Sovereignty. *Public Culture* 18(1):125–146.

Stoler, Ann Laura (editor)

2006 *Haunted by Empire: Geographies of Intimacy in North American History.* Duke University Press, Durham, NC.

Stoler, Ann Laura, and Frederick Cooper

1997 Between Metropole and Colony: Rethinking a Research Agenda. In *Tensions of Empire: Colonial Cultures in a Bourgeois World*, edited by Frederick Cooper and Ann Laura Stoler, pp. 1–56. University of California Press, Berkeley.

Stoler, Ann Laura, and Karen Strassler

2000 Castings for the Colonial: Memory Work in "New Order" Java. *Comparative Studies in Society and History* 42:4–48.

Stoller, Paul

1995 *Embodying Colonial Memories: Spirit Possession, Power and the Hauka in West Africa.* Routledge, New York.

Swanepoel, Natalie

2004 "Too Much Power is Not Good": War and Trade in Nineteenth Century Sisalaland, Northern Ghana. Unpublished doctoral dissertation, Department of Anthropology, Syracuse University, NY. Proquest Information and Learning, Ann Arbor, Michigan.

2006 Socio-Political Change on a Slave-Raiding Frontier: War, Trade and "Big Men" in Nineteenth Century Sisalaland, Northern Ghana. In *Past Tense: Studies in the Archaeology of Conflict*, edited by Tony Pollard and Iain Banks, pp. 265–293. Brill, Leiden.

Tengan, Alexis B.

2000 Space, Bonds and Social Order: Dagara House-Based Social System. In *Bonds and Boundaries in Northern Ghana and Southern Burkina Faso*, edited by Sten Hagberg and Alexis B. Tengan, pp. 87–103. Uppsala Studies in Cultural Anthropology 30. Acta Universitatis Upsaliensis.

Tibbles, Anthony (editor)

2005 *Transatlantic Slavery: Against Human Dignity.* 2nd ed. Liverpool University Press, Liverpool.

Tibbles, Anthony

2008 Facing Slavery's Past: The Bicentenary of the Abolition of the British Slave Trade. *Slavery and Abolition* 29(2):293–303.

Trigger, Bruce G.

1984 Alternative Archaeologies: Nationalist, Colonialist, Imperialist. *Man* 19:355–370.

1989 *A History of Archaeological Thought.* Cambridge University Press, Cambridge.

Trouillot, Michel-Rolph

1995 *Silencing the Past: Power and the Production of History.* Beacon Press, Boston.

UNESCO

1994 Executive Board Summary, Hundred and Forty-Fifth Session. Report by the Director-General on the Implementation of the Slave Route Project. August 5, 1994. http://unesdoc.unesco.org/images/0009/000988/098867eo.pdf. Accessed 10/21/2005.

2006a The Slave Route. Published April 2, 2006.

2006b World Heritage List. http://whc.unesco.org/en/list/.

Van Dantzig, Albert

1982 Effects of the Atlantic Slave Trade on Some West African Societies. In *Forced Migration: The Impact of the Export Slave Trade on African Societies*, edited by J. E. Inikori, pp. 187–201. Hutchinson University Library, London.

Van Keuren, Scott

2006   Decorating Glaze-Painted Pottery in East-Central Arizona. In *The Social Life of Pots: Glaze Wares and Cultural Dynamics in the Southwest, AD 1250–1680*, edited by Judith A. Habicht-Mauche, Suzanne L. Eckert, and Deborah L. Huntley, pp. 86–104. University of Arizona Press, Tucson.

Wallace, Elizabeth Kowaleski

2006   *The British Slave Trade and Public Memory.* Columbia University Press, New York.

Watson, James L. (editor)

1980   *Asian and African Systems of Slavery.* University of California Press, Berkeley.

Werbner, Richard (editor)

1998   *Memory and the Postcolony: African Anthropology and the Critique of Power.* Zed Books, New York.

Wilks, Ivor

1975   *Asante in the Nineteenth Century: The Structure and Evolution of a Political Order.* Cambridge University Press, Cambridge.

Williams, Eric

1964   *Capitalism and Slavery.* André Deutsch, London.
[1944]

Wolf, Eric R.

1982   *Europe and the People without History.* University of California Press, Berkeley.

Wright, Donald R.

1981   Uprooting Kunta Kinte: On the Perils of Relying on Encyclopedic Informants. *History in Africa* 8:205–217.

Yoffee, Norman

1993   Too Many Chiefs? (Or, Safe Texts for the '90s). In *Archaeological Theory: Who Sets the Agenda?* edited by Norman Yoffee and Andrew Sherratt, pp. 60–78. Cambridge University Press, Cambridge.

3

African Slavery

Archaeology and Decentralized Societies

Peter Robertshaw and William L. Duncan

In the global context of slavery, Africa is generally known as the continent devastated by the forced export of millions of its inhabitants to satisfy the labor demands of American plantation economies. Perhaps less well-known is the fact that between about 600 and 1900 CE, on the order of 11.5 to 14 million Africans were sold into slavery in the Islamic world, which once stretched from Spain to India (Austen 1979, cited in Segal 2001:59–60). Two million Africans were enslaved in the nineteenth century alone (Lovejoy 1983:151), with more than three-quarters of a million of these people sent to work on the plantations of Zanzibar and the East African coast, then under the control of the Sultanate of Oman. These numbers are enormous, representing an average of about ten thousand people per annum. Moreover, one late nineteenth-century writer estimated that ten people lost their lives from various causes for each person sold into slavery (Segal 2001:62, citing Hourst 1896). Given these staggering figures, it seems almost churlish to remark that there was an internal system of African slavery that offers many contrasts with the export-oriented systems of the Atlantic (Christian) and Islamic worlds. The antiquity of this internal slavery is unknown because of the difficulties, discussed below, in discerning slavery in the African archaeological record. Slavery certainly existed in Pharaonic Egypt and probably south of the Sahara in the Nubian kingdoms (Connah 2001:56–57), but whether it existed anywhere in sub-Saharan Africa prior to the development of state-level societies, generally in the mid to late first millennium CE or later, is unknown. To some degree, slavery, or at least a market and demand for slaves, and states in Africa go hand in hand, though we do not mean to imply that slavery was always an important component of all African states. Although the ethnohistorical literature indicates that slavery existed in Africa in decentralized societies, the scale of this slavery, including its antiquity and economic and cultural importance, may have been small. However, we would not be too surprised if future archaeological endeavors were to find the exception to prove the rule. The question of whether slavery was present or absent from ancient African societies is in part a matter of semantics, depending on one's definition of slavery, which we discuss below. What is clear from the contributions to this volume is that the forcible taking of captives from other communities is a feature of human societies at all levels of sociopolitical complexity, probably dating back to at least the period immediately following the last Ice Age (see Cameron, this volume). Whether or not captives are considered "slaves" would appear to be a matter of semantic niceties that one suspects would be incorrigible to the captives themselves.

In this chapter we explore various aspects of African slavery, particularly, though not exclusively, as they pertain to archaeology and to decentralized societies.[1] On one hand we explore the nature of internal African slavery, which is best known from ethnohistorical and anthropological literature; on the other, we cannot ignore the fact that what we know about this internal slavery dates to the period when the demand for African slaves for export was running at full throttle. Thus, any anthropological or archaeological examination of African slavery must be placed in its historical context—namely, the context in which many thousands of Africans were enslaved each year to quench the thirst of overseas and trans-Saharan markets. For at least the last four hundred years, if not the last thirteen hundred, the slave trade has been the sine qua non of existence for many societies in sub-Saharan Africa, particularly those of the tropics. Slavery, the slave trade, resistance to slavery, and fear of slavery were key variables in political, economic, social, and cultural change. Given this reality, the problem of how to recognize slavery in the archaeological record is no problem at all for much of Africa during the last four hundred or more years; slavery is the elephant in the room. For African archaeologists, it is not slavery's existence, but its manifestations and effects that require investigation.

A Note on Sources

The literature on African slavery, particularly the Atlantic slave trade, is very extensive. In preparing this chapter, we have relied heavily on relatively few sources, in part because of our own prior lack of experience in conducting research on African slavery, and in part because these seem to be the seminal works, particularly since our focus is the anthropological and archaeological manifestations and effects of slavery and the slave trade in and on decentralized societies. Therefore, we have felt relatively little remorse about ignoring most of the historical literature, primarily based on documentary sources, pertaining to the African termini of the Atlantic slave trade.

Until a few years ago, archaeological research on African slavery was mostly confined to the study of European trading posts and settlements on the edge of the African continent that were involved in the slave trade (for useful reviews, see Posnansky and DeCorse 1986; Mitchell 2005: Chap. 6). However, the last decade or so has seen a relative flood of research in western Africa, from Senegambia to the Chad Basin, on the effects of both the Atlantic slave trade and the Columbian exchange on African societies; the chapters in the edited volume by DeCorse (2001b) provide an excellent survey of this research (see also Stahl 2001; DeCorse 2001a), upon which we have relied heavily in preparing this chapter. An issue of *World Archaeology* devoted to slavery contained a paper by Alexander (2001) on the archaeology of Islamic slavery in Africa, which served to highlight the difficulties of identifying slavery in the archaeological record, and another by Cox et al. (2001) that used isotopic evidence to identify slavery in early Cape Town, South Africa. More recently Kusimba (2004), drawing on his own fieldwork in Kenya, has challenged East African archaeologists to come to grips with the study of slavery, particularly given its overwhelming importance for our understanding of the history of the last few centuries. In our case, Kusimba's plea has not fallen on deaf ears; we acknowledge his inspiration, as well as the value of his list of references (see also Kusimba 2006).

The anthropological literature on slavery within Africa is relatively limited, presumably because early in the twentieth century slavery mostly ceased to exist as an institution that could be readily studied by social anthropologists. We have found three edited volumes (Miers and Kopytoff 1977; Watson 1980a; Robertson and Klein 1983), all of which contain contributions from both anthropologists and historians, and a monograph (Meillassoux 1991) to be particularly useful.

As noted above, we have mostly steered clear of the historical literature that is based primarily on documentary sources; much of this is of only marginal relevance to our research as it focuses largely on European perspectives on the Atlantic slave trade. However, we found books by Lovejoy (1983) and Manning (1990) that presented useful syntheses and interesting insights. We made similar use of Segal's (2001) study of the Islamic slave trade. Finally, the volume edited by Diouf (2003) on West African strategies for resisting the slave trade contained some obvious implications for archaeology and also led us to other historical research on slavery and the slave trade in decentralized societies.

Definitions of Slavery

Cameron (this volume), while recognizing that others have expended much ink on the definition of slavery, suggests that for practical purposes we may define slavery as the involuntary transfer of individuals from one society to another; thus, slavery becomes synonymous, or almost synonymous, with captive-taking. While this simple definition serves its purpose well for many of the chapters in this volume, particularly those focused on the Americas, the varied types, scales, and complexities of both slavery and the slave trades in Africa require us to be more specific about the application of the term "slavery" on this continent. Indeed, many of the debates over slavery's definition seem to have occurred in the African literature, with some differences of opinion clearly linked to particular disciplinary perspectives. Without wishing to rehash these debates *in toto*, two of them are particularly instructive for our understanding of internal African slavery.

First, debate about to what degree African systems of slavery were "closed" rather than "open" highlights the fact that internal African slavery was often an open system in the sense that routes existed for slaves to become free members of the societies in which they had been enslaved (Watson 1980b:9–13; see also Cameron, this volume). Emancipation was often easier for women and for the children of a slave and a free person, but to correlate this emancipation simply with gender would be an oversimplification. Unlike the plantations of the Americas, where slaves were treated as chattels or merely economic units, slaves within Africa, particularly captives who were not funneled into the Atlantic and trans-Saharan export markets, generally were not simply economic units but "whole persons" with important social roles within the societies into which they had been enslaved (Kopytoff and Miers 1977:24, 28; Lovejoy 1983:5; Manning 1990: 116; for examples, see Boston 1968:162–175, 184–185; Brain 1972:14–15); for example, slaves had no kinship ties in their new societies and hence could sometimes be more trustworthy in political positions where a free person's loyalty to the state might be undermined by kinship obligations. Slaves were not merely non-kin; they were in a sense "anti-kin" and as such could be

trusted (Meillassoux 1991:138–140; for examples, see Brain 1972:15; Harms 1981:185). One implication of this is that the acquisition of slaves for internal African use was not just, or even at all, an economic decision. We offer further explanation of this observation below, but here we wish to draw attention to the fact that the openness of African slavery, but not the institution of slavery itself (Meillassoux 1991:40), may have its roots in the tangled complexity of African concepts of identity and individuality. As Kopytoff and Miers (1977:7–11) have demonstrated, there is no simple dichotomy in most African societies between freedom and slavery (or other forms of bondage) because systems of kinship and marriage ensure that nobody is entirely free to make his or her own decision about such matters as whom to marry and where to reside. Contributions to and receipts from bride-price and bride-wealth payments mean that everyone has vested "rights-in-persons." Indeed, perhaps paradoxically, a slave is a person who is free of the obligations of kinship and marriage. Thus, the route to emancipation lay with integration into the kinship system of the host society, though in some cases, at least, there were limits to this integration. The stigma of slave origins often lingered for many generations (e.g., Brown 2003; Robertson and Klein 1983:7), and in some cases such fictive kin were more expendable than real kin (see Stahl, this volume).

The second important debate pertaining to the definition of slavery revolves around the question of whether slavery should be defined by its attributes, as for example in the definition Cameron offers, or as an institution—in other words, as a mode of production based on the economic output of slaves acquired through capture (Meillassoux 1991). For Meillassoux (1991:36), "slavery, *as a mode of exploitation*, exists only where there is *a distinct class of individuals*, with the same social state and *renewed constantly and institutionally*, so that, since this class fills its functions permanently, the relations of exploitation and the exploiting class which benefits from them can also be regularly and continually reconstituted" (emphases in original). This suggests that it may be useful to distinguish societies with relatively small numbers and percentages of slaves from those where slaves can be recognized as a distinct class. Drawing upon the work of Finley (1968:310), the historian Paul Lovejoy has made precisely this distinction, drawing a contrast between societies where slavery was "incidental to the structure of the society and the functioning of the economy" and those in which slavery was an "institution" in that slaves played an *essential* economic role and thus there existed a "slave mode of production," though other modes could coexist in the same society (Lovejoy 1983:9–10). While "incidental" slavery may well have been almost ubiquitous in decentralized societies, societies in which slaves comprised a distinct class must, almost de facto, be state-level. In the latter case, it was not uncommon to encounter societies (for example, in the Sudan [the region, not the modern country]) where slaves represented 50 percent of the population (Burnham 1980:43; Lovejoy 1983:186–187; MacEachern 2001:145). In these circumstances, a constant imperative was to replenish the supply of slaves to counteract losses through death, escape, or sale; hence "the institutions of war and trade were the necessary conditions for its [slavery's] existence" (Meillassoux 1991:43). Furthermore, it follows that the victims of the imperative of replenishment would most likely have come from decentralized societies. As we shall see, the major effect of slavery on decentralized societies in Africa lay in their attempts to avoid these depredations.

Why Slavery in Africa?

Based on the American experience, the development of the institution of slavery is often seen as founded upon a shortage of labor for economic production (Nieboer 1900). Thus, it can be argued that slavery was never particularly prevalent in India because it was land, not labor, that was in short supply (Watson 1980b:11–12). However, as Goody (1980) has explained, this explanation is not a good fit for Africa. Here land was indeed abundant and labor scarce, but the productivity of labor was constrained by the available technology. People whose agriculture was based on the hoe could not generally produce significant surplus crops (Goody 1980:36). Hence, the economic value of an African in an African society, even when labor was a limiting resource, was less than that of a European in a European society practicing plow agriculture (Manning 1990:

33). It is this marginal economic value of an African slave that may explain why huge numbers of slaves were required to make a success of slavery as "a mode of exploitation" within Africa in the nineteenth century. However, this argument assumes that slaves were simply economic units, whereas, as noted earlier, slaves could fill a variety of roles as "whole persons" in African societies. Nevertheless, these observations reinforce the impression that slavery was probably an institution of minor importance in decentralized societies. With the exception of some elites in state-level societies, most Africans lacked the wealth needed to sustain many slaves, nor could they generally find buyers for any goods the slaves might produce (Manning 1990:34). Goody (1980:24, 31) also noted that it was not the ratio of arable land to labor that led to slavery, but the existence of organizational and military inequalities between neighboring societies. Moreover, it is worth noting that even where conditions of inequality encouraged warfare and raiding for booty by state-level societies against decentralized neighbors, male captives were often deemed to be worth so little that they were routinely killed on the battlefield rather than taken home to become slaves (e.g., Vansina 2004:77).

Gender, Slavery and the Slave Trade

The killing of male captives highlights the fact that slavery and the slave trade were not gender-neutral activities. Some two-thirds of the slaves exported to the American markets were males, mostly young adults (Manning 1990:22). The rise of the Atlantic slave trade from about 1650 CE until its decline in the nineteenth century provided a new market into which Africans could sell males captured in war or raids who would perhaps otherwise have been put to death. The American preference for male slaves dovetailed nicely with the preference for female slaves in Africa and the Islamic world.

Islamic societies valued female slaves to fill a variety of roles, including those of concubines, entertainers, and domestic workers. Many thousands of African women became members of rulers' harems; it is said the harem of the Fatimid rulers in Cairo contained about twelve thousand concubines (Segal 2001:39).[2] There was also an almost insatiable demand for slave eunuchs, with prices being inflated even further by the high death rates associated with castration (Segal 2001:41). However, male Africans had been sent in large numbers to Iraq from as early as the late seventh century CE. These slaves, known as the Zanj, appear to have derived from the East African coast, where archaeological evidence of settlement, let alone slaving, at this time is virtually nonexistent (but see Horton 1996:367 for an exception).

The Zanj were put to work in such harsh conditions on plantations in southern Iraq that rebellion was perhaps inevitable. It took the 'Abbasid Caliphate more than ten years to crush the major Zanj revolt of the late ninth century; thereafter, Islamic rulers were very diffident about employing large numbers of male African slaves on plantations. Of course, there were exceptions, and by the nineteenth century thousands of enslaved African men were working on plantations on the islands off the East African coast. African slaves were also used as soldiers. Indeed, it was a slave general who defeated the Crusaders. The Mamluk dynasty of Egypt in the medieval period was a dynasty of military slaves; the term *mamlūk* translates literally as "possessed" or "slave" (Segal 2001:31). Nevertheless, across much of the Islamic world it was African women rather than men who were generally preferred as slaves.

A preference for female slaves also existed within Africa itself. Women were selected primarily for their reproductive ability, as well as for their ability to work in the fields and house (Goody 1980:39–42). Slaveholders could strengthen their lineage by having more offspring, and doing it through a slave arguably avoided such troublesome matters as paying bride-wealth and having to negotiate with a bride's lineage. Indeed, it sometimes cost less to buy a slave than to pay bride-wealth (e.g., Harms 1981:180).

Marrying or becoming a concubine for one's owner or another freeperson often allowed a slave to assume a position of status within the free society. This was usually achieved after giving birth to an owner's or freeperson's child (Kopytoff and Miers 1977:31–32; Robertson and Klein 1983:6, 16; Lovejoy 1983:7). Children fathered by a freeperson were usually considered free at birth. However, Meillassoux (1983:52–53) argues that the demand for women for reproductive purposes—either to produce new slaves or to strengthen the family lineage—is overstated. He points out that, among other reasons, since the children most often became the owner's to do with as he wished, women were often not willing to give birth, and some may have practiced infanticide (ibid.). Nevertheless, female slaves were also preferred over male slaves because they were thought less apt to try to escape and easier to train, and they were able to perform manual labor in the field as well as menial domestic tasks (ibid.:58). In fact, Meillassoux argues that "in slavery, women were valued above all as workers, mostly because female tasks were predominant in production" (ibid.:49), a statement with which Robertson and Klein (1983:10) heartily concur. Indeed, there is an example of the labor of slave women, albeit owned by Europeans, leaving archaeological traces at a site in Cape Town where they washed clothes (Jordan 2005). In addition, at slack times in the agricultural cycle in West Africa, "slaves were encouraged to engage in craft activities, especially those related to textile production" (Frank 1993:394). Some female slaves, primarily in state-level societies, became administrators for their masters, and some even owned or used slaves themselves (Meillassoux 1983:58; Robertson and Klein 1983:15).

The importance of male slaves within Africa varied through time. As already noted, prior to the demand for males for the American market that swiftly accelerated in the mid-seventeenth century, or in areas lacking ready access to trade routes leading to the Atlantic ports, it was common for men captured in war to be put to death immediately (Keeley 1996:83–86; for African examples, see Evans-Pritchard 1940:128; Vansina 2004:77). This practice seems to have been particularly prevalent in decentralized societies, which, in comparison to states, lacked the manpower, facilities, and surplus production to control and feed male slaves. However, states and perhaps complex chiefdoms sometimes spared the lives of male captives, albeit briefly, so that they could be sacrificed later in religious rituals and/or displays of the rulers' power. We have one probable example of this from the African archaeological record in a region where a documentary source of the early sixteenth century describes how the servants of a coastal Manding chief in West Africa were buried alive in an earthen tumulus with their master (see McIntosh 2001:25). Excavation of a tumulus in the Senegal Valley, dated by a sole radiocarbon assay to cal. 1410–1650 CE, uncovered fifty-six skeletons buried simultaneously. Very few were children, hence the mortality profile does not fit that of an epidemic, leaving sacrifice as the most plausible interpretation. Further support derived from the fact that the teeth of the skeletons exhibited a high frequency of caries and enamel hypoplasias, indicative of nutritional deficiencies and/or poor health, such as one might expect among slaves or captives (see Martin, this volume, for a comparable study). Two mounds at another site in this region, dated to cal. AD 1020–1270, also yielded numerous simultaneous inhumations with some evidence of dental pathologies (Thilmans et al. 1980, cited in McIntosh 2001:25).

While this West African example dates prior to the development of the Atlantic slave trade, the sacrifice of male slaves, usually recently acquired, is widely documented in the nineteenth century, when the demand for slaves for the internal African market was at its peak (e.g., Austen 1977:316; Harms 1981:149; Uchendu 1977:129). In West Africa, slaves were executed as sacrifices in celebration of the royal ancestors of Dahomey and Benin (Manning 1990:118). That such executions were relatively common is evident from observers' accounts of slaves in the Asante kingdom hiding in fear of their lives whenever they heard funeral drums (Goody 1980:31). McIntosh (2001: 25) and others (e.g., Keim 1983:152) have argued that these human sacrifices were particularly potent displays of chiefly or royal power in Africa, where labor, rather than land, was in short supply (see Peregrine, this volume, for a different perspective in a North American context). An apparent royal disdain for human life, particularly that of slaves, is evident from many wide-eyed accounts of European visitors to the Buganda court in the nineteenth century; one Italian officer was told that when the king, Suna, fell ill, he had ordered a hundred people a day to be put to death to obtain his cure and that these sacrifices had continued for fifteen days (Casati 1891, vol. 2; fifty-one cited by Reid 2002:128). Meillassoux (1991:221), however, takes a more sanguine view, arguing that once the demands of merchants and

the dominant class for slaves had been met, excess captives were sacrificed to limit the potential for slaveholding by the lower classes, which would have provided them with an avenue to wealth and political emancipation, and to get rid of malcontents and excess mouths to feed. Sacrifices of female slaves were rare, and thus more potent in terms of ritual effect and ostentation (ibid.:39).

In summary, women, as well as young children who could be relatively easily integrated into a new society, were preferred as slaves in internal African slavery (see also DeBoer, this volume). Male captives were either put to death immediately, soon sacrificed, or sold (relatively cheaply) to traders for external markets, particularly after 1650. However, the rapid expansion of internal African slavery in the nineteenth century led to large numbers of male slaves being employed on plantations or at royal courts, where they contributed their talents in a variety of ways to prodigious displays of wealth and power. These were part of a short-lived and unsustainable golden age that was to be destroyed by European colonialism (e.g., Boston 1968:162–175; Reid 2002). But if slavery supported prestige economies in the states of nineteenth-century Africa, what were slavery's effects on African decentralized societies?

The Dynamics of Slave Capture in Africa

Decentralized societies were the main suppliers, albeit involuntary, of slaves. People became slaves in various ways: through warfare, raids aimed at capturing slaves, kidnapping, and exactions of tribute from conquered societies (e.g., Lovejoy 1983:83–84). Some individuals were sold into slavery as a result of court proceedings, including witchcraft accusations. Finally, people in dire straits sometimes gave themselves or sold their kin into slavery (Manning 1990:88–89), a practice that was particularly prevalent in times of drought and famine (e.g., Feierman 1974:137; Hubbell 2001:43). This last mechanism is well documented in the kingdom of Buganda in East Africa, where people were sometimes enslaved within their own society as a result of fines or debts, though often only temporarily, with the victims set free once the debt had been paid or particular services rendered (Reid 2002:118–119).

FIGURE 3.1. "Moors pursuing Negroes to enslave them." From D-H. Lamiral, *L'Afrique et le people africain considérés sous tous les rapports avec notre commerce et nos colonies* (Paris: Desenne, 1789). Reprinted as Plate 3 in *Senegambia and the Atlantic Slave Trade*, by Boubacar Barry (New York: Cambridge University Press, 1998). Reprinted with permission of Cambridge University Press.

It seems likely that most of the relatively small number of slaves held for a relatively long period in decentralized societies, which would not generally have been capable of dealing with war captives, were people who had voluntarily become slaves, as has been documented among the Kerebe of Tanzania and the Sena of Mozambique (Hartwig 1977; Isaacman and Isaacman 1977).

In those periods and regions where one can speak of a slave mode of exploitation (production), particularly the era of the Atlantic slave trade and its nineteenth-century aftermath, the constant demand for replenishment of the slave workforce led to endemic warfare and raiding, with concomitant major transformations of the decentralized societies that were targeted, as we discuss below. However, the particular characteristics of Islamic culture and society gave the Sudanic belt of Africa a trajectory of cultural change that resulted in a moving frontier of slavery. Koranic teaching distinguishes between the Dar el Islam, the land where inhabitants have submitted to the Muslim faith, and the Dar el Harb, where they have not. Although slavery is permitted in the Holy Koran and codified in Shari'a law, inhabitants of the Dar el Islam could not be enslaved except for particular crimes. However, people of the Dar el Harb could be enslaved (Figure 3.1). Moreover, Muslims were under obligation to conquer and incorporate the Dar el Harb into the Dar el Islam. Individual slaves who voluntarily accepted the Muslim faith could also improve their lot in life, though they remained slaves unless manumitted, a practice that was encouraged by the tenets of Islam. Thus, following the Arab conquest of North Africa, the inhabitants of this region, now incorporated within the Dar el Islam, pushed the boundary with the Dar el Harb southwards over the next thousand years through conquest and a virtually insatiable appetite for slaves (Cordell 2003:32–33; also see Alexander 2001:45–47 for details and a map of this moving frontier). As MacEachern (2001:147) remarks on the basis of his work in the southern Lake Chad basin, "[T]his resulted in the uninterrupted development of a slaving frontier, a frontier on which 'peripheral' populations were under threat of enslavement and behind which adoption of dominant cultural and [Islamic] religious forms allowed people at least a theoretical immunity to such enslavement." This moving frontier and its concomitant cultural transformations have been mapped primarily on the basis of documentary sources. However, despite Alexander's (2001) pessimism over the recognition of Islamic slavery in the archaeological record, archaeology has already begun to reveal patterns of cultural, political, and economic changes that occurred, particularly among societies in the Dar el Harb (e.g., Gronenborn 2001; MacEachern 2001); we explore some of these below.

Somewhat in contrast to the moving frontier of Dar el Islam is the historical trajectory of slave acquisition that has been reconstructed for the great eighteenth- and nineteenth-century states of the West African coastal regions. In order to profit from supplying slaves to the Atlantic ports, states such as Asante and Dahomey in their early days obtained captives by conquering their neighbors; thus, slaves were produced as part of the process by which states expanded their territorial control. However, as the supply of slaves from conquered regions dried up, rather than attempting to conquer regions increasingly distant from the capital, states switched to acquiring slaves from distant regions through the exaction of tribute, thus compelling their conquered neighbors to raid their own neighbors or to obtain slaves through clientship arrangements with traders and petty leaders based in distant lands

(Klein 2001:57–58). Thus, the primary mechanism for acquiring slaves shifted from warfare to raiding, kidnapping, and the rather more nebulous workings of capitalist market forces (see below).

The pattern of acquisition of captives that we have just described is sometimes referred to as the "predatory state" model or thesis whereby militaristic states and their conquered tributary neighbors descended upon regions populated by decentralized societies, primarily in the dry season, when the reduced demands of agricultural labor permitted more men to be conscripted into raiding parties (e.g., Echenberg 1971:245), in order to obtain slaves to meet the almost insatiable demands of the Atlantic export trade in the seventeenth to nineteenth centuries (Hubbell 2001:27; Klein 2001:49). This model views raided areas as "predatory landscapes" (Swanepoel 2006; see also Cameron, this volume) whose resident decentralized societies are cast in the role of passive victims (Hubbell 2001:28; Klein 2001:50). However, as both Hubbell and Klein (ibid.) emphasize, this model not only reflects the fact that far more historical research has been undertaken on state-level as opposed to decentralized societies in Africa, hence offering a "state" perspective on the process, but also ignores the inconvenient fact that oftentimes the decentralized societies occupying the predatory landscapes survived repeated raids. Success at repulsing or avoiding raids did not, however, completely stem the flow of captives from these societies, as we shall see.

In light of the formidable nature of fortified villages, which were the major obstacles to slave-raiding, predatory states and their tribute-paying allies were generally obliged to resort to other strategies to acquire slaves. Common among these was the seizure of people who ventured outside their villages, as was usually necessary to tend crops, by bands of bandits (e.g., Baum 1999:83, 111–112). In the high-stakes chess game of slave raids, decentralized societies occupying fortified villages responded by moving their fields close to the villages, intensifying their agriculture (at least where arable land was in short supply), and by venturing out to the fields only in large, armed parties (Klein 2001:56, 2003:66). Nevertheless, people were frequently seized, as happened notably both to the father of the distinguished African historian Joseph Ki-Zerbo (Hubbell 2001:25) and to Olaudah Equiano, author of the first description of the New World to be written by a slave (Edwards 1969). Moving fields close to settlements, as well as the threat of seizure while working in those fields, often induced or required people to change the crops that they grew—a change that would probably be discernible in the archaeological record (see also Stahl, this volume).

The bandits who kidnapped people working in their fields or traveling outside their settlements were not always agents of predatory states but sometimes themselves members of the very decentralized societies that were being targeted. As Hubbell (2001) has pointed out, there was much competition within these decentralized societies over access to scarce resources. Young men chafing at their limited access to the wealth and status controlled by elders were particularly prone to resort to banditry, especially the kidnapping of children from within their own settlements (Hubbell 2001:39–40; Klein 2001:60, citing work by Warnier on the Cameroon Grassfields). The kidnappers' activities were encouraged by merchants who were often able to enter fortified settlements because they carried desired commodities such as salt, cowries, iron, and weapons (Hubbell 2001:35; Klein 2001:58; see also Stahl, this volume, for discussion of the role of material culture in relation to slavery). Indeed, in times of famine and in the desperate conditions of the nineteenth century, decentralized societies pawned or sold their own members into slavery, seizing their most vulnerable members and converting judicial penalties into enslavement (Klein 2001:59–60).

Finally, it should be noted that captives were taken far from their homelands whenever possible, even when they were not sold into the Atlantic or Islamic trade, since this reduced the likelihood that they would attempt to flee. In accordance with this principle, captives in the Congo Basin were moved both up and down river, with the result being a "continual mixing of the population of the central basin" (Harms 1981: 29). European explorers saw so many captives being taken towards the Ubangi River that they incorrectly assumed that they were being consumed for food (ibid.:31).

Decentralized societies in Africa faced with the threat of well-armed slaving expeditions, often in the Sudanic belt wrapped in the cloak of jihad, exhibited a range of countermeasures. First among these was to try to get out of the way by moving settlements into relatively inaccessible regions where the cavalry and guns of slave raiders would be less effective (Bah 2003:16–18). Such regions included marshes in Benin (Soumonni 2003) and Guinea-Bissau (Hawthorne 2001), the Mandara Mountains of northern Nigeria (MacEachern 2001), and the Taita Hills of eastern Kenya (Kusimba 2004). The relocation of villages created new regional settlement patterns characterized by densely populated areas that were relatively safe from attack separated by large swaths of depopulated countryside (e.g., Hawthorne 2003:158–159).

These wholesale migrations to new areas were sometimes permanent, as in the case of the Balanta of Guinea-Bissau in the seventeenth century (Hawthorne 2001), but avoidance also took the form of moving to temporary refuges. People in the Bassar region of Togo combined both strategies in the eighteenth century, abandoning settlements on the open plains for sites within easy reach of mountains to which they could flee when an attack by slaving cavalry was imminent (de Barros 2001:71–72). One reason for the comparative success of this avoidance strategy was the fact that slave-raiding was often a seasonal activity, since in the dry season there were fewer demands for agricultural labor and travel was generally easier. Moreover, slave raiders did not necessarily return each year to the same locations (Cordell 2003:37), and when they did come, they did not linger. Usman (2003:204–205) uses the term "smash and grab" to describe slave raid operations by groups of Nupe in Nigeria in the eighteenth and nineteenth centuries.

Caves and rockshelters where people could hide, at least temporarily, were often used as refuges in many parts of Africa. In Bunyoro, Uganda, people living close to the border with the kingdom of Buganda frequently hid in caves during times of war. Excavations in one such rockshelter at Munsa uncovered many smoking pipes, as well as a few beads and potsherds, suggesting that people wiled away time here until it was safe to go home (Robertshaw, forthcoming).

These were also commonly places where one might communicate more readily with the spirit world, reached through portals in the rock; thus, those hiding from their enemies might derive spiritual solace during their time of stress. Indeed, some mountainous regions that served as refuges came to be regarded as sacred, as in the case of the Tekem Mountains in Chad, settled by the Toupouri (Bah 2003:17).

Not only could one hide in a rockshelter, but one could also defend it. Kusimba (2004, 2006) describes rockshelters in Tsavo, Kenya, that were fortified four hundred years ago, apparently to provide shelter and seclusion from raiders and warfare. The timing of their fortification coincides with the beginning of a period of active slave-raiding. These rockshelters were located in a circle around a village, but at a distance from the domestic areas. Though difficult to recognize on approach, they provided a lookout from within to observe anyone approaching. Other evidence that points to these structures as being temporary getaways is the presence of only a few artifacts. Apparently, they were used infrequently, presumably when under threat of attack (Kusimba 2004).

Kusimba (2004:81) has also pointed out that fortified settlements were built in many areas of the East African interior in approximately the seventeenth to nineteenth centuries. It is not always clear from oral traditions or documents, let alone archaeological investigations, that these fortifications were a response to heightened levels of slave-raiding, particularly in the nineteenth century, but their tendency to be located in the vicinity of established trade routes is surely no coincidence (ibid.). Most of these sites have as yet been the subject of little or no archaeological investigation.

As in East Africa, fortified settlements were also a common, and often the most effective, response to the threat of slave raids on the western side of the continent (e.g., DeCorse 1989; Baum 1999:93, 121; Bah 2003; Klein 2003; Usman 2003), as well as in parts of southeastern Africa exposed to Portuguese raiding (Pikirayi and Pwiti 1999: 80). Fortification was also commonly accompanied by population aggregation (e.g., Usman 2003:210), a process with epidemiological implications (Cordell 2003:44). With some villages

housing several thousand inhabitants, attacking forces often risked having the tables turned on them. Hubbell (2001:31) cites numerous examples of villages in the Niger Bend region successfully repulsing attacks by powerful armies. Villages in this region and elsewhere were often encircled by high *pisé* (adobe) walls that were virtually impregnable in the absence of artillery (Figure 3.2). Even if attackers succeeded in clambering over or breaching the exterior walls, they were usually faced with more-formidable obstacles, such as open courtyards to be crossed under fire, small and few doorways, narrow and twisting passages, and even barriers of living vegetation (Bah 1985, 2003:20–21; DeCorse 1989:129–131; Guèye 2003:56; Klein 2001:53–55; Usman 2003:206). The Musgu, south of Lake Chad, lived in scattered settlements whose houses could be easily set on fire, but in the face of repeated raids they designed new, less flammable architecture and grouped their houses in such a way that there were very few exterior doors. Moreover, the new dome-shaped houses looked like termite nests from a distance, with the result that they were reputedly overlooked by several slaving parties (Bah 2003: 24–25). However, other groups adopted almost the opposite strategy: houses in Cayor and Baol villages in northern Senegambia were torched by their owners to distract and slow the advance of raiding parties while the people fled, later to return and rebuild (Guèye 2003:55–56).

Both flight and settlement fortification were employed by Sisala groups in Ghana. The choice of strategy was generally based on location: those who lived at a distance from the major trade routes and were rarely exposed to raids lived in scattered villages from which they fled when necessary; those who were close to the trade routes fortified nucleated settlements with walls, palisades, and ditches (Mendonsa 2001:42–43). The rise of nucleated settlements provided a new opportunity for entrepreneurial individuals, among the otherwise politically decentralized Sisala, to establish themselves as war leaders and wealthy big men. They themselves raided for slaves and accrued wealth through trade, allowing them to acquire followers outside the kinship system (Swanepoel 2006; see also Baum 1999:126 for another example). Mendonsa (2001:39) reports that "In life such leaders received extra respect,

FIGURE 3.2. The Nalerigu defensive wall in the northern region of Ghana. Reprinted from *A History of Indigenous Slavery in Ghana: From the 15th to the 19th Century,* by Akosua Adoma Perbi (Legon, Accra: Sub-Saharan Publishers, 2004) with permission of Sub-Saharan Publishers.

dressed better, ate well, had many possessions and wives, lived in two-story houses, and had large farms and granaries," though they were not distinguished in death.

The fortification of settlements was by no means a universal response among decentralized societies exposed to the slave trade. Neither the Igbo of eastern Nigeria nor the Bobangi along the Congo River in Central Africa fortified their settlements because the threat that they faced came not from predatory states or their vassals but from within. These societies became deeply involved in both sides of the slave trade, as both captors and captives, after they were penetrated by the market forces of capitalism. The profits to be made from the sale of captives, together with the demand for European trade goods, encouraged entrepreneurial individuals and groups in these societies to become merchants in the slave trade (e.g., Harms 1981). They acquired slaves through local conflicts and raiding, but increasingly through internal judicial mechanisms that were transformed so that marginal members of society could be sold into slavery (Klein 2001: 61–65; Rashid 2003:135). In Igbo society, wid-

ows and their children were most at risk (Brown 2003:219).

Settlement relocation and fortification both imply organizational complexity and substantial use of labor. The slave trade, and perhaps the Atlantic trade in particular, seems to have acted as a catalyst for political centralization as a defensive strategy (Daaku 1970:144–181). The Wandala polity in the southern Chad Basin provides an example of this process. Relatively little is known about the archaeology of this polity, but its origins clearly lie among the small agricultural communities of the southern plains of the Chad Basin in the period from about 300 to 1200 CE. The development of the Wandala state seems to have been predicated upon its proximity to the Muslim slave-raiding Kanuri state of Bornu, which was well established by 1500 CE. Although part of Wandala's rise can be credited to its ability to dominate the export trade in iron from the southern Mandara Mountains to the Kanuri state in the north, the Wandala became more politically centralized to cope with the threat of Kanuri slave raiders. By the sixteenth century, these raiders were entering the region on horseback accompanied by a corps of Turkish gunners. A documentary source from that century describes the Wandala retreating to a mountain fortress in the face of one of these raids. However, by the end of the eighteenth century, the Wandala state had transformed itself into a powerful adversary that was able to send out an army to defeat a Kanuri invasion. Through increasing political centralization, the acquisition of firearms and armor in exchange for iron, and the incorporation of numerous people from other groups, the Wandala established themselves as a predatory, slave-trading state that acted, using MacEachern's (2001:141) term, as subcontractors for the Kanuri, supplying captives to the Islamic trade. Wandala rulers also converted to Islam in the early eighteenth century and began to make greater use of slaves domestically as well as for export (MacEachern 2001:141–143).

The Wandala case is not unusual. The Yao provide a comparable example from the other side of the continent, in Tanzania. Kusimba (2006:224), drawing on historical research by Alpers (1969), describes how entrepreneurial Yao men became "merchant chiefs" by responding to the increasing demand for slaves and ivory in the sixteenth and seventeenth centuries. Ivory obtained from local elephants was sold for guns and slaves, particularly women and children, who then belonged to their owner's lineage. Thus, men could build their kin groups into powerful factions, in part by avoiding bride-wealth obligations. Yao chiefs then engaged in predatory expansion of their territory, not only selling captives into the slave trade but also using them to carry ivory down to the coast. In the face of this terror, populations fled, and farms and villages were abandoned, precipitating the additional misery of famine. Thus, the Yao, like the Wandala, transformed themselves from targets of the slave trade into protagonists.

The Bobangi of the central Congo Basin provide another example of the rise of a class of merchants through slave trading (Harms 1981). These were fishermen who began to transport slaves up and down the rivers, and who also conducted trade in both slaves and other goods during their travels. Successful merchants acquired many slaves to paddle more canoes to expand their businesses. As they prospered, merchants would establish new villages and enter into alliances with other villages to establish commercial networks, the deal often being sealed by the burial of a male and a female slave (ibid.:135). With alliances, "an ethnic name that previously had designated a localized group of fishing people could expand to designate an entire trading alliance" (ibid.:127), and the Bobangi alliance was the largest of these. In the case of the Bobangi, these developments did not lead to political centralization in the form of a state, but rather the establishment of merchant chiefs, like those of the Yao. Such chiefdoms expanded and contracted in line with the fortunes of their rulers (ibid.:147).

The Effects of Slaving

Slave-raiding led to various reactions by indigenous African communities, including relocation to more-defensible areas, active resistance, and sometimes political centralization. However, in many cases, as with some of the Yao's neighbors, slave raids precipitated the destruction of communities, or at least their dispersal, often with a concomitant loss of ethnic identities and the forging of new ones. In Senegambia, the Floup state declined in the seventeenth century at least in part because its leaders could not "readily control a slave trade where it was so easy to become a participant" (Baum 1999:83). In the absence of a centralized state, the slave trade in this Diola region "was regulated and legitimated through a series of cults and their priests" (ibid.:177). Moreover, successful entrepreneurial slave raiders used their wealth to acquire priestly offices. They also accumulated wealth in cattle from the sale of slaves, as a result of which animal sacrifice became a more important element of the various cults (ibid.:177–178).

MacEachern's (2001) work again offers further examples, derived primarily from ethnohistorical research. He notes both the disappearance of named communities from the southern Chad Basin, though some people retained memories of their former ethnicities, and "an homogenization of plains ethnicity and culture" (MacEachern 2001:144). The latter was fueled by the adoption by elites of elements of Kanuri culture, such as court titles and functions, and by progressive conversion to Islam. There are clear archaeological implications here: MacEachern (ibid.) notes that a loss of ethnic diversity may be reflected in the varied ceramics made by communities who are now all called "Wandala."[3] In analogous fashion, the diffusion of pottery with twisted-strip roulette decoration can be linked to the expanding influence of the slave-raiding Borno empire (Gronenborn 2001:118). Similarly, it seems that female potters in the Kadiolo region of southern Mali may have originally been slaves who brought their potting skills with them when they were captured (Frank 1993).

Usman (2003:211) has also noted ceramic changes, particularly the introduction of new decorative motifs, that can be explained as responses to the aggregation of people from different ethnic backgrounds in fortified settlements in Nigeria. Moreover, he suggests that some of these changes may reflect both ethnic heterogeneity and the hegemony of one ethnic group.

Another example of ceramic change, apparently as a consequence of slaving, comes from the Middle Senegal Valley in West Africa. Ceramic assemblages from this region in the period between 1600 and 1850 CE are notable for their poor quality. This pottery was thin-walled, hastily fired, and porous, the latter being the result of the use of large amounts of organic temper that burned off during firing. Reductions in the amount of labor dedicated to pottery manufacture is evident in all stages of the process, from inadequate preparation of the clay and temper, to a limited range of vessel forms and decoration, to hasty firing. This is in marked contrast to the well-made and often highly decorated pots made in this region in earlier times and in the present day (McIntosh 2001:26–29). While McIntosh (2001:29) call for caution in linking the ceramic change to slaving, noting that this was a period of recurrent droughts, political unrest, and population movements spurred by Islamic militancy, it seems clear that slaving was indeed a factor, if not the major factor, in promoting the disruptions that McIntosh describes.

In addition to slave-raiding's effects on ethnicity, the slave trade involved trade in more than slaves. Slaving increased demand for firearms and, in the Sudanic belt and West Africa, horses (e.g., Echenberg 1971), since these were the tools of slavery. Other weapons were also desirable commodities: "swords, knives, spears, and iron-tipped arrows" (Klein 2001:59; see also Hawthorne 2003:161). The link between trade and warfare is thus clear: "States…warred to trade and traded to war" (Reyna 1990:39, quoted in MacEachern 2001:148). The acquisition of more guns also intensified the slaughter of elephants for ivory, particularly in East Africa, where decimation of elephant populations led to what must have been unexpected changes in vegetation, leading in turn to the spread of insect-borne diseases, the agents of what Kusimba (2006:230) has called "the elephant's revenge."

Other items besides guns and horses were received by African societies in exchange for slaves. Indeed, the importance of trade goods spurred the development of a distinct merchant class in some African states, as well as in some decentralized societies (e.g., Harms 1981). Chief among these imports were textiles, mostly of Indian origin until the end of the eighteenth century. Alcohol, especially rum, and tobacco, mostly from Brazil, were important imports from across the Atlantic. Money in various forms, such as cowries, copper wire, and silver coins, was also exchanged for slaves, as were a variety of other goods, including umbrellas and, of special interest to archaeologists, glass beads. The vast majority of these items were controlled by elites as prestige goods, with the plainer textiles, as well as most of the alcohol and tobacco, being used to buy the loyalty of commoners (Manning 1990: 100). However, some imports were channeled in novel ways into changing cultural practices, as has been demonstrated with cowries in the Yoruba region of Nigeria (Ogundiran 2002).

The Atlantic slave trade was also linked, albeit perhaps rather indirectly, with the import to Africa of New World crops that transformed African agriculture. In suitable growing regions, high yields of maize led to surpluses that allowed more people to engage in nonagricultural activities, while cassava became the most important staple for warding off famine in times of drought across tropical Africa. Indeed, the introduction of American crops may have led to population increases in many parts of Africa, though these were probably more than offset by the loss of people to the slave trade (Mitchell 2005:198–200).

Transformations in African agriculture were not confined to the effects of the introduction of

New World crops. The Balanta of Guinea-Bissau were a decentralized society in the sixteenth century, producing yams and maize using mostly stone and wood tools in settlements dispersed across the uplands. With little surplus production and a lack of mineral resources, they were simply unable to afford iron tools. However, when they became "part of the 'slaving frontier' of one of West Africa's most powerful states [Kaabu]" (Hawthorne 2001:2), the Balanta abandoned the uplands in favor of defensive villages in the coastal swamps. In these new surroundings they flourished by developing an intensive paddy-rice monoculture. Life in their new, densely populated villages lent itself well, with the aid of a new age grade system, to the increased demands for labor to clear mangroves and build dykes to create rice paddies. Rice, in turn, being easily stored, proved to be a lucrative trade good for which the Balanta could obtain iron tools and slaves, which promoted further expansion of their new agricultural system. However, the Balanta preferred not to have direct dealings with European traders; instead, they themselves raided for captives among neighboring societies, who were then ransomed for goods such as iron tools and cattle (Hawthorne 2003:162). Thus, Balanta became one of the most densely populated regions of West Africa in the nineteenth century, despite being occupied by an acephalous society in a region of predatory states (Hawthorne 2001).

Agricultural transformations were not always as successful as in the case of the Balanta. In the absence of external threats from slave raiders, peoples of the savanna regions of West and Central Africa obtained much of their food from sorghum and millets. However, in the face of slave-raiding, cultivation of these crops became desperately dangerous since the crops were easily seen, required lots of care, and had to be harvested at just the right time. According to Cordell (2003:41), people adapted in one of two ways, both of which have been reported in the Banda area of Ghana. The first was to abandon most agriculture in favor of hunting and gathering, while the second was to grow manioc, a plant that was easy to hide, required little care, and could be left hidden in the ground.

In contrast to Guinea-Bissau, with its dearth of iron, the Bassar region of north-central Togo was a major center of iron production in West Africa. This region has been the focus of long-term archaeological and historical research that has provided an excellent example of the complex effects of the slave trade on an African society (what follows is summarized from de Barros 2001). From about 1300 CE, there was a dramatic increase in the demand for iron artifacts in this part of the world as a result of both the rise of states among the Bassar's neighbors and later, perhaps, population increases stemming from the spread of New World crops. Iron weapons, horse paraphernalia, and body armor were required to service the military ambitions of the new states, often themselves aimed at acquiring slaves, while iron hoes were needed for agriculture. The Bassar responded by introducing induced-draft furnaces to ramp up iron production (de Barros 2001).

Their success and the wealth generated from the sale of their products led to population increases because of higher standards of living, the immigration of ironworkers from surrounding areas, and the importation of slaves as domestic laborers. Success bred success: Bassar ironworkers, freed from the necessities of agricultural labor by their slaves and by the import of foodstuffs, dedicated themselves to iron production, and by the seventeenth century they had moved to densely populated villages close to the major ore deposits. Individual villages began to specialize in particular aspects of the industry, such as smithing and charcoal production. Ironworkers often became rich men, importing not only slaves but a wide variety of prestige goods, including so many small ceramic vessels, used instead of gourds for eating and drinking, that locally made wares became increasingly uncommon (de Barros 2001).

The rise of the Atlantic slave trade in the late seventeenth century, however, exposed the Bassar, who lacked political centralization, to the acquisitive attention of neighboring states. Given that the Bassar chiefdom emerged between 1780 and 1810, it seems likely that it arose as a defensive response to slave-raiding, as de Barros (1986: 166–167) initially proposed. However, further work by de Barros and others has shown that the motive for creating the chiefdom was political rather than defensive. It was designed to resolve disputes in the large settlements to which the Bassar, as well as many refugees from other regions, had moved as a defensive measure in the late eighteenth century. Support for this interpretation derives from the fact that the first Bassar chief was selected from a foreign group, presumably to ensure impartiality in dispute resolution. The success of this new institution was reflected in continued intensification of iron production until a decline in the late nineteenth century. This decline stemmed from the more-frequent slave raids and a shifting of trade routes away from the Bassar region that preceded German colonial control by the end of the century. The disruptions caused by intensified slave-raiding in the late eighteenth century also stimulated changes in Bassar ceramics. Imported pottery became rare, so locally made wares returned to prominence, though the changes in settlement locations compelled experimentation with new sources of clay (de Barros 2001).

The Bassar experience was not unique. Just as the Bassar seem to have avoided, at least for several centuries, being the victims of slave raids by more powerful neighbors by supplying them with iron, so did the small-scale societies of the Mandara Mountains in northern Cameroon attempt to cope with the neighboring Wandala state. However, the security provided by this relationship was tenuous; on occasion the iron ore that the montagnards provided to the Wandala was made into shackles to enslave them. Nevertheless, this economic relationship seems to have helped minimize the frequency and scale of such unfortunate occurrences (MacEachern 1993).

The Roles of Slaves in African Society

Those unfortunate individuals who, despite their best efforts, found themselves enslaved in Africa filled a variety of roles and occupations. Some of this variation pertained to gender, with female slaves being far more likely to work in domestic, including sexual, contexts. Indeed, the fact that domestic tasks were overwhelmingly specified as women's work in almost all African societies contributed to the preference for female slaves (Broadhead 1983:179; Meillassoux 1983:55). However, a more important structuring principle was the complexity of the society in which they were enslaved. Decentralized societies provided slaves with little opportunity to engage in specialized occupations; most work was in the agricultural and domestic spheres. In contrast, state-level societies employed slaves in myriad occupations, some of which offered slaves opportunities to accumulate wealth and even own slaves of their own. This was particularly true in the nineteenth century, when the ruling classes put large numbers of slaves to work in their capitals, in large part as a form of personal or state aggrandizement (e.g., Boston 1968:162–175; Reid 2002). However, the nineteenth century also witnessed the zenith of plantation slavery within Africa. Slaves sent to these plantations were faced with arduous labor, miserable living conditions, and few, if any, opportunities for advancement, a situation very similar to that of African slaves in the Americas or in eighth-century southern Iraq.

As noted above, female slaves were preferred over male slaves in African decentralized societies for several reasons. They worked domestically in the home and fields, thereby releasing the free men and women of the household from some of the drudgery of everyday tasks, and they also seem to have frequently given birth to children sired by freemen. This was one route to possible manumission, particularly for the children, who could be rapidly integrated into their fathers' lineages, at least in patrilineal societies. Thus, slavery provided a man with an opportunity to avoid the requirements of bride-wealth or bride-price payments and to ensure that his children were members of his own kin group (Manning 1990: 46–47, 118–120), thus increasing his wealth-in-people, a form of wealth that tended to guarantee a more secure existence in Africa than did material wealth (Guyer 1995).

Since slaves were usually obtained from other ethnic groups, opportunities presumably existed for the transfer of cultural and technological knowledge from the slave's to the owner's society. Slaves were generally required to learn the language of their owners, assuming that they did not know it already, but it seems plausible that they could have introduced their new owners to new ways of making and doing things, even if, as seems almost certain, they brought few or no possessions with them. DeCorse (1989:137) remarks that "oral histories [from northeastern Sierra Leone] indicate that blacksmiths were so highly valued for their skill that they were singled out for capture in raids into neighboring areas. Women, the manufacturers of pottery, were also frequently taken as wives or slaves."

Although we have discovered no archaeological evidence of any specific cultural or technological transfers that occurred within the context of slavery in African decentralized societies, among the Mangbetu of northeastern Democratic Republic of Congo, "Marriage with slaves, however, facilitated culture change and technology transfer because it often transcended linguistic and geographical barriers.... The amudjaandro [female slaves] of lineage society must stand out as one of the most significant means of culture modification, even if there were many others" (Keim 1983:150). Indeed, Keim suggests that cultural exchanges of the sort promoted through slavery eventually resulted in the cultural homogenization of a large region that was thereby rendered susceptible to unification based on Mangbetu cultural principles. In a similar vein, Brain (1972:14) mentions that "Bamileke culture, therefore, was brought to [the] Bangwa [chiefdoms] by women, the wives of the chiefs and the mothers of their children, who were mostly slaves from the grassfields." We also noted earlier in this chapter the likely transfer of ceramic skills by slaves in southern Mali (Frank 1993). While these examples are encouraging, African societies were not closed systems, so transfers of knowledge were common, as is evident from archaeological data pertaining to diffusion and linguistic data pertaining to loanwords. As yet we have no way of ascertaining if some of these transfers were linked to slavery (see also Stahl, this volume).

When we turn our attention to African state-level societies, we encounter slaves in a wide variety of specialized occupations, including artisans who must have been quick to transfer skills from their natal societies to their new surroundings. Indeed, we have documentary evidence of one such transfer. Kagwa (1969:159) recounts how a Nyoro potter, supposedly captured with some three thousand of his compatriots by Ganda soldiers in the late eighteenth or early nineteenth century, so impressed the Ganda king with his ceramic skills that he was appointed the king's potter and given his own village near the royal capital.[4] While this is only one instance of prob-

able technology transfer via slavery (see also Frank 1993), other examples likely exist given the extensive list of specialized occupations of slaves that can be assembled from the literature. Moreover, transfers were not restricted to technology; various deities were introduced to the Dahomey court by a slave who rose to the prestigious position of queen mother (Bay 1983:347). However, the main period in which such transfers occurred is the nineteenth century, the time when numerous slaves were employed as artisans to embellish the royal courts, though many slaves are reported to have been engaged in the specialized production of trade goods in the eleventh century at Tegdaoust in the ancient empire of Ghana (McIntosh 2001:32).

Identifying Slavery in the African Archaeological Record

Much of what we have discussed here is derived from combining documentary, ethnohistorical, and anthropological evidence with archaeological research. It is difficult to imagine how we would have conducted this research if we had to rely solely on archaeological data, since the recognition of slavery from the archaeological record seems to be a very difficult task (for Africa, see Alexander 2001:56; Connah 2001:61; Croucher 2004; Mitchell 2005:142, 162; Welsby 1996:176). The exception that perhaps proves the rule is the discovery of an underground chamber and an iron shackle in a house in the town of Lamu on the East African coast (Donley-Reid 1984:289). Less certain evidence for slavery, but nevertheless suggestive, includes a chain link and a couple of possible irons from Shanga on the Kenya coast; they date to the late first millennium, when numerous Africans were taken to Iraq prior to the Zanj revolt (Horton 1996:367, 416).

Typically, slaves would have had few or no possessions at the time of their enslavement. Assemblages of religious artifacts, including charms and fetishes, as well as beads similar to ones used in shamanic rituals in West Africa connoting signs of anxiety and distress, have been identified in New World plantation sites and ascribed to slaves (Kusimba 2004:62; Singleton 1995: 126, 1996:568; Stine et al. 1995:60 [but see Kelly 2004:229]; Wilkie 1995:146, 1997:89). While it is conceivable that assemblages of this sort might be found in slave communities in nineteenth-century African states (but see Croucher 2004: 68), their presence seems unlikely in the close confines of the domestic slavery that was typical of decentralized societies. Moreover, in contrast to slavery in the Americas, the open system in decentralized African societies would surely have often favored rapid acculturation rather than encouraging slaves to maintain their former ethnic identities and cultural practices in secret.

Other examples of cultural remains that may indicate the presence of slaves are few. A most unusual example from Cape Town, South Africa, is the excavation of a former clothes-washing site used by female slaves; located in a streambed, the site was identified through documents and shovel test pits that yielded buttons and other detritus (Jordan 2005). Slaves and their resistance to the cultural practices of their owners might also be found in faunal remains. Bones with cut marks, indicating that they were cut for stew, as well as a collection of bowls, stood out as indigenous African cultural traits in contrast to European styles of food preparation and the use of plates at European trading sites on the Gold Coast of Africa, as well as on American plantations (though in the Gold Coast case of Elmina, the Africans were probably not enslaved) (DeCorse 1992:188). Dietary distinctions might also be predicted between slaves and their owners, with slaves condemned to eat inferior foods or choosing to consume different foods (DeCorse 1992; Singleton 1995:123). Again, such distinctions seem more likely to have been prevalent in state-level societies where slavery was institutionalized than in decentralized societies.

Another source of potential evidence is burials. Slaves are likely to have been buried in separate cemeteries, as with the Diola in the nineteenth century (Baum 1999:161), or to have received less formal burial or no burial at all in comparison with other members of society. For example, in nineteenth-century Buganda, "as a rule slaves were not honored with funerals but their corpses were thrown into the forest, a procedure consistent with the idea that a dead slave was an expended economic asset" (Reid 2002: 124). However, a graveyard in Zanzibar identified by local people as a nineteenth-century slave cemetery revealed no obvious differences, at least without excavation, from graveyards of free persons (Croucher 2004:68). Skeletons found in a cemetery in colonial South Africa show differentiation in the manner in which they were interred compared to those presumed to have belonged to a higher class; they were buried without caskets or artifacts, unlike the graves of other individuals. Isotopic studies of these presumed slaves were also instructive, revealing an abrupt change in diet during their lives. Relatively high quality tropical foods had been replaced, when the slaves reached Cape Town, by one dominated by seafood, a despised food in colonial South Africa (Cox and Sealy 1997; Cox et al. 2001).

Apart from archaeological evidence of the slaves themselves, we might also seek evidence of the slave raiders. Here again, the archaeological evidence may be elusive, as can be seen from a recent example from Ghana. Kasana is a village identified in traditions and documents as the headquarters of the slave-raiding Zabarima in the 1870s. However, excavations yielded, in the words of the archaeologist who worked there, "no positive and clear-cut evidence of raids, invasions or slavery in the archaeological data" (Boachie-Ansah 2005:50). Moreover, this conclusion contradicted the testimonies of the village's modern inhabitants, who were all too keen to identify the locations of the houses and activities of slave traders, presumably in response to an emerging tourist industry in Ghana that caters to African Americans searching for their roots (ibid.; see also Stahl, this volume).

The best archaeological evidence for behaviors associated with slavery, although not necessarily evidence of the actual presence of slaves, is probably that which we have discussed earlier in this chapter. In other words, the effects of slavery—evident archaeologically from such things as changing settlement patterns, fortifications, and refuge sites, as well as associated transformations in pottery styles—are far easier to identify than are the houses, artifacts, and burials of the slaves themselves. Indeed, just about any evidence of warfare involving societies of different levels of political complexity should alert archaeologists to the probable existence of slavery. It is these kinds of what might be termed "indirect" evidence for slavery that provide our best insights into the history of this practice in African decentralized societies (see Stahl, this volume, for further discussion of a future "archaeology of slavery as practice" that emphasizes "a genealogical approach" and "material practices of inclusion and exclusion").

Conclusions

Several conclusions about slavery in African decentralized societies, and about its archaeological manifestations, can be drawn from this discussion. Assuming that slavery existed anywhere in Africa prior to the development of states, which south of the Sahara can be broadly dated to the first millennium CE in the west and a little later in the east, it probably did not involve many people in total, and the proportion of slaves in any one society was probably small. This generalization seems to be applicable to the decentralized societies of Africa even in more-recent centuries, except for the nineteenth century, when internal slavery became rampant across much of the continent after the abolition of the Atlantic slave trade and the rise of the so-called legitimate, internal trade with slaves employed on agricultural plantations.

Where slavery existed in decentralized societies, women were preferred as slaves. Some slaves were obtained through warfare, raiding, and kidnapping, but others entered a state of servitude voluntarily because of economic hardship. Slaves undertook domestic chores, including subsistence farming, and were concubines or wives. Avenues existed for slaves and/or their children to become full and free members of society, though the stigma of slave origins might still adhere (see Stahl, this volume). Slaves were not simply economic units of labor, but people who by their presence increased the size of a man's household or lineage and thus contributed to his security and wealth. It seems unlikely that cases of this form of slavery will be identified solely on the basis of archaeological evidence, though artifactual, mortuary, and bone isotope data might provide clues.

The importance of slavery for African decentralized societies lay primarily not in their ownership of slaves, but in their role as the targets and victims of slave capture by state-level societies. In order to comprehend the scale and intensity of slavery's effects on African decentralized societies, as well as the trajectories of change—political, social, economic, cultural, and demographic—that ensued, African slavery must be examined, as has been attempted here, within the particular historical and cultural contexts of the Atlantic and Islamic slave trades.

Faced with the threat of being enslaved, African decentralized societies responded in some ways that, with the benefit of hindsight, seem predictable: they moved themselves out of harm's way; they hid; they used the terrain to their advantage, particularly by occupying steep, broken terrain when facing cavalry; they fortified their settlements. Other, perhaps less predictable, responses included increased political centralization and coordination of manpower, as well as occasional attempts at rapprochement with their attackers, such as through the provision of desirable goods, notably iron, or conversion to Islam. Indeed, in a few instances, as a consequence of their responses to the slave trade, decentralized societies became state-level societies and shifted from being victims of the slave trade to being its perpetrators.

Almost irrespective of whether the tactics employed by decentralized societies to avoid enslavement were successful or not, the effects of the tactics reverberated through all aspects of society—and hence all aspects of the archaeological record. Populations either aggregated in defended settlements or dispersed, sometimes for only very short periods, into remote, inaccessible, or hidden locations. Some regions were abandoned, and others newly settled. Societies became more politically centralized and sometimes more hierarchical, or they were scattered. As a result, ethnic identities were lost, merged, or created. Ceramic assemblages changed too, though by no means in simple lockstep with the identities with which archaeologists have often erroneously attempted to associate them. Ceramics could be used to help foster new identities, but they could also serve as repositories of information about old identities, if not vessels of resistance to the forces of change. Methods of pottery production, as well as the availability of raw materials, were also sometimes negatively impacted by the disruptions of the slave trade. Economic changes also ensued: people adjusted their subsistence to novel or changed surroundings by growing new, often American, crops and by using various forms of technological innovation and intensification, such as the terracing of hill slopes and the use of irrigation systems. In some cases, increased demand for trade goods led to increasing specialization in the extraction of raw materials and the manufacture of items for export, with the repercussions of these changes reverberating through all facets of society, as illustrated with the example of the Bassar.

Slavery and the slave trade were not the only forces of change at work in Africa over the last thousand or more years. Short-term and long-term fluctuations in climate also stimulated and demanded changes in human affairs, and there are other economic, technological, political, and cultural changes in parts of Africa that cannot be simply explained by laying them at slavery's door. While slavery has been rather neglected by African archaeologists in the past, we must be cautious now not to embrace slavery as an explanatory panacea.

From the mid first millennium CE, many decentralized societies in Africa were caught up in the whirlwinds of the world's great slave trade. They coped as best they could, sometimes becoming enslaved and scattered to the corners of the globe, but at other times adjusting, innovating, and surviving. Some even benefited during these troubled times, though always at somebody else's expense.

Acknowledgments

Many thanks to Cathy Cameron for inviting one of us (Peter Robertshaw) to participate in the Snowbird conference that was the catalyst for this volume. We also thank Ann Stahl for her generosity in sharing ideas, references, and comments on earlier drafts. The preparation and writing of this chapter challenged both of us to greatly expand our knowledge of a topic that we should have known more about at the outset. We also could, and probably should, have learned much more than we have; therefore, we humbly ask readers to forgive our sins of omission.

Notes

1. When the conference on which this volume is based was convened, its theme was the archaeology of slavery in so-called middle-range societies. This focus is reflected in the contents of this volume, which lacks any chapters that specifically address case studies of slavery in state-level societies. However, it became clear both from the precirculated papers and from conference discussions that understanding of captive-taking and slavery in middle-range societies could not be divorced from consideration of the articulation between these societies and states, at least in regions where states existed. Thus, in this chapter we have retained the focus on middle-range societies that motivated the conference, but we have ignored the already slippery state/non-state boundary in pursuing our investigations.

   We have also chosen here to refer to those societies at a level of political complexity that would not usually be called "states" as "decentralized." No term is particularly well suited to the job here, but at least we avoid the evolutionism implicit in the term "middle-range" and perhaps some of the more negative connotations of "non-state" or "stateless." In choosing the term "decentralized societies," we have been influenced by Martin Klein (2001:52), who emphasizes the general lack of coercive authority in these societies, though even this becomes moot when we consider some polities commonly labeled "chiefdoms."

2. Cairo and Egypt are, of course, situated on the African continent; therefore, on a strictly geographic basis, one should refer to this as internal African slavery. However, historically Egypt was clearly part of the Islamic world at this time, so we feel justified in considering Egypt as extra-African for the purposes of our present discussion.

3. Neither we nor MacEachern is implying here that pots and people are isomorphic. Ethnicity is merely one variable among many that are relevant to the understanding and interpretation of ceramic change.

4. Pottery manufacture is a male occupation among the Banyoro of Uganda.

References Cited

Alexander, J.
2001   Islam, Archaeology and Slavery in Africa. *World Archaeology* 33(1):44–60.
Alpers, E. A.
1969   Trade, State and Society among Yao in the Nineteenth Century. *Journal of African History* 10(3):405–420.
Austen, Ralph
1992   Egypt-Sudan Slavery Lists. In *The Human*

Commodity: Perspectives of the Trans-Saharan Slave Trade. Elizabeth Savage, ed. Pp. 232–234. London: Frank Cass.

1977 Slavery among Coastal Middlemen: The Duala of Cameroon. In *Slavery in Africa.* Suzanne Miers and Igor Kopytoff, eds. Pp. 305–333. Madison: University of Wisconsin Press.

Bah, Thierno Mouctar

1985 *Architecture militaire traditionnelle et poliorcétique dans le Soudan occidental (du septième à la fin du dix-neuvième siècle).* Yaoundé: Editions CLE.

2003 Slave-raiding and Defensive Systems South of Lake Chad from the Sixteenth to the Nineteenth Century. In *Fighting the Slave Trade: West African Strategies.* Sylviane A. Diouf, ed. Pp. 15–30. Athens: Ohio University Press.

Baum, Robert M.

1999 *Shrines of the Slave Trade: Diola Religion and Society in Precolonial Senegambia.* New York: Oxford University Press.

Bay, Edna G.

1983 Servitude and Worldly Success in the Palace of Dahomey. In *Women and Slavery in Africa.* Claire C. Robertson and Martin A. Klein, eds. Pp. 340–367. Madison: University of Wisconsin Press.

Boachie-Ansah, J.

2005 Archaeological Research at Kasana: A Search for Evidence on the Historic Slave Traffic in the Upper West Region of Ghana. *Journal of Environment and Culture* 2(1):35–57.

Boston, J. S.

1968 *The Igala Kingdom.* Ibadan: Oxford University Press.

Brain, Robert

1972 *Bangwa Kinship and Marriage.* Cambridge: Cambridge University Press.

Broadhead, Susan Herlin

1983 Slave Wives, Free Sisters: Bakongo Women and Slavery. In *Women and Slavery in Africa.* Claire C. Robertson and Martin A. Klein, eds. Pp. 160–181. Madison: University of Wisconsin Press.

Brown, Carolyn A.

2003 Memory as Resistance: Identity and Contested History of Slavery in Southeastern Nigeria, an Oral History Project. In *Fighting the Slave Trade: West African Strategies.* Sylviane A. Diouf, ed. Pp. 219–225. Athens: Ohio University Press.

Burnham, Philip

1980 Raiders and Traders in Adamawa: Slavery as a Regional System. In *Asian and African Systems and Slavery.* James L. Watson, ed. Pp. 43–72. Berkeley: University of California Press.

Casati, G.

1891 *Ten Years in Equatoria.* 2 vols. London/New York: F. Warne and Co.

Connah, Graham

2001 *African Civilizations: An Archaeological Perspective.* 2nd ed. Cambridge: Cambridge University Press.

Cordell, Dennis D.

2003 The Myth of Inevitability and Invincibility: Resistance to Slavers and the Slave Trade in Central Africa, 1850–1910. In *Fighting the Slave Trade: West African Strategies.* Sylviane A. Diouf, ed. Pp. 31–49. Athens: Ohio University Press.

Cox, Glenda, and Judith Sealy

1997 Investigating Identity and Life Histories: Isotopic Analysis and Historical Documentation of Slave Skeletons Found on the Cape Town Foreshore, South Africa. *International Journal of Historical Archaeology* 1(3):207–224.

Cox, Glenda, Judith Sealy, Carmel Schrire, and Alan Morris

2001 Stable Carbon and Nitrogen Isotopic Analyses of the Underclass at the Colonial Cape of Good Hope in the Eighteenth and Nineteenth Centuries. *World Archaeology* 33(1):73–97.

Croucher, Sarah

2004 Zanzibar Clove Plantation Survey 2003: Some Preliminary Findings. *Nyame Akuma* 62:65–69.

Daaku, Kwame Yeboa

1970 *Trade and Politics on the Gold Coast, 1600–1720: A Study of the African Reaction to European Trade.* Oxford: Clarendon Press.

de Barros, P.

1986 Bassar: A Quantified, Chronologically Controlled, Regional Approach to a Traditional Iron Production Centre in West Africa. *Africa* 56:148–174.

2001 The Effect of the Slave Trade on the Bassar Ironworking Society, Togo. In *West Africa During the Atlantic Slave Trade: Archaeological Perspectives (New Approaches to Anthropological Archaeology).* Christopher R. DeCorse, ed. Pp. 59–80. Leicester: Leicester University Press.

DeCorse, Christopher R.

1989 Material Aspects of Limba, Yalunka and Kuranko Ethnicity: Archaeological Research in Northeastern Sierra Leone. In *Archaeological Approaches to Cultural Identity.* S. Shennan, ed. Pp. 125–140. London: Unwin Hyman.

1992 Culture Contact, Continuity, and Change on

the Gold Coast, AD 1400–1900. *The African Archaeological Review* 10:163–196.

2001a *An Archaeology of Elmina: Africans and Europeans on the Gold Coast, 1400–1900*. Washington, D.C., and London: Smithsonian Institution Press.

DeCorse, Christopher R. (editor)

2001b *West Africa During the Atlantic Slave Trade: Archaeological Perspectives*. Leicester: Leicester University Press.

Diouf, Sylviane A. (editor)

2003 *Fighting the Slave Trade: West African Strategies*. Athens: Ohio University Press.

Donley-Reid, L.

1983 The Social Uses of Swahili Spaces and Objects. Ph.D. thesis, University of Cambridge, Cambridge, UK.

Echenberg, Myron J.

1971 Late Nineteenth-century Military Technology in Upper Volta. *Journal of African History* 12:241–254.

Edwards, Paul (editor)

1969 *Equiano's Travels: The Interesting Narrative of the Life of Olaudah Equiano or Gustavus Vassa the African*. London: Heinemann.

Evans-Pritchard, E. E.

1940 *The Nuer*. Oxford: Clarendon Press.

Feierman, Steven

1974 *The Shambaa Kingdom: A History*. Madison: University of Wisconsin Press.

Finley, M. I.

1968 Slavery. *International Encyclopedia of the Social Sciences* 14:307–313.

Frank, Barbara E.

1993 Reconstructing the History of an African Ceramic Tradition: Technology, Slavery and Agency in the Region of Kadiolo (Mali). *Cahiers d'Études Africaines* 131:381–401.

Goody, Jack

1980 Slavery in Time and Space. In *Asian and African Systems and Slavery*. James L. Watson, ed. Pp. 16–42. Berkeley: University of California Press.

Gronenborn, D.

2001 Kanem-Borno: A Brief Summary of the History and Archaeology of an Empire of the Central *bi'ad al-sudan*. In *West Africa During the Atlantic Slave Trade: Archaeological Perspectives (New Approaches to Anthropological Archaeology)*. Christopher R. DeCorse, ed. Pp. 101–130. Leicester: Leicester University Press.

Guèye, Adama

2003 The Impact of the Slave Trade on Cayor and Baol: Mutations in Habitat and Land Occupancy. In *Fighting the Slave Trade: West African Strategies*. Sylviane A. Diouf, ed. Pp. 50–61. Athens: Ohio University Press.

Guyer, Jane I.

1995 Wealth in People, Wealth in Things—Introduction. *Journal of African History* 36:83–90.

Harms, Robert W.

1981 *River of Wealth, River of Sorrow: The Central Zaire Basin in the Era of the Slave and Ivory Trade, 1500–1891*. New Haven and London: Yale University Press.

Hartwig, Gerald W.

1977 Changing Forms of Servitude among the Krebe of Tanzania. In *Slavery in Africa*. Suzanne Miers and Igor Kopytoff, eds. Pp. 261–285. Madison: University of Wisconsin Press.

Hawthorne, Walter

2001 Nourishing a Stateless Society During the Slave Trade: The Rise of Balanta Paddy-rice Production in Guinea-Bissau. *Journal of African History* 42:1–24.

2003 Strategies of the Decentralized: Defending Communities from Slave Raiders in Coastal Guinea-Bissau, 1450–1815. In *Fighting the Slave Trade: West African Strategies*. Sylviane A. Diouf, ed. Pp. 152–169. Athens: Ohio University Press.

Horton, Mark

1996 *Shanga: The Archaeology of a Muslim Trading Community on the Coast of East Africa*. London: British Institute in Eastern Africa.

Hubbell, Andrew

2001 A View of the Slave Trade from the Margin: Souroudougou in the Late Nineteenth-century Slave Trade of the Niger Bend. *Journal of African History* 42:25–47.

Isaacman, Barbara, and Allen Isaacman

1977 Slavery and Social Stratification among the Sena of Mozambique: A Study of the Kaporo System. In *Slavery in Africa*. Suzanne Miers and Igor Kopytoff, eds. Pp. 105–120. Madison: University of Wisconsin Press.

Jordan, Elizabeth Grzymala

2005 "Unrelenting Toil": Expanding Archaeological Interpretations of the Female Slave Experience. *Slavery and Abolition* 26(2):217–232.

Kagwa, Apolo

1969 *The Customs of the Baganda*. New York: AMS Press.

Keeley, Lawrence H.

1996 *War Before Civilization*. New York: Oxford University Press.

Keim, Curtis A.

1983 Women in Slavery among the Mangbetu c. 1800–1910. In *Women and Slavery in Africa*.

Claire C. Robertson and Martin A. Klein, eds. Pp. 144–159. Madison: University of Wisconsin Press.

Kelly, Kenneth G.
2004 The African Diaspora Starts Here: Historical Archaeology of Coastal West Africa. In *African Historical Archaeologies*. Andrew M. Reid and Paul J. Lane, eds. Pp. 219–241. New York: Kluwer Academic/Plenum Publishers.

Klein, Martin A.
2001 The Slave Trade and Decentralized Societies. *Journal of African History* 42:49–65.
2003 Defensive Strategies: Wasulu, Masina, and the Slave Trade. In *Fighting the Slave Trade: West African Strategies*. Sylviane A. Diouf, ed. Pp. 62–78. Athens: Ohio University Press.

Kopytoff, Igor, and Suzanne Miers
1977 African "Slavery" as an Institution of Marginality. In *Slavery in Africa*. Suzanne Miers and Igor Kopytoff, eds. Pp. 3–81. Madison: University of Wisconsin Press.

Kusimba, Chapurukha M.
2004 Archaeology of Slavery in East Africa. *African Archaeological Review* 21(2):59–88.
2006 Slavery and Warfare in African Chiefdoms. In *The Archaeology of Warfare: Prehistories of Raiding and Conquest*. Elizabeth N. Arkush and Mark W. Allen, eds. Pp. 214–249. Gainesville: University Press of Florida.

Lovejoy, Paul E.
1983 *Transformations in Slavery: A History of Slavery in Africa*. Cambridge: Cambridge University Press.

MacEachern, Scott
1993 Selling the Iron for Their Shackles: Wandala-montagnard Interactions in Northern Cameroon. *Journal of African History* 34:247–270.
2001 State Formation and Enslavement in the Southern Lake Chad Basin. In *West Africa During the Atlantic Slave Trade: Archaeological Perspectives (New Approaches to Anthropological Archaeology)*. Christopher R. DeCorse, ed. Pp. 131–151. Leicester: Leicester University Press.

Manning, Patrick
1990 *Slavery and African Life: Occidental, Oriental, and African Slave Trades*. Cambridge: Cambridge University Press.

McIntosh, Susan Keech, with a contribution by I. Thiaw
2001 Tools for Understanding Transformation and Continuity in Senegambian Society, 1500–1900. In *West Africa During the Atlantic Slave Trade: Archaeological Perspectives (New Approaches to Anthropological Archaeology)*.

Christopher R. DeCorse, ed. Pp. 14–37. Leicester: Leicester University Press.

Meillassoux, Claude
1991 *The Anthropology of Slavery: The Womb of Iron and Gold*. Alide Dasnois, trans. Chicago: University of Chicago Press.
1983 Female Slavery. In *Women and Slavery in Africa*. Claire C. Robertson and Martin A. Klein, eds. Pp. 49–66. Madison: University of Wisconsin Press.

Mendonsa, Eugene L.
2001 *Continuity and Change in a West African Society: Globalization's Impact on the Sisala of Ghana*. Durham, NC: Carolina Academic Press.

Miers, Suzanne, and Igor Kopytoff (editors)
1977 *Slavery in Africa*. Madison: University of Wisconsin Press.

Mitchell, Peter
2005 *African Connections*. Walnut Creek, CA: AltaMira Press.

Nieboer, H. J.
1900 *Slavery as an Industrial System*. The Hague: M. Nijhoff.

Ogundiran, Akinwumi
2002 Of Small Things Remembered: Beads, Cowries, and Cultural Translations of the Atlantic Experience in Yorubaland. *International Journal of African Historical Studies* 35:427–457.

Pikirayi, I., and G. Pwiti
1999 States, Traders and Colonists: Historical Archaeology in Zimbabwe. *Historical Archaeology* 33(2):73–89.

Posnansky, M., and C. R. DeCorse
1986 Historical Archaeology in Sub-Saharan Africa: A review. *Historical Archaeology* 20:1–14.

Rashid, Ismail
2003 "A devotion to the idea of liberty at any price": Rebellion and Antislavery in the Upper Guinea Coast in the Eighteenth and Nineteenth centuries. In *Fighting the Slave Trade: West African Strategies*. Sylviane A. Diouf, ed. Pp. 132–151. Athens: Ohio University Press.

Reid, Richard J.
2002 *Political Power in Pre-Colonial Buganda: Economy, Society and Warfare in the Nineteenth Century*. Athens: Ohio University Press.

Reyna, Stephan P.
1990 *Wars Without End: The Political Economy of a Precolonial African State*. Hanover, NH: University Press of New England.

Robertson, Claire C., and Martin A. Klein
1983 Women's Importance in African Slave Systems. In *Women and Slavery in Africa*. Claire

C. Robertson and Martin A. Klein, eds. Pp. 3–25. Madison: University of Wisconsin Press.

Segal, Ronald
2001   *Islam's Black Slaves: The Other Black Diaspora.* New York: Farrar, Straus and Giroux.

Singleton, Theresa A.
1995   The Archaeology of Slavery in North America (FN1). *Annual Review of Anthropology* 24:119–140.
1996   Plantation Life in the Southern United States. In *The Oxford Companion to Archaeology*, edited by Brian Fagan, pp. 567–569.

Soumonni, Elisée
2003   Lacustrine Villages in South Benin as Refuges from the Slave Trade. In *Fighting the Slave Trade: West African Strategies.* Sylviane A. Diouf, ed. Pp. 3–14. Athens: Ohio University Press.

Stahl, Ann Brower
2001   *Making History in Banda: Anthropological Visions of Africa's Past.* Cambridge: Cambridge University Press.

Stine, Linda F., Melanie A. Cabak, and Mark D. Groover
1995   Blue Beads as African-American Cultural Symbols. *Historical Archaeology* 30(3):49–75.

Swanepoel, Natalie
2006   Socio-political Change on a Slave-raiding Frontier: War, Trade and "Big Men" in Nineteenth Century Sisalaland, Northern Ghana. In *Past Tense: Studies in the Archaeology of Conflict.* Tony Pollard and Iain Banks, eds. Pp. 265–293. Boston: Brill.

Thilmans, G., C. Descamps, and B. Khayat
1980   *Protohistoire du Sénégal,* I: *Les sites mégalith-iques.* Dakar: L'Institut Fondamental d'Afrique Noire.

Uchendu, Victor C.
1977   Slaves and Slavery in Igboland, Nigeria. In *Slavery in Africa.* Suzanne Miers and Igor Kopytoff, eds. Pp. 121–132. Madison: University of Wisconsin Press.

Usman, Aribedesi
2003   The Ethnohistory and Archaeology of Warfare in Northern Yoruba. *Journal of African Archaeology* 1(2):201–214.

Vansina, Jan
2004   *Antecendents to Modern Rwanda: The Nyiginya Kingdom.* Madison: University of Wisconsin Press.

Watson, James L.
1980a   *Asian and African Systems of Slavery.* James L. Watson, ed. Berkeley: University of California Press.
1980b   Slavery as an Institution: Open and Closed Systems. In *Asian and African Systems of Slavery.* James L. Watson, ed. Pp. 1–15. Berkeley: University of California Press.

Welsby, Derek A.
1996   *The Kingdom of Kush: The Napatan and Meroitic Empires.* London: British Museum Press.

Wilkie, Laurie
1995   Magic and Empowerment on the Plantation: An Archaeological Consideration of African-American World View. *Southeastern Archaeology* 14(2):136–148.
1997   Secret and Sacred: Contextualizing the Artifacts of African-American Magic and Religion. *Historical Archaeology* 31(4):81–106.

4

Captivity, Slavery, and Cultural Exchange between Rome and the Germans from the First to the Seventh Century CE

Noel Lenski

The study of ancient European cultures, as with all premodern cultures, is hampered by the lack of source material. This is doubly true of the study of captivity and slavery, for captives and slaves leave very few distinctive markers of their status and even fewer of their activities in the archaeological record. In ancient Europe, for example, Roman slaves were often branded or tattooed (Jones 1987) and German slaves had their hair cropped short as a marker of status (see below), yet these physical markers leave practically no traces in the paleobiology. Osteology can demonstrate that the bodies of certain individuals were worked to extremes, but there is no proving that these were necessarily captives or slaves (Capasso 2001). Similarly, ancient built structures can usually only hint at the activities of slaves. Certain work environments in the sophisticated economy of the ancient Mediterranean are sure to have employed slaves—fullers shops, tanneries, bakeries, ceramic factories, construction sites, agricultural villas (Carandini and Filippi 1985; Schumacher 2001:116–161; Thompson 2003: 187–215)—and in certain instances slaves are positively attested in these contexts through inscriptions. But in most cases their ghosts can only be discerned lurking in the shadows: we know they were present but cannot prove it. Most revealing are the many figural representations of slaves which survive, yet here too problems of identifi-

cation inhibit strong argumentation. While those depicted in statuary as bound in fetters or in wall paintings as servants at banquets are sure to have been slaves (Dunbabin 2003; George 2000; Lenski, Working Models, in prep.), many other figures bear elements of attire or physical attributes that point toward slavery but cannot confirm it. In the ancient Mediterranean context, we do have the advantage of written material, most of it in Latin and Greek, that survives in abundance from the sixth century BCE onward and reveals the presence of slaves from the earliest records (Wiedemann 1981). This material is not only literary but also documentary, for hundreds of thousands of inscriptions and papyri (ancient paper documents) have now been recorded, and many of these pertain to captives, slaves, and freedmen (Bieżuńska Małowist 1984; Eck and Heinrichs 1993). Here too, however, problems abound: the literary sources are only as trustworthy as their authors and are bound by generic conventions that generally, though not always, wrote slaves out of the picture; the inscriptions are highly formulaic, restricted in their context, and tend to tell us very little about slaves (though very much about freedmen), and the papyri derive almost entirely from Egypt, where the climatic conditions were ideal to ensure their preservation, but where slavery also played a smaller role than in many parts of Rome's empire.

These problems are even more acute when one attempts to speak of captivity and slavery among the Romans and their Germanic neighbors. The Romans had encountered Germanic peoples by the second century BCE, engaging them in combat on a regular basis beginning with Caesar's conquest of Gaul in the 50s BCE. This means that Roman writers regularly discuss Germanic cultures, but always from their own—biased, even distorted—perspective. Only beginning in the fourth century CE do we encounter texts written by those from inside Germanic territory (see Heather and Matthews 1991:103–131 for translations). By the late fourth century, Germanic and other peoples had begun to take control of former Roman territory, and beginning in the fifth century we get a flood of texts written about Germanic culture from an insider perspective, or at least from the perspective of those who had daily contact with Germans. Even the authors of these texts, however, generally wrote in Latin and generally considered themselves ethnically and culturally Roman, albeit subject to Germanic rulers. Such texts thus reveal a society in transition—one that continued to manifest distinctively Germanic traits but that had also absorbed much that was Roman, especially Christianity. This chapter attempts to reconstruct an anthropology of captivity and slavery among the Romans and Germans using this material. It builds a picture of Rome as a state society, then turns to Roman slaveholding culture in order to set the background for the argument that follows. Next it undertakes an overview of Germanic culture and then investigates slavery among the Germans down through the fourth century CE. This forms the basis for a more detailed investigation of slavery as revealed in five Germanic law codes of the sixth through eighth centuries CE. Finally, the chapter concludes with examples of how captivity and slavery led to cultural interchange.

Rome as a State Society

Already at its first encounter with the Germans, Rome was a state society, and with the rise of autocracy under the Roman emperors—the first being Augustus, who ruled from 31 BCE to 14 CE—the power of the state only grew. Naturally the existence of a strong central state affected all levels of social praxis, including slaveholding.

The Romans had, for example, a complex and differentiated economy that was based in a sophisticated and ubiquitous monetary system. There were, thus, professional slave dealers (*mangones*) whose entire economic function was the trade in slaves (see Harris 1980; cf. Kleberg 1945), and there were spaces designated specifically as slave markets, the most famous of these in the archaeological record being that on the island of Delos. Slaves were generally sold for coined money, as attested above all in the hundreds of slave sale contracts that survive on papyri (Straus 2004). The Roman state apparatus also governed social interactions through a sophisticated and codified legal system, and this too influenced slaveholding. Roman contract law, for example, governed all aspects of slave sales, including a law of warranty that is attested both in extant jurisprudence and in slave sale contracts. And Roman law reached much deeper into master-slave-freedman relations, affecting the birth, care, feeding, punishment, acquisition, transferal, employment, inheritance, manumission, and death of slaves (Buckland 1908; Melluso 2000; Watson 1987).

The existence of a strong Roman state also spawned a powerful military machine that was able to deploy formidable force against its opponents in the form of an army of 200,000 to 400,000 soldiers (in an empire of ca. fifty million inhabitants) who were fed and paid by the central state and garrisoned in a carefully arranged fortification system. These soldiers played a crucial role both in suppressing attempts by the Germans, and other peoples, to attack and enslave Roman citizens, and also in allowing the Romans to conquer Germanic peoples and their territories, and absorb them into the Roman state, whether as captives or as resident aliens, many of whom later became citizens (Elton 1996; Goldsworthy 2003; Le Bohec 1994). The Roman state supported itself on a systematically implemented system of taxation both in coin and in kind, the records of which have survived in dizzying abundance. Among items taxed were the sales and manumissions of slaves. The state itself thus profited directly from the traffic in human capital. Finally, the Romans generated a tremendous amount of literature that offers abundant testimony to slaveholding practices. The ancient literary environment not only reflected those practices, but also critiqued them, for Greek and Latin literature offered ample space for slave characters—particularly in comedies and novels (Fitzgerald 2000; McCarthy 2000)—and included both spirited defenses of slaveholding as an ethical practice and self-reflexive, at times even vitriolic attacks on the excesses of slaveholders and even the institution of slavery (Garnsey 1996).

For purposes of this chapter, then, Rome was neither a prehistoric nor a pre-state society. It is, in this sense, a foil to most of the cultures studied in this volume. Importantly, it is also a foil to Germanic culture for much of the period treated here given that, down to the fifth century, Germanic societies were fundamentally prehistoric—in that they left almost no historical record of their own—and, before the fifth century, pre-state. The use of Roman material in a study of Germanic captivity and slavery is thus not simply a matter of necessity, it is also a source of tremendous interest. The study of slavery and captivity in these two neighboring cultures allows us to map, in ancient times, the degree to which the acquisition and retention of captives and slaves facilitated cultural interchange between a pre-state and a state society.

Rome as a Slave Society

Slavery was intimately intertwined with the Roman state apparatus precisely because it was intertwined with all aspects of Roman culture. Rome, or at least Roman Italy, was what some historians have characterized as a "slave society"—that is, a society in which at least 20 percent of the total population was enslaved and in which slaves constituted a major force of production (Hopkins 1978:99–132). Estimates of the enslaved population of Roman Italy in the first century BCE have ranged as high as 35 percent, though the current hypothesis places the figure much lower, at ca. 20 percent, or ca. 1.2 million out of a total population of ca. 5 to 7 million on the Italian peninsula (Scheidel 2005). In Rome's provinces, these numbers and percentages would have been lower. Unfortunately, any statistical hypothesis must be formulated on the basis of exiguous demographic data and must thus be viewed with caution. Even so, what data exist

point in the direction of a significant percentage of slaves. That these constituted a major force of production can be learned from the variety of trades in which slaves were engaged. Most were agricultural laborers, a fact that is abundantly attested in the writings of ancient agronomists such as Cato, Varro, and Columella (Wiedemann 1981:138–149; Schumacher 2001:91–115). We also learn of slaves in the building trades, ceramic manufacture, tanning, fulling, art production, metalwork, and other occupations (Schumacher 2001:116–161). They were also crucial to service and mercantile industries, working as household attendants, teachers, secretaries, merchants, ship captains, and even as such high-status professionals as doctors and, in limited instances, priests (see, for example, Christes 1979; Green 2007:185–205; Kudlien 1986). Slave laborers regularly worked alongside free laborers, often under the supervision of other slave overseers (*vilici*), sometimes in conjunction with slaves owned by slaves themselves in a form of quasi ownership (*peculium*). Slavery was thus a central element in the Roman world: slaves were commonplace, and they were integral to production, trade, and service economies.

More interesting for the purposes of this chapter is the question of the sources of Roman slaves. Most obvious among these was birth into slavery. According to Roman law, children followed the status of their mothers; thus children born to a slave woman were themselves slaves of the slave woman's owner. The Romans prized these "homebred slaves" (*vernae*) highly because they were the most likely to be loyal and subservient (Hermann-Otto 1994). Many abandoned children were also taken up as foundlings and enslaved. In the absence of effective birth control, unwanted children were usually exposed, especially on garbage heaps, and some of these were recovered by speculators to be raised as slaves. This we know above all from the many preserved wet-nurse contracts that were made by slave owners with lactating women in order to feed these infants up to an age at which they could survive without mother's milk (Harris 1994; Manca Masciadri and Montevecchi 1984). People could also be enslaved as punishment for a crime. Interestingly, however, the existence of a Roman state dictated that such slaves were not available for exchange in the open market. They remained, rather, "slaves of their crime" (*servi poenae*), which was considered a crime against the state and its representative, the emperor. As such, they were ultimately the emperor's property and were generally employed in imperial mines or quarries or in the imperial games—in all of which they could be exterminated in the interests of the state (Millar 1984). We will see that this constitutes a major difference with Germanic societies, in which the commission of crimes and delicts often led to enslavement, but to the individual against whom the offense was committed rather than to the state. Two further avenues to bondage commonly attested for other cultures were also closed to the Romans. At least down to 329 CE (*Theodosian Code* 5.10.1 + 11.27.1) the sale of one's own children into slavery was strictly forbidden to Roman citizens, and even beyond this date the scope of child-sale was hemmed in by legal restrictions (see Lenski, *Constantine and Slavery*, in press). Furthermore, from the third century BCE onward the Romans did not permit the enslavement of Roman citizens for debts (see Jolowicz 1961:166–170). Both customs, the prohibition on child sale and the absence of debt bondage, stood in contrast to Germanic practice.

None of the modes of acquisition discussed thus far would have impinged on the capture or sale of Germanic peoples. As what the Romans called barbarians (*barbari*) (roughly equivalent to our generic word "aliens," including the negative connotations) Germans were only likely to become slaves of the Romans through sale or capture. These last two modes of acquisition are, however, amply attested in the sources, both generally and with specific reference to Germans. That commercial traders were actively engaged in selling Germanic slaves into the empire is particularly well attested in sources for the fourth century CE. In the winter of 393–394, for example, the statesman Symmachus sent a letter from Rome to a friend then resident on the Rhine asking him to acquire twenty young male slaves, "to be selected not for their beauty but their age and health." Symmachus elected to purchase bondsmen from the German frontier because "finding slaves is easy along the border and

the price is usually tolerable" (Symmachus, *Letter* 2.78; cf. Cecconi 2002:393–400). These slaves were traded by merchants, some of them Romans and others Germans, who colluded in an interethnic traffic in human misery. A crack force of Roman mercenaries sent into German territory in 372 to capture the Alammanic king Macrianus encountered a band of such slave dealers (*scurrae*) and their "wares" and had to exterminate them lest the traders reveal the covert activities of the Roman commandos to the neighboring peoples (Ammianus 29.4.3–4). Ammianus implies that these traders were German, but the question of their ethnicity is in many ways moot, for they must actually have been bicultural, at least to the extent of being able to communicate and conduct business on both sides of the Rhine. We know fourth-century Romans also did a bustling trade in slaves with the Goths, who lived at this time north of the Danube in what is today Romania. When Emperor Julian was advised to attack the Goths as a threat to the empire in 362, he declined, saying, "[T]he Galatian merchants who sell them everywhere without regard to conditions were sufficient to deal with them" (Ammianus 22.7.8; on Galatians—i.e., residents of central Anatolia—as notorious slave merchants, see Claudian, *In Eutropium*, 1.59).

Little wonder then that, writing around 400 CE, Synesius, bishop of the North African city of Cyrene, could remark that every household with even moderate wealth possessed Gothic servants, "for this race is entirely appropriate for and most worthy of serving as slaves of the Romans" (Synesius, *De Regno*, 20). Synesius's disdainful attitude provides an excellent backdrop for an event in Gotho-Roman relations that forever changed the course of European history. In the mid 370s the Huns descended on Gothic territory from central Asia and began attacks that drove Gothic society to the brink of military and economic collapse. Several Gothic tribes asked the Romans for permission to relocate south of the Danube into Thrace (modern Bulgaria). The emperor Valens granted this request but did not provide adequate military supervision or supplies to accommodate the flood of refugees. When the Gothic fugitives became desperate for food, the Roman soldiers charged with their resettlement began exchanging food for slaves. The historian Ammianus tells us the Romans offered one dog per person, which, even if it is exaggerated, indicates the level of desperation to which the Goths were reduced and the level of disdain in which the Romans held the Goths (Ammianus 31.4.10–11, 5.1; cf. Eunapius, *Histories,* fr. 42; Jordanes, *Getica,* 26[134]). In the wake of this mistreatment, the Goths rose up in revolt in 377 and eventually defeated the Romans in a series of battles that wiped out two-thirds of the eastern army and left the emperor Valens dead. Even though they were temporarily pacified through a treaty arranged in 382 with Valens's successor, Theodosius I, this group of Goths was never fully subdued. They eventually became restive in the 390s and went on to sack the city of Rome in 410. Throughout this period of unrest, a major source of manpower for this mobile group of rebellious Goths was the fund of barbarian, and particularly Gothic, captives who fled their Roman masters to join the rag-tag army assembled from their ethnic kin (Ammianus 31.6.5–6; Zosimus 5.42.2–3). The incident illustrates well the impact of slave trading on Romano-German relations, for it was the Roman soldiers' assumption that the Goths were by their very nature enslaveable that set the match to the powder keg of the Gothic revolt.

This last point is corroborated by a fourth-century hanging lamp excavated at Panayia, in northern Greece, ca. 300 km from Gothic territory, that depicts a barbarian captive, bound and genuflecting, designed to "serve" its owner as a source of light but also as a reminder of the inherently servile nature attributed to people like the Goths by late Romans (Rhomiopoulou 2002). The readiness of Romans to objectify the barbarian as archetypal captive and even as objet d'art impinges on the final mode in which Romans acquired slaves, the mode that most profoundly affected relations between Romans and Germans: captivity. The Roman soldiers who traded dogs for Gothic slaves had not only been habituated to a culture that accepted the equation of Goths with slaves, they had been conditioned to regard the barbarians they captured as a potential source of wealth (Themistius, *Oration,* 8.114c–d, in Heather and Matthews 1991:29). Soldiers regularly took captives in the course of battle, and these could be disposed of in a variety of ways,

including enslavement. The variety of outcomes a captive might expect is well illustrated by another event from the fourth century CE. In 358 the emperor Julian attacked the Germanic Chamavi, who inhabited what is today Holland, just north of the Rhine delta. Upon subduing them, he executed some of his captives, bound others in chains to serve as slaves, and allowed yet others who had fled his initial assault to return to their lands and be resettled on terms dictated by the Romans (Ammianus 17.8.5; cf. 20.10.2). Romans thus disposed of those they subdued using a continuum of arrangements: execution, slavery, redeployment as settlers or soldiers, and even release (see the parallel situation from 409 described at Sozomen 9.5.1–7; Theodosian Code 5.6.3; Zosimus 5.22).

Taking each of these arrangements in order, some executions took place immediately, as with the Chamavi in 358, while others were postponed for public spectacles so as to make a greater impact. Captives chosen for death in the arena were often of high status or in leadership roles. Their deaths could serve as a graphic illustration of the power of the Romans over the barbarian enemy and were thus preceded by the elaborate ceremonial procession known as the triumph (Beard 2007:107–142, which includes ancient images of captives on parade). The emperor Constantine, for example, captured the Frankish kings Ascarius and Merogaisus in battle in 307 and then held them just long enough to transport them to his capital in Trier, where he had them fed to the beasts before cheering crowds (*Panegyrici Latini* 7[6].4.1–4, 6[10].2, 4[10].16.5–6; cf. Strabo, *Geography,* 7.1.4, where high-status Germanic captives are paraded in triumph but not executed). The demands of the public for victims in the arena, however, outstripped the supply of high-status captives, forcing the Romans to turn as often as not to lower-status individuals to fight and die in public spectacles: Symmachus lamented the fact that twenty-nine captives from among the Saxons who had been destined to fight in games he sponsored in 393 had committed suicide to avoid this cruel fate (cf. *Letter* 2.46 with Cecconi 2002: 307; cf. *Relatio* 47). As often as not, however, captives were destined for slavery rather than death: executions provided splendid entertainment, but slaves supplied wealth. The examples of this phenomenon are so numerous that they could fill an entire book (Welwei 2000 covers only the early Roman Republic; cf. Orosius 5.16.2 for the capture of 140,000 Germans in 102–101 BCE), but two examples can suffice for our purposes. In 368 the emperor Valentinian I undertook an expedition across the Rhine during which he captured a number of Alamanni, including a beautiful blonde-haired, blue-eyed girl who came to be known as Bissula. She was bought by a confidant and official of his named Ausonius, a man of high culture and impeccable tastes. We only know of her because Ausonius wrote a poem describing her stunning appearance and her charming combination of German and Roman habits, for he had trained the clever girl to master Latin, and no doubt the other skills necessary to pleasure her master (Ausonius, XVII, *Bissula*). At the opposite end of the spectrum, in 406 a band of Goths broke into the empire through Pannonia (modern Hungary) under the leadership of a certain Radagaisus. They descended upon Italy and wreaked havoc before being surrounded and defeated near Fiesole by the Roman general Stilicho. Those who survived were so bedraggled that they were sold off as slaves at a single gold solidus per head, about one-twentieth of the normal price for a slave at that time (Orosius 7.37.12–16; cf. Zosimus 5.26).

Mass enslavement was in fact a common result of mass captivity in the aftermath of battles (Lenski, Captivity, in press), but the case of Radagaisus's Goths is illustrative of yet another potential fate for captives: service in the Roman army. Stilicho, the general who defeated Radagaisus's Goths, was himself a German, from the tribe of the Vandals, whose father had been enrolled as a cavalry officer in the Roman army. Though we have no evidence that his family traced its entry into the empire to the experience of captivity (in point of fact, many Germans entered Roman service voluntarily), it would not have been unusual if it had. Often those who survived combat were neither executed nor sold as slaves but integrated into the Roman war machine, usually after having been divided into fighting units of a containable size and deployed to regions of the empire far from their original homelands (see, for example, *Historia Augusta Life of Probus* 14.1; cf. Welwei 1974–1977). Finally, some groups of captives, or

at least groups that surrendered to the Romans en masse, were transferred wholesale into unoccupied or under-occupied Roman territory for resettlement as agricultural laborers. The exact terms of such resettlements varied from group to group, but one constant remained: the settlers were obliged to render taxes and military service to the emperor. Though they were not enslaved in the sense of being sold off as chattels, these settlers seem to have occupied a semi-servile position that is reflected in the collective name they were given by the Romans: *laeti*, as they were called, seems not to derive from the Latin homonym *laetus* (fortunate) but rather from the Germanic word *letus* or *lidus* which means, as we shall see, a half-free or semi-servile person (Demougeot 1969; De Ste. Croix 1981:509–518).

Thus when Germans (or any other barbarians) were taken captive, they could have made no firm prediction of their eventual fate. They may not have survived the day, they may have served the Romans as slaves for years to come, they may have been sent thousands of miles from home to risk their lives as soldiers, or they may have been resettled on Roman soil as a semi-dependent tributary of the empire.

Before closing this survey of Rome as a slave society, two further issues pertinent to the discussion must be raised. First, it must be stated that the Roman slaveholding system was very liberal with manumission. Estimates of manumission rates among urban slaves in classical Rome range from 10 percent to 20 percent, and while these percentages would have been lower in the countryside, they give adequate testimony to the fact that the Romans were much more inclined to grant freedom to their slaves than were, for example, the slaveholders of the American South. Furthermore, Roman freedmen were not generally socially disadvantaged relative to free Roman citizens. On the contrary, all were granted some degree of Roman citizenship upon manumission, many nearly full citizenship, and many who had been trained in lucrative professions while enslaved attained considerable wealth and even status for themselves and their offspring (Garnsey 1981; Kirschenbaum 1987). Little wonder then that Roman freedmen are abundantly attested archaeologically by the funerary monuments, often sumptuously appointed, which they left behind (Petersen 2006). Second, the Romans did not attach any particular social stigma to the captivity of their own citizens by barbarians or brigands. From the beginning, Roman law created provisions for the possibility of capture according to which the captive Roman could regain his personal and political status and his property rights immediately upon returning home provided he had not deserted willingly to the enemy. This right of *postliminium* ensured that the legal person of a father-of-the-household (*paterfamilias*), around whom the Roman kin group revolved, merely went into abeyance during the period of captivity but was instantly restored upon his return (Sanna 2001). Captivity was thus not especially disadvantageous, at least to males, provided one could escape or be redeemed from one's captors. Even a great political figure like Julius Caesar could suffer captivity at the hands of brigands and eventually go on to become ruler of the Roman state.

Nevertheless, beginning in the third century CE the problem of captivity by barbarians, and particularly the Germans, became increasingly acute among the Romans. In this period, as we shall see, the various peoples along Rome's frontier, both Germans and others, turned increasingly aggressive. The natural outcome of the raids and wars that ensued was an increase in the capture and enslavement of Romans. Entire regions were raided for captives (as, for example, Greece by the Goths in 397 [Zosimus 5.5.5–8; Claudian, *On the Gothic Wars,* 616–622]), entire cities captured, sometimes multiple times (as, for example, Mainz, in the fourth and fifth centuries [Ammianus 27.10.1–2; Salvian, *On the Governance of God,* 6.8.39]). Unsurprisingly, these disruptions were at times taken advantage of by Roman citizens themselves. In the 260s the Goths from the northern litoral of the Black Sea sailed to the coast of Anatolia, where they disembarked and plundered as far south as Cappadocia. Long after they returned to their homeland with booty and captives, there remained behind in central Anatolia a number of captives who had fallen into the hands of fellow citizens and were kept by them in slavery (Gregory Thaumaturgus, *Canonical Epistle,* 6, trans. in Heather and Matthews 1991: 8–9). Maximus, the bishop of Turin, reported similar problems in Italy in the first decade of the

400s (*Homily* 96), and a pair of laws from 408 and 409 reveal the efforts of the central government to control such behavior. In the first (*Theodosian Code* 5.6.2 + 5.7.2 + *Sirmondian Constitution* 16) the emperor Honorius forbade the enslavement of citizens who had fled their homes in Illyricum in the wake of plundering Goths and ordered those who had ransomed captives to free them rather than retaining them as slaves, provided of course that they were compensated for the ransom. If the captive could not afford to pay, he or she was legally bound to serve his redeemer for five years. In the second law the emperor Theodosius II ordered soldiers who recovered Roman citizens and slaves from barbarians to return the former to freedom and the latter to their original masters (Theodosian Code 10.10.25; cf. *Codex Justinianus* 1.3.53 + 9.13.1). Despite the horrific ordeals these Romans must have suffered through their captivity to barbarians, they had at least two advantages: first, they could count on a still relatively strong central state apparatus that was operating, albeit with limited success, to extract them from captivity; second, the legal principle of *postliminium* and the relatively low stigma attached to captivity permitted some hope for those who were freed that reintegration back into their native society was possible upon their return (cf. *Novels of Anthemius* 3).

Germanic Society: An Overview

It is difficult, even dangerous, to generalize about "Germanic society" in antiquity, for there is no evidence that the people we now call "Germans" shared any common political unity or recognized any sense of collective identity in the period of Roman contact. "German" was a title used by Greek and, above all, Roman writers to describe the people who inhabited the territory of northern Europe generally east of the Rhine and north of the Danube as far northeast as modern Poland (Figure 4.1). Though they were vastly oversimplifying in using the blanket designation "German," the ancients were at least correct that many of these peoples were indeed united by common cultural and religious characteristics, and above all by languages that grew from the Germanic branch of the Indo-European system. Yet many of these same peoples often lived cheek by jowl with Celtic, Slavic, and even Indo-Iranian peoples in

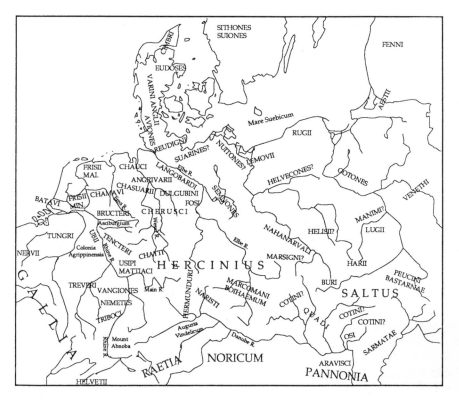

FIGURE 4.1. Germanic peoples of the first century CE.

the same territories, and they shared customary and linguistic features with them. Modern scholarship is thus not averse to speaking of "the Germans" as a collectivity, but it must always keep in mind that this broad category is an artificial and fundamentally theoretical construct.

Germanic society was at its base an iron-age culture that shared much in common with the other iron-age societies of ancient Europe. Throughout the period covered in this chapter, the Germans were agriculturalists who raised primarily barley and who practiced animal husbandry, mainly cattle rearing. They dwelt in wooden structures the largest of which were long-houses designed to shelter livestock as well as humans. In the centuries straddling the turn of the common era, these societies began to show signs of cultural contact with the Romans: settlements became larger and more consolidated, Roman trade goods and arms were used with increasing frequency, and some graves came to be distinguished by the deposition of considerable wealth. This trend continued into the second and third centuries as Roman influence became ever more apparent in the growth of villages (*oppida*), the use of Roman coined money for trade, and the frequency of burials involving weapons, many of them of Roman manufacture. This is especially true of the strip of territory ca. 100 km wide north of the Danube and east of the Rhine, where contact with the more complex and centralized Roman state was most common. Roman culture was thus influencing Germanic trade and exchange, increasing the size and complexity of dwellings and settlements, and facilitating the growth of a military segment of the society that gained intimate contact with Roman culture through direct service in Rome's auxiliary military units (Todd 1992; Wells 1999; Burns 2003).

Similar shifts can be divined in Germanic social structures, at least as far as we can discern from the sketchy evidence of our texts. The basic social unit of Germanic cultures was the clan (*sippe*), which involved up to one hundred interrelated individuals under the control of the male line. Women were explicitly subordinate to the authority (*mundium*) of their agnatic kin, as were slaves and the semi-servile *aldi* or *leti* (*lidi*) we shall encounter in the Germanic law codes (Fischer Drew 1988; Wolfram 1988:89–105). Again, contact with the more complex and expansionist Roman state seems to have fostered the growth of larger tribal groupings, headed by kinglets referred to by the Celtic loan word *reiks* and usually translated in our sources with the cognate Latin word *rex*. These units were generally fluid, with tribes regularly coming into being and disappearing, waxing and waning in size and power. Much of this resulted from an inbuilt social custom of feuding. Germanic society accepted feuding—intra- and interclan, and intra- and intertribal—as an integral element of social exchange. Indeed, Germanic law, at least as it is reflected in the late-antique codes, largely revolves around the regulation (not to be confused with the elimination) of feuding through the imposition of a system of defined compositions to be paid in money for various offenses ranging from punching to murder, and from blocking a traveler's way to stealing his horse. The historical sources make it abundantly clear, however, that the codification of such remedies was only partially successful in limiting violence, for Germanic society thrived on the recourse to force throughout this period. This is well reflected in yet another social grouping, the war-band or *comitatus* (*Gefolgschaft* in German). Powerful leaders, whether of clans or tribes, retained a body of armed male followers who attended them in offensive and defensive combat and plundering raids. Such bands were not bound by clan affinities, and the leader of a *comitatus* was thus compelled to maintain control of his group through violent domination and the careful distribution of wealth, including precious metals and, of note for this discussion, human chattels.

By the mid third century, even larger confederations of Germans began to appear, particularly the Goths along the lower Danube and the Alamanni on the upper Rhine. The latter group consisted of numerous smaller tribes that shared cultural commonalities and geographical proximity. Although Alamannic tribal groups were often in conflict, at times they united in a larger confederation to conduct warfare against external enemies, particularly the Romans (Drink-water 2007; Geuenich 1997). These Alamanni, whose name simply means "the men" or "the people," were a confederation of territorial kinglets who came together as need arose but lacked permanent transmissible central leadership structures before the sixth century.

In contrast, the Goths might more properly be characterized as a tribe that assembled a confederation around itself because of the early appearance of strong central leadership in the form of a supra-tribal king or "judge" termed the *thiudans* (Heather 1991:97–107; Wolfram 1988:91–100; cf. Heather 1996). Though this term is first attested in the fourth century, already in 250 we know of a Gothic king named Cniva who was able to assemble a massive force, attack deep into Roman Thrace, and outgeneral the Roman emperor Decius who was left dead on the battlefield in 251. The sources report explicitly that Decius's successor was in such a weak negotiating position that he was forced to permit Cniva to return to Gothic territory with all of his Roman captives (Zosimus 1.24.2). Although the Goths were pacified briefly in the late third and early fourth centuries, in the later fourth they began to challenge Roman authority again, and as we have seen, many eventually migrated en masse into the Roman empire in the wake of the Hun invasions of 376. We have also seen that this arrangement collapsed almost instantly because of the exploitation of captives, and that in 382 the Goths succeeded in carving out a semi-independent protectorate inside Roman territory. Because of ongoing tensions between the Roman state and Alaric, the new king who emerged to lead the Goths in the 390s, they began a halting migration westward that eventually resulted in the sack of Rome in 410 (Heather 1991:213–218; Kulikowski 2007:154–177). This Gothic group, by this point known as the Visigoths, then continued westward until eventually they were settled in southern Gaul by a treaty with the Romans in 418 that essentially ceded to their control the Gallic territory of Aquitaine.

The name "Visigoth" was acquired at some point during this forty-year process of ethnic formation that occurred as a response to the mutual hostilities between these barbarians and the Romans whose territory they traveled through, plundered, and settled in. The Visigoths were by no means an ethnically pure group but were rather a rag-tag agglomeration of various peoples—Germans, Huns, Alans, and even Romans, including many runaway slaves—who sought identity cohesion with this group as it snowballed its way through the empire, picking up momentum with each military success. This process, termed "ethnogenesis" by the Austrian school that has studied the Goths most intensively, thus forged a tribal state out of disparate peoples bonded together between the hammer clash of regular military conflict and the anvil of stable kingship structures (Wolfram 1988, 1997; cf. the critique of ethnogenesis theory by Gillett [2002] and Kulikowski [2007:43–70]).

A similar process seems to have occurred among other Germanic peoples at various stages of their interaction with the Roman Empire (Todd 1992:149–215). The Visigoths represented only a portion of the massive Gothic population that had once occupied the territory stretching from modern Romania in the west to the Ukraine in the east (Figure 4.2). When the Huns (Thompson 1999) occupied what is today Romania, a number of Goths remained behind and continued to live under their suzerainty. With the death of Attila in 453 and the disintegration of the Hunnic Empire, some of these Goths moved into the former Roman province of Pannonia, just west of the Danube bend. Known as the Ostrogoths, this group also found strong central leadership in the family of the Amals and particularly in the person of Theodoric, who had spent much of his youth as a hostage in Roman military service. In 499 Theodoric led an ethnically heterogeneous band of barbarians in the nominal service of the Roman state to retake Italy from another group of Germans, the Rugi. Once in Italy, Theodoric established his own Ostrogothic kingdom, which lasted down to 552. A formidable soldier and politician, he used his skills to gain regency over the Visigothic kingdom that now ruled from Toulouse. He was unable to prevent, however, the loss of most of Gaul to yet another growing tribal confederation, the Franks (Geary 1988; James 1982; 1988; Wood 1998; Zöllner 1970). These peoples of the lower Rhine remained much like the Alamanni down to the late fifth century: a cluster of interrelated tribes who regularly served with Roman armies but just as regularly attacked

them. As the Romans withdrew control from the region in the fifth century, a Frankish leader emerged in the person of Clovis (Chlodwig), who quickly began consolidating power by ruthlessly eliminating rivals and attacking his neighbors. It was Clovis who defeated the Visigothic king Alaric II, Theodoric's son-in-law, in 507 and forced the Visigoths to reconsolidate their state onto the Iberian Peninsula, where it survived down to 711. Clovis also attacked his neighbors to the southeast, another tribal kingship called the Burgundians who ruled the central Rhone down to 534. At this point Clovis's successors, the so-called Merowingian dynasts, gained control of Burgundia and with it most of Gaul, which they held until 751. Meanwhile, the Ostrogoths united under Theodoric lasted even less time, for they were attacked by generals of the Byzantine emperor Justinian and eventually relieved of power in 552. Yet Byzantine control of Italy was itself short lived, for yet another Germanic group, the Lombards, invaded Italy in 568 under yet another powerful king, Alboin, and gained control of its northern half until 774 (Christie 1995).

The late-antique and early medieval period thus witnessed an orgy of violence between the crumbling Roman Empire and a host of Germanic groups, all of whom followed a similar process of coalescence around a steady diet of warfare and, with the exception of the Alamanni, central leadership. All of this is important to this discussion for three reasons: first, it shows the degree to which Germanic societies were in a constant state of flux that involved increasing centralization and societal complexity; second, the degree of political and military instability that resulted from this state of almost constant warfare offered fertile ground for captivity and enslavement on a regular basis and a massive scale; third, the single best source for slavery in Germanic society remains the law codes that survive from these various late-antique and early medieval kingdoms. These will be surveyed in the fifth part of this chapter.

Slavery in Germanic Society through the Mid Fifth Century

To repeat a refrain found throughout this chapter, the fundamental problem with an investigation of slavery in Germanic society prior to the fifth century is that the written sources trace almost uniformly to Roman contexts and are thus heavily weighted toward the Roman perspective, which was at once limited and biased. Archaeology permits us to see beyond this conundrum, but only in hazy and piecemeal fashion. One obvious starting point for the archaeology—and one mentioned in several chapters in this volume—is the presence of defensive fortifications. Indeed, the evidence for Roman stone fortifications abounds from along the German frontier (Lander 1984). The Romans were extremely concerned with minimizing the impact of incursions by the Germans into their territories and, particularly, their population centers. The fact that some of these fortifications were designed to wall off urban centers while others were built to house exclusively military garrisons along the Rhine and Danube demonstrates at once the scale of the problem and the degree of sophistication the Romans brought to bear upon it. The Germans themselves, by contrast, left very few traces of stone structures, let alone fortifications. This need not indicate an absence of concern among the Germans for Roman attacks. More likely it shows that, because the Romans had developed elaborate and effective siege tactics, German efforts to ward off incursions using defensive fortifications were regarded as futile. Rather than defend their fixed abodes, Germanic peoples generally responded to Roman invasions by fleeing into adjacent forests or mountain fastnesses (Ammianus 17.1.7, 27.5.3, 27.10.7; cf. 31.3.7), often after having built wooden roadblocks along major thoroughfares to hinder, if not halt, the invading forces (Elton 1996:80–86). Settlement archaeology also gives some indications of the growth of slave exploitation among Germanic peoples during the period of Roman contact. The well-excavated settlement at Feddersen Wierde in extreme northern Germany shows tremendous growth in the size of elite "long-houses" to as large as 30 × 10 m by the second century CE even as much smaller huts were developed around them in plentiful clusters, apparently to house slaves (Haarnagel 1979:316–322).

Material remains also make it abundantly clear that, among the slaves held by Germanic peoples, a number may have been captives from inside the Roman Empire. Metal wares, including statuettes, drinking horns, and even weapons, have been found from Germanic territory that seem to have been manufactured in situ, but using techniques and motifs that are distinctly Mediterranean. The theory has been advanced that these may have been produced by metalsmiths captured from Roman territory and transferred by their captors as far north as Denmark (Stupperich 1997; cf. Tacitus, *Annals*, 2.62.3, for the presence of Roman traders and camp followers at the court of the Suebic king Marboduus ca. 20 CE). So too, numerous Germanic settlements from late third-century Mainfranken have yielded ceramic wares made in situ according to Roman techniques and specifications, apparently by Roman potters. It has been plausibly argued that these craftsmen had been captured during late third-century invasions into the empire and transferred into Germanic territory (Steidl 2002; cf. Steidl 2000:109). Even more telling are the shackles found at a number of sites along the Rhine associated with barbarian plunder hoards. A gravel quarry near modern Neupotz, for example, has turned up more than a thousand finely crafted metal objects that clearly formed part of a hoard plundered from Gallo-Romans by a band of Alamannic raiders in the mid third century CE. The objects were recovered from the left (i.e., Roman) bank of the river, indicating that the barbarians, who had already hacked some objects to bits for distribution, were somehow prevented from crossing back into their homeland, likely by Roman riverboat patrols. Among the objects found were two sets of iron shackles, surely meant for Roman captives. Similar hoards, also replete with shackles, have been discovered nearby at Hagenbach and other sites along the Rhine (Hannemann 2006; cf. Thompson 2003:217–244). Of even greater interest, a set of shackles was excavated from a second- or third-century CE Germanic context in Bavenstedt near Hildesheim, about 200 km east of the Rhine, that were clearly of Roman manufacture. Whether these already bound a captive, Roman or otherwise, when they were sold to their Germanic owners or were acquired to be clapped onto a slave or captive subsequent to their acquisition, they clearly attest to the interethnic nature of the slave trade in the period (Cosack and Kehne 1999).

The archaeology has also turned up related evidence in the form of epigraphy. Two funerary inscriptions from sites bordering Germanic territory, one at Cologne on the Rhine and the second from the Grand-St.-Bernard in Switzerland, attest the interment of *mangones*, slave dealers in these borderlands (*Corpus Inscriptionum Latinarum* 13.8348; *Inscriptiones Latinae Selectae* 4851). Whether these traded Germanic slaves into Roman territory or vice versa can no longer be established, though one suspects some of both occurred. Regardless, such slave dealers were apparently a common and acceptable enough feature of the Germanic cultural landscape that the Latin word *mango* entered the Germanic lexicon as a general word associated with "trade" and "trading" (Kleberg 1945; cf. Wolters 1991:80–89 on traders). Even more spectacular was the recent discovery of a victory altar unearthed in Augsburg in Bavaria. Its inscription records a raid by the Germanic Iuthungi deep into Roman Italy in which "many thousands of Italian captives" were carried off before the Germans were stopped by a Roman general in April 260 (Bakker 1993).

Yet another pertinent recent archaeological discovery has been the site of the famous Battle of the Teutoborg Forest, in which three Roman legions and their accompanying auxiliaries (ca. 20,000 to 25,000 men) were defeated over a four day battle late in 9 CE. The Romans had been led into a trap by Arminius, king of the Germanic Cherusci, a man who had himself grown up a hostage in the empire, where he had been schooled in Roman military tactics and was eventually promoted to the rank of an auxiliary commander (Tacitus, *Annals*, 1.59–62; Cassius Dio 56.18–22). After his return to his people, Arminius became a sworn enemy of the Romans and eventually set a trap for the unwary general Quinctilius Varus in the rocky and forested reaches of northern Germany. The site of the battle, which represented a major turning point in the Roman conquest of Germany, had been sought for more than eight hundred years but was only firmly identified in the late 1980s with the discovery of thousands of Roman military artifacts strewn along a 15 km corridor near Kalkriese in Osnabrück (Wells 2003). Though no definitive evidence of captive taking has been found among the artifacts (but see Van der Sanden 1996:180), it is amply attested

in the written sources for the battle. The early second-century historian Tacitus describes how, when the Roman general Germanicus returned to the battle site in 15 CE, he was guided by former prisoners who had escaped from the Germans and who "pointed out the raised ground from which Arminius had harangued his army, the number of gibbets for the captives, and the pits for the living" (Tacitus, *Annals*, 1.61). Many of these captives did not escape as quickly as Germanicus's guides, instead serving as slaves to the Cherusci and their allies over the long term, as also attested by Tacitus. In 50 CE the Roman general Lucius Pomponius defeated the Chatti, who had aided the Cherusci as allies, and rescued Roman prisoners who had been among the captives enslaved in the Teutoburg disaster forty years earlier (Tacitus, *Annals*, 12.27; cf. Cassius Dio 56.22.2a–4; Seneca, *Letter* 47.10).

While the Romans were certainly prime targets for captivity, it would be wrong to assume that the Germans refused to enslave other barbarian enemies, including fellow Germans (Thompson 1960). This, too, is attested in the sources, albeit much more rarely given that Roman writers were largely unconcerned with conflicts between barbarian peoples (see, for example, Jordanes, *Getica*, 55[280–282]). Once these captives were in German hands, there was apparently a thriving commercial traffic in slaves both within tribes and between them. Tacitus, again, tells of a group of Germanic Usipi who had been drafted into the Roman army and transported to Britain to serve there. After rebelling against their commander and taking flight in stolen military ships, they were captured by the Germanic Suebi and Frisii (from northern Germany and Holland) and eventually sold from dealer to dealer until they ended up back in Roman hands (Tacitus, *Agricola*, 28.1–5). Cassius Dio (71.13.2–4; cf. 71.11.2) reports that in the late second century the Quadi, who lived north of the middle Danube, had refused to return any Roman captives to the emperor Marcus Aurelius except those they could neither put to work nor sell to neighboring tribes. Finally, some slaves among the Germans were likely purchased directly from the Romans, especially from brigands within the empire. Two legal responses from the second century treat, respectively, a woman who had been condemned to the mines but then kidnapped by bandits and resold to the barbarians, and the sale of a privately held Roman slave similarly kidnapped and resold. Both cases arose because the victims had later been sold back into the empire (*Digest* 49.15.6, 49.15.27). One can well imagine that most such unfortunates would have remained in barbarian hands unto death. It was precisely this which Valentinian III was trying to prevent with a law of 451 forbidding parents to sell their own children to barbarians in the wake of a famine (*Novels of Valentinian* 33). These would quickly have lost cognizance of their native culture, and legal rights, and would thus have remained slaves the rest of their lives whether their Germanic purchasers kept them or resold them back into their homeland.

A similar traffic also occurred in endemic slaves as indicated in Tacitus's ethnographic work *Germany*. In the brief section of the treatise devoted to slavery Tacitus reports:

> Surprisingly, gambling for them is a serious matter, in which they engage when sober; so recklessly do they win and lose that when all is gone they stake their bodily freedom on the last and final throw. The loser willingly becomes a slave; although perhaps the younger and stronger, he suffers himself to be bound and sold. Such is their persistence in a thoroughly bad business: they themselves call it honor. Slaves of this sort they exchange in trade, to free themselves from the shame of victory. (Tacitus, *Germany,* 24)

Indeed, we have good indications from the Germanic law codes that these societies tended to accept debt slavery (Liebs 2001), which stood in contrast with what we have seen of Roman practice. If we can believe Tacitus, however, the retention of such endemic bondsmen was stigmatized, and those who acquired them felt compelled to sell off debt bondsmen acquired in wagers quickly. Even more stigmatized by the Germans was, it would seem, capture by foreigners, especially the capture of Germanic women. Cassius Dio (77.14) avers that a group of Cennian women committed suicide rather than serve as slaves after being captured by Emperor Caracalla in the early third century. Tacitus (*Germany*, 8.1) says Germanic women often incited their husbands

in battle with reminders that the females would be captured if the men suffered defeat.

What diplomatic efforts the Germans may have made to ransom their own captives we do not know. We have ample evidence, however, that the Romans regularly engaged in the business of redeeming fellow citizens from captivity among the Germans. First and foremost, the emperor and his representatives championed the cause of Roman captives in negotiations with the barbarians. To take just two examples, when Emperor Marcus Aurelius negotiated a peace with the Quadi in 169–170 CE, he insisted they begin by handing over 13,000 Roman captives and later all the captives and deserters they held (Cassius Dio 71.11.1–2; cf. 72.2.2). And when the Alamannic chief Vadomarius came to terms with Julian in 359, the emperor demanded the return of all Romans captured by his Germanic tribe. To ensure full compliance, Julian had assembled a roster of 3,000 names to be checked against those returned (Ammianus 18.2.19; Eunapius, *Histories*, fr. 19; Libanius, *Oration*, 18.78–79; cf. Drinkwater 2007:136–138). As the empire wore on and the problem of barbarian captivity grew, this ransoming activity assumed greater and greater importance. From the later fourth century, it was dominated in particular by bishops, who simultaneously had sufficient capital at their disposal and ample motivation to ransom massive numbers of prisoners. They did so in large part to fulfill the biblical injunction to "ransom captives" (Lk 4:18–19; Mt 25:34–43; cf. Osiek 1981), but also in part to build their own patronage networks among the beneficiaries of their charity (Grieser 1997:167–190; Klingshirn 1985; Lenski, Captivity, in press, n. 19). When high-prestige captives were involved, negotiations became even more delicate, as when the general Heracleius was captured by the Ostrogoths in the 490s and had to be ransomed for a huge sum. The historian Malchus (*Histories*, frg. 6.2) tells us that the emperor insisted the ransom be paid only by the members of Heracleius's family, "lest he seem to have been a slave." The situation illustrates well that the line between captives and slaves was no easier to draw in antiquity than it is in the present and that it often represented a matter of semantics. It also hammers home the fact that, while the Romans imposed no legal impediments upon those enslaved by foreigners if they returned from captivity, a certain social stigma remained, at least for high-status individuals.

Nowhere is this better illustrated than in the instance of Placidia, sister of the emperor Honorius, who was captured by the Visigoths during their invasion of Italy in 410 CE. Placidia was eventually married to the Gothic king Athaulf, and the historians Orosius (7.40.2, 43.1–8) and Jordanes (*Getica*, 31[159–160]) even go so far as to claim that Athaulf married Placidia in order to facilitate negotiations with the Romans. His fellow Goths, however, resented this peaceful posturing and murdered him. Placidia herself apparently never consented to the marriage and her concomitant role as a political pawn. Even so, when she was finally returned to her brother in 416, it was as part of a negotiated settlement that involved concessions on both sides and served as a precursor to the permanent settlement of the Goths in Aquitaine (Jordanes, *Getica*, 32[164]; cf. Orosius 7.43.12–13). Captives were thus pivotal figures in cultural, political, and social exchanges between Romans and Germans.

Placidia's case raises another question commonly treated in this volume: as a female and an object of cultural value, was Placidia representative of a specific or common type of captive among the Germans? James Brooks's (2002) seminal work has crystallized brilliantly the role played by captives from the Southwest American Borderlands in facilitating, albeit under duress, cultural exchange. Much of this was due to the fact that the captives he discusses tended to be females who, precisely because of their social inferiority, were able to introduce elements of new cultural heritage without directly threatening those who dominated them. To a certain degree this was surely true of Germanic societies as well, and there is no better example of this than Placidia, whose status as bride conditioned her role as cultural and political intermediary. In a similar instance, the princess Eudocia was captured during the Vandal sack of Rome in 455 and married off to Huneric, son of the Vandal king Geiseric, in a ploy to win kinship claims to imperial privileges and property for this Germanic kingship (Priscus, *Histories*, frg. 38–39; Theophanes, a.m., 5947, 5949, 5964). We also have abundant evidence that Frankish kings, who regularly

practiced polygamy, took slaves as wives, even if we cannot confirm that these slaves originated as captives. Though we lack the sorts of evidence at Brooks's disposal to project this scenario further down the vertical social scale, it may well be that the royal practice of marrying captives as tokens of prestige reflected a broader social praxis.

Furthermore, we can assume that Germanic warriors were more likely to kill in battle or execute male enemies and then to enslave a predominance of women and children. This certainly occurred in Roman society (examples at Scheidel 2005:72 n. 56), and we have some testimony that confirms it for the Germans as well. In the mid first century CE, Tacitus (*Annals*, 13.56) reports, the young men of the Ampsivari were exterminated by neighboring tribes while their noncombatants were shared out as plunder. At the other end of antiquity, when a group of Saxons set upon the Swabians who had settled on their former territory in the mid fifth century, they planned in advance their strategies of attack, including how to share out the women and children they intended to capture once they had killed all adult males (Gregory of Tours, *History of the Franks*, 5.15; cf. Procopius, *Wars*, 6.21.39). This being said, there is countervailing evidence indicating that there was no strong gender bias in captive taking among the Germans. Most of our sources say nothing about it, and many others make it clear that males as well as females were often subject to capture (see, for example, *Martyrium Athenogeni* 3). This probably resulted in large part from the fact that, in contrast with the Southwest Borderlands described by Brooks, the Germans had an extensive and developed system of chattel slavery with equal room for male and female slaves. Where the cultural no-man's-land of the American Southwest favored kinship slavery, Germanic slavery, at least as reflected in our meager sources from before the late fifth century, and certainly in the sources that follow, approached more closely modern notions of chattel slavery. As we shall see, the Germanic law codes of the late fifth century and following (our most detailed sources on the question) are equally concerned with male and female slaves, and as such use gendered terms for males (*servi, aldii, leti*) and females (*servae, ancillae, aldiae, letae*) as well as a neuter generic term for all slaves regardless of gender (*mancipium*) (Nehlsen 1984:219–222). When it came to taking captives from the Romans, this lack of bias was probably facilitated by the relatively sharp divide between soldier and civilian in Roman society. Because Rome had a professional army, and because it restricted access to weapons for noncombatant civilians, its male civilians were not in a strong position to resist captivity and were probably nearly as likely to be enslaved as females and children.

Before closing this section on the role of captives and slaves in Germanic societies prior to the end of the fifth century, it is worth asking what evidence we have for the employment of slaves within Germanic territory. Here the sources are, in general, textual rather than archaeological and thus once again Roman. Pride of place among them goes to Tacitus's *Germany*, which reports of the first century CE Germans:

> The other slaves they do not use as we do, with designated duties throughout the household; each one controls his own holding and home. The master requires from him, as from a tenant, some amount of grain or livestock or clothing, and only so far must the slave submit; the wife and children perform the other domestic chores. Seldom do they beat a slave or punish him with shackles and hard labor, yet they are apt to kill him: not through harsh discipline, but in a fit of rage as they would a foe, except that the deed is unpunished. Freedmen rank little higher than slaves. They rarely have any influence in the home and never in the state, excepting only those tribes ruled by kings. For there they surpass both the freeborn and the well-born; among the others, unequal freedmen are an indication of freedom. (Tacitus, *Germany*, 25; cf. Rives 1999: 217–218)

As we have already noted, Tacitus wrote for a Roman audience and with his own agenda, which was in many ways to hold the Germans up as a nobly savage foil to what he perceived as the decadence of Roman culture. Nevertheless, that his sources were good appears to be confirmed in the Germanic law codes of five and six centuries later. Taken at his word, Tacitus portrays Germanic society using slaves primarily to serve as farm tenants on independent holdings disconnected from the master's household. In contrast with the Romans, the Germans of Tacitus's day did not rely on slaves as household attendants but left domestic tasks to wives and children (cf. Tacitus, *Germany*, 20). Certainly, by the fourth century, we have evidence of slave attendants (Ammianus 18.2.13, 27.10.3–4), which may reflect a change in the Germanic practice of slaveholding that accompanied the growing social and economic complexity of fourth-century Germanic culture. Tacitus's notice on slave punishment also contrasts with Roman practice, which put greater restrictions on the murder of a slave (especially *Theodosian Code* 9.12.1); it fits well, however, with what we can learn from the Germanic law codes. A classic example of this contrast is evident in a source from the sixth century: Agathias (*Histories*, 2.7.1–5) describes how the Roman general Belisarius executed a Frankish commander fighting with his forces because the Frank had summarily murdered one of his slaves. While this harshness made perfect sense in a Roman legal context, it nearly drove Rome's Frankish allies, who saw things very differently, to rebellion. Finally, the notice on freedmen and their lack of influence, except in the king's household, is also surely meant to contrast with Roman society, but conforms to what we learn from the Germanic codes.

If slaves were primarily employed as agricultural workers, we nevertheless have good evidence that, by virtue of their status as "socially dead," Germanic slaves and captives also played liminal social roles not open to other segments of their society. In the case of the Suiones, Tacitus reports, this liminality manifested itself in the fact that this island-dwelling people was ruled by a king who used a slave to guard their communal weapons cache in order to limit feuding. More commonly, the liminal role of slaves was operative on the level of religion, particularly human sacrifice. Strabo tells us that priestesses of the Chatti predicted the future by viewing the blood of captives spilled into cauldrons and inspecting their entrails (*Geography*, 7.2.3). So, too, Tacitus (*Annals*, 13.57) reports that the Hermunduri, after defeating the Chatti in a feud over control of a sacred river, sacrificed all their captives to "Mars and Mercury," presumably some version of the Germanic gods Thor and Woden.

Much later, Jordanes reports that the Goths sacrificed their captives to their war god Woden by hanging them in trees (*Getica*, 5[41]; cf. Tacitus, *Germany*, 12.1, and Orosius 5.16.6 for hanging in trees). More commonly, it seems, slaves and captives were killed by drowning. The Germanic peoples of first-century Denmark are said by Tacitus (*Germany*, 44) to have worshipped the earth goddess Nerthus with a ritual that involved the cleaning of her sacred wagon by slaves who were then drowned in her lake (Rives [1999: 292–294] offers a bibliography on such ritual wagons, originally excavated at Dejbjerg in Jutland). So too Jordanes reports that in 410 the Visigoths, who at least in name had been Christian for three decades, buried their king, Alaric, by diverting a river in southern Italy, forcing captives to dig his grave in its bed, then redirecting its waters into the channel so as to smother the grave and drown the captives (*Getica*, 30[156–158]). Similarly, in 540 the Franks, again nominally Christian for decades, drowned captives in the Po River as a mode of divination (Procopius, *Wars*, 6.25.7–11). Slaves were entrusted with these culturally dangerous roles as intermediaries who could negotiate the ritual space between sacred and profane, but also as "disposable people" (Bales 2004) whose dangerous contact with the divine could be washed away, literally, through human sacrifice.

Connections with the "bog bodies," over 1,500 of which have been found drowned and often staked into lakes and bogs throughout northwestern Europe, are of course tempting. Unfortunately, precise relations cannot be drawn. First of all, bog bodies have been found not just in Germanic but also in Celtic and Slavic territories, making them a commonplace of north European rather than specifically Germanic culture. Second, while bogs were almost certainly used to perform ritual killings, Tacitus is surely correct in reporting that drowning in bogs was also used to punish cowards, criminals, and sex offenders (*Germany*, 12.1; cf. *Passion of St. Saba* 7.5–8.1, in Heather and Matthews 1991:116–117; *Laws of the Burgundians* 34.1). Such executions surely entailed religious elements but were unlikely to have been intended as protreptic rituals like those described in Tacitus and Jordanes. Third, while some bog bodies bear indications

of slave or at least outcast status, especially those with short-cropped hair, markers associated with many others, including long hair and elaborate clothing and ornamentation, indicate high status (Todd 1992:112–115; Turner and Scaife 1995; Van der Sanden 1996). The excavated bog bodies thus surely include some slaves, at least some of whom were ritually killed, but drowning or postmortem submersion in bogs was by no means exclusively religious, let alone exclusive to slaves.

Slavery in Germanic Society beyond the Mid Fifth Century: The Evidence of the Germanic Law Codes

Just as it is difficult to speak of "Germanic society" as any one thing, so too it is difficult to speak of Germanic law as a homogeneous, let alone essential, category. For much of the period of Germanic contact with Roman society, the locus of legal knowledge and enforcement resided in the family rather than some larger political grouping. Issues were decided according to custom, and there appears to have been no written law. Claims involving members of disparate families could come before a tribal assembly that brought together the free males or an elite subset of these to decide cases. Even with the rise of larger tribal confederations we have little evidence that central leaders, who were primarily military figures, became involved in judicial concerns. The only possible exception to this in the fourth century was the overlord of the Gothic Tervingi, whose title the Roman sources translate as "judge" (*iudex*) even if we have no further evidence of judicial authority. Apart from the extremely limited and tendentious reports of the Roman sources, we thus have no access to early Germanic law. It first speaks for itself, as it were, with the codification of customary law in the so-called "Barbarian Law Codes" of late antiquity. Between the late fifth and early ninth centuries at least a dozen of these were recorded that have been preserved down to the present. In a chapter of this length it would be impossible to cover the contents of all of these, let alone the complications of their textual history (on this see Liebs 2002; Nehlsen 1972:251–260, 358–360; and the introductions to the English translations of the Salian, Burgundian, Ripuarian, and Lombardic laws by K. Fischer Drew and T. J. Rivers). Instead we will discuss the most important codes recorded before the end of the eighth century—that is, the earliest codes. These include the Visigothic Code of Euric (*Codex Euricianus* = CE, ca. 475 CE); the Laws of the Burgundians (*Leges Burgundionum* [*LB*], 483–532 CE); the Law of the Salian Franks (*Pactus Legis Salicae* [*PLS*], 507–511 CE); the Law of the Ripuarian Franks (*Lex Ribuaria [LR]*, ca. 630); and the Lombardic Edict of Rothair (*Lex Langobardorum Rothari* [*LLR*], 643 CE).

This investigation takes into account three limitations on its methodology. First, each code represents a distinct tradition based on individual tribal customs that had been reformed through the process of ethnogenesis and the rise of central monarchies. Attempting to draw general conclusions about "Germanic" custom from the disparate codes is thus precarious, but not impossible, for in as far as the codes manifest commonalities, these can be taken to represent practices shared among the various Germanic peoples. Second, all of the codes were recorded by Germanic peoples who had already come to occupy former Roman territories in which they were a demographic minority relative to their indigenous Roman subjects. As such, the codes necessarily reflect the absorption of, and interaction with, Roman practice; most obviously, all were composed in Latin. Here, too, however, the problem can be managed, for our knowledge of Roman law and custom is extensive and can be used to cross-check the Germanic codes for what stands out as distinctive. Furthermore, the codifiers themselves clearly recognized a distinction between Roman and German legal praxis, for the Germanic codes were written to operate within a given territory alongside and concurrently with Roman codes; those who identified themselves as ethnically Roman were judged according to Roman law, and those ethnically German, according to their respective tribal code (see, for example, *LB* pref. 3, 8; *LR* 35[31].3–4). Finally, the codes are all rather later than much of the evidence presented in the remainder of this chapter. All date to a period when the respective Germanic tribes were ruled by monarchs, and when much of the responsibility for maintaining peace and order had shifted from the family to the state. Retrojecting the findings from this section onto what has gone before is thus a delicate

operation, for the Germanic peoples of late antiquity had undergone considerable transformation that surely altered their customs. Here again, however, the project is not hopeless, for the many points of intersection between the various codes point to a font of deep tradition that predated the transformations of the migration period.

The Germanic law of the codes remained largely a matter of private or family justice. Most issues they treat amount to what we would call criminal offenses, but these were invariably handled as civil affairs. Germanic society was characterized by a strong attachment to blood feud (*faida*), in which family or clan members were charged with wreaking vengeance on rival offenders by force. The law sought to impose peace and order by commuting the feud to monetary penalties. In cases short of death, this was dictated according to quite specific categories by the codes. Note for example *LR* 71[68], which lays out penalties for when an extremity that is struck off is large enough that it makes a sound when thrown against a shield across a road twelve feet wide, or the differentiation between amounts owed for the striking off of thumb versus index fingers versus third, fourth, and fifth fingers (*LLR* 63–67, 89–93). Such "compositions" also extended to property damage, again with the same degree of situational specificity. They stood in contrast with instances where an individual had been killed. In these cases the *wergeld*, or monetary worth, of the dead person had to be paid to his or her relatives, and this depended not so much on the manner of death as on the victim's relative status. Slaves, for example, almost invariably bear one-quarter the *wergeld* of ordinary free Germans (Nehlsen 1972: passim, 2001). Attaining justice entailed a large degree of self-help, for the plaintiff had to bring the defendant to court (*mallus*) without the aid of the state or tribe. Once there, the law codes assume that justice would be rendered by a representative of the state, usually a count (*grafio*) and his council. Trial procedure involved two forms of proof: first the oath (or compurgation), which was taken in formalistic fashion (any mistakes proved the guilt of the defendant) in conjunction with a series of "oath helpers," family members who also swore and assumed collective responsibility for the outcome of the trial; second was the

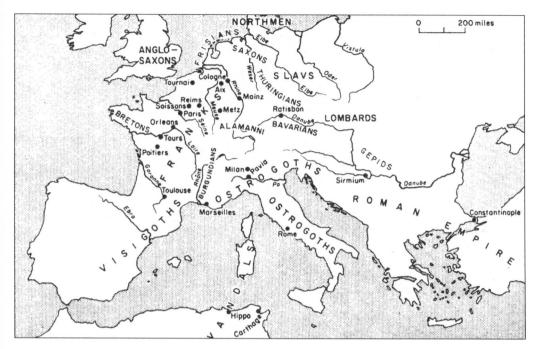

FIGURE 4.2. Germanic peoples of the sixth century CE.

ordeal, usually involving the fetching of a stone out of a boiling cauldron, then checking the burn this caused days later to see if it was "clean" or "dirty," the latter of which indicated guilt. Slaves, who were incapable of having oath helpers, were forced either to confess (or not) under torture or to submit immediately to the ordeal. This could be spared, however, if the master paid the requisite composition prior to trial in order to "save the slave's back" (*PLS* 40.2–3, 6).

Slavery is an extremely common element in all the codes, itself an indication of its prevalence in the Germanic societies of the fifth through seventh centuries (Figure 4.2). This fact can most easily be laid out in tabular form. The table that follows lists, by law code: (1) the total number of chapters (and titles, when applicable, in parentheses) extant from a given code; (2) the number of chapters (and titles) that deal in some way, even if not primarily, with enslaved or semi-servile individuals; (3) the number of these that were semi-servile (*leti* in the Frankish codes, *aldii* in the Lombardic); and (4) the percentage of chapters (and titles) in each given code dealing with slaves.

As Table 4.1 reveals, between one-quarter and one-third of the material in the Germanic codes deals with enslaved or semi-servile individuals. The only code that appears to have a significantly smaller percentage of slaves is the *PLS*, a striking fact given that this is commonly regarded as the most "Germanic" of the lot. The lower percentage can be explained, however, by the fact that the *PLS* has an extremely differentiated set of chapters, but that when one looks at the percentage of the larger titles (i.e., thematic groupings) dealing with slaves, the *PLS* falls much more squarely into line with the remaining codes at 26 percent. Slavery was thus a crucial element in Germanic legal practice and, we can assume, Germanic society.

In his *Germany* of 98 CE, Tacitus reported of the Suebi, by which he means not one tribe but, collectively, the Germanic tribes of eastern Germany (Rives 1999:282–285): "It is a characteristic of the tribe to dress their hair on the side and bind it up tight in a knot. This distinguishes the Suebi from the other Germani, and their freeborn from their slaves." This distinction appears to have carried through to late antiquity, at least among some tribes. Certainly the Franks attached special importance to their long hair as a

TABLE 4.1 Numbers and Percentages of Chapters in Germanic Law Codes Dealing with Enslaved or Semi-Servile Individuals

Code	Total chapters (and titles)	Chapters (and titles) involving slaves/semi-slaves	Chapters (and titles) involving semi-slaves	Percentage of chapters (and titles) dealing with slaves/semi-slaves
Codex Euricianus	59	18	—	30%
Lex Burgundionum (including constitutiones extravagantes)	364 (109)	122 (53)	—	33.5% (49%)
Pactus Legis Salicae (including capitularies 6 and 7)	642 (154)	92 (40)	12	14.3% (26%)
Lex Ribuaria	229 (91)	58 (29)	2 (*Litus*)	25.3% (32%)
Lex Langobardorum Rothari	388	140	35 (*Aldius*)	36.1%
Total	1,682 (354)	430 (122)	49	25.56% (34.4%)

marker of status (e.g., Gregory of Tours, *History of the Franks*, 2.41, 3.18; cf. Rives 1999:285; Wallace Hadrill 1982, 1981:156–160). Their neighbors the Burgundians also appear to have distinguished male slaves by their short hair, for *LB* 6.4 lays out stiff penalties for those who aided fugitive slaves by furnishing them with false hair (Nehlsen 1972: 224–226; though female slaves kept their hair long, see *LB* 33.2–4. 92.3–5). Apart from this, however, we know of no markings of the body or apparel that would have distinguished freeborn from slave among the Germans.

The codes also confirm that, much like the Romans, the Germans conceived of their slaves as little more than property. In many laws the slaves are treated on a par with livestock as fungible chattels (e.g., *PLS* 47.1; *LB* 4.1; *LLR* 252; CE fr. 294). More tellingly, the compositions to be paid for the theft or killing of slaves reveal their value. Ordinary slaves average between 15 and 25 solidi, equal to 0.21 to 0.35 pounds of gold or about four to six years' wages for the average laborer (e.g., *PLS* 10.6, 35.9; *LB* 4.1; *LLR* 131–134, 136). For skilled slaves prices reached 50 to 60 solidi, and for highly skilled slaves as high as 200 (e.g., *PLS* 104.10; *LB* 10.1–5; *LLR* 130, 135). These prices are remarkably consistent with what we know of prices for slaves inside Roman territory at this time (Lenski, Price of Slaves, in prep.). Of itself this fact is interesting, for it confirms from an economic perspective what we learned in the previous section: the market in slaves was international. Because the slave trade between Rome

and its Germanic neighbors seems to have been active and substantial, prices between Roman and Germanic territory were in rough equilibrium.

The codes can also help us determine the uses to which the Germans put their slaves. As just mentioned, certain slaves were definitely used as skilled craftsmen: gold, silver, iron, and bronze-smiths (*PLS* 10.6, 35.9; *LB* 10.2–4, 21.2); carpenters and masons (*PLS* 10.6; *LB* 10.5; *LLR* 145); millers and vinedressers (*PLS* 10.6, 35.9); even shoemakers (*LB* 21.2). Among the most valued bondsmen were household attendants, a luxury in the Roman world which Tacitus claimed was unheard of among the Germans of the first century CE. We have already seen that attendants are attested among Alamannic leaders in the fourth century, and the law codes offer many references to them in the fifth through seventh centuries (*PLS* 35.9. 104.11; *LB* 10.1; cf. Gregory of Tours, *History of the Franks*, 2.23–24, 3.5, 3.18, 3.21, 4.44–46, 4.49). The *Lex Langobardorum* (76–102) even draws a firm distinction between these household slaves (*servi ministeriales*), who had to have been born and raised in the master's house and thus had established quasi-kinship with the family, and the average field slave (*servus rusticanus*). This should serve as a reminder that, more than anything, the Germans employed their slaves in agriculture.

We have numerous attestations of these field slaves, several of which indicate that they were the least valued among German slaves (*PLS* 121; *LLR* 103, 279–280). We also have indications that there was considerable specialization in agricultural skills: we hear of slaves trained to herd sheep, cattle, goats, and pigs (*PLS* 10.6, 10.1, 121; *LLR* 133, 135–136), to groom horses (*PLS* 10.6–7, 35.9), and to plow fields (*LB* 10.1). Above all, in a passage quoted earlier, Tacitus (*Germany,* 25) explains that the Germans tended to grant a greater degree of independence to their field slaves than the Romans did, and some of this appears to show up in several passages of the *LLR* that speak of "tenant slaves" (*servi massarii*) who lived on separate servile holdings (*casa mancipiata*), were given considerable freedom to dispose of their produce, and supervised slaves of their own (*LLR* 132, 134, 227, 234). It is interesting, then, that the Germans did not grant legal agency to their slaves. With the exception of the *servus massarius,* who could make sales independent of the master, Germanic law forbade slaves from conducting any business transaction without the master's explicit consent (*PLS* 27.33, 124; *LB* 21; *LR* 77[74]; *LLR* 233, 235; *CE* fr. 283, 287). This stood in contrast with Roman practice, for while Roman law never fully accepted the principle of third-party agency between free men, it was more than ready to recognize that a slave could conduct business and make contracts that were binding between third parties and the master (Kirschenbaum 1987; Watson 1987:102–114). Contact with Rome and the importation of Roman slaves must then have had an effect on the differentiation of labor and the expansion of production in Germanic economies and societies. By contrast, it seems not to have altered agricultural traditions—hence the continuation of the quasi-independent *servus massarius*—nor trade practices, hence the avoidance of slaves in the mercantile sector.

A whole class of slaves was also owned by and served the king. Tacitus (*Germany,* 25), it will be recalled, reported the employment and high status of royal slaves already in the late first century CE. This continued to hold true in the Germanic tribal states, for while at times the royal slaves of the codes worked as agricultural laborers on the king's domains (cf. *LB* 38.80), often they served governmental functions, including collecting taxes and fines (*LB* 49.4, 76.1–4). They also enjoyed certain privileges, commanded much higher compositions, and bore a larger

wergeld than ordinary slaves. Indeed, in this arena they were often on a par with free Germans (*PLS* 54.2, 117.1; *LB* 2.1; *LR* 54[53], 61[58].14; *LLR* 371–373). And the Germanic codes attest to slaves of the church (e.g., *PLS* 87; *LR* 61[58].9–10; *LLR* 272), a reality that is widely attested in ecclesiastical sources. This latter, in particular, was an obvious effect of contact with Rome. As we shall see below, the Christianization of the barbarians from the fourth century onward was itself at least partially a product of cultural interaction facilitated by slaves.

It is now time to turn to the question of what the codes reveal about the ways of becoming a slave. We have already seen that there is abundant evidence that the Germans of the first four centuries of our era regularly seized captives and held them as slaves. This practice continued into the sixth century, as vividly illustrated in a passage from Gregory of Tours (*History of the Franks,* 3.11–13): in 532, the Frankish king Theuderic declined a chance for battle against the Burgundians but later had to placate his troops' thirst for plunder by granting them permission to attack the Roman city of Clermont Ferrand and "bring home with them not only every single thing which they could steal in the region…but also the entire population." The codes also discuss captivity as a mode of becoming a slave. Here again, the political and military disruptions of the period regularly led to the capture of individuals, not just of Romans but also of fellow Germans from other tribes (*LB* 21.4, *Const. Ex.* 21.2, 21.9). Moreover, those already held in slavery by one tribe were often subject to captivity during the continuous wars and raids of the period; they simply swapped servitude to one people for servitude to another (*LB* 21.5, 39.2, 56.1–2, *Const. Ex.* 21.2). Many, slave and free, also experienced captivity due to the exploitation and chicanery of their own fellow countrymen: numerous laws try to curb the sale of even free Germans into slavery as a result of kidnapping or fraud (*PLS* 39.2–5, VI *Cap.* 6; VII *Cap.* 2; *LR* 17[16]; *CE* fr. 290). Endogenous slavery was thus commonplace, even if not sanctioned.

Birth to a slave woman was also an obvious avenue to slavery. This we learn especially from laws governing sexual relations between free males and female slaves: these dictate that the offspring of such unions were to be the slaves of the maidservant's owner (*LR* 61[58].10–16; *LLR* 156, 219, 231). Furthermore, the value of the offspring of a pregnant slave woman who died or miscarried because of some injury was reckoned to her *wergeld*, indicating that the master regarded even her fetus as his property (*PLS* 104.9–11; *LLR* 334).

Slaves could also be acquired through purchase, a fact pointed to by a number of constitutions. In contrast with Roman law, however, the Germanic codes provide only very sporadic and underdeveloped warranties for the slave whose value was compromised by physical defects or defects in title (*LB Const. Ex.* 21.3, 21.9; *LLR* 230–231; *CE* fr. 288, 291). We have also seen from a passage of Tacitus (*Germany* 24) that the Germans, in contrast with the Romans, allowed the sale of oneself into slavery for debts. This possibility is amply confirmed in the codes (e.g., *PLS* VII *Cap.* 6; *CE* 300). One of the most common ways for this to occur was for a freeman to commit an offense grievous enough that he was financially incapable of satisfying the requisite composition, in which case he could become subject to enslavement by the defendant (Liebs 2001). This arrangement approximated the Roman practice of enslavement for crimes, though instead of the defendant falling to the ownership of the state, as with the Romans, he fell to the ownership of the offended party. In extreme cases, however, such as livestock rustling, incest, or performing abortions, enslavement could result immediately from the breach of cultural taboos (*LB* 47.1–2; *CE* 2–3). Interestingly, the *Codex Euricianus* (299) forbids freeborn parents to sell their children into slavery, yet another contrast with Roman law, which had begun permitting this in the early fourth century. (Tacitus [*Annals* 4.72.2] reports that in 28 CE the Frisians were forced to sell their children to meet tax dues.) Germanic contact with Romans and Roman slaves appears then to have had little effect on the process of becoming a slave in Germanic society. Capture, birth, and purchase had long been part of Germanic tradition, and the distinctive practice of self-sale was unaffected by the Roman avoidance of this mode of becoming a slave.

In Germanic law, the slave's personality was almost entirely subsumed by that of the master. This meant that any delict committed by a slave was the responsibility of the master, and the composition awarded was accordingly assessed against the master (*PLS* 40.11, 82.2, 121; *LR* 19[18], 23[22]–31[17.2]; *LB* 4.2, 4.7, 50.3–4). By the same token, any offense committed against the slave punishable by composition was credited to the master: if a slave was insulted, harmed, or even killed, the master was awarded the composition or *wergeld* (*PLS* 35.2–9; *LR* 20[19], 22[21], 25[24], 28[27]). If the slave was accused of some offense, the master was also responsible for presenting the slave to the court within a fixed period and was personally liable for fines in case of delays (*PLS* 40.9, 82.1, 88; *LR* 32[30]). Often, rather than pay a composition, the slave's master was allowed, or even required, to permit his slave to be subjected to physical punishment for delicts that a free person would have compensated through money. This generally involved beatings with rods according to a fixed schedule of blows graded according to the offense, but at times punishments entailed castration or even execution (*PLS* 12.1–2, 40.1–5; *LB* 4.2–7, 23.1, 25.2, 27.1–9, 28, 33.4, 63.1, 70.1, 73.2, 89.5, 91, 94.1–5; *LLR* 33). As in so many societies, including Roman, the slave was thus denied the positive assertion of a legal persona to defend his rights, but attributed with one for the negative purpose of punishing his offenses. Furthermore, court procedure dictated that the slave be tortured to establish guilt or innocence, another practice common in the Roman world. Because this process often so compromised the slave physically that he became useless to the master, accusers were obliged to provide the master with the slave's *wergeld* or an alternate slave prior to beating him so that, should he be proved innocent, the master would receive back both the broken slave and a replacement or his monetary worth (*PLS* 40.4–6; *LB* 7.1, 77.1). To spare himself the need to pay composition in the case where a slave murdered a free man, the master could simply turn over the slave to the plaintiff, who would kill him. This was useful in that the slave's value would have been considerably less than the *wergeld* of the victim (*PLS* 35.8, 111; *LB* 2.3, cf. 2.5–6). A similar substitution was also allowed by the Romans (noxal surrender). Thus, as regards crimes and delicts, Germanic and Roman law shared numerous similarities. The fact is, however, that these were common across many slave cultures and probably reflect nothing in the way of cultural interchange. The very basis of the Germanic law of compositions and *wergeld*—in essence, the very basis of Germanic law—was entirely foreign to Roman praxis, making a melding of the two systems unlikely before the production of the *Lex Visigothorum* in the mid seventh century.

The same can be said regarding manumission, for while the Germans seem to have practiced manumission regularly, its methods and consequences differed greatly from those of the Romans. This stemmed largely from the very central fact of manumission in all cultures: just as slavery represented "social death" (Patterson 1982), manumission represented "social rebirth" into the slaveholding culture, with all the particularity that this entailed. Because manumission created new members of the culture, it had to do so in ways that reflected the peculiarity of that culture. Thus, just as Roman manumission was a uniquely Roman social practice, Germanic manumission was as well. Indeed, Germanic manumission was not one thing but came in a variety of forms depending on the tribal state. Even so, as with other areas, commonalities across the codes point to a collective reservoir of tradition. When a master determined to manumit his slave in Germanic society, he was presented with a series of choices. He first had to choose the community into which he wished to manumit the slave, for the barbarian kingdoms accommodated both Roman and Germanic communities and the master could choose to make his former slave a member of either. Second, he had to choose what degree of freedom he wished to grant, for, as with Roman law, some freedmen gained nearly full rights in the community, others only partial. Having answered these questions, the master then chose the requisite procedure.

Such procedures were highly differentiated by culture. The Frankish custom called for the master to toss a penny (*denarius*) before the king. Using this method, a Frank symbolically and legally relinquished all patronage claims to the freedman, who became a full member of the Frankish community, owing patronage rights only to the king (*LR* 60[57], 64[61].3, 65[62].2; cf. *PLS* 26.1–2, VI *Cap.* 5.4). Franks were also permitted to free

their slaves unto Roman citizenship, in which case they used Roman methods (*LR* 64[61].1–4), or into the patronage of the church (*LR* 61[58].1). Burgundian law does not describe manumission procedure in detail but does mention that full freedom could only be gained when a freedman ceremonially offered his master twelve gold solidi, about half the value of an average slave. It also reports that manumission had to take place before seven witnesses and could involve a written charter (*LB* 57, 88; cf. *PLS* VII *Cap.* 11). The Lombards used a ceremony in which the master handed the slave to another free man, who then passed the slave on to a third, and then a fourth, who took the slave to a crossroads and gave him an arrow and whip with the words, "From these four roads you are free to choose where you wish to go." As with the Frankish penny throw, this severed all patronage ties of the master and inducted the freedman into the Lombard community. The Lombards, however, also recognized three other modes of manumission, one by which the king himself granted full freedom, a second in which the slave was "given the choice of the four roads" but not fully released from the master's patronage, and a third involving the partial manumission of a slave, who was denied the choice of the four roads and raised only to the state of an "*aldius*" (*LLR* 224, cf. 222, 225–226; and Paul the Deacon, *History of the Lombards*, 1.13). Apart from the Frankish custom of manumission in a church, which derived directly from a late Roman practice introduced by Constantine (Buckland 1908:449–450; Fabbrini 1965), none of these methods bears any resemblance to Roman practice.

The mention of an *aldius* does, however, introduce yet another area in which Germanic custom differed from Roman (Nehlsen 1972:373–376). Although the Romans did create a compromised citizenship category (Junian Latinity) for some slaves who had not been properly manumitted (Buckland 1908:533–537; Watson 1987:23–34), this halfway status was rare from the fourth century onward and was eliminated by the sixth (Weaver 1990; cf. Mellusso 2000:78–85). Germanic law, by contrast, retained a strong attachment to various forms of half-freedom that resulted not from defects in manumission but from deliberate restrictions imposed on the former slave by the master.

The Lombards, as we have just seen, referred to these half-freedmen as *aldii,* and the Franks (and Alamanni) as *leti* (also *lidi*). Lombardic *aldii* were still largely controlled by their lords, who collected compositions on their behalf, paid the bride-price for their marriages, and supervised the disposition of their property (*LLR* 28, 205, 216, 235). That their status was close to that of slaves is proven by the fact that the *Leges Langobardorum* equate them with household slaves (*servi ministeriales*) for purposes of calculating compositions. Their half-free status was also symbolically enforced by the fact that their *wergeld* and compositions were generally half those of a free man (*LLR* 76–102, 244). If male and female *aldii* married, their children took their same status, thus their half-freedom was a heritable condition (*LLR* 219). Frankish *leti* were similarly valued at half the worth of a free man (*PLS* 42.4, 77.1–2, 83.1–2, 104.9; cf. *LR* 65[62].1). Like slaves, *leti* were also liable to corporal and capital punishment in some instances where a free man would have been permitted to pay a composition (*PLS* 130.1–3). The *Lex Burgundionum* offers fewer indications of half-freedom, or rather, it seems to imply that all freedmen were only half free (*LB* 32.2, 33.2). It also indicates that Burgundians assimilated their farm tenants (*coloni orignarii*) to semi-slaves (*LB* 7.1, 38.8–11). This situation was at least in part derived from Roman practice, for the terminology *colonus originarius,* and likely the phenomenon itself, is borrowed directly from Roman legal practice. Beginning in the late third century, Roman society had begun locking *coloni originarii* into semi-servile status as well (Rosafio 2002). Our understanding of their legal and social situation remains very much unresolved (see Grey 2007), but it is not unreasonable to assume that Germanic and Roman practice among the Burgundians and other successor kingdoms in Gaul may have influenced one another toward the mutual creation of a new type of unfreedom that approximated serfdom.

Finally, a look at marriage and sexual relations rounds out this discussion of the Germanic law of slavery. From the start, Germanic practice stands out from Roman in recognizing the legal possibility of marriage between slaves. Although Roman society gave acknowledgment to long-term affective relationships between male and female, these had no legal force. Slaves in late antique Germanic society, by contrast, could marry legally (see esp. *LLR* 261; cf. Gregory of Tours, *History of the Franks,* 5.3; Nehlsen 1972: 271–272, 367–368). So too, *aldii* and *leti* were able to marry, and their offspring, as we have seen, inherited their status. Difficulties arose, however, when slaves or half-slaves wished to create unions with free men or women. Free men were allowed to marry their slave women provided they freed them first, at least according to Lombard law (*LLR* 222). This also occurred regularly in Roman society. Free Germans who married another's maidservant, however, were reduced to slavery (*PLS* 13.9, 25.3; *LR* 61[58].14–15). If the free man merely fornicated with another's slave or half-slave, even by forceful rape, he was compelled to pay a composition to her master but was not otherwise compromised (*PLS* 25.1–2; *LR* 61[58].9; *LLR* 194, 205–207; *LB* 30.1). Indeed, he could even buy and legitimate his offspring by her (*LLR* 156). Similarly, the free Frank who took another's female half-slave (*lita*) in marriage owed a composition equal to her value but remained free (*PLS* 13.10). The situation was more stringent with free women. These too were enslaved for choosing to marry a slave (*PLS* 13.8, 25.4; *PLS* VII *Cap.* 14; *LR* 61[58].16). But harsher penalties are also indicated, as in a Frankish law making the free woman who attempted to marry a slave an outlaw and granting her relatives the right to kill her with impunity (*PLS* 98.1–2; cf. *LLR* 221; *LB* 35.2–3; Gregory of Tours, *History of the Franks,* 3.29, 4.41). The same law orders the torture and execution of the slave. A Ripuarian law orders the free female the choice of killing her slave lover or living on in servitude with him, and a Lombard law orders the execution of any male slave who dares to marry a free woman (*LR* 61[58].18; *LLR* 221, cf. 193). Little wonder then that the slave male who raped a free female was to be executed (*LB* 35.1; *LR* 38[40]). Even for raping another slave woman, the male slave could be castrated if she died in the attack or given three hundred blows with rods if she lived (*PLS* 25.5–6). Here again, overlap with Roman law is superficial at best. Harsh punishments against rapists who were slaves were also ordered by the Romans, but because the Romans never acknowledged the legal right of slaves to marry, it would never have been possible for a free male to suffer enslavement for marrying another owner's slave woman. Roman women who cohabited with male slaves were, after 54 CE, to be enslaved by the master, but they too were never allowed to consider themselves married. The only point of overlap is thus that Roman free women who cohabited with their own slaves were, from the early fourth century, subject to execution (*Theodosian Code* 9.9.1).

Overall then, the Germanic law codes reflect some points of intersection and many others of divergence between Romans and Germans. On issues such as independent agricultural slave tenants, self-sale into slavery, culturally specific styles of manumission, the punishment of slaves according to compositions, and the recognition of slave marriage, the law codes demonstrate that Germanic slaveholding practices remained very tenacious, even in the face of the external influence of the Roman Empire and the internal influence of Roman citizens and captives within Germanic kingdoms. In other areas, however, cultural exchange is more evident. The equilibrium in slave prices between Germanic and Roman cultures points to the existence of a common market. The cultivation of labor differentiation and use of slaves with individuated skills sets also points to an assimilation of Roman economic and social styles. Finally, the introduction of half-free farm tenants in the Roman west may also indicate influence in the other direction if Germanic manumission practices cross-pollinated relationships of dependence among the Romans. The evidence for regular captivity between Romans and Germans also points to an avenue of cultural interchange. And the role of slaves in the Christian church and use of the church as a vehicle for manumissions points to slavery as a medium of cultural exchange.

Conclusion: Slavery and Cultural Exchange between Romans and the Germans

Captivity and slavery offered an important vector for cultural exchange. Yet, as we have seen with the Germanic laws, this avenue was only left open if the enslaving culture proved in some way receptive to the cultural knowledge carried by the slaves. The various forms of knowledge brought by captives into their new culture were only made

use of selectively depending on the needs of the master culture. Four stories prove the point. In the 50s BCE, Julius Caesar (*Gallic Wars* 6.32; cf. 6.35) needed to cross-check pledges of loyalty brought to him by several German tribes thought to be in revolt against the Romans. To do so, he interrogated captives from these tribes. In 16 CE the Roman general Germanicus launched a naval expedition on the North Sea that was scattered by a storm. Many Roman soldiers wound up captive to neighboring Germans, who sold them as far afield as Britain. Germanicus used an allied German tribe, the Angrivarii, to ransom his men, and when these ex-captives returned, they regaled their commander with tales of "wonders, of violent hurricanes, and unknown birds, of monsters of the sea, of forms half human, half beast like, things they had really seen or in their terror believed" (Tacitus, *Annals*, 2.24). The information was largely mythical—thaumatography fit only for literary retellings. But some of this hard-won local knowledge was also correct and was employed by the Romans as they prepared strategy, tactics, and operations for the invasion of Britain less than forty years later. Third, in the early fifth century, Augustine, the bishop of Hippo (Bona, Algeria), reported that he regularly questioned barbarian captives for information about which African tribes were converting in order to coordinate his efforts to spread the message of Christianity (*Letters*, 199). Finally, in the mid fifth century, Severinus of Noricum learned that a group of barbarian raiders, likely Goths, had raided his village along the middle Danube and taken several captives. He convinced a local military tribune named Mamertinus to hunt them down and free the Roman captives. In so doing, the soldiers also enslaved the marauders and brought them to Severinus, who set them free only on the condition that they return to their homeland and dissuade their fellow Germans from further captive-hunting (Eugippius, *Life of Severinus*, 4; cf. 19, 31). Each of these four figures had his own agenda: Caesar sought immediate diplomatic knowledge, Germanicus recorded tall tales interspersed with strategically important eyewitness testimony, Augustine put captive knowledge to work toward a pastoral program, and Severinus sought to use captives to infiltrate neighboring Germanic groups and thereby control the traffic in captives.

Captive knowledge was thus able to gain a purchase in the dominant culture provided it could be made useful.

Augustine's work of conversion was also carried out in barbarian territories. As already noted, the various Germanic peoples under consideration all converted to Christianity between the fourth and sixth centuries. It is thus important to note that the vehicle of conversion for the Goths, at least, was captivity. The first translation of the Bible into a Germanic language, Gothic, was undertaken by the descendant of Christian captives seized by the Goths during their invasion of Anatolia in the 250s. Ulfilas (Gothic for "Little Wolf") was directly related to a family of Christian clergy transported back to Gothic territory in the wake of these raids. His family, and no doubt other Christian captives, began the process of converting their captors in the later third century (sources in translation at Heather and Matthews 1991:133–153; cf. *Martyrium Athenogeni* 3, 7), and by the mid fourth century, the Christian population among the Gothic Tervingi was large enough that their leadership under-took a wide-scale persecution of Christians that drove Ulfilas and many followers to resettle in Roman territory just south of the Danube (Lenski 1995). Yet the Christian religion continued to grow in Gothic territory, in no small part thanks to the missionary efforts of this child of captives, who went so far as to invent an alphabet, based on the Greek alphabet, with which to begin writing Gothic and then used it to translate the Bible. Indeed, captives are known to have played a role in converting the royal house of Georgia in the Caucasus and Axum on the Horn of Africa as well (sources and discussion at Lenski, Captivity, in press). As a monotheist and socially appealing religion, Christianity had, of course, taken the Roman world by storm in the second through fourth centuries CE. It would seem that this cultural product of the Roman Empire also met with a receptive host among the Germans. It is more than telling, however, that the original vehicle for conversion among the first Germanic group to migrate into the Roman Empire in late antiquity was a captive.

References Cited

Agathias
    Agathiae Myrinaei Historiarum Libri Quinque. Ed. R. Keydell. DeGruyter, Berlin, 1967. Cf. *The Histories*, trans. J. D. Frendo, DeGruyter, Berlin, 1975.

Ammianus
    Ammianus Marcellinus. 3 vols. Trans. J. C. Rolfe. Loeb Classical Library, Harvard University Press, Cambridge, MA, 1935–1940.

Augustine, *Letters*
    Sancti Aureli Augustini Opera. Corpus Scriptorum Ecclesiasticorum Latinorum vol. 57, ed. A. Goldbacher. Tempsky, Vienna, 1887.

Ausonius
    Ausonius. 2 vols. Trans. H. G. Evelyn White. Loeb Classical Library, Harvard University Press, Cambridge, MA, 1919–1921.

Bakker, L.
1993   Raetien unter Postumus—Das Siegesdenkmal einer Juthungenschlacht im Jahre 260 n. Chr. aus Augsburg. *Germania* 71:370–386.

Bales, Kevin
2004   *Disposable People: New Slavery in the Global Economy*. Rev. ed. University of California Press, Berkeley.

Beard, Mary
2007   *The Roman Triumph*. Harvard University Press, Cambridge, MA.

Bieżuńska Małowist, Iza
1984   *La schiavitù nell'Egitto greco-romano*. Bibliotheca di Storia Antica 17. Editori Riuniti, Rome.

Brooks, James F.
2002   *Captives and Cousins: Slavery, Kinship and Community in the Southwest Borderlands*. University of North Carolina Press, Chapel Hill.

Buckland, W. W.
1908   *The Roman Law of Slavery: The Condition of the Slave in Private Law from Augustus to Justinian*. Cambridge University Press, Cambridge.

Burns, Thomas S.
2003   *Rome and the Barbarians, 100 BC–AD 400*. Johns Hopkins University Press, Baltimore.

Caesar, *Gallic Wars*
    C. Iuli Caesaris Commentariorum Libri VII de Bello Gallico. Ed. R. DuPontet. Oxford University Press, Oxford, 1991. Cf. Joseph Pearl, trans., *Caesar's Gallic War*, Barron's, Woodbury.

Capasso, Luigi
2001   *I fuggiaschi di Ercolano: paleobiologia delle vittime dell'eruzione vesuviana del 79 d.C.* L'Erma di Bretschneider, Rome.

Carandini, Andrea, and M. Rosella Filippi
1985   *Settefinestre: Una villa schiavistica nell'Etruria romana.* Panini, Modena.

Cassius Dio
        Dio's Roman History. 9 vols. Trans. Earnest Cary. Loeb Classical Library, Harvard University Press, Cambridge, MA, 1914–1927.

Cecconi, Giovanni Alberto
2002   *Commento storico al libro II dell'epistolario di Q. Aurelio Simmaco.* Giardini Editori, Pisa.

Christes, Johannes
1979   *Sklaven und Freigelassene als Grammatiker und Philologen im antiken Rom.* Franz Steiner, Wiesbaden.

Christie, Neil
1995   *The Lombards.* Blackwell, Oxford.

Claudian
        Claudian. 2 vols. Trans. Maurice Platnauer. Loeb Classical Library, Harvard University Press, Cambridge, MA, 1922.

Codex Euricianus
        Leges Visigothorum. Ed. K. Zeumer. Monumenta Germaniae Historica Leges Nationum Germanicarum I. Hannover, 1902; reprinted 2005.

Cosack, E., and P. Kehne
1999   Ein archäologisches Zeugnis zum germanisch-römischen Sklavenhandel? *Archäologisches Korrespondenzblatt: Urgeschichte, Römerziet, Frühmittelalter* 23:97–109.

Demougeot, E.
1969   A propos des lètes gaulois du iv siècle. In *Beiträge zur alten Geschichte und deren Nachleben: Festschrift für Franz Altheim,* ed. R. Stiehl and H. Stier, pp. 101–13. DeGruyter, Berlin.

De Ste. Croix, Geoffrey
1981   *The Class Struggle in the Ancient Greek World from the Archaic Age to the Arab Conquests.* Cornell University Press, Ithaca, NY.

Digest
        The Digest of Justinian. Latin text ed. T. Mommsen and P. Krueger, English trans. by A. Watson. University of Pennsylvania Press, Philadelphia, 1985.

Drinkwater, John
2007   *The Alamanni and Rome, 213–496 (Caracalla to Clovis).* Oxford University Press, New York.

Dunbabin, Katherine M. D.
2003   The Waiting Servant in Later Roman Art. *American Journal of Philology* 124:443–468.

Eck, Werner, and J. Heinrichs
1993   *Sklaven und Freigelassene in der Gesellschaft der römischen Kaiserzeit.* Wissenschaftliche Buchgesellschaft, Darmstadt.

Elton, Hugh
1996   *Warfare in Roman Europe, AD 350–425.* Oxford University Press, Oxford.

Eugippius, *Life of Severinus*
        Eugippe Vie de Saint Séverin. Sources chrétiennes 374. Ed. Philippe Régerat. Éditions du cerf, Paris, 1991.

Eunapius, *Histories*
        The Fragmentary Classicising Historians of the Later Roman Empire, vol. 2. Ed. R. C. Blockley. Francis Cairns, Liverpool, 1983.

Fabbrini, F.
1965   *La manumissio in ecclesia.* Istituto di diritto e dei diritti del oriente mediterranea, Milan.

Fischer Drew, Katherine
1988   The Family in Visigothic Law. In K. Fischer Drew, ed., *Law and Society in Early Medieval Europe,* study VII. Ashgate, London.

Fitzgerald, William
2000   *Slavery and the Roman Literary Imagination.* Cambridge University Press, Cambridge.

Garnsey, P.
1981   Independent Freedmen and the Economy of Italy under the Principate. *Klio* 64:359–371.

1996   *Ideas of Slavery from Aristotle to Augustine.* Cambridge University Press, Cambridge.

Geary, Patrick
1988   *Before France and Germany: The Creation and Transformation of the Merovingian World.* Oxford University Press, New York.

George, Michele
2000   Family and *familia* on Roman Biographical Sarcophagi. *Mitteilungen des deutschen archäologischen Insituts* 107:192–207.

Geuenich, Dieter
1997   *Geschichte der Alamannen.* W. Kohlhammer, Stuttgart.

Gillett, Andrew (editor)
2002   *On Barbarian Identity: Critical Approaches to Ethnicity in the Early Middle Ages.* Brepols, Turnhout.

Goldsworthy, Adrian
2003   *The Complete Roman Army.* Thames and Hudson, New York.

Green, Carin
2007   *Roman Religion and the Cult of Diana at Aricia.* Cambridge University Press, New York.

Gregory of Tours, *Historia Francorum*
        Gregorii episcopi Turonensis libri historiarum X. Monumenta Germaniae Historica, Scriptorum Rerum Merovingicarum 1.1. Hannover,

1951. Cf. Lewis Thorpe, trans., *Gregory of Tours: The History of the Franks*, Penguin, New York, 1974.

Grey, Cam

2007 Contextualizing *Colonatus*: The *Origo* of the Late Roman Empire. *Journal of Roman Studies* 97:155–175.

Grieser, Heike

1997 *Sklaverei im spätantiken und frühmittelalterlichen Gallien (5.–7. Jh.).* Franz Steiner Verlag, Stuttgart.

Haarnagel, Werner

1979 *Die Grabung Feddersen-Wierde: Methode, Hausbau, Siedlungs- und Wirschaftsformen sowie Sozialstruktur.* Franz Steiner, Wiesbaden.

Hannemann, Bärbel

2006 Römer in Fesseln? In Historisches Museum der Pfalz-Speyer, ed., *Geraubt und im Rhein versunken: Der Barbarenschatz.* Konrad Theiss Verlag, Stuttgart.

Harris, William V.

1980 Towards a Study of the Roman Slave-Trade. In John H. D'Arms and E. C. Kopff, eds., *The Seaborne Commerce of Ancient Rome: Studies in Archaeology and History,* Memoirs of the American Academy in Rome 36, pp. 117–40. American Academy in Rome, Rome.

1994 Child-Exposure in the Roman Empire. *Journal of Roman Studies* 84:1–22.

Heather, Peter

1991 *Goths and Romans, 332–489.* Oxford University Press, Oxford.

1996 *The Goths.* Blackwell, Oxford.

Heather, Peter, and John Matthews

1991 *The Goths in the Fourth Century.* Translated Texts for Historians. Liverpool University Press, Liverpool.

Herrmann-Otto, Elisabeth

1994 *Ex ancilla natus: Untersuchungen zu den "hausgeborenen" Sklaven und Sklavinnen im Westen des römischen Kaiserreiches.* Franz Steiner Verlag, Stuttgart.

Historia Augusta

The Scriptores Historiae Augustae. 3 vols. Trans. David Magie. Loeb Classical Library, Harvard University Press, Cambridge, MA, 1921–1932.

Hopkins, Keith

1978 *Conquerors and Slaves: Sociological Studies in Roman History,* vol. 1. Cambridge University Press, Cambridge.

James, Edward

1982 *The Origins of France from Clovis to the Capetians, 500–1000.* St. Martin's, New York.

1988 *The Franks.* Blackwell, Oxford.

Jolowicz, H. F.

1961 *A Historical Introduction to the Study of Roman Law.* Cambridge University Press, Cambridge.

Jones, C. P.

1987 Stigma: Tattooing and Branding in Graeco-Roman Antiquity. *Journal of Roman Studies* 77:139–155.

Jordanes, *Getica*

Iordanis Romana et Getica. Monumenta Germaniae Historica Auctores Antiquissimi 5.1, ed. T. Mommsen. Berlin, 1882. Cf. C. C. Mierow, trans., *Jordanes: The Origin and Deeds of the Goths,* Princeton University Press, Princeton, NJ, 1908.

Kirschenbaum, A.

1987 *Sons, Slaves and Freedmen in Roman Commerce.* Magnes Press, Jerusalem.

Kleberg, Tönnes

1945 *Mango*—A Semasiological Study. *Eranos* 43: 277–284.

Klingshirn, William

1985 Caesarius of Arles and the Ransoming of Captives. *Journal of Roman Studies* 75:183–203.

Kudlien, Fridholf

1986 *Die Stellung des Arztes in der römischen Gesellschaft: freigeborene Römer, Eingebürgerte, Peregrine, Sklaven, Freigelassene als Ärzte.* Franz Steiner Verlag, Stuttgart.

Kulikowski, Michael

2007 *Rome's Gothic Wars: From the Third Century to Alaric.* Cambridge University Press, Cambridge.

Lander, James

1984 *Roman Stone Fortifications: Variation and Change from the First Century AD to the Fourth.* British Archaeological Reports, Oxford.

Le Bohec, Yann

1994 *The Imperial Roman Army.* Hippocrene Books, New York.

Lenski, Noel

1995 The Gothic Civil War and the Date of the Gothic Conversion. *Greek, Roman and Byzantine Studies* 36:51–87.

In press Captivity and Romano-Barbarian Interchange. In Ralph Mathisen and Danuta Shanzer, eds., *Barbarians in Late Antiquity.* Ashgate, Aldershot.

In press Constantine and Slavery: *Libertas* and the Fusion of Roman and Christian Values. In G. Crifò, ed., *Atti dell'Accademia Romanistica Costantiniana XV.* Pubblicazioni Dell'Università Degli Studi Di Perugia, Perugia.

In prep. Working Models: Functional Art and Ancient Conceptions of Slavery. In Michele George, ed., *Roman Slavery and Roman Material Culture*.

In prep. The Price of Slaves in Late Antiquity.

Laws of the Burgundians (*LB*)
> *Leges Burgundionum*. Monumenta Germaniae Historica, Leges Nationum Germanicarum 2.1, ed. L. R. De Salis. Hannover, 1892; reprinted 1973. Cf. K. Fischer Drew, trans., *The Burgundian Code: Book of Constitutions or Law of Gundobad, Additional Enactments*, University of Pennsylvania Press, Philadelphia, 1949.

Law of the Ripuarian Franks (*LR*)
> *Lex Ribuaria*. Monumenta Germaniae Historica, Leges Nationum Germanicarum 3.2, ed. F. Beyerle and R. Buchner. Hannover, 1951. Cf. T. J. Rivers, trans., *Laws of the Salian and Ripuarian Franks*, AMS Press, New York, 1986.

Libanius, *Oration 18*
> *Libanius Selected Works*. Trans. A. F. Norman. Loeb Classical Library, Harvard University Press, Cambridge, MA, 1969.

Liebs, Detlef

2001   Sklaverei aus Not im germanisch-römischen Recht. *Zeitschrift der Savigny-Stiftung für Rechtsgeschichte* 118:286–311.

2002   *Römische Jurisprudenz in Gallien (2. bis 8. Jahrhundert)*. Duncker und Humblot, Berlin.

Lombardic Edict of Rothair (*LLR*)
> *Leges Langobardorum Rothari*. Monumenta Germaniae Historica, Leges Nationum Germanicarum 6, ed. F. Bluhme. Hannover, 1869. Cf. F. Beyerle, *Die Gesetze der Langobarden*, Weimar, 1947 and 2nd ed., 3 vols., Witzenhausen, 1962–1963; K. Fischer Drew, trans., *The Lombard Laws*, University of Pennsylvania Press, Philadelphia, 1973.

Malchus, *Fragmenta Historica*
> *The Fragmentary Classicising Historians of the Later Roman Empire,* vol. 2. Ed. R. C. Blockley. Francis Cairns, Liverpool, 1983.

Manca Masciadri, M., and O. Montevecchi

1984   *I contratti di baliatico*. Milan.

Martyrium Athenogeni
> *La passion inédite de S. Athénogène de Pédachthoé (BHG 197b)*. Subsidia Hagiographica 75, ed. P. Maraval. Société de Bollandistes, Brussels, 1990.

Maximus of Turin
> *Maximi Episcopi Taurinensis sermones*. Corpus Christianorum Series Latina 23, ed. A. Mutzenbecher. Brepols, Turnhout, 1962.

McCarthy, Kathleen

2000   *Slaves, Masters and the Art of Authority in Plautine Comedy*. Princeton University Press, Princeton, NJ.

Melluso, M.

2000   *La schiavitù nell'età giustinianea: Disciplina giuridica e rilevanza sociale*. Presses Universitaires Franc-Comtoises, Paris.

Millar, Fergus

1984   Condemnation to Hard Labour in the Roman Empire, from the Julio-Claudians to Constantine. *Papers of the British School at Rome* 52: 124–147.

Nehlsen, Hermann

1972   *Sklavenrecht zwischen antike und Mittelalter: Germanisches und römisches Recht in den germanischen Rechtsaufzeichnungen, I: Ostgoten, Westgoten, Franken, Langobarden*. Musterschmidt, Göttingen.

2001   Die Servi, ancillae und mancipia der Lex Baiuvariorum: Ein Beitrag zur Geschichte der Sklaverei in Bayern. In Heinz Bellen und Heinz Heinen, eds., *Fünfzig Jahre Forschungen zur antiken Sklaverei an der Mainzer Akademie*, pp. 505–521. Franz Steiner, Stuttgart, 1950–2000.

Novels of Anthemius (see *Theodosian Code*)

Novels of Valentinian (see *Theodosian Code*)

Orosius
> *Pauli Orosii Historiarum Adversum Paganos Libri VII*. Corpus Scriptorum Ecclesiasticorum Latinorum 5, ed. C. Zangemeister. Vienna, 1882.

Osiek, C.

1981   The Ransom of Captives: Evolution of a Tradition. *Harvard Theological Review* 74:365–386.

Pactus legis salicae
> *Pactus legis salicae*. Monumenta Germaniae Historica, Leges Nationum Germanicarum 4.1, ed. K. A. Eckhardt. Hannover, 1962. Cf. K. Fischer Drew, trans., *The Laws of the Salian Franks*, University of Pennsylvania Press, Philadelphia, 1991.

Panegyrici Latini
> *In Praise of Later Roman Emperors: The Panegyrici Latini*, trans. and comm. C. E. V. Nixon and Barbara Saylor Rodgers. University of California Press, Berkeley, 1994.

Patterson, Orlando

1982   *Slavery and Social Death*. Harvard University Press, Cambridge.

Paul the Deacon
> *Pauli Historia Langobardorum*. Monumenta Germaniae Historica, Scriptores Rerum Germanicarum. Hahn, Berlin, 1878.

Petersen, Lauren
2006   *The Freedman in Roman Art and Art History.* Cambridge University Press, Cambridge.

Priscus
The Fragmentary Classicizing Historians of the Later Roman Empire, vol. 2. Ed. R. C. Blockley. Francis Cairns, Liverpool, 1983.

Procopius
Procopius History of the Wars. 5 vols. Trans. H. B. Dewing. Loeb Classical Library, Harvard University Press, Cambridge, MA, 1914–1928.

Rhomiopoulou, Katerina
2002   A Roman Bronze Lamp in the Form of a Barbarian Prisoner. In C. C. Mattusch, A. Brauder, and S. E. Knudsen, eds., *From the Parts to the Whole: Acta of the 13th International Bronze Congress, May 28–June 1, 1996*, vol. 2, pp. 171–174. Journal of Roman Archaeology, Portsmouth.

Rives, James B.
1999   *Tacitus Germania.* Clarendon, Oxford.

Rosafio, Pasquale
2002   *Studi sul colonato.* Edipuglia, Bari.

Salvian, *On the Governance of God*
Salviani presbyteri massiliensis opera omnia. Ed. F. Pauly. Vienna, 1883. Cf. Jeremiah F. O'Sullivan, trans., *The Writings of Salvian the Presbyter,* New York, 1947.

Sanna, Maria Virginia
2001   *Nuove ricerche in tema di postliminium e redemptio ab hostibus.* Cagliari.

Scheidel, Walter
2005   Human Mobility in Roman Italy, II: The Slave Population. *Journal of Roman Studies* 95:64–79.

Schumacher, Leonhard
2001   *Sklaverei in der Antike: Alltag und Schicksal der Unfreien.* C. H. Beck, Munich.

Seneca
Seneca Epistles 1–65. Trans. R. M. Gummere. Loeb Classical Library, Harvard University Press, Cambridge, MA, 1917.

Sirmondian Constitutions (see *Theodosian Code*)

Sozomen
Sozomenus Kirchengeschichte. Die griechischen christlichen Schriftsteller der ersten Jahrhunderte 4, 2nd ed., ed. Joseph Bidez and Günther Christian Hansen. Akademie Verlag, Berlin, 1995. Cf. Chester D. Hartranft, trans., *The Ecclesiastical History of Sozomen*, Nicene and Post Nicene Fathers of the Church, 2nd series vol. 2, Hendrickson, Peabody, MA.

Steidl, B.
2000   Die Siedlungen von Gerolzhofen und Gaukönigshofen und die germanische Besiedlung am mittleren Main vom 1. Jahrhundert v. Chr. bis zum 4. Jahrhundert n. Chr. In Alfred Haffner and Siegmar von Schurbein, eds., *Kelten, Germanen, Römer im Mittelgebirgsraum zwischen Luxemburg und Thüringen*, pp. 95–113. Habelt, Bonn.

2002   Lokale Drehschreibenkeramik römischer Formgebung aus dem germanischen Mainfranken: Zeugnis für die Verschleppung römischer Reichsbewohner nach Germanien? *Bayerische Vorgeschichsblätter* 67:87–115.

Strabo
Strabo Geography. 8 vols. Trans. H. L. Jones. Loeb Classical Library, Harvard University Press, Cambridge, MA, 1917–1932.

Straus, Jean A.
2004   *L'achat et la vente des esclaves dans l'Egypte romaine: Contribution papyrologique à l'étude de l'esclavage dans une province orientale de l'Empire Romain.* K. G. Saur, Munich.

Stupperich, Reinhard
1997   Export oder Technologietransfer? Beobachtungen zu römischen Metallarbeiten in Germanien. In *Römer und Germanen—Nachbarn über Jahrhunderte*, ed. Clive Bridger and Claus von Carnap-Bornheim, pp. 19–24. British Archaeological Reports, Oxford.

Symmachus
Q. Aurelii Symmachi Quae Supersunt, Monumenta Germaniae Historica 6.1, ed. O. Seeck. Berlin, 1883.

Synesius, *De Regno*
Opere di Sinesio di Cirene: Epistole, Operette, Inni. Ed. A. Garzya. Unione tipografico-editrice torinese, Torino, 1989.

Tacitus, *Annals*
P. Cornelius Tacitus Annales. Ed. H. Heubner. Teubner, Stuttgart, 1983. Cf. A. J. Woodman, trans., *Tacitus: The Annals,* Hackett, Indianapolis, 2004.

Tacitus, *Germany*
Cornelii Taciti opera minora. Ed. M. Winterbottom and R. M. Ogilvie. Oxford University Press, Oxford, 1975. Cf. J. B. Rives, trans., *Tacitus Germania,* Clarendon, Oxford, 1999.

Theodosian Code
Codex Theodosianus, ed. T. Mommsen. Weidemann, Berlin, reprinted 2000. Cf. Clyde Pharr, trans., *The Theodosian Code and Novels and the Sirmondian Constitutions,* Princeton University Press, Princeton, NJ, 1952.

Theophanes
The Chronicle of Theophanes Confessor: Byzantine and Near Eastern History AD 284–813.

Trans. C. Mango and R. Scott. Oxford University Press, Oxford, 1997.

Thompson, E. A.

1960   *Slavery in Early Germany.* In M. I. Finley, ed., *Slavery in Classical Antiquity: Views and Controversies*, pp. 17–29. Heffer and Sons, Cambridge.

1999   *The Huns.* Revised by Peter Heather. Blackwell, Oxford.

Thompson, F. H.

2003   *The Archaeology of Greek and Roman Slavery.* Duckworth, London.

Todd, Malcolm

1992   *The Early Germans.* Blackwell, Oxford.

Turner, R., and R. Scaife

1995   *Bog Bodies: New Discoveries and New Perspectives.* British Museum Press, London.

Van der Sanden, Wijnand A. B.

1996   *Through Nature to Eternity: The Bog Bodies of Northwest Europe.* Batavian Lion International, Amsterdam.

Wallace-Hadrill, J. M.

1982   *The Long-Haired Kings.* University of Toronto Press, Toronto.

Watson, Alan

1987   *Roman Slave Law.* Johns Hopkins University Press, Baltimore.

Weaver, P. R.

1990   Where have all the Junian Latins Gone? Nomenclature and Status in the Early Empire. *Chiron* 20:275–305.

Wells, Peter S.

2003   *The Battle That Stopped Rome: Emperor Augustus, Arminius, and the Slaughter of the Legions in the Teutoburg Forest.* Norton, New York.

1999   *The Barbarians Speak: How the Conquered Peoples Shaped Roman Europe.* Princeton University Press, Princeton, NJ.

Welwei, Karl-Wilhelm

1974–77 *Unfreie im antiken Kriegsdienst.* 3 vols. Forschungen zur antiken Sklaverei 5, 8, 21. Franz Steiner Verlag, Stuttgart.

2000   *Sub corona vendere: Quellenkritische Studien zu Kriegsgefangenschaft und Sklaverei in Rom bis zum Ende des Hannibalkrieges.* Forschungen zur antiken Sklaverei 34. Franz Steiner Verlag, Stuttgart.

Wiedemann, Thomas

1981   *Greek and Roman Slavery.* Routledge, London.

Wolfram, Herwig

1988   *History of the Goths.* Trans. T. J. Dunlap. University of California Press, Berkeley.

1997   *The Roman Empire and Its Germanic Peoples.* Trans. T. J. Dunlap. University of California Press, Berkeley.

Wolters, Reinhard

1991   Der Waren- und Dienstleistungsaustausch zwischen dem Römischen Reich und dem Freien Germanien in der Zeit des Prinzipats. *Münsterische Beiträge zur antiken Handelsgeschichte* 10:78–132.

Wood, Ian (editor)

1998   *Franks and Alamanni in the Merovingian Period: An Ethnographic Perspective.* Boydell, San Marino, CA.

Zöllner, Erich

1970   *Geschichte der Franken bis zur Mitte des sechsten Jahrhundert.* C. H. Beck, Munich.

Zosimus

Zosime Histoire Nouvelle. 3 vols. Ed. and trans. F. Paschoud. Les Belles Lettres, Paris, 1971–1989.

5

The Impact of Captured Women on Cultural Transmission in Contact-Period Philippine Slave-Raiding Chiefdoms

Laura Lee Junker

In the twelfth through sixteenth centuries, the political landscape of the Philippine Islands consisted of numerous chiefdom-type polities of differing ethnicity, languages, and cultural practices on the eastern edge of a vast South China Sea–Indian Ocean maritime trading network that linked the Chinese and Indian empires, Southeast Asia kingdoms, Middle Eastern polities, and even East African kingdoms such as the Swahili (Hall 1985; Junker 1999a; Reid 1988). Maritime raiding expeditions were as significant as foreign trade in the political economy of these chiefdoms, with raids extending throughout island Southeast Asia and even to the Annamese and Siamese states of the mainland (Junker 2003). Slave-taking, particularly involving women captives as sources of labor and marriage partners, was an important conduit for the spread of new technologies, languages, religions, and material culture styles (Hall 1992; Junker 1999b). Contact-period Spanish documents, Chinese accounts dating back to the twelfth century, indigenous Indic-based scripts with elite genealogies, and indigenous oral traditions collected by ethnographers and travelers since the sixteenth century are rich sources of data on the cultural and historical contexts for slave capture and social integration (Junker 1998).

Historical sources suggest that maritime slave-raiding in the Philippines, as elsewhere in South-

east Asia, was widespread by at least the twelfth century AD, and captured female slaves in particular were a major source of wealth and labor for chiefs and other nobility (Tarling 1963; Vink 2003; Warren 1985). Relatively low population levels, a fragmented geography, and an abundance of rich agricultural land in Southeast Asia meant that control of people, rather than land or capital, was key to political power (Reid 1993b; Wolters 1999:164–165; see also Junker 1999a, 2003, 2006). Therefore, it was not surprising that institutionalized forms of slavery were ubiquitous in the region, and more than half of the labor force in some Southeast Asian polities was comprised of captured and debt-bonded slaves (Hoadley 1983; Warren 1985). Historical analysis shows that female slaves in the Philippines were transported from throughout the archipelago, and as far as the Vietnamese, Thai, and Sumatran coasts (Scott 1994; Warren 2002). They were rapidly integrated into local social networks as wives, agricultural workers, and/or craftswomen (particularly textiles and ceramics manufacturers)(Reid 1983a). They presumably were able to introduce new cultural practices and material forms (Salman 2005), but in ways I would argue were culturally contingent and dependent on the circumstances of capture and assimilation.

What is not well studied in Southeast Asia is how power relations involving domination and resistance, historically and culturally contingent forms of interaction, and the women themselves as social agents shaped these cultural encounters and subsequent dynamics of cultural change (Andaya 2000). Recent research on both colonial and noncolonial slavery using multivocal historical sources have shown that captives often have an unexpected degree of agency in negotiating forms of social and economic integration (e.g., Alpers et al. 2005; Larson 2000; Vink 2003) and that women, in particular, as the primary agents for enculturating future generations, are particularly significant in this process (Niemeijer 2000). Archaeological material studies have also illuminated how slaves resist ideological and social repression through subtle infusion of natal symbols and meanings, with artifact analyses often revealing hidden dimensions of social dynamics (e.g., Lightfoot 1995; Orser 2001).

In this chapter, ethnohistoric evidence is used to argue that in Southeast Asian societies supporting what historians call "open slave systems" (Reid 1983a), in which slaves are not socially and economically segregated but rapidly integrated into host communities, foreign women were strong social agents of social and cultural transformation. Ethnohistoric analysis also suggests that certain principles of social organization and common forms of social transaction in premodern Southeast Asia, such as cognatic descent, bride-service and transfers of wealth paid in bride-price by males, and status-associated polygamy, as well as the importance of female labor in agriculture, made the large-scale capture of female slaves a particularly attractive economic and social strategy for these societies. The relatively high value of women in both economic production and social reproduction also promoted rapid incorporation of foreign social identities by female slaves and their children.

Because women are known through ethnographic work and historical accounts to have been the primary earthenware pottery manufacturers and textile weavers in complex Philippine societies (Fenner 1985; Junker 1994a; Longacre and Skibo 1994; Scott 1994), the analysis of textile designs and pottery vessels in communities with historically known slave-raiding activities can provide additional insights into this process of technology and design transfer in interethnic

slave-taking. Long-term archaeological research has been carried out within the historically known Tanjay chiefdom of the twelfth through sixteenth centuries on the island of Negros in the central Philippines. The coastal polity center has been extensively excavated, and dozens of additional settlements of this period within the chiefdom's approximately 300 km² territory have been excavated and mapped (Junker 1994b, 1996, 1999a, 2002). Prehispanic burials with metal weapons, male warrior insignia, and evidence of traumatic deaths, as well as settlement fortifications and weapons in household contexts, document changing patterns of warfare and interpolity raiding since at least the twelfth century AD (Junker 1999b).

Archaeological work in Tanjay has also yielded abundant earthenware pottery from dozens of settlements and burial contexts that have allowed us to relate these changes in the scale and intensity of slave-raiding to changes in ceramics, which according to historical sources were produced largely by indigenous and captive women. Archaeologists have long recognized that variation in stylistic components of craft design generally reflect culturally influenced production norms and patterns of social interaction between craft producers (e.g., Good 2001; Hegmon 1992). In situations of cultural contact involving female captives, we would expect to see the movement of designs but not raw materials, unlike patterns characteristics of long-distance trade. In the second half of this chapter, earthenware pottery designs from the Tanjay region are examined with reference to contemporaneous large-scale maritime raiding polities such as Sulu, Cebu, and Manila in an effort to document the flow of innovative ceramic designs from likely "captive" polities to probable "captor" polities. Of significance is an upsurge in the diversity of decorative designs at all archaeologically studied polities of the fifteenth and sixteenth centuries—diversification that may reflect the historically known expansion of slave-raiding and import of foreign potters as local laborers in this period. Archaeological and historical studies discussing technological innovation during the early historic period of emerging Southeast Asia kingdoms and chiefdoms have tended to focus on male trader-raiders spreading new languages, writing systems, ideologies, and technologies. This view ignores certain features of culture contact in island Southeast Asia during the first millennium AD to mid second millennium AD rise of maritime trading and raiding polities: more women were being transported through slave-raiding than men, captured women were more likely to become permanently fixed in foreign communities, and these "foreign" women were the primary transmitters of hybrid cultural knowledge (including multilingualism) to the succeeding generation of children. It is also suggested that the assumption often made by archaeologists that technological and design innovations generally flow from larger-scale and more regionally powerful polities may not be warranted in a political landscape in which slave-raiding and transport of female craft workers is a primary component of the political economy.

Chiefly Polities and Slave-Raiding in the Philippines

The study of slave-raiding and women's labor in the prehispanic Philippine chiefdoms benefits from unusually rich and diverse sources of empirical data (see Junker 1998 and 1999a:29–53 for a summary of these sources). Due to the participation of Philippine polities in Chinese tributary trade from at least the tenth century, we have numerous Chinese sources spanning five centuries prior to European contact. Combined with contemporaneous Southeast Asian Indic-based texts and abundant Spanish contact-period records, these documents comprise a substantial historical record.[1] Many of the traditional chiefdoms, particularly the Islamic polities of the south, persisted as semiautonomous entities until the early twentieth century and continued slave-raiding activities until at least the late nineteenth century, well after the early penetration of these regions by trained ethnographers, whose writings are also valuable additions to descriptions of slave capture and impacts on the economy and social life of these societies.[2] In contrast, until recently, there has been almost no archaeological work done on slave-raiding in the Philippines (and Southeast Asia in general), and the present study builds on more-generalized archaeological investigations on warfare carried out in the Tanjay region, where a small-scale, maritime-

oriented chiefdom existed between at least the twelfth century and European contact (Junker 1999a, 2001b, 2003).

Political Landscapes in the Late Prehistoric and Early Historic Philippines

By at least the later part of the first millennium AD, the coastlines and major river valleys of the Philippine islands were occupied by numerous chiefdoms of varying complexity (Figure 5.1). Ethnographic and historic sources, along with archaeological work, document a complex cultural landscape, with the upland interior of the islands occupied by ethnically and linguistically diverse tribal swidden farming populations and mobile foraging groups who interacted through river-based trade with the larger-scale, maritime-oriented polities on the coast—a pattern of political fragmentation and economic specialization quite common to premodern Southeast Asia in general (Junker 1999a, 2002, 2003). Archaeological evidence from Philippine burial sites suggests that complex societies may have initially emerged along the coasts and inner river valleys in the island archipelago by the first millennium BC (Hutterer 1977; Junker 1999a, 2003). However, both historical and archaeological data indicate that considerably larger-scale chiefdoms and, in some cases, Islamic sultanates evolved at Manila, Cebu, Jolo (the Sulu polity), Cotabato (the Magindanao polity), and several other coastal centers in the few centuries just prior to European contact (Hutterer 1973; Junker 1994b, 1999a; Nishimura 1992; Peralta and Salazar 1974; Warren 1985).

Archaeological evidence and Chinese records show that porcelain, metalwork, and other exotic items from China, India, and Southeast Asian kingdoms were entering the Philippine archipelago by the late first millennium AD, and explicitly identified Philippine polities were launching competitive trade missions to the Chinese court by the tenth century.[3] However, foreign trade increased throughout the early second millennium AD, reaching its zenith in terms of trade volume and frequency of two-way voyaging during the late fourteenth- to mid sixteenth-century height of political development in the archipelago (Fox 1967; Hutterer 1977; Locsin and Locsin

1967; Wu 1959). The politically fragmented landscape of polities in the Philippines thus became the easternmost terminus of a vast luxury goods trade network linking empires, kingdoms, and chiefdoms ringing the Indian Ocean and the South China Sea, and scattered among the island archipelagos of Southeast Asia (Hall 1985, 1992; Wheatley 1971). This cosmopolitan maritime trading world brought Philippine traders and raiders into direct and frequent contact with foreigners and their exotic technologies, ideologies, and resources.

Despite a wealth of historical evidence and archaeological work at what are clearly maritime-oriented polity centers in the Philippine archipelago,[4] long-term and regional-scale archaeological investigations have been carried out only on the relatively small-scale chiefdom centered on the Tanjay region of Negros Island in the central Philippines (Figure 5.1). This polity never launched a trade mission to the Chinese court or figured prominently in foreign trade records, but it has yielded archaeological evidence for a thriving 30–50 hectare coastal port in the sixteenth century, vigorous foreign trade between the twelfth and sixteenth centuries, and an increasingly complex regional settlement system in the thousand years prior to Spanish contact. Archaeological work has been conducted in the 315 km^2 Tanjay region for more than twenty-five years, involving systematic regional survey within the coastal zone and associated uplands within the Tanjay River basin, as well as excavations at the coastal center of Tanjay and more than a dozen sites spanning the early second millennium BC to mid second millennium AD (see Hutterer 1981; Hutterer and Macdonald 1982; Junker 1990, 1994, 1998, 1999a for syntheses of the Bais-Tanjay Project research) (Figure 5.2).

Archaeological investigations in the Tanjay region suggest that the polity of Tanjay, like a significant number of other Philippine polities known primarily through historical sources, expanded in scale and complexity in the fifteenth and sixteenth centuries in conjunction with growing reliance on trade in foreign prestige goods (Junker 1990). The emergence of a three-tiered settlement hierarchy and a larger and more complexly organized coastal center was accompa-

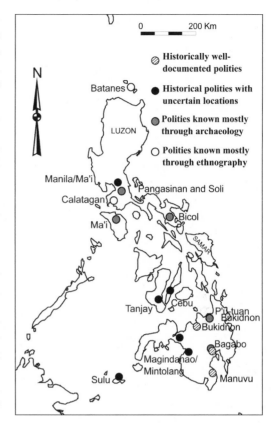

FIGURE 5.1. Locations of tenth- to nineteenth-century chiefdoms and Islamic sultanates in the Philippines, based on Chinese trade records, Spanish contact-period accounts, nineteenth- to early twentieth-century ethnographic research, and archaeological investigations. The map includes the European contact-period polity of Tanjay, which has archaeologically known prehispanic occupation layers dated from ca. AD 500 to the late 1500s.

nied by escalating status competition and wealth circulation evidenced in household and burials (Junker 1999a; Junker et al. 1994), greater emphasis on large-scale competitive feasting as shown in porcelain assemblages and feasting foods in household midden contexts (Junker 2001a), the emergence of more-specialized and centrally administered craft production systems involving both luxury goods and mundane ceramics (Junker 1994a), expanded river-based trade networks between foragers and farmers (Junker 1996, 2002), and increased indicators of conflict between rival polities or the region's culturally distinct tribal and lowland groups (Junker 2003;

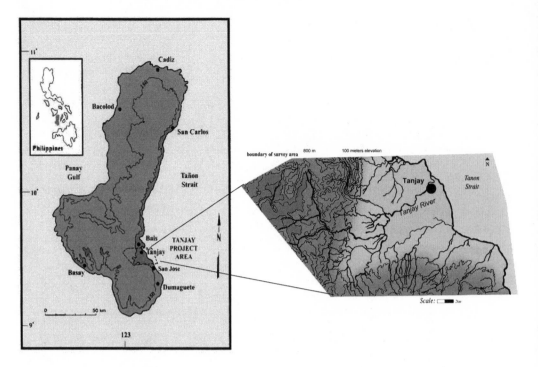

FIGURE 5.2. The island of Negros in the Philippine archipelago. Inset shows the 315 km² Tanjay coastal region.

see also Bacus 1995; Dizon, pers. comm., 2001; Hutterer 1977; Nishimura 1992).

Evidence for escalating violence and defensive tactics in the Tanjay region by the fifteenth century includes the construction of defensive fortification, the first appearance of violence in burials (detached skulls, skeletal trauma, and a mass burial), and expanded metals production (likely for weapons manufacture) (Junker 1999a:336–369, 1999b, 2001b). Although the indicators of conflict are ambiguous about whether it involved large-scale interpolity warfare or briefer and more targeted raids associated with slave-taking, of significant interest is the appearance of male burials in this period containing historically reported emblems of prowess as a maritime raider: filed and gold-pegged teeth, ornaments incorporating boar's teeth, decapitated skulls, and bronze and iron weaponry (Junker 1999b). We cannot be certain, but in the absence of historical records, the traumatic injuries in the burials suggest that in at least the instances represented, the Tanjay population were the victims of unknown aggressors.[5] If consistent with historic accounts of maritime raids, Tanjay probably lost more community members to slave-capture than to violent death (as discussed in more detail in the next section). What is significant about the Tanjay archaeological evidence is that we can study changes in economic patterns, particularly the importing or exporting of ceramic technologies and styles, that are contemporaneous with the upsurge in slave-raiding and may be directly associated with the consequent movement of ceramic-producing women between regions within the archipelago.

Slave-Raiding in the Philippines

Relatively low population levels, a fragmented geography, and an abundance of rich agricultural land in most regions of Southeast Asia meant that control of people rather than land or capital was the key to political power (see Junker 2003, 2006). Both anthropologists and historians have pointed to these demographic and ecological factors, as well as the general absence of strongly territorial unilineal descent groups, as significant in the formation of "decentralized" political structures (often termed "segmentary" polities, "galactic" polities, or "theater states") characteristic of Southeast Asian complex societies (e.g., Geertz 1973:331–338, 1980:11–25; Kiefer 1972b; Leach 1965:56–59; Tambiah 1976:69; Winzeler 1981:462; see also Junker 1999a:57–84, 2003). In the Philippines, as elsewhere in Southeast Asia, political authority relied not on control over fixed territorial bases, but on cultivating ties of personal loyalty, commanding productive labor, and expanding one's power base of followers through elaborate and continual ceremonial circulation of prestige goods (Junker 2003). In societies in which an individual's labor was a valuable asset, it is not surprising that institutionalized forms of slave-raiding would become an integral part of the social and economic fabric (Reid 1983a:156–157, 1983b:8). Many Southeast Asian precolonial cities (e.g., Angkor, Ayutthaya, Melaka, Johor, Aceh, Brunei, Manila, and Makassar) were fueled economically as much by slave-raiding as maritime trading, and slaves and their labor were the most valuable form of movable property (Mabbett 1983; Manguin 1983:210; Reid 1993b:13; Thomaz 1993:75, 82–86) (Figures 5.3 and 5.4).

There is a long-term link between the development of long-distance maritime trading systems in Southeast Asia and the rise of sea-based slave-raiding and plundering. As early as the mid first millennium AD, the Cham polities of southern Vietnam aggressively sought to maintain a monopoly on maritime trade through almost continual raiding of the coastal ports of rival trade polities, as well as seaborne piracy against trading vessels headed for these foreign ports (Hall 1985:178–181, 1992:252–260; Taylor 1992:153–157). Historical analysis has shown that maritime raiding of rival coastal trading ports and seizure of slaves increased during times of greater political fragmentation, when individual polities may have suffered a loss in direct trade revenues (Hall 1992:259). Many historically known Southeast Asian maritime trading polities protected their sea lanes by establishing special relationships with ethnically distinct seafaring populations who could either escort a foreign ship or plunder it on the ruler's command, and whose specialty was sweeping adjacent coasts to seize slaves to support the economy of coastal ports (Junker 1999a:343–345). For example, the late first millennium AD Srivijaya polity used the

"*orang laut*," a traditional seafaring group living on the islands and coasts near Palembang and Jambi and both linguistically and ethnically distinct from the Srivijayan population, as its maritime security force along its sea routes (Andaya and Andaya 1982:25; Wolters 1967:187). Slave-raiding and trading, like warfare and trade in general in human societies (e.g., Keeley 1996), were related activities since wide-ranging trade expeditions to foreign ports brought Southeast Asian peoples expanded knowledge of geography, resources, and opportunities that could be exploited through maritime raiding.

Chinese sources going back to the tenth century, Spanish contact-period records, and ethnographic accounts of the nineteenth century describe the Philippine island archipelago in which slave-raiding was a ubiquitous component of local political economies and a deeply engrained "value" in local ideologies of male prestige in the coastal Philippine chiefdoms. A thirteenth-century Chinese text provides a vivid description of probable central Philippine maritime raiders (known as the Pi-ye-sha or "painted ones," probably tattooed), who created fear along the western littoral of the Philippines and even reputedly attacked the Cham of the southern Vietnam coast in the early second millennium AD, seizing slaves and prestige goods from coastal settlements (Laufer 1907:253–255; Scott 1984:74–75). Early Spanish *relaciones* and other writings were unanimous in emphasizing that maritime raiding was perpetual and large-scale, although there was a certain seasonal periodicity and predictability to sea raids related to the labor demands of the agricultural cycle and seasonal sailing conditions (Rada 1569; Morga 1609:287). The seizure of resources (particularly slaves, but also agricultural stores, metal weaponry, and elite paraphernalia) was the primary motivating factor in the maritime and river-based raids that were launched against competing polities, upland tribal groups, and even groups outside the archipelago (e.g., Chirino 1604:305–308; Morga 1609: 292; Loarca 1582:117; see also Baumgartner 1977 and Mallari 1986). Like the "specialist-raiders" of the Srivijayan polity on Sumatra, the Iranun, Ilanun, Balangingi, and other groups developed clientage relationships with the expanding Sulu and Magindanao maritime-trading polities,

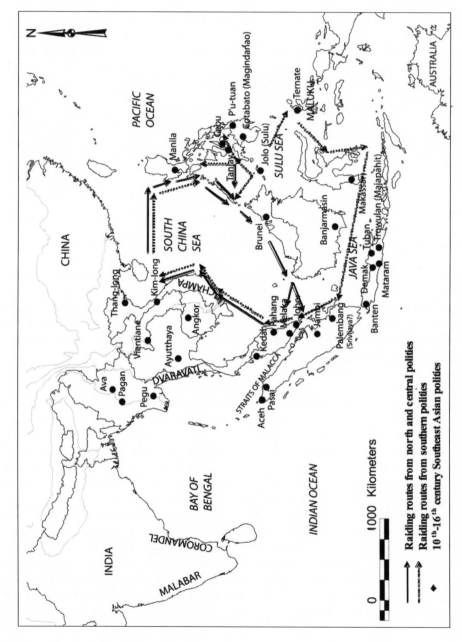

FIGURE 5.3. Locations of the primary Southeast Asian maritime trading/raiding polities of the eleventh through sixteenth centuries and major maritime raiding routes.

FIGURE 5.4. A Sulu slave-raiding ship of the eighteenth century and a Sulu chief wearing imported Chinese silk pantaloons and carrying a Sumatran bronze sword with ivory inlays.

carrying out slave-raiding expeditions that provided a constant inflow of labor to the Sulu, Magindanao, and Maranao polities to which they were attached in exchange for wealth and influence (Warren 1985:149–171, 2002). Warren (2002: 167) notes that while chiefs or other hereditary elites were most often the sponsors of such slave raids, ambitious individuals could take on the high risk and high cost of commanding a raiding vessel and enhance their chances at wealth, rank, and political ascendancy. The significance is that warriors/slave raiders often functioned independently of political leaders, as a group or as individuals, with their own economic, political, and social motivations and agendas for raiding activity. Hence, the experiences of slaves and their social integration into new communities likely varied according to the desires and ambitions of the raiding party and their social history.

James Warren's (1985, 2002) studies of slavery in the Sulu polity emphasize the significance of slave-raiding not only as an economic institution, but also in political competition to build power bases. Both Warren and Reid (1983a) suggest that competition to acquire slaves through raiding and through debt-bondage increased in general during periods of significant economic stress and political fragmentation within Southeast Asia. During such times, elite entrepreneurs within Southeast Asia kingdoms and

chiefdoms were particularly keen to augment their labor resources and political following, and even the "slaves" themselves sometimes participated willingly in creating a relationship of servitude and dependency with a powerful patron by "pawning" themselves to obtain subsistence and protection (see discussion of the debt-bondage route to slavery below). The fifteenth and sixteenth centuries saw a massive upsurge in brutal trade competition and wealth accumulation for savvy elites and would-be elites in both China and Southeast Asia in the maritime luxury goods trade, as large-scale illicit or contraband trade resisted Ming Chinese efforts to maintain the strongly regulated trade of the Sung period (Ts'ao 1962:429–432). These centuries also saw the development of generally more diffuse centers of political power rather than domination by a few large polities (Hall 1985:222–231). Not surprisingly, the fifteenth and sixteenth centuries show a well-documented expansion in slave-raiding activities as maritime-trading entrepreneurs sought to support their political expansion against rivals through both more foreign wealth and slave-producers under their control (Reid 1983a). Thailand and Java, with large and relatively stable single polities controlling their political landscape, imported comparatively modest numbers of slaves, but Bali, southern Sulawesi, Nias, and the Philippines, with politically

FIGURE 5.5. In contact-period Philippines, slaves were key to agricultural production and performed various farming and food-processing tasks. Munilo Velardo map inset, 1734.

fragmented political landscapes and significant interpolity conflict and economic competition, were slave-raiding centers within Southeast Asia (Reid 1983a:18).

Individuals seeking to expand their power bases required additional surplus to support a growing number of specialist producers and foreign traders, making slave-raiding a particularly attractive strategy for increasing the labor under their control (Junker 1999a). Captured slaves served as agricultural workers, craftsmen, oarsmen on trading and raiding expeditions, household servants, and in other economically productive capacities (e.g., Alcina 1688a:161–179; Legaspi 1569:38; Maldonado 1575:180; see also Cole 1913; Gibson 1990; Scott 1994) (see Figure 5.5). As presented in more detail below, the numbers of captured slaves and their impact on the economy and social makeup of slave-taking communities were enormous, with the Sulu sultanate importing several thousand slaves per year and using slave labor for approximately 50 percent of their agricultural and craft production workforce. It is unlikely that the smaller Philippine polities absorbed these stunning percentages of "foreigners" into their communities, but

as noted below in the detailed discussion of labor capture, even in small communities chiefs controlled slaves in the hundreds (many undoubtedly from ethnically distinct communities), making a sizeable impact on the economy and cultural diversity of the slave-raiding community which exported them. The comparatively larger surplus gained through this form of labor capture could then, in turn, be "invested" by chiefs and other rising power brokers to attract a larger warrior force through sponsoring ritual feasts and strategically distributing prestige goods. Historical and ethnographic sources suggest that captured slaves were also directly invested in bride-wealth (e.g., Ileto 1971:34–40; Santa Ines 1676:90; see also Scott 1983:141–144), allowing powerful warriors, chiefs, and other participants in slave-raiding to create affinal ties that were significant in raising a fighting force for future military actions. A larger military force and superior weaponry (obtained through local production, trading, and/or raiding) would therefore allow further expansion of raiding activities.

Not surprisingly, participation in the slave-raiding activities that were so critical to Philippine chiefly political economies was reinforced through ideologies of warrior prestige. Warriors who had undertaken a great number of raids and returned with substantial booty and captives were rewarded with social rank and status insignia that were often commensurate with that of the chiefly (*datu*) class (e.g., Alcina 1688a:14; Boxer Codex 1590b:383; Morga 1609:175). The vast majority of contact-period Philippine "myths" or "epic tales" collected by Spanish writers (see particularly work by Alcina [1688a:20–23, 77–78, 1688b:165–169, 277–278]) and oral traditions recorded by more recent ethnographers and historians (e.g., Eugenio 2001; Unabia 2000; Manuel 1958; Scott 1994:166–169) are peopled by warrior-elites or-namented in the status insignia of their rank who raid neighboring populations, foreigners, or later Europeans through a combination of daring and magical power. Spanish sources suggest that epic stories were not written in native Philippine scripts (see Scott 1984) but were presented orally in pre-war rituals and on other ceremonial occasions, similar to the emotionally inflaming pre-war speeches of Maori chiefs (Vayda 1966). In these tales, it is the taking of numerous captives that earns the greatest renown, and only second-arily the seizure of a large "booty" in gold jewelry, Chinese porcelain, and bronze gongs, and the valor displayed in slaying enemies. In one traditional Visayan "hero" epic recorded by the Spaniard Francisco Alcina (1688a:175), a raider is praised for the remarkable feat of capturing 220 men and women in a series of daring maritime and land-based raiding expeditions, but his exploits in killing enemies is downplayed.[6] This ideology of warrior prestige and supernatural power, as much as anticipated economic gain, helped flame male desire to participate in the endless raids against both neighbors and foreigners, and to concentrate their efforts on prestigious and economically lucrative slave-capture rather than human slaughter.

Slaves brought into Philippine communities were polyglot and multicultural, a fact evident in a Malay-speaking Sumatran slave who guided the return voyage to Europe after Magellan's death at the hands of a Mactan chief (Pigafetta 1521:68–70); the presence of Bornean, Sumatran, and Thai women in the noble courts of the Sulu and Manila sultanate (Legaspi 1567:55; Kiefer 1972b); and the almost Southeast Asia–wide voyages of the Iranun and Balangingi slave-raiders hired by the southern sultanates (Warren 2002:167). The implications are that the slaves would bring in new languages, new cultural practices, new religions,[7] new technologies, new styles or designs associated with crafts (textiles, metalwork, pottery, etc.), new culinary and subsistence practices, and other foreign introductions. As noted above and expanded on below, the sheer numbers of imported foreigners (up to 50 percent of the population in Sulu in the seventeenth and eighteenth centuries) and a strong tendency not to isolate slaves in separate communities but to integrate them very rapidly into local kin groups (see below) suggest that these social, economic, and cultural impacts would not be insignificant and would not be easily absorbed without often dramatic changes within the slave-taking community. The main focus in the discussion below is on the archaeologically visible introductions of new technologies, particularly those introduced by women, but it is interesting to note here some of the strong evidence that Philippine groups, particularly those most actively involved in long-distance trade and slave-raiding, exhibited these trends towards multiculturalism and cosmopolitanism in language, religion, technology, and cultural norms—likely a reflection to some degree of the continual presence of foreign slaves at various stages of cultural assimilation. Early historic texts invariably emphasize the multilingual nature of most Philippine groups, and Philippine languages are full of borrowed vocabulary both from within and outside the archipelago (Scott 1994). As emphasized by historian O. W. Wolters (1999:158–159), polyglot proficiency and "ethnic fluidity" (i.e., the ability to situationally change your self-identified ethnicity) were critical cultural features of Southeast Asian societies due to the strong emphasis on foreign trade, the enforced movement of individuals through slave-raiding, and the personalized nature of political relations. Technical, trade-related, and ritual vocabularies appear to have been the first foreign vernacular elements to enter communities through these types of contacts, and women captives were likely significant conduits for introducing not only new technologies and cosmologies, but also a vocabulary to describe them.

Economic Integration and Labor Capture

Hereditary chiefs (known as *datus*) and other individuals seeking to expand their power bases required additional surplus to support a growing number of specialist producers and foreign traders, making slave-raiding a particularly attractive strategy for increasing the labor under their control (Junker 1999a). Early Spanish accounts emphasize the tremendous economic significance of an institutionalized slave class: "These slaves constitute the main capital and wealth of the natives of these islands, since they are both very useful and necessary for the working of their farms. Thus, they are sold, exchanged, and traded, just like any other article of merchandise, from village to village, from province to province, and indeed from island to island" (Morga 1609:274). Captured slaves, both male and female, were a major source of economic wealth for chiefs and rising elites, serving their captors as agricultural workers, craftsmen, oarsmen on trading and raiding expeditions, household servants, and in other economically productive capacities (e.g., Alcina 1688a:161–179; Guitérrez 1636:207; Legaspi 1569: 38; Maldonado 1575:180; Rada 1569:50; see also Cole 1913; Gibson 1990; Scott 1994). The comparatively larger surplus gained through this form of labor capture could then, in turn, be "invested" by chiefs and other rising power brokers to attract a larger warrior force through the sponsoring of ritual feasts and the strategic distribution of prestige goods. Historical and ethnographic sources suggest that captured slaves were also directly invested in bride-price (e.g., Ileto 1971:34–40; Santa Ines 1676:90; see also Scott 1983:141–144), allowing powerful warriors, chiefs, and other participants in slave-raiding to create affinal ties that were significant in raising a fighting force for future military actions. Female slaves were also frequently added to polygamous harems of high-status individuals as secondary wives (Cole 1913), where they bore "free" children and within one generation were almost completely assimilated into the social fabric of their captor community (see below).

The economist Henry Schwalbenberg (1993) has analyzed large-scale slave-raiding in the Philippines as a well tuned strategy for redistributing labor within the archipelago. According to his model, environmental diversity, the highly variable potential productivity of local resource bases, and unevenly distributed populations would have resulted in strong differentials between regions in terms of labor productivity. The chiefdoms in particularly "rich" environments (such as the wide and rich river valleys and productive coral reef–fringed coastlines associated with the Sulu, Magindanao, and Manila polities) would enjoy relatively high labor productivity relative to chiefdoms in more limited environments with the same size labor force because the former society could easily absorb additional laborers without reaching the point where added labor costs outweighed output (in keeping with the economic principle of "declining labor output" best illustrated by Geertz's and Boserup's concept of "agricultural involution"). These ecologically favored but labor-poor polities would have had strong incentives to obtain more workers since this would increase both necessary output (i.e., to feed workers) and elite surplus to invest. Another factor in labor capture was social: given the relative lack of mobility of laborers, who were traditionally attached by strong clientage ties or bondage to regional elite, slave-raiding played an analogous role to a competitive labor market. Instead of offering higher wages, richer polities with larger warrior contingents could forcibly transfer workers from areas with lower productive potential.

That the addition to local labor forces was substantial is suggested by Spanish estimates of the numbers of slaves controlled by a typical lower-ranking chief, or *datu*, as ranging between one hundred and three hundred (e.g., Alcina 1688a: 227; Bobadilla 1640:331; Santa Ines 1676:85). Nobility in the larger-scale polities frequently controlled well over a thousand slave workers. In 1870, two upper valley Magindanao *datu*s, Datu Utu of Buayan and the sultan of Kabuntalan, are reported to have each owned several thousand slaves (Ileto 1971:35), including some obtained from distant islands through upriver trade with the coastal Magindanao sultanate (Beckett 1982:396), and others from the Mindanao interior obtained through upland raids against tribal swidden-farming groups such as the Tiruray (Schlegel 1979). In terms of sheer numbers of foreign captives, the Islamic polities of Mindanao (particularly Sulu, Magindanao, and Maranao) appear to have been the major Philippine aggressors in slaving expeditions both within and outside the archipelago in the sixteenth century (Herrera 1573:147; Sande 1578:176) and into the colonial period (Reid 1983b:31; Tarling 1963: 146; Warren 1985:147–211). Warren estimates that between 200,000 and 300,000 foreign slaves were brought into the Sulu sultanate between 1770 and 1870 (averaging 2,000–3,000 per year transported on 60 to 200 seagoing vessels), and during this period more than 50 percent of the population of Jolo Island (the capital of the Sulu sultanate), was comprised of foreign slaves (1985: 208–209). While Schwalbenberg's labor mobility model is based strictly on a generalized form of economic theory and is simplistic in its lack of attention to specific historical and social contexts in the Philippines, it is consistent with the fact that the most active slave raiders in the archipelago, and the polities with the most reliance on slave labor, are found in the regions with some of the richest terrestrial and maritime environments.

In his study of Sulu slavery, Warren (1985, 2002) argues that Sulu-captured slaves were rapidly integrated into the polity's social and economic fabric. Female slaves were used to make and sell pottery, cloth, and food at local markets or to foreign traders at the port, to perform certain types of agricultural labor, to entertain and serve in *datus'* residences, and to function as secondary wives to prominent men. Male slaves performed agricultural labor, served as oarsmen in maritime trading expeditions, procured export goods such as trepang (sea slug) and pearls, worked as woodworkers and metalsmiths, served as warriors on raids (even participating in capturing other slaves to augment a chief's workforce), and functioned as interpreters in encounters with foreigners (since the vast majority spoke languages other than Tausug). Warren (1985:221) suggests that during its height in the fifteenth through eighteenth centuries, Sulu was developing a "slave mode of production" in agriculture and crafts that freed up the local retinues of Sulu nobility to pursue their trading and raiding interests full-time, somewhat akin to what Leach describes for the Kachin of Myanmar (1965:232).

However, historian Anthony Reid points out the importance of "distinguishing between slave workers who were centrally managed and who thus made possible a scale of production not otherwise available in a household-oriented economy, and the majority whose bondage merged into a kind of serfdom or household membership" (1983b:22). Reid would reserve the former for commercial production of goods such as textiles, large-scale transport by slaves, and other maritime-trade-related production activities that occupied the bulk of the slaves at very large port cities such as Melaka, Brunei, and Johor in the fifteenth and sixteenth centuries (Reid 1983b:23; see also Kathirithamby-Wells 1993:129 and Thomaz 1993:75). Analysis of historically well-documented systems of slave labor in the Philippines suggest that most slave production was at the household level, that captured foreign slaves quickly became integrated into local kin networks, and that slaves tended to stay within their captor's community even when the possibility of return to their native locale arose. Sulu farm slaves, while cooperatively working the land of their captors, provided for their own subsistence from often distant fields and gardens assigned to them by their masters, remitting a fixed portion of the crops that passed up the tributary hierarchy, similar to taxes paid by non-slave Tausug (Figure 5.6) (Warren 1985:221–222).

Similarly, textile workers, potters, goldsmiths, carpenters, pearl divers, and other crafts specialists in the Sulu polity who produced luxury goods for elite consumption and trade (many of whom, particularly potters and textile workers, were women) were supported in the households of their captors, who provided them with raw materials and subsistence support from household stores to produce these goods full-time (Alcina 1688a:96–131; Cole 1913:85–86; Dampier 1697:297; Manuel 1971; Morga 1609:292–293; see also Fenner 1985:16–20; Scott 1994; Warren 1985: 222). The sponsored production and elite provisioning of craftspersons described by Spanish observers and early ethnographers are consistent with Earle's (1987) definition of "attached specialization," suggesting that crafts manufacture by slaves was little differentiated from that provided by "commoner" craftsmen in these societies. Significantly, many of these accounts also suggest that the craft producers, like primarily farming slaves, were allowed to produce and market some

FIGURE 5.6. Drawing of Muslim woman of unknown origin captured by Sulu raiders in 1830.

Women Slaves and Social Assimilation

It is the movement out of slave status and "foreignness"—that is, social assimilation into the captor community—that is significant in the transmission of new technologies, new styles of prestige goods such as fancy pottery and textiles, and even new languages, cosmologies or religions, and cultural practices into Southeast Asian communities, resulting in the cosmopolitan feel of maritime trading centers described by Europeans at contact. Women, as the captives who were most likely to remain in their captor communities and as the primary agents for enculturating future generations in these Philippine societies, were particularly significant in this process.

According to historical accounts, women slaves entered and assimilated into foreign communities in several ways (Junker 1999a:131–137): (1) as foreign laborers and/or potential wives who were captured in general raiding sweeps along the coastlines; (2) as foreign females specifically targeted as marriageable spouses in bride-capture; (3) as slaves controlled by other groups that were exchanged as part of bride-wealth or other social debts between communities; and (4) as women who were sent into debt-bondage slavery by their own kinsmen to satisfy debts with external trade partners or patrons. Women, like seized porcelain, gold, and other valuables, were generally divided after the raid among the male participants (ranging from chiefs and other nobility to high-status warriors and commoner or slave-status sailors) (Warren 2002). Elite female captives were sometimes allowed to arrange their own ransomed release or were retained by high-status participants as "captured" brides in chiefs' polygamous harems (Ileto 1971; Warren 2002). Most of the women captured in slave raids aimed at augmenting labor pools, particularly for the southern Philippine trading powers that were most dependent on slave labor (Ileto 1971: 35; Mednick 1965, 1977:215; Saleeby 1905; Warren 2002), were put to work in agriculture, crafts (primarily pottery and textile manufacture), and personal household service, where they became like lower-ranking kinspeople in the families which supported them. In many cases, these same women were forcibly married to young men or widowers in the kin group to make up for a deficit of marriageable females, particularly if

goods outside the quotas imposed by their owners. Numerous Spanish sources and other contact-period accounts note with puzzlement that the coastal markets were full of people identified as "slaves" who vended products for their masters but also earned small independent profits by selling additional craft items. Even more astonishing were the reports that slaves accompanying their owners as oarsmen and warriors on trading and raiding voyages were given a share of the wealth and slaves obtained in their maritime expedition similar to "freeman" warriors. They often used this profit to purchase their way out of slavery, which suggests that captives in the Philippines had a surprising degree of agency in negotiating forms of social and economic integration.

kin groups wanted to increase their social prominence and productive power through polygamous marriages for their males.

Historical accounts suggest that, in general, women slaves had fewer opportunities than men to eventually leave the captor community. Several reasons for this gender imbalance in repatriation can be offered based on the historical accounts. One factor may be that female slaves were assigned tasks closer to the household (rather than the long-distance voyaging of male captives), making escape unlikely. A second factor was that they more frequently married into the community since males provided bride-wealth, and hypergamy (i.e., marriage of lower-ranking women to higher-ranking men) was an accepted practice in the Philippines as well as throughout Southeast Asia (e.g., Andaya 1992; Geertz 1980; Ileto 1971; Leach 1965; see also Junker 1999a:294–298). In addition, women were less likely than men to be eventually manumitted or ransomed by their original kin groups or through their own wealth accumulation (see Junker 1999a:136) since men tended to be of greater political, if not economic, value in most Southeast Asian societies (Andaya 2006), and female slaves tended to be assigned work with little opportunity for accruing their own economic resources (such as farming and household service, rather than trading and raiding). Even if they had had the opportunity to escape captivity or the monetary resources to purchase their freedom, females were unlikely to move out of captor communities once they bore children due to inheritance rules that frequently allowed their children to move out of slave status at birth and become fully integrated into their father's community (Loarca 1582:185; Plasencia 1589:149). Some males left the captor community violently, however, as the more common victims of ritual human sacrifice associated with chiefly feasts in captor societies (Junker 1999a:345–347, 2001a; see also Andaya and Ishii 1992:509). Ethnographer Fay Cooper Cole observed that the early twentieth-century Bagabo of southern Mindanao differentially selected "decrepit" male slaves to sacrifice (Cole 1913:105), a choice that may be attributable to their low potential for long-term economic productivity and less likelihood that they had "become Bagabo" through marriage and producing progeny.

Spanish sources and early ethnographic accounts suggest that marriages or concubinage between female slaves and commoner or even elite members of the captor society were extremely common, and within one generation the progeny of these relationships became integrated into the slave-raiding group as "non-slave" kinsmen (see Reid 1983b:25–27; Warren 1985:227). Early Spanish writers who were concerned with gaining an understanding of the native class system in the Philippines wrote prodigiously about the social disposition and inheritance rules associated with slave-commoner or slave-elite marriages. While the details varied, they were consistent in reporting that the vast majority of children in their marriages became "freemen" and were classified as "indigenous" members of the ethnic group rather than "foreigners" (e.g., Bobadilla 1640:331–332; Plasencia 1589:148–1491; Loarca 1582:185–186). Warren (1985, 2002) and other historians (e.g., Majul 1973; Kiefer 1972b) studying the most active slave-raiding groups—such as the Sulu, Magindanao, and Maranao—have even suggested that a powerful incentive to continuous slave-raiding throughout the second millennium AD was the constant need to replenish depleted slave workforces as previously captured slaves assimilated so rapidly into these polities and moved on to more independent economic activities. Slavery in Southeast Asia therefore conformed to what Watson (1980) and Reid (1983a) refer to as an open slave system in which captured or purchased slaves are eventually assimilated into the dominant cultural group (often within a single generation) rather than prevented from doing so in order to maintain their economic and social exclusion (as in a closed slave system).

The Social Transmission of Technologies and Styles by Female Slave Artisans and Wives

We know a great deal about the organization of earthenware pottery production in the Philippines both in the prehispanic and more recent periods due to the large mass of contact-period historic records, ethnographic work, and more recent large-scale ethnoarchaeological projects on ceramic production, use, and marketing. Early Spanish documents indicate that ordinary

FIGURE 5.7. Women hand-forming earthenware vessels in 1895 in an Ifugao community (*left*, Worcester Photographic Collection, University of Michigan Museum of Anthropology), and a woman hand-forming a vessel in the town of San Nicholas, Ilocos Norte, in 2004.

household pottery was being produced in scattered centers, but more elaborate forms (including pedestaled vessels for serving feasting foods and decorated wares) were often manufactured by some of the potters in the same workshops for use in mortuary rites, as serving assemblages for ritual feasting, and as objects of wealth display (e.g., Loarca 1582:87; Pigafetta 1521:77; Chirino 1604:143; Colín 1660:167). The Sanchez dictionary (1617) suggests that fancy earthenware, such as footed plates and decorated jars, was included in what Visayans (i.e., Visayan-speaking peoples of the central Philippines) referred to as *bahandi*, or heirloom wealth, and that their manufacture required more-skilled potters than did *ginamikun*, or "ordinary household crockery."

Of significance to the present discussion is that the Spanish sources are consistent in identifying women as the primary manufacturers of earthenware ceramics, with male kinsmen primarily performing "heavy" labor such as transporting clays and other raw materials, as well as transporting the finished products and marketing them at more-distant centers. Early ethnographic accounts of the late nineteenth and early twentieth centuries (e.g., Cole 1913, 1956; Barton 1949) and my own analysis of photos in the Worcester photographic collection of ceramic production throughout the archipelago confirm that women were the primary laborers in producing earthenware for both domestic consumption and ritual use (Figure 5.7), with men

assisting in some of the large-scale raw material procurement and transportation tasks. Both European contact-period sources and early ethnographic work emphasize that male artisans were almost exclusively associated with iron and bronze production (for both tools and military weapons), goldsmithing, and boat-building (e.g., Dampier 1697:227; Sande 1577:99; see also Ileto 1971; McCaskey 1903; Peralta and Salazar 1974; Scott 1994), whereas pottery and textiles appear to have been largely the purview of women (e.g., Alcina 1668a:99; Chirino 1604:143; Colín 1660: 167; see also Fenner 1985:18–19).

More recent ethnoarchaeological studies by Longacre and his students over the last thirty years among the interior Kalinga, in Ilocos Norte, and in other areas of the Philippines have shown a more mixed gender organization of production (e.g., Longacre 1991; Longacre and Skibo 1994), with men focusing on production of more market-focused, tourist-oriented, and unique commissioned forms, while groups of kin-related women potters emphasized domestic wares for daily use in local households. Lisa Niziolek and I observed a similar gender pattern in 2004 in San Nicholas, Ilocos Norte on the island of Luzon, and in Zamboangita on the island of Negros. In these recent examples, women carried out most of the production steps in pottery manufacture (hand-modeling and paddle-and-anvil shaping, burnishing, slipping, and decoration) with the exception of the clay transport, open-air firing, and market transport of the finished vessels (which were largely done by male relatives).[8] The greater participation of men in contemporary pottery production may reflect a changing market for earthenware ceramics, which in daily household and ritual use are being rapidly replaced by metal, glass, and porcelain alternatives, while the use of traditionally manufactured earthenware has shifted in the direction of local household ornamentation (e.g., orchid holders, decorative statuary) and forms that are popular in the burgeoning tourist craft market.

If, as suggested in the ethnohistoric analysis above, women were being transported through the archipelago in large numbers from at least the twelfth through the late nineteenth centuries through slave capture, and they were being integrated into foreign communities as craft laborers or as secondary wives, and if significant numbers of those female captives were pottery specialists, then we would expect to see the transmission of pottery designs through the archipelago. The movement of local pottery design innovations into other regions would be expected to increase during periods of increased slave-raiding activity, which (as discussed earlier) were tied to expanded interpolity competition and conflict within the archipelago. Two periods in particular were identified through archaeological work in the Tanjay region and through historic sources as being times during which interethnic and interpolity raiding and violence increased within the archipelago: (1) the fifteenth to sixteenth centuries, when considerable foreign trade competition and labor shortages within expanding maritime trading polities appear to have engendered significant conflict (as archaeologically manifested in fortifications, the adoption of new weapons technologies, and an upsurge in violent deaths in burials) and large-scale slave-raiding (as reflected in historical accounts); and (2) the eighteenth and nineteenth centuries, when some polities of the southern Philippines and some societies of the island interiors not under Spanish colonial control took advantage of the weaknesses of conquered chiefdoms to the north and along the coasts to launch massive slave-raiding expeditions that brought tens of thousands of captives annually into their realms.

In both periods, we would expect that the influx of captives to have been somewhat unidirectional, largely into the larger-scale polities with greater labor deficits and larger-scale participation in the foreign voyaging and trade. In the two centuries prior to European contact, these dominant coastal maritime trading polities would have included, minimally, Manila in the north, Cebu in the central Philippines, and Sulu and Magindanao in the south; in the eighteenth and nineteenth centuries, slave-raiding and human imports were concentrated in the Islamic polities of Mindanao and the Sulu Sea region, including Sulu, Magindanao, and Maranao. Because women quickly became integrated into the social fabric of these captor societies, particularly if they joined communities as captive wives rather than slave laborers, and because ceramic designs are generally passed from mother to daughter or generally within female kin-related potting groups, we would expect foreign decorative elements and/or morphological elements to become fixed relatively rapidly into the design repertoires of the local pottery-producing community.

Archaeological Evidence for Transmission of Ceramic Design Elements in the Tanjay Region Chiefdom

In terms of archaeological evidence for transmission of ceramic designs, it is necessary to concentrate on the fifteenth- to sixteenth-century period of large-scale slave-raiding and to compare it to earlier prehispanic periods for which we have ceramic evidence, since few studies of eighteenth- and nineteenth-century earthenware exist in the Philippine archaeological literature. Several archaeologists have asserted that the indigenous decorated earthenware industry declined with the introduction of mainland Asian porcelains (Fox 1967; also see Bacus 1995), replaced by the technologically superior foreign ceramics for household status display and funerary rites. Solheim (1964), in a large reference work on "Iron Age" decorated earthenware (largely from poorly provenienced contexts and lacking associated radiometric dates), tended to support this view. He traced many highly standardized decorative designs to widely scattered sites throughout the archipelago, inferred a ca. 1000 BC to AD 800–1000 date for his types, and hypothesized that these fancy ceramics were moving through a

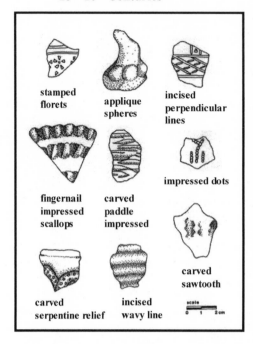

Some Decorative Motifs in the 15th-16th Centuries

stamped florets

applique spheres

incised perpendicular lines

fingernail impressed scallops

carved paddle impressed

impressed dots

carved serpentine relief

incised wavy line

carved sawtooth

scale
0   1   2 cm

Comparison of Decorative Motifs in Three Cultural Phases

AGUILAR PHASE (ca. AD 500-1000)
    impressed dots
    stamped circles
    impressed indentations on rim

SANTIAGO PHASE (ca. AD 1000-1400)
    incised perpendicular lines
    fingernail impressed

OSMENA PHASE (CA. AD 1400-1570)
    impressed dots
    impressed dashes
    fingernail impressed scallops
    incised perpendicular lines
    incised wavy lines
    fingernail impressed
    carved paddle impressed
    applique spheres on handles
    stamped florets
    stamped swirls
    burnished and red-slipped
    carved sawtooth indentations
    carved serpentine relief

FIGURE 5.8. Decorative designs on earthenware dated to the fifteenth and sixteenth centuries, recovered in habitation deposits excavated at Tanjay and other Tanjay region sites of this period (*left*), and distinct design elements found on earthenware ceramics of three periods of settlement in the region.

robust inter-island trade that was replaced in the late first millennium AD by the circulation of foreign porcelains.

However, radiometric dating of deposits with decorated earthenware in the Tanjay region (Junker 1999a:274–279) and seriation work on these decorated ceramics (Gunn and Graves 1995) suggests that many wares are contemporaneous with the second millennium AD porcelain trade rather than dated earlier. Micro-stylistic analysis by Bacus (1996) suggests that the design elements, not the vessels themselves, were moving through the archipelago. Bacus's interpretation of these patterns are that certain design elements became emblematic of membership in elite social strata and were disseminated through inter-island voyaging and consequent social interaction. Because most participants in voyages associated with trade and political alliance-building were men, this would imply that in some way male traders were disseminating information about pottery designs to local (largely female) potters or delivering ceramics that then were broadly copied within the visited community. Although Bacus's view that it was largely the designs and not the actual ceramics that were moving between polities is supported by new materials studies, I would argue that the mode of design transmission is much more likely to have involved the transport of female potters through wife-capture and slavery.

In the Tanjay region, decorated earthenware comprises between 2 and 5 percent of the total earthenware assemblage during all three of the broad phases of occupation over the thousand years prior to European contact (Figure 5.8), including the "Iron Age" Aguilar phase (ca. AD 500–1000), the Santiago phase (ca. AD 1100–1400) with Sung-period trade, and the Osmena phase (ca. AD 1400–1550) with Late Ming–period trade. However, the percentage of decorated earthenware increases significantly in settlements dated

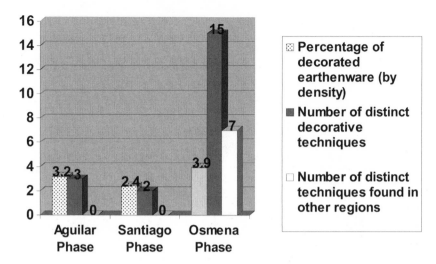

FIGURE 5.9. Percentages of decorated earthenware for each phase by density (gm/m³), number of distinct decorative techniques (see Figure 5.8), and number of distinct techniques found in other regions.

to the fifteenth to sixteenth centuries compared to earlier periods. Analysis of the household distribution of decorated wares at the coast center of Tanjay, where significant excavations have been carried out in residential zones, shows that in the fifteenth to sixteenth centuries, the Osmena phase, decorated ware was concentrated in what has been identified on the basis of house size and architectural features as an elite residential zone (Junker et al. 1994). Most significant from the standpoint of transmission of decorative styles in earthenware ceramics is that the number of distinctive decorative techniques increases dramatically in the fifteenth and sixteenth centuries (Figure 5.8). There are fifteen distinct types of design elements in this period of expanded long-distance voyaging compared to three in the late first-millennium Aguilar phase and two in the intermediate early second-millennium Santiago phase (Figure 5.9).

In previous publications on archaeological evidence from the Tanjay Project, several explanations of this increased diversity in decorated earthenware were offered. One theory is that expanding participation in ritual feasting by larger segments of the population, a function of growing status competition, led to a significant increase in the importation and production of "feasting" assemblages, including both porcelain

and decorated earthenware (Junker 2001a). Another possible explanation is increased production of decorated wares for exchange with interior tribal swidden-farming populations, related to expanding lowland demand for forest product exports for the foreign porcelain trade. This hypothesis is supported by increasing quantities of lowland decorated earthenware at upland sites in the fifteenth to sixteenth centuries (Junker 2002).

In the early stages of the Tanjay Project, microscopic analysis of clays and tempering material in the Tanjay region earthenware suggested that most of the decorated wares were locally produced in the fifteenth to sixteenth centuries, with a small number of possible extra-island imports (Junker 1982, 1994a, 1999a:274–279). Only a limited number of scanning electron microscope (SEM) and x-ray diffraction analyses were run to confirm microscope studies, but the earthenware tempering materials, in particular, closely matched those for common undecorated wares of the period in the Tanjay region. The most common ware among both decorated and undecorated pieces of the late fifteenth century and early sixteenth centuries is known as Tanjay Red ware, a hand-coiled, paddle-and-anvil finished, medium-textured, low-fired red ware with quartzite sand temper. Statistically

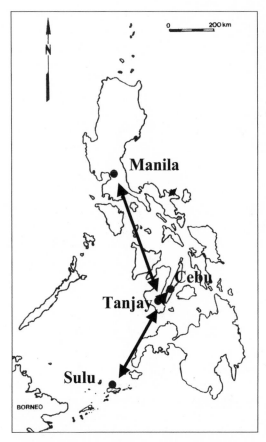

FIGURE 5.10. Four fifteenth- through sixteenth-century polity centers in the Philippine archipelago that share earthenware pottery decorative designs with Tanjay, possibly reflecting the flow of women through slave-capture and the spread of new ceramic designs.

are strikingly similar to decorated earthenware recovered at the sixteenth-century centers of Manila (Peralta and Salazar 1974), Cebu (Hutterer 1973; Nishimura 1992), and Jolo (the Sulu sultanate) (Spoehr 1973) (see Figures 5.8 and 5.10).

Recent, more detailed materials analysis on earthenware samples from the Tanjay region using inductively coupled plasma mass spectrometry (ICPMS)[9] has provided preliminary support for this initial interpretation of local origins and is consistent with Bacus's view of design imports rather than trade in foreign pots. While the ICPMS study is still in its initial stages, much of the analyzed pottery from Tanjay with these more widely disseminated designs is essentially identical chemically with nondecorated wares produced in the Tanjay region (Junker 2004). One exception is burnished and red-slipped ware, which appears to have been imported from the Manila area. Therefore, the preliminary ICPMS study suggests that most of the shared designs were transmitted as innovations between regions rather than as the result of trade in earthenware. This is consistent with the fact that clays for earthenware production and tempering materials are fairly ubiquitous in the island archipelago, and until very recently, most household and nonutilitarian earthenware were produced locally and transported relatively short distances to consumers (e.g., Hutterer and Macdonald 1982; Longacre 1991; Spoehr 1973).

I would suggest that the female potters, transported through slave-taking or possibly also inter-island marriage, were the disseminators of foreign styles as they took up their pottery-manufacturing craft in their new homelands. Marriage over long distances, while fairly common for elites in prehispanic and contact-period Philippines as part of political alliance-building (Junker 1999a:294–298), was considerably rarer for commoner classes, which would include women with pottery-making knowledge. Therefore, forced marriage through capture or the import of women as artisan-slaves is a more likely scenario. Since women tended to remain in their captor communities and would have taught their daughters to manufacture pottery, we would expect decorative innovations to have become fixed rather quickly in these captor communities.

Since no materials studies have been carried

supported spatial studies of the distribution of this type within the Tanjay River valley shows high concentrations at the coastal chiefly center of Tanjay, with a distance-dependent (i.e., socially unimpeded) flow upriver of undecorated forms to secondary centers, and more selective site size–dependent (i.e., socially restricted) distribution of more-elaborate decorated forms (Junker 1994a). This earlier work supports distribution, if not manufacture, of both decorated and undecorated earthenware of this type out of the coastal trading center of Tanjay. Most interesting of the decorated ware are seven distinct types with motifs (stamped florets, stamped shields, carved sawtooth indentations, spherical appliques) or techniques (red-slipping, fingernail impressing, carved paddle impressing) that out on pottery with these inter-island decorative styles at Manila, Cebu, and Jolo, and they are poorly dated relative to the Tanjay wares, we have no way of knowing at present whether the designs followed women being *captured from* Tanjay or being *brought to* Tanjay. However, the historical studies of slave-raiding presented earlier suggest that larger polities with richer environments and more labor shortages, like Manila, Cebu and Jolo, were more likely to be the aggressors in maritime slave-raiding. Furthermore, the archaeological evidence for a massacre event in the fifteenth century, and the archaeologically contemporaneous increase in iron production and construction of fortifications, can be interpreted as a defensive response to significant external threats. Therefore, in considering slave-raiding and the forced movement of potters as a significant factor in disseminating innovative decorative styles, we must acknowledge that the assumption that status-conferring forms of material culture design generally flow from larger centers with more elites to "emulate" may be stood on its head: such design innovations in prestige goods may in fact have originated in smaller centers among artisans who were captured and transported to these more prominent centers. It is therefore quite possible that these earthenware designs originated in Tanjay, a small and politically less significant polity, rather than in these wealthier and more prominent maritime trading polities.

Micro-stylistic studies of ceramic decoration and/or form, as well as documentation of new techniques of pottery production (e.g., use of new forming techniques, surface treatments, firing technologies), may allow us to eventually trace small-scale differences in design elements or technology within contact-period pottery-making communities in Tanjay, Jolo, Cebu, and Manila that might be attributable to innovation, contacts with other communities, or migration of foreign potters into a community through slave-capture (particularly in the fifteenth to sixteenth centuries). However, this type of detailed micro-stylistic work on earthenware ceramics has yet to be undertaken on collections from prehispanic Philippine settlements, including those from the Tanjay region. In terms of the eighteenth to early nineteenth centuries, when we see another expansion of slave-raiding within the ar-chipelago, particularly involving the southern polities outside Spanish colonial control (Warren 1985, 2002), there is significant potential for documenting these technology and design transfers through studies of textiles known historically to have been manufactured primarily by women. The Field Museum of Natural History in Chicago has a remarkable collection of nineteenth-century textiles associated with various maritime trading polities and upland groups in the Philippines, along with late nineteenth-century photographs (part of the Dean Worcester Photographic Collection) depicting these clothing pieces being worn in various ethnographic settings. Analysis of design elements on these ethnographic textiles relevant to the movement (possibly forced) of female weavers within the archipelago in this more recent period is one means by which we could further examine how fluctuations in the frequency and geographic patterns of female slave-taking affected craft systems in the slave-absorbing societies.

Conclusions

Although slavery associated with European colonization has become an increasingly frequent area of intersection of research by historians and anthropologists, indigenous forms of human bondage in places like Africa and Asia have received less attention in cross-disciplinary and cross-cultural research (Alpers et al. 2005; Reid 1983a; Watson 1980). In addition, few studies of slavery in Southeast Asia have emphasized the experiences of women captives and their social and economic impacts within slave-raiding societies (Andaya 2000; Wolters 1999:164–165). The archaeological evidence presented here is still in its preliminary stages of analysis, but a rich array of multivocal historic sources and ethnographic accounts provides a cultural context in which we can begin to examine the long-term dynamics of the incorporation of foreign female labor forces into Philippine maritime trading chiefdoms, and the consequences for technological and social change between the twelfth and nineteenth centuries AD.

A consideration of ecological features in island Southeast Asia and historical reconstructions of population factors suggest that food production strategies, particularly the agricultural intensification necessary to support the growth of complex societies, was constrained by access to labor rather than land or technological capital. Not surprisingly, historical sources and ethnographic investigations show that political authority was defined in many regions of Southeast Asia in terms of continually negotiated control over the labor of others in impermanent alliance networks that were consolidated through kinship (primarily fluid cognatic descent principles), affinal ties (expanded through polygamy), asymmetrical patron-client relationships (involving both kinsmen and non-kinsmen), debt-bondage, and captives in slave-raiding. Slave-capture, particularly of women, was a particularly attractive means for mobilizing labor at a relatively low cost for social reproduction, agriculture, key crafts such as ceramics and textiles, and politically significant activities such as trade, ritualized feasting, and military competition. The low cost/high benefit of slave-taking can be viewed in both social and economic terms: men obtaining a foreign wife or female worker through slave-capture increased their labor force while avoiding the economic obligations of bride-price and social obligations owed to affinals that often offset the labor gained by controlling female productivity. The fact that labor control, and the advantages it conferred in agricultural productivity and material support for foreign luxury goods trade, was the dominant factor fueling slave-raiding in the Philippines is attested in the stunning growth of Sulu and Magindanao, which were the most active of the slave-raiding polities and key players in maritime luxury goods trade networks well into the European contact period.

Key to the perpetuation of slave-raiding and slave-based economies in the archipelago were ethnic fluidity, social mobility, and cultural norms that conferred social legitimacy on the offspring of foreign slaves within one generation, requiring that former slaves, newly defined as *indigenes*, be continually replaced through further slave-raiding and incorporation of foreigners at the bottom of the social and economic ladder. Ideologies of warrior prestige associated with the taking of captives were also instrumental in promoting slave-raiding, most vividly captured in oral traditions and ethnographic accounts of warfare-related boasting at feasts, but

also documented archaeologically in the material accoutrements of warrior burials. In these so-called open slave systems exemplified by the Philippines and island Southeast Asia in general, the rapid social and economic assimilation of women and their importance in intergenerational dissemination of knowledge meant that innovations in technologies, styles, and cultural practices would be quickly spread between communities. That is, we would expect to see a high level of technological and cultural innovation rather than conservancy in individual communities, the rapid movement of new forms and ideas over larger regions, and a lack of clear geographically and temporally bounded "cultural traditions" (sometimes glossed by archaeologists as "ethnicity") represented by ceramic or other material "styles." Like the polyglot and cosmopolitan nature of historically described Philippine polities, we would expect that Philippine populations heavily involved in long-distance voyaging for both foreign trade and slave-raiding would be multivocal in their ceramic and textiles designs through their slave craftswomen.

Historical sources going back to Chinese records of the early second millennium AD and ethnographic work in the early twentieth century indicate that slave-raiding and intergroup conflict have been integral components of long-distance voyaging and exchange interactions for a long time within the Philippine archipelago. However, archaeological and historical evidence suggests that the fifteenth and sixteenth centuries saw a peak in conflict and interpolity raiding in the region, corresponding with the competitive expansion of foreign luxury goods trade and the rise of a number of larger-scale polities (including both Islamic and non-Islamic ones). An increased number of violent deaths in burial remains, an increased use of fortifications around major centers, expanded metals production, the appearance of "warrior" emblems and linguistic markers indicating the recognition of a distinct warrior class, and contact-period descriptions of large-scale slave-raiding all attest to this increased scale of militarism and the probability that slave-taking was a significant component of this expanded militarism.

Analysis of decorative design elements on earthenware pottery from the Tanjay region and other areas where there have been archaeological excavations around historically known polity centers shows an increased diversity of decorative styles and a larger number of shared design components between regions in the fifteenth and sixteenth centuries, just prior to European contact. Since long-distance interpolity trade in the archipelago was generally focused on luxury goods such as porcelain and metal preciosities, and it appears that it was the design elements and not the vessels themselves that were moving between centers, the interpretation offered here is that the increased diversity of shared ceramic designs is the result of more women potters being forcibly moved through the archipelago as captured slaves. It is also suggested that the polyglot and culturally diverse nature of maritime trad-

ing polities and adjacent interior societies in the Philippines at the time of contact is not solely attributable to the cosmopolitan male traders and voyagers. It is also strongly tied to the movement of captured women and, in particular, their ability to establish new technologies and ideas from their homelands over time through their unique role in enculturating children in their newly adopted societies. Because the intensity and scale of slave-raiding was higher in politically prominent and wealthy centers, women captives were likely to flow somewhat unidirectionally toward these active slaving communities. Contrary to the assumptions of many archaeologists, regionally widespread innovations seen in the archaeological record may actually be more likely to have originated in these smaller centers.

Notes

1. Although almost no actual writings have been preserved (given that people wrote on bamboo and other perishable materials), we know from other sources that Philippine lowland societies wrote in a probable Sanskrit-based script adopted from Hindu trade partners from western-lying kingdoms in island Southeast Asia and that these texts were likely chiefly genealogies and heroic tales (see Junker 1999a:30–33). It is possible that examples still exist in local archives of the southern Islamic chiefdoms or that elements of these texts have been incorporated into the Islamic *tarsilas* in the south, leaving this open as a future area of historical analysis.

2. Spanish conquest in 1570 was by no means the end of political autonomy and slave-raiding for many of the maritime polities, particularly the Islamic groups of the southern Philippines. The Sulu, Magindanao, Maranao, Bagabo, and others did not fall to foreign domination until late in the Spanish colonial period (the nineteenth century) or in some cases after American control had been asserted for several decades (Kiefer 1972a, 1972b; McKenna 1998; Warren 1985). The last remaining autonomous Islamic polity in the southern Philippines, the Sulu sultanate, surrendered to the American colonial regime in 1913, well after early fieldwork in the region by Fay Cooper Cole of the Field Museum (Cole 1913) and other ethnographers.

3. Chinese tributary trade records document at least ten distinct polities on the islands of Luzon, Mindoro, and Mindanao that carried out tribu-

tary missions to the Chinese court in the Sung, Yuan, and Ming dynasties of the early to mid second millennium AD with the aim (often successfully realized) of gaining favored trade status (Junker 1999a:189–203). These voyages involved up to three hundred people in three large ships, led by chiefly elite, accompanied by export "product samples" and gifts intended to woo Chinese trade administrators towards official recognition and the granting of trade preference. See Junker 1990, 1998, and 1999a for detailed discussion of trade voyaging and interpolity trade competition through tributary missions.

4. It should be noted that even the limited archaeological work at polity centers such as Manila, Cebu, and Jolo (the Sulu sultanate) have focused primarily on burials rather than settlement (e.g., Hutterer 1973; Jocano 1975; Nishimura 1992; Peralta and Salazar 1974; Spoehr 1973).

5. In an earlier publication, I advanced a historically and ethnographically supported interpretation that the decapitated skulls were from revenge raids by the families of victims who could not successfully complete funerary rites without taking enemy heads (Junker 1999b).

6. "Visayan" refers to several lowland societies in the central Philippines, including most likely the polities of Tanjay and Cebu, that spoke (and whose descendents still speak today) various dialects of the Visayan language.

7. At the time of contact, several of the largest polities in the Philippines were Islamic (primarily in the southern Philippines on the island of Mindanao and in the Sulu Sea, but also most likely

the Manila "sultanate"). The coastal chiefdoms on many of the other islands, as well as tribal people of the interior, had indigenous religions classified by the Spanish as pagan. Some of the captives in slave-raiding came from Buddhist and Hindu kingdoms located in both island and mainland Southeast Asia.

8. University of Illinois Chicago Ph.D. students Lisa Niziolek and Jacqueline Jackson accompanied me and participated in this brief ethnographic study in Ilocos Norte and Negros Oriental provinces. Some of the results will be incorporated into Ms. Niziolek's Ph.D. dissertation on pottery specialization in the prehispanic Tanjay chiefdom.

9. The ICPMS study is being carried out in the Materials Laboratory in the Department of Anthropology at the Field Museum of Natural History by Lisa Niziolek, a Ph.D. candidate at the University of Illinois who will incorporate the results into her dissertation.

Bibliography

Alcina, Francisco Ignacio
1688a   Historia de las Islas e Indios de las Bisayas. In *The Muñoz Text of Alcina's History of the Bisayan Islands,* book 3, part 3, edited and translated by Paul Lietz. Philippine Studies Program, University of Chicago, 1960.
1688b   Historia de las Islas e Indios de las Bisayas. In *The Muñoz Text of Alcina's History of the Bisayan Islands,* book 3, part 4, edited and translated by Paul Lietz. Philippine Studies Program, University of Chicago, 1960.
Alpers, Edward, Gwyn Campbell, and Michael Salman (editors)
2005   *Slavery and Resistence in Africa and Asia.* Routledge, London.
Andaya, Barbara
1992   Political Development between the Sixteenth and Eighteenth Centuries. In *The Cambridge History of Southeast Asia*, vol. 1: *From Early Times to c. 1800,* edited by N. Tarling. Cambridge University Press, Cambridge.
2006   *The Flaming Womb: Repositioning Women in Early Modern Southeast Asia.* University of Hawaii Press, Honolulu.
Andaya, Barbara (editor)
2000   *Other Pasts: Women, Gender and History in Early Modern Southeast Asia.* University of Hawaii Press, Honolulu.
Andaya, Barbara Watson, and Leonard Andaya
1982   *A History of Malaysia.* Macmillan, London.
Andaya, Barbara Watson, and Yoneo Ishii
1992   Religious Developments in Southeast Asia, c.

1500–1800. In *The Cambridge History of Southeast Asia,* vol. 1: *From Early Times to c. 1800,* edited by N. Tarling, pp. 508–571. Cambridge University Press, Cambridge.
Bacus, Elisabeth A.
1995   Political Economy and Interaction: Late Prehistoric Polities in the Central Philippine Islands. Ph.D. dissertation, Department of Anthropology, University of Michigan, Ann Arbor.
1996   Political Economy and Interaction Among Late Prehistoric Polities in the Central Philippines. *Bulletin of the Indo-Pacific Prehistory Association* 14:226–241.
Barton, Robert F.
1949   *The Kalingas.* University of Chicago Press, Chicago.
Baumgartner, Joseph
1977   Notes on Piracy and Slaving in Philippine History. *Philippine Quarterly of Culture and Society* 5:270–272.
Beckett, Jeremy
1982   The Defiant and the Compliant: The Datus of Mindanao Under Colonial Rule. In *Philippine Social History*, edited by A. W. McCoy and C. de Jesus, pp. 391–414. Asian Studies Association of Australia Monograph No. 7. Ateneo de Manila Press, Quezon City, Philippines.
Bobadilla, Diego de
1640   Relation of the Philippine Islands. In *Documentary Sources of Philippine History* vol. 4 (1990), edited and translated by G. Zaide, pp. 329–343. National Bookstore, Manila.
Boxer Codex
1590a   A Late Sixteenth Century Manuscript. Translated by C. R. Boxer. *Journal of the Royal Asiatic Society* (1950) 54:37–49.
1590b   The Manners, Customs, and Beliefs of Philippine Inhabitants of Long Ago (Being Chapters of a Late Sixteenth Century Manuscript). Translated by Carlos Quirino and Mauro Garcia. *The Philippine Journal of Science* (1958) 87:325–453.
Chirino, Pedro
1604   Relación de las Islas Filipinas. In *The Philippines, 1493–1898,* vol. 12, edited and translated by E. Blair and J. Robertson. Arthur H. Clark, Cleveland, 1903.
Cole, Fay Cooper
1913   *Wild Tribes of the Davao District.* Publication no. 162, Anthropology Series 13, no. 1. Field Museum of Natural History, Chicago.
1956   *The Bukidnon of Mindanao.* Chicago Natural History Museum Press, Chicago.

Colín, Francisco

1660   Labor evangelica, ministerios apostólicos de los obreros de la Compañía de Jesus: Fundación y progressos de su provincia en las Islas Filipinas. In *The Philippines, 1493–1898*, vol. 40, edited and translated by E. Blair and J. Robertson. Arthur H. Clark, Cleveland, 1903.

Dampier, William

1697   *A New Voyage Round the World*. Edited by Sir A. Gray. Argonaut Press, London, 1927.

Earle, Timothy

1987   Chiefdoms in Archaeological and Ethnohistorical Perspective. *Annual Review of Anthropology* 16:279–308.

Eugenio, Damiana

2001   *Philippine Folk Literature: The Epics*. University of the Philippines Press, Quezon City.

Fenner, Bruce

1985   *Cebu Under the Spanish Flag, 1521–1896: An Economic and Social History*. University of San Carlos Press, Cebu City, Philippines.

Fox, Robert

1967   The Archaeological Record of Chinese Influences in the Philippines. *Philippine Studies* 15(1):41–62.

Fox, Robert, and Avelino Legaspi

1977   *Excavations at Santa Ana*. National Museum Publications, Manila.

Geertz, Clifford

1973   *The Interpretation of Cultures*. Basic Books, New York.

1980   *Negara: The Theatre State in Nineteenth Century Bali*. Princeton University Press, Princeton, NJ.

Gibson, Thomas

1990   Raiding, Trading and Tribal Autonomy in Insular Southeast Asia. In *The Anthropology of War*, edited by J. Haas, pp. 125–145. Cambridge University Press, Cambridge.

Good, Irene

2001   Archaeological Textiles: A Review of Current Research. *Annual Review of Anthropology* 30: 209–226.

Gunn, Mary, and Michael Graves

1995   Constructing Seriations from the Guthe Collection, the Central Philippines: The Implications for Southeast Asian Ceramic Chronologies. *Asian Perspectives* 34(2):257–282.

Gutiérrez, Pedro

1636   The Battle of Punta de Flechas and Datu Tagal's Death. In *Documentary Sources of Philippine History*, vol. 4, edited and translated by G. Zaide, pp. 205–209. National Bookstore Publications, Manila, 1990.

Hall, Kenneth

1985   *Maritime Trade and State Development in Early Southeast Asia*. University of Hawaii Press, Honolulu.

1992   Economic History of Early Southeast Asia. In *The Cambridge History of Southeast Asia*, vol. 1: *From Early Times to c. 1800*, edited by N. Tarling, pp. 183–275. Cambridge University Press, Cambridge.

Hegmon, Michelle

1992   Archaeological Research on Style. *Annual Review of Anthropology* 21:517–536.

Herrera, Diego de

1573   Augustinian Memoranda Denouncing the Unjust Wars, In Violation of the King's Orders. In *Documentary Sources of Philippine History*, vol. 2, edited and translated by G. Zaide, pp. 145–151. National Bookstore Publications, Manila, 1990.

Hoadley, Michael

1983   Slavery, Bondage and Dependency in Precolonial Java. In *Slavery, Bondage and Dependency in Southeast Asia*, edited by A. Reid, pp. 90–117. St. Martin's Press, New York.

Hutterer, Karl L.

1973   *An Archaeological Picture of Prehispanic Cebuano Community*. University of San Carlos Press, Cebu City, Philippines.

1974   The Evolution of Philippine Lowland Societies. *Mankind* 9(4):287–299.

1977   Prehistoric Trade and the Evolution of Philippine Societies: A Reconsideration. In *Economic Exchange and Social Interaction in Southeast Asia: Perspectives From Prehistory*, edited by K. Hutterer, pp. 177–196. Michigan Papers on South and Southeast Asia No. 13. University of Michigan Center for South and Southeast Asian Studies, Ann Arbor.

1981   Bais Anthropological Project, Phase II: A First Preliminary Report. *Philippine Quarterly of Culture and Society* 9(4):333–341.

Hutterer, Karl L., and William K. Macdonald (editors)

1982   *Houses Built on Scattered Poles: Prehistory and Ecology in Negros Oriental, Philippines*. University of San Carlos Press, Cebu City, Philippines.

Ileto, Reynaldo

1971   *Maguindanao, 1860–1888: The Career of Datu Uto of Buayan*. Southeast Asian Paper no. 32. Cornell University, Ithaca, NY.

Jocano, F. Landa

1975   *The Philippines at the Spanish Contact*. Garcia Publications, Quezon City, Philippines.

Junker, Laura L.

1990 The Organization of Intra-Regional and Long-Distance Trade in Prehispanic Philippine Complex Societies. *Asian Perspectives* 29(2):167–209.

1994a The Development of Centralized Craft Production Systems in AD 500–1600 Philippine Chiefdoms. *Journal of Southeast Asian Studies* 25(1):1–30.

1994b Trade Competition, Conflict, and Political Transformations in Sixth- to Sixteenth-Century Philippine Chiefdoms. *Asian Perspectives* 33(2):229–260.

1996 Hunter-Gatherer Landscapes and Lowland Trade in the Prehispanic Philippines. *World Archaeology* 27(2):389–410.

1998 Integrating History and Archaeology in the Study of Contact Period Philippine Chiefdoms. *International Journal of Historical Archaeology* 2(4):291–320.

1999a *Raiding, Trading and Feasting: The Political Economy of Philippine Chiefdoms.* University of Hawaii Press, Honolulu.

1999b Warrior Burials and the Nature of Warfare in the Prehispanic Philippine Chiefdoms. *Philippine Quarterly of Culture and Society* 27(4): 120–161.

2001a The Evolution of Ritual Feasting Systems in Prehispanic Philippine Chiefdoms. In *Feasts: Archaeological and Ethnographic Perspectives on Food, Politics and Power*, edited by M. Dietler and B. Hayden, pp. 267–310. Smithsonian Institution Press, Washington, D.C.

2001b Warfare in the Political Economy of Prehispanic Philippine Chiefdoms. Paper presented at the 66th Annual Meeting of the Society for American Archaeology, New Orleans.

2002 Economic Specialization and Inter-Ethnic Trade Between Foragers and Farmers in the Prehispanic Philippines. In *Forager-Traders in South and Southeast Asia*, edited by K. Morrison and L. Junker. Cambridge University Press, Cambridge.

2003 Political Economy in the Historic Period Chiefdoms and States of Southeast Asia. In *Archaeological Perspectives on Political Economies*, edited by G. Feinman and L. Nicholas, pp. 223–252. University of Utah Press, Salt Lake City.

2004 Archaeological Investigations in the Tanjay Region. Unpublished lecture presented at the Archaeological Studies Program, University of the Philippines, Quezon City.

2006 Population Dynamics and Urbanism in Premodern Island Southeast Asia. In *Urbanism in the Pre-Industrial World: Cross-Cultural Approaches*, edited by G. Storey, pp. 203–230. University of Alabama Press, Tuscaloosa.

Junker, Laura L., Karen Mudar, and Marla Schwaller

1994 Social Stratification, Household Wealth and Competitive Feasting in Fifteenth–Sixteenth Century Philippine Chiefdoms. *Research in Economic Anthropology* 15:307–358.

Kathirithamby-Wells, Jelamayar

1993 Restraints on the Development of Merchant Capitalism in Southeast Asia Before c. 1800. In *Southeast Asia in the Early Modern Era*, edited by Anthony Reid, pp. 123–150. Cornell University Press, Ithaca, NY.

Keeley, Lawrence

1996 *War Before Civilization: The Myth of the Peaceful Savage.* Oxford University Press, New York.

Kiefer, Thomas

1972a *The Tausug: Violence and Law in a Philippine Moslem Society.* Holt, Rinehart and Winston, New York.

1972b The Tausug Polity and the Sultanate of Sulu: A Segmentary State in the Southern Philippines. In *Sulu Studies,* vol. 1, edited by G. Rixhon, pp. 19–64. Notre Dame of Jolo College Press, Jolo, Philippines.

Larson, P. M.

2000 *History and Memory in the Age of Enslavement.* Oxford University Press, Oxford.

Laufer, Berthold

1907 *The Relations of the Chinese to the Philippine Islands.* National Publications, Washington, D.C.

Lavezaris, Guido de

1576 Slavery Among the Natives. In *The Philippine Islands, 1493–1803,* vol. 3, edited and translated by E. Blair and J. Robertson, pp. 286–287. Arthur H. Clark, Cleveland, 1903.

Leach, Edmund R.

1965 *Political Systems of Highland Burma.* Beacon Press, Boston.

Legaspi, Miguel de

1567 Letters to Felipe II of Spain. In *The Philippine Islands, 1493–1803,* vol. 2, edited and translated by E. Blair and J. Robertson, pp. 232–243. Arthur H. Clark, Cleveland, 1903.

1569 Relation of the Filipinas Islands and of the Character and Conditions of the Inhabitants, Cebu, July 7, 1569. In *Documentary Sources of Philippine History,* vol. 2, edited and translated by Gregorio Zaide, pp. 37–42. National Bookstore Publications, Manila, 1990.

1570 Relación de las Islas Filipinas. In *The Philippine Islands, 1493–1803,* vol. 3, edited by

E. Blair and J. Robertson, pp. 54–61. Arthur H. Clark, Cleveland, 1903.

Lightfoot, Kenneth
1995   Culture Contact Studies: Redefining the Relationship between Prehistoric and Historic Archaeology. *American Antiquity* 60(2):199–219.

Loarca, Miguel de
1582   Relación de las Islas Filipinas. In *The Philippines, 1493–1898,* vol. 5, edited and translated by E. Blair and J. Robertson, pp. 32–187. Arthur H. Clark, Cleveland, 1903.

Locsin, Leandro, and Cecilia Locsin
1967   *Oriental Ceramics Discovered in the Philippines.* Rutland, Tokyo.

Longacre, William
1991   Sources of Ceramic Variability Among the Kalinga of Northern Luzon. In *Ceramic Ethnoarchaeology,* edited by W. Longacre, pp. 94–111. University of Arizona Press, Tucson.

Longacre, William, and James Skibo (editors)
1994   *Kalinga Ethnoarchaeology.* Smithsonian Institution Press, Washington, D.C.

Mabbett, I. W.
1983   Some Remarks on the Present State of Knowledge on Slavery in Angkor. In *Slavery, Bondage and Dependency in Southeast Asia,* edited by A. Reid, pp. 44–63. St. Martin's Press, New York.

Majul, Cesare
1973   *Muslims in the Philippines.* University of the Philippines Press, Quezon City.

Maldonado, Juan Pacheco
1575   Letter to Felipe II of Spain. In *Documentary Sources of Philippine History,* vol. 2, edited and translated by G. Zaide, pp. 178–184. National Bookstore Publications, Manila, 1990.

Mallari, F.
1986   Muslim Raids in Bicol, 1580–1792. *Philippine Studies* 34:257–286.

Manguin, Pierre-Yves
1983   Manpower and Labour Categories in Early Sixteenth Century Malacca. In *Slavery, Bondage and Dependency in Southeast Asia,* edited by A. Reid, pp. 209–215. St. Martin's Press, New York.

Manuel, E. Arsenio
1958   *The Maiden of the Buhong Sky.* Ateneo de Manila University Press, Quezon City, Philippines.
1973   *Manuvu Social Organization.* University of the Philippines Press, Quezon City, Philippines.

McCaskey, H. D.
1903   Iron Metallurgy in the Philippines. *The Engineering and Mining Journal* 76:780.

McKenna, Thomas
1998   *Muslim Rulers and Rebels.* University of California Press, Berkeley.

Mednick, Melvin
1977   Ilanun. In *Insular Southeast Asia: Ethnographic Studies,* Section 4: Philippines, edited by F. Lebar, pp. 209–228. HRAF Publications, New Haven, CT.

Morga, Antonio
1609   Sucesos de las Islas Filipinas. In *Readings in Philippine Prehistory,* edited by M. Garcia, pp. 270–295. Filipiana Book Guild, Manila, 1979.

Niemeijer, Hendrik D.
2000   Slavery, Ethnicity and the Economic Independence of Women in Seventeenth Century Batavia. In *Other Pasts: Women, Gender and History in Early Modern Southeast Asia,* edited by B. Andaya, pp. 219–243. Center for Southeast Asian Studies, University of Hawaii, Honolulu.

Nishimura, Masao
1992   Long Distance Trade and the Development of Complex Societies in the Prehistory of the Central Philippines: The Cebu Central Settlement Case. Ph.D. dissertation, Department of Anthropology, University of Michigan, Ann Arbor.

Orser, Charles
2001   Archaeology and Slave Resistance and Rebellion. *World Archaeology* 33(1):61–77.

Peralta, Jesus, and L. A. Salazar
1974   *Pre-Spanish Manila: A Reconstruction of the Pre-History of Manila.* National Historical Commission, Manila.

Pigafetta, Antonio
1521   First Voyage Around the World. In *The Philippines at the Spanish Contact,* edited and translated by F. Landa Jocano, pp. 44–80. Garcia Publications, Quezon City, Philippines, 1975.

Plasencia, Juan de
1589   Las costumbres de los indios Tagalogs de Filipinas. In *Documentary Sources of Philippine History,* vol. 3, edited and translated by Gregorio Zaide, pp. 145–161. National Bookstore Publications, Manila, 1990.

Rada, Fray Martin de
1569   Letter of Fray Martín de Rada to Marqués de Falces, Viceroy of Mexico. In *Documentary Sources of Philippine History,* vol. 2, edited and translated by G. Zaide, pp. 49–53. National Bookstore Publications, Manila, 1990.

Reid, Anthony
1983a   "Closed" and "Open" Slave Systems in Pre-Colonial Southeast Asia. In *Slavery, Bondage and Dependency in Southeast Asia,* edited by

A. Reid, pp. 156–181. St. Martin's Press, New York.

1983b   Introduction: Slavery and Bondage in Southeast Asian History. In *Slavery, Bondage and Dependency in Southeast Asia*, edited by A. Reid, pp. 1–43. St. Martin's Press, New York.

1988   *Southeast Asia in the Age of Commerce, 1450–1680,* vol. 1: *The Lands Below the Winds.* Yale University Press, New Haven.

1992   Economic and Social Change, c. 1400–1800. In *The Cambridge History of Southeast Asia,* vol. 1, *From Early Times to c. 1800,* edited by N. Tarling. Cambridge: Cambridge University Press.

1993a   *Southeast Asia in the Age of Commerce 1450–1680,* vol. 2: *Expansion and Crisis.* Yale University Press, New Haven.

1993b   Introduction: A Time and a Place. In *Southeast Asia in the Early Modern Era,* edited by A. Reid, pp. 1–22. Cornell University Press, Ithaca, NY.

Saleeby, Najeeb

1905   *Studies in Moro History, Law, and Religion.* Ethnological Survey Publications vol. 4, pt. 1. Bureau of Printing, U.S. Dept. of the Interior, Manila.

Salman, Michael

2005   Resisting Slavery in the Philippines: Ambivalent Domestication and the Reversibility of Comparisons. In *Slavery and Resistance in Africa and Asia,* edited by E. Alpers, G. Campbell, and M. Salman. Routledge, London.

San Bueneventura, Pedro de

1613   *Vocabulario de Lengua Tagala el Romance Castellano Presta Primera.* 2 vols. National Archives of the Philippines, Manila.

Sanchez Dictionary

1617   Sanchez Dictionary. Philippine National Archives, Manila.

Sande, Francisco

1577   Relation and Description of the Filipinas Islands. In *The Philippines, 1493–1898,* vol. 4, edited and translated by E. Blair and J. Robertson. Arthur H. Clark, Cleveland, 1903.

1578   Letter to Estevan Rodríguez de Figueroa. In *The Philippines, 1493–1898,* vol. 4, edited and translated by E. Blair and J. Robertson, pp. 174–181. Arthur H. Clark, Cleveland, 1903.

Santa Ines, Francisco de

1676   Crónica de la Provincia de San Gregorio Magno de China, Japón, etc. In *Documentary Sources of Philippine History* vol. 5, edited and translated by G. Zaide, pp. 67–93. National Bookstore Publications, Manila, 1990.

Schlegel, Stuart

1979   *Tiruray Subsistence.* Ateneo de Manila Press, Quezon City, Philippines.

Schwalbenberg, Henry

1993   The Economics of Maritime Raiding. *Philippine Quarterly of Culture and Society* 21:1–27.

Scott, William Henry

1980   Filipino Class Structure in the Sixteenth Century. *Philippine Studies* 28:142–175.

1983   *Oripun* and *Alipin* in the Sixteenth Century Philippines. In *Slavery, Bondage and Dependency in Southeast Asia,* edited by A. Reid, pp. 138–155. St. Martin's Press, New York.

1984   *Prehispanic Source Material for the Study of Philippine History.* New Day Publications, Quezon City, Philippines.

1994   *Barangay: Sixteenth Century Philippine Culture and Society.* Ateneo de Manila Press, Quezon City, Philippines.

Solheim, Wilhelm

1964   *The Archaeology of the Central Philippines: A Study Chiefly of the Iron Age and Its Relationships.* Philippine Bureau of Printing, Manila.

1982   Philippine Prehistory. In *The People and Art of the Philippines,* edited by G. Casals, R. Jose, E. Casino, G. Ellis, and W. Solheim, pp. 17–83. Museum of Cultural History, University of California, Los Angeles.

Spoehr, Alexander

1973   *Zamboanga and Sulu: An Archaeological Approach to Ethnic Diversity.* Ethnology Monograph no. 1. University of Pittsburgh, PA.

Tambiah, Stanley

1976   *World Conquerer and World Renouncer: A Study in Religion and Polity in Thailand Against an Historical Background.* Cambridge University Press, Cambridge.

Tarling, Nicholas

1963   *Piracy and Politics in the Malay World.* F. W. Chesire, Melbourne.

Taylor, Keith

1992   The Early Kingdoms. In *The Cambridge History of Southeast Asia,* vol. 1, edited by N. Tarling, pp. 137–182. Cambridge University Press, Cambridge.

Thomaz, Luis Felipe

1993   The Malay Sultanate of Melaka. In *Southeast Asia in the Early Modern Era,* edited by A. Reid, pp. 69–90. Cornell University Press, Ithaca, NY.

Ts'ao, Yung-ho

1962   Chinese Overseas Trade in the Late Ming Period. In *Second Biennial Conference Proceedings, International Association of Historians of Asia*, pp. 429–458. International Association of Historians of Asia, Taipei.

Unabia, Carmen

2000   *Bukidnon Myths and Rituals*. Ateneo de Manila University Press, Quezon City, Philippines.

Vayda, Andrew

1966   Expansion and Warfare amongst Swidden Agriculturalists. *American Anthropologist* 63: 346–358.

Vink, Marcus

2003   The World's Oldest Trade: Dutch Slavery and Slave Trade in the Indian Ocean in the Seventeenth Century. *Journal of World History* 14(2):131–177.

Warren, James F.

1985   *The Sulu Zone, 1768–1898: The Dynamics of External Trade, Slavery and Ethnicity in the Transformation of a Southeast Asian Maritime State*. 2nd printing. New Day Press, Quezon City, Philippines.

2002   *Iranun and Balangingi: Globalization, Maritime Raiding and the Birth of Ethnicity*. New Day Press, Quezon City, Philippines.

Watson, James (editor)

1980   *Asian and African Systems of Slavery*. University of California Press, Berkeley.

Wheatley, Paul

1971   *The Pivot of the Four Quarters*. Aldine, Chicago.

Winzeler, Robert

1981   The Study of the Southeast Asian State. In *The Study of the State*, edited by H. Claessen and P. Skalnik, pp. 455–467. Mouton, The Hague.

Wolters, O. W.

1967   *Early Indonesian Commerce*. Cornell University Press, Ithaca, New York.

1999   *History, Culture, and Region in Southeast Asian Perspectives*. Rev. ed. Southeast Asian Program Publications. Cornell University, Ithaca, NY.

Wu, Ching-hong

1959   A Study of References to the Philippines in Chinese Sources from Earliest Times to the Ming Dynasty. *Philippine Social Sciences and Humanities Review* 24(1–2):1–182.

6

Slavery, Household Production, and Demography on the Southern Northwest Coast

Cables, Tacking, and Ropewalks

Kenneth M. Ames

This chapter is about the role of slaves and slavery in the household and prestige economies of complex hunter-gatherers in the Greater Lower Columbia region (GLCR) (Hajda 1984) of western North America (Figure 6.1). This region is part of the southern Northwest Coast. Northwest Coast slavery is one of the best-known examples of slavery in a non-state, non-agricultural context, and is the subject of a major book (Donald 1997). Hajda (2005) examined slavery on the lower Columbia River in response to Donald. Contrasting views of the social role of Northwest Coast slaves see them either as markers of the prestige and power of their owners, or as essential labor in the production system that supported Northwest Coast elites.

Slavery is not expected in hunter-gatherer societies, and its existence in the Northwest Coast violates long held anthropological stereotypes. The category "complex hunter-gatherers" is in many ways a residual category, used for groups that do not fit the stereotypes. In documenting the scale of household production in the GLCR, this chapter seeks to establish the parameters within which slaves and their owners acted.

It is also about a common methodological and theoretical problem for archaeology: how is it possible to do the archaeology of something that either has no archaeological record or one that is inaccessible? In this case, not only is there no obvious archaeological record for slavery in the GLCR, but there is an extensive documentary record. What possible contribution can archaeology make in this matter? I present some partial answers by expanding Wylie's well-known analogies of archaeological practice, cables of evidence and tacking (Wylie 1989), to include the ropewalks where cables were once made. My core argument is that the seemingly contradictory claims about Northwest Coast slavery cannot be evaluated without recourse to archaeological evidence.

Excavations of houses in three GLCR villages dating between AD 1400 and 1855 provide the evidence presented here. These excavations were conducted within a problem orientation based on household archaeology and focused on houses' social and economic organization (e.g., papers in Sobel et al. 2006). The evidence is silent about the presence or absence of slaves, but it does provide a context for evaluating estimates of slave numbers and statements about the roles of slaves in local and regional economies and societies.

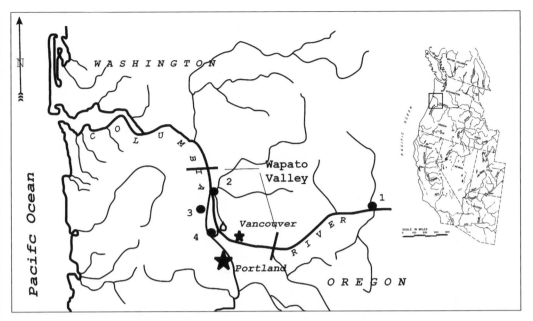

FIGURE 6.1. Map of the Greater Lower Columbia region showing locations of sites mentioned in text: 1, Clahclellah; 2, Cathlapotle; 3, Meier; 4, Site 35MU4.

Working in the Ropewalk

Rope walk *n*…1 or rope yard: a long path devoted to the manufacture of rope down which the worker carries and lays the strands.

—*Webster's International Dictionary*, 3rd ed.

The answer to the question "What can archaeology contribute to a debate based on documentary evidence and for which there is no direct archaeological evidence?" is that archaeological evidence is a crucial and otherwise unavailable frame of reference for Northwest production and, hence, of the role or lack of a role of slaves in that production. To do this requires treating the archaeological and documentary evidence as separate frames of reference (Binford 2001) or as distinct lines of evidence.

Wylie (1989) uses two nautical analogies for archaeological practice: cables and tacking. The cable analogy refers to archaeologists using multiple lines of evidence to build cables of inference; any given evidentiary thread may be weak or even fragmentary, but woven together, as a cable, they are strong. Her tacking analogy is more complex. Tacking is how sailing ships sail into the wind, making progress by zigzagging. Thus

archaeologists tack horizontally between lines of evidence, which combine multiple threads of theory and evidence; one also tacks vertically within cables between theory and evidence, and among phenomenological scales. One goal of tacking between or among lines of evidence is establishing their independence. Wylie's context for discussing independence among evidentiary lines is especially germane because it was part of a discussion of historic archaeology and archaeological and historical data as independent and mutually constraining lines of evidence.

According to Wylie, lines of evidence should be independent along three dimensions (Wylie 2002): causal, epistemological (inferential), and disciplinary, and she believes historical archaeologists often conflate these. Dating a site using radiocarbon testing and frequency seriation exemplifies all three. The physical processes underlying radiocarbon dating are completely independent of the material culture measured by frequency seriation. They are causally independent and therefore potentially epistemologically or inferentially independent. They also have disciplinary independence since the fields of physics and archaeology are institutionally and structurally distinct.

Lines of evidence can lose their inferential independence, and Wylie warns that epistemological independence may be more apparent than real (Wylie 2002). However, she is more concerned with the underlying attitudes, goals, and culture that scholars may share across disciplinary lines and that can create common biases than with the merging or blurring of distinct lines of evidence, which is the concern here.

Wylie requires that epistemological independence be established for each case rather than assumed. Pursuing the cable analogy, then, before weaving the cable, the strands must be laid out in the ropewalk, and then compared and examined. Because the strands are spread on the walk, cables are said to be "cable laid." Technically, a cable-laid rope is woven of three, three-stranded hawsers. When woven together, the individual threads can be difficult to follow or even identify. Actually, archaeologists often do not weave evidentiary cables: instead we blend evidence to the point that the sources of inferences become lost or invisible. I submit they should be very visible or, at the very least, easily teased out. One should be able to trace the strands woven into the hawsers and then woven into evidentiary cables. The purpose here, then, is not to write a blended account of lower Columbia River slavery but to do some of the ropewalk work by laying out strands of evidence and examining and testing them.

The Greater Lower Columbia Region

The GLCR encompasses the final 200 miles of the Columbia River and adjacent portions of the Pacific coastline and was one of several interaction spheres comprising the Northwest Coast culture area (Hajda 1984; Suttles 1990; Ames and Maschner 1999). Hajda defined it using local and regional patterns of social and economic interaction. The documentary record derives primarily from the accounts of explorers (such as Lewis and Clark), of individuals in the fur trade, and early settlers because we lack the voluminous ethnographic record that exists for portions of the coast farther north.

The area is topographically and ecologically diverse. At its eastern edge, the Columbia Gorge breaches the Cascade Mountain range. West of the gorge, the river passes through the Portland Basin, which Lewis and Clark called the Wapato

Valley, the name used here. Below the lowland, the river penetrates the Coast Range, a long, rugged chain of relatively low, heavily forested mountains, before entering its wide, fjord-like estuary and meeting the Pacific Ocean. The climate is maritime, with heavy rains and moderate temperatures.

Several ethnolinguistic groups occupied the GLCR at contact. Speakers of Chinookan languages were the most numerous (Hajda 1984; Silverstein 1990) with large, comparatively dense populations. Chinookan social organization and economy had much in common with other Northwest Coast societies (Hajda 1984; Silverstein 1990). The household was the basic socioeconomic unit, and the village or town the maximal unit. Households lived in large post-and-beam plank houses of western red cedar (*Thuja plicata*). Society was divided into two broad classes: free and slave (Donald 1997). Free people were subdivided into a chiefly elite and commoners. Chiefly status was based on ancestry, wealth, and widespread social and economic ties (Hajda 1984). The slave population in the late eighteenth and early nineteenth centuries may have been 20 to 25 percent of the total (Donald 1997; Hajda 1984; Mitchell 1985).

Subsistence was based on harvesting an array of terrestrial and aquatic resources, including mass harvesting of fish, most famously the five species of salmon that ran in the Columbia. Resources were hand processed, and vast quantities of food were stored (e.g., Sobel 2004), sometimes requiring large amounts of labor over short, intense time periods. Other tasks could be accomplished more slowly. In general, though, production was organized as sets of simultaneous rather than sequential, lineal tasks (Ames and Maschner 1999). Simultaneous task organization placed a priority on a household's ability to field labor.

The Fur Trade

Ongoing interaction between the peoples of the Greater Lower Columbia region and Europeans began in AD 1792, when the first ships entered the Columbia River.[1] Between 1792 and 1811, contact was primarily via the maritime fur trade. Ships bound for Chinese markets entered the river each year to trade with the Natives for hides and sometimes furs. Lewis and Clark's lengthy presence, from October 1805 through April 1806 (Moulton 1990), was the major exception to this pattern before 1811.

The continental fur trade in the region began in 1811 with the establishment of Astoria by the American Pacific Fur Company at the river's mouth. The first permanent European presence in the entire Pacific Northwest, Astoria was the center of continued year-round efforts to acquire furs. It was sold to the British North West Company in 1813 and renamed Fort George. The North West and Hudson's Bay Companies merged in 1821, keeping the Hudson's Bay Company name. After this merger, the Hudson's Bay Company maintained Fort George and in 1824–1825 built a second lower Columbia post, Fort Vancouver. Fort Vancouver was located in the Wapato Valley and was the Hudson's Bay Company headquarters for its Columbia Department, which encompassed the entire Pacific Northwest.

Northwest Coast Slavery

I draw on the work of Donald (1997), Hajda (2005), and Sobel (2004) in summarizing the salient points of slavery on the Northwest Coast. In general, slave status was usually permanent; violence was the ultimate means of origin and recruitment (individuals born as slaves were the children of captives); slaves were alienated from their natal circumstances (they were without kin and, to some extent on the coast, without gender [as a social construct]; and slaves were under a social stigma, so that in the rare case of someone escaping and returning home, they and their descendents would carry the taint of slavery. This summary description loses important nuances explored in detail by Donald (1997), Hajda (2005), and Sobel (2004).

Since slavery was usually hereditary (although originating in capture), slaves formed a distinct class or caste. In fact, slaves and non-slaves may have been the only status distinction strongly visible in many Northwest Coast households.

Most slaves were owned by elite individuals, but lower-ranked high-status individuals also might own slaves. Slave owners treated their slaves as they wished; they could be coddled, sold, or destroyed as desired. Slaves were used as assassins and bodyguards to reinforce status

and perhaps Northwest Coast chiefs' weak power (Ames 1995). Slaves were also inherited and disposed of as grave goods like any prestige item. Slave owners had rights to a female slave's children. Upon death, slaves could be thrown away (that is, their bodies could be discarded without regard to normal mortuary practice [see Ames 2005; Hajda 2005]).

In some parts of the coast, slaves might be distinguishable from their owners by the presence or absence of permanent body modifications. On the northern Northwest Coast, free women wore lip plugs or labrets. An enslaved woman could be marked by the absence of the labret but the presence of the slit for it (and, in some cases, the lower lip hanging loosely) or possibly the absence of her lower incisors (Cybulski 1993). Free people along the lower Columbia practiced frontal/occipital cranial deformation; thus slaves, all of whom originated outside the region, had round heads. The daily life of slaves, however, could differ little from that of their owners.

In some places on the coast, slaves slept in the least comfortable part of the house near the structure's single door. Ethnographic sources are ambiguous about this (Sobel 2004). What is unambiguous is that slaves were the household drudges, "hewers of wood, haulers of water," but none of the tasks performed by slaves were done by them exclusively. Donald lists twelve broad subsistence/household chores performed by slaves (Donald 1997: Tables A-6, A-7, 318–319). Any and all of these tasks were also done by free household members. Walter (2006) argues that among these various tasks, a primary role of slaves and women on the Northwest Coast was processing foods.

Estimating the numbers of slaves on the coast is a typical demographic problem in ethnohistory (see below). Donald (1997) reviewed a variety of documentary sources (Table 6.1) and estimates about 20 percent of the GLCR population to have been slaves, generally the highest on the coast. Hajda (2005) reports an even higher average figure of 24 percent for the region. Donald concludes that with the exception of a few places, including the GLCR, the numbers of slaves held at any one time on the coast were probably low but variable, with slaves ubiquitous but not numerous.

TABLE 6.1. Estimates of the Relative Frequencies of Slaves in Northwest Coast Populations

Region	Median	Minimum	Maximum	Inter-Quartile Range	Number of Groups
North 1840s	4.8	1.4	26.1	2.8–11.8	29
Central ca. 1850	5.0	1.3	7.2	2.3–5.1	26
South ca. 1850	3.7	0.3	17.3	1.8–5.1	16
Lower Columbia River	20.0	15.8	47.4	20.0–24.8	13

Source: Donald 1997.

There were four slave-trading networks (Donald 1997), two major ones and two much smaller. The major networks encompassed the northern and southern coasts, and the GLCR was at the center of the southern network. Slaves in the GLCR were acquired either through raids on distant people or through exchange (Hajda 2005). This network was part of a much larger and ancient exchange network through which flowed a variety of goods, from processed foods to prestige goods.

Slaves and slavery were an important part of the prestige and/or political economy of the Northwest Coast. Donald (1997) sees their labor as essential to producing the wealth needed by Northwest Coast elites to maintain their status. On the coast, labor transformed harvested food into wealth; feasting, exchange, and other activities transformed wealth into prestige. Chiefs did not have power over household members (Ames 1995; Donald 1997), but they did over slaves. Because slaves were the only labor the Northwest Coast elite controlled, Donald argues that they were crucial elements in the political economies of Northwest Coast households.

Alternatively, slaves were wealth or prestige goods (animate parts of the prestige technology, in Hayden's [1998] terms). Their labor was useful but not essential. They might even be an indicator of what has sometimes been seen as the "irrationality" of Northwest Coast status competition, costing more than they produced. Hajda describes chiefly status on the lower Columbia most succinctly:

Here...the local group or village consisted of one or more large houses, each with a core consisting of an extended family related through males. The most prominent household head might be considered the village "chief" or headman. His influence, like that of other household heads, depended on his ability to accumulate wealth and thereby attract followers, create kinship links through marriage, conduct raids, and provide food. Descent from a high-ranking family was necessary to assert or maintain high status, but the possession of wealth was crucial. Though numbers of wives...and sons...as well as dentalia and other property...were said to be important for chiefly status, the possession of slaves is mentioned most often.... While George Simpson's comment that "every Flat Head [lower Columbia River] Indian who owns a slave considers himself a chief"...may be an exaggeration, or perhaps reflects changes that had taken place by 1825, the existence of "chiefs" can be seen to have depended at least partially on the existence of slavery. (Hajda 2005:570)

In Hajda's view, Northwest Coast social status was a continuum, with the highest elite at one pole and slaves at the other. High status depended on the negation and degradation of others; it required the existence of slaves, not their production. She also makes the point that it is not possible to assess the contribution of slaves to household production given the available documentary sources. This is one of two specific issues this chapter explores using archaeological data. The second issue is whether the high estimated numbers of slaves for the GLCR are plausible.

The Archaeology and Prehistory of Northwest Slavery and Elites

There are two time periods on the northern coast during which slavery plausibly developed: 3500 to 1000 BC and AD 500 to 1200 (Ames 2001). The latter period is marked by intensified warfare across western North America (e.g., Chatters 2004; Lambert 2002). Possible direct evidence for slaves and slavery on the northern coast includes remains of individuals discarded at death rather than formally buried (e.g., Cybulski 1979), individuals possibly killed as captives (Cybulski 1979), and skewed sex ratios in burial populations (Ames 2005; Cybulski 1993; Ames and Maschner 1999). These data are not available for the lower Columbia River and unlikely to be since much of it is derived from excavations of human burials, which are strongly opposed by most Native peoples in the GLCR. Evidence for conflict elsewhere is also fairly direct (Ames and Maschner 1999). There is reasonably good evidence for increased labor demands as well (Ames 2001, 2005). The evidence for the evolution of elites is better, but the timing is controversial.

There is a general consensus that permanent elites based on ascription existed on the coast at least by AD 500 with some kind of vertical social differentiation (e.g., ranking based on achievement) present earlier. I argue (e.g., Ames 2005) that ascribed ranking was present by approximately 1000 BC on the northern coast, if not earlier. The archaeological data used in this chapter dates between AD 1400 and 1830, well after the consensus date for the emergence of ranking. The available documentary evidence clearly indicates the presence of both elites and slaves when the era of documentary evidence opened in 1792.

The Archaeological Evidence

The bulk of the archaeological data used here was produced by Portland State University's Wapato Valley Archaeological Project (WVAP), which was initiated in 1988. The project's research is framed by household archaeology for reasons developed elsewhere (e.g., Ames 1996, 2006; Smith 2004; Sobel 2004; papers in Sobel et al. 2006). The evidence discussed here is drawn from three archaeological sites. Analyses of materials from two of them (Meier and Cathlapotle) are ongoing, so much of what follows is preliminary.

The Sites

Meier (35CO5) is located in the Wapato Valley (see Figure 6.1 for locations of sites). Excavations conducted from 1987 to 1991 exposed portions of a large (14 × 30 m) plank house, exterior midden, and activity deposits. There were minimally two broad categories of wooden houses in the GLCR (Hajda 1994): permanent structures used during the winter or year-round, and more temporary structures. Permanent (or winter) structures also fall into two broad categories: those with open interiors, and those divided permanently by walls into compartments. The Meier house appears to have been of the former style, with no dividing walls, but it did have a cellar: a voluminous complex of open areas and pits beneath the floor (Ames et al. 1992; Ames et al. 2008). Although such pits were common elements in Chinookan houses in the Wapato Valley, they are not described by early Euroamerican travelers. The Meier complex is the largest known archaeologically in the GLCR. The house was constructed between AD 1400 and 1450, and abandoned sometime after contact, perhaps between AD 1810 and 1820 based on nineteen calibrated radiocarbon dates and trade goods (Kaehler 2002). Meier is not mentioned in any Euroamerican accounts.

Cathlapotle (45CL1) is in the Wapato Valley on the Washington State side of the Columbia River. The site contains six very large depressions marking the locations of plank houses arrayed in two rows paralleling the nearest river. Fieldwork was conducted from 1991 to 1996 and extensively sampled two structures as well as non-house deposits. The structures are designated Houses 1–6 (there is also a deeply buried House 7). Houses 1 and 4 were extensively sampled, and laboratory analyses are ongoing. Four of the six houses were divided by walls into compartments. Two houses had open interiors or lacked substantial interior dividers. All tested houses had storage pits. The site's occupation spans ca. AD 1450 to AD 1833 based on fifty-two radiocarbon dates (Ames et al. 1999) and historic trade goods (Kaehler 2002). One significant element of the chronology is the archaeological clarity of contact. Glass and ceramic trade goods appear abruptly in the deposits generally about 70 cm below the surface in deposits that are generally about 2 m deep.

Cathlapotle, one the major Chinookan towns in the Wapato Valley, is mentioned frequently in Euroamerican accounts written between 1792 and its abandonment. Its people and chief(s) had ongoing and complex relationships with the fur traders and other Euroamericans in the region. Fort Vancouver, the Hudson's Bay Company's administrative center for the entire Columbia District (Oregon, Washington, and British Columbia), was 18 miles above Cathlapotle on the Columbia River between 1824 and 1844.

Clahclellah (45SAll), located in the Columbia Gorge, was completely excavated in the 1970s by a Phase III data recovery project (Minor et al. 1989). The site was not part of the WVAP. However, Sobel (2004) included an artifact sample from Clahclellah in her analysis of artifacts from Cathlapotle, allowing us to incorporate Clahclellah into the broader project. The site contained remains of seven plank houses, exterior activity areas, and perhaps earlier mat lodges (Minor et al. 1989). The plank-house village may have been established as early as AD 1500 or as late as AD 1700, and it was abandoned by AD 1856. It is briefly mentioned in Euroamerican accounts between 1805 and 1836. Clahclellah did not have the multiple linkages to the fur trade that Cathlapotle had. The houses were arrayed in two rows facing the river. The structures are broadly similar to those at Meier and Cathlapotle, although smaller. They have subfloor pits, but the pits are not merged and hence do not form cellars or trenches.

Recruitment:
Slavery and Regional Interaction

The GLCR interaction sphere (Hajda 1984) interconnected with the Plateau interaction sphere (Hayden and Schulting 1997) and the network of regional interaction spheres comprising the Northwest Coast (Suttles 1990; Ames and Maschner 1999). A trading center near the modern city of The Dalles, at the upstream end of the Columbia Gorge, was one of the major nodes for both sets of interaction spheres (Figure 6.2). The Dalles center was adjacent to the Columbia River's premier salmon fishing locale and attracted people from great distances. The river's mouth and the Wapato Valley were also major nodes.

The coastal interaction spheres probably formed in the Early Holocene, if not earlier (Ames and Maschner 1999). At the same time, in the interior, marine shell beads and obsidian flowed north from California though the Great Basin into the eastern Columbia Plateau region. The Plateau interaction sphere crystallized by 3500 BP (Ames 2000; Ames et al. 1998; but see Hayden and Schulting 1997). Grave goods suggest exchange and interaction on the Plateau and Columbia River intensified after 1500 BP (Schulting 1995). Among the grave goods are dentalia and copper, both of which probably originated on the central and northern coast, respectively, perhaps entering the Plateau via the GLCR. Extraregional interaction on the Plateau seems to have shifted from primarily a north-south orientation to a west-to-east (coast to interior) orientation in the Late Holocene. Interaction along the coast continued to be strongly north-south, although that is an oversimplification.

Figure 6.2 overlays Donald's reconstruction of the southern Northwest Coast slave network (white lines) onto the distribution of obsidian sources represented at Meier, Cathlapotle, and Clahclellah. The location and number of sources on the map are approximate. There are more than a hundred obsidian sources in Oregon, some quite small, but others very large and diffuse (Craig Skinner, pers. comm.).

Figure 6.2 also reproduces Stern's (1998) map of the trade routes (black lines) in the northwestern United States. The major route from the south split in the Klamath Basin, with a western route entering the southern Willamette Valley and thence up the valley into the Wapato Valley. The bulk of the three sites' obsidian (76 percent, $n = 445$) is from sources along this route. The eastern route ran east of the Cascades, meeting the Columbia River not far east of The Dalles. Only 8 percent of the obsidian derives from sources either on this eastern fork or in southern Oregon and northern California. The rest (16 percent) comes from sources in the high Cascades, close to the eastern route. None is from the many sources farther east in Oregon or Idaho.

There was some east-to-west movement of obsidian into the GLCR. Ellis and Skinner (2004) examined sources for obsidian recovered from twenty-six Wapato Valley sites in an effort to reconstruct the routes followed by obsidian within the valley. Excluding Cathlapotle and Meier from their sample left fifty-four obsidian pieces, of which twenty-five (46 percent) originated from the Willamette Valley sources, twenty-two (41

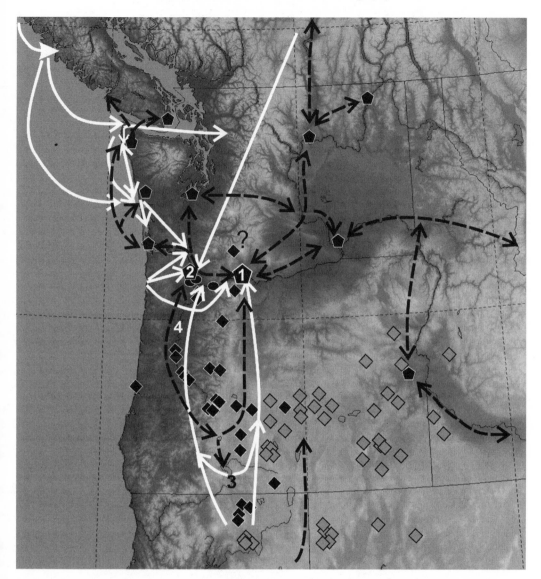

FIGURE 6.2. Map of the slave routes (white lines) and trade routes (black dashed lines) in the southern Northwest. Black diamonds indicate obsidian sources represented in samples from the Meier, Cathlapotle, and Clahclellah sites. Grey diamonds are sources not represented. Black pentagons are major trading centers. Locations and numbers are approximate. Numbers refer to locations mentioned in text: 1, The Dalles; 2, The Wapato Valley; 3, The Klamath Basin; 4, The Willamette Valley.

percent) from the sources east of the Cascades (the eastern route), and seven (13 percent) from sources farther east.

The general correspondence between obsidian sources and the southern slave routes, as provocative as it is, needs to be approached cautiously. It certainly does not mean captives trudged north carrying obsidian cores. The connection may be indirect, perhaps indicating only

that both moved north along the same ancient, well-established routes. Although obsidian was probably a prestige marker at Cathlapotle and Clahclellah (Sobel 2004), it would be premature to link the movement of slaves and obsidian together as prestige goods, which moved in a variety of directions in the region.

We currently have insufficient data from the three sites to document north-to-south linkages either along the coast or from the Canadian Plateau, although obsidian from Oregon is found archaeologically across southern British Columbia. Meier produced marine shells, including dentalia, as well as two mackerel vertebrae. It also has two nephrite adzes that might be from south-central British Columbia. Both Meier and Cathlapotle have large copper assemblages, but at present only four have been analyzed, and they are European in origin.

Slaves and obsidian appear to have moved into the GLCR primarily along the same routes from the south. Whether most slaves, like most of the obsidian, moved up the Willamette Valley route, is unknown. Both slaves and obsidian were prestige goods, but it is very premature to conclude their movement was linked. Having said that, this close correspondence is very intriguing. What is also unknown is the impact of the northern movement of slaves on the likely donor populations in Oregon and California.

Production

The developing archaeological evidence on household production in the GLCR (e.g., Smith 2004; Sobel 2004) indicates it was intense. This section reviews several lines of evidence to support that claim. Among these are the labor costs of the structures themselves during their use-lives; the available storage space within the structures as a proxy measure for the scale of storage; and the spatial organization of production, currently measured by the distributions of shaped artifacts and bone, antler, and lithic debitage.

These structures had relatively long use-lives. Both the Meier house and Cathlapotle House 1 were used, at a minimum, for 370 years (Ames 1996; Ames et al. 1992; Ames et al. 1999; Ames et al. 2008). Cathlapotle House 4 was used a minimum of 200 years. According to estimated labor costs for Northwest Coast houses using the amount of lumber in them as a proxy measure (Ames 1996; Ames et al. 1992), the Meier house is estimated to have required between ca. 40,000 and 50,000 board feet of wood. (A board foot is 12 × 12 × 1 in. and is the standard cut lumber measure in the United States, where a modern suburban house requires 10,000 to 12,000 board feet.) For other archaeologically and ethnohistorically documented Chinookan houses, I estimated between 6,200 and 147,000 board feet (Ames 1996: Table 9.3). Gahr (2006) examines in greater detail the labor costs of Northwest Coast plank houses, including those of the GLCR. She analyzes these costs through three phases in the use-life of these structures: construction, maintenance, and demise. Assuming the Meier house was constructed in a short time period (following common Northwest Coast practice, but not directly documented on the lower Columbia River), its construction involved between 1,480 and 2,579 people. That figure includes everyone involved: builders, people providing food, and so on.

Ames et al. (1992) calculated the maintenance requirements of the Meier house to be between 420,000 and 1.1 million board feet of lumber over its use-life. This estimate is based on several lines of archaeological evidence. We have not extended these estimates to Cathlapotle, but they are sufficient. Gahr (2006) examined additional lines of evidence such as the vulnerability to decay of the woods used, infestations, fire, and load stresses, and she concluded that labor estimates based on board feet underestimate labor costs for house maintenance. She further observed that her estimates of the labor costs of house construction are 20 to 48 times higher than the estimated household populations. House demise was an ever-present risk, often due to fire and a maintenance load beyond the household's labor capacity. In short, these structures demanded ongoing, high labor investments.

Available storage space is a common archaeological proxy measure for investment in storage. For example, Christakis (1999) estimated "storage potential" for recent and Bronze Age houses on Crete using the volume of domestic storage spaces and jars. Ethnohistoric and ethnographic data suggest that the primary storage space in GLCR houses, as with the Northwest Coast generally, was under the house's roof, where different foods were hung on racks and lines. This space was filled in the fall. However, a number of excavated GLCR houses have large pit complexes, or cellars, beneath their floors (Ames et al. 2008). The storage potential of the subfloor pit complexes at Clahclellah and Cathlapotle House 4 are equivalent to the most common houses in Christakis's modern and Bronze Age samples, whereas the potentials for Meier and Cathlapotle

House 1 far exceed those for all of the Cretan structures, including palaces (Ames et al. 2008). They even exceed the storage potential of the great Minoan palace of Knossos. These estimates do not include the space beneath the roof. Using the figures for the dimensions of the Meier house (Ames et al. 1992), the storage potential under the roof was 907,000 liters, and the cellar's was 127,000 liters. These figures are at best an approximation and can only suggest the scale of the available space, which may well have been smaller but still enormous.

The pit complexes are only known archaeologically, and they contain a diversity of materials (Ames et al. 2008) that Kent (1999) terms both food and non-food storage. They are rich in plant, animal, and fish remains, indicating food storage was their primary but not sole function. However, they were not filled with rubbish (Smith 2006; Ames et al. 2008). The scale of the storage potential supports a hypothesis that stored food production was geared not just for household consumption but to create a significant surplus, probably for exchange and alliance formation (that is, conversion into prestige).

Darby's analysis of wapato production provides some evidence with which to gage that possibility. Wapato (*Sagittaria latifolia*), (a.k.a. "Indian potato" or "arrowhead root") is a widely distributed wetland plant whose tubers or corms were a GLCR staple. In an exhaustive study, Darby (1996) assumed wapato provided 20 percent of the annual caloric intake for a family of five, and she estimated that a family would need 0.633 metric tons of wapato per year. Her figures also suggest the storage space needed for a family of five possessing 0.633 metric tons of wapato. Lacking estimates of the volume/weight ratio of a wapato tuber, I used volume/weight of potatoes (Alabama Cooperative Extension Service 1997). Potatoes and wapato roots are sufficiently similar for this to be appropriate (Darby 1996). Using the Meier household population estimate of 203 people (developed below) and Darby's assumption that wapato contributed 20 percent of a year's caloric intake, 26 metric tons of wapato would have been required annually. That translates to approximately 33,000 liters of storage space (assuming it was all collected at once) or 26 percent of the potential cellar space, remember-

ing the space under the roof for other foods.[2] If we combine the space under the roof and the cellar, the wapato would require 3.2 percent of the total storage potential of the Meier house.

Two final examples of the scale of production are thermally altered rocks (TAR) and acorn processing. A variety of processing features, including numerous small earth ovens at Cathlapotle and multiple hearths both inside and outside the houses at all these sites, produced TAR. The amount of TAR can be used as a rough measure of the amount of heating, which would include food processing. Meier produced 8,100 kg of TAR for a mean of 61 kg/m^3. The Cathlapotle excavations yielded much less TAR, although still a great deal: 1,900 kg or 19 kg/m^3. This difference reflects, in part, differences in our sampling, the sizes of the sites, and their depositional histories. Applying the density figures to the sites as a whole, Cathlapotle is estimated to contain over a million kg of TAR, while Meier is estimated to have more than 600,000 kg.

The final example of the scale of processing comes not from Meier or Cathlapotle but recent work at a Wapato Valley wet site (35MU 4). The site contains at least sixty baskets preserved in the intertidal zone of a distributary of the Willamette River (Figure 6.1) (Croes et al. 2007). The baskets are filled with acorns (*Quercus garryana*), which were leached by water flowing through them from an aquifer and probably the tidal flux. The sixty baskets are estimated to have the capacity to hold approximately two million acorns annually, assuming they were used simultaneously. Acorns and hazelnuts (*Corylus cornuta*) are also ubiquitous at Meier and Cathlapotle, where they were roasted in ovens. The acorns indicate the kinds of labor involved in production in the GLCR. Some of it was skilled (making the baskets), but much was not (collecting and transporting the nuts, monitoring the baskets). These several, admittedly ad hoc, estimates need much more work and refinement, but they suggest a capacity to produce significant surpluses of processed foods. They also clearly point to the role slaves potentially would play in the production of processed foods. Given that capacity, the next issue is: how was production organized?

The available evidence comes from formal (Smith 2004; Sobel 2004) and edge-wear

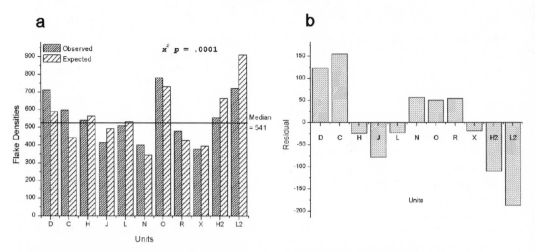

FIGURE 6.3. Chi-square analyses of flake densities in eleven excavation units within the Meier houses. Figure 6.3a shows the observed and expected densities, and also illustrates the high density of flakes throughout the deposits. Figure 6.3b shows the difference (residual) between observed and expected densities.

analyses of tools (Smith 2004). For a variety purposes, all studies of production use household segments as their analytical units. At Cathlapotle the units are based on architectural divisions (all of House 4, the three excavated compartments in House 1); at Meier they are arbitrary but correspond closely to the distribution of hearths, which are regularly spaced along the house's long axis. These house segments are also used to investigate status (Table 6.2). The assignment of high status at Cathlapotle to the southern compartment in House 1 (compartment H1d) is on firm inferential grounds; the assignment of high status to the northern section of the Meier house is probably correct, but the archaeological evidence is contradictory. The picture developed by Sobel and Smith is being altered somewhat by current work, but their basic results are robust and are summarized qualitatively in Table 6.2. Among the key points, it is evident that all house segments, including high-status ones, participated in all major productive activities: everyone did everything, or almost everyone did. They might not have done everything to the same degree, but the differences in degree are statistically significant (e.g., Smith 2004). Different household segments focused on different activities, although not exclusively (Smith 2004; Sobel 2004). Chipped lithic production within the Meier house is illustrative (Figure 6.3). While the me-

dian density of lithic waste in the eleven units sampled in the pit complex was 541 flakes/m^3, lithic debris occurs in significantly (chi–square probability $< .0001$) high densities in five units: two adjacent units in the north, and three in the central sections. These units also have high numbers of lithic cores, although cores are also found throughout the house. Lithic reduction occurred everywhere (as demonstrated by the universally high densities of flakes), but significantly more intensely in certain places. There are no special skills represented. Lithic reduction at Meier and Cathlapotle was opportunistic, relying heavily on bipolar production (Hamilton 1994).

There is no consistency across households, inferred status ranks, or between the communities as to what activities were emphasized. At Meier, land mammal hunting, for example, was emphasized by residents of the southern portion of the house, the one thought to be the low-status section. At Cathlapotle, land mammal hunting was emphasized in H1D, the highest-status house segment. There seems to have been a high-status emphasis on woodworking at Meier, but no special emphasis on it at all in either of the two sampled households at Cathlapotle. Copper working may be an exception to the lack of association between status and activity. Evidence for it is restricted to presumed low-status sections of the Meier house and Cathlapotle House 1.

Hide Production in Response to the Fur Trade

From 1792 on, English and American fur traders periodically visited the lower Columbia River to trade for elk hides and furs among other things. They were also provisioned by the Native peoples. At present there is no evidence that food production was intensified as a result of this provisioning, but it appears the processing of elk hides did increase. Called "clamons," these hides were in demand on the central and northern coasts as armor. Meier and Cathlapotle have direct and indirect archaeological evidence for hide processing, and perhaps for differential involvement in the fur trade. The evidence includes elk remains and lithic scrapers with hide-working use-wear (Smith 2004).

The faunal assemblages at Meier and Cathlapotle are dominated by deer (*Odocoileus*) and elk (*Cervus*), representing 77 percent and 81 percent of all mammals, respectively (Lyman and Ames 2005). However, at Meier only 20 percent of the cervids are elk, while at Cathlapotle 58 percent are. This difference likely reflects local ecology, but it is paralleled by the numbers of hide scrapers. At Meier 17 percent of lithic tools with analyzed edge wear (*n* = 301) are hide scrapers, compared to 47 percent (*n* = 319) at Cathlapotle. Hide scrapers were present in small numbers at both sites before contact and in much larger numbers after.

Overall, Cathlapotle and Meier appear to have been differently involved in the fur trade. The two sites have similarly sized tool assemblages (ca. 10,000 each), but Cathlapotle has a much larger assemblage of historic trade goods. Part of this is chronological. Meier was probably abandoned a decade or so before Cathlapotle, which was probably abandoned around 1833 (Kaehler 2002; Ames et al. 1999). Meier is also off the beaten track, several kilometers from the Columbia River although linked to it via small waterways. It is not clearly identified in any known fur trade–era document. Cathlapotle had regular contact with Europeans after 1792 (Sobel 2004).

The Demography of Slavery in the GLCR
Regional Demography

Precontact populations on the lower Columbia are estimated to have been large. The best current estimates are Boyd's (1999). He relies heavily

TABLE 6.2. Relative Prestige and Distribution of Productive Household Segments at Meier and Cathlapotle

	Meier North	Meier Central	Meier South	Cathlapotle H1B	Cathlapotle H1C	Cathlapotle H1D	Cathlapotle H4
Relative Prestige of Household Segment	High	Average	Low	Low	Average	High	Average
Relative Prestige of Different Activities							
Terrestrial Hunting	Low	Average	High	Average	Low	High	Average
Aquatic Hunting	High	Low	Low	High	Average	Average	Average
Woodworking	High	Low	High	Average	Average	Average	Average
Bone Working	High	Low	High	NA	NA	NA	NA
Flintknapping	Average	Average	High	Average	Low	High	Average
Hide Scraping	Low	Low	High	Average	High	Low	Average
Grinding	High	Low	High	Average	Average	High	High
Thermal Processing	Average	Low	High	Average	High	Low	Average
Copper Working	Low	Low	High	High	Low	Low	Low

on Lewis and Clark's figures, which are the best for the GLCR's population in the early nineteenth century. Boyd conservatively estimates the precontact population along the lower Columbia River (Wapato Valley and below) at approximately 14,000 (Boyd 1999: Table 6.3).[3] The estimate assumes a 33 percent "across the board mortality" from the first smallpox epidemic in the 1770s, but Boyd points out that mortality may well have been much higher. Of the 14,000, some 2,000 lived at the river's mouth, and 12,000 between the estuary and the Columbia River Gorge. Most were concentrated in the Wapato Valley. Before proceeding, a brief background on Lewis and Clark's numbers is necessary.

The explorers produced two estimates; one developed in the fall of 1805 and the second in the spring of 1806. The latter has been available in print as "Estimate of the Western Indians," but the former remained in manuscript until the 1980s (Boyd and Hajda 1987). Most GLCR population estimates (e.g., Mooney 1928; Kroeber 1939) are based on the published "Estimate," which has higher population figures than the manuscript. Boyd and Hajda (1987) postulate that the differences between the two sets of figures reflect seasonal fluctuations in population along the river, with the lower figures representing a "core" GLCR population.

The region suffered several smallpox epidemics, including the widespread epidemic in the 1770s, an 1801 epidemic, and "mortality" in 1824–1825 that was probably caused by smallpox (Boyd 1999). Dysentery afflicted the region in the mid-1840s, measles in 1848, and smallpox again in 1853. These epidemics differentially affected individual groups in the GLCR. They also were not the most devastating. Between 1830 and 1834 the GLCR experienced summer outbreaks of what Boyd (1975) shows convincingly was malaria. The Wapato Valley was especially hard hit, and Boyd (1999) estimates that 98 percent of that population was lost. For the region as a whole, he estimates an 88 percent population loss.

The only population estimate not reliant on documentary sources is Darby's (1996), which is based on carrying capacity. She calculated the human carrying capacity for Sauvie Island, a large island in the Wapato Valley. Calculating the productivity of wapato for the island along with her assumption that it provided 20 percent of the caloric intake per annum, she estimated Sauvie Island could have supported between 18,000 and 37,000 people. These extremely high figures require considerable caution since they have not been refined or tested using other resources or looking at possible limiting factors. Furthermore, hunter-gatherer populations are notorious for being below carrying capacity. Despite these caveats, Darby's numbers are useful in several ways, one of which is to suggest the possible degree of slack in the local subsistence economy. I will return to this point below.

Estimates for the numbers of slaves are also high. Mitchell (1985), Donald (1997), and Hajda (2005) draw on much the same documentary sources to estimate the number of slaves in the GLCR at 20 to 24 percent. If these numbers are even approximately accurate, they indicate slavery had a major demographic impact on the region and plausibly a major cultural impact as well, with a significant proportion of the population from somewhere else, sometimes far away. That potential impact is currently impossible to assess. Given the data on production reviewed above, the economic effects of an additional several thousand people would have been profound. The key question, of course, is whether these high frequencies were of long standing or a consequence of depopulation and/or economic changes arising from the fur trade. The region's high numbers of slaves may have replaced people lost to epidemics: not socially (that is, they were not adopted into society), but as labor. The timing of the documentary evidence is crucial for exploring this.

Hajda summarizes the critical data for Hudson's Bay Company estimates "of free and slave populations of twelve villages below the Cascades (Kennedy 1824–25)":

> The mean proportion of slaves in the population of the twelve villages was 24 percent. The range is from 16 percent for two villages on Sauvie Island to 47 percent for the village by Fort George, under Concomly's control; Kiesno's village had the second highest percentage, 31 percent slaves. The importance of owning slaves for bolstering the owner's status can be inferred from these figures. (Hajda 2005:580)

Kiesno and Concomly were the regional or "great" chiefs on the lower Columbia during the fur trade era (see Ames 1995). Hajda suggests the very high numbers at Fort George reflect fur trading posts being trading centers for trade among Native peoples as well as between Natives and Europeans. The Hudson's Bay census upon which the slavery figures are based was made shortly after the 1824–1825 "mortality" but before the catastrophic malaria outbreaks (Boyd 1999). The figures are for villages; in Boyd's view, those for the villages at the river's mouth and the estuary accord reasonably well with Lewis and Clark's estimates twenty years before, while those for the Wapato Valley are extremely low (Boyd 1999). Hajda (1984) also regards them as low but accepts the slave percentages.

Although we cannot determine whether these figures accurately reflect earlier periods, we can try to establish their plausibility, and they are all we have or are likely to have. Thus, the 24 percent figure will be used heuristically without necessarily accepting it. Applying it to Boyd's precontact population of 14,000 produces 3,353 slaves, with 475 at the river's mouth and 2,900 upstream. Applying it to Darby's high estimates yields between 4,400 and 8,900 slaves in the Wapato Valley alone. The converse is also important. If 24 percent of the population were slaves, 76 percent were free; using Boyd's figures, approximately 10,600 total were free, including 1,500 at the mouth and slightly more than 9,000 upstream.

To put the 24 percent figure in regional perspective, 4.8 percent is Donald's median figure for the frequency of slaves among groups elsewhere on the coast, which would put just 672 slaves among the lower Columbia River's 14,000 people.

Village and Household Demography

Multiple extended families comprised Northwest Coast households. Although construction histories of the excavated houses show that some persisted for centuries (Ames 1996; Ames et al. 1992; Ames et al. 1999), individual families may have been subject to a cycle of founding, growth, and eventual household death (Ames 2006; Goody 1958). These cycles have important implications for both smaller and larger houses since the proportions of producers (active adults and juveniles) and consumers (the very young and elderly) changed through time (Ames 2006). Recruitment of household members was central to the long-term prospects of any Northwest Coast household (Ames 2006). Consequently, even one or two extra pairs of productive hands might have been important for extended families or households with large numbers of consumers. Slaves were certainly all producers.

In a related argument, I have suggested (Ames 2006) that large households on the coast might have simultaneously pursued low- and high-risk economic strategies. High-risk strategies, such as whaling, seem to be associated with high status, low-risk with low status. Slave labor could be invested in what were dependable but low-risk strategies. Even seemingly small numbers of slaves might have been crucial for managing both the household cycle and subsistence risk. A key goal in household management would have maintaining household size (Ames 2006). Evaluating these hypotheses would require simulating Northwest household dynamics and subsistence practices together, which has not yet been done. However, it is possible to use the estimates developed above to roughly model the possible scale of slavery at the household level and the distribution of slaves among households, particularly since production and prestige were both based in the household. This was done using two sets of data, inferentially independent at one level but not at another, as will be seen.

The first set of data is based on Lewis and Clark's estimates. They not only estimated populations but the number of houses/group in the GLCR. Using these, Hajda (1984) calculated the mean number of household members per group (Table 6.3). There are important regional patterns. Households on the river's mouth and the adjacent coast were smaller ($n = 20$) but more numerous ($n = 286$), whereas in the Wapato Valley they were larger ($n = 58$) but fewer ($n = 158$). Applying the 24 percent figure, the mean number of slaves per household on the coast was 4 ± 1 (standard deviation) with a median of 5 (regardless of which Lewis and Clark estimate is used). In the Wapato Valley the mean was 14 ± 8 ($n = 12$). This assumes a uniform percentage. The 1824 census suggests variation among groups and households in slave numbers, perhaps on the basis of

TABLE 6.3. Estimated Slaves per Household in the GLCR

	Only Estimate or Lewis and Clark's High Estimate				Lewis and Clark's Low Estimate			
	Houses	People	People/House	Slaves/House	Houses	People	People/House	Slaves/House
Coast/River Mouth								
Total	286	5,160	18	—	31	500	16	—
Mean/Group	20	369	19	4	10	167	16	4
Median	16	225	16	4	11	200	18	4
Std. Dev.	16	304	5	1	1	58	7	2
Wapato Valley								
Total	154	7,820	51	14	127	3,060	—	—
Mean/Group	12	602	58	14	14	340	25	6
Median	6	400	50	12	6	200	25	6
Std. Dev.	13	661	31	8	15	443	7	2
GLCR Totals								
Total	502	15,780	31	—	220	4,900	—	—
Mean	18	564	38	9	17	377	22	6
Median	10	270	23	5	9	200	22	5
Std. Dev.	18	666	29	7	19	470	7	4

Source: Hajda 1984.

geography but also on the basis of status, as Hajda stresses. This pattern receives some support from Ray's (1938) ethnography of the Chinook at the Columbia's mouth. According to his informants, the average high-status individual had two or three slaves, and principal ones about six; the regional chief, Concomly, had ten to twelve. Ray's ethnography was based on interviews in the 1930s with two elderly informants about conditions almost a century earlier, so these figures need to be viewed with caution. However, it is plausible that slaves were distributed across households in a pattern common to prestige markers and wealth: the power-log distribution (Maschner and Bentley 2003). We are all familiar with these. We read newspaper reports that in some country 1 percent of the population controls 90 percent of the wealth, and the bottom 90 percent controls 1 percent of the wealth. This distribution is also the essence of the Gini indices used by researchers to demonstrate wealth and prestige differentials (Ames 2007).

To model in more detail the distribution of slaves among households within a community, I estimated household populations for the Cath-

lapotle, Clahclellah, and Meier houses (Table 6.4). The calculations are based on the assumption that all the houses at each site have been excavated or mapped. Defending that claim is deferred to other publications, but it is a strong one. To estimate household populations, I used a ratio of 2.42 m² roofed area per person. This was developed after I applied Narrol's well-known ratio of 10 m² per person, and Cook's somewhat more nuanced formula of allocating 13.92 m² for the first six people and 9.29 m² for each additional person. I previously used the latter formula (Ames 1996) with what seemed at the time satisfactory results. Both estimates yielded total and household population estimates that did not accord with Hajda's (1984) household estimates in several ways.

The index used is the mean of six population estimates for Cathlapotle made between 1792 and 1825 (Boyd 1999), which is 666 (which I think is a bit low). The resulting household estimates fit well with Hajda's household estimates for the Wapato Valley. (This is another matter deferred to a different planned publication.) I then multiplied the resulting household estimate by 0.24. I also

TABLE 6.4. Estimated Household Sizes and Slave Populations at Three Lower Columbia Sites

Sites and Households	House Area (m²)	Estimated Population	Estimated Numbers of Slaves for Different Percentages of the Population			
			24%	16%	10%	4.8%
Meier	492	203	49	33	20	10
Cathlapotle						
1A	160	66	16	11	7	3
1B	66	27	7	4	3	1
1C	113	47	11	7	5	2
1D	187	77	19	12	8	4
4	92	38	9	6	4	2
2A	128	53	13	8	5	3
2B	116	48	12	8	5	2
2C	84	35	8	6	3	2
2D	56	23	6	4	2	1
3A	131	54	13	9	5	3
3B	144	60	14	10	6	3
5	117	48	12	8	5	2
6a	108	45	11	7	4	2
6b	108	45	11	7	4	2
Total		666	160	107	67	32
Clahclellah						
1	107	44	11	7	4	2
2	101	42	10	7	4	2
3	89	37	9	6	4	2
4	72	30	7	5	3	1
5	86	36	9	6	4	2
6	65	27	6	4	3	1
7	56	23	6	4	2	1
Total		239	57	38	24	11

used three smaller estimates for the percentage of slaves: 16 percent, the estimate for the Wapato Valley cited by Hajda; 10 percent because it was intermediate between 16 percent and 4.8 percent; and 4.8 percent, Donald's median figure.

These estimates, in combination with the evidence on production discussed above, make it clear that slaves would have been a significant presence and labor source in all households at the numbers suggested by the documentary evidence. Even at 10 percent, slaves would have been significant extra labor if controlled primarily by the elite. For example, if household elites controlled a third of the total number of slaves, at Meier they would been a labor force of 19 people.

At Cathlapotle, House 1D would have had 22 slaves (33 percent of the total number estimated for the site), and House 1 at Clahclellah also would have had nineteen.

The low estimate (4.8 percent) is perhaps more revealing. If slaves were uniformly distributed, their potential labor contribution would have been trivial, with most households having fewer than four slaves and many only one or two (ignoring the potential contribution in balancing household consumers with producers). However, if slaves were unequally distributed, their potential labor contribution would have been much greater, even at low numbers. At Cathlapotle the low total estimate is 32 slaves. However, if a third

(11) were in House 1D, they would have been 13 percent of that house's estimated population of 77 individuals.

The picture is somewhat different at Clahclellah and Meier. The low estimate at Clahclellah is four slaves. If all of these were owned by House 1, the high-status household, there would have been four slaves in a household of 44. At Meier the low estimate is 10 in a household 203. If all of those were controlled by the elite, they would still have had an impact on the ability of the house's elite to generate wealth. However, the point here is somewhat different. These figures may suggest why the percentage of slaves varied geographically in the 1825 census. Small households or communities may have needed higher proportions of slaves for them to affect production levels significantly, particularly in light of the evidence for the intensity of resource processing outlined above.

Finally, whatever the actual sizes of these households, they remained stable in size and organization over the several centuries the houses were occupied. Archaeological evidence suggests that individual house sizes fluctuated before and during contact, and also provides hints of declining populations (Butler 2000; Ames et al. 1992), but house sizes seem to have been stable.

This section has relied heavily on what Henige (1998) might call "numbers from nowhere." However, they provide a sense of the potential available pool of labor, even at percentages lower than those reported in the documentary record. Arnold (1996) defines hunter-gatherer complexity as the control of non-kin labor. The estimates developed here at least hint at the potential scale of that control along the lower Columbia River.

Discussion

The high estimated numbers of slaves in the GLCR are very plausible when examined in the context of archaeological data on processing and storage. I have not addressed resource harvesting, which would probably strengthen the numbers' plausibility. There was a lot of processing; there was also a lot of tending, such as minding the acorn baskets (which are not associated with a residential site) and tending the hearths and ovens that produced all that TAR. At Cath-

lapotle, someone had to collect all the rock that became TAR (Meier sits on a Pleistocene gravel bar). At small numbers, slaves would have been productively important only if they were concentrated in particular households. Additionally, slaves may have buffered households that possessed them from the household cycle.

One unanswered question is whether these numbers are a consequence of declining post-epidemic populations or whether they predate the epidemics. The archaeological data clearly show that the production system dates to at least AD 1400 if not earlier. The data also suggest household sizes were generally stable until they were overwhelmed by disease.

Slaves entered the Greater Lower Columbia region via an extensive regional network. From the south they moved along the same ancient routes as obsidian. The reported high numbers of slaves in the GLCR imply social and cultural impacts well beyond the region itself, regardless of whether those numbers were a consequence of population decline. If this was an ancient pattern, then the issue is how those numbers were sustained; if not, then one issue is what was the impact of a suddenly increased demand for slaves in the broader region and how was it met.

Finally, we return to the issue of whether slaves were essential for supporting elite status through their production or whether they were primarily status markers. These are not mutually exclusive. However, what emerges from the archaeological evidence is that small numbers of slaves would have had little economic impact unless held by only some people. Further, the GLCR's economy was fully capable of supporting small numbers of slaves without intensification (e.g., Darby's wapato-based population estimates). Owning small numbers of slaves would not have been an economic drain.

Large numbers are another matter, particularly if they were held for long periods, and much of their labor was required for their own maintenance. However, the storage potential at Meier suggests an enormous productive potential, particularly for hunter-gatherers. From this I infer that even large numbers of slaves may not have been difficult to maintain and support.

This conclusion supports Donald's position

that slaves were essential for producing the wealth needed by Northwest Coast elites to maintain their position. However, it does not preclude Hajda's argument, which is actually based on an entirely different calculus. In that emic calculus, the existence of high status required the existence of a null or negative status (slaves), whether there was one slave or fifty. Greater numbers would have represented greater wealth and prestige, and they were no doubt needed to produce that wealth. Finally, these data counter a long held anthropological view that Northwest Coast economies were somehow "irrational," expending important resources in a pursuit of prestige to the point of impoverishment. This is obviously not the case.

Conclusions

As an anthropological category, complex hunter-gatherers are those who counter long held stereotypes of such groups. The levels of production described here are also unanticipated, even in most discussions of complex hunter-gatherers or Northwest Coast economies. The possible extent and role of slaves in this production are also unanticipated, again particularly for hunter-gatherers, just as the extent and impact of slavery and captives documented elsewhere in this book are also generally unanticipated.

We are left to wonder about the possibility and extent of slavery among other complex hunter-gathers, such as the Japanese Jomon. This is not to suggest that slavery should be assumed, but the message of this book and this chapter is that it needs to incorporated into our thinking.

Whatever success this chapter has can be attributed to two parallel threads of evidence for Northwest Coast slavery: documentary and archaeological. In the absence of the documentary record, given our stereotypes, it is extremely unlikely we would have conceived of the possibility of slavery on the coast or among hunter-gatherers. The data I have presented are silent about the presence of slaves. Where do we go from here in the absence of archaeological correlates? One obvious place is the scale of production and labor demands.

However, more broadly, we need to spend more time in the ropewalk, laying out and checking multiple lines of evidence. It is too soon for narratives. In preparing this chapter, I learned that making cables in ropewalks was hard work, and that ropewalks were dirty, unpleasant places, even dangerous. It seemed like a good analogy for a chapter on slavery and for the kind of hard work needed for an archaeology of slavery.

Acknowledgments

I would like to thank Cathy Cameron both for her invitation to participate in the conference at Snowbird and in this volume, and for her patience. The completion of this chapter was significantly slowed by other obligations. I also thank the other participants for an extremely lively and thought-provoking seminar. Craig Skinner provided important information and insights on Oregon's obsidian sources, and David Ellis gave me access to his obsidian data. My knowledge of lower Columbia River ethnohistory and demography has benefited from Bob Boyd's instruction. I thank all three. My colleagues on the Wapato Valley Archaeological Project generated much of the data used here, especially Ann Gahr, Cameron Smith, and Elizabeth Sobel. I am deeply indebted to them. David Ellis, Bob Boyd, Yvonne Hajda, and Alf Hornborg commented on an earlier draft and materially improved this chapter. I thank them. The errors, of course, are entirely mine.

Notes

1. Both Europeans and Euroamericans are termed "Europeans" here unless the distinction is necessary.
2. The calculation is: 203 people are 40.6 five-member families. At .633 metric tons/family, that is 26 metric tons (40.6 × 0.633) or approximately 28 US short tons or 56,642 lbs. A bushel of potatoes weighs 60 lbs for 944 bushels (56,642/60). A bushel is 35.239 liters, for a total of 33,267 liters (944 × 35.239). The total available subfloor space in the Meier pit complex is 127,000 liters.
3. This is an estimate of the groups along or immediately adjacent to the river, not the entire GLCR.

References Cited

Alabama Cooperative Extension System
1997   Containers and Weights of Commercial Fruits, Nuts, and Vegetables. *ACES Publications.*

Auburn University, Auburn. http://www.aces
.edu/pubs/docs/A/ANR-0829/.

Ames, Kenneth M.

1995 Chiefly Power and Household Production on the Northwest Coast. In *Foundations of Inequality*, edited by T. D. Price and G. M. Feinman, pp. 155–187. Plenum Press, New York.

1996 Life in the Big House: Household Labor and Dwelling Size on the Northwest Coast. In *People Who Lived in Big Houses: Archaeological Perspectives on Large Domestic Structures*, edited by G. Coupland and E. B. Banning, pp. 131–150. Monographs in World Prehistory vol. 27. Prehistory Press, Madison, WI.

2000 *Kennewick Man Cultural Affiliation Report*, Chapter 2: Review of the Archaeological Data. National Park Service. http://www.nps.gov/archeology/kennewick/ames.htm.

2001 Slaves, Chiefs and Labour on the Northern Northwest Coast. *World Archaeology* 33(1): 1–17.

2005 *The North Coast Prehistory Project Excavations in Prince Rupert Harbour, British Columbia: The Artifacts*. British Archaeological Reports: International Series 1342. John and Erica Hedges, Oxford.

2006 Thinking About Household Archaeology on the Northwest Coast. In *Household Archaeology on the Northwest Coast*, edited by E. A. Sobel, D. A. T. Gahr, and K. M. Ames, pp. 16–36. International Monographs in Archaeology, Ann Arbor, MI.

2007 The Archaeology of Rank. In *Handbook of Archaeological Theories*, edited by R. A. Bentley and H. D. G. Maschner. AltaMira Press, Lanham, MD.

Ames, Kenneth M., Don E. Dumond, Jerry R. Galm, and Rick Minor

1998 Prehistory of the Southern Plateau. In *Handbook of North American Indians*, vol. 12: *Plateau*, edited by D. E. Walker, pp. 103–119. Smithsonian Institution, Washington, D.C.

Ames, Kenneth M., and Herbert D. G. Maschner

1999 *Peoples of the Northwest Coast: Their Archaeology and Prehistory*. Thames and Hudson, London.

Ames, Kenneth M., Doria F. Raetz, Stephen C. Hamilton, and Christine McAfee

1992 Household Archaeology of a Southern Northwest Coast Plank House. *Journal of Field Archaeology* 19:275–290.

Ames, Kenneth M., Cameron M. Smith, and Alexander Bourdeau

2008 Large Domestic Pits on the Northwest Coast

of North America. *Journal of Field Archaeology* 33(1):1–16.

Ames, Kenneth M., Cameron M. Smith, William L. Cornett, Elizabeth A. Sobel, Stephen C. Hamilton, John Wolf, and Doria Raetz

1999 Archaeological Investigations at 45CL1 (1991–1996) Ridgefield Wildlife Refuge, Clark County, Washington: A Preliminary Report. *Cultural Resources Series 13*. U.S. Department of the Interior, Fish and Wildlife Service Region 1, Portland, OR.

Arnold, Jeanne E.

1996 The Archaeology of Complex Hunter-Gatherers. *Journal of Archaeological Method and Theory* 3(2):77–126

Binford, Lewis R.

2001 *Constructing Frames of Reference: An Analytical Method for Archaeological Theory Building Using Hunter-Gatherer and Environmental Data Sets*. University of California Press, Berkeley.

Boyd, Robert T.

1975 Another Look at the "Fever and Ague" of Western Oregon. *Ethnohistory* 22(2):135–154.

1999 *The Coming of the Spirit of Pestilence: Introduced Infectious Diseases and Population Decline among Northwest Coast Indians, 1774–1874*. University of Washington Press, Seattle.

Boyd, Robert T., and Yvonne P. Hajda

1987 Seasonal Population Movement along the Lower Columbia River: The Social and Ecological Context. *American Ethnologist* 14:309–326.

Butler, Virginia L.

2000 Resource Depression on the Northwest Coast of North America. *Antiquity* 74(285):649–662.

Chatters, James C.

2004 The Influence of the Bow and Arrow on Village Formation on the Columbia Plateau. In *Complex Hunter-Gatherers: Evolution and Organization of Prehistoric Communities on the Plateau of Northwestern North America*, edited by William C. Prentiss and Ian Knight, pp. 67–83. University of Utah Press, Salt Lake City.

Christakis, Kostas S.

1999 Pithoi and Food Storage in Neopalatial Crete: A Domestic Perspective. *World Archaeology* 31(1):1–20.

Croes, Dale R., John L. Fagan, and Maureen N. Zehender

2007 *Evaluation of Archaeological Site 35MU4, The Sunken Village Site, Multnomah County, Oregon*. Report no. 4. Department of Anthropology, South Puget Sound Community College and Archaeological Investigations Northwest Inc., Portland, OR.

Cybulski, Jerome S.

1979 *Conventional and Unconventional Burial Positions at Prince Rupert Harbour, British Columbia.* Archaeological Survey of Canada, Archive Manuscript No. 1486.

1993 *A Greenville Burial Ground: Human Remains in British Columbia Coast Prehistory.* Archaeological Survey of Canada, Canadian Museum of Civilization, Ottawa.

Darby, Melissa Cole

1996 Wapato for the People: An Ecological Approach to Understanding the Native American Use of *Sagittaria latifolia* on the Lower Columbia. Unpublished M.A. thesis, Portland State University, OR.

Donald, Leland

1997 *Aboriginal Slavery on the Northwest Coast of North America.* University of California Press, Berkeley.

Ellis, David V., and Craig E. Skinner

2004 *The Social Dimensions of Obsidian in the Portland Basin.* Paper presented at the 57th Annual Northwest Anthropological Conference, Eugene, OR.

Gahr, D. Ann Trieu

2006 Architects to Ancestors: The Life Cycle of Plankhouses. In *Household Archaeology on the Northwest Coast,* edited by E. A. Sobel, D. A. T. Gahr, and K. M. Ames, pp. 57–79. International Monographs in Archaeology, Ann Arbor, MI.

Goody, Jack (editor)

1958 *The Developmental Cycle in Domestic Groups.* University of Cambridge Press, Cambridge, England.

Hajda, Yvonne P.

1984 Regional Social Organization in the Greater Lower Columbia, 1792–1830. Unpublished Ph.D. dissertation, University of Washington, Seattle.

1994 Notes on Indian Houses of the Wapato Valley. *Northwest Anthropological Research Notes* 28(2):177–188.

2005 Slavery in the Greater Lower Columbia Region. *Ethnohistory* 52(3):563–588.

Hamilton, Stephen C.

1994 *Technological Organization and Sedentism: Expedient Core Reduction, Stockpiling, and Tool Curation at the Meier Site (35CO5).* Unpublished M.A. thesis, Portland State University, OR.

Hayden, Brian

1998 Practical and Prestige Technologies: The Evolution of Material Systems. *Journal of Archaeological Method and Theory* 5(1):1–53.

Hayden, Brian, and Rick Schulting

1997 The Plateau Interaction Sphere and Late Prehistoric Cultural Complexity. *American Antiquity* 62(1):51–85.

Henige, David

1998 *Numbers from Nowhere: The American Indian Contact Population Debate.* University of Oklahoma Press, Norman.

Kaehler, Gretchen Ann

2002 *Patterns in Glass: The Interpretation of European Glass Trade Beads from Two Protohistoric Sites in the Greater Lower Columbia River Region.* Unpublished M.A. thesis, Portland State University, OR.

Kent, Susan

1999 The Archaeological Visibility of Storage: Delineating Storage from Trash Areas. *American Antiquity* 64(1):79–94.

Kroeber, Alfred

1939 *Cultural and Natural Areas of Native North America.* Publications in American Archaeology and Ethnology 38. University of California, Berkley.

Lambert, Patricia M.

2002 The Archaeology of War: A North American Perspective. *Journal of Archaeological Research* 10(3):207–241.

Lightfoot, Kent G.

1995 Culture Contact Studies: Redefining the Relationship between Prehistoric and Historic Archaeology. *American Antiquity* 60(2):199–217.

Lightfoot, Kent G., and Antoinette Martinez

1995 Frontiers and Boundaries in Archaeological Perspective. *Annual Reviews of Anthropology* 24:471–492.

Lightfoot, Kent G., Antoinette Martinez, and Ann M. Schiff

1998 Daily Practice and Material Culture in Pluralistic Social Settings: An Archaeological Study of Culture Change and Persistence from Fort Ross, California. *American Antiquity* 63(2): 199–222.

Lyman, R. Lee, and Kenneth M. Ames

2005 Sampling to Redundancy in Zooarchaeology: Lessons from the Portland Basin, Northwestern Oregon and Southwestern Washington. *Journal of Ethnobiology* 24(2):329–346.

Maschner, Herbert D. G., and R. Alexander Bentley

2003 The Power Law of Rank and Household on the North Pacific. In *Complex Systems and*

Archaeology: Empirical and Theoretical Applications, edited by R. A. Bentley and H. D. G. Maschner, pp. 47–60. University of Utah Press, Salt Lake City.

Minor, Rick, Kathryn A. Toepel, and Steven D. Beckham

1989   *An Overview of Investigations at 45SA11: Archaeology in the Columbia Gorge.* Report no. 83. Heritage Research Associates, Eugene, OR.

Mitchell, D.

1985   A Demographic Profile of Northwest Coast Slavery. In *Status, Structure, and Stratification: Current Archaeological Reconstructions,* edited by M. Thompson, M. T. Garcia, and F. J. Kense, pp. 227–236. Archaeological Association of the University of Calgary.

Mooney, James

1928   *The Aboriginal Population of America North of Mexico.* Miscellaneous Publications 80(7). Smithsonian Institution, Washington, D.C.

Moulton, G. E. (editor)

1990   *The Journals of Lewis and Clark.* Vols. 6 and 7. University of Nebraska Press, Lincoln.

Peterson-del Mar, David

1995   Intermarriage and Agency: A Chinookan Case Study. *Ethnohistory* 42(1):1–30.

Ray, Verne F.

1938   Lower Chinook Ethnographic Notes. *University of Washington Publications in Anthropology* 7(2):29–165.

Schulting, Rick J.

1995   *Mortuary Variability and Status Differentiation on the Columbia-Fraser Plateau.* Archaeology Press, Burnaby, B.C.

Silverstein, Michael

1990   Chinookans of the Lower Columbia. In *Handbook of North American Indians,* vol. 7: *The Northwest Coast,* edited by W. Suttles. Smithsonian Institution, Washington, D.C.

Smith, Cameron M.

2004   The Social Organization of Production in Three Protohistoric Lower-Columbia River Plankhouses. Unpublished Ph.D. dissertation, Simon Fraser University, Burnaby.

2006   Formation Processes of a Lower-Columbia Protohistoric Chinookan Plankhouse. In *Household Archaeology on the Northwest Coast,* edited by E. A. Sobel, D. A. T. Gahr, and K. M. Ames, pp. 233–269.

Sobel, Elizabeth A.

2004   Social Complexity and Corporate Households on the Southern Northwest Coast, AD 1400–1840. Unpublished Ph.D. dissertation, University of Michigan, Ann Arbor.

2005   Household Prestige and Obsidian Use in the Lower Columbia River Valley: Implications Regarding Prestige and Exchange Networks on the Northwest Coast. In *Household Archaeology on the Northwest Coast,* edited by E. A. Sobel, D. A. Trieu, and K. M. Ames, pp. 159–199. International Monographs in Archaeology, Ann Arbor, MI.

Sobel, E. A., D. A. T. Gahr, and K. M. Ames

2006   *Household Archaeology on the Northwest Coast.* International Monographs in Archaeology, Ann Arbor, MI.

Stearn, Theodore

1998   Columbia River Trade Network. In *Handbook of North American Indians,* vol. 12: *Plateau,* edited by D. E. Walker, pp. 641–652. Smithsonian Institution, Washington, D.C.

Suttles, W.

1990   Introduction. In *Handbook of North American Indians,* vol. 7: *The Northwest Coast,* edited by W. Suttles, pp. 1–15. Smithsonian Institution, Washington, D.C.

Walter, M. Susan

2006   Polygamy, Rank, and Resources in Northwest Coast Foraging Societies. *Ethnology* 45(1):41–57.

Wylie, Alison

1989   Archaeological Cables and Tacking: The Implications of Practice for Bernstein's "Options beyond objectivism and relativism." *Philosophy of Science* 19(1):1–18.

2002   *Thinking From Things: Essays in the Philosophy of Archaeology.* University of California Press, Berkeley.

7

Ripped Flesh and Torn Souls

Skeletal Evidence for Captivity and Slavery
from the La Plata Valley, New Mexico, AD 1100–1300

Debra L. Martin

Studying historical forms of violence can help to create a more broad and encompassing approach to understanding the persistence of violence in a global perspective. Although less is known about the chronology and context of violence in precolonial (prehistoric) times, historians and others have begun to provide a detailed and nuanced examination of the enormously disruptive increase in violence that accompanied colonization and expansion in America (Steele 1994; LeBlanc 2003). Regarding colonial violence, Blackhawk writes that "violence becomes more than an intriguing or distressing historical subject.... It becomes an interpretive concept as well as a method for understanding these understudied worlds" (2006:5). It is these understudied worlds that this volume seeks to examine, and the chapters collectively provide a way to sharpen our focus on the role of violence and its impact on cultures. Current perspectives on violence have been too narrowly conceived, particularly as they relate to long-standing culturally sanctioned and institutionalized forms of violence (Arendt 2004).

There is a growing archaeological literature on the forms of violence that operate in pre-state societies (e.g., Guilaine and Zammit 2005), but the focus has tended to be on male warriors and on violent interactions between men in the service of retribution, gaining resources, or self-defense (Milner et al. 1991; Ferguson 1997; Walker 2001). Women and children have rarely been discussed

in these contexts. What is missing from these discussions of ancient forms of violence is the bioarchaeological counterpart to these studies. What are the effects of violence, captivity, torture, and slavery on the human body, and do these leave markers on human skeletal remains? Is there a signature of trauma, pathology, and stress that would point to violence such as forced captivity and indentured servitude? Walker (2001) and Lovell (1997) provide overviews of the various ways that human remains can reveal indications of interpersonal violence and assault injuries, but these methodological surveys lack detailed information and do not address nonlethal forms of violence specific to captivity.

In the American Southwest between AD 900 and 1350, violence and warfare were carried out in a variety of contexts, many of which included women and children. There is a growing literature on empirical support for many forms of violence in the Southwest, including raiding and abduction (Martin et al. 2001; Kohler and Turner 2006), small-scale skirmishes (Hass and Creamer 1993), witchcraft executions (Darling 1999), cannibalism (White 1992), warfare (LeBlanc 1999; Turner and Turner 1999; Lovell 2007), and massacres (Kuckelman et al. 2002). Skeletal remains have been integrated into some of these studies (notably White 1992; Turner and Turner 1999; Martin et al. 2001; Kuckelman et al. 2002), but a systematic assessment of blunt force trauma and other signs of struggle, submission, and forced captivity has not yet been made.

A handful of studies have demonstrated the utility of interrogating the human remains for information on the effects of various forms of violence with more specificity. For example, after examining head trauma for a precolonial site from Michigan (ca. AD 1300), Wilkinson and Van Wagenen (1993) showed a strong pattern of healed head wounds in a subset of the women in the burial ground. Combined with ethnohistoric information, the data led the authors to conclude that abduction and forced captivity of women in these early Iroquoian communities is the most likely scenario accounting for the pattern of nonlethal head wounds. Because women with head trauma were buried with grave goods and in a manner similar to women who were not beaten, the authors further suggest that the captives had been adopted into the group and were not considered outsiders at the time of death.

Walker (1989, 2002) analyzed human remains from precontact sites (AD 1000–1300) along the California coast and the nearby islands and found a pattern of healed head wounds in a subset of men and women. By also using regional settlement data and ethnohistoric information, he shows how ritualized fighting among men and women of high standing involved nonlethal blows to the head. Walker (1989) also demonstrated that cranial trauma was more frequent for those living on the islands than for the coastal people. He attributes this to intense competition over resources on the circumscribed islands. What is important about this study is that the skeletal evidence proves unequivocally that women were part of these ritualized violent encounters.

In a final example, Allen and her colleagues (1985) analyzed ten cases of scalping at Navakwewtaqa (AD 1200–1300) and Grasshopper Ruin (AD 1300) in the American Southwest. Some of the individuals who had been scalped exhibited depression fractures as well. One female had a depression fracture on the left frontal, and another had an ovoid-shaped hole in the left parietal, suggesting penetration by a weapon and the probable cause of death. A young female (age fifteen) exhibited a depression fracture above the left orbit as well. The authors suggest that

these individuals were victims of isolated raids (1985:30).

These studies provide models for integrating skeletal information with archaeological reconstruction to better understand ritualized, institutionalized, and sanctioned forms of nonlethal violence. In particular, activities that include raiding and abduction, forced captivity, slavery, and indentured servitude are of interest because these forms of violence have been largely invisible in the archaeological record in the American Southwest, but these activities clearly were more prevalent than previously thought (Brooks 2002; Gutiérrez 1991). Interpreting signs of violence on human remains can only be done in conjunction with a wide range of supporting evidence garnered from the archaeological and ethnohistoric record.

It is important to establish criteria for evaluating the extent and impact of forced captivity and slavery in order to open up new dialogues about the persistence of these forms of violence. The far-reaching and broad theoretical issues raised by captivity and slavery within and between ethnic groups include attempts to better understand the geographic, demographic, economic, and social factors determining captive-taking. Skeletal evidence can reveal the subgroups that were most vulnerable to capture and enslavement and answer questions regarding the targeting of women and children during raids.

These areas of inquiry situate this study within a relatively new and emerging area of scholarship, and have the potential to break new ground in understanding these and other forms of violence. Many questions can be illuminated by analyses of the human skeletal remains because the burials can reveal demographic and biological patterns within the subgroups at risk. The practices used in subduing and dominating captives leave life-long signatures on the bones, and that is the focus of this chapter.

Human remains present a robust source of empirical data for exploring slaving practices. The present study extends previous research regarding the extent to which women and children living in the La Plata River valley between AD 1000 and 1300 were targets of raiding, abduction, and forced captivity (Martin et al. 2001). Earlier studies of these human remains revealed a strong pattern of women with healed head wounds and a variety of pathologies related to physically demanding activities (Martin 1997). Information on the deleterious effects of these practices on behavior, morbidity, mortality, and social position are expanded here. This study employs several new methodologies created to distinguish the skeletal signature of abduction, forced captivity, and slavery from other things, and to extend the analysis into neuropathology in order to understand the quality of life for people who survive severe head wounds and beatings.

The Skeletal Signatures of Forced Captivity and Slavery

Although the ethnohistorical, historiographical, and narrative literature on captives and slaving in indigenous populations is plentiful, very few sources provide details about the survivors. Cameron (this volume) provides a review of the literature on the fates of captives who survive, and she finds that most become slaves or are adopted into the community, becoming involved in a wide range of tasks. Domestic work, menial tasks, food production, and child care are some of the tasks relegated to captives. They also can become retainers, servants, and porters. Sometime they act as interpreters or mediators between groups because of their language abilities. Regardless, most captives who survive abduction have only a low status within the community, making them vulnerable to a range of verbal and physical insults. Sources discussing the roles of captives rarely give detailed descriptions in terms of the healing process after torture or beatings, or captives' access to medicines or healers. Information on the long-term biological and health effects of beatings, torture, and hard labor are difficult to come by.

Bioarchaeological literature on data derived from analysis of the Atlantic slaving practices in colonial America has presented a broad brushstroke of the indelible markers that this kind of horrific activity leaves on its victims. Blakey (2001) and Rankin-Hill (1997) detail the kinds of traumatic lesions and bone markers found on enslaved and post-reconstruction African Americans as revealed from analysis of the skeletal remains. In general, there are many musculoskeletal markers of stress that suggest excessive and grueling habitual physical labor. Slaves often worked sixteen-hour days, pushing many of them beyond their physical capabilities (Starobin 1988). Enslaved individuals have higher frequencies of disease than their white counterparts (including iron-deficiency anemia, nonspecific infections, and dental disease). Martin and her colleagues (1987) and Rose (1985) analyzed a historic African-American cemetery from Arkansas, and their data reveal similar health problems for adult males and females, including early osteoporosis and chronic undernutrition.

Although edited volumes such as Morton's *Discovering the Women in Slavery* (1996) present a multifaceted picture of southern female slaves using historiography, far fewer studies provide a glimpse into the morbidity burden carried by these women. Hard work and long days are alluded to, and the additional strain of beatings and poor diet underlie chronic health problems such as anemia, respiratory ailments, and persistent low-grade infections (staphylococcus and streptococcus) (Blakey 1998).

Turning from the Atlantic slave trade to precolonial Native America, Larsen (1999) and Boyd (2005), among others, have reviewed a variety of bioarchaeological literature on the skeletal correlates of warfare, but they make no mention on the identification or analysis of war captives or slaves. These studies do demonstrate that recidivism (trauma received numerous times over the course of a lifetime) and healed fractures in males are the most frequent signatures of endemic warfare and fighting. As mentioned earlier, Wilkinson and Van Wagenen (1993) found patterns of healed (nonlethal) cranial depression fractures in higher frequencies in female skulls in a precolonial Iroquois population. Walker (1989) also documented healed cranial depression fractures from precolonial Chumash remains of both males and females.

These groundbreaking bioarchaeological studies beg the question: How frequent was captivity in ancient America? Scholars who have attempted to reconstruct precolonial and colonial patterns of captivity and enslavement note that women and children tended to be the preferred targets. For example, Patterson (1982), in a cross-cultural study of slavery, revealed that women and children were almost always the most likely victims. They were easier to capture and less likely to fight back. Regarding status in proto-historic and historic Northwest Coast tribes, Josephy (1991:65) states that "At the bottom were slaves, usually women and children who had been captured in raids on other villages, purchased, or received as gifts, or who were the offspring of a man of high rank and a slave woman."

John (1975:341) characterizes the Wichita groups during the early historic period as preferring women and children, stating that they were "generally [more] useful and more numerous.... as slaves, they enhanced the productivity of the villages and the prosperity of their owners' households. Some were eventually adopted into Wichita families." Gutiérrez (1991:185) documents several cases of Pueblo women and children enslaved by the Spanish, chronicling their daily lives of hard work, physical punishment, and marginalized status. Female captives and slaves carry the additional burden of reproduction and motherhood. Combined with the rigors of life in captivity, the added responsibilities of childbearing and child care likely contributed to health problems. As Schwartz (1996:251) states, "Compelling evidence suggests...that the work routine experienced by new mothers remained rigorous enough to jeopardize the health of slave infants." Among enslaved Africans, pregnant women were still sent to work every day, doing hard physical labor in the fields (Starobin 1988).

Hard work, physical labor, demanding activities, and long hours leave patterned marks on skeletons (Capasso et al. 1999). As muscles are strengthened and strained, they leave enlarged and often reactive areas around the place of attachment on various bones (Kennedy 1989: 134–135). Strained muscles can tear at the point of attachment, leaving bone lesions and inflammation at the site (Blakey 1998:53). Although identification and interpretation of these musculoskeletal markers can be somewhat subjective, other methods involve metric analysis of various limbs in order to understand the range of activities that may have produced the lesions (Gualdi-Russo and Galletti 2004; Cope et al. 2005).

Blakey (1998:57) presents a compelling case for identifying enslaved African Americans who regularly carried heavy loads on their heads. He presents cases from a historic African cemetery that show fractures in the first and second cervical vertebrae, and fusion from carrying heavy loads. He also discusses several cases of ring-shaped fractures at the base of the skull, also likely due to carrying extremely heavy loads on the head.

Judd (2002) provides an excellent overview of injury recidivism, arguing that it is a powerful tool for bioarchaeologists. In reviewing the clinical literature on injury recidivism in contemporary society, she notes that individuals with multiple injuries are similar in profile. In general, if an individual has been the recipient of violent actions once in their lives, they are highly likely to have repeat encounters. Recidivism is the result of culturally patterned violence that repeatedly targets the same individuals. This was demonstrated by Brinkley and Smith (2006) in their observations of violence and injury recidivism in a historic urban cemetery from England.

Fractures and broken bones clearly play a role in the identification of captives and slaves. Head wounds are among the most common in warfare as well as domestic violence (Merbs 1989). Broken noses and fractured bones of the midface likely occur in captives who fight back or attempt to flee (Martin 1997; Walker 1997). Healed broken ribs and metacarpals (finger bones) are also related to fighting and falling down (Robb 1997).

Evidence of recovery from trauma, most pertinent for this study, is likewise among the more unambiguous types of bone changes that can be easily documented. Injuries to the head leave particularly characteristic lesions that last for many, many years after the original injury has healed, thus providing a record of nonlethal blows to the head (Walker 1989). Bhootra (1985:567) states for all deaths that result from violence in contemporary society, one quarter can be attributed to head injuries. Diagnosis of violence-related trauma in the osteological record is fairly straightforward, particularly with the growth of the forensic and bioarchaeological literature on violence in the last ten years (Lovell 1997; Reichs 1998; Walker 2001; Byers 2002; Steadman 2003). The use of force leaves a distinctive and permanent record on bone when it is applied with enough power to cause tissue damage.

Depression fractures begin with a traumatic event such as a blow to the head, which ruptures

TABLE 7.1. Activities Related to Captivity and Slavery and Possible Signatures on Human Skeletal Remains

Action	Skeletal Correlates
Capture and forced abduction (combined with ambush, warfare, or raiding)	Nonlethal blows to head, healed cranial depression fractures, broken ribs, Colle's fracture Demographic targets: women and children
Desire for prestige, trade, and/or concubines	Demographic target: young, strong, reproductive-aged women
Subordination, beatings	Cranial and post-cranial fractures, recidivism, co-occurrence of trauma and pathology in various stages of healing, Colle's and Parry fractures, fractures of hand, foot, rib, arm, leg bones
Indentured service, hard physical labor, domestic or market tasks, childrearing, subsistence activities	Musculoskeletal markers, enthesiopathies, ossified ligaments, asymmetries, work-related osteoarthritis, dental pathology related to occupations
Punishment	Amputation of fingers, blood loss and nonspecific infectious disease responses, frail osteoporotic bones, early death
Not a recognized member of community	No cradle boarding, no filed dentition, no proper burial, no grave goods
Food restriction, forced poverty	Iron-deficiency anemia, nonspecific infections, children with short stature
Poor sanitation and living conditions	Nonspecific infections (staph and strep), tuberculosis, trepanematosis

blood vessels in the bone marrow and periosteum (Gurdjian 1973:94–98). A hematoma forms within six to eight hours, gradually replaced by young connective tissue that transforms into a fibrous callous. Through remodeling, this callous is gradually replaced with new bone. Depression fractures are produced by a force applied to just one side of the bone. The outer cortex of bone is clearly depressed inward, while the underlying diploe space becomes compressed. There are three characteristics of depression fractures: there are usually fine cracks that radiate from the depressed areas; within the depressed area, the inner table of bone is beveled at the edges; and the area surrounding the depression is raised as it rebounds from the pressure buildup. With healing, these signs of trauma all but disappear, but a diagnostic depression usually remains for long periods. The depression fracture stays depressed long after healing because of bone necrosis. Traumatic interruption of blood supply results in the death of bone cells and a sloughing off of dead tissue.

In summary, due to the variety of possible factors that can affect the modus operandi of various forms of abduction, forced captivity, slavery, indentured servitude, and torture, the skeletal signatures may be more or less apparent. It is the patterning of diagnostic indicators on human remains that will help identify captives and slaves (Table 7.1). The suite of variables most likely to co-occur on a single skeleton include patterned cranial and post-cranial fractures (healed or healing); violence and injury recidivism; markers of muscle hypertrophy, strain, and tearing; asymmetries in limb and hip proportions; higher frequencies of nutritional anemia, nonspecific infections, and osteoarthritis; a different pattern or lack of cultural skeletal deformation common to the community (e.g., cradleboard deformation, filed dentition); and a surplus of reproductive-aged females and/or children. Other bioarchaeological variables indicating outsider or low status could include an unusual mortuary context, unusual burial orientation or placement, and a lack of grave goods (see Ames, this volume, for detailed examples from the Northwest Coast).

Studies of Trauma and Violence in the Southwest

The Southwest provides a distinctive setting for study because of the long-term residence by ancestral Puebloans. With thousands of years of habitation in the Southwest, Pueblo groups offer insight into the mechanisms underlying adaptability and behavioral flexibility in the face of changes over time. A wealth of data already exists for many aspects of Pueblo precolonial history as reconstructed from the archaeological record (e.g., Adler 1996; Hegmon et al. 2000; Kamp 2002). Since the 1930s, thousands of sites have been excavated, and the reconstruction of health, environment, climate, trade networks, population movement, settlement patterns, housing, subsistence activities, and other facets of prehistoric Pueblo existence continue to be documented and studied. Therefore, the Southwest as a multiregional interactive area provides an unusually rich database for exploring relationships among availability of resources, resource allocation, alliance formation, risk-sharing, population density, settlement, health, and other variables likely to have had a role in the creation and reproduction of violence.

Human remains are abundant across time and space in the Southwest. Of recent interest is the occurrence of human skeletal assemblages that are disarticulated, broken, chopped, and sometimes burned, and that often show signs of dismembering. These collections (which include both children and adult males and females) have been variously interpreted to represent "cannibalism" (Turner and Turner 1999; White 1992), witchcraft retribution (Darling 1999), warfare (Wilcox and Haas 1994), anthropophagy (Kuckelman et al. 2002), or ritualized dismemberment (Ogilvie and Hilton 1993). Whatever the motivation behind these deaths and perimortem alterations of the victims' bodies, there is suggestive evidence for violent action directed against certain individuals and subgroups.

Collectively, the archaeological data on fortification and strategic location and the osteological data on victims and mass graves suggest that fighting in the form of ambushes, raids, skirmishes, or attacks by aggressors may have been the status quo in many parts of the precontact Southwest. Haas and Creamer (1993) suggest that these patterns of "chronic warfare" pushed previously egalitarian and loosely connected groups into larger, politically centralized units between AD 1100 and 1300. LeBlanc (1999, 2003) has explored the reasons for violence in the Southwest, but these largely focus on male activities and regional interactions.

The litany of injury and trauma on individual skeletal remains has been noted in the literature as well, but not always with much specificity and rarely linked to other aspects of local or regional dynamics. On one hand, there are places where virtually no intentional violence is apparent. For example, Miles (1975) analyzed 179 burials from Wetherill Mesa (AD 1200), and he states that "the relative absence of fractures of major external force indicates that these people lived a rather quiet life without frequent warfare, and that they did not sustain many serious falls from the cliffs and mesas where they lived" (1975:20). He also observes that "there were no depressed skull fractures, and no arrowheads or other foreign bodies imbedded in bone" (1975:24).

Akins (1986) likewise found little evidence of trauma in the Chaco series that she examined. Exceptions to this include a male (Number 14 from Room 33 at Pueblo Bonito) with "two holes and a gash in the frontal bone," suggesting that he died in a confrontation (1986:116–117). For skeletal remains from Chaco small sites, Akins notes a few cases of post-cranial fractures, and one female (age thirty or older) with four depression fractures on the parietal.

On the other hand, some sites have yielded evidence of strife. For the Transwestern Pipeline series (ca. AD 1200), Ogilvie and Hilton (1993) note that several adult females have post-cranial fractures in the fibula, sacrum, radius, and tibia. Several women had multiple healed fractures on their lower bodies. One female had three depression fractures on the frontal (she also had post-cranial healed fractures), and another had a perimortem fracture on the maxilla. Danforth and colleagues (1994:96) summarize evidence of trauma at Carter Ranch (ca. AD 1200) as follows: "One-quarter of 24 scorable adults had healed fractures. There are two nasal fractures, one associated with a broken mandible and the other with a broken humerus, two radius fractures, a clavicle fracture and a femur fractures. Four of the six cases can be interpreted as the result of blows." Sex of the individuals is not specified.

Stewart and Quade (1969) present one of the more thorough accounts of bone lesions from North American precontact series. They provide information on frontal lesions from Pueblo Bonito and Hawikku (together) and derived a population frequency rate of 9 percent for males and 5.8 percent for females in the Southwest. The authors state that most of the lesions they saw from the Pueblo sites are due to trauma (1969:89).

For the Pecos collection, Hooton (1930) presents a detailed inventory of cranial trauma by sex. Out of a total sample size of 581, he found 20 cases of cranial trauma, representing a 3.4 percent frequency. Of these 20 cases, 5 (25 percent) are on females, and the rest are on males (75 percent). The depression fractures are located primarily on the frontal bones, although other areas of the crania are implicated as well.

Stodder (1989:187) compiled a frequency chart for a number of archaeological populations from the Greater Southwest (New Mexico, parts of Texas, south-central Colorado). These frequencies range from 2 percent to 22 percent, with the highest percentages located at the Gallina sites. Regarding the frequency data, Stodder (1989:187) states that the fact that the Gallina sample exhibits the highest frequencies of postcranial and cranial trauma "is not surprising, as they are most often identified as warlike, with defensive architecture in relatively isolated locations"; the likewise relatively high rates of cranial injury at San Cristobal (8 percent) are primarily in the males, "suggesting that they were engaged in warfare."

Recently there has been an increased focus on various forms of violence and intentional injury, such as small-scale warfare, attacks and massacres, and endemic violence. The literature on conflict in the Greater Southwest has been growing exponentially as new theories about the roles of violence, warfare, anthropophagy, conflict, and raiding become increasingly emphasized as dominant features of the ancient Pueblo world. Haas (1990), Haas and Creamer (1993), and Wilcox and Haas (1994) provide detailed overviews of archaeological data that demonstrate evidence of sustained intervillage conflict (e.g., fortification, palisades, towers, communities positioned in strategic locations, walled villages, and sites burned at the time of abandonment). These studies conclude that violent interactions between groups increased over time, starting around AD 1150 and continuing through the 1300s. The building of defensive architecture and the stra-

tegic location of sites by the Pueblo people offer compelling circumstantial evidence to suggest that people were in a mode of constant vigilance.

LeBlanc (1999) pulled together a great deal of archaeological data pertaining to the potential role for war in the Southwest, suggesting it was commonplace over a long period of time (extending from the Basketmaker phase to the protohistoric periods). He documents the many ways that communities were constructed so that they were fortress-like. One explanation for these difficult to reach compounds is that they offered protection from being attacked or raided. Raiding and retribution for raiding—especially if it included the abduction of men, women, and children—would provide powerful incentive to fortify habitation areas.

In summary, the osteological evidence for violence is highly varied. LeBlanc (1999:83–90) and Larralde (1998:20–21) provide overviews of human remains found in several contexts suggestive of violence. In particular they present a review of the skeletal evidence for perimortem fractures, embedded stone points, burials with unusual mortuary treatment, and trophy skulls. Turner and Turner (1999) present 360 pages that catalog 76 sites believed to be candidates for either violence or "cannibalism," or both. These include disarticulated, broken, burned, and processed human remains.

These reviews present a complex picture for the prehistoric Southwest. Variability exists in the ways that injurious actions occurred across time and space. Mass slayings, individual dismemberments, burning, possible cannibalism, scalping, intentional injury, witch execution, and limited hand-to-hand combat are some of the alternative hypotheses regarding the interpretation of these findings. However, the relationship of these signs of trauma and violence on the bodies to other political, economic, and ideological currents has been less systematically explored. These cases of violence may represent relatively isolated examples, or they may be indicative of a more large-scale and integrated system of power dynamics, show of force, oppression, coercion, or conflict resolution.

Most importantly, the accumulated evidence for violence from the human remains suggests that several different kinds of strategies were operating simultaneously, resulting in a very diverse assemblage of dead bodies over time (AD 900–1300) and across space (the Greater Southwest). Although males (based on the evidence presented above) appear to have been involved in hand-to-hand combat and fighting, females and children were more likely to have been the subjects of human trafficking.

Kramer (2002) and Kohler and Turner (2006) have proposed that raiding for women may have occurred in the northern Pueblo communities, and they draw on demographic and sex ratio data to show an excess of males and a shortage of females in some places. Using regional mapping of sex ratios, they suggest that one can start to see patterns where females are under- and overrepresented in the burial populations and that an abundance of females may be related to the use of captives in a system-wide network of raiding and abduction.

Lowell (2007) presents a different (and problematic) interpretation of skewed sex ratios in the Southwest burial record at Grasshopper (PIII/IV). She proposes that because men died in warfare and raids, a population of adult females was left to find new homes in distant communities (much as modern-day refugees do in war-torn areas of the world). In addition to noting the slightly skewed sex ratios, she suggests that the type of pottery being used indicates certain gendered continuities and discontinuities in the habitation areas. However, until a more detailed examination of the skeletons is completed, it is possible that the excess of female skeletons at Grasshopper can be explained by raiding and abduction, trading, and high maternal mortality. Of course, there may also have been problems with the recovery of all available adult burials from the site. Nonetheless, it is quite possible that human trafficking in females was an active part of the regional economics, which would have contributed to the patterns examined by Lowell. Habicht-Mauche (this volume) and Junker (this volume) provide additional suggestions about the ways that captive women (as wives, concubines, and slaves) contribute to the transformation of some aspects of material culture.

Bioarchaeological support for raiding and abduction comes from a study of nonlethal violence in the form of blunt force trauma and healed broken bones in a large integrated community in the La Plata River valley near Farmington, New Mexico (ca. AD 1000–1300). Studies of the skeletal remains demonstrated a pattern of females with healed cranial depression fractures and unusual mortuary treatments (Martin 1997; Martin and Akins 2001; Martin et al. 2001). The original interpretation these women formed a subclass of either indentured servants or a lower class or clan, and were therefore relegated to hard labor and unceremonious burials. The original analysis focused on political and economic forces operating in the region. Marginalized individuals from some of the crowded political centers may have been drawn to La Plata because of its relative abundance of food and water. Intentional, nonlethal violence against these immigrant women would have kept them in subservient positions while still allowing them to tend other people's fields and households.

Brooks (2002) documented widespread forms of slavery and the extent of slave systems in the Southwest Borderlands region during the earliest colonial periods. He argues that captive women and children moved into and out of both Indian and Spanish communities as part of a complex web of trade, prestige, and cultural exchange. Although captive women and children often became somewhat integrated into the community, they also remained marginalized and subservient. Brooks presents compelling evidence for these patterns during the contact periods, but the question remains: Were the Spanish adapting to and integrating themselves into an existing local system of raiding and abduction, or was this an entirely new system? Habicht-Mauche (2000) shows that for the Pueblo-Plains region, archaeological and ethnohistoric data suggest that women may have moved across the borderlands as captives, refugees, and/or marriage partners prior to contact.

Wounded Women and Men from La Plata: A Reanalysis of the Evidence for Captivity and Slavery, AD 1100–1300

The reanalysis of data from the La Plata Valley addresses the extent to which women and children were subjects of raiding, abduction, and captivity, and the effects of these practices on behavior, morbidity, mortality, and societal position. The data strongly suggest that in addition to other forms of violence operating in the Southwest—such as warfare, massacres, anthropophagy, and witch executions—a pattern of raiding and abduction of women and children was also in play.

The La Plata River valley in northwestern New Mexico (near the Colorado border) is a permanently watered, productive agricultural area in which more than nine hundred sites have been reported. The valley was continuously occupied from AD 200 until about AD 1300. Large communities were maintained throughout the occupation. This area was lush by local and regional standards, with a high density of available resources. Agricultural potential was likewise very good, and there is ample evidence of hunted and domesticated game in the diet. This area is located in the middle of what was a large and interactive political sphere of influence, with Mesa Verde to the north and Chaco Canyon to the south. Trade items and non-utilitarian goods are present. Some researchers have suggested that this region was a "breadbasket" compared with other contemporaneous sites, in part because of its well-watered location and accessibility to major population centers to the north and south (Martin et al. 2001:196–197).

The La Plata burial collection (65 individuals) was originally analyzed in the late 1990s by Martin and colleagues (2001:13–32). Skeletal remains were examined using systematic data collection on age, sex, pathologies, metrics, and discrete traits using the Standards for Osteological Data Collection (SOD) (Buikstra and Ubelaker 1994). Pathological lesions were scored as osteoclastic/resorptive, osteoblastic/proliferative, or as trauma-related lesions. The methods for assessment and analysis of trauma on cranial and post-cranial remains followed the recommendations of Merbs (1989), Ortner and Putschar (1981), and Walker (1989). If trauma was present, it was further analyzed as to type, location, extent, and level of remodeling (healing). Cranial depression fractures were measured for width, height, and depth. All fractures were radiographed in multiple dimensions. Data from individuals also included the recording of burial location, strata, position, grave type, grave goods, and completeness and preservation.

Evidence for cranial and post-cranial trauma

TABLE 7.2. Frequency of Healed Trauma for La Plata Burial Population

	Children	Males	Females
Cranial	1/16 (6.2%)	3/13 (23.1%)	6/10 (60%)
Post-cranial	0/16 (0%)	3/15 (20%)	6/12 (50%)

from the La Plata burial series includes healed fractures and traumatic injuries in the remodeling (healing) phase (indicating injuries that were nonlethal). The cranial wounds at La Plata fit the description of depression fractures caused by blows to the head (e.g., Courville 1948; Stewart and Quade 1969; Merbs 1989; Walker 1989). Adults were analyzed for cranial and post-cranial healed traumatic injuries (Table 7.2) with only a small number (about six) that could not be included due to poor preservation and fragmentary remains. Reproductive-aged females are implicated to the greatest degree, followed by adult males and children.

A summary of individuals from this population with trauma and pathology is provided in Table 7.3. Individuals with cranial and/or post-cranial pathology related to trauma suggest different patterns for adult males and females. The ages assigned represent the midpoint age based on the age range assigned using a number of aging techniques (Bass 1981; White 1992).

For males, there are three cases of cranial trauma: one 25-year-old has a healed compression fracture of the right parietal (37599 B5), another 25-year-old has a healed fracture at the corner of the left eye (37599 B9), and a 35-year-old has a healed depression fracture on the left parietal (37601 B5). These injuries, all in males 35 and under, are suggestive of head wounds from fighting, beatings, or combat. The left parietal and left orbit could easily be the result of blows to the side of the head and eye region delivered by assailants with weapons in their right hands. The right parietal would get damaged by a blow coming from a left-handed assailant or aggression from behind.

Male post-cranial fractures include a healed Colle's fracture of the right radius and ulna (the type one gets when breaking a fall), a healed fractured right thumb, and an individual with several healed rib and vertebrae fractures. All of the

TABLE 7.3. La Plata Individuals with Trauma and Related Pathologies

Site Number Sex, Age	Trauma and Pathology
LA 37592 B6 Child, Age 15	Healed depression fracture on left side of head
LA 65030 B7 Child, Age 10	Thrown into pit structure with 33-year-old female; no pathology
LA 37599 B5 Male, Age 25	Partly healed, unreunited depression fracture on right side of head
LA 37599 B9 Male, Age 25	Healed depression fracture of left forehead and bone socket near left eye
LA 37601 B5 Male, Age 35	Healed depression fracture on the back, left side of head
LA 37599 B4 Male, Age 45	Healed fracture of right hand bone
LA 37593 B3 Male, Age 48	Healed right and left ribs, healed trauma to middle back of spine with resultant wedging of vertebrae
LA 37600 B4 Male, Age 50+	Healed Colle's fracture (distal ends of radius and ulna, usually due to breaking a fall)
LA 37592 Female, Age Unknown	Healed right lower leg bone (fibula)
LA 65030 B8 Female, Age 20	Healed broken nose, healed fractures on 1st and 2nd vertebrae at base of the back of the head
LA 37601 Female, Age 25	Healed depression fracture on left side of head and six rounded depression fractures at the center of the forehead above the eyes, healed rib fractures (two right and one left), depression fracture on right shoulder blade, three neck vertebrae with trauma-induced reaction boney growths, healed lower back fracture in lumbar vertebrae
LA 65030 Female, Age 28	Healed depression fractures on right forehead and back of the head
LA 37603 B2.1 Female, Age 30	Healed Colle's fracture near right wrist (distal end of radius, usually due to breaking a fall)
LA 65030 B9 Female, Age 33	Severe depression fracture at top of the head with involvement of several bones and uneven healing due to unreunited sutures, healed fracture on left hip
LA 37601 B10 Female, Age 38	Healed depression fracture on forehead above right eye
LA 65030 B6 Female, Age 38	Healed depression fracture on back of head, trauma to left hip, left joint arthritis and asymmetrical hip joint

post-cranial traumas are on males over 45 years old and indicate less severe trauma that could be related to combat or the occasional accident or occupational hazard. Because these cases of post-cranial fractures did not co-occur in individuals with cranial trauma, and because these individuals were elderly, it is likely their injuries were due to the normal occupational hazards of farming.

Six females (out of 10) have healed cranial trauma (largely in the form of depression fractures), and they range in age from 22 to 38. The inventory of healed nonlethal cranial wounds for the females is longer and more extensive than that of the males, with three of the six cases involving multiple head wounds. The youngest female (age 20) has a healed broken nose (65030 B8). Another young female (age 22) with cranial trauma has two depression fractures, one on the forehead and one on the back of the head (65030 B15). A 25-year-old has multiple depression fractures on the front and side of her head (37601 B4). A 33-year-old has a large, unreunited but healed series of fractures at the top of her head (65030 B9). Of the two 38-year-old females, one has a healed fracture above her right eye (37601 B10), and one has a depression fracture at the back of the head (65030 B6).

These nonlethal head fractures are quite different from that found in age-matched males. Wounds are not located on the sides of the head (as in the male pattern) but are on the top, back, and front of the head. These injuries are very similar to those documented in forensic cases of wife-beating in historic and contemporary samples (Walker 1997:161). It is primarily the face that gets struck, or the back of the head as the victim attempts to flee. Also, most of the wounds sustained by the females are not the typical circular depressions left by use of blunt force. Instead these wounds are highly variable in size, location, and depth, suggesting the use of more common and expedient implements (sticks and fists) than clubs and weapons.

A total of six females demonstrate post-cranial trauma. Two features of lower body trauma are distinctly different from the male pattern. In four out of six cases, the cranial and post-cranial fractures co-occur (strongly suggesting recidivism), and the post-cranial fractures in the females occur in younger age categories, ranging from 20 to 38.

The youngest female (age 20) has fractures in the atlas and axis of the neck vertebrae (an also a broken nose). The neck fractures could have been caused by carrying excessively heavy loads on the head (see Blakey 1998) or from blow to the upper neck from the back.

A 25-year-old (37601 B4) has several fractures (right shoulder, left humerus, upper neck) along with multiple depression fractures on the head. This female also had an active case of severe osteomyelitis that affected numerous bones of the chest and shoulder region. Parts of the sternum are thickened with osteophytic reactive bone covering all surfaces. Some parts of the bone surface appear smooth and rounded, and these areas were likely caused by lytic lesions and subsequent sclerotic processes, suggesting a chronic condition (Ortner and Putschar 1981:111). The scapulae, clavicles, and distal portion of one humerus are likewise massively remodeled and affected by the same process. Differential diagnosis relying primarily on x-ray examination suggests osteomyelitis, although the original cause of this massive infection confined to the shoulder and chest area can only be speculated upon. The right scapula near the spine and the sixth and seventh ribs show roughened, depressed areas that look like healed fractures. There appear also to be localized, trauma-induced osteophytes on the third through fifth cervical vertebrae. It is possible that this woman was struck with an object hard enough to cause not only cranial fracturing, but also lacerating wounds on the shoulders and chest area that failed to heal due to massive soft tissue damage.

Other examples of co-occurrence of cranial and post-cranial trauma on the females include a 33-year-old with fractures and asymmetries of the left hip as well as a series of healed fractures on the top of her head. The oldest female (age 38) also had an asymmetrical pelvis with osteophytes and a possible healed fracture on the left hip. She also had a circular depression fracture at the back of her head. The size and nature of these wounds suggest cases of recidivism, since they represent multiple episodic events of violent interactions combined with more-developmental (chronic) involvement of pathology in the hip region. These could have been sustained by an original dislocation of the bones from falling, followed by high levels of musculoskeletal stress and biomechanical use. Asymmetries in the body are often the result of differential use of one side or the other of the body due to the type of activity being sustained (Glassman and Bass 1986) or to compensate for an injury by relying more heavily on the side without injury.

Two cases of lower body fractures unaccompanied by head wounds were identified. One 30-year-old female had a healed fracture of the right distal radius (of the kind one can sustain while breaking a fall). She seems also to have died while pregnant or during childbirth because a term-fetus was found commingled with her skeletal remains. The other case is that of an adult female with healed fibula fractures.

One 15-year-old had a healed cranial depression fracture on the left parietal. The location and size of the circular lesion suggest a blow to the side of the head by a right-handed assailant with a blunt force weapon. Due to poor preservation, no other pathologies could be ascertained.

The frequencies of healed trauma for adults at La Plata reveal that females have about a three-fold increase in the frequency of cranial trauma over males (23 percent versus 60 percent), and a two-fold increase in post-cranial trauma (20 percent versus 50 percent). Adult frequencies greatly outnumber those for subadults, who have an overall rate of 4.7 percent for cranial trauma and no cases of post-cranial trauma.

In reviewing other factors associated with the health of adult males and females at La Plata, females had more cases of infection (30.7 percent) than males (6.2 percent), and some of these may have been related to sequelae from the injuries that produced the fractures. Females demonstrated higher frequencies of childhood growth disruption (for four out of six teeth, females had more hypoplastic lines). Females with cranial trauma also have more enamel defects than females without. For example, at Barker Arroyo site LA 65030, four females have cranial trauma and co-occurring severe or multiple hypoplastic defects, whereas the other two females from this site show no trauma and have few defects.

Other characteristics of the females with cranial trauma are that these women as a group generally exhibit more signs of anemia and systemic infection. Several of the women with cranial trauma exhibit more left/right asymmetry of 2 to 6 mm in long bone proportions (three individuals in particular are asymmetrical: LA 65030 B6, B8, and B9) and more pronounced cases of post-cranial ossified ligaments, osteophytes at joint surfaces (unrelated to general osteoarthritis or degenerative joint disease), and localized periosteal reactions (enthesiopathies). Whether these pathologies are the result of occupational stress (Capasso et al. 1999) or the sequelae of injuries that caused abnormal biomechanical problems is not clear. They do, however, indicate muscle strain and biomechanical stress. In fact, the one physical characteristic that most distinguishes several of the women with trauma is the pattern of musculoskeletal markers associated with muscle stress or habitual use of select muscle groups. For example, both females in Pit Structure 1 from site LA 65030 demonstrate asymmetrical measurements for many of the width proportions of the long bones. Particularly, the humerus, radius, and ulna are most affected. Trinkaus and colleagues (1994) examined modern, extant, and extinct groups and found that humeral bilateral asymmetry related most often to activity-related functional changes.

Another attribute of some of these women is the existence of isolated osteophytes in places that correspond to muscle insertions. Because as a group these women were generally too young to have the osteoarthritic changes associated with aging, these morphological changes could be related to habitual use of certain muscles, which can lead to the buildup of bone and changes at the site of the most biomechanical stress. Bridges (1990) examined the osteological correlates of weapon use in two precontact groups from Alabama and showed that the shift from hunting and gathering to agriculture can be correlated with nonpathological changes in morphology relating to different use of tools and weapons. Bridges noted changes in porosity and osteophytic lipping at the shoulder joints and elbow in particular. She also found bilateral asymmetry in the diameters of the radius and ulna between the groups. Although it is somewhat circumstantial evidence at this point, many of the La Plata females within the subgroup do demonstrate osteophytes and asymmetries, and therefore the most distinguishing element of their physical makeup is developmental and relates to occupation or habitual performance of certain activities.

Although the subgroup sample sizes limit a detailed quantitative analysis of musculoskeletal stress markers, it is possible to speculate on a division of labor that was by sex and possibly by class as well. Spencer and Jennings (1965), Titiev (1972), and Dozier (1970) summarize sexual division of labor for historic Pueblo Indians, suggesting that traditionally women ground corn, prepared food, gathered wood, built and mended houses, made pottery and clothing, gathered wild foods, and made baskets. Men were responsible for farming, occasional hunting, and religious and ceremonial activities. The difficult task of grinding a season's crop of corn into meal to be stored for the year belonged to the women, who might spend as many as eight to nine hours a day at the grindstone for several weeks.

In traditional subsistence societies with agricultural intensification and stratification, there is often a concomitant pressure on women to increase their productivity while simultaneously decreasing birth spacing (Harris and Ross 1987: 49). This places an enormous burden on women to partition their time, energy, and activities between the very different and competing tasks of economic labor and bearing and rearing children. Harris and Ross cite summary data (1987:50) on the number of hours that women work daily in agriculturally based villages, and it ranges from 6.7 to 10.8 hours a day (with the high end representing intensive agriculturalists). These kinds of data underscore the value that women as servants and slaves could have had in domestic, production, and child-rearing realms.

Mortuary Contexts
of La Plata Females with Head Trauma

An association emerges when the mortuary contexts of the individuals with cranial trauma are examined. Most of the burials from La Plata are flexed or semiflexed and placed in abandoned structures or storage pits. Often burials contain associated objects, usually ceramic vessels or ground stone. Every female at La Plata with cranial trauma had a mortuary context that did not follow this pattern. All were found loosely flexed, prostrate, or sprawled. Particularly at two sites, both from Barker Arroyo (LA 37601 and LA 65030), the mortuary context of females with cranial trauma reveals that unlike their age-matched counterparts without signs of trauma, they were generally haphazardly placed in abandoned pit structures without associated grave goods.

At Barker Arroyo site LA 65030, three individuals found in the lower fill of Pit Structure 1 appear to have died at approximately the same time and were interred together. These include an 11-year-old child and two adult women aged at 20 and 33. The child, who shows no signs of non-lethal trauma or pathology, is clearly associated with one of the women, most likely the 33-year-old given the age of the child and the proximity of the child to her. All are in a haphazard position (as if thrown from a higher elevation). Cause of death could not be ascertained for any of these individuals. Also in Pit Structure 1, located in the middle fill on top of the roof fall, another female, age 38, was placed facing downward in a semiflexed position with no grave offerings. In the lower fill of Pit Structure 8, a 22-year-old female also was placed in a semiflexed position with no grave offerings.

At a contemporaneous site, LA 37601, a 25-year-old female with cranial and post-cranial trauma was located in a similar position with no grave goods. Of the three males with cranial trauma, at least one 25-year-old from site LA 37599 was placed in Pit Structure 2 in a similar fashion with no grave goods. Unfortunately, the mortuary context of the other two males with cranial trauma is unknown.

To summarize the association of healed cranial trauma and mortuary context, out of a total sample size of ten adult females with crania, six show trauma and were buried without grave goods and in either sprawled or semiflexed positions (one female with cranial trauma could not be assigned to a mortuary condition). Six females had no trauma and were in flexed or semiflexed positions with associated grave goods; one female had no cranial trauma, a semiflexed burial, but no grave goods; and one female with no cranial trauma had an unknown mortuary context (see Martin and Akins 2001 for a complete discussion of the mortuary treatment of the La Plata individuals).

In contrast, for the 13 males that could be assessed for cranial trauma, six had none and were in flexed burials with grave goods, while four had no cranial trauma or grave goods and were in a variety of positions ranging from extended to flexed. Of the three males with cranial trauma, only one had grave goods, but all were in a semiflexed position. There is more variability in the relationship between cranial trauma and burial treatment for the males, with most males having no grave goods but placed in formal burial contexts in flexed or semiflexed positions.

Theorizing about the Nature of the
Wounds, Recidivism, and Chronic Morbidity

The variation in overall size and dimensions of the depression fractures suggests that any number of implements could have been used to cause

171

these fractures. Two out of three male cranial fractures are on the parietals (one on the left and one on the right, both towards the back). For females, the lesions are tend to be located around the front of the head or on the far back (occipital) portion of the head. It is difficult to verify exactly what type of implement was used in each case of cranial trauma at La Plata, but modern forensic information suggests that fractures and depression wounds of the head can be made with any number of blunt or sharp implements (Petty 1980). In their review of artifacts associated with warfare and hand combat in the Southwest, Wilcox and Haas (1994:223–224) find little evidence for the manufacture of objects to be used solely as weapons. The strongest evidence that they could garner was of two bipointed axes found with a male burial at Aztec Ruin, and wooden swordlike implements found at Chaco Canyon.

Although it is easy to envision a stone axe, hammerstone, core, chopper, or projectile point causing damage, it is equally likely that bone, antler, and wood objects could be used as well. For example, a forensic case involving cranial and post-cranial wounds similar to those at La Plata was caused by being struck repeatedly with a common wooden broomstick handle (Bhootra 1985), not unlike the size and shape of a Pueblo digging stick (Colton 1960:96). Digging sticks were most likely common in an agricultural community such as that of the Barker Arroyo sites at La Plata, and the use of such objects was primarily within the domain of men (at least in historic Pueblo societies) (Dozier 1970). Colton (1960: 98) states that sometimes wooden digging sticks also had a hoe made of hafted stone or triangular pieces of basalt or sandstone. A wide variety of stone tools such as tchamahias and axes were found in the La Plata Valley, and any of these items could have been used to cause injury.

In the reanalysis of the La Plata skeletal data for this project, current clinical techniques were drawn upon in the analysis of radiographic images of the La Plata head wounds (Martin et al. 2007). A neuropathologist (B. Crenshaw) who is a specialist in traumatic brain injuries sustained from blows to the head was consulted to obtain a partial picture of the types of traumatic brain injury that may have accompanied the individuals with head wounds. After detailed analysis of the crania in conjunction with x-ray images of the heads, the following observations can be made regarding the individuals with head wounds.

In general, for individuals who have suffered a blow to the head, a process of injury begins within the brain, divided along a temporal gradient. The primary damage occurs at impact and initiates a sequence of bluntly physical changes (Bernert and Turski 1996). The force of the blow to the skull is imparted to the underlying brain tissue. As this tissue absorbs the force, it rebounds in much the same way that a soccer ball responds when kicked: the brain bounces away from the point of impact (which is called the coup). It then strikes the inside of the skull 180 degrees from the original site of percussion. This second area of impact is called the counter coup, and in many instances it represents a region of injury more severe than those arising at the site of the blow itself. Furthermore, since the brain is inside a sealed container, it continues to rebound along multiple axes, essentially ricocheting from one interior boney wall to another. As it bounces, the soft tissue of the brain rotates with the chaotic lines of force, precipitating a secondary trauma called shearing. In shearing, deep axonal damage is inflicted inside the subcortex when neurons are stretched and compressed by the radiating shock waves.

Unlike primary changes, which occur within a relatively brief period of time, the secondary damage occurs in response to the primary insult and may extend for a prolonged, indefinite time. For instance, the brain may swell afterward in reaction to the physical trauma, much as an external contusion will swell. But since the brain is enclosed, the consequent edema causes increased intracranial pressure that squeezes the soft neuronal tissue against the inside of the skull with damaging force. Similarly, blood vessels may be ruptured by the blunt trauma. They then bleed unrestrictedly, causing local edema, with its attendant problems, and flooding interstitial regions with liquids that are supposed to be contained and that interfere with proper neuronal function (Hohlrieder et al. 2003). The hemorrhage may also cause hypoxia to areas downstream of the ruptured vessels because the tissues that are supposed to be irrigated have lost their blood supply and may therefore be compromised by the want of oxygen. Finally, the trauma initiates a cascade of neurotoxic, excitatory chemicals that accelerate neuronal degeneration by mechanisms that are incompletely understood (Bernert and Turski 1996).

The range of behavioral changes that can result from head trauma is notable, beginning with a transient loss of consciousness and extending— if the force of the trauma is sufficient—to a more or less prolonged coma from which the victim may abruptly wake up as magically as if rising from the dead. Further categories of behavioral change can be discriminated into those involving specific alterations to a componence skill (i.e., change in language, change in motor skill) and those involving alterations to the overall state of mind. Into this latter category is placed the most common change in mental status found after head injury: impairment of concentration.

After a closed head injury, victims may still be able to establish a focus on something interesting, but they cannot sustain their concentration for usable lengths of time. The mind wanders off target, and the individual becomes distractible: unable to inhibit his reactivity to other events that wander into his awareness. There may be impairment to levels of arousal as well. People who have had concussions, for instance, find that they may suddenly lose consciousness, as if someone turned off a switch, or that their mental clarity starts to fog over, or that mental acuity is blunted as if under the subtle, pervasive influence of intoxication (sometimes referred to as non-epileptic seizures). Similarly, the onset of epileptic seizures, which can introduce profound alterations in mental status, is a relatively common consequence of head injury (Diaz-Arrastia et al. 2000), as are changes in endemic mood: the risk of depression among individuals who have sustained traumatic head injury can approach 20 percent (Holsinger et al. 2002).

Changes in social/emotional behaviors are also common, and often there are dysinhibitions in aggression and/or sexual appetite (Janusz et al. 2002; Milders et al. 2003; Stone et al. 2002; Thornhill et al. 2000.). In this context, it is worth noting that several of the La Plata skeletons have what appears to be a sequence of healed wounds inflicted at different times, which may be congruent with these problems of social competence.

People who are aggressive in a social context, for instance, and who are not paying attention to social cues or are misreading them when they do notice, are at greater risk than usual of receiving further head injuries (recidivism). The same set of risks may be in place for those who are incompetent in sexual mores.

Finally, blows to the head can cause alterations in particular aspects of instrumental thinking that tend to be associated with the local region of the coup and the counter coup. For instance, a depression fracture to the left temporal/parietal region may impair speech production and weaken the individual's right arm, while leaving her left arm wholly unaffected. Two females at La Plata (37592 B6 and 37601 B4) have blunt force trauma in the region of the left temporal/parietal bones, and one of these individuals (37601 B4) has smaller overall dimensions of the right humerus versus the left.

Vision can be compromised by a blow to the back of the head. One of the La Plata females (65030 B6) had a large cranial depression fracture in the occipital region. For all of the La Plata females with head injuries, the size, location, depth, and severity suggest that these women were likely suffering from various forms of facial paralysis, impaired memory and attention, compromised expressive and receptive language use, damaged visual-spatial organization, and disrupted vision (Gallagher and Holland 1970; Katz and Alexander 1994; Katzen et al. 2003).

Based on an analysis of the gross presentation of the injuries on the female crania in conjunction with the radiographic images, there is ample evidence that these wounds, although "healed," were severe enough to damage the skeletal tissue and to indicate that some of these women would have had the above-noted neurological problems. These individuals were probably set even further apart from other group members, and perhaps made more vulnerable to beatings, because of behavior that was aberrant or from an inability to focus on tasks, communication, or problem-solving. This analysis of the likelihood of traumatic brain injury, lasting a lifetime after the initial head wound, provides a sense of the range of neurological symptoms, behavioral changes, and morbidity burden suffered by these victims of violence. Thus, the La Plata females with significant healed cranial depression fractures not only carried out harder physical labor, but they likely suffered from lifelong behavioral changes that would have further reinforced their marginalized existence and low status within the community. The injuries sustained by the La Plata women suggest serious long-term behavioral implications—from non-epileptic seizures to memory loss and an inability to focus on tasks—for them and, consequently, for their children.

Strategic Social Violence and Slavery at La Plata

It was likely difficult to maintain unanimity across diverse (economically, linguistically, and ideologically) Pueblo communities in the precontact Southwest. One among several courses of action may have been abduction and captivity of some individuals as part of a larger political strategy. Sectarian-driven raiding and abduction, and captivity and slavery, constitute a form of strategic social violence that can aid in the maintenance of systems of economic exchange and resource redistribution, as well as cross-ethnic interchanges (see Habicht-Mauche, this volume).

A phrase from Taussig's essay on understanding deeply embedded violence goes something like this: the deeper you dig, the dirtier it gets (2004:269). In some ways, the reanalysis and application of new methods and interpretations have permitted an increasingly nuanced interpretation of violence at La Plata. Violence and fear of injury may have played a significant role in oppressing individuals who clearly lived and died within the community, but who stood apart on many levels. Young, reproductive-aged females carry the unequal burden of traumatic injuries in this group. The location and size of the cranial injuries in females covered a larger area, involved more bony elements, often occurred in multiples, and caused internal (endocranial) damage in some cases. Furthermore, the co-morbidity factors of cranial and post-cranial trauma, infections, and decreased life expectancy (there were very few females represented in the older age categories) suggest suboptimal conditions for these adult females. Females with these health problems are more likely to have been in mortuary contexts described as haphazardly thrown or discarded and with no associated grave offerings. As

a group, they were younger when they died than females who had traditionally prepared graves.

An examination of other attributes suggests that these women were in fact regional and not from a distinctively different ethnic group. Most of them have occipital or lambdoidal flattening consistent with the use of cradleboarding during infancy (a strong ancestral Pueblo behavioral characteristic). Only one female with a compression fracture (37601 B10) did not show flattening. It is not unusual in Pueblo groups to have some individuals without cradleboarding (Renaud 1927; Morris 1939), but it may indicate migration or adoption of outside peoples into the Pueblo group. Isotopic analysis was conducted on rib samples from several women with cranial fractures and compared with the other adult males and females. For the sample of thirteen adults, there were no statistically significant differences between males and females, or between individuals with and without evidence of traumatic injury. This suggests that the women with trauma were somewhat local, or at least they came from an environment similar to that at La Plata. Unfortunately, cranial metrics and cranial and post-cranial discrete traits could not be used to characterize the subgroups because of the small sample size.

Why would this subgroup of traumatized women be largely young adults? Spouse abuse and domestic violence can be ruled out because there are other adult females who demonstrate no trauma and who were placed in prepared graves in a flexed position with grave goods. Also, the association of women with injuries and a young child in close proximity suggests that their children were also part of the underclass, and when they died, the child died as well. Witch executions detailed by Walker (1998) and Darling (1999) likewise do not fit the pattern seen at La Plata (bones with cut marks, burning, and dismemberment).

The most parsimonious explanation is that these women represent captive or enslaved women. At La Plata, a more secure economy may have led to increased population density, decreased mobility, increased political centralization, and the need for more routes of exchange and prestige-garnering with the region's competing population centers. Whether this pattern of enslaved captives was widespread or regionally localized is not yet clear. There are cases of females in similar mortuary configuration (women and sometimes children thrown into abandoned structures) at other Southwest sites (e.g., Dolores, Arroyo Hondo, and Homolovi), but analysis of these has not yet been undertaken.

Junker (this volume) demonstrates the ways that women captives were utilized as sources of marriage partners, labor, and wealth in the twelfth- to sixteenth-century Philippine Islands. Of interest here is that one of the motivating factors explored by Junker involves the notion that people (versus land or material goods) were the key capital that could be controlled by those in power, and her model is one that presents intriguing possibilities for the ancient Southwest as well.

Individuals who survived violent interactions are crucial to track in the expanding research agenda on violence in the ancient Southwest. Nonlethal injuries in general need to be studied much more systematically and in conjunction with all the other lines of evidence regarding conflict and violence. This one case study suggests that this area of analysis could yield a richer and more nuanced database that should be integrated into existing interpretations.

As Hegmon and her colleagues (2000) point out, regional interaction in the Southwest needs to be much better understood, particularly in the ways that geographically separate communities could, and probably did, exchange goods, services, and slaves. Captured women could have served not only as additional labor but also as objects of prestige, trade, and alliance. Collectively, the archaeological data on fortification and strategic location and the osteological data on victims are highly suggestive of endemic warfare in the form of ambushes, raids, skirmishes, and attacks by groups of aggressors in many parts of the Pueblo world between AD 950 and 1350. Haas and Creamer (1993) have suggested that these patterns of "chronic warfare" pushed previously egalitarian and loosely connected groups into larger, politically centralized units between AD 1100 and 1300. The socioeconomic, political, and environmental stress caused by this transition likely would have impacted regional interaction spheres.

Human trafficking in the form of raiding, abduction, slavery, and captivity has been an understudied form of strategic political maneuvering in pre-state populations (Cameron, this volume). That these forms of social violence were common and ubiquitous in the pre- and protohistoric periods throughout the Americas is becoming more widely accepted (Ames 2001; Arkush and Allen 2006; Gallay 2002; Kohler and Turner 2006). Human skeletal remains can provide one of the strongest sources of empirical evidence for testing hypotheses about social and institutionalized violence in pre-state societies. Linking the biological effects of violence to the complex suite of cultural and political factors that promote violence as a socially sanctioned and legitimate category of behavior is a difficult task.

A signature of forced captivity and slavery on human skeletal remains probably does exist and could be useful in adding biological, demographic, and behavioral information to the reconstruction of archaeological contexts. This analysis of the La Plata Valley skeletal data addresses the extent to which women, men, and children were subjects of institutionalized, culturally sanctioned abduction and captivity, and the effects of these practices on behavior, morbidity, mortality, and societal position. These data suggest that in addition to other forms of violence known to be operating in the Southwest, a pattern of trafficking in women and children was also in play. Today, human trafficking, forced servitude, captivity, and slavery in a multitude of forms are alive and well in large parts of the world, and anthropologists can lead the way in understanding what motivates and drives these systems, how violence is embedded in historical and political-economic frameworks, and what the cultural logic behind these practices might be.

It seems highly plausible that as the La Plata Valley communities grew and prospered in relation to those in other regions, raiding and abduction of women and children from lesser communities would have been a strategic and politically expedient way to increase productivity and economic wealth. Reproductive-aged females would have been the most advantageous group to exploit because they could aid in domestic tasks and food production as well as in child-rearing. Although Brooks (2002) suggests that captives during the colonial period were often absorbed into the community and sometimes provided with relatively good treatment, the system was built on a permanent structure of inequality, subordination, and ownership. The nature of captivity in the protohistoric/historic communities was one of slave networks and human trafficking that sustained political-economic relationships between the Navajo, the Pueblo, and the Plains communities. Brooks's research suggests that captive-taking provided networks and bonding for these groups who may have otherwise resorted largely to violent means for obtaining power and resources. His examination focuses more on how captivity functioned and the cultural logic that sustained it over broad regions and across hundreds of years than on the actual moment of abduction and its sequelae. Evidence of the actual act of taking captives and of the range of biological and behavioral consequences for the captives can be better understood by interrogating human remains and their contexts. The information derived from the La Plata study provides important empirical data on the human costs of maintaining a political-economic system that used women as prestige objects, beasts of burden, and/or trade goods.

Note

The chapter title is borrowed from Capozzoli (1997: 313).

References Cited

Adler, Michael A. (editor)
1996   *The Prehistoric Pueblo World, AD 1150–1350.* University of Arizona Press, Tucson.

Akins, Nancy J.
1986   *A Biocultural Approach to Human Burials from Chaco Canyon, New Mexico.* Reports of the Chaco Center no. 9. National Park Service, Santa Fe, NM.

Allen, Wilma F., Charles F. Merbs, and Walter H. Birkby
1985   Evidence for Prehistoric Scalping at Nuvak-wewtaqa (Chavez Pass) and Grasshopper Ruin, Arizona. In *Health and Disease in the Prehistoric Southwest*, edited by Charles C. Merbs and R. J. Miller, pp. 23–42. Anthropological Research Papers no. 34. Arizona State University, Tempe.

Ames, Kenneth M.
2001   Slaves, Chiefs and Labour on the Northern Northwest Coast. *World Archaeology* 33(1):1–17.

Arendt, Hannah
2004   From "On Violence." In *Violence in War and Peace*, edited by Nancy Scheper-Hughes and Philippe Bourgois, pp. 236–243. Blackwell, Malden, MA.

Arkush, Elizabeth N., and Mark W. Allen (editors)
2006   *Archaeology of Warfare: Prehistories of Raiding and Conquest.* University of Florida Press, Gainesville.

Bernert, H., and L. Turski
1996   Traumatic Brain Damage prevented by the Non-N-Mythyl-D-Aspartate Antagonist 2,3-Dihydroxy-6-Nitro-7-Sulfamoylbenzo[f] quinoxaline. *Proceedings of the National Academy of Science* 93(11):5235–5240.

Bhootra, B. K.
1985   An Unusual Penetrating Head Wound by a Yard Brook and Its Medicolegal Aspects. *Journal of Forensic Sciences* 30:567–571.

Blackhawk, Ned
2006   *Violence Over the Land: Indians and Empires in the Early American West.* Harvard University Press, Cambridge, MA.

Blakey, Michael L.
1998   The New York African Burial Ground Project: An Examination of Enslaved Lives, a Construction of Ancestral Ties. *Transforming Anthropology* 7(1):53–58.

2001   Bioarchaeology of the African Diaspora in the Americas: Its Origins and Scope. *Annual Review of Anthropology* 30:387–422.

Boyd, Donna C.
2005   Skeletal Correlates of Human Behavior in the Americas. *Journal of Archaeological Method and Theory* 3(3):189–251.

Bridges, Patricia S.
1990   Osteological Correlates of Weapon Use. In *A Life in Science: Papers in Honor of J. Lawrence Angel*, edited by Jane Buikstra, pp. 87–98. Scientific Papers 6. Washington, D.C., Center for American Archaeology.

Brinkley, M. B., and M. J. Smith
2006   Culturally Determined Patterns of Violence: Biological Anthropological Investigations at a Historic Urban Cemetery. *American Anthropologist* 108:163–177.

Brooks, James F.
2002   *Captive Cousins: Slavery, Kinship, and Com-*

munity in the Southwest Borderlands. School of American Research Press, Santa Fe, NM.

Buikstra, Jane, and Douglas Ubelaker

1994   Standards for Data Collection from Human Skeletal Remains. Arkansas Archaeology Survey Research Series no. 44. Western Newspaper Company, Indianapolis.

Byers, Steven N.

2002   Forensic Anthropology. Allyn and Bacon, Boston.

Capasso, Luigi, Kenneth A. R. Kennedy, and Cynthia A. Wilczak

1999   Atlas of Occupational Markers on Human Remains. Edigraphital S.P.A., Teramo, Italy.

Capozzoli, Maureen McCarthy

1997   A Rip into the Flesh, A Tear into the Soul: An Ethnography of Dissection in Georgia. In Bones in the Basement: Post-Mortem Racism in Nineteenth-Century Medical Training, edited by Robert L. Blakely and Judith M. Harrington, pp. 313–339. Smithsonian Institution Press, Washington, D.C.

Colton, Harold S.

1960   Black Sand: Prehistory in Northern Arizona. University of New Mexico Press, Albuquerque.

Cope, Janet M., Alison Berryman, Debra L. Martin, and Dan Potts

2005   Robusticity and Osteoarthritis at the Trapeziometacarpal Joint in a Bronze Age Population from Tell Abraq, UAE. American Journal of Physical Anthropology 126:391–400.

Courville, C. B.

1948   Cranial Injuries among the Indians of North America: A Preliminary Report. Los Angeles Neurological Society 13:181–219.

Danforth, M. E., Della C. Cook, and S. G. Knick III

1994   The Human Remains from Carter Ranch Pueblo, Arizona: Health in Isolation. American Antiquity 59:88–101.

Darling, J. Andrew

1999   Mass Inhumation and the Execution of Witches in the American Southwest. American Anthropologist 100:732–752.

Diaz-Arrastia, Ramon, Mark Agostini, Alan B. Frol, Bruce Mickey, James Fleckenstein, Eileen Bigio, and Paul Van Ness

2000   Neurophysiological and Neuroradiologic Features of Intractable Epilepsy after Traumatic Brain Injury in Adults. Archives of Neurology 57(11):1611.

Dozier, Edward P.

1970   The Pueblo Indians of North America. Holt, Reinhart and Winston, New York.

Ferguson, Brian

1997   Violence and War in Prehistory. In Troubled Times: Violence and Warfare in the Past, edited by Debra L. Martin and David W. Frayer, pp. 321–355. Gordon and Breach, Amsterdam.

Gallagher, Michela, and Peter Holland

1970   The Amygdala Complex: Multiple Roles in Associative Learning and Attention. Proceedings of the National Academy of Sciences 91: 11771–11776.

Gallay, Alan

2002   The Indian Slave Trade. Yale University Press, New Haven, CT.

Glassman, D. M., and William M. Bass

1986   Bilateral Asymmetry of Long Arm Bones and Jugular Foramen: Implications for Handedness. Journal of Forensic Science 31:589–595.

Gualdi-Russo, E., and L. Galletti

2004   Human Activity Patterns and Skeletal Metric Indicators in the Upper Limb. Collegium Antropologogicum 28:131–143.

Guilaine, Jean, and Jean Zammit

2005   The Origins of War Violence in Prehistory. Blackwell, Malden, MA.

Gurdjian, E. S.

1973   Head Injury from Antiquity to the Present with Special Reference to Penetrating Head Wounds. C. C. Thomas, Springfield, IL.

Gutiérrez, Ramón A.

1991   When Jesus Came, the Corn Mothers Went Away. Stanford University Press, Stanford, CA.

Hass, Jonathan

1990   Warfare and the Evolution of Tribal Polities in the Prehistoric Southwest. In The Anthropology of War, edited by Jonathan Haas, pp. 171–189. School of American Research Press, Santa Fe, NM.

Haas, Jonathan, and Winifred Creamer

1993   Stress and Warfare among the Kayenta Anasazi of the Thirteenth Century AD. Field Museum of Natural History, Chicago.

Habicht-Mauche, Judith A.

2000   Pottery, Food, Hides and Women: Labor, Production and Exchange within the Protohistoric Plains-Pueblo Frontier Economy. In The Archaeology of Regional Interaction: Religion, Warfare and Exchange across the American Southwest and Beyond, edited by Michelle Hegmon, pp. 209–231. University of Colorado Press, Boulder.

Harris, Marvin, and E. B. Ross

1987   Death, Sex, and Fertility: Population Regulation in Preindustrial and Developing Societies. Columbia University Press, New York.

Hegmon, Michelle, Kelly Hays-Gilpin, Randall H. McGuire, A. Routman, and Sara H. Schlanger

2000   Scale, Interaction and Regional Analysis in

Late Pueblo Prehistory. In *The Archaeology of Regional Interaction: Religion, Warfare and Exchange across the American Southwest and Beyond,* pp. 99–118, University of Colorado Press, Boulder.

Hohlrieder, Matthias, Josef Hinterhoelzl, Hanno Ulmer, Christiane Lang, Wolfgang Hackl, Andreas Kampfl, Arnulf Benzer, Erick Schmutzhard, and Robert Gassner

2003   Traumatic Intracranial Hemorrhages in Facial Fracture Patients: Review of 2195 Patients. *Intensive Care Medicine* 29:1095–1100.

Holsinger, Tracey, David C. Steffens, Caroline Phillips, Michael J. Helms, Richard J. Havlik, John C. S. Breitner, Jack M. Guralnik, and Brenda L. Plassman

2002   Head Injury in Early Adulthood and the Lifetime Risk of Depression. *Archives of General Psychiatry* 59:17–22.

Hooton, Ernest A.

1930   *The Indians of Pecos Pueblo: A Study of Their Skeletal Remains.* Papers of the Southwestern Expedition 4. Yale University Press, New Haven.

Janusz, Jennifer A., Michael W. Kirkwood, Keith Owen-Yeats, H. Gerry Taylor

2002   Social Problem–Solving Skills in Children with Traumatic Brain Injury: Long Term Outcomes and Prediction of Social Competence. *Child Neuropsychology* 8:179–194.

John, Elizabeth A. H.

1975   *Storms Brewed in Other Men's Worlds.* University of Nebraska Press, Lincoln.

Josephy, Jr., Alvin M. (editor)

1991   *America in 1492: The World of the Indian Peoples Before the Arrival of Columbus.* Vintage Books, Random House, New York.

Judd, Margaret

2002   Ancient Injury Recidivism: An Example from the Kerma Period of Ancient Nubia. *International Journal of Osteoarchaeology* 12:89–106.

Kamp, Katheryn A. (editor)

2002   *Children in the Prehistoric Puebloan Southwest.* University of Utah Press, Salt Lake City.

Katz, D., and M. Alexander

1994   Traumatic Brain injury: Predicting Course of Recovery and Outcome for Patients Admitted to Rehabilitation. *Archives of Neurology* 51(7): 661.

Katzen, Timothy J., Reza Jarrahy, Joseph B. Ebay, Ronald Matthias, Daniel R. Margulies, and Harry K. Shawinigan

2003   Craniofacial and Skull Base Trauma. *Journal of Trauma* 54:1026–1034.

Kennedy, Kenneth A. R.

1989   Skeletal Markers of Occupational Stress. In *Reconstructions of Life from the Skeleton,* edited by Mehmet Yasar Iscan and Kenneth A. R. Kennedy, pp. 129–160. Alan R. Liss, New York.

Kohler, Timothy A., and Kathryn Kramer Turner

2006   Raiding for Women in the Prehistoric Northern Pueblo Southwest? A Pilot Examination. *Current Anthropology* 47:1035–1045.

Kramer, Kathryn

2002   *Sex Ratios and Warfare in the Prehistoric Puebloan Southwest.* Unpublished master's thesis, Washington State University, Department of Anthropology, Pullman.

Kuckelman, Kristin L., Ricky R. Lightfoot, and Debra L. Martin

2002   The Bioarchaeology and Taphonomy of Violence at Castle Rock and Sand Canyon Pueblos, Southwestern Colorado. *American Antiquity* 67:486–513.

Larralde, Signa

1998   The Context of Early Puebloan Violence. In *Deciphering Anasazi Violence,* edited by Peter Yochio Bullock, pp. 11–33. HRM Books, Santa Fe, NM.

Larsen, Clark Spenser

1999   *Bioarchaeology: Interpreting Behavior from the Human Skeleton.* Cambridge University Press, Cambridge.

LeBlanc, Steven A.

1999   *Prehistoric Warfare in the American Southwest.* University of Utah Press, Salt Lake City.

2003   *Constant Battles: The Myth of the Peaceful, Noble Savage.* St. Martin's Press, New York.

Lovell, Nancy C.

1997   Trauma Analysis in Paleopathology. *Yearbook of Physical Anthropology* 40:139–170.

Lowell, Julia C.

2007   Women and Men in Warfare and Migration: Implications of Gender Imbalance in the Grasshopper Region of Arizona. *American Antiquity* 72(1):95–124.

Martin, Debra L.

1997   Violence Against Women in a Southwestern Series (AD 1000–1300). In *Troubled Times: Violence and Warfare in the Past,* edited by Debra L. Martin and David Frayer, pp. 45–75. Gordon and Breach, New York.

Martin, Debra L., and Nancy J. Akins

2001   Unequal Treatment in Life as in Death: Trauma and Mortuary Behavior at La Plata (AD 1000–1300). In *Ancient Burial Practices in the American Southwest,* edited by D. R. Mitchell and J. L. Brunson-Hadley, pp. 223–248. University of New Mexico Press, Albuquerque.

Martin, Debra L., Nancy J. Akins, Bradley Crenshaw, and Pamela K. Stone

2007   Inscribed on the Body, Written in the Bones: The Consequences of Social Violence at La Plata. In *Multidisciplinary Approaches to Social Violence in the Prehispanic Southwest*, edited by Patricia Crown and Deborah Nichols. University of Arizona Press, Tucson.

Martin, Debra L., Nancy J. Akins, Alan H. Goodman, H. Wolcott Toll, and Alan C. Swedlund

2001   *Harmony and Discord: Bioarchaeology of the La Plata Valley*. Museum of New Mexico Press, Santa Fe.

Martin, Debra L., Ann L. Magennis, and Jerome C. Rose

1987   Cortical Bone Maintenance in an Historic Afro-American Cemetery from Cedar Grove, Arkansas. *American Journal of Physical Anthropology* 74:255–264.

Merbs, Charles F.

1989   Trauma. In *Reconstructions of Life from the Skeleton*, edited by Mehmet Yasar Iscan and Kenneth A. R. Kennedy, pp. 161–190. Alan R. Liss, New York.

Merbs, Charles F., and Robert J. Miller (editors)

1985   *Health and Disease in the Prehistoric Southwest*. Anthropological Research Papers no. 34. Arizona State University, Tempe.

Milders, Maarten, Sandra Fuchs, and John R. Crawford

2003   Neuropsychological Impairments and Changes in Emotional and Social Behavior Following Severe Traumatic Brain Injury. *Journal of Clinical Experimental Neuropsychology* 25:157–172.

Miles, J. S.

1975   *Orthopedic Problems of the Wetherill Mesa Populations*. Publications in Archaeology 7G. Wetherill Mesa Studies, National Park Service, Washington, D.C.

Milner, George R., Eric Anderson, and V. G. Smith

1991   Warfare in Late Prehistoric West-Central Illinois. *American Antiquity* 56:581–603.

Morris, Earl H.

1939   *Archaeological Studies in the La Plata District*. Carnegie Institution, Washington, D.C.

Morton, Patricia (editor)

1996   *Discovering the Women in Slavery: Emancipating Perspectives on the American Past*. University of Georgia Press, Athens.

Ogilvie, Marsha D., and Charles E. Hilton

1993   Analysis of Selected Human Skeletal Material from Sites 423-124 and -131. In *Across the Colorado Plateau: Anthropological Studies for the Transwestern Pipeline Expansion Project*, vol. 18: *Human Remains and Burial Goods*, edited

by N. P. Hermann, pp. 97–128. Office of Contract Archaeology and Maxwell Museum of Anthropology, University of New Mexico, Albuquerque.

Ortner, Donald J., and W. G. J. Putschar

1981   *Identification of Pathological Conditions in Human Skeletal Remains*. Smithsonian Institution Press, Washington, D.C.

Patterson, Orlando

1982   *Slavery and Social Death*. Harvard University Press, Cambridge, MA.

Petty, C. S.

1980   Death by Trauma: Blunt and Sharp Instrument and Firearms. In *Modern Legal Medicine, Psychiatry, and Forensic Science*, edited by W. J. Curran, A. L. McGarry and C. S. Petty, pp. 100–121. Davis, Philadelphia.

Rankin-Hill, Lesley M.

1997   *A Biohistory of Nineteenth Century Afro-Americans*. Bergin and Garvey, Westport, CT.

Reichs, Kathleen J.

1998   *Forensic Osteology*. C. C. Thomas, Springfield, IL.

Renaud, E. B.

1927   Undeformed Prehistoric Skulls from La Plata, Colorado, and Cañon del Muerto, Arizona. *University of Colorado Studies* 16(1):5–36.

Rice, Glen E., and Steven A. LeBlanc

2001   *Deadly Landscapes: Case Studies in Prehistoric Southwest Warfare*. University of Utah Press, Salt Lake City.

Robb, John

1997   Violence and Gender in Early Italy. In *Troubled Times: Violence and Warfare in the Past*, edited by Debra L. Martin and David Frayer, pp. 111–144. Gordon and Breach, New York.

Rose, Jerome

1985   *Gone to a Better Land: A Biohistory of a Rural Black Cemetery in Post-Reconstruction South*. Arkansas Archaeological Survey Press, Fayetteville.

Schwartz, Marie Jenkins

1996   "At Noon, Oh How I Ran": Breastfeeding and Weaning on Plantation and Farm in Antebellum Virginia and Alabama. In *Discovering the Women in Slavery: Emancipating Perspectives on the American Past*, edited by Patricia Morton, pp. 241–259. University of Georgia Press, Athens.

Spencer, R. F., and Jesse D. Jennings

1965   *The Native Americans: Prehistory and Ethnology*. Harper and Row, New York.

Sponsel, L. E.

2001   Response to Otterbein. *American Anthropologist* 102(4):837–841.

Starobin, Robert S.
1988   *Black in Bondage.* Marcus Wiener, Princeton, NJ.

Steadman, Dawnie Wolfe
2003   *Hard Evidence.* Prentice Hall, Upper Saddle River, NJ.

Steele, Ian K.
1994   *Warpaths: Invasions of North America.* Oxford University Press, New York.

Stewart, Ted D., and L. G. Quade
1969   Lesions of the Frontal Bone in American Indians. *American Journal of Physical Anthropology* 30:89–110.

Stodder, Ann L. W.
1989   Bioarchaeological Research in the Basin and Range Region. In *Human Adaptation and Cultural Change in the Greater Southwest,* edited by A. H. Simmons, Ann L. W. Stodder, A. L. Dykeman, and P. A. Hicks, pp. 167–190. Research Series no. 32. Arkansas Archaeological Survey, Wrightsville.

Stone, Valerie, Leda Cosmides, John Tooby, Neal Kroll, and Robert Knight
2002   Selective Impairment of Reasoning about Social Exchange in a Patient with Bilateral Limbic System Damage. *Proceedings of the National Academy of Sciences* 99(17):11531–11536.

Taussig, Michael
2004   Terror as Usual: Walter Benjamin's Theory of History as a State of Siege. In *Violence in War and Peace,* edited by Nancy Scheper-Hughes and Philippe Bourgois, pp. 269–271. Blackwell, Malden, MA.

Thornhill, Sharon, Graham Teasdale, Gordon Murray, James McEwen, Christopher Roy, and Kay Penny
2000   Disability in Young People and Adults One Year after Head Injury. *British Medical Journal* 320:1631–1635.

Titiev, Mischa
1972   *The Hopi Indians of Old Oraibi.* University of Michigan Press, Ann Arbor.

Toll, H. Wolcott, III
1993   The Role of the Totah in Regions and Regional Definitions. Unpublished paper presented at the Fifth Occasional Anasazi Symposium, San Juan College, Farmington, NM.

Toll, Mollie S.
1993   The Archaeobotany of the La Plata Valley in Totah Perspective. Unpublished paper presented at the Fifth Occasional Anasazi Symposium, San Juan College, Farmington, NM.

Trinkaus, Eric, S. E. Churchill, and Christopher B. Ruff
1994   Postcranial Robusticity in *Homo,* Part 2: Humeral Bilateral Asymmetry and Bone Plasticity. *American Journal of Physical Anthropology* 93:1–4.

Turner, Christy G., III, and Jacqueline A. Turner
1999   *Man Corn: Cannibalism and Violence in the Prehistoric American Southwest.* University of Utah Press, Salt Lake City.

Walker, Philip L.
1985   Anemia Among Prehistoric Indians of the American Southwest. In *Health and Disease in the Prehistoric Southwest,* edited by Charles F. Merbs and Robert J. Miller, pp. 139–164. Anthropological Research Papers no. 34. Arizona State University, Tempe.
1989   Cranial Injuries as Evidence of Violence in Prehistoric Southern California. *American Journal of Physical Anthropology* 80:313–323.
1997   Wife Beating, Boxing and Broken Noses: Skeletal Evidence for the Cultural Patterning of Violence. In *Troubled Times: Violence and Warfare in the Past,* edited by Debra L. Martin and David Frayer, pp. 145–180. Gordon and Breach, New York.
2001   A Bioachaeological Perspective on the History of Violence. *Annual Review Anthropology* 30:573–596.

Walker, William H.
1998   Where Are the Witches of Prehistory? *Journal of Archaeological Method and Theory* 5(3):245–308.

White, Tim D.
1992   *Prehistoric Cannibalism at Mancos 5MTUMR-2346.* Princeton University Press, Princeton, NJ.

Wilcox, David R., and Jonathan Haas
1994   Competition and Conflict in the Prehistoric Southwest. In *Themes in Southwest Prehistory,* edited by George J. Gumerman, pp. 211–238. School of American Research Press, Santa Fe, NM.

Wilkinson, Richard G., and Karen M. Van Wagenen
1993   Violence Against Women: Prehistoric Skeletal Evidence from Michigan. *Midcontinental Journal of Archaeology* 18:190–216.

8

Captive Wives?

The Role and Status of Nonlocal Women
on the Protohistoric Southern High Plains

Judith A. Habicht-Mauche

James F. Brooks (2002:35), in his landmark book, *Captives and Cousins: Slavery, Kinship and Community in the Southwest Borderlands,* argues that during the colonial period along the Spanish Southwest–Southern Plains borderlands, "native and colonizing peoples came to share some understanding of the production and distribution of wealth and status" that "involved a convergence in patriarchal notions about the socially productive value and exchangeability of women and children." According to Brooks (2002:31), these "practices joined to form a 'slave system' in which victims symbolized social wealth, performed services for their masters, and produced material goods under the threat of violence." He also argues, however, that this system of slavery differed from others in colonial North America because captive women and children on both sides of the exchange often became socially integrated, although marginally, within their host communities through such kinship-based practices as marriage, concubinage, adoption, and/or the Spanish practice of *compadrazago* (godparenting). As a result, Brooks (2002:34) points out, "the hapless women and children who became slaves also became the main negotiators of cultural, economic, and political exchange between groups" and participated in major transformations of gender, power, and status relationships within their host societies.

But to what degree were Spanish colonizers adapting to and integrating themselves within an existing Native system of captive-taking, prestige-building, and cross-cultural exchange that had deep roots along the Southwest–Southern Plains frontier? The reports of the earliest Spanish chroniclers (Gallegos 1927; Hammond and Rey 1940, 1953; Hodge 1907), combined with extensive archaeological evidence from both the Southwest and Southern Plains (Baugh 1982, 1984; Habicht-Mauche 1991; Kidder 1958; Spielmann 1982, 1991; Vehik 2002; Wedel 1950, 1982), indicate that these two regions of southern North America were linked by a broad network of cross-cultural trade and interaction that appears to date back to the end of the late precontact period, intensifying significantly after AD 1450. This interaction focused on the exchange of regional products such as bison hides, meat, and fat from the Plains for the agricultural produce and craft specialties of the Rio Grande Pueblos such as maize, ceramics, and cotton cloth. Prestige items such as exotic lithics, shell beads, and turquoise jewelry also changed hands.

In addition, archaeological and ethnohistorical evidence suggests that people, especially women, also may have moved across this indigenous interethnic frontier. It is quite likely that at least some of these women were incorporated into southern High Plains society as captives taken in raids by nomadic bison-hunting groups on their settled agricultural neighbors. But as

Catherine Cameron points out in the introduction to this volume, captive-taking is often part of a much broader web of intersocietal relations that includes a complex mix of trade, warfare, and "moving bodies." Other processes that could have moved people, more or less willingly, across this interethnic landscape include the negotiation of marriage alliances and the temporary or permanent migration of refugees. The presence of these captive women, wives, and refugees may have facilitated further intercultural interactions across the Southwest–Southern Plains frontier, especially if these women were allowed to maintain contact with their natal villages and were able to exploit their potential as cultural intermediaries. As foreigners they may have been active agents of culture change, bringing with them new technologies, foodways, and other novel ways of being in the world. However, their presence also may have disrupted traditional systems of kinship, status, gender relations, and divisions of labor, leading to major transformations in the organization of production and the structure of social reproduction among these Plains groups.

In this chapter, I present archaeological evidence for the presence of nonlocal women at sites dating to the protohistoric period (AD 1500–1700) on the southern High Plains. These sites are associated with a major shift along the western margins of the Southern Plains from more generalized, mixed hunting-gathering-farming economies to those based on the intensive hunting of bison and the specialized production and exchange of bison products, especially tanned hides. Archaeological and ethnohistoric data suggest that the accumulation and distribution of processed bison hides played an increasingly important role in male prestige-building activities on the southern High Plains during this transitional period. Because women were the primary producers of men's wealth, in the form of processed bison hides, the exchange of women and the control of women's labor may have become a central feature of men's competitive status-building efforts. In particular, ambitious men may have actively recruited nonlocal women's labor through increased raiding and captive-taking, the negotiation of interregional marriage alliances, and the patronage of Pueblo refugee families. These trends, along with the

major demographic and economic changes that were taking place at this time, tended to undercut traditional patterns of matrilineal kinship, marriage, status, and labor. These transformations in the structure of gendered social relations and status within southern High Plains society, which began largely prior to sustained European contact, are what made the development of the colonial borderlands slave system described by Brooks (2002:34), with its "shared patriarchal structures of power and patrimony," possible.

Protohistoric Plains-Pueblo Interaction

When telling a story, one is often encouraged to begin at the beginning, but often beginning in the middle is more satisfying and effective. Such a strategy allows the narrator to move alternatively forward and backward in time, explaining the origins of events or processes, as well as their resolution or transformation. Marvin Smith (1987) has referred to this approach to studying culture change during the late precontact and early colonial periods in North America as the "indirect historical approach." Unlike the "direct historical approach" (Steward 1942) used by early cultural historians, the indirect historical approach does not assume a continuity of people, social structures, or cultural norms from present to past, but rather seeks to illuminate the dynamics of shifting social formations, ethnic identities, and cultural change through time. Ann Stahl (1993) has proposed a similar "comparative approach" to analogical modeling in archaeology that is attentive to the points of similarity as well as disjuncture that may inform on how the past differed from the present. Beginning at a known historical moment or baseline, one compares and contrasts eyewitness testimonies with contemporary and earlier archaeological data and later historical and ethnographic accounts in order to reconstruct the events or processes in question within their broader social and historical contexts.

My baseline for examining the cultural and economic impact of nonlocal women on Southern Plains society is the protohistoric period, from the end of the fifteenth century through the seventeenth century. It was during this period, around the middle of the sixteenth century, that the first Spanish explorers began to penetrate the far corners of what would become the northwestern frontier of New Spain: the North American Southwest and Southern Plains. The accounts of these early reconnaissance missions and aborted colonization attempts provide us with a tantalizing glimpse of a world that was on the cusp of being rapidly and irrevocably transformed by conquest, colonization, and economic globalization, but was still largely untouched by these events. These accounts are sometimes frustratingly vague or silent on certain issues of interest, such as indigenous captive-taking practices or the social status and economic roles of native women, and they are clearly colored by the peculiar motivations and perspectives of each European observer. Nonetheless, when combined with contemporary archaeological evidence and later ethnographic and historical sources, they provide an important window on the peoples of the Southwest–Southern Plains frontier during a time of dramatic social and demographic transformation.

Documents dating from the time of Francisco Vásquez de Coronado's initial *entrada* in 1540 to the first successful colonization of the province of New Mexico by Juan de Oñate at the turn of the seventeenth century (Gallegos 1927; Hammond and Rey 1940, 1953; Hodge 1907; Peréz de Luxán 1929; Schroeder and Matson 1965) provide us with the earliest recorded descriptions of the Native peoples of the southern High Plains and their interactions, both friendly and violent, with the Pueblo villagers of the Rio Grande Valley. According to these accounts, the badlands and high flat plains of the Llano Estacado, which extended east of the Rio Grande Valley and southern Rocky Mountains, were the domain of various groups of highly mobile bison-hunting nomads who lived in portable hide tents that they carried from place to place on the backs of dogs. These accounts also describe the periodic trading visits of nomadic Plains bison hunters to eastern frontier pueblos such as Pecos, Taos, Picurís, and San Marcos (Gallegos 1927; Hammond and Rey 1953; Hodge 1907). During the course of these visits, specialized, processed bison products—such as dried meat, hides, and rendered fat—were exchanged for the agricultural produce and craft specialties of the settled villagers, especially maize, ceramics, and cotton cloth (Forbes 1994; Hammond and Rey 1940).

Archaeological evidence from both the Southwest and Southern Plains mirrors the ethnohistoric accounts and documents the important economic and social ties that linked these two regions of southern North America in the century immediately preceding European conquest. In sixteenth-century and later deposits from the frontier Pueblo site of Pecos, A. V. Kidder (1932, 1958) noted the presence of a complex of materials that indicated contact with bison-hunting groups to the east, including a Plains-style tool kit notable for its association with the processing of bison hides and consisting of snub-nosed end scrapers, two- and four-edged beveled knives, and bison bone end scrapers. The presence of exotic lithic raw materials, such as Alibates agate from quarries along the Canadian River in Texas, was also indicative of contact and trade with nomadic peoples to the east (Kidder 1958). In addition, Snow (1981) reports a marked increase in the amount of eastern freshwater shells recovered from Rio Grande Pueblo sites beginning in the fifteenth century.

Numerous finds of southwestern materials and artifacts have been recovered from various archaeological contexts throughout the Southern Plains. Pueblo pottery, obsidian, turquoise, Pacific Coast shells, and other materials of southwestern origin first occur in notable quantities on sites of the late prehistoric Antelope Creek phase, located along the Canadian River in the northern Texas Panhandle and dating to between AD 1200 and 1500 (Baerreis and Bryson 1966; Krieger 1946, 1947; Lintz 1984, 1991; Moorehead 1931). More extensive evidence of interregional contact and trade have been recovered from a series of archaeological complexes associated with highly specialized bison-hunting groups who occupied the western margins of the Southern Plains, ranging from the mixed grass prairie of western Oklahoma to the high plains of the Texas Panhandle, during the protohistoric period (AD 1450–1700) (Baugh 1986, 1994; Habicht-Mauche 1992; Hofman 1984; Hughes 1989; Johnson et al. 1977). Scattered evidence of contact between Plains Village groups and the Southwest—in the form of small quantities of Rio Grande pottery, obsidian, shell jewelry, and turquoise—has been noted as far north and east as central Kansas (Wedel 1950, 1982). The variety, abundance, and widespread distribution of southwestern trade goods on sites throughout the Southern Plains, and extending into the Central Plains, reflect a dramatic increase in the frequency and intensity of Plains-Pueblo interactions beginning around the mid fifteenth century.

The archaeological record suggests that more than just things may have moved across the protohistoric Southwest–Southern Plains frontier. People, too, particularly women, may have flowed through this system: some by choice, some by necessity, and others through force and violence. Their presence may be glimpsed in the ubiquitous, yet unassuming, remains of small Pueblo-style cooking pots found on sites throughout the southern High Plains dating between AD 1450 and 1700.

Bison Hunters
on the Southern High Plains

Pueblo-style pots are found on sites associated with two relatively poorly known archaeological complexes on the protohistoric southern High Plains, referred to as the Tierra Blanca and Garza complexes (Habicht-Mauche 1992; Hughes 1989; Johnson et al. 1977). Sites attributed to the Tierra Blanca complex are concentrated in the northern Llano Estacado region of the Panhandle Plains in Texas. Settlements appear to have been particularly dense along the upper tributaries of the Red River in Randall and Armstrong counties, but isolated sites suggest that Tierra Blanca territory may have extended north of the Canadian River into the Oklahoma Panhandle and eastward into New Mexico. Radiocarbon dates and ceramic cross-dating indicate a general time span from about AD 1450 to around 1650 for the complex (Hughes 1978; Katz and Katz 1976; Spielmann 1982).

These dates partially overlap with the latest Antelope Creek phase dates in the area. The Antelope Creek people lived in permanent villages and practiced a mix of hunting, gathering, and farming. Overlap in the dating of these complexes suggests that the expansion of highly mobile bison-hunting nomads onto the southern High Plains may account for some of the evidence for increased competition and violence that characterizes late Antelope Creek phase sites (Lintz 1991; Vehik 2002). Competition between

these groups may have been partially responsible for the eventual abandonment of the area by Plains Village farmers.

Ethnohistoric evidence strongly suggests that the Tierra Blanca complex can be directly associated with nomadic bison-hunting groups identified as "Querechos" in the mid sixteenth-century Coronado documents (Hammond and Rey 1940), as "Vaqueros" or "Vaquero Apaches" in the Oñate documents around the turn of the seventeenth century (Hammond and Rey 1953), and as various bands of Plains Apaches in the eighteenth century (Forbes 1994; Habicht-Mauche 1992). The Tierra Blanca complex is probably associated with Athapaskan-speaking groups who were moving southward along the western margins of the Great Plains during the fifteenth and sixteenth centuries (Gunnerson 1956; Habicht-Mauche 1992; Wilcox 1981). These migrant groups introduced a more highly mobile and efficient bison-oriented lifeway to the southern High Plains, displacing or absorbing the local Plains Village groups with whom they came into contact.

Sites attributed to the Garza complex are concentrated along the upper forks of the Brazos River, as these cut through the eastern escarpment of the lower Llano Estacado (Booker and Campbell 1978; Boyd et al. 1993; Johnson 1987; Johnson et al. 1977; Northern 1979; Parker 1982; Parsons 1967; Runkles 1964; Runkles and Dorchester 1987; Wheat 1955; Word 1963, 1965, 1991). Other sites associated with the Garza complex have been identified in the Colorado-Concho area of central Texas (Treece et al. 1993) and along the middle Pecos River, between Roswell, New Mexico, and the junction of the Rio Grande (Holden 1938; Lorrain 1968; Parry and Speth 1984). Currently available radiocarbon, archaeomagnetic, and obsidian hydration dates all suggest that the Garza occupation of the southern High Plains most likely fell between AD 1500 and 1700. Cross-dating of imported glaze-painted ceramics from the Rio Grande Pueblos of New Mexico would appear to confirm this general time range.

Ethnohistoric evidence suggests that the Garza complex can be associated with the other major group of bison-hunting nomads encountered by the Coronado expedition on the southern High Plains during the mid sixteenth century and referred to in those accounts as the "Teyas" (Habicht-Mauche 1992). The Teyas were said to be the enemies of the Querechos and could be distinguished physically by their practice of painting or tattooing their eyes, a custom later associated with the historic Wichita and other Plains Caddoan groups. Like the Querechos, they lived in skin tents, had dog transport, and hunted bison on the open plains. However, some enigmatic passages in the accounts suggest that these "painted Indians" also may have occupied more substantial, semi-sedentary settlements, with grass houses sheltered in the canyons at the edge of the Llano Estacado and may have practiced some limited horticulture.

The linguistic identity of the Teyas has been the subject of some debate among ethnohistorians (Gunnerson 1956; Habicht-Mauche 1992; Hickerson 1990; Riley 1997; Blakeslee et al. 2002). However, the combined weight of current archaeological and documentary evidence strongly suggests that the Teyas were most likely a Plains Caddoan group with strong cultural ties to contemporaneous groups living in western Oklahoma and central Kansas (Habicht-Mauche 1992; Vehik 1986, 1992). However, in contrast with their linguistic cousins to the north and east—many of whom continued to practice a mixed farming, hunting, and gathering economy with roots in the Plains Village Tradition—the Teyas appear to have adopted a more mobile, bison-oriented lifestyle. This strategy may have allowed these peripheral Plains Caddoan groups to compete more successfully, at least over the short term, with Athapaskan-speaking nomadic groups who were expanding onto the southern High Plains during the late fifteenth and sixteenth centuries.

The fate of the Teyas is somewhat unclear both archaeologically and ethnohistorically, but it seems quite likely that they were ultimately displaced or absorbed by expanding Plains Apache populations during the eighteenth century, part of a process that Anderson (1999) has referred to as the "Apacheanization" of the Southwest–Southern Plains frontier. As noted above, the Teyas were described in the Coronado accounts as being enemies of the Querechos, suggesting that there may have been some level of violent competition between these nomadic groups for control of the bison-hunting territory of the

southern High Plains during the sixteenth century. Castañeda, one of the chroniclers of the Coronado expedition, noted that "The Teyas whom the army met…are known by the people of the towns as their friends. The Teyas often go to the latter's pueblos to spend the winter, finding shelter under the eaves" (Hammond and Rey 1940: 258). However, he also reports local accounts of the Teyas as aggressive and violent raiders who were responsible for destroying and forcing the abandonment of several large Galisteo Basin pueblos during the early sixteenth century.

Thus relations between the Rio Grande Pueblos and their nomadic neighbors at this time seem to have fluctuated between friendly alliance and trade, and hostile raiding and violence. As Cameron points out in the introduction to this volume, systems of captive-taking and slavery are often strongly correlated with endemic intersocietal warfare and violence among non-state societies. Archaeological and documentary evidence for a marked increase in interaction and violence along the Southwest–Southern High Plains frontier beginning around AD 1450 should alert us to look more carefully for archaeological indicators of captive-taking among these competing, yet highly interdependent groups.

Archaeological evidence suggests that the Tierra Blanca and Garza complexes do not represent self-sufficient, generalized hunter-gatherers, but rather highly specialized commodity producers whose economy focused on the intensive exploitation, processing, and exchange of bison products. Bison, and to a lesser extent pronghorn antelope, appear to dominate the faunal assemblages at most sites (cf. Boyd et al. 1993). In general, small lowland animals such as rabbits and turtles appear to have been ignored or used only as a secondary food source. Most of the bison bones are highly fractured, suggesting that they were systematically processed for marrow extraction and bone grease manufacture (Brooks and Flynn 1988; Johnson et al. 1977; Runkles 1964; Treece et al. 1993; Word 1991). Scattered postholes, interpreted as the remains of racks and scaffolds for drying meat and dressing hides, have been identified at several Garza complex sites (Boyd et al. 1993; Northern 1979). Tools associated specifically with hide-processing activities—such as small, snub-nosed end scrapers,

FIGURE 8.1. Sherds of striated utility ware pottery (Tierra Blanca Plain) from various protohistoric sites in the Texas Panhandle. Top row shows variety with fingernail punctate decoration.

two- and four-edged bevel knives, serrated metapodial fleshers, and a wide variety of bone awls—occur with increasing frequency on sites dated after AD 1450 throughout the Southern Plains, including those associated with the Tierra Blanca and Garza complexes (Creel 1991; Schultz 1992). At several Garza Complex sites, unifacially retouched scrapers outnumber every other formal tool category (Boyd et al. 1993). In contrast, the typical farm implements associated with Plains Village communities, such as bison scapula hoes and tibia digging sticks, are conspicuously absent, as are clearly associated macrobotanical remains of corn or other cultigens (cf. Spielmann 1982:295–297). Ground-stone implements, most likely used for plant processing, have been recovered from a few sites. Clear evidence for permanent house structures is lacking for both complexes, although possible tipi rings and associated features have been identified at the Tierra Blanca type-site (Spielmann 1982) and at the Longhorn site associated with the Garza complex (Boyd et al. 1993).

Of Pots and Women

Evidence of trade between Tierra Blanca and Garza complex peoples and Pueblo farmers from the Rio Grande region of New Mexico includes the widespread distribution of small amounts of southwestern obsidian, turquoise jewelry, and Pacific shell ornaments at sites throughout the southern High Plains. In addition, sherds of both decorated and undecorated Pueblo-style pottery have been recovered from sites associated with each of these complexes (Habicht Mauche 1988; Habicht-Mauche 1991). The remains of Rio Grande–style glaze-painted ollas dominate the decorated ceramic assemblages from these sites. Visual and petrographic examination of samples of glaze-painted sherds from Tierra Blanca and Garza complex sites indicates that all of these vessels were imported directly from the Rio Grande Valley (Leonard 2006). Production sources in the Galisteo Basin, Pecos, and the Salinas District seem to predominate, which is not surprising since these areas are the ones most often described in early historical documents as engaging in trade with bison-hunting Plains nomads. However, a high degree of homogeneity characterizes the sources of glaze-painted pottery from any given site, suggesting that particular groups of Plains nomads may have maintained long-standing and exclusive trade partnerships with particular individuals or families within specific Rio Grande pueblos. Leonard (2006) argues that the social relationships sustained by these trade partnerships may have been at least as important, if not more important, than the actual material goods that flowed through this system.

Even more intriguing are the ubiquitous remains of small, squat Pueblo-style cooking jars with faintly striated exteriors and darkly smudged interiors on protohistoric sites throughout the southern High Plains (Figure 8.1). Sometime around the beginning of the sixteenth century, smooth-surfaced utility ware pottery began to replace indented corrugated and smeared indented corrugated types throughout much of the upper and middle Rio Grande Valley. The exteriors of these vessels are frequently covered with diagnostic scratches or "striations" produced by a soft finishing tool (e.g., a corn cob or fingers) as it was dragged across the surface of the damp vessel. Interiors are often smudged black and have a smooth, burnished, almost glossy finish. Subtle changes in vessel form also occurred at this time, with jars generally becoming squatter and more globular. Smooth, inflected contours tended to replace composite forms that had a sharp break, or corner point, between the rim and the shoulder (Figure 8.2).

These trends have been most clearly documented in utility ware assemblages from north-central New Mexico. The most detailed published analysis of this ceramic type is Kidder and Shepard's (1936:316–317) description of the striated utility pottery from Pecos Pueblo, which was found associated stratigraphically with late glaze-painted pottery dating to the sixteenth and seventeenth centuries. Striated utility pottery has also been recovered from contexts dating from the late fifteenth through seventeenth centuries at sites near Albuquerque (Lambert 1954; Tichy 1939), in the Galisteo Basin (Reed 1954; Habicht-Mauche 1988), and at Kuapa in the Santa Domingo Basin west of the Rio Grande. The type name Rio Grande Striated has been adopted to encompass all of the protohistoric striated utility ware pottery from this core area of north-central New Mexico (Baugh and Eddy 1987).

The remains of pottery that is stylistically and technically similar to Rio Grande Striated has also been found on protohistoric sites located throughout the southern High Plains of Texas and extending into the mixed grass prairies of western Oklahoma (Figure 8.3). The type

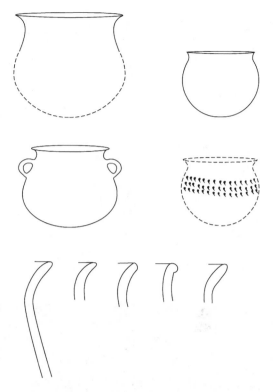

FIGURE 8.2. Tierra Blanca Plain vessel forms and rim profiles.

name Tierra Blanca Plain has been used to identify Pueblo-style faint striated utility ware pottery found on the Southern Plains (Baugh and Eddy 1987; Habicht-Mauche 1988, 1991). The core area for the distribution of Tierra Blanca Plain is the northern Llano Estacado, where it occurs regularly on sites attributed to the Tierra Blanca complex. On Tierra Blanca complex sites, Pueblo-style striated utility pottery is either the only ceramic type recovered or is found in association with imported Rio Grande glaze-painted pottery. The distribution of Tierra Blanca Plain may extend northward as far as the Oklahoma Panhandle, where a single, whole striated utility ware vessel has been reported (Dale 1972).

Pottery found on a number of Garza complex sites from the south Texas Plains include a mix of Plains-style types, such as Edwards Plain and Little Deer Plain, which are distinguished technologically by distinct marks of the paddle and anvil thinning technique, and Pueblo-style striated utility wares, which were made using the southwestern technique of coiling and scraping.

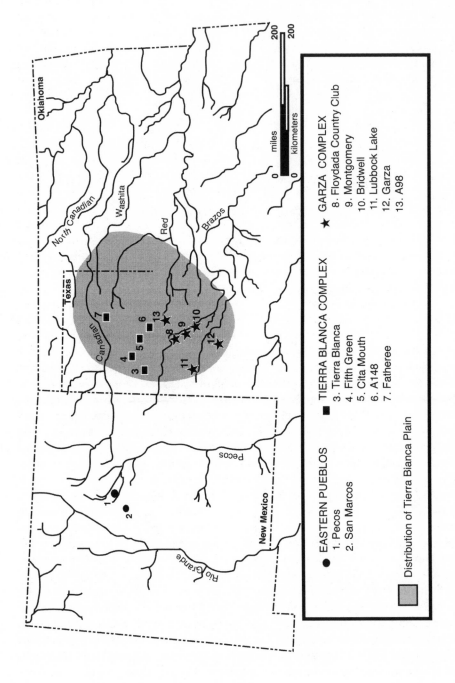

FIGURE 8.3. Map of the distribution of Tierra Blanca Plain pottery in relationship to the Garza and Tierra Blanca complex sites discussed in text.

At some of the larger residential base camps in the canyons along the eastern edge of the Llano Estacado, these plain wares have been found in association with imported decorated pottery from the Southwest. Rio Grande glaze wares account for between 14 to 50 percent of the pottery recovered from sites in Blanco Canyon, along the eastern edge of the Llano Estacado (Baugh 1984). Most of the Rio Grande glaze wares from Garza complex sites are stylistically associated with the late glaze period (Glazes E and F), which dates to between AD 1500± and 1700, and, as noted above, they were manufactured at a variety of Rio Grande frontier pueblos.

I have conducted detailed attribute analyses and petrographic studies on samples of Tierra Blanca Plain pottery from three Tierra Blanca complex sites and three Garza complex sites (Habicht-Mauche 1988, 1991). The Tierra Blanca complex sites—Cita Mouth (A288), Fifth Green (A1363), and Tierra Blanca (A264)—are all located in the northern Llano Estacado, on or near small tributary streams of the Prairie Dog Town Fork of the Red River. The Garza complex sites—Montgomery (41FL17), Bridwell (41CB27), and Floydada Country Club (41FL1)—are all located in the bottomlands of Blanco Canyon, along a 20 to 30-mile stretch of the White River, a tributary of the Brazos, in southern Floydada and northern Crosby counties. Blanco Canyon cuts into the eastern edge of the caprock escarpment of the lower Llano Estacado. The striated utility ware pottery from these southern High Plains sites was compared with similar collections of Rio Grande Striated pottery from Pecos and San Marcos pueblos in New Mexico (Habicht-Mauche 1988, 1991).

The attribute analyses revealed that striated utility ware vessels from both the Southwest and Southern Plains had been made using similar forming and finishing techniques. These small, squat, wide-mouthed globular jars, with gently everted rims, were made by building up the sides of the vessel using thin coils, which were then annealed and thinned using a hard, sharp-edged tool, such as a gourd rind. Exterior surfaces were smoothed using a soft, pliable tool while the clay was still wet, giving the surface a slightly gritty texture marked by fine overall striations. Interior surfaces were burnished with a hard tool, such as

a pebble, that obliterated most signs of thinning and gave the surface a smooth, compact texture. After firing, the interiors of most pots appear to have been rubbed with some sort of plant fiber in order to seal the pores of the vessels and make them watertight. This practice gave the interiors of these pots a distinctly black and somewhat glossy appearance. Exteriors were coated with greasy black soot, indicating that these vessels were used predominately for cooking over open fires.

The most significant differences between the southwestern and Southern Plains examples of faint striated utility pottery were the average size and size range of vessels. The Southern Plains examples were generally smaller and showed less variation in size compared to the sample from the Rio Grande Pueblos. Conspicuously absent were the larger pots that were probably used in the Rio Grande Pueblos for public feasting activities (Potter 2000; Spielmann 1998). In contrast, the smaller striated utility ware jars from the Southern Plains were probably used exclusively for household cooking activities. Handles are significantly more common on the Southern Plains examples than on those from the Rio Grande Pueblos. Nomadic Plains groups may have preferred vessels with handles because they facilitated transport by allowing vessels to be tied to packs. These differences may reflect minor adaptations made by Pueblo-trained potters to meet the local needs and particular cultural "tastes" (see Stahl 2002) of Plains consumers while at the same time essentially reproducing their own embodied technological traditions.

In general, the striated utility wares from the Southern Plains also show less standardization in production. This pattern is most clearly exemplified by looking at variability in lip form. A much greater diversity of lip forms characterize the southern High Plains assemblages, and these lip variants tend to concentrate at specific sites, perhaps marking the work of specific potters or potting groups. The southern High Plains samples are also characterized by greater overall variability in surface treatment and paste color compared to the Rio Grande Pueblo collections (Habicht-Mauche 1991). The Southern Plains pattern is more indicative of nonspecialized potters who only produced a few vessels at a time as needed, using a diversity of available materials. In contrast, the Rio Grande samples seem to represent the more standardized output of part-time specialists (Costin 1991).

Despite these differences in the overall variability of the samples, the detailed similarities in technical attributes recorded for the two regional assemblages suggest that the makers of all these cooking pots were part of a shared "community of practice" (Wenger 1998), characterized by a distinct technological style or embodied tradition that required the use of specific tools and mastery of specific motor skills (Lechtman 1977; Lemonier 1986). Such technological traditions tend to be very conservative within nonindustrial potting communities since they are imbedded in formal cognitive systems that are passed from one generation of artisans to the next (Capone 2006; Lave and Wenger 1996). In addition, such techniques—since they require the performance of a step-wise series of embodied practices (a.k.a. "production steps" or *chaîne operatoire*)—would have to have been learned by carefully observing potters at work rather than simply copying existing prototypes (Costin 1991). The latter process would result in recognizable "translation errors" as similar forms and textures were rendered using different tools, manual skills and techniques, and cognitive structural models (Hardin 1984).

Petrographic analysis indicates that most of the Pueblo-style striated utility ware vessels recovered from the Tierra Blanca and Garza complex sites were made on the southern High Plains using a variety of locally available materials (Habicht-Mauche 1988, 1991). Potters from both complexes appear to have favored the loosely consolidated sands and calcareous sandstones of the Ogallala Formation that are locally abundant throughout the Llano Estacado as temper. However, it appears the potters also experimented with a variety of other locally available lithic materials.

In sum, both the attribute analyses and the petrographic studies strongly indicate that Pueblo-style cooking pots were being made locally on the southern High Plains throughout the fifteenth and sixteenth centuries. Traditionally, Native American pottery was made and used predominately by women, particularly in the context of domestic food preparation, storage, and service activities. This was true ethnographically for groups in both the Southwest and Southern Plains. These women potters usually learned to make pottery as young girls by watching and working with other women in their local group: their mothers, sisters, aunts, and neighbors. Therefore, the ubiquitous presence of locally made, Pueblo-style pottery on the southern High Plains provides strong evidence for the presence of nonlocal Pueblo women potters at these sites.

But who were these Pueblo women, and how did they come to be present among the nomadic bison-hunting groups that roamed the protohistoric southern High Plains? What role did these women play within the larger political economy of the Southwest–Southern Plains frontier regional system, and how did their presence transform the structure of gendered social relations? In order to answer these questions, we will first need to explore how local strategies for negotiating economic inequality and social status among both Eastern Pueblo and Southern Plains societies came increasingly to depend on the mobility and exchangeability of women during the protohistoric period. We will then explore the impact that these nonlocal women had—whether as captives, wives, or refugees—on the changing structure of southern High Plains society.

Negotiating Status Through Trade

This increase in contact and interaction, especially between the Eastern Pueblo farming peoples of the Southwest and the nomadic bison hunters of the southern High Plains, appears to have coincided with a period of increasing environmental, demographic, and social stress in both regions. In the Southwest, the late prehistoric, or Pueblo IV, period (AD 1275 to 1400) was marked by a series of demographic upheavals that resulted in the formation of a radically new social landscape. Massive migrations led to the displacement and reorganization of local communities and regional social networks, with some areas becoming completely depopulated while others received substantial influxes of new populations. In areas such as the Rio Grande Valley, where these migrant populations tended to concentrate, people from diverse ethnic, linguistic, and cultural backgrounds were forced to come together and remake their social worlds.

The proliferation and spread of new social and religious institutions and their associated rituals restructured relationships between the individual, society, and the cosmos, leading to major transformations in notions of community, individual, and corporate identity and the nature of leadership and power in Pueblo society (Duff 2002; Habicht-Mauche 1993, 2006).

In the Rio Grande Valley, a new form of community, the nucleated town, began to emerge around the turn of the fourteenth century. These towns consisted of large apartment-style roomblocks arranged around open plazas that were the sites of large public performances and religious rituals. The physical appearance of these communities projects a sense of mundane sameness, of equality, harmony, and corporate integration that masks the frictions and factionalism that are a normal part of day-to-day life in the pueblos (Brandt 1994; Ortiz 1969; McGuire and Saitta 1996). Archaeological data suggest that many of these early nucleated towns were highly unstable and were often partially or wholly abandoned over the course of only two or three generations (Mera 1940). Under these circumstances certain kin groups may have found it advantageous to aggressively assert ritually sanctioned claims to land and leadership positions (Levy 1992). Large nucleated communities grew up around these powerful core kin groups and the corporate agricultural lands they controlled. Other families attached themselves to the most successful and stable of these communities, but their social and economic positions were always more socially marginal and economically precarious.

Jerrold Levy (1992) has argued that this status hierarchy was reinforced by the need to manage scarce and sometimes unpredictable resources. Thus, although cooperation and sharing were highly valued features of Pueblo society, resources could not always be distributed evenly, since in times of extreme scarcity there was often too little to support everyone. As a result, lower-ranking, marginal households would have had to seek more diverse and flexible alternatives for survival. One strategy may have been to periodically increase their emphasis on hunting and gathering activities in order to supplement farming. Another alternative may have been to specialize in certain household crafts, such as pottery making or the weaving of cotton cloth. These craft products could then be exchanged for food among inhabitants of the pueblos to supplement individual household agricultural production.

Marginal families also may have been more aggressive in seeking formal trade alliances with nomadic bison-hunting groups from the Plains. Although dried bison meat may have been a useful supplemental food source, a much more valuable commodity obtained through the Plains trade would have been processed deer and bison hides, which were used extensively by the Pueblos for both clothing and ritual costuming (Spielmann 1989). Hides, like other craft products, could be exchanged with other Pueblo households for surplus agricultural produce, which in turn could be exchanged with bison-hunting groups for more hides.

One way to cement these trade alliances would have been through formal marriage exchanges. Historically, Eastern Pueblo groups tended to marry partners from within their own community or from a closely related village. This marriage pattern was probably strongly preferred by the high-ranking core kin groups in each community, since it would tend to concentrate corporate rights to the best land and most important religious offices in the hands of a few prominent families. However, despite this strong preference for village and ethnic endogamy, marriages to non-Pueblo partners—especially the Jicarilla, Ute, and Navajo—were far from rare ethnographically and seem to have had a long history (Hill 1982; Parson 1964).

During the protohistoric period, similar interethnic marriages may have been the basis for establishing formal trade partnerships such as those described ethnographically between the Tewa Pueblos and the Jicarilla (Ford 1972). These relationships linked families from different ethnic communities over multiple generations. Trade partners and their families were expected to visit each other regularly, especially on the occasion of local feast days and rituals. These visits were accompanied by mutual gift-giving and other forms of both immediate and delayed reciprocity. The patterning of Rio Grande glaze ware distribution on protohistoric southern High Plains sites, which is marked by a homogeneity and exclusivity of sources within each site, suggests that such trade partnerships were well established by the turn of the sixteenth century (Leonard 2006).

At the same time, marriage exchanges may have facilitated the short- or long-term migration of Pueblo households to the Plains, where they could have joined their bison-hunting affinal kin and trade partners. This may have been a reasonable and viable strategy, especially for some low-ranking and economically marginal families, especially during times of extreme stress. During the seventeenth century, Spanish officials in New Mexico reported that groups of Pueblo Indians, usually from one of the eastern frontier communities, such as Pecos, Taos, or Picurís, occasionally abandoned their towns to join Apache groups living on the Plains. Economically marginal families may have suffered the most under the burdens of the Spanish *encomienda* system and would have had the least to lose by abandoning their homes and farmlands. Accounts of the Spanish *reconquesta* of New Mexico in 1696 also give us a glimpse of this strategy at work (Forbes 1994:264–297). Unable to expel the invaders, many of Pueblo inhabitants of the Rio Grande Valley fled their homes, seeking shelter either among the more remote Western Pueblos or with Apaches and other nomadic tribes living in the surrounding mountains and plains. The decision to flee to neighboring groups rather than stay and either fight or appease the Spanish probably split communities along status lines and reflected long-standing differences in the personal interests and alliance-building strategies of low- versus high-ranking households.

Thus, the survival of some domestic groups among the Eastern Pueblos may have come to depend in part on the mobility and exchangeability of their women. Marriage exchanges would have built strong trade partnerships and kinship alliances with specific groups of Plains nomads who could be counted on to provide a reliable supply of dressed hides that could be exchanged for surplus agricultural products. In turn, these connections would have facilitated the acceptance and assimilation of refugee Pueblo families among southern High Plains groups during times of extreme hardship. Contrary to this analysis, Speth (1991) has argued that it is more common cross-culturally for hunter-gatherer women to marry men from the agricultural or pastoralist groups with whom they interact than the reverse, a pattern referred to as "hypergyny." While I do not dispute the empirical accuracy of this observation, I do believe that as a generalization it tends to mask the ways in which differences in rank and social circumstances strongly influence individual marriage choices. Marriage is more than just mate selection; it is a social contract between kin groups and a strategy for negotiating aspects of labor, production, and social reproduction that may be more important than the simple management of biological reproduction. If women tended to "marry up" within the protohistoric Plains-Pueblo regional system, such strategies may well have included the occasional marriage of lower-ranking Pueblo women to higher-ranking Plains men.

The sixteenth and seventeenth centuries were also a time of dramatic demographic, social, and economic change on the southern High Plains. These trends include the complete demise of the mixed farming-hunting-gathering economies that had flourished in the valleys of the Canadian and Red rivers for nearly three hundred years; the rapid spread of more-specialized economies that focused almost exclusively on the intensive hunting of bison and processing of bison products; increasing intergroup competition and violence; and a significant expansion in the intensity and scope of interregional interaction and trade.

Susan Vehik (2002) argues that long-distance trade among the more sedentary late prehistoric Plains Village groups initially developed in response to the prestige good requirements of stratified Mississippian-influenced societies living along the eastern margins of the Southern Plains during the thirteenth century. She contends that these contacts stimulated Plains Village leaders to enhance their own social status through competitive exchanges of exotic materials, especially high-quality lithics. The collapse of stratified societies in the east and the expansion of more-nomadic and highly specialized bison-hunting groups in the west during the late fifteenth century tended to accentuate these trends, particularly as immigrant nomadic groups came into conflict with resident Plains Village groups over access to the bison herds and other critical resources. Political leaders and competitors for leadership on the southern High Plains may have exploited the social disruptions and demographic upheavals of these times to further enhance their own individual wealth, power, and prestige.

Trade, in this context, would have provided ambitious men with the means to accrue the resources and wealth necessary to participate in increasingly competitive status-building activities. Joseph Jablow (1950), in his classic analysis of historic Plains trade relations, defined two different kinds of trade, which he referred to as ceremonial and individual trade. Individual trade was undertaken by both men and women, but was largely the arena of women. This trade focused on the complementary exchange of domestic and subsistence-related goods, such as the exchange of bison meat for corn. Individual exchanges were routine, business-like transactions that took place without much pomp or ceremony (Peters 1995). In contrast, ceremonial trade was primarily the province of men, who surrounded their exchanges of exotic, high-value manufactured goods with elaborate rituals and competitive displays. Fictive adoptions and exogamous marriages, usually negotiated by high-ranking men, also were associated with highly ritualized gift exchanges that established powerful bonds of obligation and alliance between individuals and families across potentially hostile interethnic boundaries. Nonsubsistence items such as personal ornaments and high-quality lithic materials probably played a more important role in such competitive transactions and alliance-building activities because of their potential for being converted into visible symbols of status and for being accumulated as objects of wealth.

Well-made bison robes and tanned hides were also probably important high-status items that circulated regularly through this system. Hides, which are durable, storable, and easily transportable, may have shifted from being relatively mundane items produced primarily for domestic use during late prehistoric times to highly specialized commodities whose conspicuous consumption, distribution, and exchange came to mark individual wealth and status during the protohistoric period. Finely made robes and hides may have come to be valued not only for their functional utility but for what their quantity and quality suggested about the competency and power of both hunter (man-husband) and processor (woman-wife) (e.g., Spector 1993).

The earliest Spanish accounts of various expeditions to the southern High Plains during the mid sixteenth and early seventeenth centuries would seem to support such an interpretation. These accounts record several instances where large quantities of dressed hides were presented as formal, diplomatic gifts to the Spanish by the male leaders of various nomadic bison-hunting groups encountered on the High Plains (Hammond and Rey 1940, 1953, 1966). In one instance an advance group of the Coronado party, upon entering a large settlement of the Teyas located along the eastern edge of the Llano Estacado, were formally presented "with a pile of tanned skins and other things and a tent as big as a house" (Hodge 1907:332). When the general arrived with the rest of his men, chaos broke out as the soldiers began looting the stockpile of hides and other gifts to divide among themselves. This severe breach of Native protocol and the expected ritualized formalities of ceremonial exchange caused understandable confusion and consternation among the Teyas. Some women were reported to have been reduced to tears, while others joined in the looting, attempting to recover what they could of their stolen goods. Other encounters, such as those between Oñate's men and the Vaquero Apaches (Hammond and Rey 1953) went much more smoothly, with gifts being exchanged between leaders on both sides, creating a context for peaceful diplomatic and economic interactions.

The intensification of hide production for exchange would have entailed a major shift in the organization of labor on the southern High Plains, especially along gender lines. During the late prehistoric period, women would have been principally responsible for the gathering of wild plants and gardening. Among Plains Village groups, such as the late prehistoric Antelope Creek phase people of the Canadian River valley, farming was primarily the arena of women, who would have controlled the distribution and use of agricultural products and other domestic items both within their own households and through individual exchange (Peters 1995). With the demise of Plains Village farming economies on the southern High Plains, the focus of women's labor would have shifted from farming to hide production.

With this shift, women may have no longer controlled the products of their own labor to the degree that they had in the past. As Weist (1983) notes, women's status, cross-culturally, is determined less by how hard they work or the specific kind of work that they do than by the degree to which they are able to assert control over the fruits of their efforts. Dressed hides, though largely the product of women's labor, increasingly may have been co-opted by their male partners and family members for use in competitive exchanges and alliance-building activities (Klein 1983). Thus, men's power and status within southern High Plains society was increasingly determined during the protohistoric period by their ability to control women's labor and to appropriate the products of that labor (Collier 1988).

Roberts (1984) has made a similar observation regarding the changing role and status of Maraka women in the West African textile industry at the end of the nineteenth century. West African textiles, like Plains bison hides, were critical to ritualized exchanges that determined social relations and status. As market demand for high-status dyed textiles increased, men began to usurp women's traditional monopoly of indigo production, thus transforming the reciprocal labor and property relationships that previously linked the joint interests of husbands and wives within household economies. As a result of these changes, male household heads emerged as patriarchs, and women became increasingly secluded and less able to control specific aspects of the household economy. These social changes had little to do with technological innovations or even major changes in the structure of women's work, but had more to do with a loss of control by women over specific resources and products of their labor within a shifting regional political economy. Interestingly, the availability of slave labor may have been critical to this transformation in the gendered relations of production in Maraka society.

Similarly on the southern High Plains, the shift from subsistence farming to commodity-based hide production would have put women

and men in a highly interdependent, but potentially antagonistic, relationship to one another. In this context the interests of men, their wives, and their wives' families may not always have coincided. The most closely related descendent groups to the protohistoric occupants of the southern High Plains are probably the Eastern Apache and the Wichita. Historically, both of these groups were organized matrilineally, with economic production and social reproduction centered around a core group of related women (Goodwin 1942; Opler 1936; Schmitt and Schmitt 1953). Marriages were negotiated between kin groups, with husbands generally going to live with and work for their wives' families. Thus, a married man's interest in promoting his own status within such a context would inevitably have been in conflict on some level with his social and economic obligations to his wife and her kin. In addition, he would have had to compete with his wife's male kin, particularly her brothers, for control of the products his wife's and her children's labor for use in competitive status-building activities (Collier 1988). This situation gives women a certain level of social power, giving them the opportunity to play the interests of their husbands and brothers against each other to the best advantage of themselves and their children.

However, within a society where women's labor was increasingly being converted into men's status through the medium of dressed hides, the most successful men were those who could increase the size of their domestic female workforce while minimizing their social and economic obligations to those workers and their kin. Processing hides was labor-intensive work, with each bison robe representing about 70 woman-hours of labor (Moore 1991). This effort potentially conflicted with other economic and domestic tasks performed by Plains women, such as foraging, farming, preparing food, making pottery, and rearing children. These tasks were performed most efficiently when they could be divided among a group of women working together within the same domestic group. Nineteenth-century accounts of the Plains fur and hide trade indicate that a single woman was capable of producing only about a dozen dressed hides per season, significantly fewer than the number of animals a man could kill, even without the aid of horses or guns. However, this ratio could be substantially increased if multiple women worked cooperatively within the same domestic group. Jablow (1950:20) reports that a Blackfoot chief once boasted "that his eight wives could dress a hundred and fifty skins in the year whereas a single wife could only dress ten." Thus by working collaboratively within the same household, these women could nearly double their productive output of dressed skins (Collier 1988).

There were several ways that Plains men could have increased their access to and control over women's labor while at the same time minimizing their social and economic obligations to affinal kin. The two most common strategies used by nomadic Plains men during the nineteenth century were the practice of sororal polygyny and the incorporation of captive women into domestic groups as "slaves" or lower-ranking "chore wives" (Weist 1980, 1983). However, other practices that also may have emerged include the negotiation of interethnic marriage alliances or adoptions, and the patronage or exploitation of refugee groups.

Sororal polygyny, the practice of one man marrying multiple sisters and/or close matrilineal cousins, had obvious advantages for both husbands and wives. For men, these larger households represented more wives and daughters to produce goods, such as tanned hides, that were needed to participate in status- and alliance-building activities. Wives benefited from this situation by having a group of women to share chores with, and the power of women in these situations may also have been enhanced because sisters or cousins could present a more united front to their husbands. The practice of sororal polygyny is reported to have increased significantly among nomadic Plains groups during the late nineteenth century in response to the market demands of the Euroamerican hide trade (Weist 1983). Moore's (1991) analysis of the 1880 U.S. census of the Cheyenne suggests that approximately 20 to 25 percent of the households recorded were polygynous. Although we lack clear archaeological or ethnohistoric evidence for the practice of sororal polygyny on the southern High Plains during the sixteenth and seventeenth centuries, it would have been a culturally acceptable strat-

egy that could have been used by ambitious men to increase their status.

Women and children captured in hostile raids on the Rio Grande Pueblos and other agricultural groups living along the margins of the southern High Plains would have provided an additional source of labor for ambitiously expanding Plains domestic units. Cameron (this volume) notes that there appears "to be two entwined avenues for the creation of power that are key to creating contexts in which captive-taking is practiced." The first is where power is directly related to the number of followers a leader can recruit, and the second is where captive-taking satisfies a need for labor, increasing the production of surplus goods that bring wealth, status, and power to the captors. These strategies are not necessarily exclusive, and in the context of the Pueblo-Plains regional system both impulses may have led to increased competition, violence, and raiding along the Southwest–Southern Plains frontier.

An increase in raiding and captive-taking around the turn of the sixteenth century may be one explanation for the sudden and widespread presence of locally made Pueblo-style cooking pots on protohistoric sites attributed to nomadic bison-hunting groups on the southern High Plains. As noted above, the chroniclers of the Coronado expedition in the mid sixteenth century reported that raiding by the seminomadic Teyas had been responsible for the destruction and abandonment of several large towns in the Galisteo Basin. Interestingly, Garza complex sites, which are arguably associated with Coronado's Teyas, have a more diverse mix of locally and nonlocally made Pueblo-style striated utility pottery than Tierra Blanca complex sites. Almost all of the striated utility pottery identified as being made in the Rio Grande Valley appears to have come from pueblos in the Galisteo Basin, including some towns known to have been abandoned in the 1520s (Habicht-Mauche 1988). It is intriguing to imagine captive Pueblo women and refugees bringing these humble possessions with them to the Plains and later teaching their daughters and nieces to make and use similar pots in their new homes.

Because these captives were forcibly alienated from their local kin groups, they brought to their captors fewer of the economic and social burdens of traditional marriage or adoption. Nevertheless, the social position of these captives within Plains society appears to have been somewhat ambiguous and mutable. Therefore, it is unclear whether it is appropriate to refer to captives in this protohistoric context as "slaves." Brooks (2002:32) follows Meillassoux (1991:343) in defining slavery as "a social system based on the exploitation of a class of producers or persons performing services, renewed mainly through acquisition." Patterson (1982:5), on the other hand, defines a slave, however recruited, "as a socially dead person" alienated from all rights or claims of birth and ceasing to belong to any legitimate social order. Although these captive women on the Plains clearly were an exploited class of producers, it is not at all clear that they were always "non-persons" with no claims on the local social order.

Woolf (1997) has speculated that in many non-state societies, captives or slaves may have been somewhat analogous to children. Like infants, captives or slaves entered the community without an established social identity, as "non-persons." But those who survived and persevered would gradually build up a set of social relations with the members of their household and wider community that were based on shared interest and experience. Thus the ambiguity that surrounds interpretations of captive status in non-state societies may be partly the result of our historical and ethnographic view of specific captive cases at diverse points in the life history of their captivity and social integration.

The most detailed first-hand accounts of the captive experience come from the narratives of Euroamerican women captured and held by nomadic Plains groups during the nineteenth century (Kestler 1990). Of course, these women's understanding and perception of their experiences as captives would have been profoundly different from that of Native women, but their stories do provide us with some insight into how captives were treated and how they were integrated into their host groups. In virtually all of these narratives, the women report that immediately after capture they were treated particularly brutally and were subjected to extreme physical hardship and deprivation. This treatment might be interpreted as a strategy to reinforce the cap-

tives' sense of isolation and dependency and to break down their existing social identity. Captives also appear to have been traded from group to group as chattel, with a negotiable value. However, once captives were settled within a particular community, their experiences could be quite diverse depending on their personal qualities and the nature of the domestic context in which they found themselves. In some cases, captives do appear to have been treated as expendable "non-persons" who were physically deprived and abused, and more or less worked to death. In other cases, however, captives appear to have been integrated more fully into the economic and social life of the domestic unit and community.

For example, Sarah Ann Horn, who spent about a year and half in 1836–1837 as a captive among the Comanches, reported that:

> There were three branches of the family in which I lived, residing in separate tents. One branch consisted of an old widow woman and her two daughters, one of whom was also a widow. The next was the son of the old woman, who claimed me as his property, and the third was a son-in-law of the old woman. In the family to which I belonged there were five sons, no daughters. It was my task to dress the buffalo skins, to make them up into garments and moccasins, to cut up and dry the buffalo meat, and then pound it for use, and to do all the cooking for the family. (Kestler 1990:257)

Interestingly, Sarah Horn makes no mention of a wife in the tent of her captor, and the tasks she performed for this household were the normal ones expected of any wife. With five sons and no daughters, this household was clearly in need of a female caretaker. Sarah reports being well treated by her captor's mother, although less so by his sisters. The overall impression is that she was being treated as a full member of this extended domestic unit, most likely as the son's wife, with all the rights, responsibilities, and petty family jealousies attendant to that position in that particular society.

More often captive women would have been brought into households as secondary or lower-ranking "chore wives" whose treatment would have been dependent on how well they were able to get along with the other females in the domestic group. Wives may have encouraged their husbands to take in captive women to share the workload of the household without lessening the social status of the noncaptive wife or reducing her husbands' obligations to her kin. Husbands would have been able to increase the size and productive capacity of their households without adding to their load of local social and economic obligations.

Along with looking to the Rio Grande Pueblos as a potential source of captives, some Southern Plains men during the protohistoric period may have chosen to solidify their trade partnerships with particular families in the pueblos by negotiating formal marriage alliances or adoptions. Such alliances would have ensured that they and their dependents would have regular access to the agricultural produce critical to their survival, as well as to exotic resources such as obsidian, turquoise, and Pacific shells that may have been increasingly valued as diplomatic gifts and status objects. Such practices are well attested to in the historic record of the fur and hide trade in North America, going back to the earliest recorded contact between Native Americans and European traders. For generations, "potentially hostile native groups had secured channels of trade through marriages and adoptions. Even during war peaceful exchange was carried on by individuals who crossed between enemies over bridges of kinship" (West 1998:81). There is some archaeological evidence to suggest that such practices on the Plains may extend back into the late prehistoric period (Hanna 1984). And this practice may be another plausible explanation for the Pueblo-style cooking pots found on the protohistoric southern High Plains.

As noted above, over time the status of captives may have transformed into that of adopted children or wives who, in turn, may have been able to reassert their kinship ties to their home community and act as valuable transcultural interlocutors. So the distinction between marriage and captive-taking in terms of the social statuses or roles of those involved may have been somewhat fuzzy in the context of day-to-day practice and may be difficult to distinguish in the archaeological record.

For Pueblo women who went to live on the Plains, whether through arranged marriages or capture, life would have been potentially difficult and dangerous. Isolated on a daily basis from the support of their kin, these women would have been extremely vulnerable to potential abuse or abandonment, especially as captives or lower-ranking wives in polygynous households. To a large extent their fate probably depended on their abilities to get along with the other women in the families to which they found themselves attached, and their skills in demonstrating their social and economic worth to the men who controlled and benefited from their labor.

A final strategy that may have been used by men on the protohistoric southern High Plains to increase the size and productive capacity of the residential groups under their control may have been to take in refugee families that may have abandoned the Rio Grande Pueblos during times of extreme economic stress. Collier (1988: 74) argued that among the Cheyenne and other historic High Plains groups, high-ranking men often took in widows, orphans, and other "strays" whose products they could appropriate to give away as part of status-building exchanges. These social "strays" would have been completely dependent on their patrons, having few other social attachments within the residential group, and as such they could have been subjected to exploitation that bordered on slave labor. Pueblo refugees who came to live on the Plains most likely were from low-ranking, marginal kin groups who had little in the way of social capital to draw on in their own communities. Under these circumstances, seeking the support and patronage of higher-ranking Plains men may have seemed a reasonable alternative during particularly hard times. However, this practice was probably predicated on the previously discussed practices of captive-taking and negotiated intergroup marriage and adoptions, since Pueblo refugees would most likely have attached themselves only to extended domestic units to which they already had an existing kin-based relationship.

The success of this strategy from the refugees' perspective may have varied considerably with specific circumstances, since patronage and support, as noted above, could easily degenerate into exploitation and abuse. During the Pueblo Revolt and subsequent Reconquest period at the end of the seventeenth century, several hundred refugees from Taos and Picurís were said to have fled New Mexico to live among the Apaches north of the Arkansas River in an area the Spanish referred to as El Cuartelejo. Over the succeeding decades, as the political situation in Spanish-controlled New Mexico stabilized, many of these refugees returned to their homes in the Taos Valley, but in 1706 a number of Picurís natives complained to New Mexico governor Cuervo y Valdez that others remained involuntarily among the Apaches. According to the governor, they asked the Spanish to send a military expedition to free their relatives and bring them back to New Mexico. Cuervo y Valdez reported to the Spanish Crown that these renegade Picurís Indians "had sought refuge" among the Apaches, but "many of them being able-bodied men, they were made captives and held as slaves and obliged to do all kinds of work" (Hackett 1937:383). The governor did send a military party to El Cuartelejo, and the expedition was successful in negotiating the release of seventy-four Picurís natives. However, others may have chosen to remain among the Apaches voluntarily, for as Brooks (2002:58) notes, the Cuartelejo Apaches continued to claim kinship with the Picurís in later times.

Shifting Status of Local and Nonlocal Women on the Protohistoric Southern High Plains

It is possible that Pueblo women came to be present on the protohistoric southern High Plains as the result of social and economic strategies that linked the peoples of the Southwest–Southern Plains frontier during the sixteenth and seventeenth centuries. These strategies included captive-taking, the negotiation of interethnic marriage alliances and adoptions, and the flight of Pueblo refugees to the Plains during times of extreme hardship. These women brought with them their own family and cultural traditions about how to make pottery and the proper way to cook food. They taught these new technologies and foodways to their daughters, their nieces, and their adopted in-laws. In so doing, they left telltale, enduring traces of their presence and influence in the remains of their simple little cooking pots, found across the length and breadth of the protohistoric southern High Plains.

By integrating these women and their children into the domestic units under their control, ambitious Plains men were able to increase their access to women's labor and appropriate the products of that labor for their own status-building activities. In some instances, local women may have been able to use these practices to their advantage to enhance their own status by turning over the more mundane household tasks and daily drudgery to younger and lower-ranking women in the household. This would have freed elder women and senior wives to focus on the more detailed sewing and elaborate decorating of skins and clothing that added to their quality and value as exchange goods (Moore 1974). A woman's skill and artistry in this arena commanded respect and added to her prestige (Collier 1988; Kehoe 1983).

In the long run, however, the presence of these nonlocal women would have disrupted local women's traditional social networks and had a significant impact on the role and status of women in protohistoric southern High Plains society. With the demise of farming economies on the High Plains, women no longer were the primary producers of subsistence goods. Instead they were workers who transformed the products of the hunt, obtained by men, into food (bison meat) and durable wealth (hides). Women may have continued to control the distribution of meat and other food within their own households through individual exchange, but they probably had less control over the distribution of hides, which by the sixteenth century appear to have become central to the ritualized gift exchanges that defined men's status. Traditionally, men in these matrilineal societies would have sought to marry women from the most prosperous and high-ranking kin groups. A man's success and status were tied to that of his in-laws, to whom he owed his labor and support. However, the intensification of hide production for exchange, both to acquire food and to negotiate status, changed to some degree the social calculus that defined the relative status of husbands and wives. As men developed strategies for competitively recruiting women's labor from outside the residential group, the role and status of women as the core of social relations within the residential group diminished.

Some archaeological evidence suggests that the status of women on the southern High Plains may have been declining during the sixteenth and seventeenth centuries. In comparison to their late prehistoric Plains Village counterparts, protohistoric Garza complex women appear to have had less access to exotic, high-status exchange goods, especially high-quality lithic material and personal ornaments such as turquoise jewelry and Pacific shell beads (Habicht-Mauche 2005).

In making this argument for the shifting status of women in the context of the development of the Southwest–Southern Plains frontier economy, I do not mean to reinvent the nineteenth-century Euroamerican stereotype of Plains women as "chattel, enslaved as beasts of burden and beaten into submission by overbearing male masters" (Albers 1983:3). Women certainly would have benefited from the labor they provided in support of the ambitious status-building activities of their menfolk, and in so doing would have gained a level of social power and prestige in their own right. Protohistoric nomadic groups on the southern High Plains probably retained significant vestiges of their matrilineal pasts, which would have continued to allow women to negotiate their interests and those of their children against those of their brothers and husbands. The experience of any particular woman probably varied according to her social connections, age, status, and personal history within the local group. Certainly the experience of local women would have been different from those of nonlocal women, and those of senior wives would have been different from those of junior wives or captives. Anecdotal historical evidence suggests that, on occasion, even captive women were able to capitalize on their unique positions as cultural intermediaries to negotiate positions of relative security for themselves and their offspring (Brooks 1996, 2002).

Nevertheless, the arenas where social power and status could be negotiated on the southern High Plains were shifting in favor of men. Women were becoming valued less for the social connections they engendered and more as exchangeable units of labor and production. From this perspective, the fewer social ties and obligations they brought with them, the better. The gradual emergence of this view of at least some women—particularly nonlocal, captive women—as mobile and exchangeable units of labor is what fueled the development of the Southwest Borderlands slave system in the seventeenth and eighteenth centuries. Remains of those unassuming little Pueblo cooking pots on the protohistoric southern High Plains suggest that elements of that system were already in place by the turn of the sixteenth century.

References Cited

Albers, Patricia
1983   Introduction: New Perspectives on Plains Indian Women. In *The Hidden Half: Studies of Plains Indian Women*, edited by P. Albers and B. Medicine, pp. 1–28. University Press of America, Washington, D.C.

Anderson, Gary Clayton
1999   *The Indian Southwest, 1580–1830: Ethnogenesis and Reinvention.* University of Oklahoma Press, Norman.

Baerreis, David A., and Reid A. Bryson
1966   Dating the Panhandle Aspect Cultures. *Bulletin of the Oklahoma Anthropological Society* 14:105–116.

Baugh, Timothy G.
1982   *Edwards I (34BK2): Southern Plains Adaptations in the Protohistoric Period.* Studies in Oklahoma's Past no. 8. Oklahoma Archaeological Survey, Norman.

1984   Southern Plains Societies and Eastern Frontier Pueblo Exchange During the Protohistoric Period. In *Collected Papers in Honor of Harry L. Haddock*, edited by N. L. Fox, pp. 157–167. Papers of the Archaeological Society of New Mexico no. 9.

1986   Culture History and Protohistoric Societies in the Southern Plains. In *Current Trends in Southern Plains Archaeology*, edited by T. G. Baugh, pp. 167–187. Memoir 21. *Plains Anthropologist* 31(114), part 2.

1994   Holocene Adaptations in the Southern High Plains. In *Plains Indians, AD 500–1500*, edited by K. H. Schlesier, pp. 264–289. University of Oklahoma Press, Norman.

Baugh, Timothy G., and Frank W. Eddy
1987   Rethinking Apachean Ceramics: The 1985 Southern Athapaskan Ceramics Conference. *American Antiquity* 52(4):793–798.

Blakeslee, D. J., D. K. Boyd, R. Flint, J. A. Habicht-Mauche, N. P. Hickerson, J. T. Hughes, and C. L. Riley

2002   Bison Hunters of the Llano in 1541: A Panel Discussion. In *The Coronado Expedition from the Distance of 460 Years*, edited by R. Flint and S. C. Flint, pp. 164–186. University of New Mexico Press, Albuquerque.

Booker, R., and J. Campbell

1978   An Excavation Report on Site 41LU6: Slaton Dump Site. *Bulletin of the Southern Plains Archeological Society* 4:19–37.

Boyd, D. K., J. Peck, S. A. Tomka, and K. W. Kibler

1993   *Data Recovery at Justiceburg Reservoir (Lake Alan Henry), Garza and Kent Counties, Texas: Phase III, Season 2.* Reports of Investigations 88. Prewitt and Associates, Inc., Austin, TX.

Brandt, Elizabeth

1994   Egalitarianism, Hierarchy, and Centralization in the Pueblos. In *The Ancient Southwestern Community*, edited by W. Wills and R. Leonard, pp. 9–23. University of New Mexico Press, Albuquerque.

Brooks, James F.

1996   "This Evil Extends Especially…to the Feminine Sex": Negotiating Captivity in the New Mexico Borderlands. *Feminist Studies* 22(2): 279–309.

2002   *Captives and Cousins: Slavery, Kinship, and Community in the Southwest Borderlands.* University of North Carolina Press, Chapel Hill.

Brooks, Robert L., and Peggy Flynn

1988   34TX-71: A Late Prehistoric Bison Processing Station in the Oklahoma Panhandle. *Plains Anthropologist* 33(122):467–487.

Capone, Patricia

2006   Rio Grande Glaze Ware Technology and Production: Historic Expediency. In *The Social Life of Pots: Glaze Wares and Cultural Transformation in the American Southwest, AD 1250–1680*, edited by J. A. Habicht-Mauche, S. L. Eckert, and D. L. Huntley, pp. 216–231. University of Arizona Press, Tucson.

Collier, Jane Fishburne

1988   *Marriage and Inequality in Classless Societies.* Stanford University Press, Stanford, CA.

Costin, Catherine L.

1991   Craft Specialization: Issues in Defining, Documenting, and Explaining the Organization of Production. In *Archaeological Method and Theory*, vol. 3, edited by M. B. Schiffer, pp. 1–56. University of Arizona Press, Tucson.

Creel, Darrell

1991   Bison Hides in Late Prehistoric Exchange in the Southern Plains. *American Antiquity* 56: 40–49.

Dale, Vincent

1972   A Unique Vessel from the Oklahoma Panhandle. *Bulletin of the Oklahoma Anthropological Society* 21:187–189.

Duff, Andrew I.

2002   *Western Pueblo Identities: Regional Interaction, Migration, and Transformation.* University of Arizona Press, Tucson.

Forbes, Jack D.

1994   *Apache, Navaho, and Spaniard.* 2nd ed. University of Oklahoma Press, Norman.

Ford, Richard I.

1972   Barter, Gift, or Violence: An Analysis of Tewa Intertribal Exchange. In *Social Exchange and Interaction*, edited by E. N. Wilmsen, pp. 21–45. Anthropological Papers no. 46. Museum of Anthropology, University of Michigan, Ann Arbor.

Gallegos, Lumero Hernan

1927   *The Gallegos Relation of the Rodriquez Expedition to New Mexico.* Translated and edited by G. P. Hammond and A. Rey. El Palacio Press, Santa Fe, NM.

Goodwin, Grenville

1942   *The Social Organization of the Western Apache.* University of Chicago Press, Chicago.

Gunnerson, Dolores A.

1956   The Southern Athabascans: Their Arrival in the Southwest. *El Palacio* 63:346–365.

Habicht Mauche, Judith A.

1988   An Analysis of Southwestern-Style Utility Ware Ceramics from the Southern Plains in the Context of Protohistoric Plains-Pueblo Interaction. Ph.D. dissertation, Harvard University, Cambridge, MA.

Habicht-Mauche, Judith A.

1991   Evidence for the Manufacture of Southwestern-Style Culinary Ceramics on the Southern Plains. In *Farmers, Hunters, and Colonists: Interaction Between the Southwest and the Southern Plains*, edited by K. A. Spielmann, pp. 51–70. University of Arizona Press, Tucson.

1992   Coronado's Querechos and Teyas in the Archaeological Record of the Texas Panhandle. *Plains Anthropologist* 37(140):247–259.

1993   *The Pottery from Arroyo Hondo Pueblo, New Mexico: Tribalization and Trade in the Northern Rio Grande.* Arroyo Hondo Archaeological Series vol. 8. School of American Research, Santa Fe, NM.

2005   The Shifting Role of Women and Women's

Labor on the Protohistoric Southern High Plains. In *Gender and Hide Production*, edited by L. Frink and K. Weedman, pp. 37–55. Altamira Press, Walnut Creek, CA.

2006 The Social History of Southwestern Glaze Wares. In *The Social Life of Pots: Glaze Wares and Cultural Transformation in the American Southwest, AD 1250–1680*, edited by J. A. Habicht-Mauche, S. L. Eckert, and D. L. Huntley, pp. 3–16. University of Arizona Press, Tucson.

Hackett, Charles Wilson (editor)

1937 *Historical Documents Relating to New Mexico, Nueva Vizcaya and Approaches Thereto, to 1773*, vol. 3. Publication no. 330. Carnegie Institution of Washington, Washington, D.C.

Hammond, George P., and Agapito Rey (editors and translators)

1940 *Narratives of the Coronado Expedition, 1540–1542*. Coronado Historical Series vol. 2. University of New Mexico Press, Albuquerque.

1953 *Don Juan de Oñate: Colonizer of New Mexico, 1595–1628*. University of New Mexico Press, Albuquerque.

1966 *The Rediscovery of New Mexico, 1580–1594*. Coronado Historical Series, vol. 3. University of New Mexico Press, Albuquerque.

Hanna, Margaret G.

1984 Do You Take This Woman? Economics and Marriage in a Late Prehistoric Band. *Plains Anthropologist* 29(104):115–129.

Hardin, Margaret A.

1984 Models of Decoration. In *The Many Dimensions of Pottery: Ceramics in Archaeology and Anthropology*, edited by S. E. van der Leeuw and A. C. Pritchard, pp. 573–601. Albert Egges Van Giffen Instituut voor Prae-en Protohistorie, Cingvla VII, Universiteit van Amsterdam, Amsterdam.

Hickerson, Nancy P.

1990 Jumano: The Missing Link in South Plains Prehistory. *Journal of the West* 29(4):5–12.

Hill, W. W.

1982 *An Ethnography of Santa Clara Pueblo, New Mexico*. University of New Mexico Press, Albuquerque.

Hodge, Fredrick W. (translator)

1907 The Narrative of the Expedition of Coronado by Pedro de Castañeda. In *Spanish Explorers in the Southern United States, 1528–1543*, edited by F. W. Hodge, pp. 281–387. Charles Scribner's Sons, New York.

Hofman, Jack L.

1984 The Western Protohistoric: A Summary of the Edwards and Wheeler Complexes. In *Prehistory of Oklahoma*, edited by R. E. Bell, pp. 347–362. Academic Press, Orlando, FL.

Holden, W. C.

1938 Blue Mountain Rock Shelter. *Bulletin of the Texas Archeological and Paleontological Society* 10:208–221.

Hughes, Jack T.

1978 Archeology of Palo Duro Canyon. *Panhandle-Plains Historical Review* 51:35–58.

1989 Prehistoric Cultural Developments on the Texas High Plains. *Bulletin of the Texas Archaeological Society* 60:1–55.

Jablow, Joseph

1950 *The Cheyenne in Plains Indian Trade Relations, 1795–1840*. Monographs of the American Ethnological Society 19. J. J. Augustin, New York.

Johnson, Eileen

1987 *Lubbock Lake: Late Quarternary Studies on the Southern High Plains*. Texas A&M University Press, College Station.

Johnson, Eileen, Vance T. Holliday, Michael J. Kaczor, and Robert Stuckenrath

1977 The Garza Occupation at the Lubbock Lake Site. *Bulletin of the Texas Archaeological Society* 48:83–109.

Katz, Paul R., and Susana R. Katz

1976 *Archeological Investigations in Lower Tule Canyon, Briscoe County, Texas*. Archeological Survey Report no. 16. Texas Historical Foundation, Texas Tech University, Texas Historical Commission, Office of the State Archeologist.

Kehoe, Alice

1983 The Shackles of Tradition. In *The Hidden Half: Studies of Plains Indian Women*, edited by P. Albers and B. Medicine, pp. 53–76. University Press of America, Washington, D.C.

Kestler, Frances R.

1990 *The Indian Captivity Narrative: A Woman's View*. Garland Publishing, New York.

Kidder, Alfred V.

1932 *The Artifacts of Pecos*. Papers of the South West Expedition no. 6. R. S. Peabody Foundation for Archaeology. Phillips Academy, Andover. Yale University Press, New Haven.

1958 *Pecos, New Mexico: Archaeological Notes*. Papers of the Robert S. Peabody Foundation for Archaeology vol. 5. Phillips Academy, Andover.

Kidder, Alfred V., and Anna O. Shepard

1936 *The Pottery of Pecos*, vol. 2. Papers of the South West Expedition no. 7. Phillips Academy, Andover. Yale University Press, New Haven.

Klein, Alan

1983   The Political Economics of Gender: A Nineteenth Century Plains Indian Case Study. In *The Hidden Half: Studies of Plains Indian Women*, edited by P. Albers and B. Medicine, pp. 143–174. University Press of America, Washington, D.C.

Krieger, Alex D.

1946   *Culture Complexes and Chronology in Northern Texas, with Extension of Puebloan Datings to the Mississippi Valley*. Publication no. 4640. University of Texas, Austin.

1947   The Eastward Extension of Puebloan Datings Toward Cultures of the Mississippi Valley. *American Antiquity* 12:141–148.

Lambert, Marjorie F.

1954   *Paa-ko, Archaeological Chronicle of an Indian Village in North Central New Mexico*. Monograph no. 19, parts 1–5. Archaeological Institute of America. School of American Research, Santa Fe, NM.

Lave, J. and E. Wenger

1996   Practice, Person, Social World. In *An Introduction to Vygotsky*, edited by H. Daniels, pp. 143–150. Routledge, London.

Lechtman, Heather

1977   Style in Technology—Some Early Thoughts. In *Material Culture: Styles, Organization, and Dynamics of Technology*, edited by H. Lechtman and R. S. Merrill, pp. 3–20. West, St. Paul, MN.

Lemonnier, P.

1986   The Study of Material Culture Today: Towards an Anthropology of Technical Systems. *Journal of Anthropological Archaeology* 5:147–186.

Leonard, Kathryn

2006   Directionality and Exclusivity of Plains-Pueblo Exchange During the Protohistoric Period (AD 1450–1700). In *The Social Life of Pots: Glaze Wares and Cultural Transformation in the American Southwest, AD 1250–1680*, edited by J. A. Habicht-Mauche, S. L. Eckert, and D. L. Huntley, pp. 232–252. University of Arizona Press, Tucson.

Levy, Jerrold

1992   *Orayvi Revisited: Social Stratification in an "Egalitarian" Society*. School of American Research Press, Santa Fe.

Lintz, Christopher

1984   The Plains Villagers: Antelope Creek. In *Prehistory of Oklahoma*, edited by Robert E. Bell, pp. 325–346. Academic Press, Orlando, FL.

1991   Texas Panhandle-Plains Interactions from the Thirteenth through the Sixteenth Century.

In *Farmers, Hunters, and Colonists: Interaction Between the Southwest and the Southern Plains*, edited by K. A. Spielmann, pp. 89–106. University of Arizona Press, Tucson.

Lorrain, D.

1968   Excavations at Red Bluff Shelter (Sotol Site) 41CX8 Crockett County, Texas. *Transactions of the 4th Regional Archeological Symposium for Southeastern New Mexico and Western Texas*, pp. 18–39. Midland, TX.

McGuire, Randall H., and Dean Saitta

1996   Although They Have Petty Captains, They Obey Them Badly: The Dialectics of Prehispanic Western Pueblo Social Organization. *American Antiquity* 61(2):197–216.

Meillassoux, Claude

1991   *The Anthropology of Slavery: The Womb of Iron and Gold*. University of Chicago Press, Chicago.

Mera, H. P.

1940   *Population Changes in the Rio Grande Glaze-Paint Area*. Technical Series Bulletin 9. Laboratory of Anthropology, Santa Fe, NM.

Moore, John H.

1974   Cheyenne Political History, 1820–1894. *Ethnohistory* 21(4):329–359.

1991   The Developmental Cycle of Cheyenne Polygyny. *American Indian Quarterly* 15(3):311–328.

Moorehead, Warren K.

1931   *Archaeology of the Arkansas River Valley*. Publication no. 2. Department of Archaeology, Phillips Academy, Andover. Yale University Press, New Haven.

Northern, M. J.

1979   Archaeological Investigations of the Montgomery Site, Floyd County, Texas. M.A. thesis, Texas Tech University.

Opler, Morris E.

1936   A Summary of Jicarilla Apache Culture. *American Anthropologist* 38:202–223.

Ortiz, Alfonso

1969   *The Tewa World: Space, Time, and Becoming in a Pueblo Society*. University of Chicago Press, Chicago.

Parker, Wayne

1982   *Archeology at the Bridwell Site*. Crosby County Pioneer Memorial, Crosbyton, TX.

Parry, W. J., and J. D. Speth

1984   *The Garnsey Spring Campsite: Late Prehistoric Occupation in Southwestern New Mexico*. Technical Report 15. Museum of Anthropology, University of Michigan, Ann Arbor.

Parson, Elsie Clews

1964   The Social Organization of the Tewa of New

Mexico. *American Anthropological Association Memoirs* 36:3–309.

Parsons, M. L.

1967 *Archeological Investigations in Crosby and Dickens Counties, Texas During the Winter, 1966–1967.* Archaeological Program Report 7. Texas State Building Commission, Austin.

Patterson, Orlando

1982 *Slavery and Social Death: A Comparative Study.* Harvard University Press, Cambridge, MA.

Peréz de Luxán, Diego

1929 *Expedition into New Mexico Made by Antonio Espejo 1592–1583 as Revealed in the Journal of Diego Peréz de Luxán, a Member of the Party.* Translated by G. P. Hammond and A. Rey. Quivira Society, Los Angeles.

Peters, Virginia Bergman

1995 *Women of the Earth Lodges: Tribal Life on the Plains.* Archon Books, North Haven, CT.

Potter, James M.

2000 Pots, Parties, and Politics: Communal Feasting in the American Southwest. *American Antiquity* 65(3):471–492.

Reed, Erik K.

1954 Test Excavations at San Marcos Pueblo. *El Palacio* 61(10):323–343.

Riley, Carroll L.

1997 The Teya Indians of the Southwestern Plains. In *The Coronado Expedition to Tierra Nueva,* edited by Richard Flint and Shirley Cushing Flint, pp. 320–343. University Press of Colorado, Niwot.

Roberts, Richard

1984 Women's Work and Women's Property: Household Social Relations in the Maraka Textile Industry of the Nineteenth Century. *Comparative Studies in Society and History* 26:229–250.

Runkles, Frank A.

1964 The Garza Site: A Neo-American Campsite near Post, Texas. *Bulletin of the Texas Archaeological Society* 35:101–125.

Runkles, Frank A., and E. D. Dorchester

1987 The Lott Site (41GR56): A Late Prehistoric Site in Garza County, Texas. *Bulletin of the Texas Archeological Society* 57:83–115.

Schmitt, Karl, and Iva O. Schmitt

1953 *Wichita Kinship: Past and Present.* University Book Exchange, Norman.

Schroeder, Albert H., and Dan S. Matson

1965 *A Colony on the Move: Caspar Castaño de Sosa's Journal, 1590–1591.* School of American Research, Santa Fe.

Schultz, Jack M.

1992 The Use-Wear Generated by Processing Bison Hides. *Plains Anthropologist* 37(141):333–351.

Smith, Marvin T.

1987 *Archaeology of Aboriginal Culture Change in the Interior Southeast: Depopulation During the Early Historic Period.* Ripley P. Bullen Series. University Press of Florida, Gainesville.

Snow, David H.

1981 Protohistoric Rio Grande Pueblo Economics: A Review of Trends. In *The Protohistoric Period in the North American Southwest, AD 1450–1700,* edited by D. R. Wilcox and W. B. Masse, pp. 354–377. Anthropological Research Paper no. 24. Arizona State University, Tempe.

Spector, Janet D.

1993 *What This Awl Means: Feminist Archaeology at a Wahpeton Dakota Village.* Minnesota Historical Press, St. Paul.

Speth, John D.

1991 Some Unexplored Aspects of Mutualistic Plains-Pueblo Food Exchange. In *Farmers, Hunters, and Colonists: Interaction between the Southwest and the Southern Plains,* edited by K. A. Spielmann, pp. 18–37. University of Arizona Press, Tucson.

Spielmann, Katherine A.

1982 *Inter-societal Food Acquisition Among Egalitarian Societies: An Ecological Study of Plains/Pueblo Interaction in the American Southwest.* Ph.D. dissertation, University of Michigan. University Microfilms, Ann Arbor.

1989 Colonists, Hunters, and Farmers: Plains-Pueblo Interaction in the Seventeenth Century. In *Columbian Consequences,* vol. I, edited by D. H. Thomas, pp. 101–113. Smithsonian Institution Press, Washington, D.C.

1991 *Farmers, Hunters, and Colonists: Interaction Between the Southwest and the Southern Plains.* University of Arizona Press, Tucson.

1998 Ritual Influences on the Development of Rio Grande Glaze A Ceramics. In *Migration and Reorganization: The Pueblo IV Period in the American Southwest,* edited by K. A. Spielmann, pp. 253–261. Anthropological Research Papers no. 51. Department of Anthropology, Arizona State University, Tempe.

Stahl, Ann B.

1993 Concepts of Time and Approaches to Analogical Reasoning in Historical Perspective. *American Antiquity* 58(2):235–260.

2002 Colonial Entanglement and the Practices

of Taste: An Alternative to Logocentric Approaches. *American Anthropologist* 104(3): 827–845.

Steward, Julian H.
1942   The Direct Historical Approach to Archaeology. *American Antiquity* 7:337–343.

Treece, A. C., C. Lintz, W. N. Trierweiler, J. M. Quigg, and K. A. Miller
1993   *Cultural Resource Investigations in the O. H. Ivie Reservoir, Concho, Coleman, and Runnels Counties, Texas,* vol. 4: *Data Recovery Results from Ceramic Sites.* Technical Report 346-IV. Mariah Associates, Inc., Austin.

Tichy, Marjorie Ferguson
1939   The Archaeology of Puaray. *El Palacio* 46(7): 145–163.

Vehik, Susan C.
1986   Oñate's Expedition to the Southern Plains: Routes, Destinations, and Implications for Late Prehistoric Cultural Adaptations. *Plains Anthropologist* 31(111):13–33.

1992   Wichita Culture History. *Plains Anthropologist* 37:311–332.

2002   Conflict, Trade, and Political Development on the Southern Plains. *American Antiquity* 67(1):37–64.

Wedel, Waldo R.
1950   Notes on Plains-Southwestern Contacts in the Light of Archaeology. In *For the Dean: Essays in Anthropology in Honor of Byron Cummings,* edited by E. K. Reed and D. S. King, pp. 99–116. Hohokam Museum Association, Tucson.

1982   Further Notes on Puebloan-Central Plains Contacts in Light of Archaeology. In *Pathways to Plains Prehistory: Anthropological Perspectives of Plains Natives and Their Pasts,* edited by D. G. Wycoff and J. L. Hofman, pp. 145–152. Memoir no. 3. Oklahoma Anthropological Society. Contributions no. 1. Cross Timbers Heritage Association, Duncan, OK.

Weist, Katherine M.
1980   Plains Indian Women: An Assessment. In *Anthropology on the Great Plains,* edited by W. R. Wood and M. Liberty, pp. 255–271. University of Nebraska Press, Lincoln.

1983   Beasts of Burden and Menial Slaves: Nineteenth Century Observations of Northern Plains Indian Women. In *The Hidden Half: Studies of Plains Indian Women,* edited by P. Albers and B. Medicine, pp. 29–52. University Press of America, Washington, D.C.

Wenger, E. C.
1998   *Communities of Practice: Learning, Meaning, and Identity.* Cambridge University Press, Cambridge.

West, Elliott
1998   *The Contested Plains: Indians, Goldseekers, and the Rush to Colorado.* University Press of Kansas, Lawrence.

Wheat, Joe Ben
1955   Two Archaeological Sites Near Lubbock, Texas. *Panhandle-Plains Historical Review* 28: 71–77.

Wilcox, David R.
1981   The Entry of the Athapaskans in the American Southwest: The Problem Today. In *The Protohistoric Period in the North American Southwest, AD 1450–1700,* edited by D. R. Wilcox and W. B. Masse, pp. 213–256. Anthropological Research Papers no. 24. Arizona State University, Tempe.

Woolf, Alex
1997   At Home in the Long Iron Age: A Dialogue between Households and Individuals in Cultural Reproduction. In *Invisible People and Processes: Writing Gender and Childhood into European Archaeology,* edited by J. Moore and E. Scott, pp. 68–74. Leicester University Press, London.

Word, James H.
1963   Floydada Country Club Site 41-FL-1. *Bulletin of the South Plains Archeological Society* 1:37–63.

1965   The Montgomery Site in Floyd County, Texas. *Bulletin of the South Plains Archeological Society* 2:55–102.

1991   The 1975 Field School of the Texas Archaeological Society. *Bulletin of Texas Archeological Society* 60:57–106.

9

Unwilling Immigrants

Culture, Change, and the "Other" in Mississippian Societies

Susan M. Alt

Archaeological studies of alien people within societies tend to focus on willing immigrants, or the dynamics and interactions within multi-ethnic communities (for an example, see Lightfoot et al. 1998; Lyons and Papadopoulous 2002; Stein 2005b). But there were "others" in many ancient societies who were unwilling immigrants, introduced to a new community through engagements with violence and capture. I refer to such people as unwilling immigrants for two reasons. First, in eastern Native North American societies, captives were often integrated into societies as members rather than as despised enemies. Second, and more importantly, such captives had the same potential to stimulate culture change as did willing immigrants.

Because all people participate in and create culture (Archer 1996; Bourdieu 1990; Wolf 1984), to understand a culture, it is necessary to understand all of the participants. Captives cannot be ignored or considered extraneous persons of little import, or we risk not only mischaracterizing societies, but also fail to understand culture and how it changes.

The possibility that Mississippian people engaged in captive-taking has seldom been considered. This is problematic, because as others in this volume point out, taking and keeping captives does not seem to have been an unusual occurrence through time or across space (see the chapters by Brooks and Cameron, this volume). Hence, by ignoring captives, we are also ignoring important mechanisms for culture change.

Indeed, I propose here to lay the groundwork for a new model of Mississippian society that shifts focus from political organization to social-demographic history.

Elsewhere I have discussed my approach in terms of the "hybridity" of early Cahokia (Alt 2006a, 2006b). In this chapter I review the evidence that led me to infer that captive-taking was in fact an integral part of the dynamics of Mississippian societies. Turning first to imagery and burial practices, I next review "Morning Star" practices and other early Mississippian evidence that unwilling immigrants constitute a heretofore unexamined basis for rethinking the broad outlines of Mississippian cultural history.

Why Movements of People Matter

The movement of people was once considered a prime motivator for culture change, but the early migration and diffusion theories were problematic and eventually fell out of favor (Burmeister 2000). The culture historical characterizations of migration were unsatisfactory in their all-or-nothing approach to culture change. People were said to have adopted new traits in imitation of others. Later models, most coming from work on culture contact situations or colonialism, invoked concepts such as assimilation, acculturation, syncretization, and creolization (see, for example, Cusick 1998; Deagan 1983, 1996; Ferguson 1992; Loren 2003; Silliman 2005). These concepts were incorporated into ways of looking at interactions between people that tried to be more nuanced and agentive. Analysts began recognizing that there were not simply donors and receptors of cultural traits, but that interactions were more subtle, and that all people involved were somehow altered, not just those who could be identified as subordinate in some way. Then again, most studies still looked for traits, or elements of traits, that were adopted or preexisting elements that were combined or given new meanings.

Studies of Mississippian societies during the past few decades have typically focused on the local political development of particular regions (e.g., Anderson 1994; Dye 2006a; King 2003b). More recently, some have considered processes of immigration as integral to understanding particular developmental trajectories (for example, Alt 2006b; Blitz 1999; Cobb 2005; Cobb and Butler 2000, 2002, 2006; Goldstein 1991; Hally and Langford 1988; King 2003a; Pauketat 2003; M. Williams 1994; S. Williams 1990; Williams and Shapiro 1990). Few of these studies, however, have fully considered what the presence of migrants might mean in terms of culture change (although see Alt 2006a, 2006b; Cobb 2005; Cobb and Butler 2006; Pauketat 2003). Moreover, none have considered the importance of indigenous practices of captive-taking, adoption, and slavery.

Migration studies worldwide suggest that the presence of foreigners within societies can lead to moments of transformation (see, for example, Alt 2006b; Bhabha 1994; Cobb and Butler 2006; Cusick 1998; Deagan 1996; Hannerz 1987; Lekson 1999; Pollock 1999; Postgate 1992; Silliman 2005; Soja 1996; Stein 2002, 2005a). People affect other people, and when introduced to new beliefs and ideas, people react in a variety of ways. They may adopt something newly encountered, aggressively cling to the familiar, or perhaps find a compromise between the old and the new. Such encounters may even lead to moments of innovation (Alt 2006a, 2006b). Whatever the case, all parties engaged in encounters with difference are affected.

The concept of hybridity as proposed by Bhabha (1994) adds a new dimension to such studies by focusing attention on how interactions between different peoples can open the potential for true innovation, not just novel combinations of preexisting elements. Hybridity is a spatial process whereby new cultural forms arise from "third spaces" (something like liminal spaces) that are created through encounters with difference (see, for example, Bhabha 1994; Hannerz 1987; Lefebvre 1991; Soja 1996). In a sense, the interactions of different people open a space where the typical rules of engagement are renegotiated. In this space it is then possible for something totally new to appear—something more than a mix of different parts, something never before done, which cannot be broken down into familiar parts. In other words, in this space people can invent; they can act in ways they never have before.

It is this process of hybridity that can help make sense of novel cultural changes. Although originally identified through studies of colonial encounters, where differences between people and societies were very obvious, this process also occurs in routine and momentous encounters everywhere. There are always differences between people, and thus hybridity exists in all such encounters, even at the scale of everyday practices.

Mississippian Societies, Warfare, and Captives

The earliest records of European and Native American contact contain numerous accounts documenting occasions where contact-era "Mississippian" societies raided each other or Europeans and took captives. Examples come from accounts of the Narváez expedition of 1528 and the De Soto *entrada* of 1539–1543, during which raiders mistreated or killed Native men but took women and children captive (Clayton et al. 1993).

In the case of the Narváez expedition, the Natives attacked the Europeans, killing most of the men save Juan Ortiz, who was taken captive in 1528 and tortured by a chief named Hirrihigua. Ortiz spent the next twelve years living with southeastern Indians (before later joining the De Soto expedition).

Ortiz's experience differed from that of many other captives, who were often adopted to become full members of the abductor's society (see Peregrine, this volume). This does not seem to have been the case for Ortiz, because only he had to obey all of the chief's orders and suffer physical abuse perpetrated by him (Clayton et al 1993: 103–104). This suggests that his status was more like that of a slave than of an individual adopted into the group. Eventually the chief's daughter helped Ortiz escape to a nearby town, which led to his encounter with de Soto (Clayton et al. 1993).

As further detailed by Ames, Brooks, DeBoer, Habicht-Mauche, Martin, and Peregrine (this volume), there is no lack of evidence for captive-taking in other Native North American contexts during the historic period. Various groups across the continent waged war, raided, and took captives. The Jesuit *relaciones* (documents written from 1610 to 1791; see Thwaites 1896–1901) describe similar episodes of captive-taking in the northern Eastern Woodlands among, for instance, the Iroquois, Menominee, and Huron. The reported incidents reveal that captives could be tortured, killed, or adopted into the raiding tribe (Thwaites 1896–1901). The particulars of such encounters varied, but the practice of captive-taking was in fact a fairly common occurrence.

The more difficult task is to identify evidence from the deeper past indicating that societies four or five hundred years earlier, such as those of the Mississippians, also took captives. Mississippian societies have been identified as mound-building, agricultural chiefdoms located from eastern Oklahoma to the East Coast in the southern half of what is now the United States (Figure 9.1). Sites were identified based on the presence of platform mounds, plazas, and shell-tempered pottery and a reliance on corn agriculture. To some degree, the study of Mississippian polities has been the study of chiefdoms: how they developed, functioned, and collapsed (see, for example, D. Anderson 1994; Pauketat 2007). Mississippian culture is thought to have been based on a set of commonly held beliefs and religious practices (called the Southeastern Ceremonial Complex [Galloway 1989; King 2007; Reilly and Garber 2007]) which underwrote the chiefdom organizations.

Researchers have recently recognized that there was a great deal of diversity in the particular histories, practices, and beliefs of various Mississippian polities, some of which may have been the results of episodes of warfare (e.g., Alt 2001;

Dye 2006b; Emerson et al. 2008; Pauketat, in press; Wilson et al. 2006). Mississippian people did engage in warfare, raids, and other violent acts against each other (Bridges et al. 2000; Dye 1995; Emerson 2007; Lambert 2002; Milner 1998; Milner, et al. 1991; Pauketat 1999, 2007b). This is attested to by palisaded and burned villages at places like Orendorf in Illinois, Snodgrass in Missouri, and Aztalan in Wisconsin, as well as human bodies with evidence of weapon-induced trauma (Barrett 1933; Conrad 1989, 1991; Milner 1999; Price and Griffin 1979). Depending on the time and place, evidence of violence can be clear and overwhelming, such as the mutilated bodies found at the non-Mississippian village site of Crow Creek in South Dakota (Willey and Emerson 1993). Elsewhere, the evidence is only considered suggestive (see, for example, Goldstein 1997).

Material evidence for some violent acts, such as captive-taking, can be even more difficult to pin down. When nonlocal people have been identified in a population, archaeologists have usually assumed that the immigrants were willing, perhaps brought in as part of voluntary exogamous marriage practices (e.g., Brashler et al. 2000; Gibbons and Dobbs 1991). However, given widespread evidence of warfare and violence in pre-Columbian populations, nonvoluntary practices of incorporation are probably equally likely.

Captive-taking in North American societies was generally a very low-tech affair that involved moving people across space with little in the way of material evidence left behind. Other than typical weapons of violence, a (very perishable) captive collar may be the only identified artifact directly associated with captive-taking (for an example, see Willoughby 1938).

There are, nonetheless, reasons to suspect captives were taken by Mississippian peoples. Captives, as well as other alien persons, may be indicated by things such as nonlocal material culture, poorly made or hybrid pottery styles, different dietary signatures, and the presence of physical trauma or unusual burial treatments (e.g., the chapters by Cameron, Habicht-Mauche, and Martin, this volume). Using such material evidence to identify the presence of captives assumes either that resistance from captives would be visible in material culture, as described by

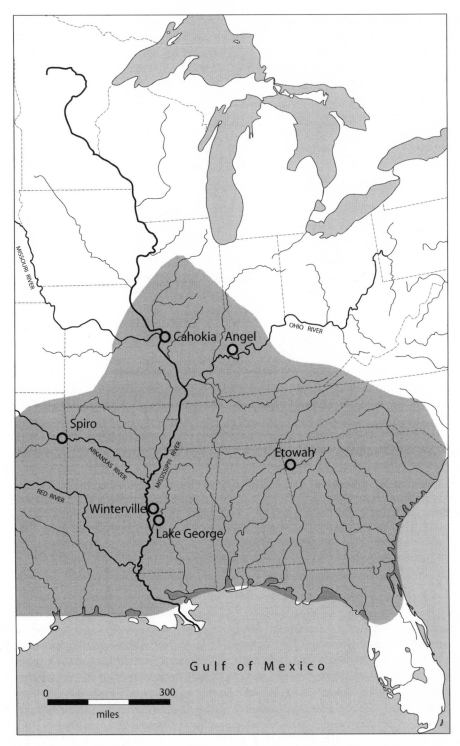

FIGURE 9.1. Map showing the extent of Mississippian settlement and locations of sites mentioned in text.

Ferguson (1992) for African-American slaves in the South, or that captives' unfamiliarity with local technology would result in seemingly incompetently made products. However, as suggested by Brumfiel (1996), overt resistance may have been unlikely if a person's status and/or well-being depended on the quality of the product. Also, as noted by Peregrine (this volume), Iroquois captives apparently willingly assumed the roles of the people they replaced. Another possible marker of alien individuals is a visible learning curve in productive activities, but then this can also mark nonlocal wives, apprentices, and children. Therefore, although such material can indicate captives, to be at all convincing there would need to be multiple lines of evidence.

Unusual dietary signatures are perhaps among the best markers for the presence of foreigners within a community. For instance, the consumption of corn products was highly variable across the Midwest and Southeast, and these differences are visible and retrievable via bone chemistry studies (Buikstra et al. 1994; Hedman et al. 2002; Lynott et al. 1986; Schurr 1989, 1992). It is also likely that a subpopulation of low-status individuals would receive different foods (see, for example, Swanton 1979), and over enough time this, too, is visible in bone chemistry (Ambrose, pers. comm.). In any case, individuals with anomalous bone chemistry exist in several Mississippian populations and, when combined with other lines of evidence, provide compelling evidence of captives (see, for example, Hedman et al. 2002; Schurr 1992).

Mississippian Warrior and Captive Carvings

A suite of images related to the Southeastern Ceremonial Complex featuring warriors, birdmen, and falcon dancers have been interpreted as materializations of supernatural or mythological characters, projecting ideologies of warfare (Brown 2007; Dye 1995, 2004, 2006b, 2007; Lankford 2007; Reilly 2007). These include carved redstone smoking pipes made at Cahokia that depict warriors and captives or execution victims (Brown 1996; Brown 2007; Dye 1995, 2004, 2006b, 2007; Lankford 2007; Reilly 2007). The Conquering Warrior and Resting Warrior pipes, found at Spiro but made at Cahokia, and the Guy

Smith figure from Illinois show characters outfitted with weapons and shields, and dressed in protective padded body wear and head coverings. Two of the redstone figures show warriors holding and killing captives. The Conquering Warrior pipe depicts a warrior slicing into the face of a captive with a stone mace (this is sometimes called the "human sacrifice" effigy pipe [Emerson 2007; Reilly 2004]).

Other non-Cahokian carved effigy smoking pipes more particularly emphasize the captive status of certain individuals. The first is the Kneeling Prisoner effigy pipe from Mississippi. This pipe depicts a bound male individual who is kneeling and bowed, his body parallel to the ground. A second bound-captive pipe found at the Winterville site in Mississippi depicts a less stylized, more realistic looking prisoner (Figure 9.2) (Brain 1986; Dye 2004). Another pipe from Arkansas also depicts an individual kneeling and bound, with his arms very clearly tied at the elbows. As Emerson (2007) notes, the captives appear to wear headgear similar to that depicted on the warrior pipes, which serves to identify them as warriors. I would also note that in a convention reminiscent of Mesoamerican captive images, the captives are depicted naked to emphasize their vulnerability.

For present purposes, I assume that, whether citing supernatural characters or not, the figures were created based on actual experiences and may further represent characters who were impersonated by real people (Brown 2006, 2007; Hall 1997; Pauketat 2008). In fact, leaders often seem to have "adopted" the personae of mythical characters, suggesting that they were potentially linked with heroes in deed (Hall 1997). Given Native American customs and beliefs regarding adoption, it is likely that people who assumed a mythic persona were perceived as having the potential to carry out some of the same kinds of actions as the mythic character.

Therefore, even if the carved pipes depict mythical moments, they still reveal things people believed did or could happen. Thus, they seem to show that Mississippian people took captives. Of course, these carved stone figures, made around Cahokia and Winterville and traded to other places, depict only male captives. Yet many Eastern Woodland captive narratives from the

FIGURE 9.2. Stone pipe recovered from the Winterville site depicting a kneeling and bound captive. Note the rope around the upper arm.

historic period describe the capture and adoption of women and children, and the killing of male prisoners (see the chapters by DeBoer and Peregrine, this volume). Moreover, physical evidence from the Cahokia area (discussed later in this chapter) suggests that female captives were sacrificed, even though this practice is not depicted on the Cahokia redstone figures.

Mississippian Burial Evidence

In a variety of ways, burials can provide other lines of evidence for Mississippian captives by pointing to odd population profiles, individuals with unusual social identities, nonlocal DNA, or anomalous isotopic readings; that is to say, both missing persons or captives introduced to a society may skew a burial population in revealing ways. Hollinger (2005) identified captives at the Wever site in Iowa based on the presence of broken human bones in pits rather than in the cemetery with the bulk of the population. And then again, too few young females and juveniles in a mortuary profile may indicate a society experiencing excessive raiding. This was the case at the

Crow Creek massacre site, in South Dakota, where the few remains of young women led researchers to conclude that the young women had either escaped or were taken captive (Emerson 1999; Willey and Emerson 1993). On the other hand, an unusually large number of women and children in a population could indicate the presence of captives, which may be the case at the early Mississippian Schild site, in Illinois, or at the later Mississippian Lake George site, in Mississippi, where an unusual number of juveniles were found buried with adults (Raff et al. 2006: Williams and Brain 1985). Because captives were often treated roughly and brought across a long distance (raids were not generally conducted close to home), they likely experienced high death rates (see Patterson 1995).

The Schild case is bolstered by DNA evidence from several "mother and child" paired burials. As it turns out, the five tested pairs were, in fact, not biologically related (Raff et al. 2006). Given the prevalence of adoption in some societies, this may be a reminder that Native American relationships were not as dependent on biology as Western re-

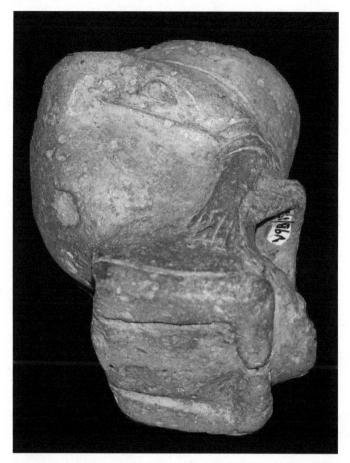

FIGURE 9.3. Pipe fragment (made of shell-tempered clay) from the Angel site depicting a bound captive. Note bindings around arm at the elbow. Photograph courtesy of Staffan Peterson, Glen Black Laboratory.

lationships. The burials may also be the enactment of a belief that children needed caretakers in death, or that children represented rebirth and renewal for other deceased individuals (for example, the Natchez sacrificed infants at the death of a chief) (Raff et al. 2006; see also Swanton 1998). Then again, this finding may be evidence of captive children.

Unusual burials at some Mississippian sites suggest recent arrivals who continued to practice nonlocal customs. Doubtless, some individuals who were captured and adopted into a community could have become nearly invisible in the host community, whereas others may have retained their traditional practices (Alt 2001; Emerson and Hargrave 2000). At the fortified Angel site in Indiana, two different burial pro-

grams were distinguished using bone isotopes. By comparing burial programs with isotopic signatures, and in some cases material culture, Mark Schurr (1992) determined that Fort Ancient people (non-Mississippian agriculturists) lived with the Mississippian people at the Angel site, and that the Fort Ancient people retained their natal burial practices (Schurr 1992).

In fact, additional evidence at the Angel site suggests that some people may not have arrived there willingly. Of the five human form effigy pipes recovered from the site, two depict kneeling and bound captives (Figure 9.3) (Black 1967; Peterson, pers. comm.). Found perhaps 150 m away from one of the pipes was a suggestive set of burials (Figure 9.4). Burial 20/W-11-A was that of an adult male (approximately fifty years old)

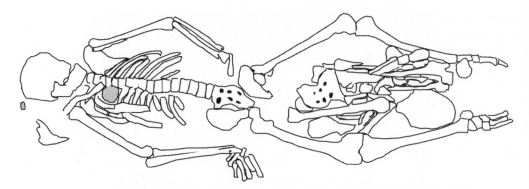

FIGURE 9.4. Composite drawing of Burial 20/W-11-A with Burial 21/W-11-A at the Angel site. The extended burial was an older male individual, and the bundle burial between his knees was a nonlocal female.

placed extended on his back. His legs, however, were positioned with bent knees in a bow-legged position so that the bundle burial of a twenty-seven-year-old woman (Burial 21/W-11-A) could be placed between his legs (Black 1967; Schurr 1989). A fire was built atop this burial, the flames scorching the legs of the male. Possibly associated with this burial were a bone bead and a slate disk of types not common to the site (Black 1967: 202–203).

The female member of this pair has a very unusual isotopic signature compared to that of the corn-eating Angel population (Schurr 1989, 1992). Although the male had an isotopic $\delta^{13}C$ value of −8.2, and the population average was −8.6, the $\delta^{13}C$ signature for the female was an aberrant −20.6, compatible with that of hunter-gatherers. The reading could be skewed due to burning; however, Schurr believes the burning was insufficient to cause the anomalous value (pers. comm., 2006). Given the nonlocal material found near these burials, and the anomalous isotopic readings, it seems likely that the woman was not from Angel (or even a nearby Fort Ancient community, where $\delta^{13}C$ values average −9.6 to −11.8).

Although this woman may have been a non-local wife, the unusual burial position seems to suggest that she was subordinate unlike any other person buried at the site, thus perhaps an unwilling immigrant. Better examples of such unwilling female immigrants are known from a series of unusual burials at Cahokia's Mound 72. In fact, these women may provide evidence of a program of capture for sacrifice, revealing the historical importance of captives in Mississippian societies that culminated in what was known historically through the stories and sacrificial practices associated with the worship of the Morning Star.

The Morning Star Story and Ritual

Of the Native American stories and rituals that reference captive-taking and human sacrifice, I focus here on the Morning Star sacrifice and the Red Horn (or Morning Star) myth because of their possible connections with Mississippian peoples. Such connections are evidenced by cave paintings dated to the early Mississippian period (ca. AD 1000–1100), by anecdotal evidence of Morning Star platforms, and by the sacrificial victims from the Cahokia region. While I do not believe that correlations between early Mississippian imagery and later recorded native stories and practices mean that either practices or beliefs survived for centuries unchanged, some evidence suggests continuities between later oral histories and early Mississippian ideologies (see Brown 2007).

The Red Horn story is a culture hero myth told among the northern midwestern and Siouan-speaking Ho-Chunk and Iowa peoples. In their stories, Red Horn has various names that call attention to his different aspects as a hero. "Red Horn" refers to his long braid of red hair, but he is also called "He-who-wears-human-heads-as-earrings" because of the heads that appear from time to time on his earlobes, or "He-who-is-hit-with-deer-lungs" because of events in his childhood (Hall 1997). Red Horn is also thought to be a manifestation of the Morning Star and thus related to the ceremony described below (Radin 1948).

In the Ho-Chunk and Iowa versions of the story, Red Horn has a companion or brother who also has supernatural powers. After defeating a group of giants in a series of contests, Red Horn takes a giantess champion from the defeated group to be his second wife. The giantess, who is in effect a captive wife, has a child with Red Horn, as does his first wife (Hall 1997; Radin 1948). These children also possess supernatural powers. In subsequent contests with the giants, Red Horn himself is taken captive and killed, but years later his sons retrieve his head and resurrect him (Hall 1997).

These stories, which reference the taking of a wife from an enemy group and the eventual capture of Red Horn himself, are also thought to reference aspects of adoption ceremonies that followed captive-taking (Hall 1991, 1997). This is in part because one of Red Horn's other names, He-who-is-hit-with-deer-lungs, is connected to the calumet ceremony, an adoption ceremony (Hall 1997). More importantly, the death and rebirth of Red Horn parallel the experience of an adopted person who takes on the spirit and life of the deceased (Hall 1991, 1997). As described by Peregrine (this volume), the Iroquois would adopt a captive to replace a lost family member, believing the captive did not just take over the lost person's life, but actually became that individual.

The Red Horn story cycle was thought by Radin (1948) to be related to the Morning Star ritual based on references to similar symbolic features in both. While Red Horn stories reference battles, capture, death, and adoption, the Morning Star ritual was centered on the taking of a captive to be used as a sacrifice, best known from accounts of the Skiri Pawnee.

The last known Morning Star sacrifice among the Skiri Pawnee occurred in 1838. The ceremony traditionally involved the sacrifice of a young woman or, infrequently, a male victim. The ceremony was not practiced regularly but was initiated when several criteria were met, beginning with a dream by a male member of the tribe that was deemed significant (Brooks 2002; Hall 1997). The ceremony could only occur if Venus,

the morning star, was visible, and only if a religious specialist verified that the time and situation were appropriate. All events related to the ritual were carried out according to a specific formula, including the particulars of the capture of an enemy woman who would be sacrificed after being treated with great care and respect (Hall 1997; Linton 1926; Murie 1989; Weltfish 1977).

At the designated time, the ritually painted captive would be led to a large, raised wooden platform and tied to a frame, facing east. After the appropriate actions by the priests and participants, the captive was shot through the heart with an arrow by the man who had captured her (Brooks 2002; Hall 1997). In some accounts, all men of the village then shot arrows into her body to symbolize the mythical arrow that united the Morning Star and Evening Star in a sacred union and led to the conception of the first child.

Early Mississippian Evidence of the Morning Star Practices

At least two cave paintings have been interpreted as representations of Red Horn stories, one in the Gottschall Rock Shelter, Wisconsin, and the other in Picture Cave, Missouri (Diaz-Granados and Duncan 2004; Duncan and Diaz-Granados 2000; Salzer and Rajnovich 2000). In both cases the art was securely dated to the terminal Late Woodland or early Mississippian period (ca. AD 1000) via radiocarbon assay. Painted on the walls in both cases are images of an individual with a long red braid, wearing human heads on his ears in the case of Picture Cave, or similar decorations on his nipples in Gottschall (as described for Red Horn's son). In Gottschall, there are images interpreted as giants as well as pictures of other characters mentioned in the stories. Also recovered from Gottschall was a carved stone head with lines on its face that match those on the face of a painted Red Horn character. This all suggested that the cave was, in fact, a shrine to Red Horn (Salzer and Rajnovich 2000).

Picture Cave contains multiple panels of images that seem to reference several Red Horn characters and depict different episodes of the saga (Diaz-Granados and Duncan 2004). In this case, the main character wears "Long Nosed God" earrings thought to indicate the Morning Star hero (Brown 2007). Earrings (usually made of shell, copper, or bone) that look just like those in the paintings have been recovered from select Mississippian sites (Hall 1991).

Besides representations of the Morning Star hero, there is other possible evidence from the Mississippian period of the Morning Star ritual. For example, a marine-shell bowl recovered from Craig Mound at Spiro is engraved with the image of an individual tied to a wooden frame being shot with arrows by warriors (Hall 1997: Plate 165; Phillips and Brown 1975:164; Reilly 2007). The designs around the image have been interpreted as sacrificed people who became stars after death (Hall 1997:90).

It is possible that we have evidence of Morning Star ceremony platforms or scaffolds. Near the large early Mississippian complex of Cahokia, "truss trenches" have been proposed as locations for footings of large platforms (Wittry et al. 1994). The spotty occurrence of such features could coincide with the sporadic nature of Morning Star sacrifices. For example, a set of truss trenches interpreted to have supported a substantial platform that faced east is known from the early Mississippian period Grossmann site (Alt 2006a). Interestingly, Grossmann also had an anomalous burial of a young adult female, which I have interpreted as a possible Morning Star sacrifice. The burial was located inside a temple rather than in a cemetery, as would have been customary. Her body was oriented in the same way as the truss trenches, and she had an offering burned over her heart (the heart was reportedly exposed in later Morning Star sacrifices). And this is not the only potential female sacrifice in the region. The body of another woman was found face down in the bottom of a post pit at the East St. Louis site, and it appears her arms and legs were bound before she was tossed into the pit (Eve Hargrave, pers. comm.).

The most compelling evidence for captives comes from Mound 72 at Cahokia. This small, inconspicuous mound is located toward the southern end of Cahokia's central mound complex and was excavated by Melvin Fowler between 1967 and 1971 (Fowler 1999). It appears that Mound 72 was the location of a series of dramatic mortuary events dating to the earliest Mississippian phase of Cahokia's history (Porubcan 1983, 2000). Pauketat (2004) suggests that certain events at Mound 72 focused on the ascension of a new leader (or leaders) through rituals of adoption and impersonation, based on the construction history of the mound and the placement of bodies and materials in relation to one another. Brown (2006) suggests that burials in Mound 72 were tableaus of the Red Horn or Morning Star myth. Certainly, the central burial of a male on a falcon-shaped bead blanket appears to reference the Red Horn story, and the organization of various other burials appears to be related to a telling of this same story or a series of related mythic tales. In this case, the telling of the story seemingly involved a new leader adopting the mythic heroic persona once embodied by the dead leader. In effect, it was a shifting of a supernatural identity from the deceased to the living, which also involved transmission of authority and leadership (Hall 1997).

Approximately 272 individuals were recovered from the sections of Mound 72 that were excavated (more burial pits remain undisturbed). Some of these people were buried with extreme care and were associated with elaborate wealth items. Others buried in the mound have been characterized as sacrificial victims who were killed in order to accompany a leader in death. Details recovered from the remains of the sacrificial victims suggest that they were not local people.

The largest burial pit had been lined with sand (which was often used to separate sacred and secular realms) and contained the bodies of 53 young women who have been interpreted as sacrificial victims (Rose 1999). It has been suggested that the four headless and handless men buried nearby (Figure 9.5) are representations of the four guardians who are part of the Morning Star myth (Brown 2006; Pauketat 2004). Other pits of burials contained 19, 22, and 24 burials, each group buried with great care. In these cases, all individuals appear to have been young adult women. In yet another pit burial, male and female victims had been clubbed before being tossed into their burial pit (Rose 1999).

Several characteristics distinguish the female burials from the rest of the burial population in Mound 72. Isotopic analysis revealed significant differences in the individuals' dietary signatures. A sample of three high-status individuals and

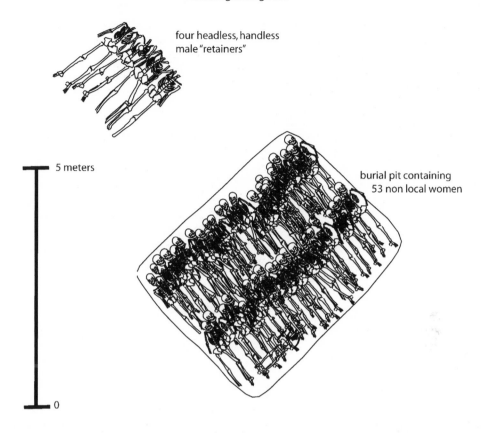

four headless, handless
male "retainers"

5 meters

burial pit containing
53 non local women

0

FIGURE 9.5. Composite drawing of a pit of nonlocal sacrificed women and the headless, handless "guardians" excavated at Mound 72, Cahokia.

four low-status individuals was tested by Ambrose and Krigbaum (2003). The samples from the executed women revealed dietary signatures significantly different from those of other Cahokia residents, presumably indicating that many of the Mound 72 women were nonlocal.[1]

The female sacrifices in Mound 72 were further identifiable as a distinct population based on dental characteristics. Rose (1999) was able to examine dentition from 109 individuals and found significant differences based on three independent traits from the litter burials, six traits from what he called "the mid-rank burials," and four traits from the litter sacrifices (Rose 1999: 83). The results suggested to Rose that the sacrificed women were not from Cahokia.

Three other facts are of great interest in interpreting the origins of the female sacrificial burials in Mound 72. First, the sacrificed women had less evidence of hyperostosis, a condition that might indicate physical blemishes, than individuals in other burial groups, suggesting to Rose that attractive or particularly healthy individuals were chosen as sacrifices. In addition, as could best be determined, all of the women were of reproductive age. Third, all of these victims were of a similar size. Measurements of the femur ball found that in 79.6 percent of the cases the femur heads were within 3 mm of each other. Overall, the population in the pits of sacrificed women in Mound 72 appears very distinct, selected with specific characteristics in mind. This was not the case for any of the other burial groups in this mound or for comparable skeletal populations from Cahokia.

The relationship between details of the pit of female burials and particulars of the Morning Star sacrifice should be noted. In the Morning Star ritual, captured, healthy women of reproductive age were sacrificed. More importantly, the sacrificed women were usually kept for a period of time (in some cases up to a year) during which they were treated with great respect and care. Interestingly, the nonlocal female sacrifices in Mound 72 were treated with much greater respect than the local sacrifices. This makes sense, since historically the Morning Star sacrifices commemorated the rebirth and renewal of the land. The Mound 72 burials did not, however, present evidence of death by arrows (it is commonly suggested the victims were strangled).

Discussion

Historic accounts, as well as Native American myths and stories, attest to practices of taking captives who became wives, adopted kin, or slaves as well as victims of violence (see, for example, the Jesuit *relaciones* [Thwaites 1896–1901]). Descriptions of practices such as the Morning Star ritual recount sacred events that required captives to perform a necessary sacrifice (Hall 1997). Stories such as the Red Horn myths describe battles and the taking of wives from defeated giants (Radin 1948). Artwork on cave and rockshelter walls and on carved stone pipes depicts battles, violence, and captive-taking. Bodies and burials provide evidence of displaced individuals, and of sacrificial events. I believe these different lines of evidence combine to strongly suggest that there were in fact "unwilling immigrants" at Mississippian towns. So why does this matter?

The taking in of others, as willing or unwilling immigrants, would have provoked changes within communities. This fact now seems particularly important for explaining the beginning of Cahokia. Recent studies are again focusing on willing immigrants, pointing out that the growth of Cahokia can only be accounted for by an influx of new people with more distant origins (Alt 2006a, 2006b; Pauketat 2003). In accordance with a general theory of hybridity, this influx of people was not, and could not, have been without consequence. The existence of these willing immigrants has suggested to me that Cahokia is best viewed as a cultural "melting pot" rather than as a homogenous and closed society, as it is more typically viewed (Alt 2006a, 2006b).

As a melting pot, Cahokia would have been the site of multiple encounters with difference. The influx of new immigrants would not only have exposed Cahokians and the relocated foreigners to new customs and beliefs, but more importantly, these interactions between people with different habits and beliefs would have opened the spaces where innovation was possible (see Bhabha 1994). And much of the new Mississippian culture was innovative. Presumably, this culture would have morphed through the divergent encounters of Mississippians at places such as Angel Mounds, Winterville, Spiro, and elsewhere.

We know this even in more recent American history. As commodified and dehumanized as African slaves were in America, certain practices now considered quintessentially American can be considered hybridized practices originating in the meetings of Euroamericans and Africans (Ferguson 1992). Even under the extreme conditions of American slavery, dominated people were able to affect the dominators and change cultural practices in ways that were not predictable or even observable as they occurred. We also know that histories of violence and domination affect societies in other ways.

Given "melting pot" environments at places like Cahokia, Angel, Winterville, and Spiro, what then would be the implications of yet another category of person, the captive? Given processes of hybridity, influxes of a large number of alien people can create environments conducive to innovation and more overt change. However, the cycling of a few, even marginalized, persons into a community is not without effect. Perhaps it is this third group, the captives, that helped propel a melting pot into a political force.

The taking, killing, or adopting of captives would have affected those doing the taking of bodies and lives as well as those made captive. These are encounters with differences that have radical outcomes for all involved. Accommodations of new roles—that of captor, captive, adopter, or adoptee—and the interactions of persons assuming those roles would have opened third spaces, generating new kinds of interactions, and new relationships of power and powerlessness. There would have been transformations from one person's identity to another, or even from life to death. These moments would have permitted, if not encouraged, new cultural forms, new social relationships, and altered ideologies. With the suspension of the normal rules of engagement that is typical of encounters with others, there comes permission, if not a mandate, to create, or re-create, normalcy. As individual people moved from one role to another, such experiences transformed identities and, ultimately, the societies themselves.

For instance, whether or not men or women were captured, killed on the spot, sacrificed, or subordinated in life, such events must have affected gendered relations differently in different Mississippian communities. Captive women, whether adopted, slave, or sacrifice, would have provided reminders of female vulnerability in the face of male violence. Killed male captives provided a reminder of the cost of violent encounters. Captives of any gender would have provoked sensibilities of uncertainty for all; rarely is one group perpetually the attacker or the attacked.

More than likely, community identity and concepts of social persons would have been less fixed, and more fluid, than commonly assumed. Mississippian adoptions and impersonations of mythical beings suggest that conceptions of personhood varied significantly in accordance with ritual as well as with warring and captive-taking practices. Since identity and gender are at the heart of social organization, what if they were both reconfigured as part of Mississippian rituals and subtly altered through encounters with unwilling immigrants?

Mississippian people did not live in isolated communities, unaware of and unaffected by others. Evidence of warfare and violence against those seen as "others" belies that image, as does evidence of executed alien individuals. For this reason, we cannot conceive of Mississippian lifeways as simple adaptations. They were the products of complex and conflicted histories, always becoming and changing through processes of hybridity, always in a process of becoming through encounters with violence and others: the willing and unwilling immigrants of the Mississippian world.

Note

1. An earlier study of isotopic signatures from Mound 72 produced more variable results, but Ambrose and Krigbaum (2003) attribute this difference to the improved testing techniques used in their later study.

References Cited

Alt, S. M.
2001   Cahokian Change and the Authority of Tradition. In *The Archaeology of Traditions: Agency and History Before and After Columbus*, edited by T. Pauketat, pp. 141–156. University Press of Florida, Gainesville.
2006a   Cultural Pluralism and Complexity: Analyzing a Cahokian Ritual Outpost. Ph.D. dissertation, University of Illinois, Urbana-Champaign.
2006b   The Power of Diversity: Settlement in the Cahokian Uplands. In *Leadership and Polity in Mississippian Society*, edited by B. M. Butler and P. D. Welch, pp. 289–308. Occasional Paper no. 33. Center for Archaeological Investigations, Southern Illinois University, Carbondale.
Ambrose, S. H., and J. Krigbaum
2003   Bone Chemistry and Bioarchaeology. *Journal of Anthropological Archaeology* 22:193–199.

Anderson, D. G.
1994   *The Savannah River Chiefdoms: Political Change in the Late Prehistoric Southeast*. University of Alabama Press, Tuscaloosa.
Archer, M. S.
1996   *Culture and Agency: The Place of Culture in Social Theory*. Cambridge University Press, Cambridge.
Barrett, S. A.
1933   *Ancient Aztalan*. Bulletin of the Public Museum of the City of Milwaukee.
Bhabha, H. K.
1994   *The Location of Culture*. Routledge, London.
Black, G. A.
1967   *The Angel Site: An Archaeological, Historical, and Ethnological Study*. Indiana Historical Society, Indianapolis.
Blitz, J. H.
1999   Mississippian Chiefdoms and the Fission-Fusion Process. *American Antiquity* 64:577–592.
Bourdieu, P.
1990   *The Logic of Practice*. Stanford University Press, Stanford, CA.
Brain, J. P.
1986   *Winterville: Late Prehistoric Culture Contact in the Lower Mississippi Valley*. Archaeological

Report 23. Mississippi Department of Archives and History, Jackson.

Brashler, J. G., E. B. Garland, M. B. Holman, W. A. Lovis, and S. R. Martin

2000 Adaptive Strategies and Socioeconomic Systems in Northern Great Lakes Riverine Environments: The Late Woodland of Michigan. In *Late Woodland Societies: Tradition and Transformation across the Midcontinent*, edited by T. E. Emerson, D. L. McElrath, and A. C. Fortier, pp. 543–579. University of Nebraska Press, Lincoln.

Bridges, P. S., K. P. Jacobi, and M. L. Powell

2000 Warfare-Related Trauma in the Late Prehistory of Alabama. In *Bioarchaeological Studies of Life in the Age of Agriculture: A View from the Southeast*, edited by P. M. Lambert, pp. 35–62. University of Alabama Press, Tuscaloosa.

Brooks, J. F.

2002 *Captives and Cousins: Slavery, Kinship, and Community in the Southwest Borderlands*. University of North Carolina Press, Chapel Hill.

Brown, A. J.

1996 *The Spiro Ceremonial Center*, Part II. Memoirs of the Museum of Anthropology 29. University of Michigan Press, Ann Arbor.

Brown, J. A.

2006 Where's the Power in Mound Building? An Eastern Woodlands Perspective. In *Leadership and Polity in Mississippian Society*, edited by B. Butler and P. D. Welch, pp. 197–213. Center for Archaeological Investigation, Southern Illinois University, Carbondale.

2007 On the Identity of the Birdman Within Mississippian Period Art and Iconography. In *Ancient Objects and Sacred Realms*, edited by F. K. Reilly III and J. F. Garber, pp. 56–106. University of Texas Press, Austin.

Brumfiel, E. M.

1996 Quality of Tribute Cloth: The Place of Evidence in Archaeological Argument. *American Antiquity* 61(3):453–462.

Buikstra, J. E., J. Rose, and G. R. Milner

1994 A Carbon Isotopic Perspective on Dietary Variation in Late Prehistoric Western Illinois. In *Agricultural Origins and Development in the Midcontinent*, edited by W. Green, pp. 155–170. Report no. 19. Office of the State Archaeologist, University of Iowa, Iowa City.

Burmeister, S.

2000 Approaches to an Archaeological Proof of Migration. *Current Anthropology* 41(4):539–553.

Clayton, L. A., V. J. Knight, and E. C. Moore

1993 *The DeSoto Chronicles: The Expedition of Hernando de Soto to North America in 1539–1542*. University of Alabama Press, Tuscaloosa.

Cobb, C. R.

2005 Archaeology and the "Savage Slot": Displacement and Emplacement in the Premodern World. *American Anthropologist* 107(4):563–574.

Cobb, C. R., and B. M. Butler

2000 Mississippian Diasporas and Upland Settlement in the Lower Ohio Valley. Paper presented at the Southeastern Archaeological Conference, Macon, GA.

2002 The Vacant Quarter Revisited: Late Mississippian Abandonment of the Lower Ohio Valley. *American Antiquity* 67(4):625–641.

2006 Mississippian Migration and Emplacement in the Lower Ohio Valley. In *Leadership and Polity in Mississippian Society*, edited by B. M. Butler and P. D. Welch, pp. 328–344. Occasional Paper 33. Southern Illinois University, Carbondale.

Conrad, L. A.

1989 The Southeastern Ceremonial Complex on the Northern Middle Mississippian Frontier: Late Prehistoric Politico-Religious Systems in the Central Illinois Valley. In *The Southeastern Ceremonial Complex: Artifacts and Analysis*, edited by P. Galloway, pp. 93–113. University of Nebraska Press, Lincoln.

1991 The Middle Mississippian Cultures of the Central Illinois Valley. In *Cahokia and the Hinterlands: Middle Mississippian Cultures of the Midwest*, edited by T. E. Emerson and R. B. Lewis, pp. 119–163. University of Illinois Press, Urbana.

Cusick, J. G. (editor)

1998 *Studies in Culture Contact: Interaction, Culture Change and Archaeology*. Occasional Paper 25. Southern Illinois University, Carbondale.

Deagan, K.

1983 *Spanish St. Augustine: The Archaeology of a Colonial Creole Community*. Academic Press, New York.

1996 Colonial Transformations: Euro-American Cultural Genesis in the Earliest Spanish Colonies. *Journal of Anthropological Research* 52(2):135–160.

Diaz-Granados, C., and J. R. Duncan

2004 Reflections of Power, Wealth and Sex in Missouri Rock Art Motifs. In *The Rock Art of Eastern North America*, edited by C. Diaz-

Granados and J. R. Duncan, pp. 145–159. University of Alabama Press, Tuscaloosa.

Duncan, J. R., and C. Diaz-Granados
2000   Of Masks and Myths. *Midcontinental Journal of Archaeology* 25(1):1–26.

Dye, D. H.
1995   Feasting With the Enemy: Mississippian Warfare and Prestige Goods. In *Native American Interactions: Multiscalar Analyses and Interpretations in the Eastern Woodlands*, edited by K. E. Sassaman and M. S. Nassaney, pp. 289–316. University of Tennessee Press, Knoxville.
2004   Art, Ritual, and Chiefly Warfare in the Mississippian World. In *Hero, Hawk, and Open Hand: American Indian Art of the Ancient Midwest and South*, edited by R. Townsend, pp. 191–206. Yale University Press, New Haven, CT.
2006a   Combat Weaponry at Picture Cave: Some Iconographic Themes. Paper presented at the Southeastern Archaeological Conference, Little Rock, AR, November 8–11.
2006b   The Transformation of Mississippian Warfare: Four Case Studies from the Mid-South. In *The Archaeology of Warfare: Prehistories of Raiding and Warfare*, edited by E. N. Arkush and M. W. Allen, pp. 101–147. University Press of Florida, Gainesville.
2007   Ritual, Medicine, and the War Trophy Iconographic Theme in the Mississippian Southeast. In *Ancient Objects and Sacred Realms: Interpretations of Mississippian Iconography*, edited by F. K. Reilly III and J. F. Garber, pp. 152–173. University of Texas Press, Austin.

Emerson, T. E.
1982   *Mississippian Stone Images in Illinois*. Circular no. 6. Illinois Archaeology Survey, Urbana.
1999   The Langford Tradition and the Process of Tribalization on the Middle Mississippian Borders. *Midcontinental Journal of Archaeology* 24:3–56.
2007   Cahokia and the Evidence for Late Pre-Columbian War in the North American Continent. In *North American Indigenous Warfare and Ritual Violence*, edited by R. J. Chacon and R. G. Mendoza, pp. 129–148. University of Arizona Press, Tucson.

Emerson, T. E., S. M. Alt, and T. R. Pauketat
2008   Locating American Indian Religion at Cahokia and Beyond. In *Religion in the Material World*, edited by L. Fogelin. Occasional Paper no. 36. Center for Archaeological Investigations, Southern Illinois University, Carbondale.

Emerson, T. E., and E. A. Hargrave
2000   Strangers in Paradise? Recognizing Ethnic Mortuary Diversity on the Fringes of Cahokia. *Southeastern Archaeology* 19(1):1–23.

Emerson, T. E., and R. E. Hughes
2000   Figurines, Flint Clay Sourcing, the Ozark Highlands, and Cahokian Acquisition. *American Antiquity* 65(1):79–101.

Emerson, T. E., R. Hughes, M. Hynes, and S. U. Wisseman
2003   The Sourcing and Interpretation of Cahokia-Style Figures in the Trans-Mississippi South and Southeast. *American Antiquity* 68(2):287–314.

Ferguson, L.
1992   *Uncommon Ground: Archaeology and Early African America, 1650–1800*. Smithsonian Institution Press, Washington, D.C.

Fowler, M. L.
1999   *The Mound 72 Area: Dedicated and Sacred Space in Early Cahokia*. Reports of Investigation no. 54. Illinois State Museum Society, Springfield.

Galloway, P. (editor)
1989   *Southeastern Ceremonial Complex: Artifacts and Analysis/The Cottonlandia Conference*. University of Nebraska Press, Lincoln.

Gibbon, G. E., and C. A. Dobbs
1991   The Mississippian Presence in the Red Wing Area, Minnesota. In *New Perspectives on Cahokia: Views from the Periphery*, edited by J. Stoltman, pp. 281–306. Prehistory Press, Madison, WI.

Goldstein, L.
1991   The Implications of Aztalan's Location. In *New Perspectives on Cahokia: Views from the Periphery*, edited by J. Stoltman, pp. 209–228. Monographs in World Prehistory 2. Prehistory Press, Madison, WI.
1997   Aztalan, a Middle Mississippian Village. *The Wisconsin Archaeologist* 78(1):223–248.

Hall, R. L.
1991   Cahokia Identity and Interaction Models of Cahokia. In *Cahokia and the Hinterlands*, edited by T. E. Emerson and L. R. B., pp. 3–34. University of Illinois Press, Urbana.
1997   *An Archaeology of the Soul: North American Indian Belief and Ritual*. University of Illinois Press, Urbana.

Hally, D. J., and J. Langford
1988   *Mississippian Period Archaeology of the Georgia Valley and Ridge Province*. Laboratory of Archaeology Series, Report 25. University of Georgia, Athens.

Hannerz, U.

1987   The World in Creolization. *Africa* 57(4):546–559.

Hedman, K., E. Hargrave, and S. H. Ambrose

2002   Late Mississippian Diet in the American Bottom: Stable Isotope Analysis of Bone Collagen and Apatite. *Midcontinental Journal of Archaeology* 27(2):237–272.

Hollinger, R. E.

2005   Conflict and Culture Change in the Late Prehistoric and Early Historic American Midcontinent. Unpublished Ph.D. dissertation, University of Illinois, Urbana-Champaign.

King, A. A.

2003a   *Etowah: The Political History of a Chiefdom Capital.* University of Alabama Press, Tuscaloosa.

2003b   Over a Century of Explorations at Etowah. *Journal of Archaeological Research* 11(4):279–306.

2007   *The Southeastern Ceremonial Complex: Chronology, Content, Contest.* University of Alabama Press, Tuscaloosa.

Lambert, P. M.

2002   The Archaeology of War: A North American Perspective. *Journal of Archaeological Research* 10(3):207–241.

Lankford, G. E.

2007   Some Cosmological Motifs in the Southeastern Ceremonial Complex. In *Ancient Objects and Sacred Realms*, edited by F. K. Reilly III and J. F. Garber, pp. 8–38. University of Texas Press, Austin.

Lefebvre, H.

1991   *The Production of Space.* Blackwell, Oxford.

Lekson, S. H.

1999   *The Chaco Meridian: Centers of Political Power in the Ancient Southwest.* AltaMira Press, Walnut Creek, CA.

Lightfoot, Kent G., Antoinette Martinez, and Anne Schiff

1998   Daily Practice and Material Culture in Pluralistic Settings: An Archaeological Study of Culture Change and Persistence from Fort Ross, California. *American Antiquity* 60:199–222.

Linton, R.

1926   The Origin of the Skidi Pawnee Sacrifice to the Morning Star. *American Anthropologist* 28(3):457–466.

Loren, D. D.

2003   Refashioning a Body Politic in Colonial Louisiana. *Cambridge Journal of Archaeology* 13:231–237.

Lynott, M. J., T. W. Boutton, J. E. Price, and D. E. Nelson

1986   Stable Isotope Evidence for Maize Agriculture in Southeast Missouri and Northeast Arkansas. *American Antiquity* 51(1):51–65.

Lyons, C. I., and J. K. Papadopoulos

2002   *The Archaeology of Colonialism: Issues and Debates.* Getty Research Institute, Los Angeles.

Milner, G. R.

1998   Archaeological Evidence for Prehistoric and Historic Intergroup Conflict in Eastern North America. In *Deciphering Anasazi Violence*, edited by P. Y. Bullock, pp. 69–91. HRM Books, Santa Fe, NM.

1999   Warfare in Prehistoric and Early Historic Eastern North America. *Journal of Archaeological Research* 7(2):105–151.

Milner, G. R., E. Anderson, and V. G. Smith

1991   Warfare in Late Prehistoric West-Central Illinois. *American Antiquity* 56(4):581–603.

Murie, J. R.

1989   *Ceremonies of the Pawnee.* University of Nebraska Press, Lincoln.

Patterson, T. C.

1995   *Toward a Social History of Archaeology in the United States.* Harcourt Brace and Company, Orlando, FL.

Pauketat, T. R.

1999   America's Ancient Warriors. *MHQ: The Quarterly Journal of Military History* (Summer):50–55.

2003   Farmers With Agency: Resettlement, Mississippianization and Historical Processes. *American Antiquity* 68:39–66.

2004   *Ancient Cahokia and the Mississippians.* Cambridge University Press, Cambridge.

2007   *Chiefdoms and Other Archaeological Delusions.* AltaMira Press, Walnut Creek, CA.

In press Wars, Rumors of Wars, and the Production of Violence. In *Warfare in Cultural Context: Practice, Agency and the Archaeology of Violence*, edited by A. E. Nielsen et al. Amerind Foundation, Dragoon, and University of Arizona Press, Tucson.

2008   Founders, Cults and the Archaeologies of Wa-Kan-da. In *Memory Work: The Archaeologies of Material Practice*, edited by B. Mills and W. H. Walker. School of American Research Press, Santa Fe, NM.

Phillips, P., and J. A. Brown

1975   *Pre-Columbian Shell Engravings from the Craig Mound at Spiro, Oklahoma.* Peabody Museum Press, Cambridge, MA.

Pollock, S.

1999   *Ancient Mesopotamia: The Eden That Never Was.* Cambridge University Press, Cambridge.

Porubcan, P. J.

1983   Human and Non-Human Surplus Display

and Mound 72, Cahokia. Master's thesis, University of Wisconsin-Madison.

2000   Human and Nonhuman Surplus Display at Mound 72, Cahokia. In *Mounds, Modoc, and Mesoamerica: Papers in Honor of Melvin L. Fowler*, edited by S. R. Ahler, pp. 207–225. Scientific Papers vol. 28. Illinois State Museum, Springfield.

Postgate, J. N.

1992   *Early Mesopotamia: Society and Economy at the Dawn of History*. Routlege, London.

Price, J. E., and J. B. Griffin

1979   Snodgrass Site of the Powers Phase of Southeast Missouri. Anthropological Papers 66. Museum of Anthropology, University of Michigan, Ann Arbor.

Radin, P.

1948   *Winnebago Hero Cycles: A Study in Aboriginal Literature*. Waverly Press, Baltimore.

Raff, J., D. Cook, and F. Kaestle

2006   The Madonna and Child Trope: Mortuary Practices in Illinois. Paper presented at the Midwest Archaeological Conference, Urbana, IL, October 12–14.

Reilly, F. K., III

2004   People of Earth, People of Sky: Visualizing the Sacred in Native American Art of the Mississippian Period. In *Hero, Hawk, and Open Hand: American Indian Art of the Ancient Midwest and South*, edited by R. Townsend, pp. 125–138. Yale University Press, New Haven, CT.

2007   The Petaloid Motif: A Celestial Symbolic Locative in the Shell Art of Spiro. In *Ancient Objects and Sacred Realms*, edited by F. K. Reilly III and J. F. Garber, pp. 39–55. University of Texas Press, Austin.

Reilly, F. K., III, and J. F. Garber (editors)

2007   *Ancient Objects and Sacred Realms: Interpretations of Mississippian Iconography*. University of Texas Press, Austin.

Rose, J.

1999   Mortuary Data and Analysis. In *The Mound 72 Area: Dedicated and Sacred Space in Early Cahokia*, edited by M. L. Fowler, J. Rose, B. Vander Leest, and S. R. Ahler, pp. 63–84. Illinois State Museum Society, Springfield.

Salzer, R. J., and G. Rajnovich

2000   *The Gottschall Rock Shelter: An Archaeological Mystery*. Prairie Smoke Press, St. Paul, MN.

Schurr, M. R.

1989   The Relationship Between Mortuary Treatment and Diet at the Angel Site. Ph.D. dissertation, Indiana University, Bloomington.

1992   Isotopic and Mortuary Variability in a Middle Mississippian Population. *American Antiquity* 57(2):300–320.

Silliman, S. W.

2005   Culture Contact or Colonialism? Challenges in the Archaeology of Native North America. *American Antiquity* 70:55–74.

Soja, E. W.

1996   *Thirdspace*. Blackwell, Oxford.

Stein, G. J.

2002   From Passive Periphery to Active Agents: Emerging Perspectives in the Archaeology of Interregional Interaction. *American Anthropologist* 104:903–916.

2005a   *The Archaeology of Colonial Encounters*. School of American Research Press, Santa Fe, NM.

2005b   Introduction: The Comparative Archaeology of Colonial Encounters. In *The Archaeology of Colonial Encounters*, edited by G. J. Stein, pp. 3–32. School of American Research Press, Santa Fe, NM.

Swanton, J. R.

1979   *The Indians of the Southeastern United States*. Smithsonian Institution Press, Washington, D.C.

1998   Indian Tribes of the Lower Mississippi Valley and Adjacent Coast of the Gulf of Mexico. Dover, New York.

Thwaites, R. G.

1896–   *The Jesuit Relations and Allied Documents:*
1901   *Travels and Explorations of the Explorations of the Jesuit Missionaries in New France, 1610–1791: The Original French, Latin and Italian Texts, With English Translation*. Burrows Bros. Co., Cleveland.

Weltfish, G.

1977   *The Lost Universe: Pawnee Life and Culture*. University of Nebraska Press, Lincoln.

Willey, P., and T. E. Emerson

1993   The Osteology and Archaeology of the Crow Creek Massacre. *Plains Anthropologist* 38:227–269.

Williams, M.

1994   The Origins of the Macon Plateau Site. In *Ocmulgee Archaeology*, edited by D. J. Halley, pp. 130–137. University of Georgia Press, Athens.

Williams, M., and G. Shapiro

1990   Paired Towns. In *Lamar Archaeology: Mississippian Chiefdoms in the Deep South*, edited by M. Williams and G. Shapiro, pp. 163–174. University of Alabama Press, Tuscaloosa.

Williams, S.

1990   The Vacant Quarter and Other Late Events in the Lower Valley. In *Towns and Temples Along the Mississippi*, edited by D. H. Dye and

C. A. Cox, pp. 170–180. University of Alabama Press, Tuscaloosa.

Williams, S., and J. P. Brain
1985   *Excavations at the Lake George Site, Yazoo Country, Mississippi, 1958–1960.* Papers of the Peabody Museum, Harvard University, Boston.

Willoughby, C. C.
1938   A Mohawk (Caughnawaga) Halter for Leading Captives. *American Anthropologist* 40(1): 49–50.

Wilson, G. D., J. B. Marcoux, and B. Koldehoff
2006   Square Pegs in Round Holes: Organizational Variation Between Moundville and Cahokia.

In *Leadership and Polity in Mississippian Society,* edited by B. M. Butler and P. D. Welch, pp. 43–72. Center for Archaeological Investigation, Southern Illinois University, Carbondale.

Wittry, W. L., J. C. Arnold, C. O. Witty, and T. R. Pauketat
1994   *The Holdener Site: Late Woodland, Emergent Mississippian and Mississippian Occupations in the American Bottom Uplands.* American Bottom Archaeology FAI-270 Site Reports 26. University of Illinois Press, Urbana.

Wolf, E.
1984   Culture: Panacea or Problem? *American Antiquity* 49(2):393–400.

10

Social Death and Resurrection
in the Western Great Lakes

Peter N. Peregrine

Slavery is widely reported in the ethnographic and ethnohistoric literature of the western Great Lakes of North America, yet the status and role of slaves, indeed the very nature of slavery itself, seem unclear. For example, Bacqueville de la Potherie's 1722 history of New France repeatedly refers to "slaves" among the indigenous peoples of the western Great Lakes, but the term appears to be used interchangeably with "captive" (see, e.g., Blair 1911 2:37, 49, and footnotes; also Kinietz 1965:205, cf. 255), whereas Nicholas Perrot's somewhat earlier description of the same peoples makes no mention of slaves or slavery (see Figure 10.1).[1] Are these differences due to each author's particular knowledge and perspective? Or is slavery in the western Great Lakes of a sort that these Europeans did not easily recognize or understand? My answer to both questions is yes.

Slavery in the western Great Lakes region seems to have taken a form that appeared unusual, even unique, to the European explorers who first witnessed it, but is common in nonstate societies (as discussed by Cameron in the introduction to this volume and described in the chapters by DeBoer, Habicht-Mauche, and Bowser). In the western Great Lakes the taking of captives was an integral part of indigenous warfare in which captives-*cum*-slaves played a central role. Once captured, individuals no longer existed as "true" human beings: they were alienated from both their own group and that of their captors. Their future depended wholly on the choice their captors made to either sacrifice

or adopt them. It is interesting that the captive's time as a slave was very short; captives were either killed or adopted within a few days of their capture. Once killed, they no longer existed, and once adopted, they existed as new individuals, no longer slaves. Perhaps it was this brevity of slavery, and its utter transformation through death or adoption, that confused European observers.

Captives as Slaves

Orlando Patterson (1982) offers a useful discussion of slavery that sheds light on my perspective. Patterson (1982:1–2) argues that slavery relies upon physical and psychological control, but, more significantly, it is rooted in the fact that a slave is completely alienated from his or her kin group and culture. Slaves experience, in a very real sense, social death (Patterson 1982:5–7). They have no genealogical roots and have, as Patterson (1982:6) puts it, "ceased to belong independently to any formally recognized community." This is precisely the case for captives in the western Great Lakes.

The following passage provides a useful example of the physical and psychological control placed on captives, and how they became "socially dead." It describes the events that occurred upon the arrival of a war party with captives to an Illinois village in the late seventeenth century (also see Figure 10.2):

> During this time the prisoners are outside the cabin (for it is a maxim with them never to admit slaves into their cabins unless they have

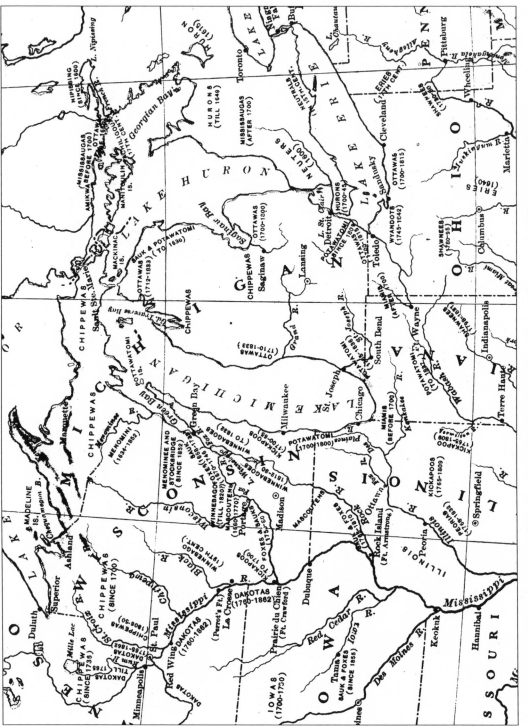

FIGURE 10.1. Map of the western Great Lakes region showing the locations of peoples and places mentioned in text (from Blair 1911).

FIGURE 10.2. Detail from Francesco Bressani's 1657 map, *Nova Francia Acurata Delineatio*, showing the torture of a captive. Original held by the National Archives of Canada.

been granted their lives). These sing their death song, holding in one hand a stick ten or twelve feet long, filled with feathers from all the kinds of birds that the warriors killed on the road. This is after having them sing at the doors of the cabins of all those who have most recently had relatives killed.

The old men and party leaders assemble and decide to whom these slaves shall be given. This settled, they lead one of them opposite the door of the cabin of the one to whom they give him, and bringing along some merchandise, they enter and say that they are delighted that the young men have brought back some men to replace, if they desire it, those whom the fate of war has taken away. For this offer great thanks are returned. A little later these people assemble and decide what they will do with the prisoner who has been given to them, and whether they wish to give him his life, a thing rarely done among the Illinois. When he is a man, they admit him and send for the principal men of the village who have brought them the prisoners. They thank these and give them some merchandise. When they want

him put to death, they bring him back to the cabin of the most considerable of those who have offered him, giving the captive to them, with a kettle and a hatchet which they have colored red to represent blood. From there he is taken to others, and according to their decision he dies or lives. When he is condemned to die, it is always by fire. I have never seen any other kind of torment used by this nation.

They plant a little tree in the earth, which they make him clasp; they tie his two wrists, and with torches of straw or firebrands they burn him, sometimes for six hours. When they find his strength far gone, they unfasten him and cut his thumbs off, after which they let him, if he wishes, run after those who are throwing stones at him, or who wish to burn him. They even give him sticks which he holds with great difficulty. If he tries to run after anybody, they push him and he falls on his face, at which they hoot. He sometimes furnishes a whole hour's diversion to these barbarians. Finally he succumbs under the strain of his torments, and sometimes drops down motionless. The rabble run to get firebrands, which they poke into the most sensitive parts of his body; they trail him over hot embers, which brings him back to life, at which they renew their hooting, as if they had performed some fine exploit. When they are tired of their sport, an old rascal cuts his flesh from the top of the nose to the chin and leaves it hanging, which gives him a horrible appearance. In this state they play a thousand tricks on him, and finally stone him or cut open his stomach. (Deliette 1934:383–386)

It is not difficult to see physical control here given that the captive "slaves" were tied, tortured, and killed by their captors. More interesting is the implicit psychological control. The captives knew that their future was almost certainly death, and they were forced to acknowledge it by singing their "death songs" and carrying staffs that physically recount their journey in captivity. While many seventeenth-century manuscripts note the stoicism of Indian captives facing death, I believe the psychological trauma they underwent must have been severe, perhaps debilitating (hence the appearance of stoicism). Clearly these captive "slaves" were both physically and psychologically controlled by their captors.

The captive "slaves" were also socially dead. Again, they carried staffs to physically identify their journey away from their homes and to the captor's village. More importantly, they were stripped of their humanity. They were treated as chattel, given as gifts, and, if rejected, killed. In torture they were cruelly shown their utter powerlessness, their lack of allies or friends of any kind, and were stripped of the very marks of their humanity: their thumbs and their face. Indeed, more than socially dead, they were made inhuman.

It is not unusual for captives to become slaves, as many of the chapters in this volume discuss. Indeed Patterson (1982:106–115) offers an entire section on captives. However, the situation Patterson describes is quite different from the one that appears to have obtained in the western Great Lakes and, indeed, in many parts of North America (see the chapters by DeBoer and Habicht-Mauche, this volume). He notes that captives typically find themselves subject to "immediate massacre, torture and sacrifice…;

ransom; prisoner exchange; temporary imprisonment; serfdom; impressments into the victor's army; colonization; and simple release" (Patterson 1982:106). While the first and second were common (if singular) experiences for captives in the western Great Lakes, there was another common experience not mentioned by Patterson here: adoption.

Patterson (1982:63) argues that while the ethnographic literature does suggest adoption of slaves, "It would be a great mistake…to confuse these fictive kin ties with the claims and obligations of real kinship." I disagree, at least in regard to the indigenous peoples of the western Great Lakes. Captives were not only adopted, but they took on the statuses, roles, and even names of deceased persons. They were, quite literally, resurrected from social death.

Social Death and Resurrection

As the example above makes clear, the rituals of captivity and torture practiced by the peoples of the western Great Lakes had the effect of socially (and, in many cases, physically) killing the captive. Their purpose was to objectify the captive, to destroy his or her humanity, to transform the captive into a being without possession of a personal history, a culture, or even a body they could control. (And this is why torture is so important: not to inflict pain, but to destroy the individual's tie to his or her body). Through rituals of captivity and torture, captives were dispossessed of their history, culture, and bodies, with ownership assumed by the captors, who could then either mold them into a new form or discard them.

One way captors molded captives into a new form was as a replacement for a deceased person. This was possible because the captive no longer existed as an individual and thus could be shaped, through ritual, into another person to replace one who had died. We can see this destruction and reconstruction of the individuality of captives in the following excerpt from Cadillac's memoir on the peoples living around Fort Michilimackinac in the 1690s:

If they capture any prisoners they pinion them so tightly that the bonds cut into their flesh. Then they travel night and day until they are out of danger and safe from their enemies.

When they are near their own village they send men ahead to give the news of all that has happened during the campaign, after which preparations are made for welcoming the warriors and haranguing them before they enter the place. At the same time arrangements are made for the entrance of the prisoners, which always begins with from three to four hundred blows with sticks, making them fall flat on their faces a hundred times before they enter the cabin of triumph which has been prepared for them.

As soon as they are within, they are told to dance and chant their death song. The chant is both proud and mournful; they recite what they have done during their lives, especially the number of persons they have killed, with their names and the names of their tribes, the place and how they did the deed. Sometimes they are made to sit and sometimes to get up and always to chant, especially when anyone of importance comes into the cabin to see them. But while they are singing in this way one man pulls out a finger-nail, another puts one of their fingers in the pipe he is smoking; at intervals a firebrand is held to their flesh, which is burned down to the bone; some cut off pieces of their flesh, which they cook and eat immediately, sucking their fingers afterward as if they had eaten something exquisite. Thus they amuse themselves for two or three days, after which the old men, the war chiefs, and the principal men of the village assemble to determine the life or death of these unfortunates.

Their death or life generally depends upon the women, for this reason. Some of them have lost a husband or sons in the war, and if seeing a handsome prisoner, or more often actuated merely by whim or caprice they ask for them to replace the dead, the council never refuses them. As soon as they are declared free they are unbound and the women or girls who have saved them lead them to their cabins. They wash their wounds, oil them, and make them look as well as they can; and a few days later a feast is given in the cabin at which the strangers are adopted as children of the house, as brothers, sons-in-law, or other relatives.

From this time they are treated kindly and no one insults them any more. But the most surprising thing is that they are the first to go to war against their own tribe, and kill or take prisoners their father, uncles, or other relatives indifferently, as if they were nothing at all to them, thinking more of the second life which has been given them than of the life they received from their fathers and mothers, whom they often see burned and torn in pieces because they were hard-hearted enough not to set them at liberty after capturing them; for, as I have already said, the life or death of the slaves depends either on the council or the women. The council gives some of them to the French commandant and others to various tribes, to confirm and ratify their alliances. As soon as they have handed them over they cease to have control of them, and their life or death depends on their new masters or the tribe to which they are presented. (Cadillac 1962:28–30)

The destruction and reconstruction of the captive's persona is clear here, a transformation that I refer to as the captive's social death and resurrection. The first paragraph describes the captive's flight from his or her home village, and the beginning of the "discipline" (see Foucault 1977) used to transform the captive into a malleable being.[2] In the second paragraph we read that the captive was forced to tell his or her personal history while being tortured. Here the captive's past and present were simultaneously destroyed. Their past deeds and present body were both the subject of torture, and both were physically consumed by their captors (either eaten or smoked). One can imagine that, after two or three days of this torture, the captive would surely be dehumanized and socially dead. He or she would no longer exist as an individual with a past and a present, but only as an object for the "amusement" of his or her captors.

The third and fourth paragraphs describe what I call the captive's social resurrection. If chosen for adoption, the torture ended, the captive's physical wounds were healed, and, in a few days, a ceremony of adoption was held. In this ceremony the captive's psychological wounds were healed, and he or she was given a new persona and a new history—that of a person in the captor's society who has died. The captive became, quite literally, the dead person resurrected. This was made possible by all that had gone before. Through torture, the captive was stripped of his or her humanity, and through adoption humanity was restored, but in a new form, a form once possessed by a person now dead. In a very real sense, the captive was resurrected into a new being.

The Purpose of Social Resurrection

What is the purpose of this social resurrection, and how can we explain its ubiquity among the peoples of the western Great Lakes? Even a cursory survey of the literature on slavery will show that most scholars view slavery's primary purpose as economic (e.g., Finley 1968). In this sense, social resurrection would replace lost labor. When individuals die, their value to society as labor to produce resources dies with them. Through adoption, the deceased person's labor could be replaced. It is a simple calculus, perhaps too simple for anthropologists who recognize the complexity of "stone age" economics (Sahlins 1972).

A more nuanced approach, such as that put forward by Igor Kopytoff and Suzanne Miers (1972:56), posits that slaves were "adopted" into a society for a range of purposes: "Acquired persons were valuable as economic, social, and political capital, as a type of wealth that could be easily converted from one use to another and that had the incomparable advantage of being also self-supporting and self-reproducing." Kopytoff and Miers see slavery primarily as a continuum of "rights-in-persons," and adoption itself as a continuum of more complete incorporation into the captor society, often taking place over several generations. From this perspective (and echoing Patterson's caution about slave adoption mentioned above), understanding slave-taking and use must focus on the particular local conditions within which it occurs (Kopytoff and Miers 1972:61–66). Within a kin-based society, however, Kopytoff and Miers (1972:29) suggest that "adopted" slaves were most valuable as producers of more kin-group members. Certainly this must have been the case among the peoples of the western Great Lakes. Labor would have always been valuable, and therefore acquiring labor through a captive

to replace labor lost through a death seems not only logical but necessary to sustain the society. Yet such a cold calculus does not seem to explain the many rituals and the profound impact social resurrection seems to have had on the individuals and societies involved. What else might have been going on?

In a careful examination of captive-taking and adoption among the Seneca, Anthony Wallace (1969) suggests that social resurrection eased the trauma of loss. As he puts it, "Death aroused the most violent reactions, [which] could only be forestalled by replacing the lost object with an adopted substitute" (Wallace 1969:76–77). Indeed Wallace (1969:102) suggests that the primary aim of warfare between the Seneca and neighbors in the Ohio Basin and Great Lakes region was to obtain prisoners to replace the dead. There appear to be two primary purposes here. First, as Wallace argues, is a psychological one: to ease the pain of loss. And Wallace provides several excellent examples described by the Seneca in their own words (e.g., Wallace 1969:31–32).

There also seems to have been a religious basis to captive adoption. Robert Hall (1997) has argued that captive adoption is part of a larger religious complex involving ceremonies of "soul release." For example, Hall (1997:42–43) describes a series of rituals among the Fox and Sauk in which the soul of a dead person is released from its bonds with other kin through the substitution of another soul in its place: the soul of a captive.

Perhaps a better way of viewing captive adoption is through the lens of alliance theory, by which I mean both the rather narrow perspective of Lévi-Strauss (e.g. 1969), where the incest prohibition is seen to force individuals to marry outside their immediate kin group and thereby form alliances with other kin groups, and also the broader application of alliance theory in structural anthropology as a whole (e.g., Hage and Harary 1984). The broader application of alliance theory sees society as a web of relationships based on kinship, gift-giving (e.g., Mauss 1954), association memberships, and the like. Each individual has a key role within this web, as they are essentially nodes that link other members of the society to one another. Death takes away that individual's node and thus severs links, perhaps unique or otherwise important ones.

From the perspective of alliance theory, death is a key problem faced by all human societies, and societies have developed a wide range of mechanisms to deal with it. In the Great Lakes region, for example, the widespread practice of holding "feasts of the dead" in which the belongings of deceased individuals are given as gifts to relatives, friends, and allies of the deceased is seen as one mechanism through which social links severed by death were reestablished (e.g., Trigger 1976). Hall (1997) describes a wide range of similar mourning rituals that served a similar purpose among peoples of the Mississippi Valley. I suggest that the adoption of captives into the roles of deceased persons—social resurrection—also served to reestablish a social node taken away by death.

What, then, was the purpose of social resurrection? Its basic purpose appears have been to maintain society in a time of crisis caused by death. Captive-taking, torture, and resurrection eased psychological traumas and maintained essential labor but, more importantly, reestablished bonds that were severed through death. I believe the case studies in this volume support my assertion, and one of the overall themes I see in the volume's chapters is that captive-taking occurs most frequently where there is a labor bottleneck, as in seasonal needs for fish processing on the Northwest Coast discussed by Ames, or where there has been a dramatic population decline or movement, as discussed by several authors here, particularly Bowser. Both conditions obtained in the western Great Lakes. Captive-taking also appears to have been common where there was political fragmentation or competition, and where political authority was rooted in the control of people rather than land. This is discussed in some detail by Robertshaw and Junker. Again, these conditions also obtained in the western Great Lakes.

In 1649 the Iroquois Confederacy, led by the Seneca, attacked and effectively annihilated the Huron, their primary economic rivals in the fur trade. The destruction of the Huron created a crisis in the western Great Lakes. Refugee Hurons and Algonquians (e.g., Ottawa and Potawatomi) from western Ontario and Michigan fled to the lee side of Lake Michigan, into what is today Michigan's Upper Peninsula and the state of Wisconsin, to escape Iroquois raiding parties. Here polities were fragmented, and labor, not land, was the key to political power. Captives provided an influx of valuable labor that was used not only for agriculture and hunting, but also for procuring valuable animal furs and for participating in long-distance trade expeditions. Just as Europeans quickly realized that neither slavery nor wage labor was well suited to the capture and trade of fur-bearing animals (see, e.g., Kardulias 1990), so the peoples of the western Great Lakes may have realized that slavery would not provide an effective labor force for the fur trade.

Captives also offered the possibility, through adoption, of establishing or reestablishing bonds of alliance between kin groups disrupted by death and flight. In this context the social death and resurrection of captives make perfect sense, as does the apparent reciprocal nature of captive-taking. While I cannot say from where the captives were being obtained, it seems clear that they were not from distant societies, but rather places within a few days' walk of captors' villages. The villages from which captives were taken likely took captives in return, in a reciprocal exchange of violence and people.[3] This seems similar to what Habicht-Mauche describes as taking place between Pueblos and Plains peoples in the Southwest. And, as she describes, it seems that bonds of alliance, forged through captives, are one purpose behind the violence.

Such reciprocal violence must surely change the societies involved in it, and this seems to have been the case in the western Great Lakes. Already disrupted at the time of their first ethnographic description, the peoples of the western Great Lakes continued to fragment, both socially and politically. By the late 1600s, for example, villages in the Fox River valley of Wisconsin are described as being multilingual and multiethnic (e.g., Thwaites 1896–1901, 55:199–201). They were palisaded, and residents are described as living in perpetual fear of attack. Despite the efforts of eighteenth- and nineteenth-century leaders such as Tecumseh and Black Hawk, stabilization of the social fabric and reunification of indigenous polities never occurred. Captive-taking appears to have developed into full-scale slave trading by the early 1800s (see, for example, Blair 1911, 2: 197), and reciprocal raiding into endemic warfare

(Blair 1911, 2:184). By the 1830s, the peoples of the western Great Lakes effectively had become dependents of the U.S. government. In this case, social death and resurrection did not provide a solution to social disruption, but seem only to have perpetuated it.

The Archaeology of
Social Death and Resurrection

One of the key questions addressed by this volume is how we might identify and do research on slavery through the archaeological record. As can be seen from the excerpts provided above, the ethnohistoric record provides an imperfect picture of social death and resurrection in the western Great Lakes. Might the archaeological record improve this picture? Might it allow us to trace the origins and evolution of these interesting social practices? Sadly, I believe the answer to both questions is no.

A primary quandary concerns what material evidence of social death and resurrection we might expect to find. Social death occurs in the context of capture and torture. Evidence for these practices might be present in the archaeological record, and Alt provides some striking examples from Mississippian sites in her contribution to this volume. Another example is the thirteenth-century site of Aztalan, located west of Milwaukee, Wisconsin, which has midden deposits containing a large number of fragmented human remains. These have been interpreted as the material residue of cannibalistic feasts (Barrett 1933). One might interpret this to be evidence for the cannibalistic practices associated with the captive torture and sacrifice described in the ethnohistoric literature (e.g., Goldstein and Freeman 1997:239–240). Nevertheless, scholars are divided on the interpretation of cannibalism at Aztalan, and even whether the fragmentary remains represent secondary burial treatment rather than cannibalism. And one might reasonably question whether an interpretation based on ethnographic descriptions of cultures three hundred years removed from the archaeological deposits are appropriate in the absence of strong linking data. Here such data are lacking, as they are for Cahokia and other Middle Mississippian sites.

Physical markers of captive status are unlikely.

Captives in the western Great Lakes remained so only briefly, and the ethnographic literature provides no mention of archaeologically recoverable markers of captivity. DeBoer suggests in his contribution to this volume that restraints or special ropes for binding and transporting captives might be recoverable, but despite the ethnographic descriptions and depictions of such objects, I know of none recovered from the archaeological record. Resurrection would surely be invisible archaeologically because the captive who replaced a deceased member of the society would have taken on his or her status, role, and material possessions. The captive and the deceased would appear identical archaeologically. However, the captive and the deceased would not be identical physically, and this is one area that might provide archaeological evidence of social death and resurrection.

Captives resurrected into a role in a foreign society may appear as biological isolates within that society. This, of course, would depend on the degree of interaction, especially intermarriage, between the captive and captor's societies. However, a captive would likely display at least some physical markers of his or her origin, even where intermarriage is common. One set of markers might be stable isotopes, particularly if captives were born in communities where a very different diet was consumed. In the western Great Lakes this might occur between groups whose diets included large amounts of fish or shellfish, and those whose diets included large amounts of maize. It is interesting that Alt (this volume) reports on these differences among those sacrificed in Mound 72 at Cahokia and other unusual burials at Mississippian sites (also see Price et al. 2007 for similar findings at Aztalan). The other set of markers might be genetic, identifiable both as unique physical traits and discrete variations in the individual's nuclear or mitochondrial DNA. Martin's chapter in this volume shows the potential value of this approach. Unfortunately, few stable isotope or DNA studies have been performed on skeletal collections from the western Great Lakes (e.g., Thurston Myster and O'Connell 1997:246–276), and given the current sociopolitical climate in which indigenous groups predominantly oppose such studies, they are unlikely to occur in the near future.

Conclusions

It seems clear from ethnohistoric documents that slavery was ubiquitous among the indigenous peoples of the western Great Lakes, but it seems equally clear that archaeological evidence for slavery is scant. The relative paucity of archaeological evidence is, in part, due to the form slavery took in the prehistoric and early historic western Great Lakes, a form which included the adoption of slaves into the captor's society. Adoption, which I have here called social resurrection, transformed captives into full members of the captor's society, thus making captives indistinguishable from other members of the society, at least in terms of the material remains they might contribute to the archaeological record. We have an interesting irony here. Slavery was ubiquitous in the western Great Lakes, but the form it takes makes it almost impossible to recognize archaeologically.

Although we may not be able to easily recognize social death and resurrection in the archaeological record, its very ubiquity serves as a valuable lesson for us as archaeologists. Because kin relations structured the indigenous societies of the western Great Lakes, death caused significant disruptions to the social fabric. Resurrection through a substitute not only allowed the social fabric to be repaired but provided the additional benefits of easing both the labor shortage and psychological trauma that death caused. Slavery is certainly rooted in power and power relations, but I think it is important to note that as archaeologists trying to understand slavery in non-state societies, we ignore kinship at our peril. Slavery among the peoples of the western Great Lakes was as much about kinship and social relations as it was about economics and power relations. Social death and resurrection in eastern North America took place in the context of kin relations, and we must understand them in that context if we hope to understand them at all.

Acknowledgments

I wish to thank Cathy Cameron for inviting me to the Snowbird conference on slavery, from which this chapter and volume derived, and for her unwavering support and encouragement. Her comments have been insightful and valuable, and this is a much better chapter because of her efforts. I also wish to thank the other participants at the conference, as well as Jim Skibo, Dave Anderson, and Alf Hornborg, for their suggestions and efforts in support of this volume. Thanks to you all.

Notes

1. The peoples of the western Great Lakes include Algonquian-speaking groups such as the Fox/Sauk, Illinois, Kickapoo, Menominee, Miami, Ojibwa (Chippewa), Ottawa, and Potawatomi; the Siouan-speaking Ho-chunk (Winnebago); and the Iroquoian-speaking Huron. I refer to these peoples in generic terms as "peoples of the western Great Lakes" throughout much of the chapter. This is because in the early contact period these peoples lived in fluid and often multiethnic communities. In addition, descriptions of Native life given by early European explorers are often either generic or imprecise about the particular group or groups involved. Thus, one often cannot tell for sure which particular group is being described. Where an attribution seems clear, I include it in the text.

2. It is interesting to note that the capture and torture of both men and women are described in the ethnographic literature (e.g., Blair 1911, 3:197; Kinietz 1965:85), and it appears that both men and women were adopted. Whether either sex was adopted or killed with greater frequency than the other is impossible to gauge from the existing narratives. Children are also sometimes mentioned as captives, but I have found no descriptions of their torture or killing. Indeed Gabriel Sagard, who lived among the Huron in 1623–1624, notes that children "they rarely kill, but save them and keep them for themselves, or make presents of them to others who have previously lost some of theirs in war and think as much of the substitutes as if they were their own children" (Kinietz 1965: 85).

3. It should be noted that this reciprocal exchange only obtained among the peoples of the western Great Lakes. Elsewhere, for example in areas within range of Iroquoian raiders, the exchange was purely one-sided, with the Iroquois taking far more captives than the Erie, Huron, or Potawatomi peoples within their reach. Thus the image of captive-taking in the western Great Lakes is one generated from within what might be called

a "periphery" of the larger Iroquoian or colonial American world.

References Cited

Barrett, Samuel A.
1933   *Ancient Aztalan*. Bulletin 13 of the Milwaukee Public Museum.

Blair, Emma Helen (editor)
1911   *The Indian Tribes of the Upper Mississippi Valley and Region of the Great Lakes*. 2 vols. Arthur H. Clark, Cleveland.

Cadillac, Sieur Antoine de Lamothe
1962   The Memoir of Lamothe Cadillac (ca. 1697). In *The Western Country in the Seventeenth Century*, edited by Milo Milton Quaife, pp. 3–83. Citadel, New York.

Deliette, Sieur Pierre
1934   De Gannes Memoir (Memoir Concerning the Illinois Country, ca. 1702)., In *The French Foundations, 1680–1693,* pp. 302-395, edited and translated by Theodore Pease and Raymond Werner. Collections of the Illinois State Historical Library (Springfield), vol. 23.

Finley, Moses I.
1968   Slavery. *International Encyclopedia of the Social Sciences*, vol. 14, pp. 307–313. Macmillan, New York.

Foucault, Michel
1977   *Discipline and Punish: The Birth of the Prison.* Pantheon, New York.

Goldstein, Lynne, and Joan Freeman
1997   Aztalan: Middle Mississippian Village. *The Wisconsin Archaeologist* 78:223–249.

Hage, Per, and Frank Harary
1984   *Structural Models in Anthropology.* Cambridge University Press, Cambridge.

Hall, Robert L.
1997   *An Archaeology of the Soul.* University of Illinois Press, Urbana.

Kardulias, P. Nick
1990   Fur Production as a Specialized Activity in a World System: Indians in the North American Fur Trade. *American Indian Culture and Research Journal* 14(1):25–60.

Kinietz, Vernon (editor)
1965   *The Indians of the Western Great Lakes*. University of Michigan, Ann Arbor.

Kopytoff, Igor, and Suzanne Miers
1972   Introduction: African "Slavery" as an Institution of Marginalization. In *Slavery in Africa*, edited by S. Miers and I. Kopytoff, pp. 3–81. University of Wisconsin Press, Madison.

Lévi-Strauss, Claude
1969   *The Elementary Structures of Kinship*. Beacon, Boston.

Mauss, Marcel
1954   *The Gift*. Free Press, Glencoe, IL.

Muller, Jon
1997   *Mississippian Political Economy*. Plenum, New York.

Patterson, Orlando
1982   *Slavery and Social Death*. Harvard University Press, Cambridge, MA.

Price, T. Douglas, James H. Burton, and James B. Stoltman
2007   Place of Origin of Prehistoric Inhabitants of Aztalan, Jefferson Co., Wisconsin. *American Antiquity* 72(3):524–538.

Sahlins, Marshall
1972   *Stone Age Economics*. Aldine, New York.

Starna, William, and Ralph Watkins
1991   Northern Iroquoian Slavery. *Ethnohistory* 38(1):34–57.

Thurston Myster, Susan, and Barbara O'Connell
1997   Bioarchaeology of Iowa, Wisconsin, and Minnesota. In *Archaeology and Bioarchaeology of the Northern Woodlands*, edited by Elizabeth Benchley et al., pp. 215–302. Arkansas Archaeological Survey Research Series 52.

Thwaites, Reuben G. (editor)
1896–   *Jesuit Relations and Allied Documents*. Bur-
1901   rows Brothers, Cleveland.

Trigger, Bruce G.
1976   *The Children of Aataentsic: A History of the Huron People to 1660*. McGill-Queens University Press, Montreal.

Wallace, Anthony F. C.
1969   *The Death and Rebirth of the Seneca*. Vintage, New York.

11

Wrenched Bodies

Warren R. DeBoer

In his 1961 opus, *Indians of North America*, Harold Driver downplayed the importance of wife-capture:

> The frequency and importance of marriage by capture or abduction of the bride was vastly exaggerated by 19th century anthropologists. In aboriginal North America, the majority of tribes sometimes captured women in warfare and kept them as wives. On the whole, however, the percentage of wives acquired in this fashion was small and had little effect on customary marriage practices. (Driver 1961:269)

McLennan's classic, *Primitive Marriage* (1865), in which marriage by capture was given a pivotal role in connubial history, had obviously lost favor and would seem to have joined other titillating outcasts such as cannibalism in the dustbin of Victorian psychosexual fantasies. Just a few years later, however, Driver appeared less certain about his earlier assessment and intimated a situation more in line with the South American results presented by Brenda Bowser in this volume.

> Ten years ago, I started a map showing where women taken captive in war were raised in status to wife. Although I never completed the map, I did not find a single negative instance in more than 100 ethnic units. Intertribal and interlanguage marriages were common and probably universal. (Driver 1966:144)

A practice that is common yet ineffectual is a curious one that warrants a look. I will approach the matter by looking over a wide area, centered on the Americas, rather than focusing on a singular case, even one claimed to be diagnostic or illustrative.

I have not tried to locate Driver's unfinished map, but his student, Joseph Jorgensen, has given us a survey of capture among, as indicated in his subtitle, *172 Western American Indian Tribes* (Jorgensen 1980). I realize that wide-ranging comparisons based on cultures reduced to assemblages of traits are no longer welcome in many anthropological circles, but Jorgensen marshals such an impressive array of data that the result is likely to detect real patterns. Two of these patterns and one noteworthy nonpattern are isolated in Table 11.1. First note that raiding for women occurred in 62 percent of the sampled "ethnic units." Most groups raiding for women, however, did not take slaves. That is, Jorgensen distinguished raiding for women from raiding for slaves and found the former to have been the more common practice. Secondly, the middle register of Table 11.1 shows that raiding for women increased with the extent of polygyny. This correlation is not surprising, but its basis is left unspecified. It could indicate that the capture of women enabled polygyny or, alternatively, that polygyny and its attendant hoarding of local women forced some men to seek wives elsewhere. The bottom register of Table 11.1 addresses whether polygyny was fueled by the need to harness female labor in hide preparation, a thesis recently explored in Frink 2005. This relationship is neither supported nor disconfirmed by Jorgensen's data, suggesting that the workings

TABLE 11.1. Correlations among Raiding, Polygyny, and Hide Processing in Western North America

	Raid for Slaves	Don't Raid for Slaves	
Raid for Women	42	59	101 .62
Don't Raid for Women	3	58	61 .38
	45 .28	117 .72	162

p < .01

	<10% Polygynous	11–25% Polygynous	26–50% Polygynous
Raid for Women	64	33	4
Don't Raid for Women	58	11	2

p < .01

	Only Women Process Hides	Men and Women Process Hides
Raid for Women	28	73
Don't Raid for Women	15	56

p < .21

Note: Probabilities based on Fisher's Exact Test.
Source: Jorgensen 1980: *top*, from Maps 187 and 188; *middle*, from Map 126; *bottom*, from Map 99.

of bison-based economies of the Great Plains, where this thesis was adumbrated (Jablow 1950: 20–21), may not apply west of the Rockies.

Although Jorgensen, unlike Driver, does find "negative instances" in which women were not raided for, the practice of abducting foreign or enemy women was evidently common and widespread, as Driver surmised. This practice is also presumably ancient and cannot be facilely blamed on the "people with history." Speculating rashly, one might even argue that the practice was a primordial one. On the basis of global comparisons of genetic data, Cavalli-Sforza suggests that more than a preference for patrilocality is needed to account for the distribution of Y chromosome mutations that can only be described as provincial in comparison to those of female-transmitted mtDNA. As he puts it, in words that might be lifted from McLennan, "in times past, when women were scarce it was usual to kidnap them from other groups" (Cavalli-Sforza 2000: 82).

Whatever its deep history, the shunting of female bodies across landscapes has many implications that remain under-addressed. Given that "people travel well," how is cultural integrity maintained, given permeable boundaries through which "the most potent flows must have been the movement of peoples, who embody energy, power, matter, genes, and cultural information" (Kowalewski 1995:151)? Can gender-linked components of this circulation be detected? Such detection will require much finer-grained distinctions than customarily made in material culture inventories. For example, gross distinctions such as hollow versus slab mortars or crutched versus straight-ended digging sticks will not do. Do such fleshy flows raze fences or merely raise them higher? Do boundaries mark or create interfaces? What happens to traditions in societies where every tenth mother is a foreigner? With respect to enculturation, are imported bodies, at best, imperfect copies or, in contrast, the best copycats? It would seem that archaeology, with its large case file on changing material culture over time, ought to play a central role in this interrogation.

This has not been the case. No diagnostic traces exist for those thousands of captives who parented new generations of captors, who processed the maize or manioc needed for daily meals or competitive feasts, who cleaned fish, processed hides, and gathered firewood, who served as concubines or catamites and who, on a moment's whim, could be beaten like dogs, who sang defiant death songs at the stake, and who, unless used as burial retainers, departed with hardly a trace. The following discussion explores ways in which captives may gain some overdue recognition. It begins by considering captivity in terms of the formal and spatial dimensions basic to all archaeological inference.

Bodies from the Borderlands

Proximity exerts a strong influence on the likelihood of interaction of any kind, including marriage (Harrison and Boyd 1972; Rogerson et al.

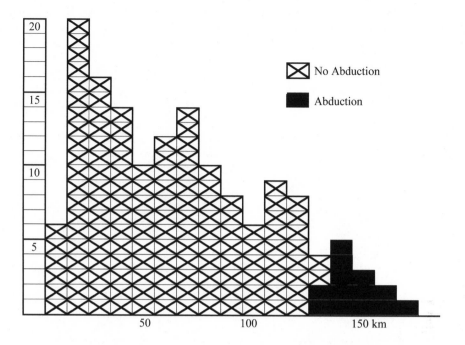

FIGURE 11.1. Hypothetical distribution of distances at which wives were obtained.

1993). Based on the Tukanoan marriage data given by Jackson (1976), Figure 11.1 plots this ordinary and somewhat unromantic state of affairs. Note the "exogamous zone" hugging the origin. Beyond this, marriage frequency declines with distance, following a typical saw-toothed profile that reflects the uneven distributions of Tukanoan as well as other real world populations. The figure also indicates that sites of wife-abduction, ritualized or otherwise, are likely to occur at the borders of the area from which spouses are recruited. From the standpoint of potential captives, such distancing, along with fortified or concealed settlements, can be seen as protective measures. From the perspective of raiders, the spatial logic differs by emphasizing:

> the desirability of getting captives as far away from their homes as possible; first, because if this were not effected, the captive's relatives would constantly attempt (her) recapture, and second, the nearness to home would tend to keep the captive restless and eager to run away or even to attempt the lives of her master. (MacLeod 1928:645)

Although addressing captives in general, MacLeod's diagnosis presumably encompasses captive wives. There is confirming evidence.

The cases compiled in Table 11.2 indeed tend to follow the plot charted in Figure 11.1. A dozen of the over one hundred marriages recorded by Julian Steward (1970) and Isabel Kelly (1964) are attributed to wife-abduction, although it is likely that some of these were of the ritualized kind described by Little (1881:34–35). Whether ritualized or not, they tend to fall, as expected, at the margins of the overall marriage catchment. Other ethnographic cases have abduction frequencies ranging from a low 1 percent of all marriages (central Australia) to a much higher 17 percent for the Telefolmin of New Guinea. The high value given for the Makuna of the Colombian Amazon is matched by the Yanomami (Early and Peters 2000: Table 19.10) and the cognate Yanamamö (Chagnon 1992:106–107), while among the Mayoruna of the Peru-Brazil borderlands, nearly half of all marriages included a captive spouse (Fields and Merrifield 1980:3). With exceptions (e.g., the Telefolmin), abductions are, as expected, phenomena of the perimeter.

TABLE 11.2. Sources of Wives, Number of Marriages, and Number and Percentage of Those Marriages Resulting from Abductions

	Same Settlement	Local Group	Adjacent Group	Distant Group	Totals
Shoshoneans (Great Basin)	M = 14	M = 62	M = 55	M = 9	M = 140
	A = 0	A = 2 (3%)	A = 4 (7%)	A = 6 (67%)	A = 12 (8%)
Makuna (Colombian Amazon)	M = 0	M = 24	M = 11	M = 6	M = 41
		A = 0	A = 1 (9%)	A = 5 (83%)	A = 6 (15%)
Telefolmin (New Guinea)	M = 30	M = 9	M = 11	M = 8	M = 58
	A = 2 (7%)	A = 1 (11%)	A = 5 (45%)	A = 2 (25%)	A = 10 (17%)
Central Australia	M = 346	M = 50	M = 4	M = 3	M = 403
	A = 0	A = 1 (2%)	A = 1 (25%)	A = 2 (67%)	A = 4 (1%)
Number of Marriages	390	145	81	26	642
Number of Abductions	2	4	11	15	32
Percentage of Marriages Resulting from Abductions	1%	3%	14%	58%	5%

Note: M = marriage; A = abduction.
Sources: For the Shoshoneans, Steward 1970; for the Makuna, Århem 1981; for the Telefolmin, Craig 1969; and for central Australia, Tindale 1953.

Sites of Capture

At what distance are potential captives sought? What distance works effectively to discourage escape and to guarantee severance from the familiar world of one's native land? The kilometer scale attached to the Tukanoan case in Figure 11.1 is of little help in this regard as the abductions are largely hypothetical. The Shoshonean plot in Figure 11.1 is scaled according to valley source, but it is difficult to estimate actual distances from this information. Steward, however, did mention one woman who fled back to her home across a hundred kilometers of basin and range (Steward 1970:160). For the Tukanoans, including the Makuna listed in Table 11.2, Jackson (1976) and Arhem (1981) intimate that captive wives come from 30 km to more than 80 km away, but no specific examples are given.

The distances separating captor and captive presumably vary according to the character of the terrain, the political landscape, and the means of transport. In order to examine these matters, I have cobbled together three sets of observations. The first consists of a composite array of Native North American cases drawn from the Jesuit Relations as well as a rather undirected library search (Appendix 11.1). As sufficiently interesting to be written about, these cases are probably tilted toward the dramatic rather than the hum-

drum. Despite bias, they nonetheless yield distance estimates that are highly patterned. The upper graph in Figure 11.2 indicates a mode at 200 to 300 km and a range that reaches 1,200 km. Also noteworthy is that the "strike zone" of raids based on canoe and foot travel surpasses that of equestrians. Unlike American horses, which went extinct in the terminal Pleistocene, canoes are fully aboriginal in North America, as are networks of well-worn trails and portages.

The data presented in Appendix 11.2 and graphed at the bottom of Figure 11.2 are a bit more specific in that they chronicle captive-seeking raids carried out in the Ucayali and Urubamba basins of the Peruvian Amazon. Over three centuries, the Conibo, inhabitants of the Ucayali mainstream, launched large, well-armed flotillas seeking *indios bravos*, or wild Indians, to pillage and enslave (DeBoer 1986). From the Conibo point of view, these raids were civilizing missions that saved captives from a life of savagery. As a counter-measure, the Remo, Amahuaca, Machiguenga, and other "savages" victimized by these raids retreated to deep forest away from navigable streams, moved often to avoid becoming fixed targets, and laid booby traps on trails leading to their settlements (Marcoy 2001, 2:128; Biedma 1989:185). Another stratagem was bribery or, perhaps more aptly, tribute. Manioc and

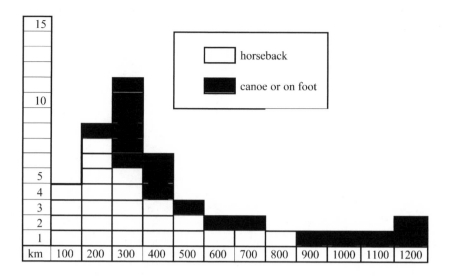

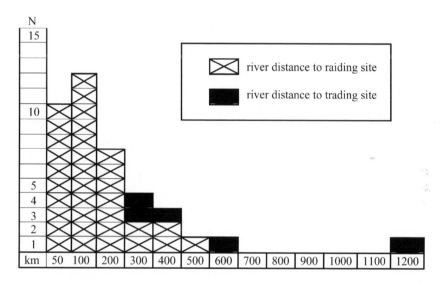

FIGURE 11.2. Distances to sites of capture for cases itemized in Appendix 11.1 (*top*) and Appendix 11.2 (*bottom*).

banana gardens were planted near the mouths of tributaries or on islands on main rivers. The understanding was that passing marauders could take the produce they wanted while sparing the gardeners (Zarzar and Román 1983:65; Camino 1977). The graph of distances between the home turfs of raider and raided again displays a sink near the origin, a modal raiding distance at about 75 km, followed by a lengthy falloff to 500 km. Markets or missions, where captives could be exchanged for other goods, tended to occur at greater distances (Figure 11.2, bottom).

The third data set is taken directly from Donald's 1997 survey of Northwest Coast slavery, amended by the addition of intergroup distances (typically along coasts or up rivers) as estimated from Donald's tables and maps. Although "slaves were supposed to come from some distance away so that they could not escape and return home" (Collins 1974:127), Donald stresses that

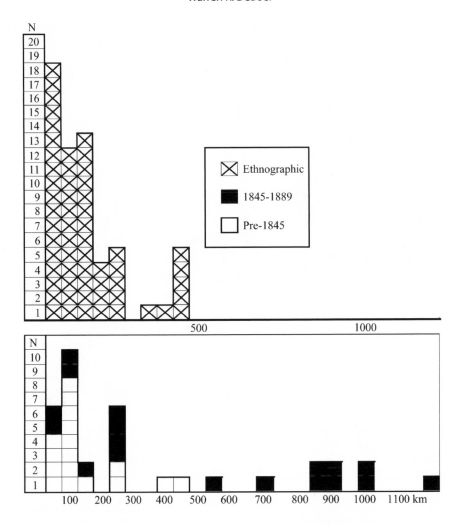

FIGURE 11.3. One-way distances covered in slave-taking raids on the Northwest Coast. Upper graph based on ethnographic testimony; lower graph based on earlier historic accounts (Donald 1997).

Northwest Coast groups primarily fought, married, and traded with their neighbors (Donald 1997:119). If so, one would expect a more localized pattern of raiding than found in the two preceding cases. Such hostile neighborliness is indeed indicated in Figure 11.3, particularly the top graph, which plots ethnographic accounts of who raided whom. The pre-1845 reports and those dating to the period 1845–1889, although represented by smaller samples, pertain to specific captive-taking events and thus might be more reliable than ethnographic accounts of "how it used to be." At any rate, the pre-ethnographic cases follow the familiar pattern of a depressed raid frequency near the origin followed by a modal peak at about 75 km. Yet another factor that needs to be taken into account is that many of the truly long-distance raids of the 1845–1889 period, carried out in war canoes 40 ft in length, may have been atypical in that they were embedded within trading voyages to Fort Victoria (Donald 1997:108).

These imperfect materials gleaned from several regions of the Americas suggest that captives, including abducted wives, commonly came from 50 km away or more, sometimes much more. Furthermore, if abduction, like other forms of wife acquisition, were reciprocated, then even a low frequency of such occurrences (a few percent) would have the effect of producing a largely seamless terrain across which human bodies flowed, disseminating and mixing both genetic and cultural chunks of information.

Kill or Let Live

Captives were chosen. To risk a sweeping statement, women and children were the chosen ones. Certainly the cases assembled in the appendices support this claim, and it is easy to marshal more evidence. Thus Goody (1980:20–21) reminds us that the earliest sign for "slave" in proto-literate tablets of the Near East can be read "slave girl," or better, "foreign woman." Trexler, following Lerner's thesis on the origins of patriarchy, boldly asserts that "the institution of slavery originated in the conquest of women" (Trexler 1995:13). Manumissions granted at the Temple of Delphi favored women over men two to one (Hopkins 1978: Table I.2). Among the ancient Germans, women and children were captured, while men were butchered or sold to the Romans (Thompson 1960:195). As might be expected from stereotypes, Viking policy was "to take the women prisoners and make the men who were not killed serfs" (Brøndsted 1965:269). In Mohave raids, Kroeber (1967:752) states that a main objective was the capture of girls or young women. A census of the Carolina colonies taken in 1706 tilted toward a predominance of females among Indian slaves, while the Black slave population, selected for hard field labor, displayed the 5:3 sex ratio generally postulated for the Atlantic slave trade (Craton 1974:197).

The reasons for targeting women were varied. Local shortages resulting from demographic fluctuations or polygyny on the part of prominent or wealthy senior men could have been prompters (but see Ayres 1974). In turn, multiple wives, captive or not, lent prestige and progeny to the husband, increased household productivity, or, alternatively, maintained productivity while reducing demands on senior wives. Among Shoshoneans, genuine (as opposed to ritual) abduction was apparently a last resort, but nonetheless was socially favored over a secret affair with a married woman (Steward 1970:164, 196). The Makuna regarded wife-capture as a perfectly

legitimate practice, one fully in accord with the cultural stereotype that affinal relations were inherently hostile and remote. Furthermore, abduction was one of the only ways for a Makuna man lacking an exchangeable sister to obtain a wife (Arhem 1981:55). Because Guaycuruan women were fiercely anti-natalist and considered the raising of children to be a tedious task beneath their standing, captive women played a critical role in reproducing the Guaycuruan population (Hemming 1978:33). Wife-capture also circumvented bride-price or bride-service (Socolow 1992:87; cf. Ayres 1974).

With respect to the transport costs involved in captive-taking, Keeley gives another common assessment of why women and children were preferred: "the most likely reason is that enemy warriors were unlikely to accept captivity without attempting violent escapes or revenge; thus holding them captive required levels of vigilance and upkeep that most tribal societies were unable or unprepared to provide" (Keeley 1996:84). One could add the comment of a Hasinai raider that men, being "swifter of foot," were simply more difficult to catch (Griffith 1954:129). Obviously, raiding parties preferred captives who could move themselves, if possible as load-bearers or canoe paddlers, and sought to avoid infirm, unruly, or otherwise uncooperative captives. Among the Iroquois, "old people and the children who would not have been able to follow their captors" were either killed on the spot or dispatched later on the trail (Starna and Watkins 1991:39–40). Adult men were transported in the portable form of scalps. If living and intact bodies were needed for sacrifice, male victims drawn from local regions were preferred (Jesuit Relations [hereafter JR] 60:645). Although young women and children were more likely to be spared, survival was not guaranteed. In an 1868 raid into Texas, for example, a Comanche war party jettisoned several captives on the trail, including a Mrs. Johnson who was scalped and left for dead, her eighteen-year-old sister who was raped and killed, and her baby, who had its brains bashed out for crying (Wilbarger 1991 [1889]:633–636). Among the seventeenth-century Ottawa, a captured woman who refused to march had her head bashed in or was burned on the spot (Kinietz 1965:199). If one accepts Lamberville's lurid account of 1682, an Iroquois

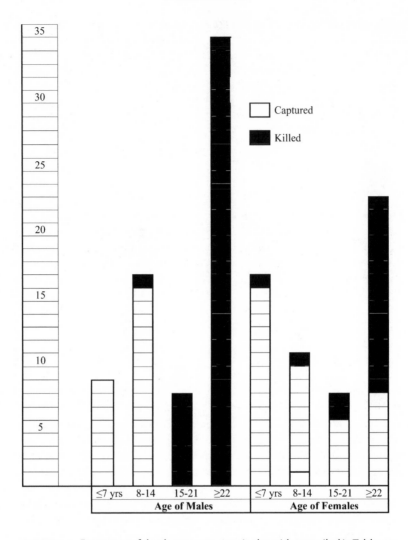

FIGURE 11.4. Frequency of death versus capture in the raids compiled in Table 11.3.

force, en route back to their own country, tied troublesome captives, "men and women, to the stakes, and, as fast as their flesh became roasted, cut it off and devoured it" (JR 62:11). Gang rape is also reported (Noyes 1993:70; cf. Chagnon et al. 1970:345–346).

More-systematic information on the selection of captives can be gleaned from Heard (1973) and Wilbarger (1889) for North America and from Socolow (1992) for South America. As summarized in Table 11.3, this evidence indicates that, as expected, adult captives tended to be females, whereas male and female children were about equally represented. Among Plains equestrians,

young boys became horse-tenders (Brooks 2002: 179) and, if adopted, came to bolster the fighting force of their captors (John 1975:341). Boys also served as particularly appropriate gifts in diplomatic exchanges (Wade 2003:229) and, as prized items, were shunted through trade networks spanning the Americas (Rushforth 2003; also Appendix 11.1, Cases 14 and 31). Adult males, in contrast, were apparently unattractive captives. As shown in Table 11.3, nearly three times as many women were present in above-age-fifteen cohorts. Among Araucanians of the Argentinean frontier, the capture of foreign women is said to have been accompanied by "male-centered

TABLE 11.3. Ages and Fates of Captives in the Argentinean and Texas Frontiers and North America

	Age at Capture—Argentinean Frontier						
	<6	10–19	20–29	30–39	40–49	50+	Total
Male	69	19	2	0	1	0	91
	76%	21%	2%		1%		
Female	88	63	40	39	5	0	235
	38%	27%	17%	17%	2%		
Total	157	82	42	39	6	0	326

	Age at Capture—Texas Frontier						
	<6	6–10	11–15	16–20	21–25	26–30	>30	Total
Male	14	28	23	5	0	0	1	71
Female	13	19	14	8	7	1	0	62
Total	27	47	37	13	7	1	1	133

	North America		
	Captured	Killed	Total
Male	23	42	65
Female	36	19	55
Total	59	61	120

p < .01

Note: Data on captives taken in Indian raids on the Argentinean frontier during the early nineteenth century from Socolow 1992; data on nineteenth-century Texas frontier and North America based on cases compiled by Heard (1973) and Wilbarger (1991 [1889]).

myths about the sexual skills of foreign women," with Spanish women, particularly blondes (*rubias*), prized for their erotic talents (Socolow 1992:87; cf. Gow 1993:334). Table 11.3 also reveals that in raids for which victims were identified, males were more likely to be killed. The latter fact is unremarkable given that males are typically the fighters. Requiring some fiddling in order to make these data comparable, Figure 11.4 illustrates these disparities. The results recall the formula "the enemy cut off many heads and carried off many women" (Vargas Llosa 1989:43).

If raiders discriminate in the selection of captives, then recurrent raiding should have detectable effects on the demography of both raided and raiding groups. Figure 11.5 was generated by applying the relative death and abduction frequencies given in Table 11.3 and the mortality estimates resulting from intergroup conflict presented in Table 11.4 to a population of 200. The top pyramid in Figure 11.5 pertains to the group that loses individuals in raids through death and abduction, whereas the bottom pyramid pertains to the group that gains captives. The two pyramids illustrate the effect that the captive-taking can have on the sex and age structures of both raiding and pillaged populations. These contrasts, of course, assume that captive-taking is asymmetric, much as in the pilot study offered by Kohler and Turner (2006). If the practice were reciprocated, these differences might well be nullified. If other technical improprieties and problematic assumptions are permitted, we can push this exercise a bit further. A regularly pillaged population should show a depression in that segment of the population below age fifteen, numerous deaths of adult male defenders, and a dearth of females of prime reproductive age. For successful raiders, in contrast, there should be a surfeit of captured children and women. If things

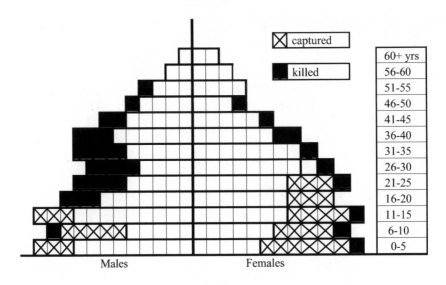

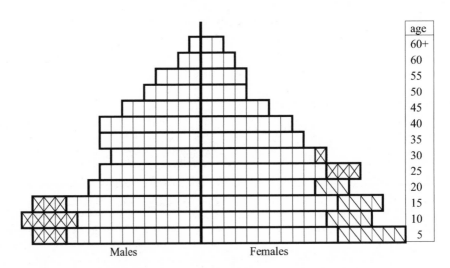

FIGURE 11.5. Population pyramids showing depletion of captive-giving group (*top*) and supplement to captive-taking group (*bottom*).

got nasty, some traumatized captives might have entered the burial record, as Martin (1997, this volume) has argued. Sex ratios alone, however, are particularly subject to equifinality, in which different processes lead to identical results (Figure 11.6).

Table 11.4 lists a number of burial collections from North America for which evidence on age, sex, and trauma have been recorded to varying degrees of completeness. Some of these collections, such as those from Pecos and the Green River sites of Indian Knoll, Ward, and Carlson

Annis, were initially analyzed decades ago and display some aberrant age and sex distributions, but they continue to be reassessed by biological anthropologists. Other collections may relate to captive-taking and deserve notice. The entry "SW Victims" is a composite consisting of those variously brutalized Southwest remains analyzed by Turner and Turner (1999) in which male victims predominate. The "Crow Creek" (Willey and Emerson 1993) and "Larson Massacre" (Owsley et al. 1977) collections from South Dakota, respectively of late prehistoric and protohistoric

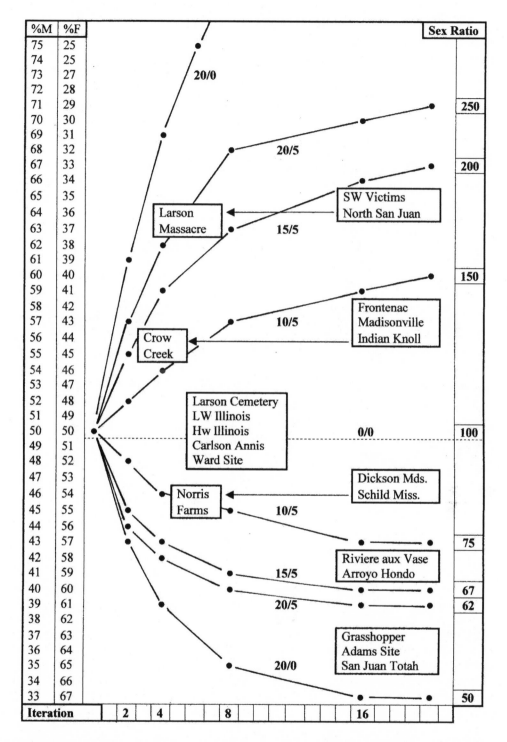

FIGURE 11.6. Changing sex ratios (vertical axes) as a function of the number of captive-taking raids (horizontal axis). The lines plot changes in sex ratio from an initial value of parity (100) through progressive iterations under varying raiding scenarios. For example, 20/5 specifies that Group A loses 20 percent of its women to Group B but gains 5 percent of Group B's women in retaliatory raids. Sex ratios above the parity value of 100 pertain to Group A; those below, to Group B. Boxed entries are taken from Table 11.4. As shown in the cases of the Larson Massacre and Crow Creek, the same sex ratios are interpretable in terms of very different raiding histories.

TABLE 11.4. Selected Attributes of Burial Samples from North America

| | *n* | M | F | Sex Ratio | Trauma | | Sex Ratio % 15–30 yrs | Percentage ≤ 15 yrs |
					Male Female	Female		
SW Victims	558	123	63	195	123 100%	63 100%	—	34%
Northern San Juan	61	39	22	177	—	—	—	—
Larson Massacre	71	31	19	163	31 100%	19 100%	13/5 260%	28%
Frontenac Island	135	54	41	132	6 11%	0	18/14 129%	28%
Madisonville	335	70	55	127	—	—	21/30 70%	34%
Indian Knoll	792	281	227	124	23 8%	2 1%	160/100 160%	36%
Crow Creek	337	99	82	120	—	—	60/25 240%	46%
Pueblo Grande	361	87	77	113	—	—	26/34 76%	51%
Koger's Island	380	38	35	109	7 45%	9 26%	8/17 47%	36%
Larson Cemetery	621	118	118	100	—	—	32/46 70%	37%
Late Woodland Illinois	376	85	85	100	16 19%	5 6%	—	39%
Hopewell Illinois	528	169	168	100	—	—	26/38 68%	33%
Carlson Annis	354	108	110	98	7 6%	3 3%	52/44 118%	38%
Ward Site	433	118	120	98	16 14%	9 8%	—	45%
Dickson Mounds	234	75	84	89	—	—	13/38 34%	32%
Norris Farms	262	53	63	84	18 34%	18 29%	12/18 67%	55%
Schild Miss.	245	60	74	81	2 3%	1 1%	19/20 95%	40%
Rivière aux Vase	307	73	98	74	4 5%	15 15%	14/40 35%	33%
Arroyo Hondo	105	14	21	67	1 7%	—	7/3 233%	58%
Grasshopper	594	101	162	62	—	—	33/54 61%	57%
Adams Site	380	89	168	53	—	—	24/40 60%	20%
San Juan Totah	41	14	27	52	—	—	—	—
	7,232	1,899	1,919	99	141 18%	81 10%	538/566 95%	42%

Sources: Turner and Turner 1999 for Southwest victims; Kohler and Turner 2006 for the Totah and Northern San Juan; Owsley et al. 1977 for the Larson Massacre; Ritchie 1945 for Frontenac Island; Drucker 1997 for Madisonville; Johnston and Webb 1961 for Indian Knoll; Willey and Emerson 1993 for Crow Creek; Sheridan 2001 for Pueblo Grande; Bridges et al. 2000 for Koger's Island; Owsley and Bass 1979 for Larson Cemetery; Perino 1973 for Illinois Late Woodland; Buikstra 1976 for Illinois Hopewell; Mensforth 1990 and 2001 for Carlson Annis; Powell 1996 for the Ward site; Harn 1980 for Dickson Mounds; Milner and Smith 1990 for Norris Farms; Goldstein 1980 for Schild; Wilkinson 1997 for Riviere aux Vase; Palkovitch 1980 for Arroyo Hondo; Whittlesey and Reid 2001 for Grasshopper; and Wray et al. 1987 for the Adams site.

age, are interpreted to evince death-dealing attacks. Although women were perhaps carried off from Larson, Crow Creek suggests a catastrophic, unsparing mortality. Rivière aux Vase, a late prehistoric site in Michigan, is unusual in the preponderance of remains belonging to young adult females, many displaying signs of brutal treatment (Wilkinson 1997). The two San Juan entries are paired in complementary fashion, the Northern San Juan purportedly serving as a source for captives entering the Totah region to the south (Kohler and Turner 2006). The low sex ratio at Grasshopper has recently been attributed to an influx of refugees fleeing conflicts elsewhere, but the alternative possibility of large-scale taking of captives cannot be excluded (Lowell 2007). The cemetery at the Adams site, a protohistoric Seneca occupation, also yielded a surplus of young females that the excavators explain "in terms of the inclusion of a sizable number of female war captives or refugees" (Wray et al. 1987:247). In fact, the Alhart site, 50 km to the west, with its burned longhouses, decapitated males, and dearth of females has been identified as the donor population (Englebrecht 2003:115). As an aside, other Seneca cemeteries of the early historic period also provide evidence for an African female who had been afflicted with non-Native tropical yaws as a child and a Caucasian male who was apparently shot with bow and arrow just before burial beneath a richly attired Seneca man. Both of these foreigners were likely captives (Englebrecht 2003:147).

Only a few of the collections itemized in Table 11.4 are statistically anomalous in a manner that might suggest, or is compatible with, captive-taking. There is no reason, however, to suggest that these cases are unrepresentative or subject to systematic distortions. The proportion of individuals less than 15 years of age, although not an especially illuminating index, averages 42 percent, a figure in accord with Sobolik's more extensive survey of southwestern skeletal series (Sobolik 2002: Table 7.3). Despite the widely varying sex ratios, the composite ratios of 99 for the sample at large and 95 for the 15–30 age cohort are unremarkable. These exercises, more suggestive than demonstrative, nonetheless indicate that biological anthropology can shed much

light on captive-giving and captive-taking in the archaeological record.

Rites of Capture

In his original formulation of *les rites de passage*, Van Gennep (1960 [1908]) devoted several pages to wife-capture. Although remaining noncommittal with respect to its role in the history of marriage, Van Gennep enlisted the practice as a useful example of his general theory. Recent studies continue to view captivity in a rite-of-passage framework (see Peregrine, this volume). In his work on the Iroquois, Richter (1992:69) implies as much when he divides the capturing process into stages reminiscent of Van Gennep: the gauntlet and the prospect of further torture; a probationary period during which the servant-slave performs menial tasks for his master; and the "social death" (see Patterson 1982) in which selected survivors had to quickly shed prior identities and learn to act as proper Iroquois. In his analysis of Iroquois adoption practices, Lynch (1985) finds a similar model embedded in mythology. Abler and Logan (1988), however, give the most detailed assessment of what can be called the rite of capture. Their discussion forms the basis for Figure 11.7.

Abler and Logan isolate certain repetitive motifs occurring in captivity accounts: the tying of the captive with a special rope, the ripping out of nails and crushing of fingers to disable the bow hand, running the gauntlet, and bestowal of a new name. In some narratives, the captive is led from house to house and, holding a rattle, forced to sing his death song (Richter 1992: Plate 7). If surviving these ordeals, the captive was offered to a longhouse that had recently lost one of its members. Acceptance of the offer was tantamount to adoption, and members of that longhouse decided the captive's fate. If calls for revenge dominated deliberations, the captive, with face painted red and black, was sentenced to prolonged torture followed by burning at the stake. The charred corpse was cleaned, butchered into pot-sized parts, boiled as part of a soup, and consumed. As Abler and Logan detail, the archaeological evidence supporting such cannibalistic feasts is substantial, although this evidence has not received the same forensic scrutiny that

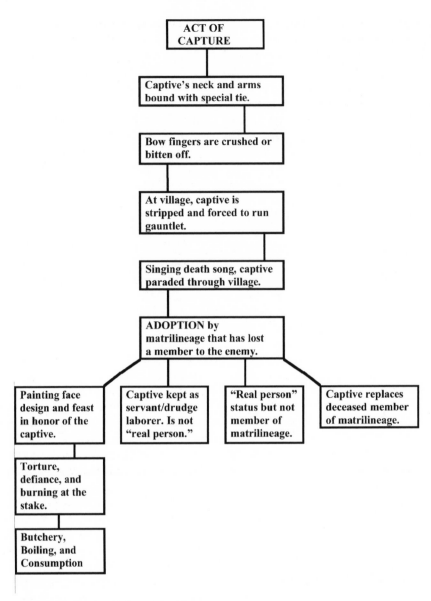

FIGURE 11.7. Flowchart plotting the courses followed by Iroquois captives from time of capture (*top*) to the various outcomes (*bottom*).

has been focused on, for example, claims for cannibalism in the prehistoric Southwest.

A second possibility was servitude, making the captive a "child of nothingness," a social nonperson to be used as hostage, concubine, or drudge put to work gathering firewood, fetching water, cleaning fish, pounding maize, cooking, sewing, dressing hides, paddling canoes, and tending fields (Englebrecht 2003:162). Physical abuse was common and, as described in Appen-

dix 11.1, Case 11, could result in death. The appellation "dog" was common for such captives. In fact, the same term was used for "dog" (or "pet," "domesticated animal") and "captive/slave" in several languages: *tshen* in Mohawk (Starna and Watkins 1991:49), *awakǎn* in Ojibway (Baraga 1992: 56–57), *apoyba* in Alabama (Sylestine et al. 1993: 45), *wayaka* in Dakota (with the second meaning "to champ, as a horse" [Riggs 1992:547]), and, far to the south, *nahua* or *iná* in Shipibo-Conibo, meaning "captive," "pet," or "uncivilized" in general. Both Erikson (2000) and Fausto (1999) have addressed this pet-captive nexus in Amazonia, where among some groups "captive" and "slave" are also glossed together with "son-in-law," a conjunction reflecting the onerous demands typically placed on a daughter's husband (Ferguson 1995:386).

From the standpoint of most captives, adoption was presumably preferred to either death or a dog's life. In what Lynch (1985) calls assimilative adoption, the captive assumed the name, identity, and social roles of a deceased individual. Anthony Wallace has gone so far as to state that "the common aim of all Iroquois war parties was to bring back persons to replace the mourned-for dead" (Wallace 1970:102). Known as the Requickening Ceremony among the Iroquois, cognate practices were widely dispersed throughout the Northeast. The following description from 1636 pertains to the Algonquian Nipissing:

> When he who has passed away has been raised from the dead—that is, when his name has been given to another, and presents have been offered to his relatives—then it is said that the body is cached, or rather, that the dead is resuscitated. (JR 9:277)

A letter written at the village of the Peoria in 1692 could just as well apply to Iroquois practice:

> When there is any dead man to be resuscitated, that is to say, if any one of their warriors has been killed, and they think it is a duty to replace him—to give to those of his cabin one of their prisoners, who takes the place of the deceased; and this is what they call "resuscitating the dead." (JR 67:141)

Wives could also be so adopted or recruited out of servitude.

A variant form of adoption among the Iroquois, one that Lynch labels "associative adoption," did not involve full incorporation into a matrilineage, nor did it require the complete shedding of one's former identity. It did, however, bestow a status of trust upon the individual. Such associate status could also be conferred upon an entire nation, a famous case being the Oneida adoption of the Tuscarora in 1714. In a very real sense, the procedures for processing individual captives could be extended to entire peoples. Thus, after the destruction of their towns in 1649, the collectivity of Huron captives was "cut up in parts and scattered about." This dismemberment of an entire polity, an act that the Iroquois called *wehaitwatsha*, accounted for the Huron "barrios" that the Jesuits noted in many Iroquois settlements (compare Appendix 11.1, Cases 12 and 33). The contemporary accounts of these incorporative policies, whether of individuals or peoples, tend to emphasize the need for warriors, those rare captives who later became chiefs, and males in general. The Jesuits were especially diligent in recording agonizing torture scenes in which adult males were the usual victims. As we have seen, however, most adopted captives were female, many becoming wives. It is not at all unlikely that by the 1660s, a majority of Five Nations children had Huron or Algonquian mothers (Donald 1997:262).

Like Captor, Like Captive

In 1642, Father Jogues, captured by the Mohawk, was hoisted and bound on the platform reserved for torturing captives. Facing a glorious martyrdom, he recounts how the torture began with his left thumb being slowly severed by an Algonquian woman, herself a captive (VanDerBeets 1994:15). Father Bressani, who left us an account of his own capture and torture by the Iroquois in 1644, observed with dismay that "Huron and Algonquian prisoners were the first to make me suffer in order to please the Iroquois" (Levernier and Cohen 1977:29). Similar stories of captives who, once adopted, came to identify with their captors are numerous and attest to the effectiveness of what might be called reculturation. Cadillac was astonished that captive boys brought up among the Ottawa "were the first to go to war against their tribe, killing or taking prisoner their fathers or uncles" (Kinietz 1965:256). Also having an unsettling impact in their time were the sagas of Mary Jemison ("the white woman of the Seneca"), Cynthia Ann Parker (mother of the celebrated Comanche Quanah Parker), and others who ended up "going Indian" to the extent of refusing rescue. In a singular study, Norman Heard (1973) attempted to assess the degree of assimilation of Euroamericans held captive by Native Americans. Although Heard's measures, expressed as percentages, are more impression-istic than rigorous (as if assimilation could be re-duced to a single number), his results expectedly show that the degree of assimilation decreases with the age at captivity and increases with the duration of captivity. Socolow's 1992 study, in which loss of Native language is used as a mea-sure of assimilation, suggests the same pattern. In his 1738 recommendations for successful captive-taking in the Upper Amazon, the Jesuit Pablo Maroni advised catching captives as children and raising and training them over a period of years until longings for home and thoughts of escape were totally eliminated (Jiménez de la Espada 1889–1892, 27:73). Beyond these normative state-ments about making "good captives," it is difficult to venture. Let us say that, in terms of getting the adoptee to act the part of one who has embraced his or her new identity, these stringent enculturing measures worked quite well, even if one suspects that the acquired identity was often a mask (see Richter 1992:72; White 1991:326–327).

Masks suggest disguise, which in turn threatens subterfuge. Keeping captives undisguised was apparently policy in French Louisiana. Accoring to Gallay (2002:310–311), Indian slaves could be readily identified on the basis of hairstyles, tattooing, and head shapes (resulting from cradling practices). Furthermore, these salient markers were said to discourage escape. Among the Cueva of the Darién, slaves were marked by the extraction of their upper incisors (Trimborn 1949:202). The cemetery at Ganondagan, a site occupied by the Seneca during the 1670s and 1680s, contained two burials with skulls flattened in the manner typifying the Cherokee (Englebrecht 2003:161). The Seneca regularly raided deep into the South (see Appendix 11.1, Case 27). On the Northwest Coast, head flattening and labret styles could pinpoint the origin of most foreigners, captive or otherwise (MacLeod 1928: 647; Hajda 2005). Among the Conibo of the Upper Amazon, female captives, if young enough, went through the *ani shreati* and the associated clitoridectomy expected of all Conibo girls (De-Boer 2001). Head flattening had to wait until captives had children (Zarzar and Román 1983:61). The significant aspect of these body modifications is that they are permanent and thereby hard to forge. In comparison, behavior is much more

a matter of putting on the act. Elsewhere, I have pointed out that among Shipibo-Conibo the daughters of captive women became competent and conventional, if not creative, potters (De-Boer 1990). Ordinarily captives are not the ones likely to test the limits of cultural canons.

By pursuing explicit pro-natalist policies that recruited the reproductive potential of young women and converted males from enemies to sacrificial victims or allies, neither Iroquois nor Algonquian captors were interested in prolonging the legacy of captivity, and, in theory, captive origins did not cast a genealogical shadow. This sort of studied amnesia was not universal in the Americas. Among the rank-conscious Kiowa, the stigma of captivity was not easily erased (Mishkin 1940:43), although the German-American captive "Kiowa Dutch" became a prominent warrior and intercultural liaison, and Kicking Bird, leader of the Kiowa peace faction during the tumultuous 1870s, was descended from a Crow captive. In northern California, where some groups practiced slavery in a manner mimicking the Northwest Coast, the slave stigma, although not formally hereditary, could carry over to the next generation, meaning that "sons of slaves had lower status than sons of ordinary people" (Bean 1978:681). On the Plateau, the "tainted" ancestry of descendants of captives often surfaced during quarrels (Kennedy and Bouchard 1998:239). On the Upper Ucayali of Peru, captive skeletons in the closet were mentioned primarily as taunts or insults—that is, as "fighting words" (DeBoer 1990:93). Even terminal rites of passage might not provide an escape. Among the Lushootseed, captives joined their own kin after death, but "those born into slavery went to the afterworld of their masters, where they remained slaves forever" (Miller 1999:89). More generally, Northwest Coast slaves could be destroyed, much like other property, upon the death of titleholders. One understanding of this practice was that those so sacrificed served as "death companions" (Donald 1997:168–170).

Finally, a case can be mentioned in which identification of captive with captor took an extreme form. The Shipibo and Conibo of the Peruvian Amazon regarded the Cashibo and other "backwoods" Indians with the disdain reserved for peoples whose only hope of becoming civilized was through adoption (i.e., capture) and subsequent indoctrination into Shipibo-Conibo *haut kultur.* The story of the Cashibo Bolivar Odicio, as relayed by Gray (1953) and Frank (1990), dramatizes some of the curious twists that this civilizing mission could take. At the age of three, Bolivar was captured in a Shipibo raid, and he spent his youth among his captors. He became fully assimilated to Shipibo culture and, having spent part of his teens in the jungle town of Iquitos, also gained familiarity with the ways of Peruvians. As a young adult, Bolivar returned to his own people, the Cashibo, where he became a zealous missionary for Shipibo culture, advocating facility in the Shipibo language, the making of Shipibo designs, the building of Shipibo-style houses, and so on. From his base on the Aguaytía River, a major tributary of the Ucayali, Bolivar would also occasionally assume the role of Peruvian patron, dispensing metal tools to his Cashibo followers, who worked for his lumbering business in return marrying several Shipibo and Cashibo women; sending his son to Lima for schooling; and hosting a first generation of visiting engineers, oil men, and anthropologists. When the Cashibo of the Sunguruyacu refused to comply with his civilizing projects, Bolivar organized a slaving raid of the kind that the Shipibo traditionally launched against the Cashibo. He gathered his "Shipibo-ized" followers and led a devastating attack on the recalcitrant villages, burning the *malocas* (multifamily houses), killing warriors, and capturing women and children. Bolivar, one of those hybrid characters at home in the interstices, died in 1947, presumably proud of his sobriquet, *El Cashibo Civilizador.*

Captives as Curers

The 1530s junket of Cabeza de Vaca across the northern reaches of New Spain might be better considered a kind of relay in which Cabeza and his companions, all captives, were shunted from one Native group to another. Important to their survival was maintaining a novel identity. The light skins of the Spaniards and the black skin of the slave Esteban were quick to lose their weirdness, but by the end of the expedition, Cabeza and Esteban were adept at posing as powerful curers bearing potent medicines (Bartlett 1998). This famous case reminds us that utility of captives extended beyond that of ready sacrificial victims, no-account drudges, handy translators and guides, breeding stock, or assimilative success stories. However asymmetric relations of power and emulation might be, interactions are perforce two-way. Blau (1966) has suggested that the False Face Society, stereotypically Iroquois, originated among the Hurons during the great epidemics of the 1630s and shortly afterwards was introduced to the Iroquois proper by Huron captives and refugees. During the same period, a complex of curing paraphernalia including bone sucking tubes, shell rattles, and ceramic effigy pipes appeared at Neutral sites, coincident with a major influx of shell-tempered pottery (Fitzgerald 2001:44). It is known that the Neutral were attacking the Mascouten at this time and returning with hundreds of captives (see Appendix 11.1, Cases 4 and 5), and these captives were arguably the carriers of the observed innovations in curing and potting. In 1657, Huron captives reintroduced pottery to the Mohawk, who had ceased ceramic production (Englebrecht 2003:163). The Jesuit Relations are sprinkled with allusions to the spread of new curing ceremonies and procedures that were much in demand in the face of European diseases. The Huron acquired particularly potent medical charms (*oky*) from Algonquian shamans (JR 17:211). The charms most in demand were body parts taken from the monstrous serpent called *onniont,* and the Huron claimed that only the Algonquians knew how to obtain them (JR 33:215–217). LeMoyne recorded the following among the Onondaga:

> The woman, being troubled by an inflammation, saw herself apparently cured in a dream by men of another nation, who were captives in Onnontague. They were summoned, and ordered to administer to the patient the best drugs of the medicine men of *their* country. (JR 47:183)

This pattern of attributing secret powers—medicinal, sexual, or otherwise—to captives was widespread. Among the Tukanoans of the northwest Amazon, the Makú, otherwise judged to be an inferior and servile class of "jungle Indians," were also believed to be dangerous sorcerers who used powerful medicines and poisons (Neves 1998:115). The disparaging attitudes that the Shipibo and Conibo had toward the peoples they took captive have already been discussed, but it seems a certain uneasiness accompanied the arrogance, as intimated by some notes jotted down in 1871. In that year, on a mission to find a part of the world where the Confederate slave-cotton economy could rise again, Galt described a Conibo who was famous for:

> murdering Cashibos whenever any of his family got sick, ascribing their illness to the awful sorcery of these *infieles*. He makes raids now and then among these Cashibos, taking the women and the children away after stealing whatever the poor wretches may have to live on. Recently he killed three Cashibos for exerting a spell on some of his children who were sick. (Galt 1872:296)

On the basis of my experience among them, the Conibo still respect the knowledge that the Cashibo and Campa have of the forest and its plant medicines, and are still wary of the skills in sorcery that only savages can master (contra Gow 1993). At the same time, the Conibo would never doubt the abject inferiority of these forest groups, these *nahua*, in other respects. Appendix 11.2 indicates that *correrías*, as raids for captives and booty are locally called, have continued into recent times. Conibo and Shipibo genealogies collected in the 1960s and 1970s also attest to captive-taking a generation ago (Bodley 1967: Table 5; DeBoer 1986). Given the Conibo reticence in discussing such matters, the actual incidence of such raids was probably higher.

Taking Stock

Along the way, the initial focus of this chapter on wife-capture has blurred. This is not because information is wanting; rather, evidence is abundant and indicates that we are dealing with a real practice of some significance, certainly more than a Victorian fantasy. Rather, the blurring comes about because of the pervasive yet overlapping and embedded character of the practice. Marriage by capture, even though excluded from most accounts of kinship systems, was, in fact, a common option. In geographical terms, it can be placed at the perimeter of the marriage catchment, the zone where conventional marriages by exchange interfinger with abduction. Although

some small-scale raids had abduction as a primary goal, more common was the larger multi-purpose raid in which captives, booty, and war honors could be obtained. Captive-taking is consequently intermeshed with warfare.

In terms of captive selection, the American evidence is overwhelming. Children and young women were favored, while warriors were killed on the spot or reserved for later torture and often death. To make an unpleasant comparison, captives were treated somewhat like livestock. Unruly and otherwise unreasonable males were slaughtered. In contrast, the reproductive potential of females was preserved, while young boys could be raised to be warriors. These investments in the future took on added significance given the demographic catastrophes resulting from disease, warfare, and attendant dislocations. In some cases, this endemic raiding was pursued symmetrically. For example, Iroquois raided various Algonquian groups and vice versa, and all participants came to have a mutual understanding of the protocols of captivity: running the gauntlet, the ideal of facing torture stoically, and adoption in which a captive replaced and came to act the part of an enemy. The raids of the Shipibo-Conibo, in contrast, tended toward the asymmetric (as also discussed by Robertshaw and Duncan, this volume). On occasion, the Cashibo successively raided the Shipibo and retreated into the forest with a captive or two, but, in general, the backwoods groups lacked the manpower and, after guns were introduced, the weaponry to pose a serious threat. One could say that Shipibo and Conibo annually hunted the backwoods groups, killing the males and carting off the females. Again, however, abducted women became wives, and their children were Shipibo and Conibo in both behavior and appearance.

As observed earlier, the movement of most captives was probably tethered, just exceeding the "escape distance." In some cases, however, displacements were global. In the early 1700s, the Jesuit Grelon, working in Chinese Tartary, met a "Huron woman whom he had known in Canada. She had been sold as a slave and traded from group to group until reaching that place" (JR 59: 309). Although this case is extreme and can be questioned on other grounds, the shunting of captives must have created a vast rhizomatic network of information exchange. How this exchange differed from the various agencies of conventional diffusion has yet to be understood. Furthermore, if the few estimates for the frequency of marriage through capture are generally applicable, then the dissemination of genetic information, or gene flow, must have been substantial. This raises numerous questions about the reliability of phylogenies based on DNA samples labeled "Apache" or "Conibo" when such groups were constituted through the incorporation of others (Weber 2005:74).

Occasionally, the influx of captives left a clear archaeological signature. We have seen this in Iroquoia, where "Mohawk" sites bear "Huron" ceramics. Oddly, however, the clinal genetic maps produced by unbounded mating at the local level need not be expressed in cultural maps. As vulnerable and marginal members of their adopted society, captives were unlikely to flaunt their pedigree or advertise their differences. In the case of the Shipibo-Conibo, captives often became *slavish* imitators or, as in the case of Odicio Bolivar, militant propagandists for the Shipibo way of life. A clever analyst might even suggest that the more permeable cultural boundaries are to body flows, the sharper and more salient those cultural boundaries become in terms of material signals.

Finally, as the section "Captives as Curers" is meant to suggest, captors may regard their charges with simultaneous disdain and fear, and as generally inferior in most matters but threateningly potent in others.

Appendix 11.1 A Selective Chronicle of Captive-Taking in North America

1. 1540. Captives from Quivira and Harahey at Pecos Pueblo (Bolton 1949:188–191).
2. 1541. Casquins and Spaniards attack the Pacaha, taking women and children back to Casqui to serve as field hands. The Pacaha said to hamstring their captives to prevent escape (Dye 1994:47).
3. 1642. Mohawk torture five men to death but "boys, girls, and women are kept as slaves" (VanDerBeets 1994:326).
4. 1641–1642. Neutral make war on the Mascouten, taking 270 captives over two years (JR 21:195).
5. 1643. A Neutral army attacks a large Mascouten village. Many men killed and 800 women and children taken captive (JR 27:25).
6. 1646. Montagnais attack Bersiamites. Seven men killed, 13 or 14 captives taken, mostly children (JR 28:35).
7. 1651. Iroquois destroy the Neutral. "The number of captives was exceedingly large, especially of young women, whom they reserve in order to keep up the population of their own villages" (JR 36:177).
8. 1651. Iroquois attack the Nipissing. "The poor women and children were, as usual, dragged away into captivity" (JR 36:189).
9. 1652. In their raids upon the Montagnais, the Iroquois "kill the men, and drag the women and children into a horrible captivity" (JR 37:11).
10. 1655. In Esopus (Munsee) attack on New Amsterdam, about 50 Dutch killed and "over one hundred, mostly women and children," taken into captivity (Ruttenber 1992:122).
11. 1657. LeJeune comments that "the Iroquois have three classes of captives. The first are those who, having willingly submitted to the yoke of the conquerors and elected to remain among them, have become heads of families after the death of their masters, or have married. Although they live a tolerably easy life, they are looked upon as slaves and have no voice, either active or passive, in public councils. The second class are those who have fallen in slavery after having been the richest and most esteemed in their own villages, and who receive no other reward from their masters, in exchange for their ceaseless labor and sweat, than food and shelter. But the fate of the third class is much more deplorable; it consists chiefly of young women or girls, who, because they have not yet found a husband among the Iroquois, are constantly exposed to the danger of losing their honors or their lives through the brutal lechery or cruelty of their masters or mistresses. Every moment is one of dread for them; their rest is never free from anxiety and danger; the only punishment for even their slightest faults is death; and their most harmless action may be considered a fault. When an Iroquois has split the head of his slave with a hatchet, they say 'It is a dead dog; there is nothing to be done but to cast it upon the dunghill'" (JR 43:295).
12. 1660. Iroquois Five Nations have perhaps 1,200 "pure-bloods" and a much larger assortment of captives incorporated from the Huron, Petun, Neutral, Erie, and various Algonquian groups (Lalemont, JR 45:207).
13. 1670. The Wisconsin Mascouten complain to

Allouez that the Iroquois and Dakota "are eating them" (JR 54:224).

14. 1673. Illinois raid far to south and west to obtain captives. Marquette is given a captive boy as a gift (JR 59:127).

15. 1674. Cree arrive at Sault Ste. Marie with 80 Dakota prisoners (JR 58:263).

16. 1680. From Illinois, LaSalle hears of the Pani to the west who raid the Padouca. As captives, the latter are, in turn, passed on to the Osage and other groups (Hyde 1959:25).

17. 1682. The Michigamea present LaSalle with a boy captured from the Pani (Wiegers 1988:190).

18. 1682. Seven hundred Illinois captives brought back to Onondaga. "They killed and ate over 600 on the spot, without counting those whom they burned along the road. They saved the children who could live without the milk of their mothers whom they had killed. They tied living men and women to the stakes, and, as fast as their flesh became roasted, they cut it off and ate it" (JR 62:11).

19. 1689. Tonti witnesses Illinois war party returning with several Osage captives (Wiegers 1988:191).

20. 1692. Apaches attack the Wichita villages, "killing as many men as they could and capturing women and children" (Hyde 1959:46).

21. 1699. Combined Shawnee and Chickasaw force attacks Cahokia. Ten men killed and about a hundred women and children taken captive (Kellogg 1917:351).

22. 1706. Chickasaw raid Choctaw, taking 300 women and children captive (Gallay 2002:238).

23. 1713. James Knight guided westward from Hudson's Bay by Thanadelthur, a Slavey captured by Cree (Newman 1987:288).

24. 1713. Acolapissas attack Natchitoches, killing 17 and taking 50 women and girls captive (John 1975:202).

25. 1718. Comanche and Ute raid Jicarilla, killing 60 and taking 64 women and children to be exchanged at Santa Fe (Hyde 1959:67).

26. 1719. As Caddoans have a reputation for eating captives, Spaniards claim that the trade in Padoucah slaves is a form of charity that rescues women and children from cannibalism (Hyde 1959:79).

27. 1719. On their annual long-distance raid to the south, Iroquois attack Catawba and take many prisoners (Jennings 1984:278).

28. 1723. Comanche raid the Jicarilla and carry off many women and children (Kenner 1994:33).

29. 1723. Spanish-Indian force attacks Apache *ranchería*, killing 35 men and capturing 20 women and children (John 1975:259).

30. 1724. Bourgmont finds captured Comanche boy and young woman among the Kansa (John 1975: 219; Bannon 1974:136).

31. 1728. A Pawnee boy, seized by the Assiniboin and then traded to the Cree, is given to Vérendrye on the north shore of Lake Superior. At this time, the Cree are also raiding the Blackfoot and the Gros Ventre, whom they call *aya hciyiniw*—that is, "strangers" or "slaves" (Wood 1980:20).

32. 1729. With respect to the Natchez uprising: "They did not kill the other women, those who were not pregnant or not nursing, but made them slaves, and treated them with every indignity during the two or three months that they were their masters. The least miserable were those who knew how to sew, because they kept them busy making shirts, dresses, etc. The others were employed in cutting and carrying wood for cooking, and in pounding the corn of which they make their sagamite" (Le Petit, JR 68:169).

33. 1731. "The Foxes are in existence by grace only of adopted captives and returned Fox prisoners" (Jones 1939:5).

34. 1732. Iroquois attack Fox village in Wisconsin, carrying off 14 young men and 140 women and children (Edmunds and Peyser 1993:167).

35. 1739. Ietans (Plains Apache?) on the upper Arkansas have Arikara captives that they obtained on the Missouri (Hyde 1959:100).

36. 1747. Comanche-Ute raid on Abiquiu yields 23 women and children (Brooks 2002:64).

37. 1754. Female captives taken from Blackfoot and Gros Ventre said to be common among Cree traders at Hudson Bay (Ewers 1994:326).

38. 1755. "Only 20 captives were taken by Indians from amongst the remnants of Braddock's force at Monongahela. Eight of these were female and allowed to live, because women and girls were deemed fertile, useful, and unthreatening. Twelve were soldiers and were tortured to death" (Colley 2004:180).

39. 1750s. According to Ian Steele, some 2,700 settlers were seized in Indian raids on the frontiers of Pennsylvania, Maryland, and Virginia. Among these, males were 19 times more likely to be killed than females" (cited in Colley 2004:147).

40. 1750s. Description of Wichita: "Male captives might be pressed into service as scouts…but more useful and numerous were captive women and children; as slaves they enhanced the productivity of the villages and the prosperity and prestige of their owners' households. Some were eventually adopted into Wichita families; some captive women became wives or concubines and bore children to swell the ranks of the nation" (John 1981:341).

41. 1760. Comanche raid Taos. Sixty women and children taken captive (Brooks 2002:64).

42. 1779. Lipans raid Tonkawas, killing four and capturing four, a 30-year-old woman, a 10-year-old girl, and two 7-year-old boys (John 1975:534).

43. 1779. Anza's expedition against the Comanche kills 87 (58 men, 29 women) and captures 34 women and children (John 1975:590).

44. 1780. Spanish attack Mimbres Apache. Three men and three women killed, one woman and three children captured (John 1975:603).

45. 1784. Piegan chief tells David Thompson that women are captured in order to replenish losses suffered during the smallpox epidemic of 1781 (Ewers 1994:326).

46. 1787. In Comanche raid on Lipan, 16 men are killed, 47 women and children are taken captive (Kenner 1994:33).

47. 1788. Spanish force from Tucson kills 54 Apache, captures 125 (John 1975:749).

48. 1792. Ecueracapa leads large Comanche force against Apache, killing 11 warriors and capturing 17 women and children (Kenner 1994:60).

49. 1799. Hidatsa raid Lemhi Snake at Three Forks, taking many "young women and older children, including Sacajawea" (Hyde 1959:176).

50. 1835. Comanche take 39 captives, of which 22 are women (Brooks 2002:265).

51. 1841. Comanche raid deep into Mexico, taking 19 women and 22 children captive (Brooks 2002:266).

52. 1851. Tonto Apache (?) raid the Oatman party. Two men, two women, and three children killed. The two young Oatman sisters are taken and later traded to the Mohave (Dunn 1969:137–138). Olive Oatman later reports that seven Cocopa women were fellow captives (Kroeber and Kroeber 1994:50; also see Braatz 2003:254).

53. 1853. Thomas Fitzpatrick on the Kiowa: "The prisoners captured contribute to keeping up the numbers of the tribe. The males thus taken are most commonly adopted into the tribe, and soon become the most expert leaders of war parties and the most accomplished marauders. The females are chosen as wives and share the duties and pleasures of the lodge" (and) "So intermingled amongst this tribe have most of the Mexican captives become that it is somewhat difficult to distinguish them. They sit in council with them, hunt with them, go to war with them, and partake of their perils, and but few have any desire to leave them" (Robinson 1997:23).

54. 1855. Ute chief Walker buried with four Paiute captives, a woman and three children (Dunn 1969:314).

55. 1856. Cheyenne raid on Babbitt party. Two men and a child killed. Mrs. Wilson is taken captive but "killed when she proved unable to ride fast enough to keep up with them" (Chalfant 1989:42).

56. 1856. In follow-up raid to above, Babbitt and two other men killed (Chalfant 1989:42).

57. 1856. In Cheyenne raid, a woman is killed and her four-year old son taken captive (Chalfant 1989:42).

58. 1856. Another Cheyenne raid: Two men, one woman, and one child killed. A young woman is taken captive (Chalfant 1989:42).

59. 1864. In Cheyenne raid on the Platte, two men are killed and two women, each with a young son, are taken captive (Rister 1940:121).

60. 1865. Cheyenne attack Laramie Station. Four men and one woman killed; two children taken captive (Afton et al. 1997:301).

61. 1865. In Kiowa raid, a woman and two boys are taken captive (Rister 1940:161).

62. 1866. Kiowa raiders kill James Box and his ten-year-old son. Wife and four children carried into captivity. These captives are ransomed shortly afterwards, and Satanta boasts that "stealing white women more lucrative than stealing horses" (Robinson 1997:48).

63. May 1865–August 1867. In Kiowa-Comanche raids on the Texas frontier, 162 settlers killed, 24 wounded, and 43 captured (estimates from Mayhall 1962:105).

64. 1868. In raid by Cheyenne Dog Soldiers, three women and a baby are taken captive (Rister 1940:159).

65. 1868. Cheyenne-Arapaho raid into Kansas. Two women and two children are taken captive (Afton et al. 1997:312).

66. 1868. A woman and her two daughters are abducted by Kiowa (Rister 1940:167).

67. 1869. Cheyenne raid near Saline, Kansas. Two women and a baby are taken captive (Rister 1940:162).

68. 1869. Cheyenne raid on Soloman: 13 civilians killed, two women and a baby taken captive (Afton et al. 1997:318).

69. 1869. Man killed and his wife and six children taken captive on Kiowa raid into Texas. Shortly thereafter, captives ransomed for $100 each (Hoig 1993:270).

70. 1870. Comanche White Horse leads raid into Texas. Gottlieb Koozier is killed, and his wife and children are captured (Robinson 1997:109).

71. 1874. Cheyenne raid on the Smoky Hill. Father, mother, and two others of the Germaine family killed; four daughters are carried off into captivity (Mooney 1979:213).

APPENDIX 11.2 Captive-Taking Raids in the Ucayali and Urubamba Basins of the Peruvian Amazon
This appendix incorporates material in DeBoer 1986.

Date	Raider	Target	Remarks	Reference
1. 1665	Shipibo	Campa	captives used as drudges	Biedma 1989:27
2. 1681	Conibo	various	captives exchanged at Laguna mission	Biedma 1987:40
3. Sept. 1686	Conibo	40 Campa captured	22 canoes carrying 66 warriors	Ortíz 1974, 1:77
4. Nov. 1686	Conibo	Piro	8 Piro killed; girl and boy taken captive	Ortíz 1974, 1:94
5. 1686	Conibo	Remo		Jiménez de la Espada 1889–1892, 30:144
6. 1689	Piro	Comabo	abduction of women	Jiménez de la Espada 1889–1892, 30:148
7. 1690	Conibo	Amahuaca and Remo	raid composed of 60 warriors	Jiménez de la Espada 1889–1892, 30:150
8. 1750	Piro	Machiguenga and Campa	captives exchanged at Quillabamba	Zarzar and Román 1983:73
9. Sept. 1790	Conibo	Mayoruna Amahuaca Remo	large convoy en route to Omaguas to trade captives for tools	Izaguirre 1922–1929, 8:130–131, 250
10. 1820s	Conibo	Remo	women become wives, boys traded	Maurtua 1906, 12:345–346
11. 1834	Shipibo Conibo	Remo Capanahua Campa	mission Indians at Sarayacu; acquired in raids	Larrabure i Correa 1905–1909, 11:57
12. 1842	Shipibo Conibo	Amahuaca	taken to Sarayacu as captives	Larrabure i Correa 1905–1909, 8:485
13. 1846	Shipibo Conibo	Remo on the Abujao		Marcoy 2001, 2:8
14. 1846	Shipibo	Cashibo on the Aguaytía		Marcoy 2001, 2:373
15. 1851	Conibo	Amahuaca		Herndon and Gibbon 1854:196
16. 1859	Shipibo Conibo	Remo	female captives kept; males traded for European goods	Larrabure i Correa 1905–1909, 9:95
17. 1860	Conibo	Remo Amahuaca	captives in Conibo household	Raimondi 1966:77
18. 1863	Shipibo	Cashibo on the Aguaytía	women and children captured; men killed	Amich 1975:372
19. 1865	Conibo	Mayoruna	small concealed settlements attributed to raids	Larrabure i Correa 1905–1909, 2:252
20. 1868	Shipibo Conibo	Remo Amahuaca	attacked on the Tamaya	Larrabure i Correa 1905–1909, 5:140
21. 1871	Shipibo Conibo	Remo Amahuaca	captives become wives or servants	Galt 1872:286

APPENDIX 11.2 (cont'd.)   Captive-Taking Raids in the Ucayali and Urubamba Basins of the Peruvian Amazon

Date	Raider	Target	Remarks	Reference
22. 1871	Conibo	Cashibo	captives made to paddle canoes	Galt 1872:288
23. 1871	Piro	Campa	children taken from the Unini	Galt 1872:340
24. 1871	Conibo	Campa Machiguenga	raid tributary groups on the Urubamba for women and children	Galt 1872:391
25. Sept. 1874	Conibo	Amahuaca	raiders in flotilla of 31 canoes	Izaguirre 1922–1929, 10:124
26. 1874	Piro	Campa on Uru-bamba		Izaguirre 1922–1929, 10:99
27. 1874	Piro	Amahuaca	raid on the Parucancha	Izaguirre 1922–1929, 10:238
28. 1875	Piro	Amahuaca	taken from Sepahua	Izaguirre 1922–1929, 10:239
29. 1876	Conibo	Amahuaca		Larrabure i Correa 1905–1909, 9:172
30. 1877	Shipibo	Amahuaca	taken from Tamaya	Amich 1975:421
31. 1883	Conibo	Amahuaca Campa	two month (July–August) raid of 50 canoes	Samanez y Ocampo 1980:812–882
32. 1886	Shipibo Conibo	Amahuaca Campa	most families have captives from these groups	Larrabure i Correa 1905–1909, 12:474–475
33. late 1800s	Conibo	Cashibo	taken from Sunguruyacu	Stahl 1928:150
34. 1900	Conibo	Campa	women and children	Portillo 1901:28
35. 1904	Conibo	Amahuaca		Larrabure i Correa 1905–1909, 4:344
36. 1911	Conibo	Remo		Izaguirre 1922–1929, 10:431
37. 1987	Atalaya slavers	Campa	women kept; children and men sold	García et al. 1998: 122–123; Hvalkof and Veber 2005

Literature Cited

Abler, Thomas, and Michael Logan
1988   The Florescence and Demise of Iroquoian Cannibalism: Human Sacrifice and Malinowski's Hypothesis. *Man in the Northeast* 35: 1–26.

Afton, Jean, David Fridtjof, and Andrew E. Masich
1997   *Cheyenne Dog Soldiers*. University Press of Colorado, Niwot.

Amich, José
1975   *Historia de las misiones del convento de Santa Rosa de Ocopa*. Editorial Milla Batres, Lima, Peru.

Arhem, Kaj
1981   Bride Capture, Sister Exchange, and Gift Marriage among the Makuna. *Ethnos* 1(1–2):47–63.

Axtell, James
1981   *The European and the Indian: Essays in the Ethnohistory of Colonial North America*. Oxford University Press, New York.

Ayres, Barbara
1974   Bride Theft and Raiding for Wives in Cross-Cultural Perspective. *Anthropological Quarterly* 47(3):238–252.

Bannon, John Francis
1974 *The Spanish Borderlands Frontier, 1513–1821.* University of New Mexico Press, Albuquerque.

Baraga, Frederic
1992 *A Dictionary of the Ojibway Language.* Minnesota Historical Society Press, St. Paul.

Bartlett, Richard A.
1998 Cabeza de Vaca, Alvar Nuñez. In *The New Encyclopedia of the American West,* edited by Howard R. Lamar, p. 149. Yale University Press, New Haven, CT.

Bean, Lowell John
1978 Social Organization. In *Handbook of North American Indians,* vol. 8: *California,* edited by Robert F. Heizer, pp. 673–682. Smithsonian Institution, Washington, D.C.

Biedma, Manuel
1989 *La conquista franciscana del Alto Ucayali.* Centro de Estudios Teológicos de la Amazonia, Iquitos, Peru.

Blau, Harold
1966 Function and the False Faces: A Classification of Onondaga Masked Rituals and Themes. *Journal of American Folklore* 79:561–580.

Bodley, John Harry
1967 Development of an Intertribal Mission Station in the Peruvian Amazon. M.A. thesis, Department of Anthropology, University of Oregon, Eugene.

Bolton, Herbert E.
1949 *Coronado, Knight of Pueblos and Plains.* University of New Mexico Press, Albuquerque.

Braatz, Timothy
2003 *Surviving Conquest: A History of the Yavapai People.* University of Nebraska Press, Lincoln.

Bridges, Patricia S., Keith P. Jacobi, and Mary Lucas Powell
2000 Warfare-Related Trauma in the Late Prehistory of Alabama. In *Bioarchaeological Studies of Life in the Age of Agriculture,* edited by Patricia Lambert, pp. 35–62. University of Alabama Press, Tuscaloosa.

Brøndsted, Johannes
1965 *The Vikings.* Penguin Books, Baltimore, MD.

Brooks, James F.
2002 *Captives and Cousins: Slavery, Kinship, and Community in the Southwest Borderlands.* University of North Carolina Press, Chapel Hill.

Buikstra, Jane
1976 *Hopewell in the Lower Illinois Valley.* Scientific Papers 2. Northwestern University Archeological Program, Evanston, IL.

Camino, Alejandro
1977 Trueque, correrías, e intercambios entre los Quechuas andinos y los Piros y Machiguengas de la montaña Peruana. *Amazonia Peruana* 1(2):123–142.

Cavalli-Sforza, Luigi L.
2000 *Genes, Peoples, and Language.* North Point Press, New York.

Chagnon, Napolean A.
1992 *Yanomamö: The Last Days of Eden.* Harcourt Brace Jovanovich, San Diego, CA.

Chagnon, Napoleon A., James Need, Lowell Weitkamp, Henry Gershowitz, and Manuel Ayres
1970 The Influence of Cultural Factors on the Demography and Pattern of Gene Flow from the Makiritare to the Yanomama Indians. *American Journal of Physical Anthropology* 32:339–349.

Chalfant, William Y.
1989 *Cheyennes and Horse Soldiers.* University of Oklahoma Press, Norman.

Colley, Linda
2004 *Captives: Britain, Empire, and the World, 1600–1850.* Anchor, New York.

Collins, June M.
1974 *Valley of the Spirits: The Upper Skagit Indians of Western Washington.* University of Washington Press, Seattle.

Craig, Ruth
1969 Marriage among the Telefolmin. In *Pigs, Pearlshells, and Women: Marriage in the New Guinea Highlands,* edited by Robert M. Glasse and Mervyn J. Meggitt, pp. 176–197. Prentice-Hall, Englewood Cliffs, NJ.

Craton, Michael
1974 *Sinews of Empire: A Short History of British Slavery.* Anchor Books, Garden City, NY.

DeBoer, Warren R.
1986 Pillage and Production in the Amazon. *World Archaeology* 18(2):231–246.
1990 Interaction, Imitation, and Communication as Expressed in Style: The Ucayali Experience. In *The Uses of Style in Archaeology,* edited by Margaret W. Conkey and Christine A. Hastorf, pp. 82–104. Cambridge University Press, Cambridge.
2001 The Big Drink: Feast and Forum in the Upper Amazon. In *Feasts: Archaeological Perspectives on Food, Politics, and Power,* edited by Michael Dietler and Brian Hayden, pp. 215–239. Smithsonian Institution Press, Washington, D.C.

Donald, Leland
1997 *Aboriginal Slavery on the Northwest Coast of*

North America. University of California Press, Berkeley.

Driver, Harold

1961 *Indians of North America.* University of Chicago Press, Chicago.

1966 Geographical-Historical versus Psycho-Functional Explanations of Kin Avoidances. *Current Anthropology* 7(2):131–182.

Drooker, Penelope Ballard

1997 *The View from Madisonville.* Memoir 31. Museum of Anthropology, University of Michigan, Ann Arbor.

Dunn, J. P., Jr.

1969 *Massacres of the Mountains.* Capricorn Books, [1866] New York.

Dye, David H.

1994 The Art of War in the Sixteenth-Century Central Mississippi Valley. In *Perspectives on the Southeast,* edited by Patricia B. Kwachka, pp. 44–60. University of Georgia Press, Athens.

Early, John D., and John F. Peters

2000 *The Xiliana Yanomami of the Amazon.* University Press of Florida, Gainesville.

Edmunds, R. David, and Joseph L. Peyser

1993 *The Fox Wars: The Mesquakie Challenge to New France.* University of Oklahoma Press, Norman.

Englebrecht, William

2003 *Iroquoia: The Development of a Native World.* Syracuse University Press, Syracuse, NY.

Erikson, Philippe

2000 The Social Significance of Pet-Keeping among Amazonian Indians. In *Companion Animals and Us,* edited by Anthony L. Podberscek, Elizabeth S. Paul, and James A. Serpell, pp. 7–26. University of Cambridge Press, Cambridge.

Ewers, John C.

1994 Women's Roles in Plains Indian Warfare. In *Skeletal Biology in the Great Plains: Migration, Warfare, Health, and Subsistence,* edited by Douglas W. Owsley and Richard L. Jantz, pp. 325–332. Smithsonian Institution Press, Washington, D.C.

Fausto, Carlos

1999 Of Enemies and Pets: Warfare and Shamanism in Amazonia. *American Ethnologist* 26(4): 933–956.

Ferguson, R. Brian

1995 *Yanomami Warfare: A Political History.* School of American Research Press, Santa Fe, NM.

Fields, Harriet L., and William R. Merrifield

1980 Mayoruna (Panoan) Kinship. *Ethnology* 19:1–28.

Fitzgerald, William R.

2001 Contact, Neutral Iroquoian Transformation, and the Little Ice Age. In *Societies in Eclipse,* edited by David S. Brose, C. Wesley Cowan, and Robert C. Mainfort, Jr., pp. 37–48. Smithsonian Institution Press, Washington, D.C.

Frank, Edwin

1990 Pacificar al hombre malo, o escenas de la historia aculturativa Uni desde la perspectiva de las víctimas. *Amazonia Indígena* 10:17–25.

Frink, Lisa (editor)

2005 *Gender and Hide Production: Archaeological, Biological, and Ethnological Perspectives.* Altamira Press, Walnut Grove, CA.

Gallay, Alan

2002 *The Indian Slave Trade: The Rise of the English Empire in the American South, 1670–1717.* Yale University Press, New Haven, CT.

Galt, F. L.

1872 Diary of F. L. Galt, doctor to the expedition exploring the headwaters of the Amazon in eastern Peru. Manuscript files, Smithsonian Institution, Washington, D.C.

García Hierro, Pedro, Søren Hvalkof, and Andrew Gray

1998 *Liberation through Land Rights in the Peruvian Amazon.* Document No. 90. International Work Group for Indigenous Affairs, Copenhagen.

Gennep, Arnold Van

1960 *The Rites of Passage.* University of Chicago Press, Chicago.

Goldman, Irving

1975 *The Mouth of Heaven: An Introduction to Kwakiutl Religious Thought.* John Wiley and Sons, New York.

Goldstein, Lynne G.

1980 *Mississippian Mortuary Practices.* Scientific Papers 4. Northwestern University Archeological Program, Evanston, IL.

Goody, Jack

1980 Slavery in Time and Space. In *Asian and African Systems of Slavery,* edited by James L. Watson, pp. 16–42. University of California Press, Berkeley.

Gow, Peter

1993 Gringos and Wild Indians. *L'Homme* 33:327–347.

Gray, Gloria

1953 Bolivar Odicio, El Cashibo Civilizador. *Peru Indígena* 4:146–154.

Griffith, William J.

1954 *The Hasinai Indians of East Texas as Seen by Europeans, 1687–1772.* Philological and

Documentary Studies vol. 11, no. 3. Middle American Research Institution, Tulane University, New Orleans.

Hajda, Yvonne P.

2005 Slavery in the Greater Lower Columbia Region. *Ethnohistory* 52(3):563–588.

Harn, Alan D.

1980 The Prehistory of Dickson Mounds: The Dickson Excavation. Reports of Investigation 35. Illinois State Museum, Springfield.

Harrison, G. A., and A. J. Boyd

1972 Migration, Exchange, and the Genetic Structure of Populations. In *The Structure of Human Populations,* edited by G. A. Harrison and A. J. Boyd, pp. 128–145. Clarendon Press, Oxford, UK.

Heard, J. Norman

1973 *White Into Red: A Study of the Assimilation of White Persons Captured by Indians.* Scarecrow Press, Metuchen, NJ.

Hemming, John

1978 *Red Gold: The Conquest of the Brazilian Indians.* Harvard University Press, Cambridge, MA.

Herndon, William L., and Lardner Gibbon

1854 *Expedition to the Valley of the Amazon.* Robert Armstrong, Washington, D.C.

Hoig, Stan

1993 *Tribal Wars of the Southern Plains.* University of Oklahoma Press, Norman.

Hopkins, Keith

1978 *Conquerors and Slaves.* Cambridge University Press, Cambridge.

Hvalkof, Søren, and Hanne Veber

2005 Ashéninka del Gran Pajonal. In *Guía etnográfica de la Alta Amazonía,* vol. 5, edited by Fernando Santos and Frederica Barclay, pp. 75–289. Smithsonian Tropical Research Institute, Balboa, Panama.

Hyde, George E.

1959 *Indians of the High Plains.* University of Oklahoma Press, Norman.

Izaguirre, Bernardino

1922– *Historia de las misiones franciscanas y narración de los progresos de la geografía en el oriente del Perú.* 12 vols. Tallares tipográficos de la Penitenciaria, Lima.

Jablow, Joseph

1950 *The Cheyenne in Plains Indian Trade Relations, 1795–1840.* University of Washington Press, Seattle.

Jackson, Jean

1976 Vaupés Marriage: A Network System in the Northwest Amazon. In *Regional Analysis,* edited by Carol A. Smith, vol. 2, pp. 65–93. Academic Press, New York.

1983 *The Fish People.* Cambridge University Press, Cambridge.

Jennings, Francis

1984 *The Ambiguous Iroquois Empire.* W. W. Norton, New York.

Jiménez de la Espada, Marcos

1889– *Noticias auténticas del famoso Río Marañon y*
1892 *misión apostólica de la Compañia de Jesus de la provincia de Quito en los dilatados bosques de dicho río.* Boletín de la Sociedad Geografica de Madrid, vols. 26–30.

John, Elizabeth A. H.

1975 *Storms Brewed in Other Men's Worlds.* Reprint, University of Nebraska Press, Lincoln, 1981.

Johnston, Francis E., and Charles E. Snow

1961 The Reassessment of the Age and Sex of the Indian Knoll Skeletal Population. *American Journal of Physical Anthropology* 19(3):237–244.

Jones, William

1939 *Ethnography of the Fox Indians.* Bulletin 125. Bureau of American Ethnology, Smithsonian Institution, Washington, D.C.

Jorgensen, Joseph G.

1980 *Western Indians: Comparative Environments, Languages and Cultures of 172 Western American Indian Tribes.* W. H. Freeman, San Francisco.

The Jesuit Relations (JR)

1896– *The Jesuit Relations and Allied Documents.* Ed-
1901 ited by Reuben Gold Thwaites. 73 vols. Burrows Brothers, Cleveland, OH.

Keeley, Lawrence H.

1996 *War before Civilization.* Oxford University Press, Oxford, UK.

Kellogg, Louise P.

1917 *Early Narratives of the Northwest, 1634–1699.* Charles Scribner's Sons, New York.

Kelly, Isabel T.

1964 Southern Paiute Ethnography. Anthropological Papers 69. University of Utah, Salt Lake City.

Kennedy, Dorothy I. D., and Randall T. Bouchard

1998 Northern Okanagan, Lakes, and Colville. In *Handbook of North American Indians,* vol. 12: *Plateau,* edited by Deward E. Walker, Jr., pp. 238–252. Smithsonian Institution, Washington, D.C.

Kenner, Charles L.

1994 *The Comanchero Frontier: A History of New Mexican–Plain Indian Relations.* University of Oklahoma Press, Norman.

Kidder, Alfred V.

1958   *Pecos, New Mexico: Archaeological Notes.* Papers of the Robert S. Peabody Foundation, vol. 5. Andover, MA.

Kinietz, W. Vernon

1965   *The Indians of the Western Great Lakes, 1615–1760.* University of Michigan Press, Ann Arbor.

Kohler, Timothy A., and Kathryn Kramer Turner

2006   Raiding for Women in the Pre-Hispanic Northern Pueblo Southwest? A Pilot Examination. *Current Anthropology* 47(6):1035–1945.

Kowalewski, Stephen A.

1995   Large-Scale Ecology in Aboriginal Eastern North America. In *Native American Interactions,* edited by Michael S. Nassaney and Kenneth E. Sassaman, pp. 147–172. University of Tennessee Press, Knoxville.

Kroeber, Alfred L.

1967   *Handbook of Indians of California.* California Book Co., Berkeley.

Kroeber, Alfred L., and G. B. Kroeber

1994   *A Mohave War Reminiscence, 1854–1880.* Dover, Mineola, NY.

Larrabure i Correa, C.

1905– *Colección de leyes, decretos, resoluciones i otros*
1909   *documentos oficiales referentes al Departamento de Loreto.* 18 vols. Imprenta de la Opinión Nacional, Lima.

Levernier, James, and Hennig Cohen (editors)

1977   *The Indians and Their Captives.* Greenwood Press, Westport, CT.

Little, James A.

1881   *Jacob Hamblin, a Narrative of his Personal Experience as a Frontiersman, Missionary to the Indians, and Explorer.* Faith-Promoting Series for Juveniles. Church of Latter-day Saints, Salt Lake City.

Lowell, Julia C.

2007   Women and Men in Warfare and Migration: Implications of Gender Imbalance in the Grasshopper Region of Arizona. *American Antiquity* 72(1):95–124.

Lynch, James

1985   The Iroquois Confederacy and the Adoption and Administration of non-Iroquoian Individuals and Groups prior to 1756. *Man in the Northeast* 30:83–99.

MacLeod, William C.

1928   Economic Aspects of Indigenous American Slavery. *American Anthropologist* 30(4):632–650.

McLennan, John F.

1970   *Primitive Marriage: An Inquiry into the Origin*
[1865]   *of the Form of Capture in Marriage Customs.* University of Chicago Press, Chicago.

Marcoy, Paul

2001   *Viaje a través de America del Sur.* 2 vols. Instituto Francés de Estudios Andinos, Lima.

Martin, Debra L.

1997   Violence against Women in the La Plata River Valley (AD 1000–1300). In *Troubled Times: Violence and Warfare in the Past,* edited by Debra L. Martin and David W. Frayer, pp. 45–75. Gordon and Breach Publishers, New York.

Maurtua, Victor M.

1906   *Juicio de límites entre el Perú y Bolivia.* 12 vols. Imprenta de Heinrich, Barcelona.

Mayhall, Mildred P.

1962   *The Kiowas.* University of Oklahoma Press, Norman.

Mensforth, Robert P.

1990   Paleodemography of the Carlson Annis (Bt-5) Late Archaic Skeletal Population. *American Journal of Physical Anthropology* 82:81–100.

Miller, Jay

1999   *Lushootseed: Culture and the Shamanic Odyssey.* University of Nebraska Press, Lincoln.

Milner, George R., and Virginia G. Smith

1990   Oneota Skeletal Remains. In *Archaeological Investigations of the Morton Village and Norris Farm 36 Cemetery,* edited by Sharron K. Santure, Alan D. Harn, and Duane Esarey, pp. 111–148. Reports of Investigations no. 45. Illinois State Museum, Springfield.

Mishkin, Bernard

1940   *Rank and Warfare among the Plains Indians.* University of Washington Press, Seattle.

Mooney, James

1979   *Calendar History of the Kiowa Indians.* Smithsonian Institution Press, Washington, D.C.

Neves, Eduardo Goes

1998   Paths in Dark Waters: Archaeology as Indigenous History in the Upper Rio Negro Basin, Northwest Amazon. Ph.D. dissertation, Department of Anthropology, University of Indiana [UMI 9966081].

Newman, Peter C.

1987   *Company of Adventurers.* Penguin Books, Harmondsworth, UK.

Noyes, Stanley

1993   *Los Comanches.* University of New Mexico Press, Albuquerque.

Ortíz, D.

1974   *El Pachitea y el Alto Ucayali.* Imprenta Editorial San Antonio, Lima.

Owsley, D. W., H. E. Berryman, and W. M. Bass

1977   Demographic and Osteological Evidence for

Warfare at the Larson Site, South Dakota. *Plains Anthropologist Memoir* 13:119–131.

Owsley, D. W., and W. M. Bass

1979   A Demographic Analysis of Skeletons from the Larson Site, Walworth County, South Dakota. *American Journal of Physical Anthropology* 51:145–154.

Palkovitch, Ann M.

1980   *The Arroyo Hondo Skeletal and Mortuary Remains.* School of American Research Press, Santa Fe, NM.

Patterson, Orlando

1982   *Slavery and Social Death.* Harvard University Press, Cambridge, MA.

Perino, Gregory H.

1973   The Late Woodland Component at the Pete Klunk Site, Calhoun County, Illinois, the Koster Mounds, Greene County, Illinois, and the Late Woodland Component at the Schild Sites, Greene County, Illinois. In *Late Woodland Site Archaeology in Illinois,* vol. 1, edited by James A. Brown, pp. 58–206. Bulletin 9. Illinois Archaeological Survey, University of Illinois, Urbana.

Portillo, P.

1901   *Las montañas de Ayacucho y los rios Apurimac, Mantaro, Tambo, Ene, Perene, y Alto Ucayali.* Imprenta del Estado, Lima.

Powell, Mary L.

1996   Health and Disease in the Green River Archaic. In *Of Caves and Shell Mounds,* edited by Kenneth C. Carstens and Patty Jo Watson, pp. 119–131. University of Alabama Press, Tuscaloosa.

Raimondi, Antonio

1966   *Viajes por el Perú.* Editorial Universitaria, Lima.

Richter, Daniel

1992   *The Ordeal of the Long House.* University of North Carolina Press, Chapel Hill.

Riggs, Stephen R.

1992   *A Dakota-English Dictionary.* Minnesota Historical Society Press, St. Paul.

Rister, Carl Coke

1940   *Border Captives: The Traffic in Prisoners by Southern Plains Indians, 1835–1875.* University of Oklahoma Press, Norman.

Ritchie, William A.

1945   An Early Site in Cayuga County, New York. *Research Records of the Rochester Museum of Arts and Sciences,* No. 7. Rochester, NY.

Robinson, Charles M.

1997   *Satanta.* State House Press, Austin, TX.

Rogerson, Peter A., Richard H. Weng, and Ge Lin

1993   The Spatial Separation of Parents and Their Adult Children. *Annals of the Association of American Geographers* 83(4):656–671.

Ruff, Christopher

1981   A Reassessment of Demographic Estimates for Pecos Pueblo. *American Journal of Physical Anthropology* 54:147–151.

Rushforth, Brett

2003   "A little flesh we offer you": The Origins of Indian Slavery in New France. *William and Mary Quarterly* 60(4):136–160.

Ruttenber, E. M.

1992   *Indian Tribes of Hudson's River to 1700.* Hope Farm Press, Saugerties, NY.

Samanez y Ocampo, José B.

1980   *Exploración de los rios peruanos Apurimac, Eni, Tambo, Ucayali, y Urubamba, 1883–1884.* Sesator, Lima.

Sheridan, Susan Guise

2001   Morbidity and Mortality in a Classic-period Hohokam Community. In *Ancient Burial Practices in the American Southwest,* edited by Douglas R. Mitchell and Judy L. Brunson-Hadley, pp. 191–222. University of New Mexico Press, Albuquerque.

Sobolik, Kristin D.

2002   Children's Health in the Prehistoric Southwest. In *Children in the Prehistoric Puebloan Southwest,* edited by Kathryn A. Kamp, pp. 125–151. University of Utah Press, Salt Lake City.

Socolow, Susan M.

1992   Spanish Captives in Indian Societies: Culture Contact along the Argentine Frontier, 1600–1835. *Hispanic American Historical Review* 72: 73–99.

Stahl, Eurico

1928   Cunibos del Ucayali. *Boletín de la Sociedad Geográfica de Lima* 45:139–166.

Starna, William A., and Ralph Watkins

1991   Northern Iroquois Slavery. *Ethnohistory* 38(1): 34–57.

Steward, Julian

1970   *Basin-Plateau Aboriginal Socio-Political* [1938] *Groups.* University of Utah Press, Salt Lake City.

Sylestine, Cora, Heather K. Hardy, and Timothy Montler

1993   *Dictionary of the Alabama Language.* University of Texas Press, Austin.

Thompson, E. A.

1960   Slavery in Early Germany. In *Slavery in the Ancient World,* edited by Moses I. Finley, pp. 191–203. W. Heffer and Sons, Cambridge, UK.

Tindale, Norman B.

1953   Tribal and Inter-tribal Marriage among the

Australian Aborigines. *Human Biology* 25: 169–190.

Trexler, Richard C.
1995   *Sex and Conquest: Gendered Violence, Political Order, and the European Conquest of the Americas.* Cornell University Press, Ithaca.

Trimborn, Hermann
1949   *Señorío y barbarie en el Valle de Cauca.* Instituto Gonzalo Fernández de Oviedo, Madrid.

Turner, Christy G., and Jacqueline A. Turner
1999   *Man Corn: Cannibalism and Violence in the Prehistoric American Southwest.* University of Utah Press, Salt Lake City.

VanDerBeets, Richard
1994   *Held Captive by Indians: Selected Narratives.* University of Tennessee, Knoxville.

Vargas Llosa, Mario
1989   *The Storyteller.* Farrar Straus, New York.

Wade, Maria F.
2003   *The Native Americans of the Texas Edwards Plateau, 1582–1799.* University of Texas Press, Austin.

Wallace, Anthony F. C.
1970   *The Death and Rebirth of the Seneca.* Alfred A. Knopf, New York.

Weber, David J.
2005   *Bárbaros: Spaniards and Their Savages in the Age of Enlightenment.* Yale University Press, New Haven, CT.

White, Richard
1991   *The Middle Ground.* Cambridge University Press, New York.

Whittlesey, Stephanie M., and J. Jefferson Reid
2001   Mortuary Ritual and Organizational Inferences at Grasshopper Pueblo, Arizona. In *Ancient Burial Practices in the American Southwest,* edited by Douglas R. Mitchell and Judy L. Brunson-Hadley, pp. 68–96. University of New Mexico Press, Albuquerque.

Wiegers, Robert P.
1988   A Proposal for Indian Slave Trading in the Mississippi Valley and Its Impact on the Osage. *Plains Anthropologist* 33:187–202.

Wilkinson, Richard G.
1997   Violence Against Women: Raiding and Abduction in Prehistoric Michigan. In *Troubled Times: Violence and Warfare in the Past,* edited by Debra L. Martin and David W. Frayer, pp. 21–43. Gordon and Breach, Amsteldjik, The Netherlands.

Wilbarger, John W.
1991   *Indian Depradations in Texas.* Texas A&M
[1889] University Press, College Station.

Willey, P., and Thomas E. Emerson
1993   The Osteology and Archaeology of the Crow Creek Massacre. *Plains Anthropologist Memoir* 27:227–270.

Wood, W. Raymond (editor)
1980   *The Explorations of the La Vérendryes in the Northern Plains, 1738–1743, by G. Hubert Smith.* University of Nebraska Press, Lincoln.

Wray, Charles F., Martha L. Sempowski, Lorraine P. Saunders, and Gian Carlo Cervone
1987   The Adams and Culbertson Sites. *Research Records of the Rochester Museum of Arts and Sciences,* No. 19, Charles F. Hayes III, general editor. Rochester, NY.

Wright, Robin M.
1991   Indian Slavery in the Northwest Amazon. *Boletim do Museu Paraense Goeldi* 7:149–179.

Zarzar, Alonzo, and Luis Roman
1983   *Relaciones intertribales en el Bajo Urubamba y Alto Ucayali.* Centro de Investigación y Promoción Amazónica, Documento 5. Lima, Peru.

12

Captives in Amazonia: Becoming Kin in a Predatory Landscape

Brenda J. Bowser

No captives are taken except women and small children
who are treated as full members of the group.
LIPKIND 1948:188

Enemy men and women alike were slaughtered and decapitated,
and the trophy heads thrown into carrying baskets. Children were captured
and brought back to be raised as Mundurucú [group members].
MURPHY AND MURPHY 2004 [1974]:106

Captives were adopted into the kinship system and thereby assumed
the same rights and privileges as members born into the community.
MEGGERS 1996:144

And they all lived happily ever after.
MODERN REINTERPRETATION OF BROTHERS GRIMM TALES

Amazonia has a long history of indigenous captive-taking. Historical and ethnographic accounts vividly document endemic warfare, head-hunting and cannibalism, slavery, retaliatory raiding for insult, murder, and witchcraft, and the widespread capture of people, including men, women, and children, beginning prior to European penetration and continuing, in some cases, to the present day. Colonial and post-colonial experiences of capture have taken many forms, with native peoples being drawn through physical force, coercion, incentive, and lack of viable alternatives into new institutions of colonialism and nationalism, including the *encomienda* and mission systems, military conscription, slave-raiding and slave-trading, debt peonage, capture for hacienda work, forced seasonal labor, government labor contracts issued to tribute and tax collectors, and the abduction of families and rape of women by soldiers during international border disputes. Indigenous peoples have been both victims and collaborators in these systems, which extended into recent times and, in many ways, are ongoing. They are part of the social memory and lived experiences of people today, documented in oral and written histories. The ubiquity of predation—creating a predatory landscape—and its profound effects on indigenous peoples throughout Amazonia are unquestionable.

Although warfare and captive-taking in Amazonia have figured prominently in ethnographies and theoretical debates in anthropology, surpris-

FIGURE 12.1. Amazonian societies discussed in text.

ingly little attention has been given to the lives of captives, particularly women and children, who were presumably integrated as kin into indigenous Amazonian societies. Rather, the implications for captives' lives have been minimized: the potential for violent incorporation, the potential inequalities introduced by bringing enemy or outsider women and children as captives into kin-based societies where rights of social personhood are dependent on kinship, how the structural constraints of kinship were renegotiated, and the possibility that captive people were incorporated into ambiguous or weak social locations in their captor societies, making them more vulnerable to abuses of many kinds—domestic violence, sexual abuse, relations of servitude, witchcraft accusations, and even human sacrifice. Yet, ethnographic accounts provide glimpses into all of these processes (Figure 12.1). Similarly, while a great deal has been written about Amazonian warfare, less attention has been given to the strategies that indigenous peoples have employed to manage conflict, seek refuge from predatory violence, and rebuild their communities—including the possibility that strategic captive-taking, ironically, may be part of conflict management. These issues have archaeological relevance, as archaeologists seek to recognize and contextu-

alize the experiences of captives, to understand the historical processes that give rise to captive-taking, and to identify the relevant archaeological evidence. Here, the question that serves as my point of departure is simple: How have men, women, and children been incorporated as captives into indigenous societies in Amazonia, and have they ever achieved full rights of social personhood? Addressing this question contributes toward a fuller understanding of how these "invisible citizens" (see Cameron, this volume) may be acknowledged, materialized, and theorized as part of the archaeological record.

Anthropological Approaches to Captives in Amazonia: An Overview

Captive-taking has long been an important "ethnographic fact" in Amazonian anthropology, and each successive paradigm has accounted for it. *The Tropical Forest Tribes,* volume 3 of the *Handbook of South American Indians* (Steward 1948d), distilled the subject to a single focus as a derived culture trait of a homogeneous culture that had diffused throughout Amazonia. Lowie (1948:35) wrote succinctly about the treatment of war prisoners: "Captive women were usually taken in marriage and children reared as ordinary tribal members." Lévi-Strauss (1948b:340) presaged the primary anthropological agenda for analysis of captive women when he wrote in the *Handbook* about the exchange of women and intertribal relationships in the Upper Xingu River region of Brazil: "Intermarriages resulted from these half-warlike, half-friendly relations." Lévi-Strauss (1963 [1958]) formulated his influential perspective on the abduction of women in the Brazilian Amazon as one aspect of the symmetric "exchange of women" between kinship groups and a vital element of social reproduction. His structuralist theory of matrimonial exchange came to dictate and shape ethnographic studies of social organization in Amazonia. These studies have focused to a considerable extent on analyzing systems of marriage, descent, and alliance, categorizing the abduction of women as marriage (see Arhem 1981; Descola and Taylor 1993; Jackson 1975; Kensinger 1984; Viveiros de Castro 1996). Chagnon's ethnography, *Yanomamö: The Fierce People*, originally published in 1968, drew attention to the stark reality of Yanomamo practices of abducting women. Chagnon was clearly influenced by Lévi-Strauss in his analysis of these abductions, which he situated squarely in terms of Yanomamo marriage and alliance. However, he emphasized its importance in biological reproduction rather than social reproduction, building the foundations of human behavioral ecology and inciting heated debate in anthropology (Chagnon 1979, 1988, 1992, 1996, 1997; Chagnon and Irons 1979; Cronk et al. 2000). In his analysis of "ceremonial" bride-capture as a relict of violent abductions in Tukanoan societies of the Colombian Amazon, Barnes (1999) revived a nineteenth-century view that theorized bride-capture as an evolutionary stage of marriage, when hordes of men could obtain women as wives only by capturing them from matrilineal groups; theoretically, this led, in turn, to the development of patrilineality as societies advanced to higher stages (see Engels 1972 [1884]:78, 100, 112; McLennan 1865).

Cultural ecological approaches of the 1960s, 1970s, and 1980s explained capture of women for marriage, the enslavement and killing of war captives, and endemic warfare as constituents of a culture of male dominance that served to reduce population pressure and create buffer zones where limited natural resources could become replenished (e.g., DeBoer 1981; Harris 1984; Meggers 1971, 1996; Bennett Ross 1984:97–98; cf. Chagnon 1997:91–97). Carneiro's (1970) influential theory of environmental or social circumscription as a necessary precondition for the origin of the state took a Marxist perspective on Amazonian captive-taking, explaining the emergence of class distinctions as the result of warfare and the incorporation of war captives into positions of slavery as circumscribed groups competed over resources in environmentally rich areas. Some Amazonianists have taken more straightforward materialist approaches to explain the abduction of women as an instrumental means to increase men's control over productive labor and serve men's status-striving (e.g., DeBoer 1986:237–238; Harner 1972:80); a way for men to obtain a valuable resource (women) while avoiding the cost of bride-payment in Western goods (Ferguson 1995:51–52); or an economic strategy of resource accumulation categorized with other forms of "plunder" from a neo-Marxist world-systems perspective (Hornborg 1998:171).

In sum, captive-taking has been a variable of central importance in the history of Amazonian anthropology, and it has been explained mainly in terms of generalizable, endogenous cultural and environmental factors. However, captives, particularly women, have been defined and analyzed primarily as objects of acquisition rather than subjects of interest—a perspective that is decidedly androcentric.

More recently, Amazonian anthropology has taken a "historical turn" (Viveiros de Castro 1996:192) with the recognition of the Amazonian landscape as a mosaic of historical, cultural, and environmental specificities where the effects of colonialism were more acute at different times and in different places, and could be highly localized. A new synthesis of history, anthropology, and human ecology has led to a growing interest in regional ethnohistory that elucidates the interactions between indigenous peoples and Western society, the tremendous depopulation and displacement of Native peoples that resulted from colonial and post-colonial encounters, and the reconstruction of new values, hybrid identities, and senses of community and place (e.g., Basso 1995; Hill 1988; Hornborg 2005; Rival 2002, 2006; Reeve 1985, 1988; Viatori 2005, 2007; and Whitten

1976, 1985; see also Brooks 2002 and Stein 2005). This paradigmatic shift de-centers the topic of captive women in Amazonia, but it integrates exogenous factors by encompassing the premise that indigenous practices of captive-taking were embedded in specific historical processes of Western encounters, yet rooted in indigenous ideologies of predation (see Rival 2002; Santos-Granero 2007; Taylor 1996; Viveiros de Castro 1996). Undoubtedly, these practices were transformed in response to institutions of colonialism and nationalism. Generally, historical documents and oral traditions support the received wisdom that native peoples began to capture, rather than kill, enemy men along with enemy women and children to sell or trade in escalating numbers to slave-traders, missionaries, plantation owners, and others (e.g., see Chernela 1993:24; Gray 1997:189; Rival 2002:32–33; Stanfield 1998:1–18; Wright 1991).

Strategic captive-taking became integral to the reworking of community, identity, and sense of place in many ways. One recurrent theme is the reconstitution of society by people seeking refuge from predatory violence in depopulated areas. These were often marginal lands (although marginality may be defined ecologically, geographically, or in terms of historical factors of predation) where people rebuilt kinship and community by incorporating diverse others, including captives (e.g., see Basso 1995:18–23, 197–199, 230–231 on the Xinguano of Brazil; Chagnon 1992:106–111 on the Yanomamo of Venezuela; and Rival 2002:30 on the Huaorani [Waorani] of Ecuador). This view of a predatory landscape provides a different perspective on marginal areas than cultural ecological approaches, one that DeBoer recognized when he incorporated ethnohistory into his discussions of buffer zones (DeBoer 1981:373) and "backwoods resistance" (DeBoer 1986:239) in the Peruvian Amazon (see also Bennett Ross 1984:96–98 on the Achuar). Wife-capture was a strategy by which men could escape from the obligations of supporting their fathers-in-law in reciprocal feuding (e.g., see Descola 1996b [1993]:176, 178 on the Achuar) because men who captured wives from distant places circumvented the perpetual indebtedness of bride-service and matrilocality, as Murdock (1949:206–207) pointed out some time ago (see

also Arhem 1981; DeBoer, this volume; Habicht-Mauche, this volume). In other examples, captive children were taken to be raised like sons (e.g., Whitten 1984:205) and daughters (e.g., Valero 1996 [1965]:113), but specifically to be marriage partners for their captors' children. In some cases, precarious alliances made the process of arranging marriages dangerous, and in others, marriage partners were lacking because groups had been decimated by predation and dispersal. Thus, incorporating captives as new members into refugee societies, capturing distant women as wives, and bringing up captive children to be future spouses of one's own children—all of these were strategies for rebuilding society and, ironically, avoiding conflict.

The Standard Model of Amazonia

With few exceptions, anthropologists and historians have written about the lives of indigenous men, women, and children taken captive in Amazonia with startling detachment and brevity, perhaps a sentence or two. In some accounts, captives are invisible altogether, despite the importance of captive-taking culturally, historically, and theoretically. This precedent, arguably, was established in the *Handbook of South American Indians* (1948), in which practices of abduction and the incorporation of captives into society were given considerably less attention than warfare, human sacrifice, anthropophagy, and the preparation of trophies made from human body parts—all described in detailed, though equally dispassionate, accounts. Raiding or abduction conducted specifically to obtain wives was not distinguished from practices of taking women as war captives, even though a few subsections on marriage and law mention raids to capture women and sanctions or payments for "stealing" wives. On the other hand, the practice of taking war captives is documented systematically in organized subsections devoted to warfare for many societies, with particular attention paid to whether men were sometimes captured or always killed. There are few details concerning the fates of war captives, especially women and children, who survived and remained within their captors' societies. The following passage by William Lipkind, based on his own fieldwork in 1937, encapsulates many of the elements of the predatory landscape of Amazonia that were of primary interest to early anthropologists.

> The Carajá are good fighters and have maintained themselves since prehistoric times in a territory surrounded on all sides by warlike enemies. Their usual tactics are waiting outside an enemy village at night and attacking at dawn. They use the bow and arrow and club, and are skilled wrestlers. They cut off a foot bone of a dead enemy and carry it back to their village; this places them in control of the ghost, who now becomes a caretaker of the village and is impersonated in a special dry-season ceremony. At one such ceremony there were two Tapirapé ghosts, three Chavante, one Cayapó, and one Neo-Brazilian. Present-day warfare is largely with the Chavante, the Cayapó, and the Canoeiro. Now and then a Neo-Brazilian may be killed by stealth to avenge a personal grievance. No captives are taken except women and small children who are treated as full members of the group. (Lipkind 1948:188)

The *Handbook* is also the source of influential generalizations made by Robert Lowie (1948) and Julian Steward (1948a) about indigenous practices of capture in Amazonia. Together, they defined the cultural stereotype of the "Tropical Forest culture" of Amazonia. Lowie characterized the culture traits of Tropical Forest peoples, and Steward established the framework for explaining the distribution of these traits as a standard aboriginal pattern that had diffused throughout the tropical forests of the Amazon Basin and its peripheries. Lowie (1948:35) minimized the variation in practices of indigenous captive-taking and established the "standard pattern" of Amazonian culture. He summarized captive-taking with characteristic brevity in a two-sentence subsection devoted to treatment of prisoners: "Slavery has already been mentioned. Captive women were usually taken in marriage and children reared as ordinary tribal members, but the cannibalistic *Tupinamba*, though taking captives, always killed and ate them sooner or later." Steward explained the distribution and variability of Tropical Forest culture traits in terms of environmental adaptation, cultural evolution, and diffusion. According to his scenario, the standard pattern of egalitarian horticulturalists originated in the Circum-Caribbean area, spread to the environmentally richest areas of Amazonia along the coast and the floodplains of major rivers, and then diffused throughout the tropical forest regions of Amazonia. The standard pattern persisted throughout most of the tropical forest, with some localized differences, including a few remnant groups of "pre-agricultural" hunter-gatherers who remained in marginal savannah environments.

In sum, the standard pattern of captive-taking was defined as one of endemic raiding, the killing of enemy men, and the incorporation of captive women and children into the kinship structure of largely egalitarian societies. Variation from the standard pattern was attributed to incipient social complexity in dense, settled populations or the diffusion of these traits from more complex neighboring societies. In the Guianas, where dense populations developed in environmentally rich areas, war captives were characterized ambivalently as slaves or serfs who were "incorporated into the tribe," comprising a "kind of lower class" together with "sons-in-law and unattached men" attached to chiefs, but not regarded by anthropologists as a true social class (Lowie 1948: 32–33; Steward 1948a:887–888, 893). Slavery of war captives or conquered peoples in the Mojos-Chiquitos region of eastern Brazil and among the Chiriguano in eastern Bolivia was attributed to the diffusion of Andean influences (Lowie 1948: 32–33).

Archaeological Perspectives

Archaeologists have contributed to these debates, building from the standard model, although captive-taking has not been the subject of archaeological investigations in Amazonia. Meggers (1996), following Lowie (1948) and Steward (1948a), argued that slavery of war captives among the Omagua could be understood as an environmental adaptation in rich floodplain areas along major rivers. From this perspective, slavery served as a buffer that allowed the dominant society to maximize food production during good years, but to kill expendable slaves as a population control measure during lean years. Otherwise, she expected that the standard Tropical Forest pattern would apply throughout

Amazonian societies located in less productive ecological zones, where "captives were adopted into the kinship system and thereby assume the same rights and privileges as members born into the community" (ibid., 144). Roosevelt (1991:416) dealt a swift blow to the possibility that captives might present an archaeological problem in the complex chiefdoms of lower Amazonia, stating briefly that "Captive slaves appear to have been few in number and often were incorporated into the societies' genealogical systems" among chiefly nobility in Amazonia.

DeBoer (1986, 1990, 2000) proposed that feasting would provide archaeological evidence of Shipibo-Conibo captive-taking in the Peruvian Amazon. Historically, the Conibo raided other groups in the same river basin, taking the girls and women as wives, and the boys for servitude or sale as slaves (DeBoer 1986). Victimized groups dispersed and fled to interior areas away from the main stretches of river, which were dominated by the Conibo. DeBoer argues that success in raiding would have led to higher rates of polygyny in Conibo villages, and that competitive feasting would have been made possible by the influx of female labor, with the women producing the beer served at feasts, and their husbands consequently gaining status as hosts. Among the possible archaeological correlates of large-scale feasting are large pots for brewing and storing manioc beer, large pottery bowls for serving and drinking beer, and ceramic vaginal plugs used in puberty ceremonies (DeBoer 1986, 2000).

DeBoer cautions that pottery made by captive wives and their descendants is likely to conform to the basic stylistic standards of their captor group rather than appear as a "foreign" style (DeBoer 1986:242–243, 1990, 2007). His caution is based primarily on impressions of pottery forms and decorative styles, including ethnographic observations by Lathrap (1970, 1983); the absence of obviously intrusive pottery styles in the archaeological record of the Shipibo-Conibo (DeBoer 1986:242); and the painted styles of ethnographic pottery made by one abducted woman (DeBoer 1990:93) and the descendants of a few abducted women (DeBoer 1986, 1990) in Shipibo-Conibo villages. However, recent studies of pottery-making suggest that subtle attributes of technological style, such as methods used to build and shape pots, are likely to remain conservative during the lifetime of a potter and to be transmitted intergenerationally, reflecting the context of her early learning and socialization, even though her painted style may change when she enters a new community and conform with more visible attributes of pottery-making in the new group (e.g., see Duff 2002; Gosselain 2000; Habicht-Mauche, this volume; Stark 1998; cf. Bowser 2002:118–130). Therefore, captive women may be implicated in the archaeological record by the use of a "foreign" technological style on vessels with a "local" decorative style. Additionally, more recent studies of Amazonian pottery show that subtle differences in the painted style of vessels made by women from different groups living in the same village may conform to similar design standards yet still be distinguished through careful quantitative analyses (Bowser 2000, 2002; Bowser and Patton 2008). Therefore, more rigorous ceramics research may help distinguish the pottery of foreign women. The subject warrants further investigation.

Today, where archaeologists and other anthropologists once envisioned a homogeneous Amazonian Tropical Forest culture, with differences based on an environmental dichotomy of rich floodplains and poor tropical forest environments, they now see diversity. By the 1970s, "the image of Amazonian homogeneity was eroding in the face of more detailed studies of the human ecology, history, and prehistory of Amazonian peoples" (Heckenberger 2005:12–13). Nevertheless, a rising awareness in contemporary archaeological studies of the extent to which colonial captive-taking and other intrusions impacted indigenous lives (e.g., see Heckenberger 2005:74, 155, 180) has overshadowed the subject of captives within Amazonian societies, silencing and even denying their experiences. Thus, it is an opportune time to reconsider the ubiquity and variability of indigenous practices of captive-taking as our understanding of the complexity and variation of archaeological societies in Amazonia grows.

Ubiquity of Captive-Taking

Despite its shortcomings as a product of its time, the *Handbook of South American Indians* remains the most comprehensive resource for assessing the ubiquity and variability of indigenous practices of capture in Amazonia. An encyclopedic compilation of the mostly piecemeal historic and ethnographic information available at the time of its publication in 1948, the *Handbook* is thus an important resource for gleaning insights from (and about) anthropological understandings of captives in Amazonia.

Clearly, the practice of taking war captives was a widespread phenomenon in Amazonia. In Table 12.1, I have summarized the information about captives in the tropical forests of Amazonia, including the adjoining coastal regions, upland margins, and other related areas, based on the *Handbook*. Captive-taking is reported from every major region, and for almost one-third (30 of 103, or 29 percent) of the 103 "tribes" or "tribal divisions" categorized variably by Steward and his colleagues on the basis of language family, geography, and cultural relationships. War captives were executed in cannibalistic rituals, kept as slaves or servants, incorporated into the social group, bought, or sold. By contrast, only four groups (4 percent) reportedly took no war captives: one society (Tucuna) engaged in warfare but did not take captives, and three groups (seminomadic Makú hunter-gatherers) did not take captives or engage in warfare but rather were themselves subjected to raiding, capture, and servitude by other groups. For the remaining cases (67 percent), the authors provide no information about captive-taking, but the high frequency of documented warfare and reciprocal raiding suggests that captive-taking was endemic.

Variability in Captive-Taking

As a starting point, it is important to consider that captives in Amazonia were incorporated into "multiple social locations" (see Brooks 2002:6) that are understandable less as categories of slave, servant, or kin than as a continuum of social rights of personhood. Generally, captives experience a loss of social personhood that is complete at the time of their capture, leaving them completely vulnerable. As disposable persons, they have no rights, including the right of life, other than those bestowed upon them by their captors. For this reason, it is useful to shift from examining the meanings of categories of servitude to examining how the captives' rights of social personhood come to be meaningfully ascribed through the process of incorporation into a community, and considering what rights of social personhood captives have compared to other people in the same category. Therefore, it is important to give attention not only to the categories into which captives are placed by anthropologists, but also to the categories into which they were placed by captor societies, and to examine the social equivalencies of those categories and the continuum of rights of social personhood that pertain.

Slavery

Generally, anthropologists have thought that "true" slavery was not widespread among indigenous groups throughout Amazonia prior to early European contact and later colonial encounters, but that some such societies did exist, mostly around the margins of complex chiefdoms, state-level societies, or expanding empires. Whether Amazonian captives should be categorized as "slaves" rather than "serfs," "servants," or "a kind of a lower class" has been a matter of definition and some debate (e.g., see Lowie 1948:32–33; Steward 1948a:887–888, 893; Steward 1948c:528; see also Jackson 1983:162). These categories were important to early anthropologists, who viewed these distinctions as critical to identifying stages of cultural evolution so that societies could be arrayed along a continuum from primitive to civilized. From this perspective, "more advanced" societies incorporated war captives as a distinct category of people, a social class, whereas "less advanced" tribal societies incorporated captives into the kinship structure of their egalitarian societies. Thus, indigenous people who captured women and children and incorporated them into society were "primitive," but those who enslaved men, women, and children were more "advanced," and indigenous and colonial peoples who bought captives to serve as slaves were "civilized." My goal here is not so much to debate these categories of meaning, but to recognize the fact that the categories themselves derive from Western historical traditions and are not readily applicable to indigenous Amazonian societies.

By "true" slavery, many people think of the hereditary, large-scale systems of slavery that

Patterson (1982:353) calls "slave societies" or "societies in which the social structure was decisively dependent on the institution of slavery," although "dependence was often, but not necessarily, economic." However, it is useful to think of slavery as a relationship of servitude involving, at its most basic level, two people. Defined broadly, slavery is a relationship of servitude that involves the deprivation of liberty, lack of rights over one's body, and ownership or commodification of human bodies for labor, sexual access, reproduction, or other purposes. The relationship may be based on the subordination of members of one social group by members of a different and dominant social group or institution, or it may arise among members of the same social group through social differentiation (Patterson 1982:38–39). Slavery encompasses varied forms of human servitude, including chattel slavery (ownership of a person), debt peonage, indentured labor, and certain forms of marriage. Slavery and other relationships of servitude may be entered into willingly or unwillingly, be permanent or temporary over the lifetime of the subordinated individual, be transferable by the dominant individual, and be heritable or not heritable by kin. All forms of human servitude sanction corporeal punishment under specified circumstances. All relationships of servitude are based on a differential of power, encoded in statutory or customary law, and governed according to cultural principles of appropriate behaviors that structure interactions between and among dominant and subordinated individuals, defining their respective rights and responsibilities. To a certain degree, slavery is distinguishable from other forms of human servitude by the extent to which subordinated individuals can negotiate within these power structures and sever the bonds of servitude; in general, slavery is the most oppressive, restrictive, and durable form of servitude, and granted the fewest rights of social personhood. Whether or not captives were "slaves" is therefore partly an issue of degree.

The Tupinamba and Yuquí cases, though differing markedly in the social organization and scale of the societies under consideration, provide examples of the hereditary enslavement of captives and their incorporation as "kin" in Amazonia.

Tupinamba

Tupinamba slavery of war captives encompassed most of the variation in practices of captive-taking documented in Amazonia (see Table 12.1). Although Tupinamba slavery was dismissed by Lowie because "though taking captives, [they] always killed and ate them sooner or later," it really is the archetype of slave systems in Amazonia. Tupinamba slavery derives its historical legitimacy from the fact that it was recorded so early and fully at the time of early European contact, with detailed accounts dating back to the mid-1500s (Métraux 1948d). It bears many strong resemblances to complex practices of indigenous slavery in native North America, which Brooks (2002:14) describes as a "great captive exchange complex that operated throughout the continent [and]…combined sacred and secular exchange imperatives: sacrificial subjects, kin replacements for those lost in war, and forcible seizures of women and children for marriage and adoption" (see also the chapters by Ames, DeBoer, and Peregrine, this volume).

The name "Tupinamba" has been applied historically to culturally related groups of Tupi-Guarani speakers of the Brazilian coastal region at the mouth of the Amazon River (Métraux 1948d). Tupinamba settlements were large, palisaded villages on hilltops where people lived in longhouses built around a central plaza. Settlements consisted of four to eight longhouses divided into separate compartments for each family; each longhouse held an extended family of twenty to thirty families, housing up to two hundred occupants. Captive-taking reportedly was a main purpose of war, with captives incorporated into the social structure as kin, substitutes for kin, or slaves.

Captives were submitted to a long ritual of social death (sensu Patterson 1982:5–7), beginning in battle, where captives were claimed by the warrior who touched them first. Captives were then led home, exhibited and paraded in villages along the way, traded for "feathers or other ornaments" (Métraux 1948d:113), and submitted to other public rituals of insult and torture. Captive men to be sacrificed endured the same treatment for days in the village of their captors before they were clubbed to death, shattering their skulls, then quartered, roasted, and

TABLE 12.1. Summary of Information on Captives in Amazonia in the *Handbook of South American Indians* (Steward 1948)

	Took War Captives	War Captives Killed, Cannibalized, and/or Sacrificed	War Captives Kept as Slaves	War Captives Bought, Sold, or Traded	War Captives Incorporated into Families	Stole or Raided for Wives	References
Coastal and Lower Amazonian Tupí							
Guaraní	Y	Y				Y	Métraux 1948a:86
Tupinambá	Y: m, w	Y: m, w	Y: m	Y	Y: m, w		Métraux 1948d
Carajá	Y: w, c, not men		Y	Y	Y		Lipkind 1948:188
Shipaya	Y: c	Y					Nimuendajú 1948f:235–236
Yuruna	Y: m, w, c	Y: m					Nimuendajú 1948f:220
Arara	Y: c						Nimuendajú 1948f:224
Maué	Y						Nimuendajú 1948c:251
Mura	Y		Y			Y	Nimuendajú 1948d:261–262
Pirahã	Y: w, c				Y: w, c		Nimuendajú 1948d:268
Mundurucú	Y: w, c, not men				Captive children never raised.		Horton 1948:278
Parintintin	Y	Y					Nimuendajú 1948a:291
Apiacá	Y	Y			Y: Captive children raised to 12 or 14 and then killed.		Nimuendajú 1948b:319
Upper Xingú	Y	Y					Lévi-Strauss 1948b:339
Matto Grasso and Eastern Bolivia							
Cozárina	Y: m, w, c		Y: m		Y: w Captive boys work.		Métraux 1948c:349–355
Guaporé River	Y		Y		Y: Pay tribute.		Lévi-Strauss 1948b:375
Chiquito	Y				Y: Marry in.		Métraux 1948e:385
Mojo	Y		Y				Métraux 1948e:418
Chiriguano	Y	Y	Y		Y	Y	Métraux 1948f:480–481
Montaña	Y: w, c, not men				Y: w, c		Steward 1948c:528
Arawakan	Y: w, c				Y		Steward and Métraux 1948:546

TABLE 12.1. (cont'd.) Summary of Information on Captives in Amazonia in the *Handbook of South American Indians* (Steward 1948)

	Took War Captives	War Captives Killed, Cannibalized, and/or Sacrificed	War Captives Kept as Slaves	War Captives Bought, Sold, or Traded	War Captives Incorporated into Families	Stole or Raided for Wives	References
Panoan (Shipibo/Conibo/Piro)	Y:w, c		Y	Y	Y:w	Y	Steward and Métraux 1948:582–583, 585–587
Jívaro	Y:w, c				Y:w, c		Steward 1948c:528
Zaparoan	Y				Y	Y	Steward and Métraux 1948:645–646
Quijo	Y:w, c		Y		Y		Steward 1948c:528
Tupí	Y		Y		Y		Steward 1948c:528, 1948a:890
Western Amazon							
Tupí (Upper Amazon-Omagua/Cocama)	Y:w, c, not men	Y	Y:w, c				Métraux 1948g:687,697–698, 700–701
Arawakan (Left, Middle Amazon)	Y		Y	Y			Métraux 1948g:710
Tucuna	N						Nimuendajú 1948e:721
Witatoan	Y	Y: old people	Y		Y		Steward 1948b:756–757
Uaupés-Caquetá (Cubeo)	Y:w, c		Y:w, c				Goldman 1948:786
Guianas and Lower Left Amazon Tributaries							
Arawakan	Y		Y	Y			Gillin 1948:849,852–853
Cariban	Y		Y	Y	Y:m		Gillin 1948: 849,852–853
Macú (Makú, Maku) (various)	N						Métraux 1948b:866

Note: Y = yes; N = no; m = men; w = women, c = children; blank = unspecified.

consumed in a public feast. Captive women and children were expected to watch and participate in the feast.

Captives were incorporated into Tupinamba social structure as wives or husbands, but in ambiguous social locations. Captured women could be taken as secondary wives, subordinate to the first wife. Following patrilineal rules of descent, the children of a captive woman and her captor husband were categorized as full members of the captor society. However, a woman was more likely to be killed for adultery if she "was a captive or without a family to revenge her" (ibid., 112). In this sense, a captive wife was located in a socially similar manner as other wives with few or no kin. However, was she simply treated like other wives with few kin, or was she in an ambiguous location, more like substitute kin? I would argue the latter. Many captive wives were eventually sacrificed "unless they belonged to an influential man who had become fond of them" (ibid., 113). When a captive woman died, her skull was crushed, like those of captives who had been enslaved or sacrificed, whether she had died a natural death or was killed. Thus, captive wives did not achieve full rights of social personhood but were categorized as captives in perpetuity, even in death.

A captive man could be taken as a husband by a Tupinamba woman, but ambiguously, as a substitute husband for the widow of a warrior killed before his capture. Although he wore the ornaments, used the hammock, and lived in the house of the deceased husband, this was not so much a privilege as a requirement to ritually cleanse them of the embodied spirit of the dead husband. The substitute husband was thus allotted the risks of doing so during a liminal period of great danger. The widow was expected to keep her new husband from escaping from the village. If she became pregnant by him, the child was regarded as a member of the enemy group, and she was expected to give up the child for sacrifice and cannibalism to her relatives. In some cases, the mother would not give up the child, and it was a source of shame for her and her family. Some women even ran away with their captive husbands.

Slaves slept with the head of the extended family and his relatives in the middle of the house or another location of high status. Men who were slaves were obligated to work for their owners "like a son-in-law." They were allotted garden land, grew their own food, and hunted for themselves. Slaves performed agricultural work, domestic labor, and domestic service for their owners. They were subjected to greater insult and abuse than other group members, and they could be sacrificed.

Men's rites of passage and positions of status in many ways depended on taking, owning, and sacrificing prisoners. A chief had an entourage of slaves and sons-in-law who worked for him, and as many as thirty wives, including captured women. A man's transition to marriageable age required him to conduct the public sacrifice of a war captive, although the captive could be given to him by his father, uncle, or brother-in-law (which helps explain why captives were killed "sooner or later"). A man's bride-service included avenging the death of his in-laws and offering a captive to his brother-in-law to kill, "thereby increasing his prestige by a change of his name" (ibid., 111). Prestigious flutes were made from the long bones of enemy men killed in battle or sacrifice. A man was entitled to marry his brother's widow by the rules of levirate, but only after he had taken a prisoner to ritually cleanse the grave, wear the ornaments, and use the hammock of his deceased brother to exorcise evil spirits. Thus, the Tupinamba social and economic structure was dependent on captive-taking during war.

The Tupinamba readily sold their war captives and slaves to Europeans after contact, leading to a rapid integration of their slave system with that of the Europeans (ibid.). Some Tupinamba were reportedly "sad" to see their slaves treated badly and would visit them, but when colonial authorities prevented them from killing war prisoners, the Tupinamba would open the graves and smash the skulls of war captives who had died. The incongruity of an emotional attachment to captives and their rapid commodification, as well as the importance of marking their captive status in death, underscore the ambivalence of their incorporation into Tupinamba society and their lesser rights of social personhood.

Similar practices of enslaving captives were recorded elsewhere in Amazonia among other Tupi-Guarani speakers, especially the Omagua, a complex chiefdom with chiefs, chiefly classes, and slaves. They expanded far into western Amazonia as major slave-traders on the rivers from the sixteenth century into the 1930s (Carvajal 1934; DeBoer 1986; Fritz 1922; Meggers 1996), as did Carib- and Arawakan-speaking groups in the Guianas (Lowie 1948:35) and elsewhere (e.g., see Heckenberger 2005:63). These similarities suggest that other complex, widespread systems of slavery may have existed in Amazonia, as they did elsewhere in the Americas, prior to the decimation of populations and reorientation of systems of captive-taking that accompanied European penetration of the region.

Yuquí

The Yuquí are mobile hunter-gatherer bands of the Bolivian Amazon who speak a Tupi-Guarani language (Stearman 1989). Yuquí are thought to be a remnant group of Guarani horticultural foragers who had institutionalized slavery. The Yuquí differ significantly from other hunter-gatherer groups in greater Amazonia because they historically took captives in warfare, whereas other forager groups, including the Makú (see Table 11.1), Ache (Hill and Hurtado 1996), and Seriono (Holmberg 1969 [1950]:10–11, 157–160), while under siege and engaged in warfare, were the source of captives rather than being captor societies themselves. Furthermore, the Yuquí differ significantly from the expected pattern of captive-taking in Amazonia in that they historically captured men as well as women, and their captives were incorporated as "slaves" in a system of hereditary servitude with well-explicated rules of descent, as among the Tupinamba. According to principles of patrilineal descent, the children of a male slave and a free Yuquí woman were born and lived as slaves, whereas the children of a female slave and a free Yuquí man were free. However, the slave heritage of a free descendant could be invoked as a basis for ridicule, servitude, or sacrifice. Slaves were expected to gather firewood, tend the fires at night, and help track and carry game, but they were rarely permitted to hunt; they slept on the ground rather than in hammocks, they ate leftover food, and they were thinner. Slaves, and sometimes the free descendants of slaves, were sacrificed to accompany the dead; captives were sometimes taken specifically for this purpose. In sum, captives and the free descendants of captives incorporated as "kin" into Yuquí society had fewer rights of social personhood than other members of their captor society.

Marriage and Adoption as Kin

The few brief glimpses afforded by ethnographies indicate that the initial process of incorporating captives into Amazonian societies as kin could be violent. Constituting a kind of social death marked by dehumanizing rituals, this process involved stripping away an individual's social personhood, although for some it could be slowly regained. Many captives were not integrated at all: they often were killed or died of neglect or injuries soon after capture. Even after "adoption" or "marriage" or otherwise being integrated into a society, a captured person might be categorized as a subordinate individual or otherwise experience fewer rights of social personhood. In many ways, captives were socially located like orphans, without close kin to protect them. The following are selective examples from ethnographies that illustrate practices of marriage and adoption as kin by capture in Amazonia.

Yanomamo

The Yanomamo of Venezuela and Brazil are in many ways a classic Amazonian "big man" society of horticultural foragers (Chagnon 1992, 1997). Chagnon's ethnographic fieldwork among the Yanomamo was conducted from the 1950s into the 1990s. Small-scale raiding was endemic, motivated by witchcraft accusations, disputes over women, and obligations of retaliatory violence. Men were killed in raids, and women and children were abducted. People lived in small, palisaded villages that were moved frequently; short-distance residential movements were made to open new garden land for swidden cultivation, and long-distance residential movements were provoked by warfare and politics. Chagnon's detailed demographic data document the profound effects of warfare and captive-taking in people's lives: one-quarter of adult men died in warfare (Chagnon 1992:6), and 12 to 17 percent of wives were women who had been captured in raids (106). The demographic data also provide a measure of the importance of refuge areas in reducing violence, including the abduction of women.

His ethnographic data are not silent on the issue of violence against captured women and children, but instead give us important, though brief, glimpses of their incorporation into society and transition to social personhood (see also Valero 1996 [1965]).

Captured women were incorporated into the group violently, raped by men in the raiding party and then by men in village before eventually being given away as wives. Although they were sometimes pursued and retrieved by men from their original village in retaliatory raids, former captives were often subject to ridicule, abuse, and rejection for having been with the enemy group. Captive wives, like other Yanomamo women without kin in the village, were more likely to be abused by their husbands, and captured children were more likely to be tormented and abused not just by adults, but also other children. Eventually, however, some older captured women became intermediaries between warring groups of Yanomamo, which may have earned them status and respect.

Settlement biographies point to imbalances of power and show how people responded in their patterns of settlement, raiding, and captive-taking (Chagnon 1992:106–111, 1997:80–91). Preferred areas of settlement were lowland areas, where some large villages had as many as three to four hundred people. These areas were characterized by more chronic warfare, elaborate alliance patterns with large and regular feasts among allies, and abductions or coercion of women from smaller, weaker neighboring villages. Some of these small, besieged groups sought refuge by pioneering new settlements in unoccupied, ecologically marginal foothills and mountains. In these areas, people lived in smaller villages of forty to eighty people. Men raided other small villages in the uplands, but not the lowland villages. These areas provided at lease some refuge and generally were safer places; mortality rates due to warfare were lower in upland areas than in the preferred lowland areas, fewer men participated in lethal violence (21 vs. 44 percent), and the percentage of captured wives in their villages was lower (12 vs. 17 percent) (ibid., 107). Concomitantly, rates of polygyny were lower (106). These findings are consistent with the Shipibo-Conibo model (DeBoer 1986) in which larger villages, greater evidence of feasting, and higher rates of polygyny in core versus marginal areas may be correlates of the abduction of women during times of warfare in precontact Amazonian societies.

Waorani

Waorani people are seminomadic horticultural foragers who live in the tropical lowlands of eastern Ecuador in the upper Amazon Basin (Robarchek and Robarchek 1998). They are the most violent society ever recorded by anthropologists; close to 100 percent of the men living in the 1960s had participated in the killing of at least one person in raids (ibid., 1, 132–133.). Historically, most raids were motivated by disputes over marriage arrangements, witchcraft accusations, and obligations of reciprocal revenge in long-term feuds, but some raiding parties were formed by groups of young men specifically to capture wives.

The abduction of women was marked by violence and mortality, with women more likely to be killed than captured in raids; according to life-history data on sixty-three Waorani women, 30 percent had been killed and 3 percent had been captured in raids (ibid., 132–134). Abducted women taken as wives by Waorani men do not survive very long in their captors' households. "Although the prospects of long-term survival of these captured women were not great (they were usually killed within a few months), for a time, at least, they were incorporated into Waorani households" (ibid., 98). Some captive women survived long enough to bear children, however; these children and their descendants are identified as kin in Waorani genealogies (ibid., 99), but the degree to which they became fully accepted as Waorani is not clear.

Achuar

The Achuar are horticultural foragers who live in the tropical lowlands of Ecuador and Peru in the upper Amazon Basin (Bowser 2000, 2002; Patton 1996, 2000). Raiding and the abduction of women were endemic threats in Achuar territory into the 1970s (see Descola 1996a [1986]; Harner 1972), although these practices had begun to abate regionally by the 1930s (Harner 1972:204). Today, a few older women in Achuar villages are still living as the wives of their captors.

Descola (1996b [1993]), who conducted field-work among the Achuar in the 1970s, provides a brief glimpse into the rape and psychological abuse involved in "the taming of women" who had been abducted as wives. He quotes Wajari, an Achuar man whose wife Senur and her children had been captured in a raid seven or eight years prior to their conversation:

> At first, it is important to get very angry. I told her, "If you do not come along with me, I shall kill you on the spot." She was frightened and followed me. In the early days I never let her out of my sight; I even accompanied her when she went to piss or shit; and I went with her when she fetched manioc from the garden. I never left her side. She cried a lot, never spoke and wanted to run off to her brother. So I threatened to kill her and she kept quiet. I wanted her to forget Yurank [Senur's husband, who had been killed in the raid when she was captured], so I made love to her as soon as possible. She didn't want to, she used to cry and hit me with her fists; but women are like us: they can't live without sex, so I "worked" on her a lot, [and] she soon got used to me. (ibid., 184–185)

Descola (ibid., 175) asserts that within a few years, "the abductions and enforced adoptions, initially acts of violence, are in time overcome, and the hostility of the past fades into a domestic intimacy that sometimes proves even more harmonious than it would have been were it the fruit of free consent." However, given that "all the men consider they have the right to beat wives who displease them" and are "selectively violent" (ibid., 191) against orphan women who lack kin, particularly brothers and fathers, to protect them (178, 187, 191), one might question how often captive wives, like orphans, live in harmonious domestic intimacy without male kin to protect them against abusive husbands. The female voice, however, is absent on this subject.

Tukanoans

The Tukanoan region of Colombia and Brazil in northwest Amazonia is characterized by a high degree of multilingualism, linguistic exogamy, and patrilineal, patrilocal territorial groups (see Arhem 1981; Barnes 1999; Chernela 1993; Gold-man 1963; C. Hugh-Jones 1979; S. Hugh-Jones 1993; Jackson 1975). Following Lévi-Strauss, anthropological studies in this region have focused on captive-taking in terms of social structure and the symmetries of reciprocal exchange of women between opposing groups. Men marry women from other language groups with which they have long-term relationships of intermarriage, such as brother-sister exchange, that establish expectations for a wife given by one group to be reciprocated by the opposite group, either in simultaneous exchange or in the future. Historically, disputes over women, particularly one promised or "owed" but not given when a request was made by a rightful claimant, provided the motivation for raids to seize women as wives in compensation. Such raids were also undertaken by men who did not have a sister or other female relative to exchange. The degree to which force might be used in the abduction, or violence in retribution, depended on several factors, including the balance of power between the two groups, the history of their relationships, the likelihood of negotiating a settlement agreement to release the abducted women or provide others as reciprocal marriage partners, and the geographical and social distance between them (see also De-Boer, this volume). Some women who were forcibly abducted were released after negotiations; however, the ethnographies provide few details of abducted women's lives or their treatment by their captors.

Death Companions

Like the Yuquí captives, slaves, and descendants of slaves discussed above, the individuals sacrificed as death companions among other groups in the Amazonian region tended to be people in weak social locations: orphans without kin, fatherless rather than motherless, and girls rather than boys. Although there are very few ethnographic accounts of these practices, such consistencies suggest that captives sacrificed as death companions may have served as substitute kin. At the very least, these accounts again show that a person without parents or other strong kin ties in Amazonian kin-based societies, whether a captive or natal member of the group, was more vulnerable to neglect and abuse, and a more disposable member of society.

Historically, orphan children sometimes were buried alive in the graves of dead or dying adults, especially important men, as sacrificial offerings among the Ache, hunter-gatherers of eastern Paraguay (Hill and Hurtado 1996), as well as the Waorani (Robarchek and Robarchek 1998: 134) and the Zápara (Tyler 1894:481), horticultural foragers of the upper Amazon in Ecuador and Peru. The rituals, beliefs, and demographics of child sacrifice are best documented by Hill and Hurtado for the Ache (1996:68–69, 157, 163–164, 166, 434–439). Women were accompanied in death less often than men. Almost all of the individuals sacrificed as death companions were orphan children, especially fatherless girls, ranging in age from infancy to twelve or thirteen years old. Orphans also were stigmatized and neglected and significantly more likely than other children to die from infanticide, homicide, or neglect, especially if they were fatherless girls (434–439). Young boys, widows, and the infirm also were sacrificed. Children sometimes were buried with hands and feet bound, tied to the chest of the dead or dying adult, or stepped on to kill them; those who struggled or tried to escape were sometimes killed and then buried. The band chose by consensus the person to be sacrificed. Adults could offer or suggest their own or other children, and the old or infirm sometimes volunteered themselves or were chosen for sacrifice by others. A dying man could request that his own child be buried with him as a grave companion, or his wife could offer one of their children, although it was understood that other adults could intercede and offer to care for the child, literally engaging in a tug-of-war to pull the "sacrificial offering" away from the person about to put the child into the grave. In this way, children offered in sacrifice could be saved by their godparents, aunts, and grandparents. However, orphan children without kin to defend them were more likely to be sacrificed.

Witchcraft Accusations

In the Peruvian Amazon, captive children have occupied a social location similar to that of orphans and others with no or few kin. Captive and orphaned children have been frequently accused of witchcraft and executed among Peruvian Arawakans. Historical and ethnographic accounts compiled and analyzed by Santos-Granero (2004: 276) show "the marked tendency is for children devoid of kinship relations (orphans, war captives) to be accused" as well as other people in weak social locations: "the most defenseless member of a community, usually a girl child, especially if it is an orphan or captive taken in a raid" (Weiss 1975:295, cited in Santos-Granero 2004:275), "orphans, widows, and destitutes" (Batlle 1905, cited in Santos-Granero 2004:276), the *desplazado* (or displaced) (Santos-Granero 2004:291), generally fatherless rather than motherless orphans, and generally girls rather than boys. Accusations of child witchcraft increased dramatically during two periods of social change and violence. Such accusations soared between the 1880s and 1930s with the large-scale displacement of Peruvian-Arawak populations by colonists, waves of epidemics that killed thousands of Native people, a massive earthquake, and deep divisions and suspicion created when indigenous people converted to a Christian faith. Since the 1990s, there has been a resurgence of sorcery accusations, especially against children and others who are known or thought to be sympathizers of terrorist organizations exerting control in the region.

Children suspected by a shaman of becoming witches may be regularly starved, beaten, and submitted to cleansing rituals such as ingestion of tobacco and other herbal purgatives to induce vomiting. Children accused of actually practicing witchcraft are starved, beaten, and subjected to treatments to make them cry, such as rubbing chile peppers in their eyes or "smoking" them: hanging them upside down, tying them to a smoking rack, or confining them in a room over a smoky fire. If the child's "victim" does not die, the child is beaten, cleansed, and released. Some accused witches and their families are expelled from the community, and others escape. If the victim dies, the child is condemned to death by bludgeoning, drowning, stoning, being shot with arrows, being buried or burned alive, or being tied to a tree and left for jaguars or ants. The child's body is burned and/or thrown into the river, and the child's possessions may be burned as well. One fatherless nine-year-old girl was condemned to be burned alive or shot with arrows (although she escaped) after a shaman identified her as responsible for the chief's brother's death from stomach pains. When a man who had recently converted to Adventism became sick, his young daughter was accused, confined, starved, beaten, and finally bludgeoned to death and thrown in the river by her brother after a shaman (prior to his own conversion) determined her to be the witch responsible for her father's illness. Historically, children suspected or accused of sorcery also were traded for manufactured goods or sold as slaves or servants to colonists. In historical practices that continue today, they are sometimes given as orphans to missionaries or other assistance groups, or they and their families are expelled from their communities.

Santos-Granero attributes the historical surges of witchcraft accusations to the extraordinary tensions of social change during apocalyptic times. Among Peruvian Arawaks, the people most likely to embrace social change are those who "have little power within their settlements, (who) ally themselves to foreign agents of change to gain leverage against current holders of political power" (2004:301):

> By directing accusations toward children and women belonging to families that had embraced change, or who themselves manifested an inordinate interest in the new ideologies and modes of behavior, Peruvian Arawak shamans and leaders sought to contain change. Thus, selective accusations of child witchcraft can be seen as forms of social control and defense of existing power relations; namely those linking village headmen and local shamans to their constituencies or clienteles. (ibid., 299)

In general, he argues, "Witchhunts take place in contexts of rapid social change, social disruption, and personal stress" (ibid., 298) and are aimed at maintaining the existing social order and political structure. In these contexts, witchcraft accusations are levied against "enemies within," people who are perceived as being different, especially people with different origins, ideas, and theologies, including those marginal people who threaten the existing social order because they have embraced social change.

Here, the archaeological implication is that captives, orphans, and other marginalized people may emerge more visibly in the archaeological record as "foreigners" and, like orphans and other marginalized people, as victims of abuse, torture, and execution during times of extraordinary social upheaval wrought by the challenges and divisiveness of warfare, new ideologies, intrusive sociopolitical powers, or potent, imminently apocalyptic or devastating events in the physical world, like the archaeological cases at Cahokia (Alt, this volume) and in the prehistoric American Southwest (Martin, this volume).

Conclusions

Captives in Amazonia must be understood as part of a larger predatory landscape of expansions and migrations, warfare and reciprocal raiding, and inequities of power at all scales, together with the tremendous displacement of people that results and the strategies that people employ for negotiating this landscape. Because new identities are constructed as relationships are reworked, these processes reveal how the rights of group membership and social personhood may be negotiated and redefined, as well as the principles of kinship upon which equalities and inequalities are built: the fracture lines in society that distinguish "us" versus "them" as well as those with lesser, or greater, rights of social personhood. The ways in which captives are incorporated into society—their transitions from captive to kin and their multiple social locations—are instructive.

The predatory landscape in Amazonia is a social one structured primarily by kinship. Captives, orphans, and other *dezplazados* share similar locations because they have been displaced from their kin by war and death. In Amazonia, rights of social personhood are not inalienable, guaranteed by birth or marriage in a kin-based society, but are actively maintained through relationships of geographically close kin. Abducted men, women, and children may be incorporated through marriage and adoption, and given new social locations within the predatory landscape, but the new labels of husband, wife, son, and daughter encompass a broad spectrum of rights of social personhood. Captives may be incorporated into new social locations, but having been displaced from the support of kin—now dead, or in enemy territory—they may never occupy the same social location as other men, women, and children who live in their natal social landscape of kin and affines. As such, many captives are subject to physical and social abuse that other people in the same social category are spared. These unincorporated or reincorporated "others" may be detected directly in the archaeological record as foreign victims of trauma or sacrifice based on archaeological studies of DNA, bone chemistry, and physical injuries, or indirectly through studies of pottery styles and technology, polygyny, feasting, warfare, and settlement patterns.

Bibliography

Arhem, Kaj
1981   *Makuna Social Organization: A Study in Descent Alliance and the Formation of Corporate Groups.* Uppsala Studies in Cultural Anthropology 4. Stockholm.

Barnes, R. H.
1999   Marriage by Capture. *Journal of the Royal Anthropological Institute* 5(1):57–73.

Basso, Ellen B.
1995   *The Last Cannibals: A South American Oral History.* University of Texas Press, Austin.

Batlle, Antonio
1905   Memoria de la prefectura apostólica de San Francisco del Ucayali. In *Colección de las leyes, decretos, resoluciones i otros documentos oficiales referentes al departamento de Loreto*, vol. 9, edited by C. Larrabure i Correa, pp. 245–248. Oficina Tipográfica de la Opinión Nacional, Lima.

Bennett Ross, Jane B.
1984   Effects of Contact on Revenge Hostilities among the Achuara Jivaro. In *War, Culture, and Environment*, edited by R. Brian Ferguson, pp. 83–109. Academic Press, New York.

Bowser, Brenda J.
2000   From Pottery to Politics: An Ethnoarchaeological Study of Political Factionalism, Ethnicity, and Women's Domestic Pottery in the Ecuadorian Amazon. *Journal of Archaeological Method and Theory* 7(3):219–248.

2002   *The Perceptive Potter: An Ethnoarchaeological Study of Pottery, Ethnicity, and Political Action in Amazonia.* Ph.D. dissertation, Department of Anthropology, University of California, Santa Barbara. University Microfilms, Ann Arbor, MI.

Bowser, Brenda J., and John Q. Patton
2008   Learning and Transmission of Pottery Style: Women's Life Histories and Communities of Practice in the Ecuadorian Amazon. In *Cultural Transmission and Material Culture: Breaking Down Boundaries*, edited by Miriam Stark, Brenda J. Bowser, and Lee Horne. University of Arizona Press, Tucson.

Brooks, James F.
2002   *Captives and Cousins: Slavery, Kinship, and Community in the Southwest Borderlands.* University of North Carolina Press, Chapel Hill.

Carneiro, Robert L.
1970   A Theory of the Origin of the State. *Science* 169:733–738.

Carvajal, Gaspar de
1934   *The Discovery of the Amazon, according to the Account of Friar Gaspar de Carvajal and other documents*, compiled by Jose Toribio Medina. Edited by H. C. Heaton. American Geographical Society, New York.

Chagnon, Napoleon A.
1968   *Yanomamö: The Fierce People.* Holt, Rinehart, and Winston, New York.

1979   Kin Selection and Conflict: An Analysis of a Yanomamö Ax Fight. In *Evolutionary Biology and Human Social Behavior: An Anthropological Perspective,* edited by Napoleon A. Chagnon and William Irons, pp. 86–132. Duxbury Press, North Scituate, MA.

1988   Life Histories, Blood Revenge, and Warfare in a Tribal Population. *Science* 239:985–992.

1992   *Yanomamö: The Last Days of Eden.* Harcourt Brace & Company, Orlando, FL.

1996   Book Review of *Yanomami Warfare: A Political History* by R. Brian Ferguson. *American Anthropologist* 98:670–672.

1997   *Yanomamö.* 5th ed. Wadsworth, Belmont, CA.

Chagnon, Napoleon A., and William Irons (editors)
1979   *Evolutionary Biology and Human Social Behavior: An Anthropological Perspective.* Duxbury Press, North Scituate, MA.

Chernela, Janet M.
1993   *The Wanano Indians of the Brazilian Amazon: A Sense of Space.* University of Texas Press, Austin.

Cronk, Lee, Napoleon L. Chagnon, and William Irons (editors)
2000   *Human Behavior and Adaptation: An Anthropological Perspective.* Aldine de Gruyter, New York.

DeBoer, Warren R.

1981 Buffer Zones in the Cultural Ecology of Aboriginal Amazonia: An Ethnohistorical Approach. *American Antiquity* 46:364–377.

1986 Pillage and Production in the Amazon: A View through the Conibo of the Ucayali Basin, Eastern Peru. *World Archaeology* 18(2): 231–246.

1990 Interaction, Imitation, and Communication as Expressed in Style: The Ucayali Experience. In *The Uses of Style in Archaeology*, edited by Margaret Conkey and Christine Hastorf, pp. 82–104. Cambridge University Press, Cambridge.

2000 The Big Drink: Feast and Forum in the Upper Amazon. In *Feasts: Archaeological and Ethnographic Perspectives on Food, Politics, and Power*, edited by Michael Dietler and Brian Hayden, pp. 215–239. Smithsonian Institution Press, Washington, D.C.

Descola, Phillippe

1996a *In the Society of Nature: A Native Ecology in*
[1986] *Amazonia.* Cambridge University Press, Cambridge.

1996b *The Spears of Twilight: Life and Death in the*
[1993] *Amazon Jungle.* The New Press, New York.

Descola, Phillippe, and Anne-Christine Taylor (editors)

1993 La Remontée de l'Amazone: Antropologie et histoire des sociétés amazoniennes. *L'Homme* (special issue) vol. 33, nos. 126–128.

Duff, Andrew I.

2002 *Western Pueblo Identities: Regional Interaction, Migration, and Transformation.* University of Arizona Press, Tucson.

Engels, Frederick

1972 *The Origin of the Family, Private Property and*
[1884] *the State.* International Publishers, New York.

Ferguson, R. Brian

1995 *Yanomami Warfare.* School of American Research Press, Santa Fe, NM.

Fritz, Samuel

1922 *Journey of the Travels and Labours of Father Samuel Fritz in the River of the Amazons between 1686 and 1723.* Edited by George Edmundson. Hakluyt Society, London.

Gillin, John

1948 Tribes of the Guianas. In *Handbook of South American Indians,* vol. 3: *The Tropical Forest Tribes*, edited by Julian H. Steward, pp. 799–860. Smithsonian Institution Bureau of American Ethnology Bulletin 143. U.S. Government Printing Office, Washington, D.C.

Goldman, Irving

1948 Tribes of the Uaupés-Caquetá Region. In *Handbook of South American Indians,* vol. 3: *The Tropical Forest Tribes,* edited by Julian H. Steward, pp. 763–798. Smithsonian Institution Bureau of American Ethnology Bulletin 143. U.S. Government Printing Office, Washington, D.C.

1963 *The Cubeo.* University of Illinois Press, Urbana.

Gosselain, Olivier P.

2000 Materializing Identities: An African Perspective. *Journal of Archaeological Method and Theory* 7(3):187–217.

Gray, Andrew

1997 Freedom and Territory: Slavery in the Peruvian Amazon. In *Enslaved Peoples in the 1990s: Indigenous Peoples, Debt Bondage and Human Rights,* pp. 183–215. Document 83. Anti-Slavery International, International Work Group for Indigenous Affairs, Copenhagen.

Harner, Michael J.

1972 *The Jivaro.* Anchor Books, Garden City, New York.

Harris, Marvin

1984 A Cultural Materialist Theory of Band and Village Warfare: The Yanomamo Test. In *Warfare, Culture, and Environment,* edited by R. Brian Ferguson, pp. 111–140. Academic Press, New York.

Heckenberger, Michael J.

2005 *The Ecology of Power: Culture, Place, and Personhood in the Southern Amazon, AD 1000–2000.* Routledge, New York.

Hill, Jonathan D. (editor)

1988 *Rethinking History and Myth: Indigenous South American Perspectives on the Past.* University of Illinois Press, Urbana.

Hill, Kim, and A. Magdalena Hurtado

1996 *Ache Life History: The Ecology and Demography of a Foraging People.* Aldine de Gruyter, New York.

Holmberg, Allan R.

1969 *Nomads of the Long Bow: The Seriono of East-*
[1950] *ern Bolivia.* Natural History Press, Garden City, NY.

Hornborg, Alf

1993 Panoan Marriage Sections. *Ethnology* 32(1): 101–108.

1998 Ecosystems and World Systems: Accumulation and Ecological Process. *Journal of World-Systems Research* 4:169–177.

2005 Ethnogenesis, Regional Integration, and Ecology in Prehistoric Amazonia. *Current Anthropology* 46(4):589–607.

Horton, Donald

1948 The Mundurucú. In *Handbook of South*

American Indians, vol. 3: *The Tropical Forest Tribes,* edtied by Julian H. Steward, pp. 271–282. Smithsonian Institution Bureau of American Ethnology Bulletin 143. U.S. Government Printing Office, Washington, D.C.

Hugh-Jones, Christine

1979   *From the Milk River: Spatial and Temporal Processes in Northwest Amazonia.* Cambridge University Press, Cambridge.

Hugh-Jones, Stephen

1993   Clear Descent or Ambiguous Houses? A Re-Examination of Tukanoan Social Organisation. In *La remontée de l'Amazone: Antropologie et histoire des sociétés amazoniennes,* edited by Phillippe Descola and Anne-Christine Taylor, pp. 95–120. *L'Homme* (special issue) vol. 33, no. 126.

Jackson, Jean

1975   Recent Ethnography of Indigenous Northern Lowland South America. *Annual Review of Anthropology* 4:307–340.

1983   *The Fish People: Linguistic Exogamy and Tukanoan Identity in Northwest Amazonia.* Cambridge University Press, New York.

Kensinger, Kenneth M. (editor)

1984   *Marriage Practices in Lowland South America.* University of Illinois Press, Urbana.

Lathrap, Donald W.

1970   *The Upper Amazon.* Praeger, New York.

1983   Recent Shipibo-Conibo Ceramics and Their Implications for Archaeological Interpretation. In *Structure and Cognition in Art,* edited by Dorothy K. Washburn, pp. 25–39. Cambridge University Press, Cambridge.

Lévi-Strauss, Claude

1948a   Tribes of the Right Bank of the Guaporé River. In *Handbook of South American Indians,* vol. 3: *The Tropical Forest Tribes,* edited by Julian H. Steward, pp. 371–380. Smithsonian Institution Bureau of American Ethnology Bulletin 143. U.S. Government Printing Office, Washington, D.C.

1948b   Tribes of the Upper Xingú River. In *Handbook of South American Indians,* vol. 3: *The Tropical Forest Tribes,* edited by Julian H. Steward, pp. 321–348. Smithsonian Institution Bureau of American Ethnology Bulletin 143. U.S. Government Printing Office, Washington, D.C.

1963   *Structural Anthropology.* Translated by Claire
[1958] Jacobson and Brooke Grundfest Schoepf. Basic Books, Garden City, NY.

Lipkind, William

1948   The Carajá. In *Handbook of South American Indians,* vol. 3: *The Tropical Forest Tribes,* edited by Julian H. Steward, pp. 179–191. Smithsonian Institution Bureau of American Ethnology Bulletin 143. U.S. Government Printing Office, Washington, D.C.

Lowie, Robert H.

1948   The Tropical Forests: An Introduction. In *Handbook of South American Indians,* vol. 3: *The Tropical Forest Tribes,* edited by Julian H. Steward, pp. 1–56. Smithsonian Institution Bureau of American Ethnology Bulletin 143. U.S. Government Printing Office, Washington, D.C.

Meggers, Betty J.

1971   *Amazonia: Man and Culture in a Counterfeit Paradise.* Aldine, Chicago.

1996   *Amazonia: Man and Culture in a Counterfeit Paradise.* Rev. ed. Smithsonian Institution Press, Washington, D.C.

Métraux, Alfred

1948a   The Guaraní. In *Handbook of South American Indians,* vol. 3: *The Tropical Forest Tribes,* edited by Julian H. Steward, pp. 69–94. Smithsonian Institution Bureau of American Ethnology Bulletin 143. U.S. Government Printing Office, Washington, D.C.

1948b   The Hunting and Gathering Tribes of the Rio Negro Basin. In *Handbook of South American Indians,* vol. 3: *The Tropical Forest Tribes,* edited by Julian H. Steward, pp. 861–868. Smithsonian Institution Bureau of American Ethnology Bulletin 143. U.S. Government Printing Office, Washington, D.C.

1948c   The Paressí. In *Handbook of South American Indians,* vol. 3: *The Tropical Forest Tribes,* edited by Julian H. Steward, pp. 349–360. Smithsonian Institution Bureau of American Ethnology Bulletin 143. U.S. Government Printing Office, Washington, D.C.

1948d   The Tupinamba. In *Handbook of South American Indians,* vol. 3: *The Tropical Forest Tribes,* edited by Julian H. Steward, pp. 95–133. Smithsonian Institution Bureau of American Ethnology Bulletin 143. U.S. Government Printing Office, Washington, D.C.

1948e   Tribes of Eastern Bolivia and the Madeira Headwaters. In *Handbook of South American Indians,* vol. 3: *The Tropical Forest Tribes,* edited by Julian H. Steward, pp. 381–424. Smithsonian Institution Bureau of American Ethnology Bulletin 143. U.S. Government Printing Office, Washington, D.C.

1948f   Tribes of the Eastern Slopes of the Bolivian Andes. In *Handbook of South American Indians,* vol. 3: *The Tropical Forest Tribes,* edited by Julian H. Steward, pp. 465–506. Smithsonian

Institution Bureau of American Ethnology Bulletin 143. U.S. Government Printing Office, Washington, D.C.

1948g   Tribes of the Middle and Upper Amazon River. In *Handbook of South American Indians*, vol. 3: *The Tropical Forest Tribes*, edited by Julian H. Steward, pp. 687–712. Smithsonian Institution Bureau of American Ethnology Bulletin 143. U.S. Government Printing Office, Washington, D.C.

McLennan, John F.

1865   *Primitive Marriage: An Inquiry into the Original of the Form of Capture in Marriage Ceremonies*. Black, Edinburgh.

Murdock, George P.

1949   *Social Structure*. Macmillan, New York.

Murphy, Yolanda, and Robert F. Murphy

2004   *Women of the Forest*. Columbia University
[1974]   Press, New York.

Nimuendajú, Curt

1948a   The Cawahíb, Parintintin, and Their Neighbors. In *Handbook of South American Indians*, vol. 3: *The Tropical Forest Tribes*, edited by Julian H. Steward, pp. 283–298. Smithsonian Institution Bureau of American Ethnology Bulletin 143. U.S. Government Printing Office, Washington, D.C.

1948b   The Cayabí, Tapanyuna, and Apiacá. In *Handbook of South American Indians*, vol. 3: *The Tropical Forest Tribes*, edited by Julian H. Steward, pp. 307–320. Smithsonian Institution Bureau of American Ethnology Bulletin 143, U.S. Government Printing Office, Washington, D.C.

1948c   The Maué. In *Handbook of South American Indians*, vol. 3: *The Tropical Forest Tribes*, edited by Julian H. Steward, pp. 245–254. Smithsonian Institution Bureau of American Ethnology Bulletin 143. U.S. Government Printing Office, Washington, D.C.

1948d   The Mura and Pirahá. In *Handbook of South American Indians, Vol. 3, The Tropical Forest Tribes*, edited by Julian H. Steward, pp. 255–270. Smithsonian Institution Bureau of American Ethnology Bulletin 143. U.S. Government Printing Office, Washington, D.C.

1948e   The Tucuna. In *Handbook of South American Indians*, vol. 3: *The Tropical Forest Tribes*, edited by Julian H. Steward, pp. 713–727. Smithsonian Institution Bureau of American Ethnology Bulletin 143. U.S. Government Printing Office, Washington, D.C.

1948f   Tribes of the Lower and Middle Xingú River. In *Handbook of South American Indians*, vol. 3:

The Tropical Forest Tribes, edited by Julian H. Steward, pp. 213–244. Smithsonian Institution Bureau of American Ethnology Bulletin 143. U.S. Government Printing Office, Washington, D.C.

Patterson, Orlando

1982   *Slavery and Social Death: A Comparative Study*. Harvard University Press, Cambridge, MA.

Patton, John Q.

1996   *Thoughtful Warriors: Status, Warriorship, and Alliance in the Ecuadorian Amazon*. Ph.D. dissertation, Department of Anthropology, University of California, Santa Barbara. University Microfilms, Ann Arbor, MI.

2000   Reciprocal Altruism and Warfare: A Case from the Ecuadorian Amazon. In *Human Behavior and Adaptation: An Anthropological Perspective*, edited by Napoleon A. Chagnon, Lee Cronk, and William Irons, pp. 417–436. Aldine de Gruyter, New York.

Reeve, Mary-Elizabeth

1985   Identity as Process: The Meaning of Runapura for Quichua Speakers of the Curaray River, Eastern Ecuador. Ph.D. dissertation, University of Illinois at Urbana-Champaign.

1988   *Cauchu Uras*: Lowland Quichua Histories of the Amazon Rubber Boom. In *Rethinking History and Myth: Indigenous South American Perspectives on the Past*, edited by Jonathan D. Hill, pp. 19–34. University of Illinois Press, Urbana.

Rival, Laura M.

2002   *Trekking through History: The Huaorani of Amazonian Ecuador*. Columbia University Press, New York.

2006   Amazonian Historical Ecologies. *Journal of the Royal Anthropological Institute* 12 (supp. 1): S79–S94.

Robarchek, Clayton, and Carole Robarchek

1998   *Waorani: The Contexts of Violence and War*. Harcourt Brace, Fort Worth, TX.

Roosevelt, Anna C.

1991   *Moundbuilders of the Amazon: Geophysical Archaeology on Marajo Island, Brazil*. Academic Press, New York.

Santos-Granero, Fernando

2004   The Enemy Within: Child Sorcery, Revolution, and the Evils of Modernization in Eastern Peru. In *In Darkness and Secrecy: The Anthropology of Assault Sorcery and Witchcraft in Amazonia*, edited by Neil L. Whitehead and Robin Wright, pp. 272–305. Duke University Press, Durham, NC.

2007   Of Fear and Friendship: Amazonian Sociality

beyond Kinship and Affinity. *Journal of the Royal Anthropological Institute* 13:1–18.

Stanfield, Michael E.

1998   *Red Rubber, Bleeding Trees: Violence, Slavery, and Empire in Northwest Amazonia, 1850–1933.* University of New Mexico Press, Albuquerque.

Stark, Miriam

1998   Technical Choices and Social Boundaries in Material Cultural Patterning: An Introduction. In *The Archaeology of Social Boundaries,* edited by Miriam Stark, pp. 1–11. Smithsonian Institution Press, Washington, D.C.

Stearman, Allyn M.

1989   *Yuquí: Forest Nomads in a Changing World.* Holt, Rinehart and Winston, New York.

Stein, Gil J. (editor)

2005   *Archaeology of Colonial Encounters: Comparative Perspectives.* School of American Research Press, Santa Fe, NM.

Steward, Julian H.

1948a   Culture Areas of the Tropical Forests. In *Handbook of South American Indians,* vol. 3: *The Tropical Forest Tribes,* edited by Julian H. Steward, pp. 883–899. Smithsonian Institution Bureau of American Ethnology Bulletin 143. U.S. Government Printing Office, Washington, D.C.

1948b   The Witotoan Tribes. In *Handbook of South American Indians,* vol. 3: *The Tropical Forest Tribes,* edited by Julian H. Steward, pp. 749–762. Smithsonian Institution Bureau of American Ethnology Bulletin 143. U.S. Government Printing Office, Washington, D.C.

1948c   Tribes of the Montaña: An Introduction. In *Handbook of South American Indians,* vol. 3: *The Tropical Forest Tribes,* edited by Julian H. Steward, pp. 507–534. Smithsonian Institution Bureau of American Ethnology Bulletin 143. U.S. Government Printing Office, Washington, D.C.

Steward, Julian (editor)

1948d   *The Tropical Forest Tribes,* vol. 3 of the *Handbook of South American Indians.* Smithsonian Institution Bureau of American Ethnology Bulletin 143. U.S. Government Printing Office, Washington, D.C.

Steward, Julian H., and Alfred Métraux

1948   Tribes of the Peruvian and Ecuadorian Montaña. In *Handbook of South American Indians,* vol. 3: *The Tropical Forest Tribes,* edited by Julian H. Steward, pp. 535–656. Smithsonian Institution Bureau of American Ethnology Bulletin 143. U.S. Government Printing Office, Washington, D.C.

Taylor, Ann Christine

1996   The Body's Souls and Its States: An Amazonian Perspective on the Nature of Being Human. *Journal of the Royal Anthropological Institute* 2:201–215.

Tyler, Charles Dolby

1894   The River Napo. *Journal of the Royal Geographical Society* 3(6):476–484.

Valero, Helena

1996   *Yanoáma: The Story of Helena Valero, a Girl*
[1965]   *Kidnapped by Amazonian Indians.* Kodansha International, New York.

Viatori, Maximilian

2005   *The Language of "Authenticity": Shifting Constructions of Zápara Identity, the Politics of Indigenous Representation, and the State in Amazonian Ecuador.* Ph.D. dissertation, University of California, Davis. University Microfilms, Ann Arbor, MI.

2007   Zápara Leaders and Identity Construction in Ecuador: The Complexities of Indigenous Self-Representation. *Journal of Latin American and Caribbean Anthropology* 12(1):104–133.

Viveiros de Castro, Eduardo

1996   Images of Nature and Society in Amazonian Ethnology. *Annual Review of Anthropology* 25:179–250.

Weiss, Gerald

1975   Campa Cosmology: The World of a Forest Tribe in South America. *Anthropological Papers* 52(5):217–588.

Whitten, Norman

1976   *Sacha Runa: Ethnicity and Adaptation of Ecuadorian Jungle Quichua.* University of Illinois Press, Urbana.

1984   Marriage among the Canelos Quichua of East-Central Ecuador. In *Marriage Practices in Lowland South America,* edited by Kenneth M. Kensinger, pp. 194–220. University of Illinois Press, Urbana.

1985   *Sicuanga Runa: The Other Side of Development in Amazonian Ecuador.* University of Illinois Press, Urbana.

Wright, Robin

1991   Indian Slavery in Northwest Amazon. *Boletim do Museu Paraense Emílio Goeldi* 7(2):149–179.

Epilogue

Captive, Concubine, Servant, Kin

A Historian Divines Experience in Archaeological Slaveries

James F. Brooks

Traveling between St. Louis and Santa Fe in the 1820s, the American trader Josiah Gregg frequently noted the presence of Mexican captives within the Comanche and Kiowa bands that bartered mules and horses with his merchant caravans. Mostly women and children, their social status seemed ambiguous to Gregg, whose primary point of comparison would have been African chattel slaves in the U.S. South. But these Mexicans were not—he thought—enslaved. One woman, "whose particularities of features" struck him forcibly as "not being Indian," hailed originally from Matamoros and had been married to a Comanche since her capture some years before. She claimed not, he said, "to entertain the least desire of returning to her people" (Gregg 1844: 207–210).

Gregg termed her condition "voluntary captivity," an ambiguous expression that reflected a conceptual challenge to the binary world of freedom and slavery from which he hailed—and one that provides a point of entry for my comments on this important volume. Continuing his commentary, the curious American described the case of another Mexican woman, seized from Chihuahua, who when offered her freedom in return for the 1,000 peso ransom raised by her father, "preferred to remain with her masters, rather than encounter the horrible ordeal of ill-natured remarks to which she would inevitably be exposed on being returned to civilized life." She explained that the Comanches "had disfigured her by tattooing, that she was married and

perhaps 'enceinte' [*sic*] (pregnant); and that she would be more unhappy returning to her father under these circumstances than by remaining where she was." Of the six Mexican "voluntary captives" Gregg met in this incident, only one, a "stupid boy about fifteen years of age who had been roughly treated on account of his laziness," accepted the traveling Americans' intervention. For Gregg, the others' decision to remain with their captors represented an easy choice in a hard land, and perhaps the better one, given the disdain that most Americans then held for Mexican family and social life (Gregg 1844:207–210). But we now know that his snapshot of Southern Plains captivity was taken on a particularly sunny day, and that for many hundreds of victims of Comanche, Kiowa, and Apache raiding bands, life felt anything but voluntary (Brooks 2000, 2002b; DeLay 2008; Rivaya-Martinez 2006).

Like Gregg's Mexican women and children, the shadowy people who fascinate the archaeologists herein display remarkable range in their condition and experience, from war captive to sexual concubine, from abject drudge to quasi kinswoman. Yet certainly we can say that if "freedom" means to be numbered among the inalienable roots and branches of distinct cultural communities, the people we seek to identify and interpret archaeologically were indeed unfree (Ste. Croix 1988). As so many Mexican captives among the Comanches would learn in time, no matter what one's level of prestige or social integration, an unfree person faced always the possibility of estrangement, abuse, and alienation. Since the very notion of "belonging" depends heavily on existence of an opposite—locally specific expressions of "not belonging"—and since slavery is essentially a condition antithetical to kinship, I am convinced that the world has long embraced, and continues to embrace, many "slaveries" that deserve the name (Meillassoux 1991). The volume at hand takes crucial steps toward manifesting this belief.

Above all, slaves in the past and present are, ironically, culturally indispensable "disposable people" (Bales 1999, 2005). Slaves' very presence and helplessness assures "those who belong" of their status and privilege. Yet this fundamental aspect of the unfree experience seems colored by gradations-in-practice of the "slaveries" we see treated in these small- to middle-range societies. Working at an even finer level of specificity, the authors in this volume have attempted to detect the range of action and agency within these shades of unfreedom. Such efforts will, we hope, help us to grasp the degree to which captive-slave-quasi-kin might "have profoundly influenced developments in language, social organization, ideology, and technology" (Cameron, this volume). This last question, I'll suggest below, has significant currency in the contemporary world.

Today, even such seemingly straightforward cases as Gregg's "voluntary captives" seem less easy to toss off as quirky local practice in the quixotic past. This volume makes clear that the dilemmas facing his small group of Mexicans on the Southern Plains ran deep in time and spanned continents. From the practice of indigenous slavery in West Africa and its articulation with the Atlantic world (Stahl) to coastal slave-raiding by city-states of the China-Philippine-South Asia circuit (Junker), from the cultural expression of power and vulnerability in slave tortures and executions among Iroquois (Peregrine) or Northwest Coast peoples (Ames) to the reciprocal slave trade between Rome and Germany (Lenski), and finally to the living survivors of wife-snatching on the upper Amazon (Bowser), the widespread practice of small-scale to middle-range "slaveries" is increasingly linked to painful conversations about slavery reparations and human trafficking today (McGill 2003).

At the acute core of these debates is the question of agency: not simply that of slave masters and human traffickers (were and are they but agents of larger economic forces?), but that of the "victims" themselves (do we condescend when we look for individual agency within pervasive systems exploitation, or might victims sometimes shape the outcome of their victimization in self-actualizing ways?) (Johnson 2003; Vance, forthcoming). Thus our immediate question—did forms of slavery play significant roles in the economic and cultural histories of ancient middle-range societies? —conceals an urgency beyond its immediate intellectual goal. If the exploitation of (especially) women and children through forms of human bondage played a central role in diverse cases of emerging social complexity—an argument as old as Engels (1884)—does its persistence today suggest that normative abuse of the world's most vulnerable people lies at the deep heart of those indigenous and folk cultures that popular imagination has long praised as more egalitarian than Western societies?

We needn't look far to find modern stories that evoke in piercing detail the experiences that characterized the lives of the nameless women and children who reside in these archaeological cases. Veena Das (1997) has shown that for the tens of thousands of women and children caught up in the ethnoreligious violence of the Indo-Pakistani border wars, decisions to remain with one's captors or within a "host" society always held the double torment of deracination or public shame. Abducted and forcibly assimilated women and children were the figurative currency in what Das calls "transactions in the construction of pain." A woman's "choice" lay either to remain with the captors who raped and forced motherhood upon her, or to test the slim chance that her natal family might accept her back, despite the fact that she literally embodied an offense to family and nation. In either case, grief obtained. Captives' "agency" lay only and simply in the women's "power to endure" by numbing themselves to alternative dreams or becoming skilled wielders of gallows humor (Das 1997; Goldstein 2003).

The nameless Mexican women whom Gregg interviewed surely inhabited a similar world, if one transitional between indigenous forms of coercive kin-making and later nationalistic projections of dominance and dishonor onto the victims' bodies and lives. The women of the thirteenth-century ancestral Pueblo communities of the La Plata Valley surely suffered similar psychological torments, as well as the perhaps daily beatings that their remains today bespeak. Amid relative environmental abundance there existed a cohort of physically abused and over-worked women. Their remains suggest hard labor at grinding stones and violence at the hands of their "own" people (Martin, this volume). At some distance, on the Southern Plains, their sisters, whose hands shaped the "squat Pueblo-style cooking jars" or scraped the bison hides so central to survival, might likewise have simply endured lives that allowed no option for contemplation (Habichte-Mauche, this volume). To research and write the archaeologies of enslaved peoples in these societies, we must inhabit a space wherein the absence of state forms—or rather, the presence of rough parities of power among neighboring indigenous groups or between those indigenes and the colonial peoples with whom they engaged—is expressed in thorny, gender-inflected dialectics of negotiation and exploitation, conflict and accommodation.

When no single people possessed the power to subjugate others completely, the time-honored slave-studies paradigm of "domination and resistance" becomes analytically untenable. Whether in Bandha villages of the Ghanaian hinterlands or fishing communities along the Vietnamese coast, the anxieties of daily life probably fluctuated between constant wariness and shrewd bartering, sudden bursts of predation and frantic defense. Time and again in this volume we see defensively oriented settlement patterns—high-place fortifications, palisaded enclosures, or aggregated villages—that suggest however much people feared the loss of crops or livestock, they dreaded more the loss of their wives and children. These patterns appear, tellingly, as often among people whose main efforts lay in raiding their neighbors for captives as among those they targeted (Junker, Robertshaw and Duncan, Lenski, Peregrine, this volume). Reciprocating cycles of captive-raiding, slave-marketing, and kin-incorporation etched a vast latticework of mutual hostility and interdependence across these local landscapes (DeBoer, this volume). The studies presented here require an alternative narrative, one that folds victimizer and victim into the same universe of potential life histories, irrespective of modern sensibilities.

Such a standpoint, of course, is perilous. If domination and resistance allowed us either to condemn the brutalities of Euroamerican slaveholders' exploitation of Africans or to celebrate those same peoples' ability to resist and persist against overwhelming odds, a victimizer/victim dialectic forefronts the agency of indigenous peoples in ways that today prove politically problematic. Our Africanist colleagues have done much to alert us to such issues; Susan Rasmussen's (1999) work on Taureg slavery, Sharon Hutchinson's (1996) on Nuer militarization, and Michael Fleisher's (2000) on Kura cattle-raiding show how historically powerful pastoral (and historically slave-holding) peoples may find themselves decidedly marginal in modern nation-states, and how each may have their pasts deployed to justify ongoing political and economic exploitation.

The work from which Gregg's story emerged harbors similar risk. In recent years I have argued that peoples such as the Comanches, Kiowas, Apaches, Pawnees, and Pueblos had been seizing captives, assimilating slaves, or coercively adopting kinspeople long before the advent of Euroamericans in the Southwest. With the arrival of Spanish colonial slavery in the seventeenth century, this custom found its first commercial rewards: Spanish *padres* and governors alike utilized the practice of *rescate*, or ransom, to add neophytes and domestic workers to their households, often purchasing captives from Apache and Comanche raiders. By the nineteenth century the slave system of the Southwest had expanded into Mexico, with powerful pastoralists such as the Comanches and Kiowas plundering villages and haciendas for their horses, mules, and cattle, as well as the labor to manage them (Brooks 1996, 1999, 2000, 2002b).

In the Southwest, I suggest, a "borderlands political economy" organized much of inter-ethnic life. Through the seizure and exchange of human captives and livestock, Indian groups and Euroamerican settlers came to share an understanding of the production and distribution of wealth as conditioned by social relations of power. This mutual understanding depended much on the ability of colonizing and indigenous men to agree that their women and children were simultaneously their most cherished relations *and* their most contestable of resources. Much of my work has attempted to define the peculiar structures of constraint and opportunity that some victims experienced in the captive-exchange system of the Southwest Borderlands, wherein Indian and colonizing men vied to seize and assimilate each others' women and children in a broadly shared contest over patriarchal prestige and community honor. More than a few such captives found their multilingual and intercultural skills valued and respected in their "host" societies. Through their victimization, some attained a social status and economic autonomy they might never have dreamed possible in their natal homes. Many others, however, suffered gruesome mutilation, death, or lives of abject misery. This violent and volatile constellation of emotional, cultural, and material exchange produced a history by which the peoples of the Southwest—Comanches, Kiowas, Apaches, Utes, Navajos, Pueblos, and Spaniards—were drawn, in the words of the poet, "closer and closer apart" (Hope 1955:20–21).

Apart from the tribal and place names above, I suspect that the slave raiders of the Roman-German borderlands, or those who captained the slaving boats of the Haida and Tlingit, or even the spiritual leaders at Cahokia who determined the need for captive sacrifice in mortuary theater could all agree that their economies functioned in roughly similar choreography. All was in motion, and the identities that fix so easily in archaeological sequences would likely appear incomprehensibly simple-minded to the peoples who lived these complex lives.

Yet the very mixed-ness of these histories can suggest—especially to critics of the manner in which Indian tribes today receive "preferential" treatment under the federal trust relationship—that the "tribes" thus codified were far from "essential" cultural entities. Rather, in their brilliant, and often violent, strategies for survival, they became part of a wider world of mixed-descent peoples who ought *not* attain special legal standing in the neoliberal nation nor the status of "victims" of European expansion (cf. Hale 1997). If similarly aggressive political economies orga-

nized life among the peoples of Africa, Southeast Asia, the Northwest Coast, the Ohio Valley, the protohistoric Southwest, the St. Lawrence borderlands of North America, and across Rome's northern Marches, we can sense a tempest in the offing. The credibility of the Western canon depends to no small degree on the stability of these protagonists' identities: if all was in flux, how do we tell the barbarous from the civilized?

I would further caution that many victims' stories within borderlands dialectics should be viewed in the context of a highly militarized and masculinized economy that rested on what Maria Mies (1988) has termed a "predatory mode of appropriation," with men's control over social and biological reproduction the quarry. The obvious modern extension is to cases of interethnic conflict in which women and children remain objects of male contestation, but brutally so, in that the "kin-building violence" of forcible adoption and exogamy is replaced with the "exclusionary violence" of rape and murder. Some of my recent writing seeks to identify the particular sets of historical forces and circumstances that account for transpositions in these two faces of the patriarchal construction and preservation of local communities by extending across cultural borderlands in South Africa, the Russian trans-Caucasus, western Canada, and the Argentine Pampas; in another, about which I'll say more below, I take a microhistorical approach to the catastrophe at the Hopi pueblo of Awat'ovi in 1700 (Brooks 2001, 2008, in prep.).

These projects entail multiple horizons of analysis, among which one brought me back to disturbing links between deep patterns of violence against women and forms of early slavery (Lerner 1987). This, of course, depends precisely upon the kind of careful work the contributors to this volume have done in the field and lab, and the bold theoretical extensions we see reflected in their writing. In each of this volume's chapters, it seems impossible to ignore the fact that the violence of these slaveries proved central to the vigor of many of the societies in question.

In an essay precedent to her work in this volume, Debra Martin notes that "violence might have contributed as much to the maintenance and growth of population as it did to its decline" (Martin 2000:293). This crucial observation—

that terrible violence often fostered sociodemographic gain among indigenous peoples who we prefer to believe acted without such brutal calculus—places women's experience at the center of social dynamics among small- to middle-scale societies in the past. We know from the few extant accounts of captive women who lived among the Comanches and Kiowas that labor indeed figured in their abductions and productive deployment. All noted that they "were set to work tanning hides," which by the nineteenth century had become the principal item of commerce with Euroamerican buyers. Hide-processing was notoriously hard work, and evidence for its intensification has been found in the skeletal remains of Plains Indian women in at least one case (Reinhard et al. 1994). Captive women's labor would have freed their captors' wives from the burdens of an increasingly insatiable market. Enslaved Indian women in colonial New Mexico were likewise set to weaving in *obrajes* maintained by governors such as Luis de Rosas, as were the Navajo slaves charged with producing "slave blankets" in nineteenth-century New Mexican households. That they were usually defenseless against sexual assault and thereby available for productive "biological work" was an ancillary dividend.

A painful irony emerges here, in that the violent traffic in women and children across societies seems to also underlie cultural vitality. Habichte-Mauche makes a convincing case that women's role in the coerced production of material culture may well have predated the advent of commodity capitalism in the Southwest. Thinking of the reciprocal human exchanges of later years, one wonders if the presence of paddle-and-anvil incised wares fashioned from local micaceous clays in Taos Valley pithouses hints at the presence of Plains Indian women in ancestral Pueblo households, either through exogamous marriages or abductions. We might ask also if the fifteenth-century Chama Valley ceramic tradition of Potsowi Incised, so similar to Plains wares of the period but for its coiled construction, derived from movements (voluntary or otherwise) of Plains women into that region. Habichte-Mauche cautiously notes that her evidence might be read as Plains-Pueblo marriage alliances, as migrating Pueblo families, or as Plains Indian captures of Pueblo women. Regardless, her work

confirms that interregional relations grew increasingly vigorous in the protohistoric eras, and that we would do well to attend to the place of violence against women as one element in those dynamics (Brooks 2002a; Plog 2004). Stahl's chapter on West Africa resonates time and again with the Southwest story, and work on East African women's slave narratives has brought voices to the experiences we will never hear elsewhere (Wright 1993).

Finally, gendered violence and painful transactions in women seem intensely central to the catastrophe at Awat'ovi Pueblo in the autumn of 1700—and to the survival of its remnant peoples. Although Spanish accounts of the internecine massacre placed its cause in Awat'ovi's friendly reception of returning Franciscan missionaries, many Hopi oral histories situate the origins of the crisis in sexual transgressions within and across village boundaries. These stories abound with promises of women to those pueblo warriors from Shungopovi, Shipaulovi, Oraibi, Walpi, and Hano who would assist in the sack: "the women and maidens you take; the men and old women you may kill" (Voth 1905). Women's productive and reproductive capacities allowed some to be spared in this case (and in so many others, when we extend our analysis to other intercultural borderlands). Surviving Awat'ovi women brought the Mamzrau ritual to Walpi and the Sand, Rabbit, Coyote, and Butterfly clans to Oraibi. Others may have found "voluntary captivity" among Navajo outfits in the nearby Jeddito Wash, for David Brugge has collected traditions indicating that the Navajo Tobacco, Deer, Rabbit, and Tansy Mustard clans descended from clan mothers who fled Awat'ovi (Brugge 1999:8–9). Here the "power to endure" was underwritten by the victims' cultural repertoires and reproductive abilities.

Women as objects of violence, agents of intercultural exchange, and actors in the renewal of families and communities were ubiquitous across the Southwest, and anywhere men of differing cultural heritage found that dialectics of conflict and accommodation might redound to their communities' benefit. The haunting liminality of women's position within these dynamics of flow and closure is inescapable, as is so evident in the story of the Mexican woman who, despite the chance to rejoin her father in Chihuahua, found her face tattooed with symbols that marked her simultaneously as Comanche and "barbarian," and her womb likewise embracing the evidence of her violation and her hope for a future. With yet so much to learn, I wish to conclude with Patricia Albers's observation from her studies of Plains ethnology that the reciprocal abduction of women among Indians of the region harbored "the grounds for conflict, but…also embodied (quite literally) the terms of reconciliation.… The capture of women and children," she argues, "was both a quintessential element of war, and a fundamental opportunity for peace" (Albers 1993: 128). It is in this fearsome paradox—where the enslavement of women and children hints also at the alternative political formations to which Albers gestures—that we might hope to situate the ongoing study of slavery in archaeology.

References Cited

Albers, Patricia C.
1993 Symbiosis, Merger, and War: Contrasting Forms of Intertribal Relationship Among Historic Plains Indians. In *The Political Economy of North American Indians,* edited by John H. Moore, pp. 94–132. University of Nebraska Press, Lincoln.

Bales, Kevin
1999 *Disposable People: New Slavery in the Global Economy.* University of California Press, Berkeley and London.
2005 *Understanding Global Slavery: A Reader.* University of California Press, Berkeley and London.

Brooks, James F.
1996 "This Evil Extends Especially…to the Feminine Sex": Negotiating Captivity in the New Mexico Borderlands. *Feminist Studies* 22(2): 279–309.
1999 Violence, Justice, and State Power in the New Mexico Borderlands, 1780–1880. In *Power and Place in the North American West,* edited by Richard White and John Findlay, pp. 28–53. University of Washington Press, Seattle.
2000 Served Well by Plunder: *La Gran Ladronería* and Producers of History Astride the Río Grande. *American Quarterly* 52(1):23–58.
2001 Life Proceeds from the Name: Indigenous Peoples and the Predicament of Hybridity. In *Clearing a Path: Theorizing the Past in Native American Studies,* edited by Nancy Shoemaker. Routledge, London.
2002a Violence, Exchange, and Renewal in the American Southwest. *Ethnohistory* 49(1):205–218.
2002b *Captives and Cousins: Slavery, Kinship, and Community in the Southwest Borderlands.* University of North Carolina Press, Chapel Hill.
2008 Seductions and Betrayals: *La frontera gauchesque,* Argentine Nationalism, and the Predicaments of Hybridity. In *Small Worlds: Method, Meaning, and Narrative in Microhistory,* edited by James Brooks, Christopher DeCorse, and John Walton, pp. 247–263. SAR Press, Santa Fe, NM.
In prep. Mesa of Sorrows: Archaeology, Prophecy, and the Ghosts of Awat'ovi Pueblo. W. W. Norton and Co., New York.

Brugge, David
1999 *The Navajo-Hopi Land Dispute.* University of New Mexico Press, Albuquerque.

Das, Veena
1997 Language and Body: Transactions in the Construction of Pain. In *Social Suffering,* edited by Arthur Kleinman, Veena Das, and Margaret Lock. University of California Press, Berkeley.

Das, Veena (editor)
1990 *Mirrors of Violence: Communities, Riots, and Survivors in South Asia.* Oxford University Press, Delhi.

DeLay, Brian
2008 *The War of a Thousand Deserts: Indian Raids and the U.S.-Mexican War.* Harvard University Press, Cambridge, MA.

Donald, Leland
1997 *Aboriginal Slavery on the Northwest Coast of North America.* University of California Press, Berkeley.

Engels, Frederick
1884 *The Origins of Marriage, Private Property, and the State.* Reprint, Pathfinder Press, New York, 1972.

Farmer, Paul
2003 *Pathologies of Power: Health, Human Rights, and the New War on the Poor.* University of California Press, Berkeley.

Fleisher, Michael L.
2000 *Kuria Cattle Raiders: Violence and Vigilantism on the Tanzania/Kenya Frontier.* University of Michigan Press, Ann Arbor.

Goldstein, Donna M.
2003 *Laughter Out of Place: Race, Class, Violence and Sexuality in a Rio Shantytown.* University of California Press, Berkeley.

Gregg, Josiah
1844   *The Commerce of the Prairies.* Edited by Milo Milton Quaife. University of Nebraska Press, Lincoln, 1966.
Habichte-Mauche, Judith
2000   Pottery, Food, Hides, and Women: Labor, Production, and Exchange across the Protohistoric Plains-Pueblo Frontier. In *The Archaeology of Regional Interaction: Religion, Warfare, and Exchange across the American Southwest and Beyond,* edited by Michelle Hegmon. University Press of Colorado, Boulder.
Hale, Charles R., Jr.
1996   Mestizaje, Hybridity, and the Cultural Politics of Difference in Post-Revolutionary Central America. *Journal of Latin American Anthropology* 2(1):34–61.
1997   Cultural Politics of Identity in Latin America. *Annual Review of Anthropology* 26:567–590.
Hope, A. D.
1955   *The Wandering Islands.* Canberra, Australia.
Hutchinson, Sharon E.
1996   *Nuer Dilemmas: Coping with Many, War, and the State.* University of California Press, Berkeley.
Johnson, Walter
2003   On Agency. *Journal of Social History* 37(1):113–124.
Lerner, Gilda
1987   *The Creation of Patriarchy.* Oxford University Press, London.
Martin, Debra
2000   Bodies and Lives: Biological Indicators of Health Differentials and Division of Labor by Sex. In *Women and Men in the Prehispanic Southwest,* edited by Patricia L. Crown, pp. 267–300. SAR Press, Santa Fe, NM.
McGill, Craig
2003   *Human Traffic: Sex, Slaves and Immigration.* Vision Books, London.
Meillassoux, Claude
1991   *The Anthropology of Slavery.* University of Chicago Press, Chicago.
Mies, Maria
1988   Social Origins of the Sexual Division of Labor.

In *Women: The Last Colony,* edited by Mies et al., pp. 67–82. Zed Books, London.
Plog, Stephen
2004   Social Conflict, Social Structure and Processes of Culture Change. *American Antiquity.*
Rasmussen, Susan
1999   The Slave Narrative in Life History and Myth. *Ethnohistory* 46(1):67–108.
Reinhard, K. J., L. Tieszen, K. L. Sandness, L. M. Beiningen, E. Miller, A. M. Ghazi, C. E. Miewald, and S. V. Barnum
1994   Trade, Contact, and Female Health in Northeast Nebraska. In *In the Wake of Contact: Biological Responses to Conquest,* edited by C. S. Larsen and G. R. Milner, pp. 63–74. Wiley-Liss, New York.
Rivaya-Martinez, Joaquin
2006   Captivity and Adoption among the Comanche Indians, 1700–1875. Ph.D. dissertation, University of California, Los Angeles.
Rubin, Gayle
1975   The Traffic in Women: Notes on the "Political Economy" of Sex. In *Toward an Anthropology of Women,* edited by Rayna Reiter. Monthly Review Press, New York.
Rushforth, Brett
2003   "A Little Flesh We Offer You": The Origins of Indian Slavery in New France. *William and Mary Quarterly* 3(60):777–808.
Ste. Croix, G. E. M. de
1988   Slavery and Other Forms of Unfree Labour. In *Slavery and Other Forms of Unfree Labour,* edited by Léonie Archer, pp. 19–32. Routledge, London.
Vance, Carole (editor)
Forthcoming *Ethnography and Policy: What Do We Know About "Trafficking"?* SAR Press, Santa Fe, NM.
Voth, Henry R.
1905   *Traditions of the Hopi.* Field Columbian Museum 96, Anthropological Series 8.
Wright, Marcia
1993   *Strategies of Slaves and Women: Life-Stories from East/Central Africa.* Lilian Barber Press, New York.

Contributors

Susan M. Alt
Department of Anthropology
Indiana University
Student Building 130
Bloomington, IN 47405

Kenneth M. Ames
Department of Anthropology
Portland State University
Portland, OR 97207

Brenda J. Bowser
Department of Anthropology
California State University, Fullerton
P.O. Box 6846
Fullerton, CA 92634-6846

James F. Brooks
School for Advanced Research
P.O. Box 2188
Santa Fe, NM 87504-2188

Catherine M. Cameron
Department of Anthropology
University of Colorado
233 UCB
Boulder, CO 80309-0233

Warren DeBoer
Department of Anthropology
CUNY, Queens College
65-30 Kissena Blvd.
Flushing, NY 11367

William L. Duncan
Department of Anthropology
University of California, Santa Cruz
361 Social Science 1
Santa Cruz, CA 95064

Judith A. Habicht-Mauche
Department of Anthropology

University of California, Santa Cruz
1156 High Street
Santa Cruz, CA 95064

Laura Lee Junker
Department of Anthropology
University of Illinois at Chicago
2102 BSB, M/C 027
1007 W. Harrison St.
Chicago, IL 60607

Noel Lenski
Department of Classics
University of Colorado
248 UCB
Boulder, CO 80309-0248

Debra L. Martin
Department of Anthropology and
    Ethnic Studies
University of Nevada, Las Vegas
Las Vegas, NV 89154-5003

Peter N. Peregrine
Department of Anthropology
Lawrence University
P.O. Box 599, 115 S. Drew Street
Appleton, WI 54912-0599

Peter Robertshaw
Department of Anthropology
California State University
5500 University Parkway
San Bernardino, CA 92407-2397

Ann B. Stahl
Department of Anthropology
University of Victoria
P.O. Box 3050
STN CSC
Victoria, BC
Canada V8W 3P5

Index